Computer Accounting with Peachtree Complete® 2008 for Microsoft® Windows®

Release 15

12th Edition

Carol Yacht, M.A.

McGraw-Hill Irwin

Boston Burr Ridge, IL Dubuque, IA Madison, WI New York San Francisco St. Louis
Bangkok Bogotá Caracas Kuala Lumpur Lisbon London Madrid Mexico City
Milan Montreal New Delhi Santiago Seoul Singapore Sydney Taipei Toronto

McGraw-Hill Irwin

The McGraw-Hill Companies

About the Author:

Carol Yacht is a textbook author and accounting educator. Carol contributes regularly to professional journals and is the Accounting Section Editor for *Business Education Forum*, a publication of the National Business Education Association. She is the author of Peachtree, Microsoft Office Accounting, QuickBooks, Dynamics-GP (Great Plains), and Excel textbooks; and the accounting textbook supplement, Carol Yacht's General Ledger and Peachtree CD-ROMs (www.mhhe.com/yacht). Carol taught on the faculties of California State University, Los Angeles; West Los Angeles College; Yavapai College; and Beverly Hills High School. Since 1978, Carol has included accounting software in her classes to help students master accounting.

Carol Yacht is an officer of the American Accounting Association's Two-Year College section and recipient of its Lifetime Achievement Award. She is a member of Microsoft's Academic Alliance Advisory Board, served on NBEA's Computer Education Task Force, worked for IBM Corporation as an education instruction specialist, and is a frequent speaker at state, regional, and national conventions. Carol earned her MA degree from California State University, Los Angeles; BS degree from the University of New Mexico, and AS degree from Temple University.

COMPUTER ACCOUNTING WITH PEACHTREE COMPLETE 2008, RELEASE 15.0,
12th EDITION
Carol Yacht

Published by McGraw-Hill/Irwin, a business unit of The McGraw-Hill Companies, Inc., 1221 Avenue of the Americas, New York, NY 10020.

1 2 3 4 5 6 7 8 9 0 QPD/QPD 0 9 8
ISBN-13: 978-0-07-337939-5
ISBN-10: 0-07-337939-5

Editorial director: *Stewart Mattson*
Executive editor: *Steve Schuetz*
Editorial assistant: *Christina Lane*
Project manager: *Dana M. Pauley*
Production supervisor: *Gina Hangos*
Senior designer: *Cara Hawthorne*
Associate marketing manager: *Dean Karampelas*
Media project manager: *Suresh Babu, Hurix Systems Pvt. Ltd.*

www.mhhe.com

Software Installation

Installing the Software includes the following.

Comment: Peachtree Complete Accounting 2008, Release (Build) 15 Educational Version, was used to write the textbook. All the illustrations and Peachtree printouts were done using Windows Vista. You may install the CD that is packaged with the textbook on individual computers or in a multi-user environment. **If you have an earlier version of Peachtree installed (Peachtree Complete Accounting 2007 or lower), see Deleting Peachtree page xii.**

System Requirements: Recommended System Configuration

- 1 GHz Intel Pentium III (or equivalent) for single user and 1.8 GHz Intel Pentium 4 (or equivalent) for multiple concurrent users.
- 512 MB of RAM for single user and 1GB for multiple concurrent users.

Minimum System Requirements

- At least 1 GHz Intel Pentium III (or equivalent).
- 256 MB of RAM for single user and 512 MB for multiple concurrent users.
- Microsoft Windows Vista (all versions); Windows XP SP2 or Windows 2000 SP3.
- 1 GB of disk space for installation.

- Internet Explorer 6 required (provided on CD; requires an additional 70 MB); Internet 7.0 supported.
- Microsoft .NET Framework CLR 2.0 (provided on CD; requires an additional 280 MB).
- At least high color (16bit) SVGA video; supports 800X600 resolution with small fonts. Optimized for 1024 x 768.
- Online features require Internet access with at least a 56 Kbps modem.
- CD-ROM drive.
- Printers supported by Windows Vista/XP/2000.
- Mouse or compatible pointing device.
- Microsoft Excel, Outlook, and Word integration requires 2000, 2002, 2003, or 2007.
- Adobe Reader 7.0 required provided on CD (requires an additional 90 MB hard disk space to install).
- *External media for Chapter 1-18 backups*: One USB drive; Zip™ drive disk; CD-R; or, DVD-R. (CD-RW or DVD-RW required for backing up to CD-R or DVD-R.) *Or,* ten blank, formatted disks. The author suggests that you reformat floppy disks.

- *Optional requirement:* Microsoft Excel, Outlook and Word integration requires 2000 and higher.

Multi-User

- Multi-user mode is optimized for Windows 2000 Server or Windows Server 2003 client-server networks, and Windows 2000/XP peer-to-peer networks. The maximum number users are 5 or 10.
- The author suggests ghosting the installation; see page xi, Computer Lab Installation.

INSTALLING ON A SINGLE COMPUTER

This section gives you instructions for installing Peachtree Complete Accounting 2008 (PCA) software. *You may need to check with your instructor to see if Peachtree has already been installed in the classroom or computer lab*. The site license for using the software is included on the Help menu. From Peachtree's menu bar, select Help; License Agreement. The Peachtree License Agreement appears.

Peachtree Complete Accounting 2008 Educational Version Install

Follow these steps to install PCA 2008 on an individual computer (non-networked). These steps are consistent with the Windows Vista operating system. If you are using a different version of Windows, your steps will differ slightly.

Step 1: Put the Peachtree Complete Accounting 2008 CD in the CD drive. If an AutoPlay window appears, click Run autorun.exe to select it.

Step 2: At the Welcome to Peachtree Accounting window, select Install Peachtree Accounting. If necessary, click Continue.

Step 3: When the window prompts to exit all Windows programs, do that, then click Next >.

Step 4: The License Agreement window appears. Select Agree; click Next >.

Step 5: If the Change Firewall Detected window appears, read the information; click Yes. The Change Firewall Settings window appears. Read the information. Take the necessary steps described; click OK. (*Hint:* If you need to disable anti-virus software, do that.) Click OK. The Setup Status window shows the installation progress.

Step 6: The Serial Number window appears. Type the Serial number shown on the CD envelope. Compare your Serial Number window to the one shown on the next page.

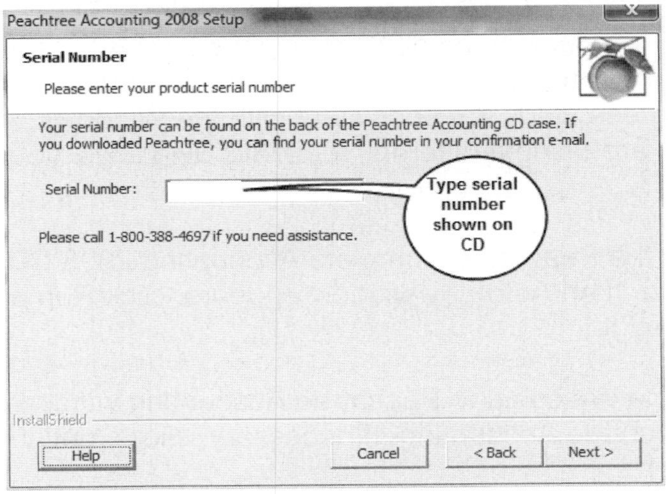

Step 7: Click 

.

Step 8: The Standalone or Network window appears. Make the appropriate selection. Yes is the default for individual computers.

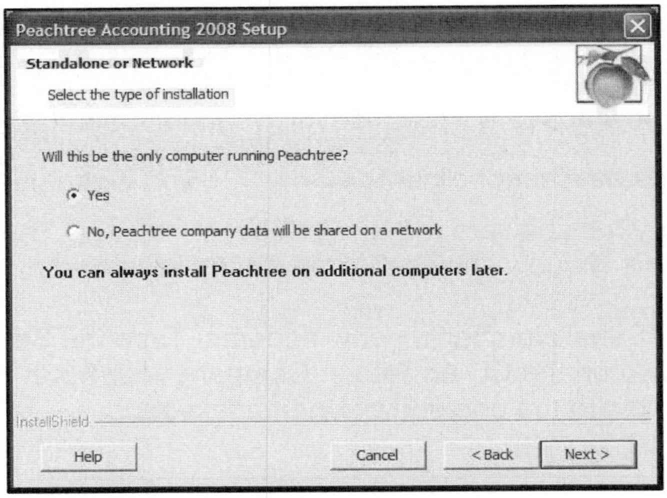

Step 9: Click 

.

Step 10: The Peachtree Company Data Location window appears. Yes is the default for individual computers. The author suggests accepting the default.

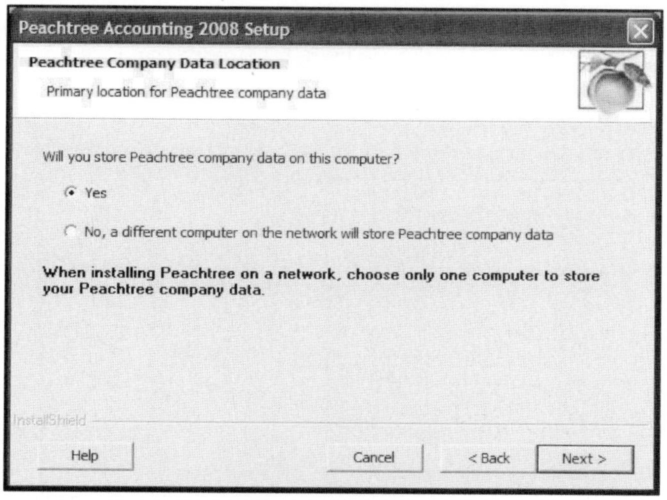

Step 11: Click 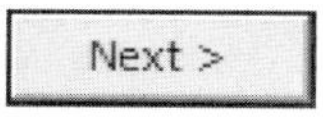

.

Step 12: The Set Peachtree Program Files Location window appears. Accept the default or click Browse to set another location.

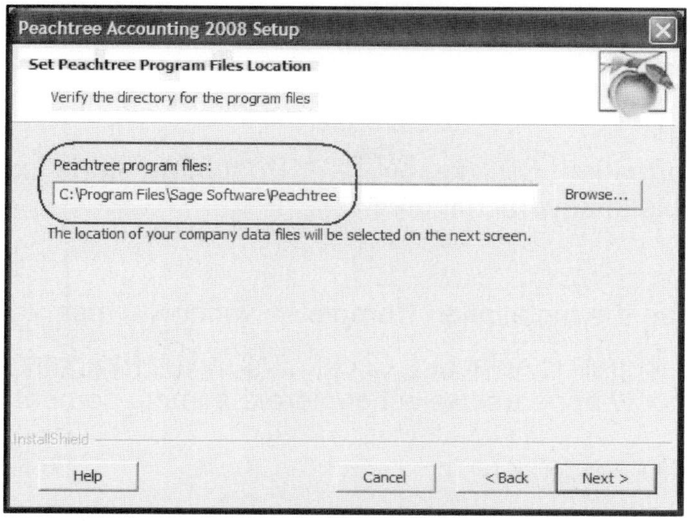

Step 13: Click Next >. The Peachtree Company Data Location window appears. Read the information. Accept the default or click Browse to set another location.

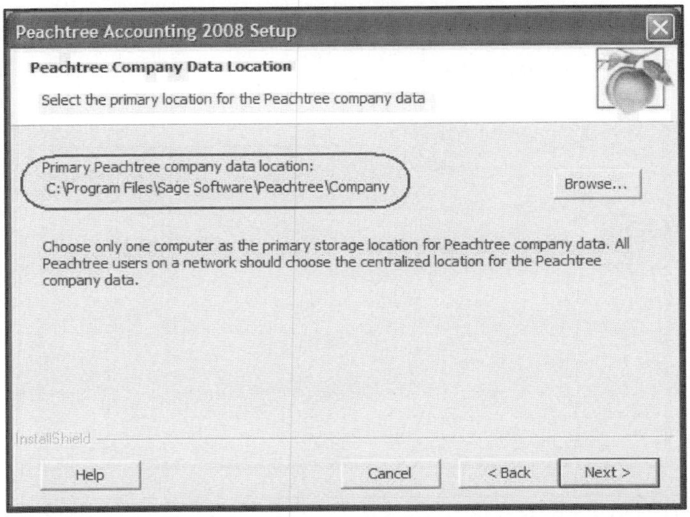

> **Comment**
>
> If a System Requirements window warns RAM is not large enough or processing speed is too slow, you may continue installation but Peachtree 2008 may run slower. Minimum system requirements are shown on pages iii-iv.

Step 14: Click Next >. The Summary window appears. Review this information. Click Install. Peachtree starts to install. This will take several minutes.

Step 15: Read the Installation Completed window. Observe that Start Peachtree is selected. Click Finish. Peachtree's startup window appears. Select explore a sample company.

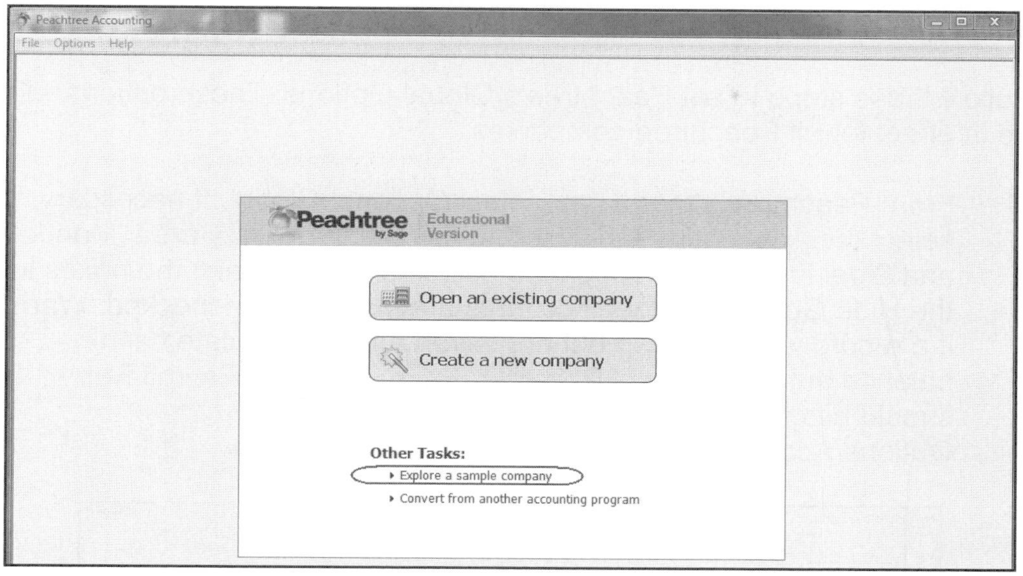

Step 16: The Explore a Sample Company window appears. The default is Bellwether Garden Supply.

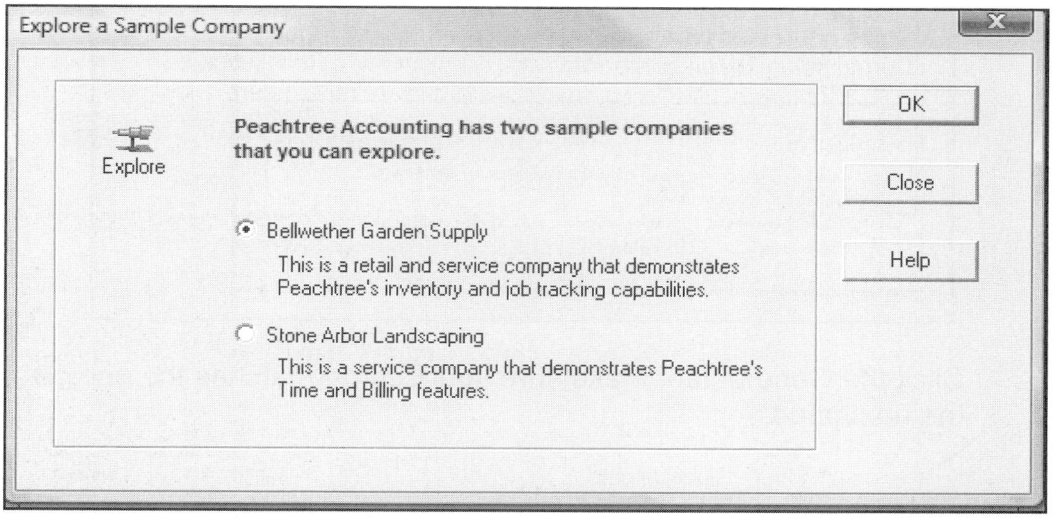

Step 17: Click OK. After a few moments the Bellwether Garden Supply opens.

Setting Global Options

Follow these steps to set Peachtree's Global Options. These options will be in effect for all Peachtree companies.

1. From Peachtree's menu bar, select Options; Global. If necessary, select the Accounting tab. (*Hint:* In the Decimal Entry area, Manual and 2 decimal places should be selected in each field; the boxes in the Hide General Ledger Accounts area *must* be unchecked; Warn if a record was changed but not saved and Recalculate cash balance automatically in Receipts, Payments, and Payroll Entry should be checked.) Compare the Maintain Global Options/Accounting window to the one shown below.

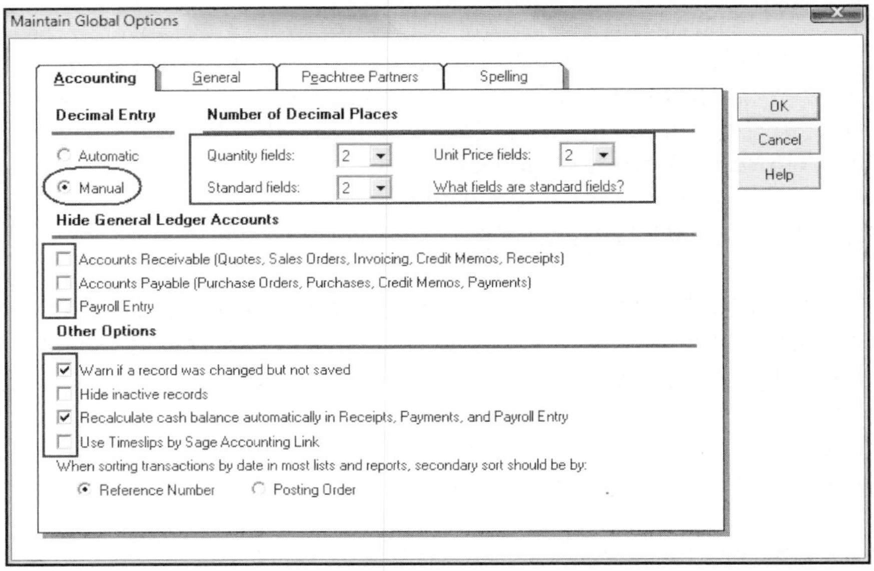

2. Click the General tab. Make sure your screen matches the one on the next page.

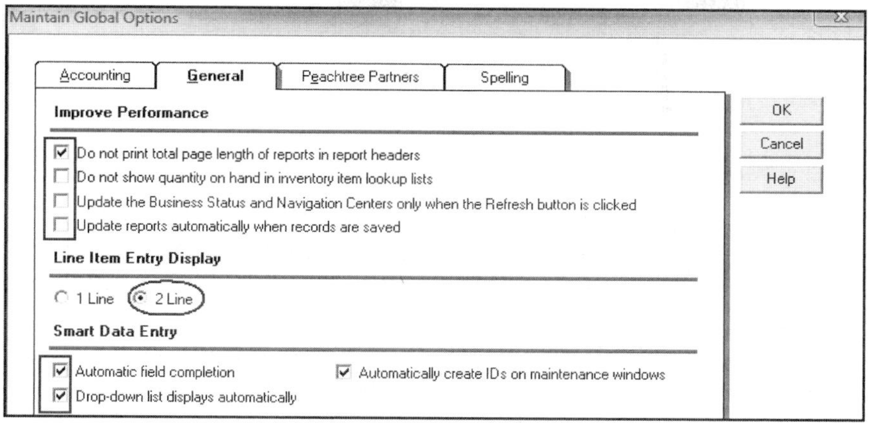

3. Click 

. The selections made in global options are now set for each Peachtree company.
4. From Peachtree's menu bar, click File, Exit. You are returned to the Peachtree Complete Accounting 2008 Install window. Click Exit. You are returned to the desktop.
5. Remove the CD from your drive.

COMPUTER LAB INSTALLATION

Before computer lab installation, make sure all former versions of Peachtree are deleted. Refer to page xii; Deleting Peachtree. For detailed steps, refer to Appendix A, Troubleshooting, pages 702-705.

1. Peachtree Complete Accounting 2008-Education Version should be installed locally. Do *not* put on server.

2. Install software on local workstation then ghost (replicate) install.

INSTALLING MICROSOFT INTERNET EXPLORER

To use PCA 2008, Microsoft Internet Explorer 6.0 SP1 (or higher) should be installed on your computer. If you do *not* have Internet Explorer 6.0 SP1, you can install it from the CD included with the textbook. (Put the CD into your CD drive, and browse to the location of the IE6SP1 folder, then open the ie6setup.exe file.)

Peachtree uses components of the Microsoft Internet Explorer Web browser. Peachtree's HTML Help viewer also uses Microsoft Internet Explorer components.

Peachtree does **not** require that Internet Explorer be your default Web browser. However, Peachtree does require that IE be installed on your computer. Also, an Internet connection is *not required* to run Peachtree. However, an Internet connection is recommended to take advantage of Peachtree's online and Internet-related features.

INSTALLING ADOBE ACROBAT READER

Electronic versions of the Peachtree manuals are automatically installed during the standard Peachtree setup process. To display or use these manuals, you must have Adobe Acrobat reader installed on your computer. Adobe Acrobat Reader can be installed from the Peachtree Complete Accounting 2008 CD or downloaded for free at www.adobe.com. Follow these steps to install Adobe Acrobat Reader from the Peachtree Complete Accounting 2008 CD included with the textbook.

1. Insert the Peachtree Complete Accounting 2008 CD in your CD-ROM drive. The Welcome to Peachtree Accounting window appears. Click Browse CD.
2. Double-click on the Acrobat folder.
3. To install Adobe Acrobat, click on the AdbeRdr70_enu_full.exe file.
4. Follow the prompts to install Adobe Acrobat Reader 7.0.
5. Click Exit on the Welcome to Peachtree Accounting window.
6. Remove the Peachtree Complete Accounting 2008 CD.

DELETING PEACHTREE

Use Control Panel's, Uninstall a program selection (Add/Remove programs in Windows XP) to uninstall Peachtree. After removal, you may want to delete the Sage Software folder at C:\Program Files\Sage Software. If you remove the Sage Software folder, all company data files are removed.

For detailed steps for removing Peachtree 2007 and earlier versions of Peachtree, refer to Appendix A, Troubleshooting, page 702-705.

Preface

Computer Accounting with Peachtree Complete Accounting 2008, Release 15, 12th Edition, teaches you how to use Peachtree Complete Accounting 2008 software. Peachtree is widely used by individuals, businesses, and accountants. For more than 30 years, Peachtree by Sage (www.sagesoftware.com) has produced award-winning accounting software. More than 2.6 million small and mid-sized business customers in North America rely on Peachtree and Sage Software products.

System Requirements: Recommended System Configuration

- 1 GHz Intel Pentium III (or equivalent) for single user and 1.8 GHz Intel Pentium 4 (or equivalent) for multiple concurrent users.
- 512 MB of RAM for single user and 1GB for multiple concurrent users.

Minimum System Requirements

- At least 1 GHz Intel Pentium III (or equivalent).
- 256 MB of RAM for single user and 512 MB for multiple concurrent users.
- Microsoft Windows Vista (all versions); Windows XP SP2 or Windows 2000 SP3.
- 1 GB of disk space for installation.
- Internet Explorer 6 required (provided on CD; requires an additional 70 MB); Internet 7.0 supported.
- Microsoft .NET Framework CLR 2.0 (provided on CD; requires an additional 280 MB).
- At least high color (16bit) SVGA video; supports 800X600 resolution with small fonts. Optimized for 1024 x 768.
- Online features require Internet access with at least a 56 Kbps modem.
- CD-ROM drive.
- Printers supported by Windows Vista/XP/2000.
- Mouse or compatible pointing device.
- Microsoft Excel, Outlook, and Word integration requires 2000, 2002, 2003, or 2007.
- Adobe Reader 7.0 required provided on CD (requires an additional 90 MB hard disk space to install).
- *External media for Chapter 1-18 backups*: One USB drive; Zip™ drive disk; CD-R; or, DVD-R. (CD-RW or DVD-RW required for backing up to CD-R or DVD-R.) *Or,* ten blank, formatted disks. The author suggests that you reformat floppy disks.

- *Optional requirement:* Microsoft Excel, Outlook and Word integration requires 2000 and higher.

Multi-User

- Multi-user mode is optimized for Windows 2000 Server or Windows Server 2003 client-server networks, and Windows 2000/XP peer-to-peer networks.

NEW *The software, Peachtree Complete Accounting 2008, Educational Version, is included with the textbook.* For software installation instructions, see pages iii-xii, Software Installation.

> **Read Me:**
> Install the software, Peachtree Complete Accounting 2008 Educational Version, included with the textbook, in the computer lab. This ensures software compatibility between the school and students' off-site installation. The site License Agreement is included on Peachtree's Help menu.

NEW *Textbook website at www.mhhe.com/yacht2008.*

PEACHTREE COMPLETE ACCOUNTING 2008

Each textbook includes a copy of the software, Peachtree Complete Accounting 2008, Educational Version. A software site license is included for installation on individual or networked computers. (From Peachtree's Help menu, select License Agreement.) Install the software included with the textbook in the school's computer lab to ensure compatibility with the software that your students install on their home or office computers.

NEW *PowerPoint slides for Chapters 1 - 18 on the textbook's website at www.mhhe.com/yacht2008.*

NEW *Read Me reminders and troubleshooting tips in the textbook and on the website.*

Computer Accounting with Peachtree Complete 2008, 12th Edition, shows you how to set up service, merchandising, nonprofit, and manufacturing businesses. When the textbook is completed, you have a working familiarity with Peachtree Complete Accounting 2008 software.
The Part 1, 2, 3, and 4 introductions include a chart showing the chapter number, backup name, size in kilobytes of each file backed up or saved, and page numbers where each backup is made.

Some of the **new features** included in *Computer Accounting with Peachtree Complete 2008, 12e*, are:

- **NEW!** Software installation, including serial number, at the beginning of textbook, pages iii-xii.
- Site License Agreement included on Help Menu for standalone and multi-user installations.
- **NEW!** All instructions, screen captures, and detailed steps are consistent with the Windows Vista operating system, Windows XP SP2, and Windows 2000 SP3.
- **NEW!** Navigation Bar includes Business Status; Customers & Sales; Vendors & Purchases; Inventory & Services; Employees & Payroll; Banking; Company.
- Navigation interface to access information and record transactions; drill down to lists, reports, setup windows, and graphs.
- Enhanced Excel Integration.
- **NEW!** Comparative budget spreadsheet creator.
- **NEW!** Create letter templates wizard.
- **NEW!** Sales tax wizard.
- Improved audit trail and internal controls.
- Daily customer balances on sales and customers windows.
- **NEW!** Custom date-range filtering and enhanced report options.
- Restore Wizard lets you restore An Existing Company or A New Company.
- Smart sort for account identification.
- Auto-complete text fields and spell check.
- Internal accounting review.
- **NEW!** E-mail reports, financial statements, and add attachments.
- **NEW!** Design tools for report customization.
- Easy-to-use checkbook register.
- Vendor payment terms are tracked in the cost of sales account, Purchase Discounts.
- **NEW!** Automatically create IDs.
- Set up 11 **new** service, retail, nonprofit, and manufacturing businesses from scratch.

PART 1: EXPLORING PEACHTREE COMPLETE ACCOUNTING 2008

There are two sample companies included with the software: Bellwether Garden Supply and Stone Arbor Landscaping. Bellwether Garden Supply is a retail business and service company that demonstrates inventory and job tracking capabilities. Stone Arbor Landscaping is a service company that demonstrates time and billing.

In Part 1 of the textbook, you complete eight chapters that demonstrate how Peachtree is used. This introduces you to the procedures that will be used with all the chapters of the textbook.

NEW *Chapter 1, Introduction to Bellwether Garden Supply, includes Peachtree's Navigation Centers and Restore Wizard for opening new or existing companies.*

NEW *Chapter 2, Vendors, shows you how to view accounts payable lists and reports from the Vendors & Payables Navigation Center as well as custom date filtering.*

NEW *Chapter 3, Customers, shows you how to view customer lists and reports from the Customers & Sales Navigation Center as well as custom date filtering.*

NEW *Chapter 5, General Ledger, Inventory, and Internal Control, shows you Peachtree's new budget feature and easy export to Export. Chapter 5 also includes Peachtree's internal controls and audit trail.*

PART 2: PEACHTREE COMPLETE ACCOUNTING 2008 FOR SERVICE BUSINESSES

Chapters 9, 10, Project 1, and Project 1A are included in this section of the textbook. The work completed in Chapter 9 is continued in Chapter 10. The accounting cycle is completed for the fourth quarter of the year.

NEW *In Chapter 9, Maintaining Accounting Records for Service Businesses, you set up two service companies—Jon Haney Design and Student Name, Designer—with Peachtree's simplified chart of accounts. You use Peachtree's new Company Setup Wizard and list feature to drill down to original entries. You also use Peachtree's enhanced account reconciliation.*

Chapter 10, Completing Quarterly Activities and Closing the Fiscal Year, shows you how to complete adjusting entries, print financial statements, and close the fiscal year.

Exercises 9-1 through 10-2 include three months of transactions, account reconciliation, adjusting entries, financial statements, and Peachtree's closing procedure.

NEW *Project 1, Mary Albert, Accountant, is a comprehensive project that reviews what you have learned in Chapters 9 and 10.*
Project 1A, Student-Designed Service Business, shows you how to design a service business from scratch. You set up the business, choose a chart of accounts, create a Balance Sheet, write business transactions, complete the computer accounting cycle, and close the fiscal year.

PART 3: PEACHTREE COMPLETE ACCOUNTING 2008 FOR MERCHANDISING BUSINESSES

Chapters 11, 12, 13, 14, Project 2, and Project 2A are included in this section of the textbook. Students set up two merchandising businesses in Chapter 11—Susan's Service Merchandise *and* Student Name Sales & Service. The work started in Chapter 11 is continued in Chapters 12, 13 and 14.

In Chapter 11, Vendors & Purchases, use Peachtree's accounts payable system; record inventory purchases and payments from vendors; set up vendor defaults to automatically track purchase discounts; and use vendor credit memos for purchase returns.

In Chapter 12, Customers & Sales, use Peachtree's accounts receivable system; record cash and credit sales and receipts from customers; set up customer defaults; use credit memos for sales returns.

Chapter 13, Inventory & Services, shows you how to use Peachtree's inventory system.

NEW *Chapter 14, Employees, Payroll and Account Reconciliation, shows how to use Peachtree's payroll system and reconcile accounts. Peachtree's payroll includes automatic payroll tax calculations. Example payroll tax withholding tables are included with the educational version software. Account reconciliation shows you how Peachtree's Accounts Payable, Accounts Receivable, Inventory, and General Ledger systems work together. Chapter 14 includes bank statements for both the checking account and payroll account.*

NEW *Project 2, Stanley's Sports, is a comprehensive project that incorporates what you have learned in Chapters 11 through 14.*

Project 2A, Student-Designed Merchandising Business, asks you to create a merchandising business from scratch.

PART 4: ADVANCED PEACHTREE COMPLETE ACCOUNTING 2008 APPLICATIONS

Chapters 15, 16, 17, 18, Project 3, Project 4, and Project 4A are included in this section of the textbook. Chapter 15, Customizing Forms, shows you how to use Peachtree's design tools. Chapter 16, Import/Export, shows you how to export data from Peachtree Complete Accounting 2008 to a word processing program. Chapter 17, Using Peachtree Complete Accounting 2008 with Microsoft Excel and Word, shows you how to use Peachtree with two Microsoft Office 2000 or later applications. In Chapter 18, Write Letters, Use Templates, and Peachtree Online, you work with Peachtree's templates.

NEW *Chapter 15, Customizing Forms, new design tools for report customization.*

NEW *Chapter 18, Write Letters, Use Templates, and Peachtree Online, includes Peachtree's Write Letters and templates feature.*

NEW *Project 3, Verde Computer Club, is a nonprofit business.*

NEW *Project 4, BJW Manufacturing, Inc., is the culminating project in your study of Peachtree Complete Accounting 2008.*

Project 4A, Student-Designed Project, instructs you to write another month's transactions for one of the four projects completed.

CONVENTIONS USED IN TEXTBOOK

As you work through *Computer Accounting with Peachtree Complete 2008, 12e*, you should read and follow the step-by-step instructions. Numerous screen illustrations help you to check your work.

The following conventions are used in this text:

1. Information that you are to type appear in boldface; for example, Type **Supplies** in the Account ID field.
2. Keys on the keyboard that should be pressed appear in brackets; for example, <Enter>.
3. Unnamed buttons and picture icons are shown as they actually appear on the screen.

Examples: 

(Next button)

(Display icon)

PEACHTREE'S GLOBAL OPTIONS

Follow these steps to set global options for Peachtree. These options will be in effect for all Peachtree companies. Software Installation, Setting Global Options, pages x-xi, also includes these steps.

1. Start Peachtree.

2. Open any company. For example, see pages 11-14 for detailed steps to open the sample company, Bellwether Garden Supply.

3. From Peachtree's menu bar, select Options; Global. If necessary, select the Accounting tab. (*Hint:* In the Decimal Entry area, Manual and 2 decimal places should be selected; the boxes in the Hide General Ledger Accounts area *must* be unchecked; Warn if a record was changed but not saved and Recalculate cash balance automatically in Receipts, Payments, and Payroll Entry should be checked.) Compare the Maintain Global Options/Accounting window to the one shown below.

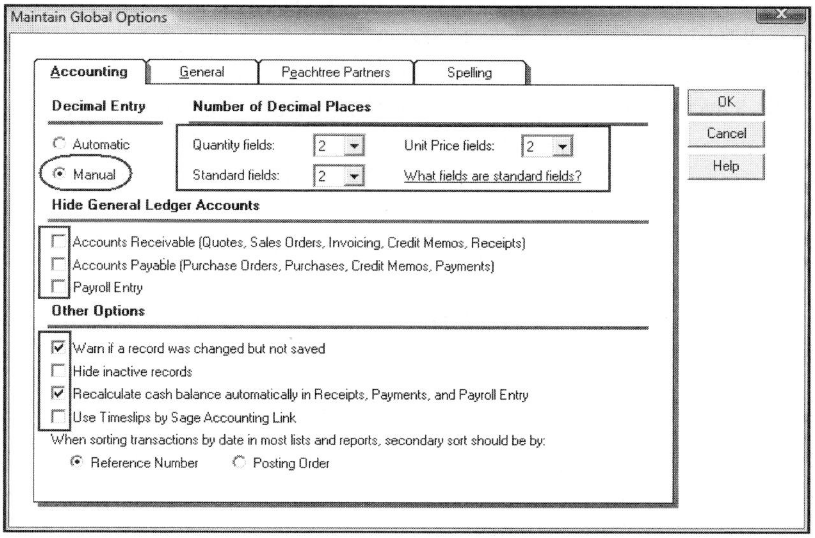

4. Click the General tab. Make sure your screen matches the one below.

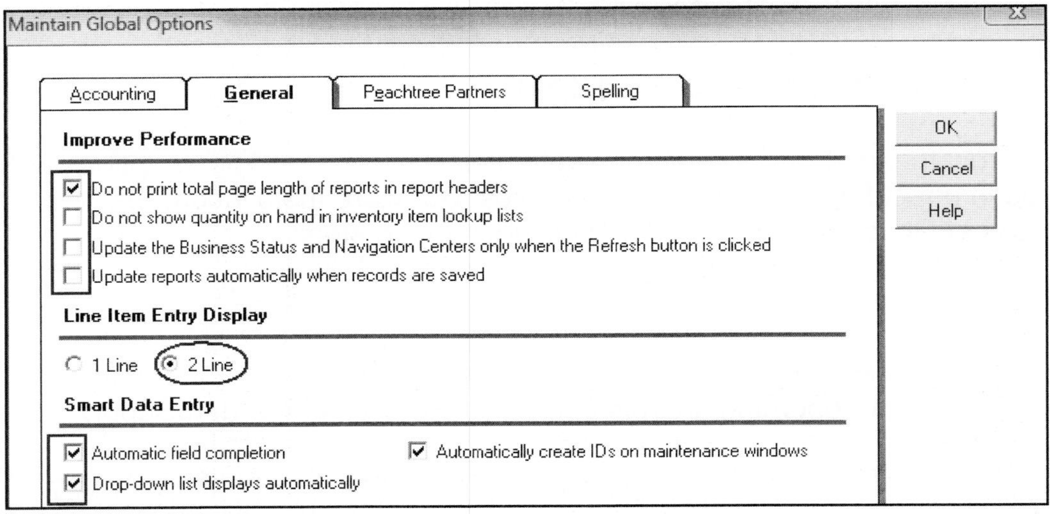

5. Click 

. The selections made in global options are now set for each Peachtree company that is used.

The textbook ends with three appendixes: Appendix A, Troubleshooting; Appendix B, Review of Accounting Principles; and Appendix C, Glossary. The glossary is also included on the textbook website at www.mhhe.com/yacht2008.

Index: Each chapter in the textbook ends with an index. The index at the end of the textbook is an alphabetic listing of the chapter indexes.

Carol Yacht, Author
Computer Accounting with Peachtree Complete Accounting 2008, 12e
www.mhhe.com/yacht2008
carol@carolyacht.com

Acknowledgments

I would like to thank the following colleagues for their help in the preparation of this book: Stewart Mattson; Steve Schuetz; Beth Woods, CPA; Sharon Clarke, Accountant; and Matt Lowenkron. A special thank you to the following accounting professors.

Diane Ardans, American River College
Robert S. Beattie, Hudson Valley CC
Linda Bolduc, Mt. Wachusett College
Marianne Bradford, NC State University
Ashley Burrowes, Univ. of Wisconsin
Judye Cadle, Tarleton State University
Vickie Campbell, Cape Fear CC
Susan Crosson, Santa Fe Community Coll.
Robert Dansby, Columbus Tech. Institute
Alan Davis, Comm. Coll. of Philadelphia
Dave Davis, Vincennes University
Roger Dimick, Lamar Inst. of Technology
George Dorrance, Mission College
Philip Empey, Purdue University-Calumet
David R. Fordham, James Madison Univ.
Stephen Fogg, Temple University
Michael Fujita, Leeward Community College
Bill Gaither, Dawson Community College
Joyce Griffin, Kansas City Kansas CC
Bill Guidera, Texas State Technical College
Jean Guttman, University of So. Maine
Norma Hall, Manor Junior College
Jim Hale, Vance-Granville Community Coll.
Mark Henry, Victoria College
Geoffrey Heriot, Greenville Tech. College
Jeff Jackson, San Jacinto College
Robert Jackson, Ivy State Tech College
Bob Johnson, Jefferson College
William Lambert, University of Houston
Judy Kidder, Mohave Community College
Alex Kogan, Rutgers University
Linda Kropp, Modesto Junior College
Bruce Lindsey, Genesee Community Coll.
Susan Looney, Mohave Community Coll.
Susan Lynn, University of Baltimore
Charles McCord, Portland Comm. College
Jack Neymark, Oakton Community College
Nancy O'Connor, Whittier Adult School
Sara Lagier, American Business College
Pat Olson, Moraine Park Technical College
Vincent Osaghae, Chicago State University
Michael Papke, Kellogg Community College
Timothy Pearson, West Virginia University
Simon Petravick, Bradley University
Joel Peralto, Hawaii Community College
Gerald Peterka, Mt. San Jacinto College
Tom Pinckney, Trident Technical College
Mildred Polisky, Milwaukee Area Tech. College
Robert Porter, Cape Fear Community College
Susan Pope, University of Akron
Charlotte Pryor, University of Southern Maine
Iris Lugo Renta, Interamerican University
Betty J. Reynolds, Arizona Western College
Monique Ring, So. New Hampshire University
Annalee Rothenberg, Tacoma Community Coll.
Diane Sandefur, Elliott Bookkeeping School
Art Shroeder, Louisiana State University
Joann Segovia, Minnesota State University
Donald Schwartz, National University
Warren Smock, Ivy Tech State College
Charles Strang, Western New Mexico Univ.
Tom Sentman, Skadron College
Marilyn St. Clair, Weatherford College
Marie Stewart, Newport Business Institute
Maggie Stone, Pima Community College
Mel Sweet, University of Connecticut
Laurie Swinney, University of Nebraska
Greg Thom, Parkland Community College
Tom Turner, Des Moines Area Community Coll.
Jamie Vaught, Southeast Community College
Mazdolyn Winston, Calhoun Community Coll.
W. Brian Voss, Austin Community College
Bruce Whitaker, Dine College
Michele Wiltsie, Hudson Valley Comm. Coll.

I would also like to extend a special thank you to my students and appreciation to the many professors who stay in touch.

Table of Contents

The Timetable for Completion shown on the next page is a guideline for in-class lecture/discussion/ demonstration and hands-on work. Work *not* completed in class is homework. In most Accounting classes, students can expect to spend approximately 2 hours outside of class for every hour in class.

TIMETABLE FOR COMPLETION		Hours
Part 1: Exploring Peachtree Complete Accounting 2008		
Chapter 1	Introduction to Bellwether Garden Supply	2.0
Chapter 2	Vendor Transactions	1.0
Chapter 3	Customer Transactions	1.0
Chapter 4	Employees	1.0
Chapter 5	General Ledger, Inventory, and Internal Control	1.0
Chapter 6	Job Cost	2.0
Chapter 7	Financial Statements	1.0
Chapter 8	Stone Arbor Landscaping: Time & Billing	1.0
	Subtotal Part 1	10.0
Part 2: Peachtree Complete Accounting 2008 for Service Businesses		
Chapter 9	Maintaining Accounting Records for Service Businesses	2.5
Chapter 10	Completing Quarterly Activities and Closing the Fiscal Year	2.0
Project 1	Mary Albert, Accountant	2.5
Project 1A	Student-Designed Service Business	2.0
	Subtotal Part 2	*9.0*
Part 3: Peachtree Complete Accounting 2008 for Merchandising Businesses		
Chapter 11	Vendors & Purchases	3.0
Chapter 12	Customers & Sales	2.5
Chapter 13	Inventory & Services	2.0
Chapter 14	Employees, Payroll, and Account Reconciliation	2.0
Project 2	Stanley's Sports	3.5
Project 2A	Student-Designed Merchandising Business	3.0
	Subtotal Part 3	*16.0*
Part 4: Advanced Peachtree Complete Accounting 2008 Applications		
Chapter 15	Customizing Forms	1.0
Chapter 16	Import/Export	1.0
Chapter 17	Using Peachtree Complete Accounting 2008 with Excel and Word	1.0
Chapter 18	Write Letters, Use Templates, and Peachtree Online	1.0
Project 3	Verde Computer Club	1.0
Project 4	BJW Manufacturing, Inc.	3.0
Project 4A	Student-Designed Project	2.0
	Subtotal Part 4	*10.0*
	TOTAL HOURS: PARTS 1, 2, 3, 4	**45.0**

Part 1

Exploring Peachtree Complete Accounting 2008

Part 1 introduces the basic features of Peachtree Complete Accounting 2008. The purpose of Part 1 is to help you become familiar with the software rather than test accounting knowledge. Beginning with Chapter 9, computer accounting skills are reviewed in more depth. In Chapters 9-18 and Projects 1-4A, eleven businesses are set up from scratch. Part 1 introduces you to Peachtree and the two sample companies that are included with the software.

Part 1 includes eight chapters:

Chapter 1: Introduction to Bellwether Garden Supply
Chapter 2: Vendor
Chapter 3: Customers
Chapter 4: Employees
Chapter 5: General Ledger, Inventory, and Internal Control
Chapter 6: Job Cost
Chapter 7: Financial Statements
Chapter 8: Stone Arbor Landscaping: Time & Billing

The instructions in this book were written for Peachtree Complete Accounting 2008 (abbreviated PCA). PCA requires Windows Vista, XP SP2 or Windows 2000 SP3. Multi-user mode is optimized for Windows 2000 Server or Windows Server 2003 client-server networks, and Windows 2000/XP peer-to-peer networks.

Windows[1] uses pictures or ***icons*** to identify tasks. This is known as a ***graphical user interface*** (***GUI***). The graphical user interface is also called the ***user interface***. For example, PCA uses common icons or symbols to represent tasks: a file folder, a trash can for deleting, an hourglass to show that the program is waiting for a task to be performed, a printer, etc. Your keyboard with a ***mouse***, ***trackball*** or other pointing device is used to perform various tasks.

[1] Words that are boldfaced and italicized are defined in the Glossary. The Glossary is on the textbook's website at www.mhhe.com/yacht2008.

Software design can be described by the acronym ***WIMP*** -- Windows, Icons, Menus, and Pull-downs.

In the chart below, the size of the backups made in Part 1 are shown. In Chapters 1-8, textbook steps explain how to back up to Peachtree's default hard drive location for Bellwether Garden Supply at C:\Program Files\ Sage Software\Peachtree\Company\BCS\[backup name]; *and* for Stone Arbor Landscaping at C:\Program Files\Sage Software\ Peachtree\ Company\!PDG\[backup name].

You can specify a hard drive or network location; or, back up to external media, such as, a USB drive, CD-RW drive, DVD-RW drive, or Zip drive. (Part 1 backups are too large for one floppy disk. If using floppy disks for backups, you need two or more blank formatted disks for each backup.)

Chapter	Backup Name	Kilobytes[2]	Page Nos.
1	bgs[3]	3,255 KB	18-21
	Chapter 1	3,235 KB	40-41
	Exercise 1-2	3,240 KB	49-50
2	Chapter 2	3,302 KB	81-82
	Exercise 2-2	3,300 KB	88-89
3	Chapter 3	3,345 KB	121-122
	Exercise 3-2	3,363 KB	127
4	Chapter 4	3,396 KB	145-146
	Exercise 4-2	3,392 KB	151
5	Chapter 5	3,408 KB	182-183
	Exercise 5-2	3,411 KB	188
6	Chapter 6	3,457 KB	199-200
	Exercise 6-2[4]	3,459 KB	204
7	No backups in Chapter 7	--	--
8	Chapter 8	1,876	239-240

Read Me: Windows Vista—Problem Backing Up to USB Drive

Because of Windows Vista operating system security features, you need to backup to your desktop first. Then copy the backup file from your desktop to the USB drive. Refer to Appendix A, Problem Backing Up to USB Drive or Other External Media, pages 700-702 for detailed steps.

[2]Your backup sizes may differ.

[3]This is the first backup and includes starting data for Bellwether Garden Supply.

[4]This back up file is used in Part 4, Chapters 15, 16, 17, and 18. If necessary, backup to external media. Do *not* delete the Exercise 6-2.ptb file.

Chapter 1 Introduction to Bellwether Garden Supply

SOFTWARE OBJECTIVES: In Chapter 1, you use the software to:

1. Start Peachtree Complete Accounting 2008 (PCA).[1]
2. Explore the sample company, Bellwether Garden Supply.
3. Back up Bellwether Garden Supply data.
4. Restore data with Peachtree's restore Wizard.
5. Operate Peachtree's menus, drop-down lists, toolbar, and navigation bar.
6. Work with Windows Explorer.
7. Make three backups: 1) Back up starting data for Bellwether Garden Supply; 2) back up Chapter 1 data; and 3) back up Exercise 1-2.[2]

WEB OBJECTIVES: In Chapter 1, you do these Internet activities:

1. Use PCA to link to Peachtree's website at www.peachtree.com.
2. Go to the PRESS list and select Recent Press Releases.
3. Link to two Peachtree press releases and write an essay about each one.
4. Use your Internet browser to go to the book's website at www.mhhe.com/yacht2008.
5. Complete the first web exercise in Part 1.

Peachtree Complete Accounting 2008 (PCA) is similar to other programs that use Windows. If you have used other Windows programs, you will see the similarities in the menus and windows, entering and saving data, and selecting icons. If you are not familiar with Windows, using PCA will help you become familiar with the Windows operating system.

---

[1] If Peachtree Complete Accounting 2008 is not installed see Software Installation, pages iii-xii. The sample companies must be installed to complete Chapters 1–8.

[2] Refer to the chart on page 2 for the size of backup files.

MOUSE AND KEYBOARD BASICS

One of the first decisions you need to make is whether you want to use your mouse or keyboard. The instructions in this book assume that you are using a mouse. When the word click is used in the instructions, it means to use the mouse, but you can also use the keyboard. The instructions below explain how to use the mouse or keyboard.

Using the Mouse

- To single click: position the mouse cursor over the selection and click the left mouse button once.
- To double-click: position the mouse cursor over the selection and click the left mouse button twice, quickly.
- Use the right mouse button the same way as the left mouse button.

Using the Keyboard

- If there is an underlined letter in the menu or option you want to select, hold down the **<Alt>**[3] key and the underlined letter to make the selection.
- If you have already held down the **<Alt>** key and the underlined letter and more selections appear with underlined letters, just type the underlined letter to select the item.

Using Shortcut Keys

Shortcut keys enable you to perform common operations by using two or more keys together. The tables on the next page show the shortcut keys.

[3]The angle brackets are used around words to indicate individual keys on your keyboard; for example, **<Alt>** is for the Alternate key, **<Enter>** for the Enter/Return key, **<Ctrl>** is for the Control key, **<Esc>** is for the Escape key.

<Ctrl> + <Letter> Shortcuts	
<Ctrl> + <X>	Cut
<Ctrl> + <C>	Copy
<Ctrl> + <V>	Paste
<Ctrl> + <E>	Erase
<Ctrl> + <N>	New Company
<Ctrl> + <O>	Open Company
<Ctrl> + <B>	Back Up Company
<Ctrl> + <R>	Restore Company
<Ctrl> + <P>	Print purchase orders, quotes, invoices, payments or reports
<Ctrl> + <F>	Find
<Ctrl> + <D>	Find Next
Function Key Shortcuts	
<F1>	Displays the online Help
<Ctrl> + <F4>	Closes the current window
<Alt> + <F4>	Closes the application window
<Ctrl> + <F6>	Moves to the next window
<Shift> + <Ctrl> + <F6>	Moves to the previous window
<F10>	Toggles the menu bar
<F5>	Saves the current record in maintenance windows

PCA'S STARTUP WINDOW

Peachtree's startup window gives you a number of options.

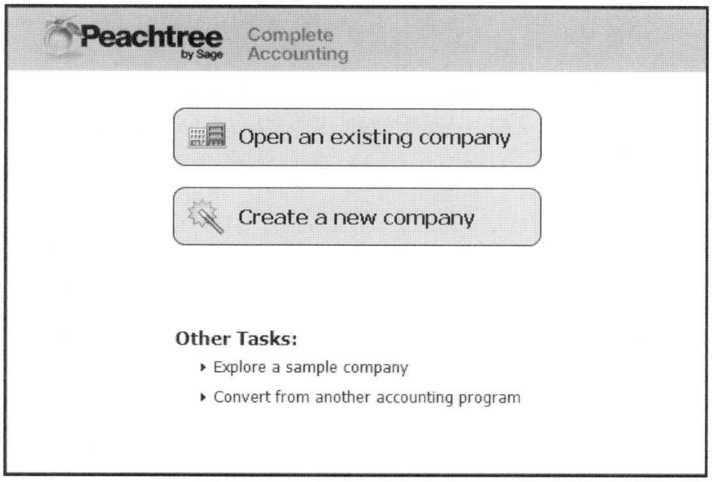

From the startup window, you can Open an existing company, Create a new company, Explore a sample company, and Convert from another accounting program.

Observe that the top-left of the Peachtree Accounting window has three menu-bar options—

.

You can also exit from the startup window by selecting File; Exit; *or*, clicking on the  on the upper right-hand side of the Peachtree Accounting window.

> **Comment**
>
> The illustrations in this textbook were done with Windows Vista and Peachtree Complete Accounting 2008, Educational Version.

THE WINDOWS ENVIRONMENT

One of the benefits of Windows is that it standardizes terms and operations used in software programs. Once you learn how to move around PCA, you also know how to use other Windows applications.

To learn more about the Windows environment, let's look at a PCA window. The Peachtree Accounting window on the next page shows the parts of a PCA window, the ***Business Status Center*** (the ***dashboard***), and the menu bar for Bellwether Garden Supply.

For now, let's study the parts of the window shown on the next page. Some features are common to all software programs that are written for Windows. For example, in the upper right corner there is the Minimize  button, Double Window  button, and the Exit or Close  button. The title bar, window border, and mouse pointer are also common to Windows programs. Other features are specific to PCA: menu bar, toolbar, Navigation Bar, and Navigation Centers.

PCA includes a Navigation Bar on the left side of the window with seven selections: Business Status; Customers & Sales; Vendors & Purchases; Inventory & Services; Employees and Payroll; Banking; and Company. The Navigation Bar selections open PCA's Navigation Centers. For example, the Business Status selection opens the Business Status Navigation Center page. The content of the Navigation Center pages differ depending on the selection from the Navigation Bar.

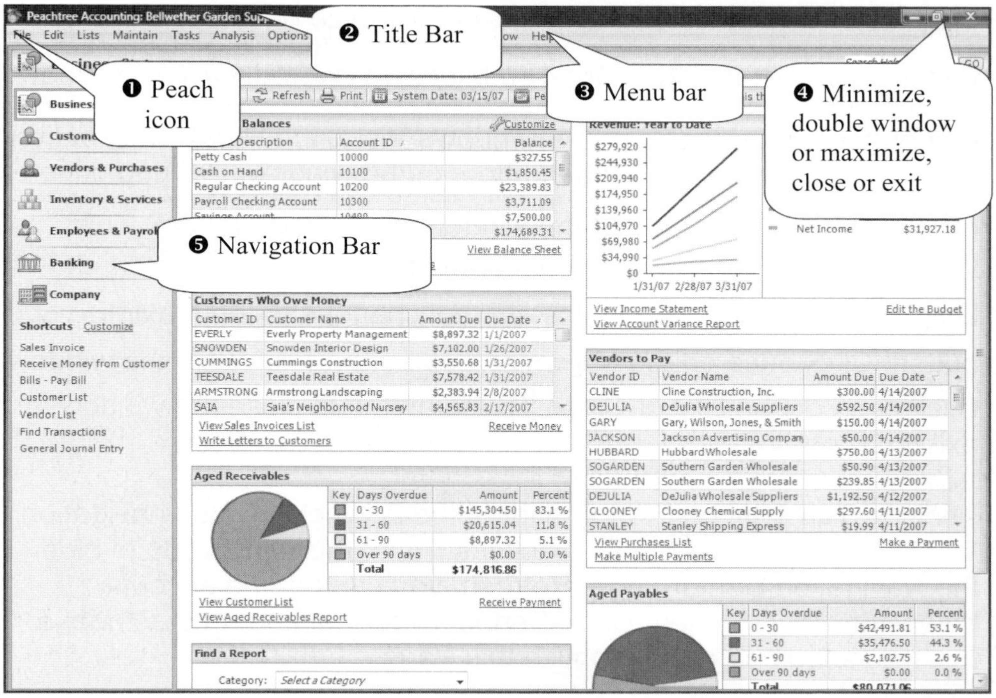

❶ Peach icon: Click on the Peach icon and a menu appears with options such as: Restore; Move, Size, Minimize, Maximize, Close.

❷ ***Title Bar***: The bar is at the top of the window. When a company is open in PCA, the name of the company is displayed on the Title Bar. If your window is minimized, you can put your mouse on the Title Bar, click and hold the left mouse button and drag the window around the ***desktop***. The title bar shows Peachtree Accounting: Bellwether Garden Supply.

❸ Menu Bar: In PCA 2008, Educational Version, there are ten menu bar selections. If your menu bar selections have underlined letters, that means you can make a selection by typing **<Alt>** and the underlined letter. For example, if you press the <Alt> key then press the <F> key, the menu bar shows underlined letters as well as the drop-down menu. You can also click with your left-mouse button on the menu bar headings to see a submenu of options.

❹ Minimize, Double Window, or Maximize, and Close or Exit buttons: Clicking once on Minimize reduces the window to a button on the ***taskbar***. In Windows Vista, the (Start) button and taskbar are located at the bottom of the window. Clicking once on Double Window returns the window to its previous size. This button appears when you maximize the window. After clicking on the Double Window button, the symbol changes to the Maximize button. Click once on the Maximize button to enlarge the window. Click once on the Exit or Close button to close the window, or exit the program.

❺ Toolbar: The gray bar[4] to the right of the Business Status navigation button shows the following selections: Hide, this allows you to hide the Navigation Center page; Refresh, you can update account balances; Print, System Date; Period for accounting records; Make this the default page; Customize this Page.

❻ Navigation Bar: Peachtree's Navigation Bar includes seven selections. These selections open the Navigation Center pages.

TYPICAL PCA WINDOWS

When you select a Navigation Bar button, the Navigation Center appears. On the next page the Maintain Customers/Prospects window is shown.

[4]Window colors may differ. Check with your instructor if you have a question.

You can enter information into the Maintain Customers/Prospects window by using your mouse to click on icons or by typing. The illustration below is the Maintain Customers/Prospects window, one that is typical of PCA. There are four sections on this window: ❶ the icon bar, ❷ Previous or next record, ❸ drop-down lists (down arrow), ❹ tabs.

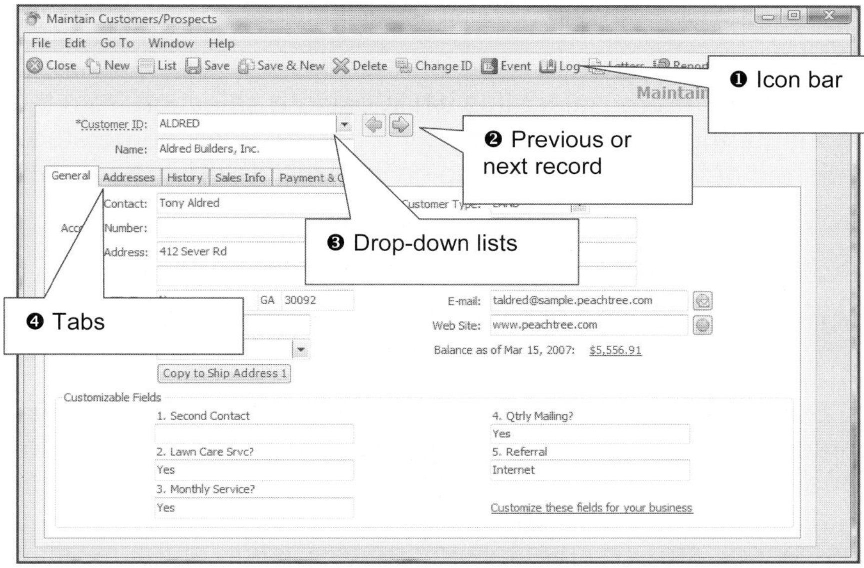

❶ ***Icon bar***[5]: The icon bar shows pictures of commands or additional information that pertains to the window. Some icons are common to all windows while other icons are specific to a particular window. The icons included in the Maintain Customers/Prospects window are:

Close: This closes the window without saving any work that has been typed since the last time you saved.

New: New record or customer.

List: List of customers.

[5]Notice that familiar business items are used for icons: disk for Save, an X for Delete, a calendar for Event.

Save: This saves information you have entered such as addresses, telephone numbers, contacts for vendors, customers, employees, etc.

Save & New: Save the record and go to a new, black record.

Delete: If you select this while using a selection from the Maintain menu, the record (customer, vendor, etc.) will be deleted. When you're finished deleting, select Close, in order to delete the records.

Change ID: When a customer record is displayed on the window, you may change the information for that customer.

Event: Select this button in various maintenance windows to create an event. The Create Event window allows you to schedule an event for a customer/prospect, vendor, or employee/sales representative. You can also use the Event log to record notes about telephone calls, meetings, letters, etc. You use this to create a listing of future activity as well.

Log: This shows you events recorded for an individual over a range of time that you specify. You can ***filter*** this list to see only certain types of activities and whether they're completed or not. You can mark activities as completed by placing a mark in the far left column. Double-clicking on any of the ***line items*** will take you to the Create an Event window. Line items appear on many of Peachtree's windows. On color monitors, a magenta line is placed around the row (line item) you select.

Letters: Select this button to process a mail merge for the currently opened record.

Reports: If you click on the down-arrow on the Reports icon, you can select the following customer reports—Aged Receivables; Customer Transaction History; Customer Ledger; Items Sold to

Customers; Job Ledger; Quote Register; Sales Order Register; Ticket Listing by Customer. (In this example, Maintain; Customers/ Prospects, Aldred Builders, Inc. is selected as the customer.)

 Help: This icon is displayed on most windows. Selecting this icon gives you information specific to the current window. The fields of the window are often listed at the bottom of the help message. When you have a question about how to use Peachtree, clicking on the Help icon often answers it.

❷  Previous or Next Record: Click on either the left arrow for the previous record; or the right arrow for the next record.

❸ ***Drop-Down List***: The down arrow means that this field contains a list of information from which you can make a selection. Many of PCA's windows have drop-down lists that appear when you click on a down arrow next to a field. You can press **<Enter>** or click on an item to select it from the list.

❹ ***Tabs***: The tabs that are shown in the Maintain Customers/Prospects window are General, Sales Defaults, Terms and Credit, Payment Defaults, Custom Fields, and History. Once a customer is selected, you can select one of these folders to display information about a customer.

THE SAMPLE COMPANY: BELLWETHER GARDEN SUPPLY

Bellwether Garden Supply is one of the sample companies included with PCA. You get a sampling of features that are developed in greater detail as you complete this book. The purpose of using the sample company is to help you become familiar with the software.

GETTING STARTED

Follow these steps to start Peachtree Complete Accounting 2008 (PCA):

1. Start PCA. If Peachtree Complete Accounting 2008 is not installed on your computer, refer to Software Installation, pages iii-xii, for installing the Peachtree Complete Accounting CD that is included with this textbook.

2. When Peachtree Complete Accounting 2008 (PCA) was installed, an icon was created for Peachtree. To start, place the mouse pointer on the Peachtree icon and double-click with the left mouse button. (Or, click Start, All Programs, Peachtree Complete Accounting Educational Version 2008. Then, select Peachtree Complete Accounting Educational Version 2008.)

3. The Peachtree Accounting window appears. From the startup window, you can Open an existing company; Create a new company; Explore a sample company; Convert from another accounting application; or Exit Peachtree.

4. Click Explore a sample company.

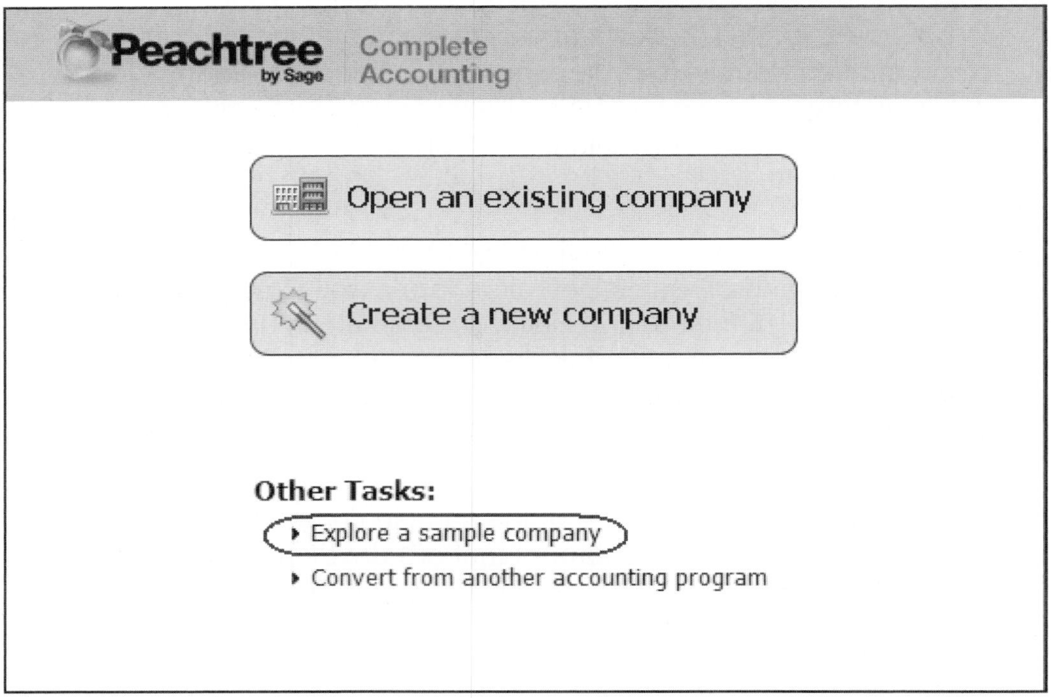

5. The Explore a Sample Company window appears. PCA 2008 has two sample companies: Bellwether Garden Supply and Stone Arbor Landscaping. In Chapters 1 – 7, you use Bellwether Garden Supply to explore Peachtree. Then, in Chapter 8, you use Stone Arbor Landscaping to see how Peachtree's time and billing feature works. Make sure that Bellwether Garden Supply is selected. Click 

.

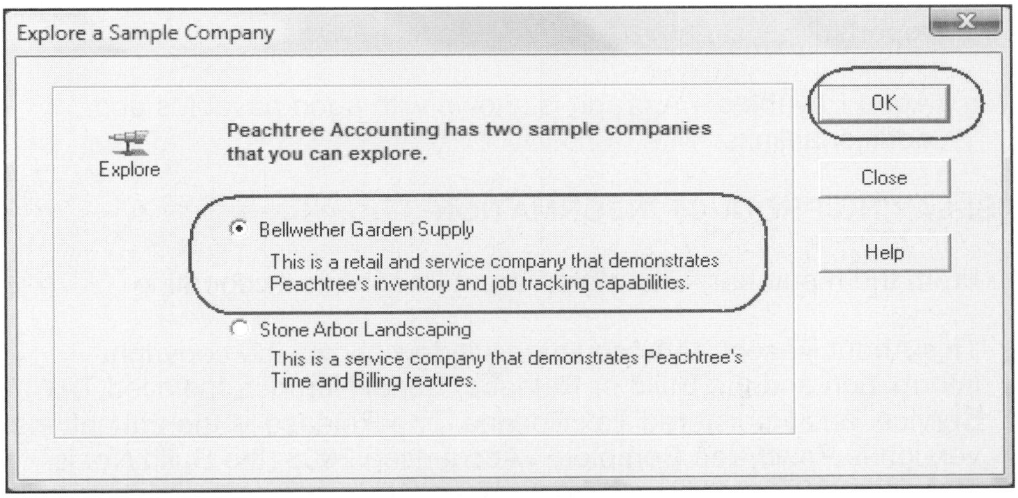

6. The Business Status window appears. The Business Status page, also known as the ***Home page***, is separated into seven areas. Each area has underlined links:

   a. Account Balances – observe the links from this area are View Account List; Reconcile Accounts and Import Bank Statements; View Balance Sheet. In Peachtree, you can link to reports from the Navigation Centers *or* from the menu bar.

   b. Customers Who Owe Money – A customer list is shown with links to customers and reports.

   c. Aged Receivables – Links include View Customer List; View Aged Receivables Report; and Receive Payment.

d. Find a Report. Observe that fields are included for Category, Report, and Description. (If necessary, scroll down the Home page.)

e. Revenue: Year to Date. A graph shows the first quarter of 2008's revenue and links to View Income Statement; Edit a Budget; and View Account Variance Report.

f. Vendors to Pay – A vendor list is shown with links to vendors and reports.

g. Aged Payables – A graph is shown with aged payables and additional links.

DISPLAYING PRODUCT INFORMATION

1. From the menu bar, click Help; About Peachtree Accounting.

   This About Peachtree Accounting window shows the copyright information and the Build or Release, Serial Number, Installed Tax Service, and Registered Tax Service. The Release of the educational version is Peachtree Complete® Accounting 2008; the Build No. is 15.0.00.1690E, and the Serial Number is Educational Version. If you are using the commercial version of Peachtree, your Release, Build, and Serial Number will differ. The Installed Tax Service and Registered Tax Service could also differ.

   To see if software or text updates have been made, periodically check the Textbook Updates link on the book's website at www.mhhe.com/yacht2008. Compare your About Peachtree Accounting window to the one shown on the next page.

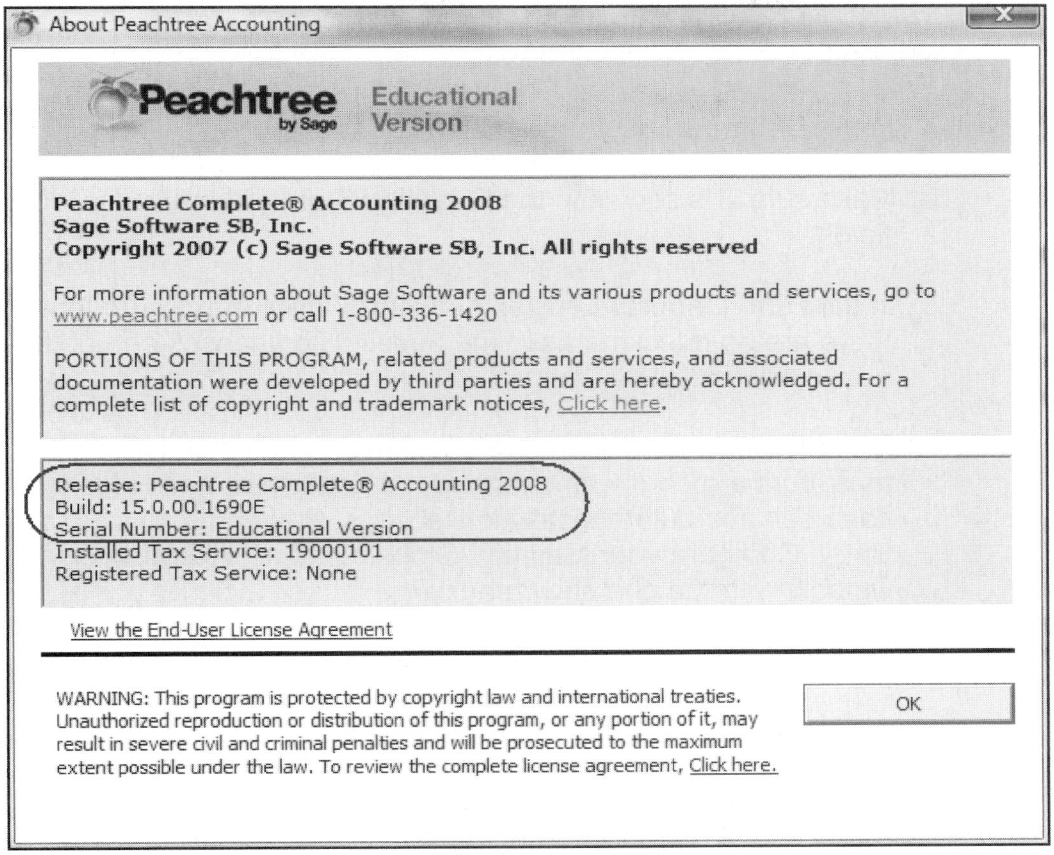

2. Click OK to close the Product Information window.

SETTING GLOBAL OPTIONS

Peachtree's ***global options*** are in effect for all Peachtree companies. On pages x-xi, steps are shown for setting global options. They are repeated here so you can make sure they are set. All companies in Chapters 1-18 require these global options. (Peachtree's global options are also shown in the Preface, pages xix-xx.)

1. From the menu bar, select Options; Global.

2. The Maintain Global Options window appears. The Accounting tab is selected.

   a. In the **Decimal Entry** area, select Manual.

   b. Make sure 2 is shown in the Quantity, Standard and Unit Price fields.

   c. In the **Hide General Ledger Accounts** area, make sure that there are no checkmarks in the boxes. (To uncheck one of the boxes, click on it.)

   d. In the **Other Options** area, a checkmark should be placed next to Warn if a record was changed but not saved; and Recalculate cash balance automatically in Receipts, Payments, and Payroll Entry. Compare your Maintain Global Options; Accounting tab window with the one shown below.

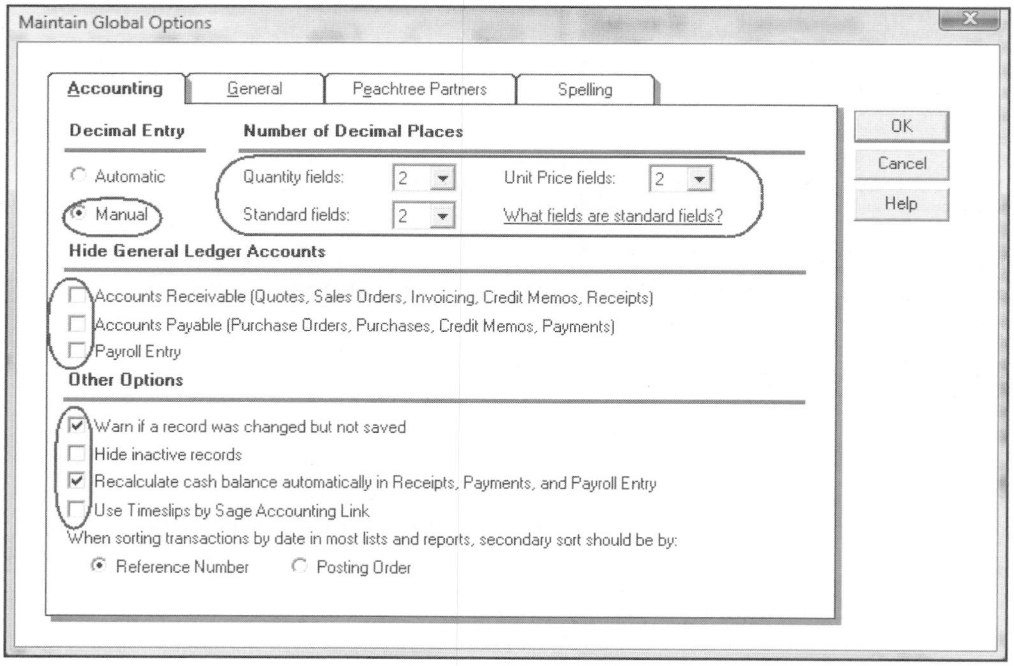

3. Click on the **General** tab. Make sure the Maintain Global Options; General window shows the following selections.

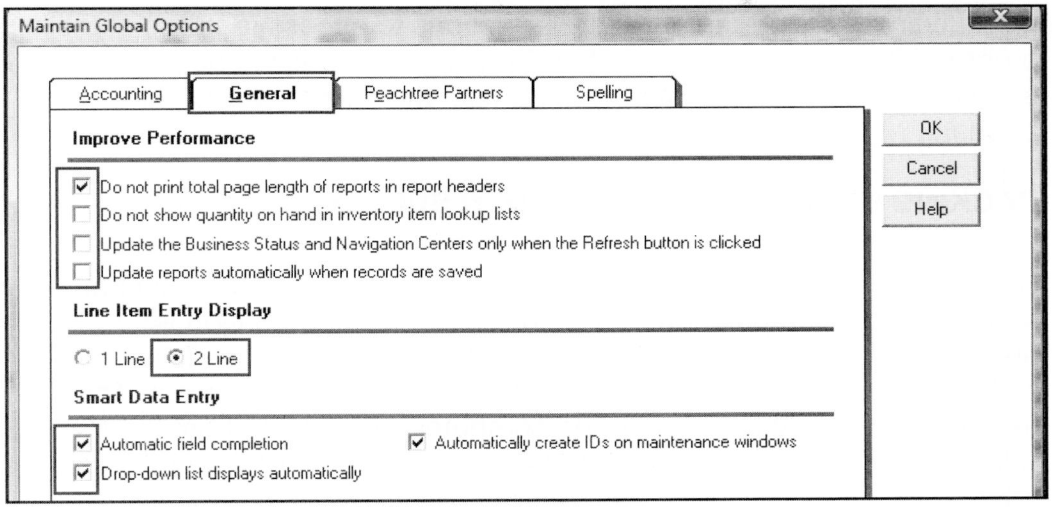

4. Click OK to save the global options, which will be in effect for all Peachtree companies.

The Navigation Bar and Navigation Center Pages

The ***Navigation Bar*** appears at the left side of the Peachtree main window and offers access to seven pages called ***Navigation Centers***. The Navigation Centers provide information about and access to the Peachtree program. The Navigation Bar's seven selections are shown below.

When you click the section representing one of the seven Navigation Centers, the panel to the right of the Navigation Bar displays information related to that area of the program. In this textbook, you use both PCA's Navigation Centers and menu bar selections to access features of the program. The individual Navigation Centers are identified as pages; for example, if you select Customers & Sales, the Customers & Sales page appears.

BACKING UP BELLWETHER GARDEN SUPPLY

Before making changes to Bellwether Garden Supply, you should back up the sample company data. When using PCA, information is automatically saved to the hard drive of the computer. In a classroom setting, a number of students may be using the same computer. This means that when you return to the computer lab or classroom, your data will be gone. ***Backing up*** means saving a copy of your data to a hard drive, network drive, or external media. Backing up insures that you can start where you left off the last time you used Peachtree.

Comment

The author suggests backing up the sample company. Since the backup requires 5.58MB, you need to back up to the hard drive, network drive, Zip disk, CD (CD-RW drive), DVD (DVD-RW drive) or USB drive. In the textbook, backing up to a drive other than the hard drive or network drive is called backing up to ***external media***. The instructions that follow assume you are backing up to the hard drive.

When a back up is made, data is saved to the current point. To distinguish between backups, a different backup name (file name) should be used. Use Peachtree's ***restore*** feature to retrieve information that was backed up.

In the business world, backups are unique to each business: daily, weekly, monthly. Think of your backups this way and you will see why individual backups at different points in the data are necessary. *You should never leave the computer lab without backing up your data.*

Follow these steps to back up Bellwether Garden Supply:

The text directions assume that you are backing up to a hard drive location. You can also back up to a network drive location or some other specified location. *If you have a CD-RW drive, DVD-RW drive, Zip disk drive, or USB drive, you can back up to external media. One CD-R, DVD-R, or Zip disk can be used for all backups in the textbook (Chapters 1 through 18).* For Windows Vista, back up to the desktop or other hard drive location first, then copy to external media. The chart on page 2 (Part 1 opener) shows the size of each backup file in Chapters 1-8 (Part 1 of the textbook).

1. From the Navigation Bar, click **Company**. In the Data Maintenance list, link to Back up. The Back Up Company window appears. If necessary, uncheck the box next to Include company name in the backup file name.

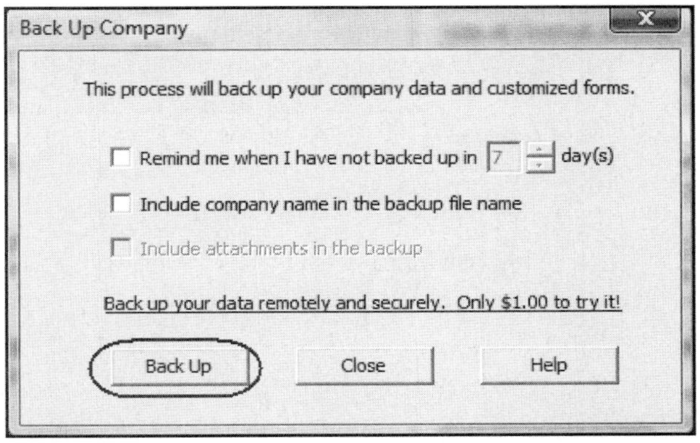

2. Click Back Up. The Save Backup for Bellwether Garden Supply as window appears.

3. The Save in field shows the default location for your backup (BCS). If you do *not* change the Save in location, you are saving to the hard drive. Click on the down-arrow in the Save in field. The list that displays shows you the location on your hard drive for the sample company files.

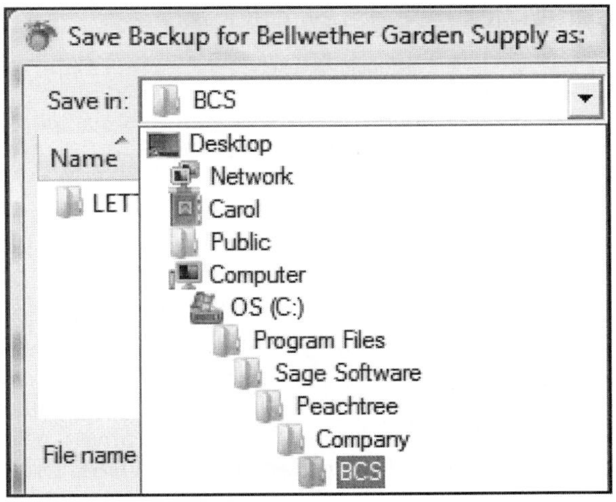

4. Since you are backing up to the default hard drive location, follow these steps.[6] Observe that the Save in field shows BCS (or the appropriate drive letter) and that the File name field shows the default name. In the File name field, highlight the default file name and then type **bgs** as the file name.

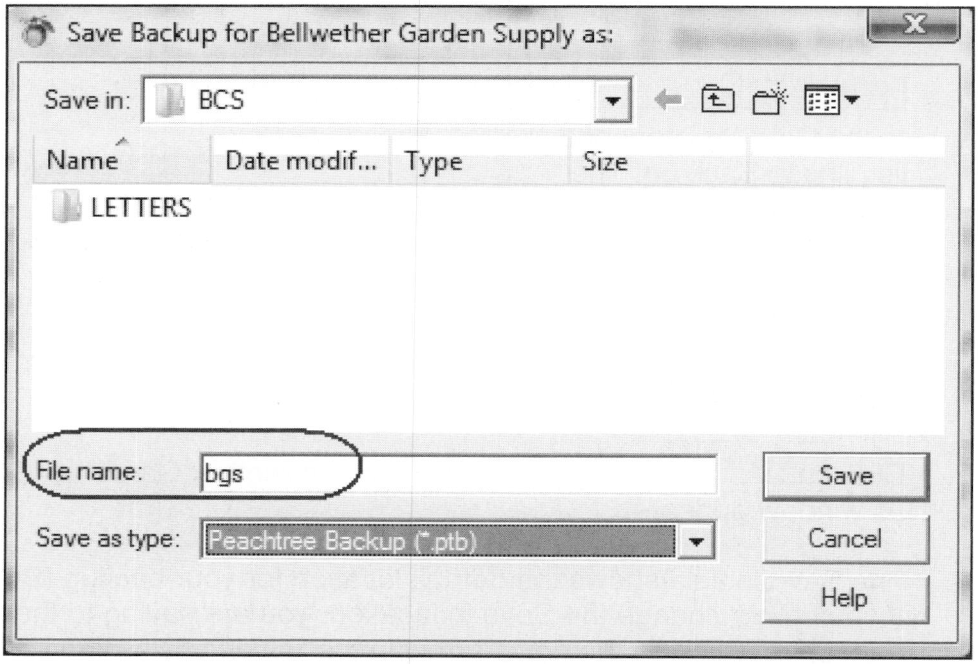

Observe that the Save as type field shows that you are making a Peachtree Backup (*.ptb), which is abbreviated ptb. This is the standard default for Peachtree backups.

[6]If you are backing up to a different location, go to the appropriate drive letter. If you having difficulty backing up to USB media (thumb or flash drive), refer to Appendix A, Troubleshooting, pages 700-702—Problem Backing Up to USB Drive or Other External Media.

Comment

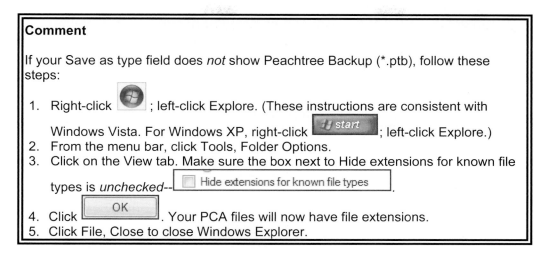

If your Save as type field does *not* show Peachtree Backup (*.ptb), follow these steps:

1. Right-click ; left-click Explore. (These instructions are consistent with Windows Vista. For Windows XP, right-click 

; left-click Explore.)
2. From the menu bar, click Tools, Folder Options.
3. Click on the View tab. Make sure the box next to Hide extensions for known file types is *unchecked*-- 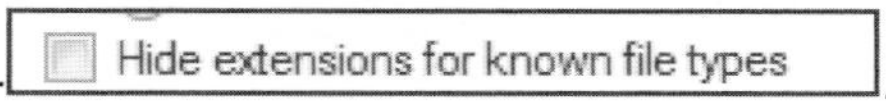

.
4. Click 

. Your PCA files will now have file extensions.
5. Click File, Close to close Windows Explorer.

5. Click 

.

6. A window appears that says This company backup will require approximately 5.58MB.

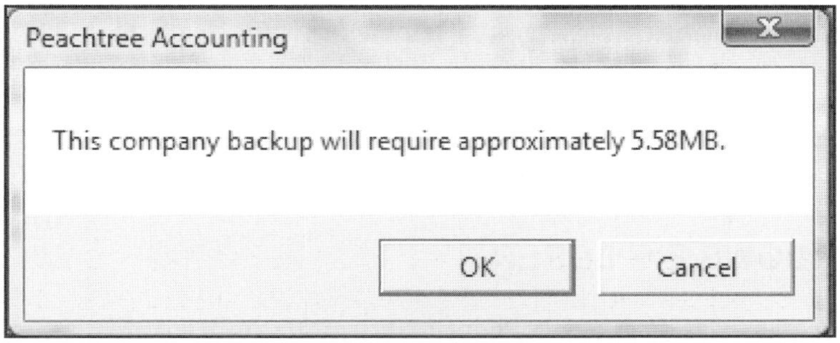

7. Click 

. When the Back Up Company scale is 100% complete, you have successfully backed up the sample company. You are returned to Bellwether Garden Supply's menu bar.

Follow these steps to see the size of the backup file.

1. Right-click ; left -click Explore. (*Hint:* This textbook was written with Microsoft Word 2007 and Windows Vista. If you are using a different Windows operating system, your start button differs.)

2. Select drive C (or the location where you backed up Bellwether Garden Supply). For example, if you backed up to the default location, select C:\Program Files\Sage Software\Peachtree\ Company\ BCS\bgs.ptb.

   The Name of the file is bgs.ptb; the size of the file is 3,255 KB;[7] and File Type is PTB File. Compare this information to the bcs folder on your hard drive, network drive, Zip disk, or CD.

BDDETAIL.DAT	3/14/2006 4:36 PM	DAT File	67 KB
bgs.ptb	6/22/2007 4:15 PM	PTB File	3,255 KB
BOMHIST.DAT	3/14/2006 1:00 PM	DAT File	50 KB

   Refer to the chart on page 2 for back up sizes. Peachtree backs up to the current point in the data. Since Bellwether's data is too large to fit on one floppy disk, the author suggests backing up to a hard drive location or external media (USB flash drive; CD; DVD; or Zip disk.)

Follow these steps to exit Peachtree:

1. Close any opened windows. From Windows Explorer, click File; Close.

2. From Peachtree's menu bar, click File; Exit. You are returned to the Windows desktop.

USING WINDOWS EXPLORER

The instructions on pages 18–21 show how to use Peachtree's Back Up feature. Peachtree's Back Up feature works with Restore, which is shown on pages 26–30. *What if your instructor prefers that all of the company files be copied or saved?*

1. The Windows desktop should be displayed.

2. Right-click ; left-click Explore. Windows Explorer appears.

---

[7]The size of your backup file may differ.

3. Select drive C. Then, open the folder for Bellwether Garden Supply: C:\Program Files\Sage Software\ Peachtree\ Company\BCS (this is the default location for Peachtree; your location may differ).

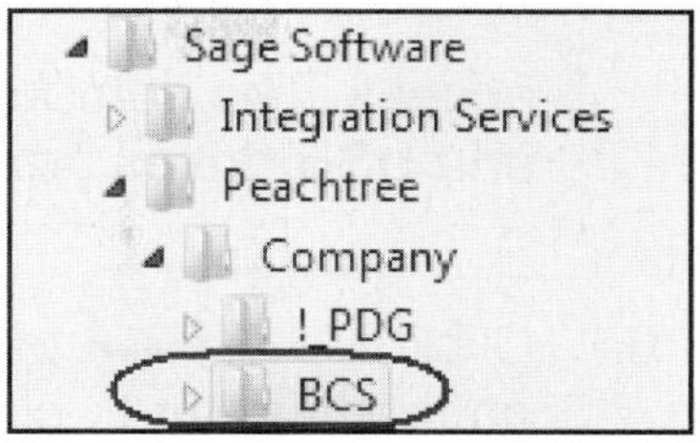

4. Right-click on the BCS folder. A drop-down menu appears. Left-click on Properties.

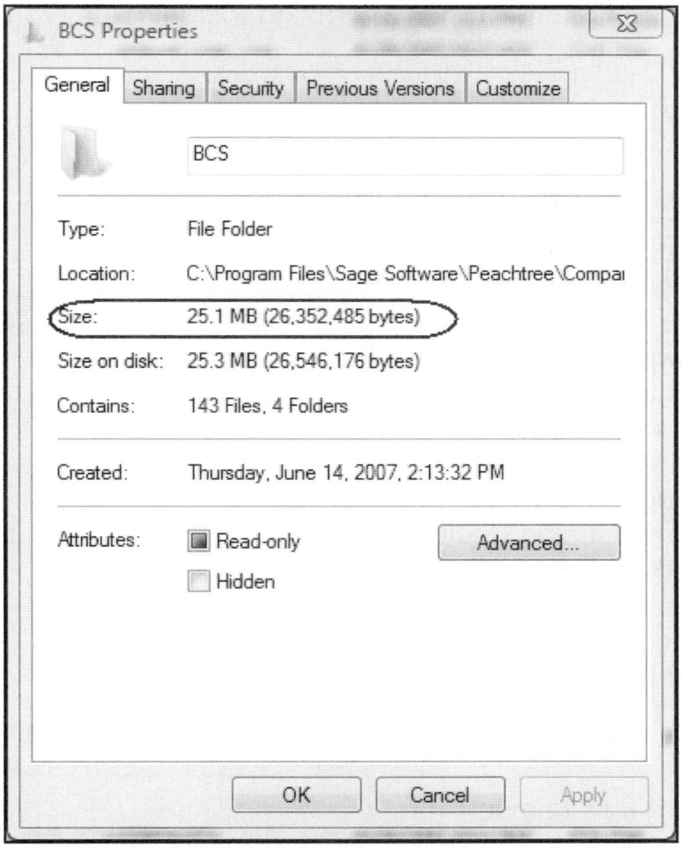

5. Observe that the size of the BCS folder is 25.1 MB (or 26,352,485 bytes). The size of your BCS folder may differ. If you want to copy the entire folder to a disk, you need to have a Zip drive, CD-RW, or DVD-RW drive. The steps shown for Copying the BCS folder to a CD-RW or DVD-RW Drive (on pages 24-25) explain how to do that. In order to use the program, Peachtree folders need read and write

access. The computer's hard drive, Zip drives, CD-RW, DVD-RW, and USB drives are read/write.

6. Click  to close the BCS Properties window. Click  on the title bar to close Windows Explorer.

Copying the BCS Folder to a CD-RW or DVD-RW Drive

Follow these steps to copy the BCS folder to a CD or DVD-RW drive. Depending on the software you are using to copy data, your instructions may differ.

1. If necessary, click File; Exit to exit Peachtree and return to the desktop. Put the CD/DVD-R disk in the drive (or other external media in the appropriate drive). In this example, the BCS folder is copied to a DVD-R. (Depending on the external media used, your steps may differ.)

   If you are copying files to a DVD, a window may appear that asks if you want to burn files to disc using Windows or Add Files using other software (for example, using Roxio Creator Data.) Make the appropriate selection. (In this example, Burn files to disc using Windows is selected.)

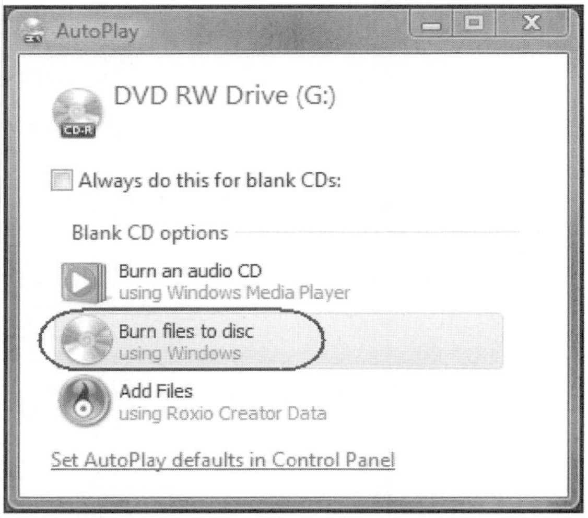

2. Click Burn files to disc.

3. Type **Bellwether** for the Disc title. Click  . Once the DVD is formatted, locate the BCS folder on the hard drive. The default location is C:\Program Files\Sage Software\Peachtree\Company\BCS. Click on BCS to select it. (Your date modified will differ.)

4. Click 

. The Copying 141 items (25.1 MB) window appears. When the files are copied, the Files Currently on the Disc (1) shows the BCS File folder.

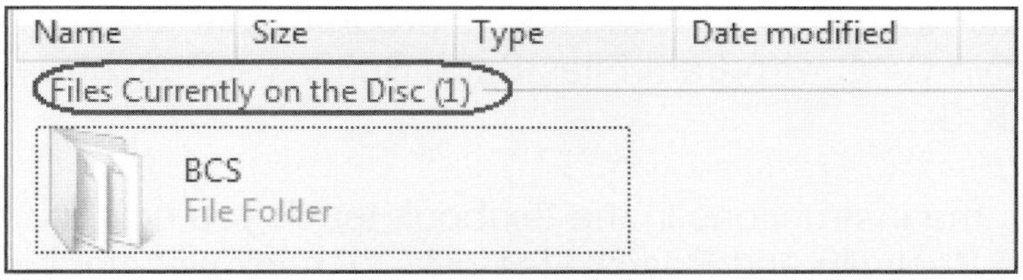

   Observe that the Folders list (on Windows Explorer's left pane) shows that the DVD RW Drive (G:) is labeled Bellwether. The contents of the BSC folder are also shown—double-click on the drive to show its contents. (The author's DVD RW drive is identified as G. Your drive letter may differ.)

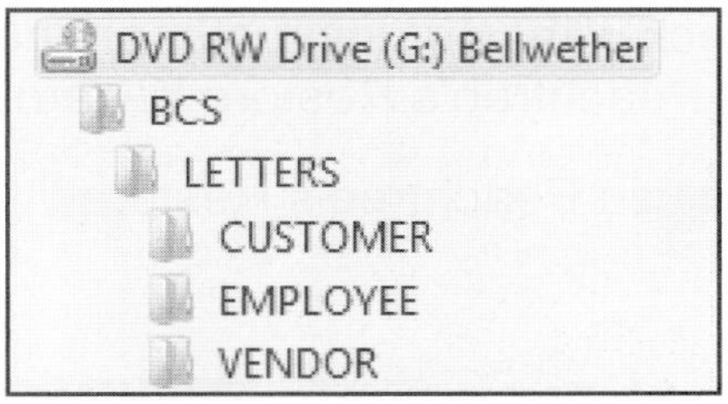

5. Right click on the CD RW or DVD RW drive; left-click Eject. A Preparing to Eject window appears. After a few moments the drive door opens. Remove the CD or DVD.

6. Close Windows Explorer.

7. To check that the file was copied, place the CD/DVD or other external media is in the appropriate drive. Right-click on the BCS folder; left-click Properties. The BCS Properties window should look similar to the one shown on page 23.

8. Click 

on the title bar to close the windows.

9. Remove the CD, DVD, or other external media.

When you copy the BCS folder from drive C to a CD/DVD RW drive or other external media, you are copying all the files contained in the folder.

Remember, backing up files compresses the data (or makes the file smaller). Copying the entire folder allows you to have all the BCS files on external media. When you want to return to where you left off, you can use Windows Explorer to copy and paste these files from your CD/DVD (or other external media) to Peachtree's program path and Bellwether's folder on drive C– C:\Program Files\Sage Software\ Peachtree\ Company\BCS.

Remember, the instructions in the textbook teach you how to use Peachtree's Back Up and Restore features. Check with your instructor for his or her preference.

USING PEACHTREE'S RESTORE WIZARD

In order to start where you left off the last time you backed up, use Peachtree's Restore Wizard. Your instructor may prefer that you use Windows Explorer to copy/paste instead of Peachtree's Restore feature. You may need to check with your instructor on the preferred method. This textbook shows Peachtree's Restore Wizard.

Follow these steps to use Peachtree's Restore Wizard.

1. Start Peachtree.

2. On the startup window, click 

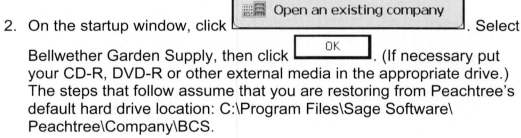

. Select Bellwether Garden Supply, then click 

. (If necessary put your CD-R, DVD-R or other external media in the appropriate drive.) The steps that follow assume that you are restoring from Peachtree's default hard drive location: C:\Program Files\Sage Software\ Peachtree\Company\BCS.

   If Bellwether Garden Supply is *not* listed as a Peachtree company, refer to the Read Me box on the next page.

Read Me: What if Bellwether Garden Supply is *not* shown as an existing company *or* when you select Explore a sample company?

Some schools delete subdirectories from the hard drive; for example, you have a back up file but the company, in this case Bellwether Garden Supply, is *not* listed as a Peachtree company. Follow these steps to restore a company from a backup file.

1. If necessary, click File; Close Company to go to the Startup window. To double-check that Bellwether is *not* listed, select Open an existing company. Make sure Bellwether Garden Supply is *not* listed in the Company Name list. Click 

.
2. The startup window shows three menu bar options—

. Select File; Restore.
3. Browse to the location of your backup file.
4. Restore *A New Company*. Compare your Select Company window with the one shown below step 6 on page 28. Continue with step 7.

3. From the Navigation Bar, click 

. In the Data Maintenance list, link to Restore.

4. The Restore Wizard – Select Backup File window appears. The window below shows Peachtree's default location.

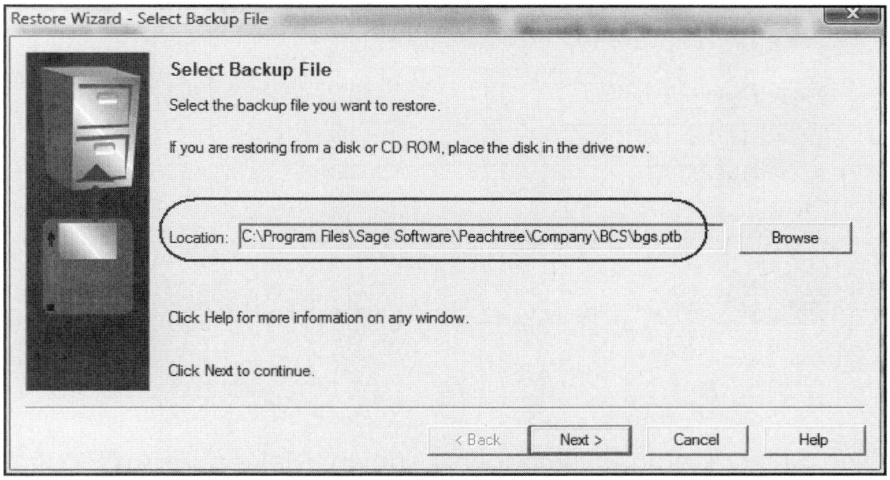

If you are restoring from external media, read the Steps for Restoring from External media on the next page.

Steps for Restoring from External Media

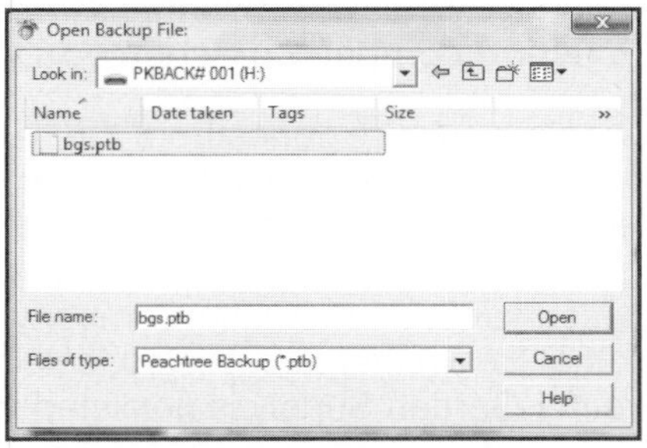

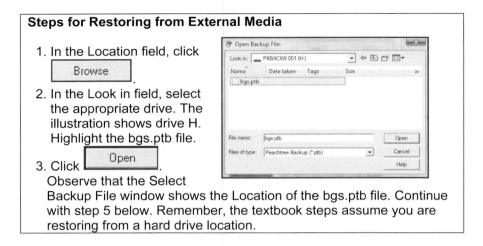

1. In the Location field, click 
.
2. In the Look in field, select the appropriate drive. The illustration shows drive H. Highlight the bgs.ptb file.
3. Click 
.
Observe that the Select Backup File window shows the Location of the bgs.ptb file. Continue with step 5 below. Remember, the textbook steps assume you are restoring from a hard drive location.

5. On the Restore Wizard – Select Backup File window, click 
.

6. The Select Company window appears. Observe that An Existing Company is the default. The Company Name field shows Bellwether Garden Supply and the Location shows Bellwether's location.

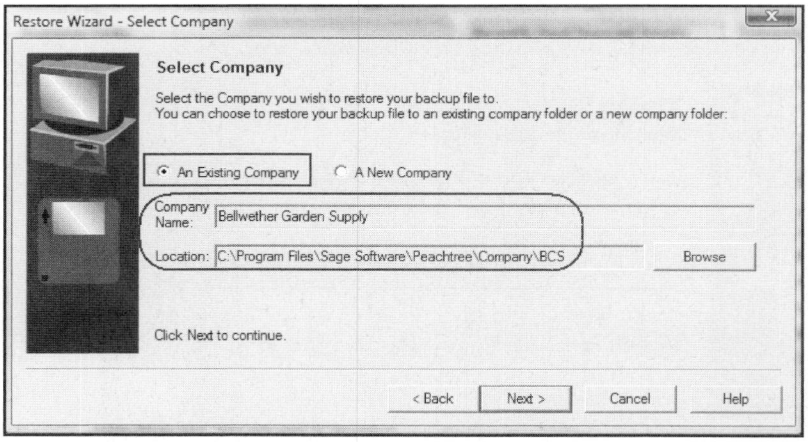

7. The Select Company window is shown. Make sure An Existing Company is selected. Read the information on the Select Company window; click 
.

8. The Restore Options window appears. Make sure that the check mark is next to Company Data.

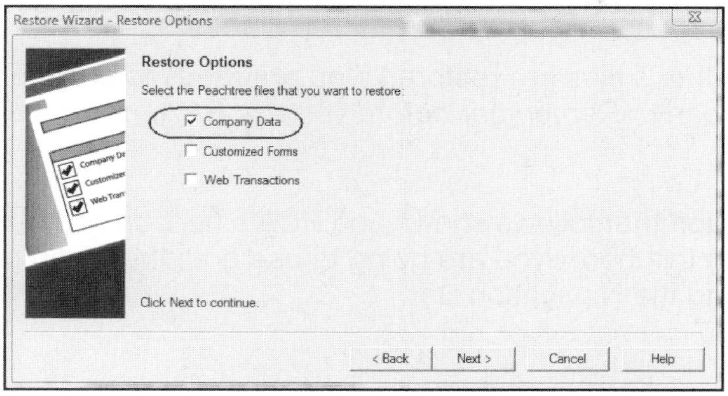

9. On the Restore Options window, click .

10. The Confirmation window appears. Remember, the textbook steps assume that you are restoring from the Peachtree default hard drive location (C:\Program Files\Sage Software\ Peachtree\ Company\ BCS\bgs.ptb). If you are restoring from external media, the From field will show the appropriate drive letter. Compare your Confirmation window to the one shown below.

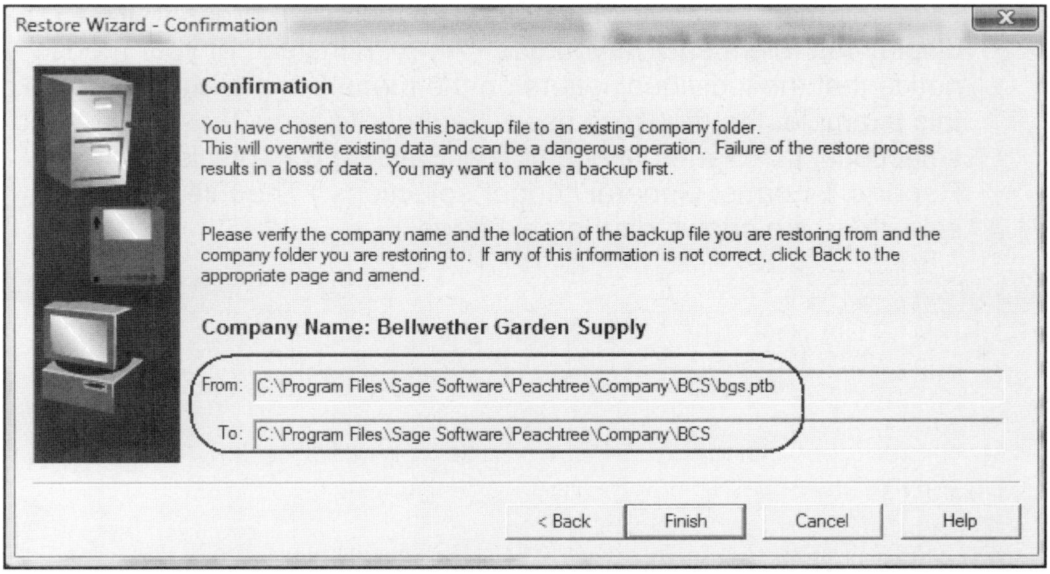

11. Read the information on the Confirmation window, then click 

. Your backup data starts to restore. When the scale is 100% complete, the Bellwether Garden Supply data is restored.

Once Bellwether's files are restored, you are ready to continue using the sample company. *Remember before you exit PCA, make a backup of your work.*

The information that follows shows you PCA's horizontal menu bar selections. In this book, you are going to use *both* the menu bar selections and the Navigation Bar.

MENU BAR

PCA's menu bar has 11 selections: File, Edit, Lists, Maintain, Tasks, Analysis, Options, Reports & Forms, Services (this selection is active on the commercial version and inactive on the educational version), Window, and Help.

In this textbook, menu bar selections *and* Navigation Bar selections are shown.

Follow these steps to explore the menu bar.

1. From the menu bar, click File to see its menu, *or*, press <Alt> + F to display the File menu. If you use <Alt> + F instead of your mouse, notice that the individual letters on the menu bar are underlined. In this example, the mouse is used. (In order to show these File menu selections, the General Ledger Trial Balance was displayed from Reports & Forms; General Ledger selections.) The File menu selections are shown on the next page.

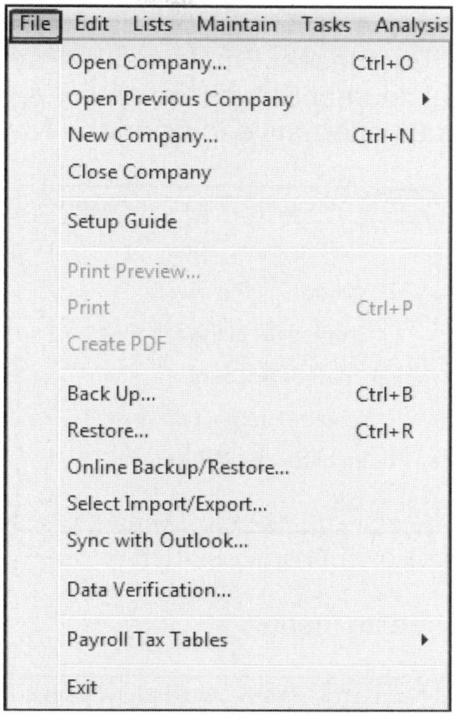

The File menu allows you to open a company, open the previous company, create a new company, close company, go to the setup guide, print preview, print, create a PDF (Adobe Acrobat) file, Back Up, Restore, Online Backup/Restore (on commercial version), select import/export, sync with Outlook, data verification, load and edit payroll tax tables, and exit.

Menu choices that are followed by an ***ellipsis*** (…) are associated with ***dialog boxes*** or windows that supply information about a window. An arrow (►) next to a menu item (Open Previous Company and Payroll Tax Tables) indicates that there is another menu with additional selections.

To cancel the drop-down menu, click File or **<Esc>**.

2. The Edit selection shows Find Transactions.

3. Click Lists to see its menu. The Lists selection shows Customers & Sales, Vendors & Purchases, Employees & Payroll, Chart of Accounts, General Journal Entries, Inventory & Services, and Jobs. The Lists menu is an alternative to using the Navigation Bar.

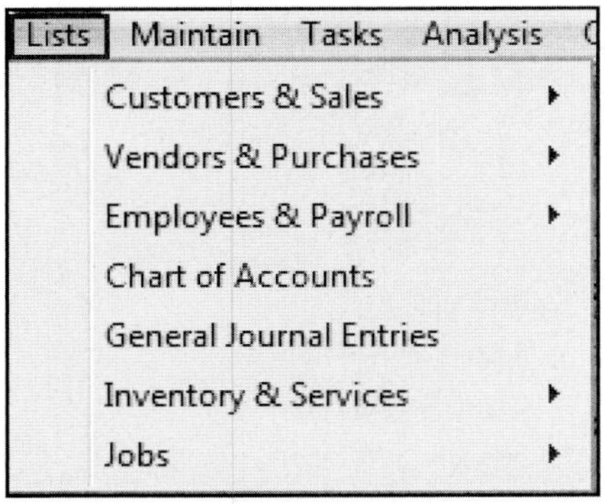

4. Click Maintain to see its menu.

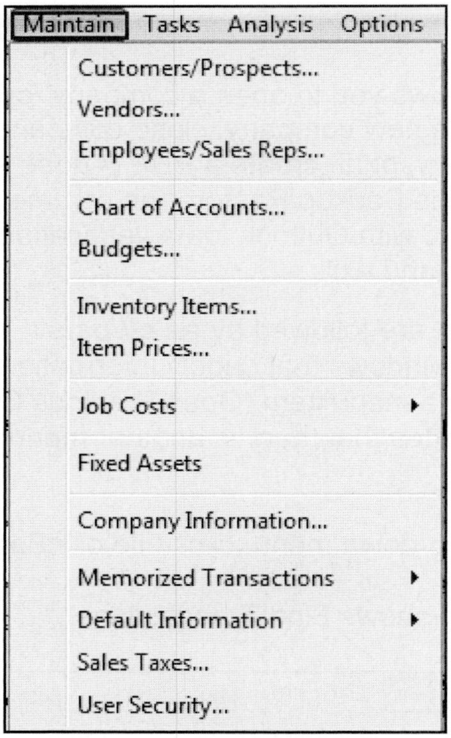

The Maintain menu allows you to enter, view, or edit required information for your company's customers or prospects, vendors, employees or sales reps, chart of accounts, budgets, inventory items, item prices, and job costs. You can also edit company information; enter memorized transactions; or go to ***default*** information, sales tax codes, and user security (passwords). Defaults are commands that PCA automatically selects. Default information automatically displays in windows. You can change the default by choosing another command.

5. Click Tasks to see its menu.

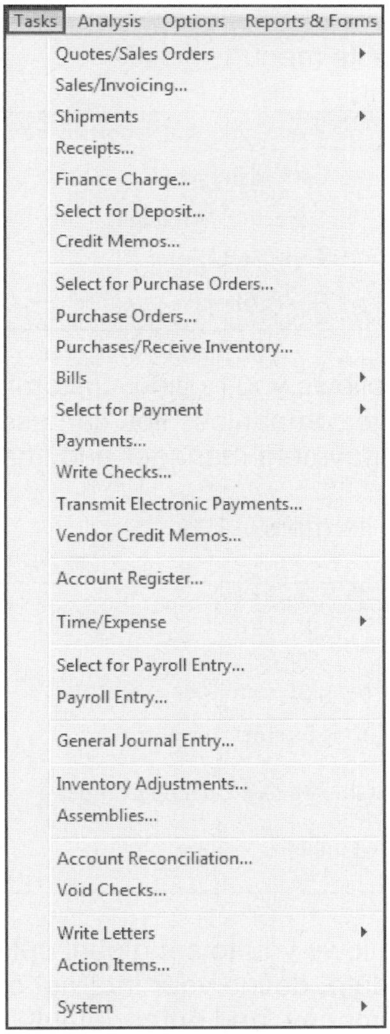

The Tasks menu allows you to enter quotes and sales orders, sales invoices, shipments, receipts, finance charges, select for deposit, issue credit memos, purchase orders, purchases of inventory, select bills to pay, make payments, write checks, transmit electronic payments, issue vendor credit memos, display account registers, record time and expenses, record payroll information, and make general journal entries. You can also make inventory adjustments, assemblies, reconcile bank statements (account reconciliation), void checks, and enter action items. With the System selection, another menu displays with choices such as post and unpost (available with batch posting), change the accounting period, use the year-end wizard, and purge old or inactive transactions.

6. Click Analysis to see its menu.

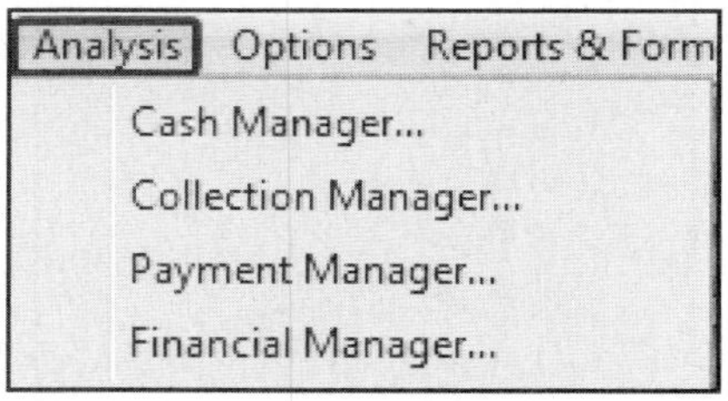

The Analysis menu allows you to view customized graphics developed for specific companies. You can use the cash manager, collection manager, payment manager and financial manager.

7. Click Options to see its menu.

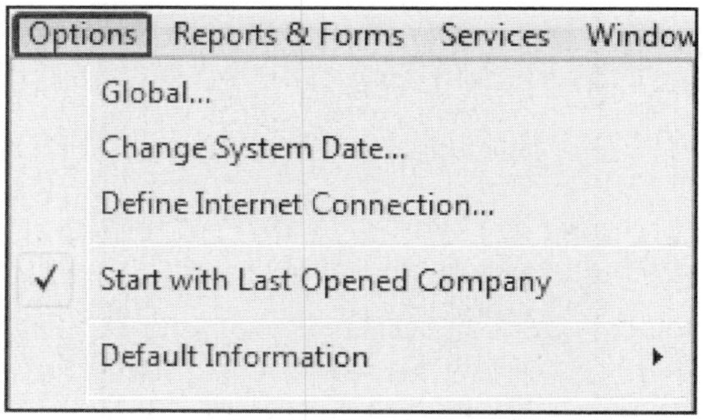

The Options menu allows you to set global options for a company, change the system date, define your Internet connection, start with the Last Opened Company, and enter default information.

The checkmark next to Start with Last Opened Company means that each time you start Peachtree, the last company you worked with will open.

8. Click Reports & Forms to see its menu.

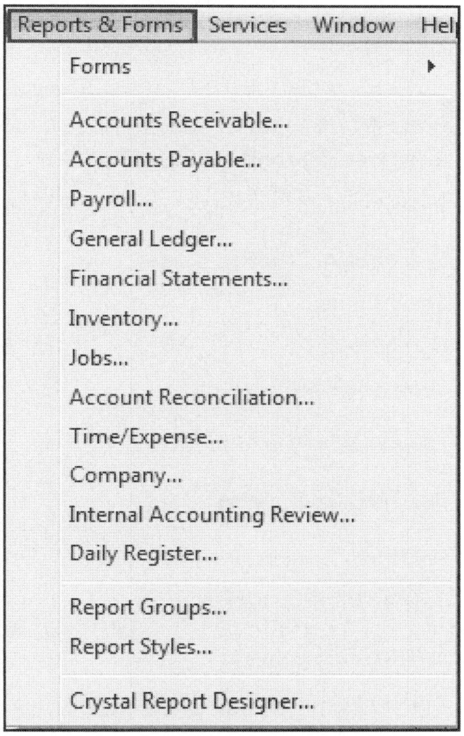

The Reports & Forms menu allows you to ***queue*** reports for printing or display reports. You can also create and edit the format for forms, reports, financial statements, and other reports.

9. The Services menu is inactive in the educational version of PCA. On the commercial version of Peachtree Complete 2008, the Services menu has selections for Check for Updates, My Peachtree Account, Checks and Forms, Credit Card Processing, Bill Pay, Customer Support, Payroll Solutions, Peachtree Web Accounting, Product Comparison, Industry Specific Solutions, Mid-sized Businesses, More Products & Services, Peachtree Web Transaction Center, PeachSync Wizard.

10. Click Window to see its menu. The Window menu allows you to close all windows at once.

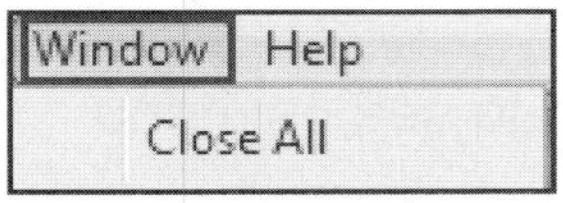

11. Click Help to see its menu.

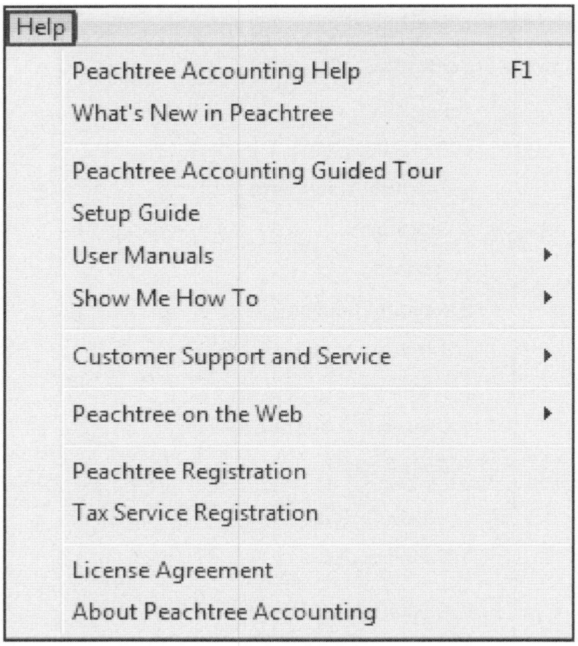

The Help menu allows you to open a window of context-sensitive help, run tutorials for PCA and Windows, and display file statistics (part of the Customer Support and Services selection). Select About Peachtree Complete Accounting to display product information. Detailed steps for displaying product information are shown on pages 14-15.

BECOMING AN EMPLOYEE OF BELLWETHER GARDEN SUPPLY

Before adding yourself as an employee of Bellwether Garden Supply, let's learn how to use the Navigation Bar to open the Maintain Employees & Sales Reps window. The Navigation Bar is displayed on the left side of the Peachtree Accounting window. The selections include: Business

Status, Customers & Sales, Vendors & Purchases, Inventory & Services, Employees & Payroll, Banking, and Company.

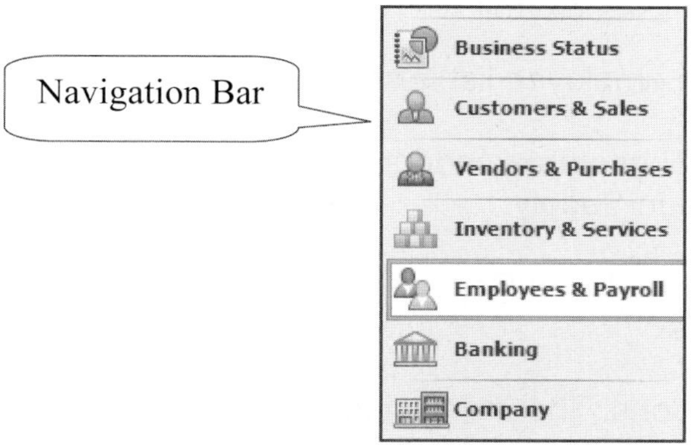

Follow these steps to use the Navigation Bar to add yourself as an employee.

1. On the Navigation Bar, select 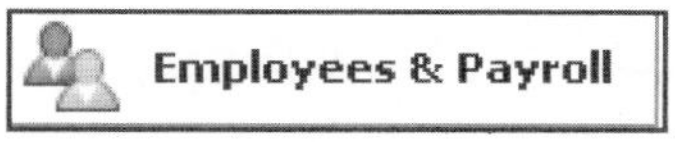

. The Employees & Payroll page appears.

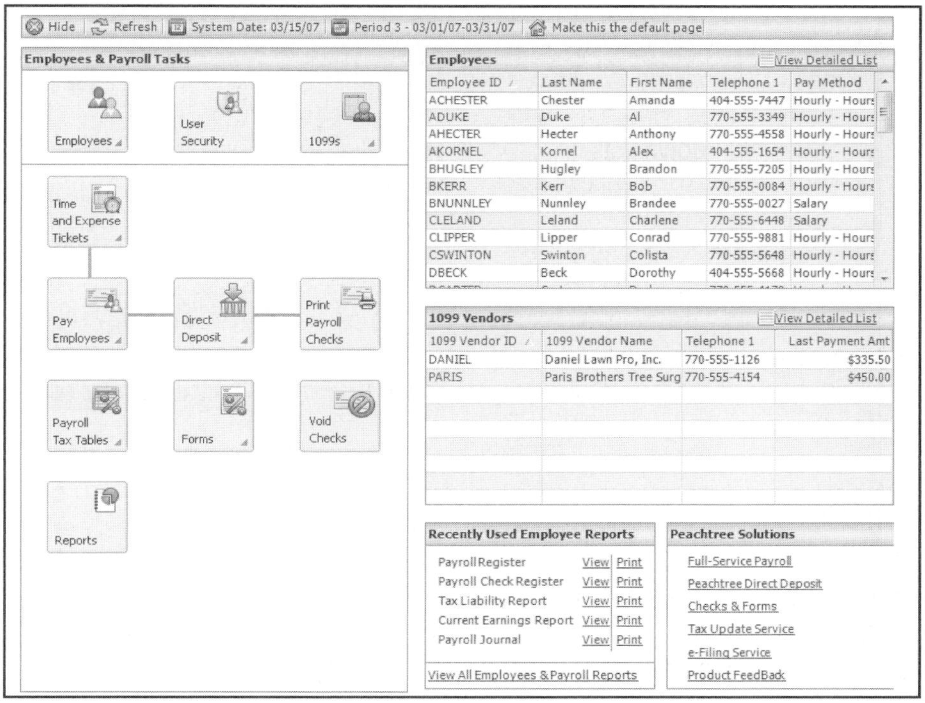

The Employees & Payroll page is organized into five sections.

a. Employees & Payroll Tasks: The flowchart shows how Peachtree processes payroll.

b. Employees: The employee list is shown.

c. 1099 Vendors: These are vendors who receive 1099's from Bellwether Garden Supply.

d. Recently Used Employee Reports. This section includes links to payroll reports.

e. Peachtree Solutions. These links include Peachtree's third-party suppliers.

2. Click 

; New Employee. The Maintain Employees/Sales Reps window appears.

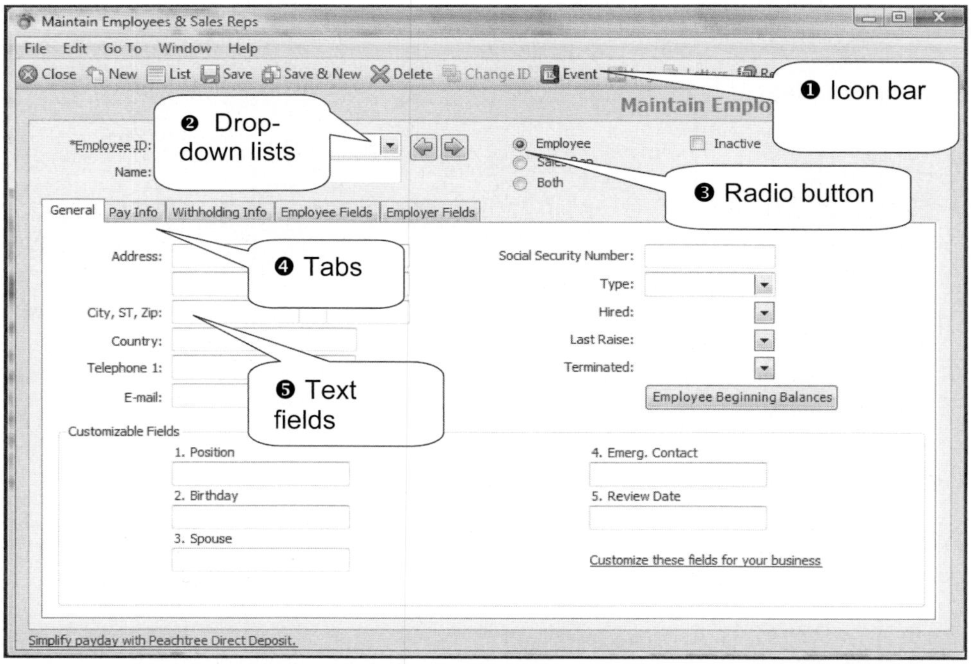

❶ The icon bar at the top of most windows shows graphical representations of commands or functions that are accessible from the window.

❷ Drop-down lists: Click on the down-arrow to see lists. On the Maintain Employees & Sales Reps window, employee IDs are shown. When you are in the text portion of the field, the cursor changes to an I-bar and a question mark <I?>. Type a question mark **<?>** in the field, or click the right mouse button, to display lists.

❸ ***Radio Button*** *or* ***Option Button:*** These buttons allow you to select one by clicking with the mouse or using the space bar. The default is Employee shown by the radio button next to Employee.

❹ Tabs are common to most PCA windows. They provide a subtitle to the various windows that store and organize information. Here, for example, the information you can choose to track is subdivided into five categories: General, Pay Info, Withholding Info, Employee Fields, and Employer Fields.

❺ Text fields are rectangles or fields where information is typed.

Adding Yourself as an Employee

Follow these steps to add yourself as an employee.

1. Type an Employee ID code for yourself in the Employee ID field. For example, type **CYACHT** (type *the first initial of your first name and your full last name in all capital letters);* and press **<Enter>**.[8]

2. In the Name field, type your first name, press **<Enter>**; type your middle initial, if any, press **<Enter>**, then type your last name. Press **<Enter>** two times.[9]

---

[8]All ID codes are case-sensitive which means that cyacht and CYACHT are considered different codes. Capital letters sort before lowercase letters.

[9]You can use **<Enter>** or **<Tab>** to move between fields. Use **<Shift>+<Enter>** or **<Shift>+<Tab>** to move back a field. You can also hold the **<Alt>** key and press the underlined letter of a text box to move between fields.

3. In the Address field, type your street address. There are two lines so you can enter an ATTENTION line or P.O. Box, if necessary. If you are using just one line for your address, press **<Enter>** two times to go to the City, ST, Zip fields.

4. In the City, ST Zip field, type your city, state (two-digits), and zip code, pressing **<Enter>** after each.

5. None of the other information is required. You work with the other fields in Chapter 14, Payroll, Employees and Account Reconciliation. Click 

.

   To check that your Employee ID has been added, click on the down-arrow in the Employee ID field.

6. Click 

to return to the Employees & Payroll page.

BACKING UP CHAPTER 1 DATA

Follow these steps to back up Chapter 1 data:

1. From the Navigation Bar, click 

; link to Back up. Make sure that the box next to Include company name in the backup file name is *unchecked*.

2. Click 

.

3. Save to the default location; *or,* if you are backing up to a network drive or external media, make the appropriate selection in the Save in field.[10] Type **Chapter 1** in the File name field. Compare your Save Backup for Bellwether Garden Supply as window with the one shown on the next page.

---

[10] If you are having difficulty backing up to USB media (thumb or flash drive), refer to Appendix A, Troubleshooting, pages 700-702—Problem Backing Up to USB Drive or Other External Media.

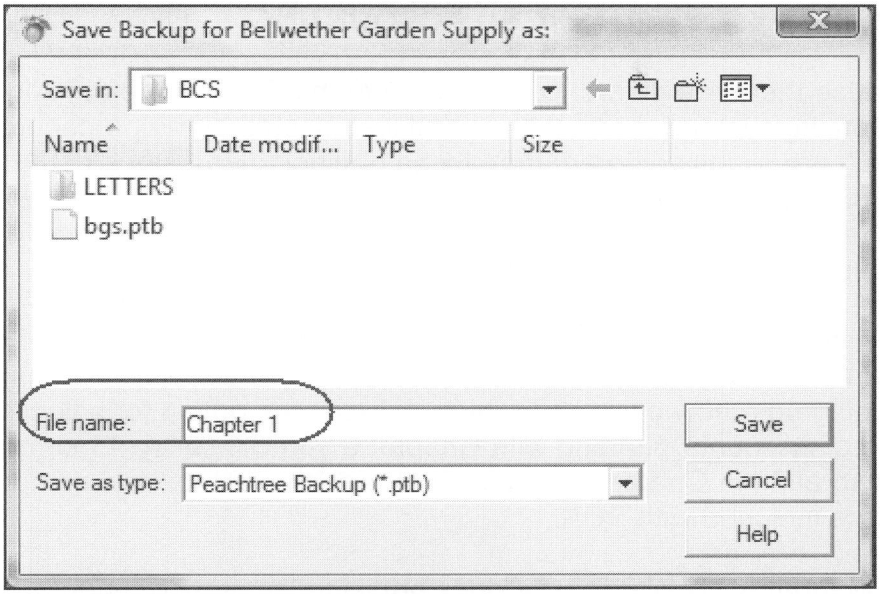

If you are saving to external media, your Save in field will differ.

4. Click 

.

5. When the window prompts that This company backup will require approximately 5.53MB, click 

. When the Back Up Company scale is 100% complete, you have successfully backed up to the current point in Chapter 1. You are returned to the menu bar.

Read Me: Windows Vista—Problem Backing Up to USB Drive

Because of Windows Vista operating system security features, you need to backup to your desktop first. Then copy the backup file from your desktop to the USB drive. Refer to Appendix A, Problem Backing Up to USB Drive or Other External Media, pages 700-702 for detailed steps.

6. Click File, Exit to exit Peachtree.

MANUAL VS. COMPUTERIZED ACCOUNTING

Because there are differences between manual and computerized accounting systems, notice in several instances that the procedures used in PCA are slightly different than those outlined in the steps of the manual accounting cycle. The steps of the manual accounting cycle shown in most accounting textbooks differs slightly from PCA's computer accounting cycle.

The differences between the Manual and Computer Accounting Cycle are shown on the next page. The first step of the Computer Accounting Cycle is setting up a new company, which includes the option for selecting a Chart of Accounts. Starting with Chapter 9 you will set up 11 companies from scratch. In Chapters 1-8 you work with the two sample companies that are included with PCA.

The Manual Accounting Cycle does not include creating a new company. In manual accounting, the chart of accounts is the same as the accounts in the general ledger.

Step five of the manual cycle shows a worksheet. There is no worksheet in the computerized cycle. In PCA you can complete account reconciliation. Account reconciliation automates bank reconciliation. Another important difference is that in the Computer Accounting Cycle, the adjusting entries are journalized and posted before printing the financial statements.

In the computerized cycle, Step 10, change accounting periods, is similar to closing the month manually except that the temporary accounts maintain balances so a post-closing trial balance is not available. PCA tracks income and expense data for an entire year. At the end of the year, all revenue and expense accounts are closed to equity. In all Peachtree companies (including sole proprietorships), a retained earnings account is needed so that posting to the general ledger can be done.

The table on the next page compares the manual accounting cycle to the computer accounting cycle.

MANUAL ACCOUNTING CYCLE	PCA's COMPUTER ACCOUNTING CYCLE
1. Analyze transactions.	1. Create a new company *or* restore A New Company.
2. Journalize entries.	2. Analyze transactions.
3. Post to the ledger.	3. Journalize entries.
4. Prepare unadjusted trial balance.	4. Post to the ledger.
5. Prepare worksheet.	5. Print general ledger trial balance (unadjusted).
6. Prepare financial statements: income statement, statement of changes in owner's equity, and balance sheet.	6. Account reconciliation: reconciling the bank statement.
7. Adjust the ledger accounts: journalize and post adjusting entries.	7. Journalize and post adjusting entries.
8. Close the temporary accounts: journalize and post the closing entries.	8. Print the general ledger trial balance (adjusted).
9. Prepare post-closing trial balance.	9. Print financial statements: balance sheet, income statement, statement of cash flow, and statement of changes in financial position.
10. Reverse entries (optional).	10. Change accounting periods.
11. Interpret accounting information	

INTERNET ACTIVITY	
The ***Internet*** is a worldwide electronic communication network that allows for the sharing of information. The ***World Wide Web*** (WWW) or Web is a way of accessing information over the Internet. To read about the differences between the Internet and the World Wide Web go online to www.webopedia.com/DidYouKnow/Internet/2002/Web_vs_Internet.asp . To make an Internet connection, your computer must be equipped with a ***modem***. The word modem is an abbreviation of **Mo**dulator/**Dem**odulator. A modem is a device that translates the digital signals from the computer into analog signals that can travel over telephone lines. There are also DSL (digital subscriber lines), wireless, and cable modems, as well as T-1 lines for faster connections.	
1.	Start PCA. Open Bellwether Garden Supply. If necessary, connect to your Internet browser.
2.	From Bellwether's menu bar, select Help; Peachtree on the Web, Product News to go to online to www.peachtree.com/peachtreeaccountingline/. *You must be connected to the Internet.*
3.	Websites are time and date sensitive. When using the Internet, be aware that changes will likely take place. For purposes of this assignment, link to Peachtree's press releases. When you place your cursor over Press, the cursor changes to a hand symbol (); then select Recent Press Releases. The Press Release page appears. The website address is http://www.sagesoftware.com/newsroom/news/index.cfm .
4.	Select two links from the Recent Press Releases page. Using a word processing program, write an essay about each site you selected. Remember to include the website address of each link. Your summary for each site selected should be no more than 100 words or less than 75 words.
5.	From your Internet browser, go to the textbook's website at www.mhhe.com/yacht2008. Link to Student Edition.
6.	In the Course-wide Content list, link Internet Activities; then link to Part 1 Internet Activities for Chapter 1-8. Open or save. (You can also choose Chapter 1, then link to Internet Activities. (In the Choose a Chapter field, if you select Chapter 1 observe that other chapter-specific links are available; for example, Multiple Choice Quiz, True or False, PowerPoint Presentations and Going to the Net Exercises.) Also observe that Course-wide Content includes a Glossary link.
7.	Complete the first activity, ACCOUNTING MONOPOLY – Chapter 1. This is a group activity. Check with your instructor regarding this assignment.

SUMMARY AND REVIEW

SOFTWARE OBJECTIVES: In Chapter 1, you used the software to:

1. Start Peachtree Complete Accounting 2008 (PCA).
2. Explore the sample company, Bellwether Garden Supply.
3. Back up Bellwether Garden Supply data.
4. Restore data with Peachtree's restore Wizard.

5. Operate Peachtree's menus, drop-down lists, toolbar, and navigation bar.
6. Work with Windows Explorer.
7. Make three backups: 1) Back up starting data for Bellwether Garden Supply; 2) back up Chapter 1 data; and 3) back up Exercise 1-2.

WEB OBJECTIVES: In Chapter 1, you did these Internet activities:

1. Used PCA to link to Peachtree's website at www.peachtree.com.
2. Went to the PRESS list and selected Recent Press Releases.
3. Linked to two Peachtree press releases and wrote an essay about each one.
4. Used your Internet browser to go to the book's website at www.mhhe.com/yacht2008.
5. Completed the first web exercise in Part 1.

GOING TO THE NET

Comment

The textbook website at www.mhhe.com/yacht2008 has a link to Textbook Updates. Check this link for updated Going to the Net exercises.

Access the Career Development website at
www.net-temps.com/careerdev/index.htm?type=careertalk&channel=fin&topic=careers
Read the article Careers in Accounting & Finance.

1. What three skills are essential for those seeking careers in accounting and finance?

2. What is the preferred educational background for an accountant?

3. List five career opportunities in accounting and finance.

True/Make True: Write the word True in the space provided if the statement is true. If the statement is not true, write the correct answer.

1. Shortcut keys enable you to use Peachtree's mouse.

____

____

2. Peachtree's Restore Wizard allows you to restore existing companies only.

____

____

3. Peachtree's graphical user interface is similar to other programs that use the Windows operating system.

____

____

4. If there is an underlined letter in the menu or option you want to select, hold down the **<Alt>** key and the underlined letter to make the selection.

____

____

5. In this book, the angle brackets are used to indicate individual keys on the keyboard; for example <Tab>.

6. You can close the application you are working with by single clicking with the mouse on the close button ().

7. You can access seven Navigation Center pages from the Navigation Bar.

8. In PCA, some icons are common to all windows while other icons are specific to a particular window.

9. The Navigation Bar is located at the bottom of most Peachtree windows.

10. The extension used for Peachtree backups is .XLS.

____

____

Exercise 1-1: Follow the instructions below to complete Exercise 1-1:

1. Start PCA. Open the sample company, Bellwether Garden Supply.
2. Follow these steps to restore your data from the end of Chapter 1:
   a. From the Company page, link to Restore. (The backup file was made pages 40-41.)
   b. The Select Backup File window appears. If the Location field is correct, click Next >; *or*, if your backup file resides in a different location, follow the steps in the Read Me box below.

> **Read Me:**
>
> If your back up file is located on external media, *or* if the Location field does *not* show C:\Program Files\Sage Software\Peachtree\company\BCS\Chapter 1.ptb in the Location field, click Browse, then follow these steps.
>
> 1. The Open Backup File window appears. In the Look in field, select the appropriate location of your backup file.
> 2. Highlight the Chapter 1.ptb file.
> 3. Click Open, then Next >. Continue with step c below.

   c. From the Select Company window make sure that the radio button next to An Existing Company is selected. The Company name field shows Bellwether Garden Supply; the Location field shows C:\Program Files\Sage Software\Peachtree\ Company\ BCS (or the appropriate location on your computer). Click Next >.

d. The Restore Options window appears. Make sure that the box next to Company Data is *checked*. Click 

.

e. The Confirmation window appears. Check the From and To fields to make sure they are correct. Click 

. When the Restore Company scale is 100% complete, your data is restored and you are returned to the menu bar.

f. If necessary, remove the external media.

3. Continue using PCA and complete Exercise 1-2.

Exercise 1-2: Follow the instructions below to complete Exercise 1-2:

1. Add Bob Wood as a new employee.

Employee ID:	BWOOD [use all caps]
Name:	Bob Wood [user upper and lower case]
Address:	1341 Brockton Road
City, ST Zip:	Norcross, GA 30093

2. Print the Employee List. (Select 

. In the Employees area, link to View Detailed List. Click 

, then make the selections to print. If necessary, click on Employee ID to display the list in alphabetical order.)
3. After printing the Employee List, close the Employee List window.

4. Follow these steps to back up Exercise 1-2:

a. Click 

; link to Back up.

b. Click 

.

c. Accept the default for backing up to the hard drive or make the selections to back up to another location. Type **Exercise 1-2** in the File name field.

d. Click Save.

e. When the window prompts that This company backup will require approximately 5.53MB, click OK. When the Back Up Company scale is 100% complete, you have successfully backed up to the current point. You are returned to the menu bar.

> **Read Me: Windows Vista—Problem Backing Up to USB Drive**
>
> Because of Windows Vista operating system security features, you need to backup to your desktop first. Then copy the backup file from your desktop to the USB drive. Refer to Appendix A, Problem Backing Up to USB Drive or Other External Media, pages 700-702 for detailed steps.

5. Exit Peachtree.

CHAPTER 1 INDEX

Chapter 2 Vendors

SOFTWARE OBJECTIVES: In Chapter 2, you use the software to:

1. Restore data from Exercise 1-2. (This backup was made on pages 49-50.)
2. Enter a purchase order.
3. Enter and post a vendor invoice in the Purchases/Receive Inventory window.
4. Go to the Payments window to pay a vendor.
5. Print a check in payment of the vendor invoice.
6. Analyze payments and vendor credit memos.
7. Make two backups: back up Chapter 2 data; and back up Exercise 2-2.[1]

WEB OBJECTIVES: In Chapter 2, you do these Internet activities:

1. Use your Internet browser to go to the book's website at http://www.mhhe.com/yacht2008.
2. Complete the Internet activity for Accounting Students.
3. Use a word processing program to write a summary about the website(s) that you visited.

In Chapter 2 you learn about how Peachtree works with vendors. The first thing you do is select 

from the Navigation Bar to go to the Vendors & Purchases Navigation Center.

When Bellwether Garden Supply orders and receives inventory from vendors, Account No. 12000, Inventory, is debited. Accounts Payable and the vendor account are credited.

Vendors offer Bellwether a ***purchase discount*** for purchase invoices paid within a discount period. Purchase discounts are cash discounts

[1]Refer to the chart on page 2 for the size of backup files.

from vendors in return for early payment of an invoice; for example, 2% 10, net 30 days. If Bellwether pays an invoice within 10 days, they can deduct two percent from the invoice amount. Otherwise, the net amount is paid within 30 days. In this chapter, you learn how PCA handles accounts payable transactions with vendors.

GETTING STARTED

Follow these steps to start PCA:

1. Start Peachtree.

2. Open the sample company, Bellwether Garden Supply. From PCA's startup window, there are two ways to open Bellwether:

   a. Click 

; select Bellwether Garden Supply, 

.
   b. *Or*, in the Other Tasks list, select Explore a sample company; Bellwether Garden Supply, 

.

In this textbook, it is assumed Bellwether Garden Supply is included with the PCA 2008 installation. Bellwether's hard drive location is C:\Program Files\Sage Software\Peachtree\Company\BCS. BCS is the shortened named that Peachtree assigns to Bellwether. If the BCS folder was deleted, you can restore the file from your backup. See the Read Me box on page 27 for detailed steps. The Restoring Data from Chapter 1 section below assumes Bellwether can be opened from Peachtree's startup window.

RESTORING DATA FROM EXERCISE 1-2

On pages 49 and 50, Exercise 1-2 is backed up (saved). In order to begin where you left off, restore the Exercise 1-2.ptb file. Restoring allows you to start where you left off at the end of Chapter 1.

Follow the steps on the next page to restore the Exercise 1-2.ptb file.

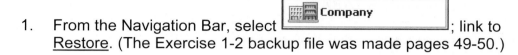

1. From the Navigation Bar, select [Company]; link to Restore. (The Exercise 1-2 backup file was made pages 49-50.)

2. The Select Backup File window appears. If the Location field shows C:\Program Files\Sage Software\Peachtree\Company \BCS\Exercise 1-2.ptb, click [Next >]. *Or, if your backup file is located on external media, read the information in the Read Me box below.*

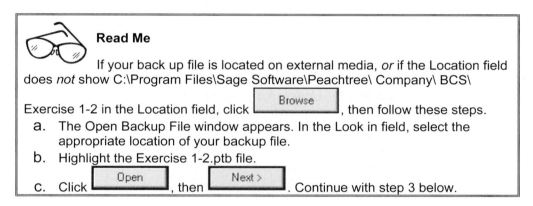

> **Read Me**
>
> If your back up file is located on external media, *or* if the Location field does *not* show C:\Program Files\Sage Software\Peachtree\ Company\ BCS\ Exercise 1-2 in the Location field, click [Browse], then follow these steps.
>
> a. The Open Backup File window appears. In the Look in field, select the appropriate location of your backup file.
> b. Highlight the Exercise 1-2.ptb file.
> c. Click [Open], then [Next >]. Continue with step 3 below.

3. From the Select Company window make sure that the radio button next to An Existing Company is selected. The Company name field shows Bellwether Garden Supply; the Location field shows C:\Program Files\Sage Software\Peachtree\Company\BCS. (*Hint:* Look at your title bar, it should show Peachtree Accounting: Bellwether Garden Supply.) Click [Next >].

4. The Restore Options window appears. Make sure that the box next to Company Data is *checked*. Click [Next >].

5. The Confirmation window appears. Check the From and To fields to make sure they are correct. Click [Finish]. When the Restore Company scale is 100% complete, your data is restored and you are returned to the Company page.

6. If necessary, remove the external media.

ACCOUNTS PAYABLE TASKS

Vendor transactions are a five-step process:

1. Maintain Vendors: Set up a new vendor.
2. Purchase Orders: Order items from one of Bellwether's vendors.
3. Purchase Invoices: Receive inventory or services from one of Bellwether's vendors. Apply a purchase order to a purchase invoice.
4. Payments: Pay a vendor or record a cash purchase. (PCA also includes vendor credit memos.)
5. Print Checks: Print a check for payment to a vendor or for expenses.

Before you begin adding accounts payable transactions, examine the Vendors & Purchases page. Follow these steps to do that.

1. From the Navigation Bar, select 

. The Vendors & Purchases Navigation Center appears. Compare yours with the one shown below.

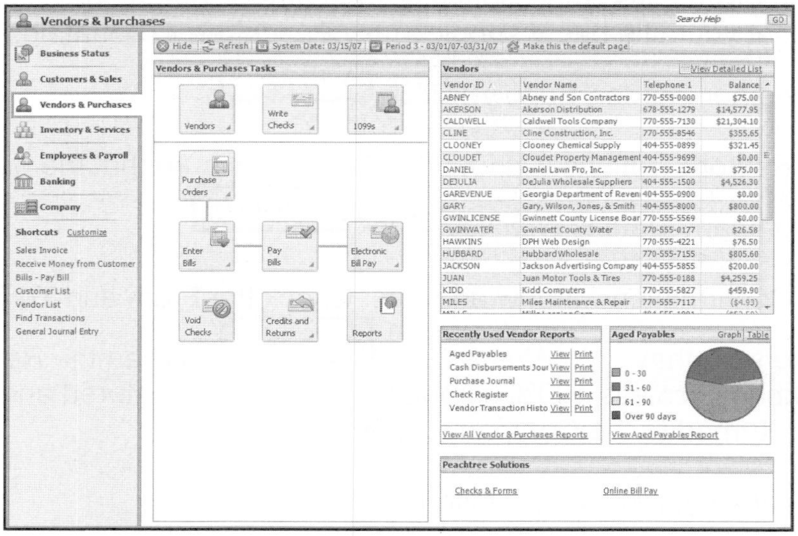

The Peachtree Vendors & Purchases Navigation Center displays information and access points related to the company's vendors. It includes a summary of vendor information, access to recently used vendor reports, and an overview of the company's aged payables. In addition, the Navigation Center shows the flow of vendor-related tasks. You can also link or drill down to various areas.

2. In the Vendors area, click ABNEY. The Maintain Vendors window appears with information about Abney and Son Contractors.

3. Click 

to return to the Vendors & Purchases page.

The Purchase Order Window

Purchase orders are used to place an order from a vendor. When you post a purchase order, you do not update accounting information. In an accrual-based accounting system, the accounting information is updated when you receive the items from the purchase order.

Changing Global Settings for Accounting Behind the Screens

Peachtree is a double-entry accounting system. There is a selection in Options/Global that allows you to hide general ledger accounts. This is called Accounting Behind the Screens. The PCA windows in this book show the general ledger accounts. To check the Accounting Behind the Screens settings, follow the steps shown below.

1. From the menu bar, click Options, then Global. The Accounting tab is already selected. The boxes in the section Hide General Ledger Accounts *must* be unchecked. (If necessary, click on the boxes to uncheck them.)

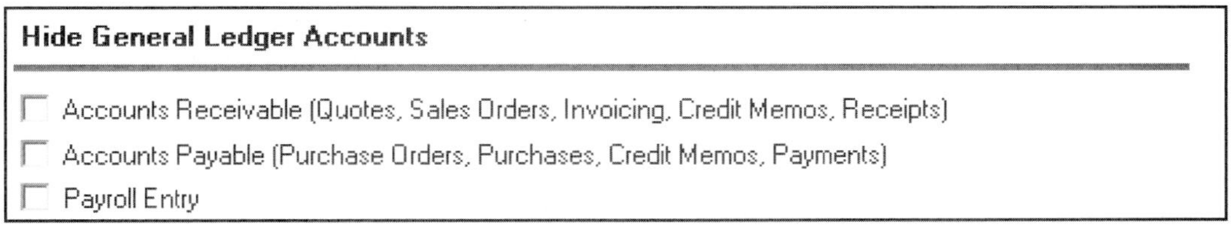

2. Observe that two boxes need to be checked in the Other Options section: Warn if a record was changed but not saved and Recalculate cash balance automatically in Receipts, Payments, and Payroll Entry. Make sure *both* of these Other Options boxes are checked.

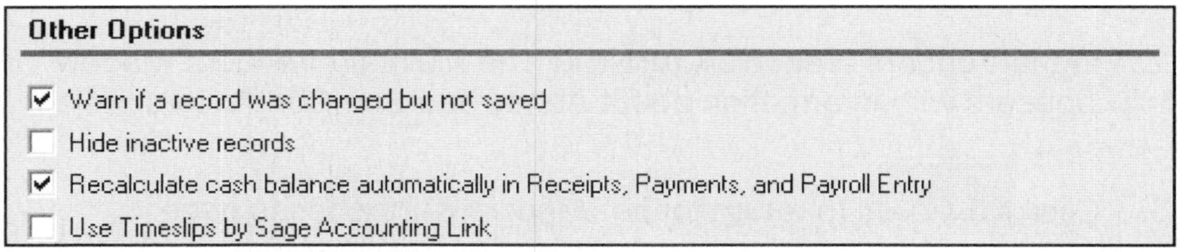

3. Click on the General tab. Make sure your Line Item Entry Display has 2 Line selected; and that the Smart Data Entry area has all three boxes checked.

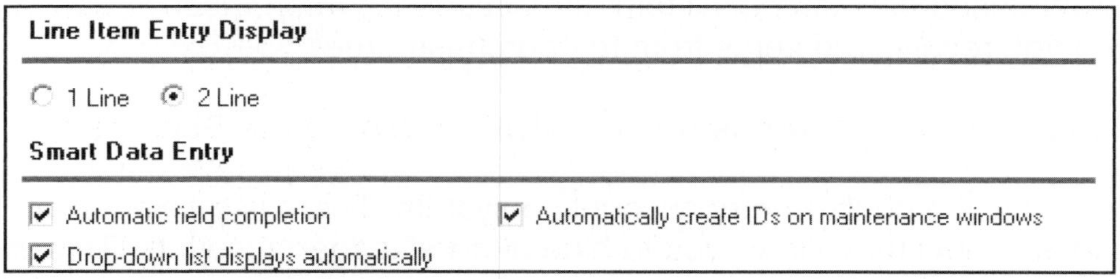

4. Click 

.

5. From the Vendors & Purchases page, select 

; New Purchase Order. The Purchase Orders window displays.

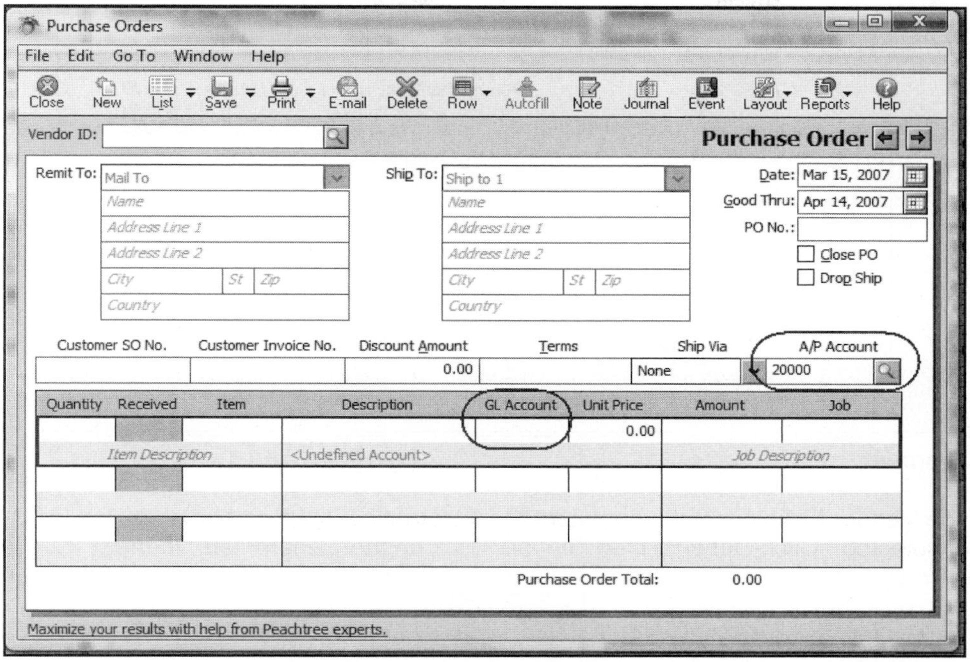

If your Purchase Orders window does *not* show an A/P Account lookup field 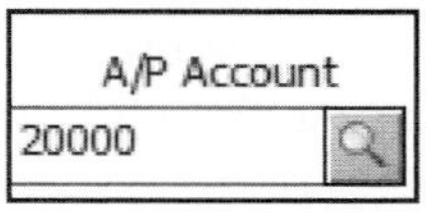

or a GL Account 

field, the option to hide general ledger accounts is selected. Uncheck the Hide General Ledger Accounts boxes in Options; Global. (*Hint: See the instructions on pages 57-58, steps 1 -4, for changing the global settings.*)

6. Your cursor is in the Vendor ID lookup field. Type **A** (use capital A). ABNEY displays in the lookup field.

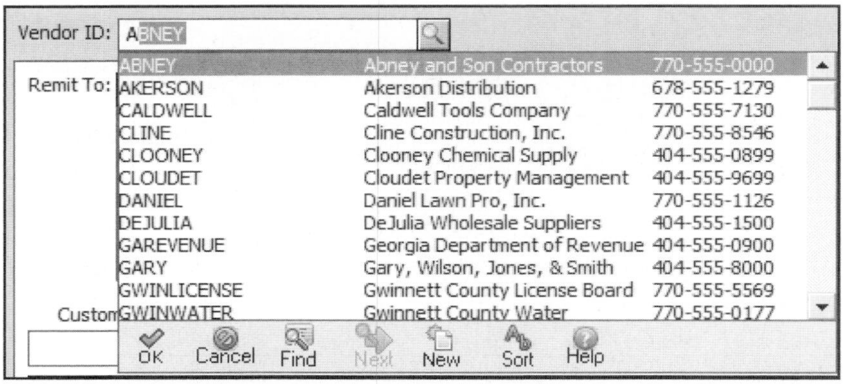

> **Comment**
>
> If the Vendor ID field is not completed, the Automatic Field Completion option is *not* selected. Click Options, then Global. Click on the General tab. In the Smart Data Entry section, make sure that a check mark is placed next to Automatic field completion. Click  when you are finished.

7. Click on the Date field. Highlight the date, then type **28** and press **<Enter>**. Your cursor moves to the Good Thru field. Press **<Enter>** to accept the default. Your cursor moves to the PO No. field.

8. Click on the Quantity column. Type **20** as the Quantity.

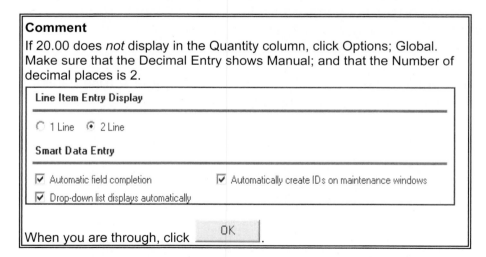

> **Comment**
>
> If 20.00 does *not* display in the Quantity column, click Options; Global. Make sure that the Decimal Entry shows Manual; and that the Number of decimal places is 2.
>
> 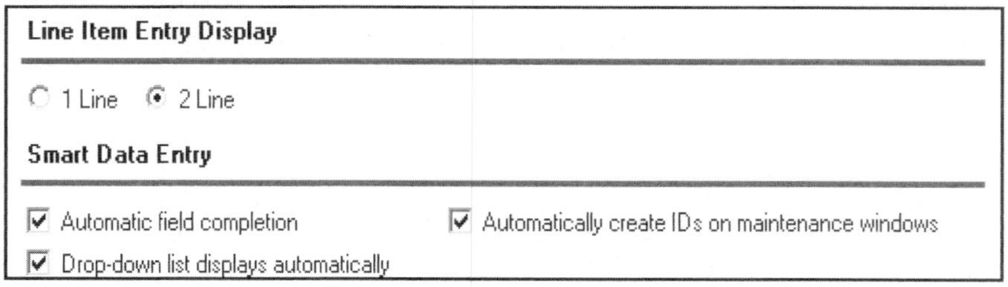
>
>
> When you are through, click  .

9. Press **<Enter>**. Your cursor is in the Item column.

10. Click once on the magnifying-glass icon in the Item column. Double-click on AVRY-10150 Bird Bath - Stone Gothic 2pc. The Description column is automatically completed.

11. Press the **<Enter>** key and your cursor moves to the GL Account column. Notice that Account No. 12000 is automatically selected. Account No. 12000 is the Inventory account. The word Inventory is also displayed on the line below the Description. (*Hint:* If Inventory is *not* shown, refer to step 1, page 57.)

12. Press the **<Enter>** key to go to the Unit Price column. The 51.95 unit automatically displays.

13. Press the **<Enter>** key to go to the Amount column. Peachtree calculates the quantity times the unit price and enters the result in the Amount column (20 X $51.95 = $1,039.00).

14. Press the **<Enter>** key to go to the Job column. The Job column is also a lookup field. It contains a list of the jobs and their descriptions. Since Bellwether does not apply this purchase to a job, press the **<Enter>** key to skip this field. Complete the following information:

Quantity: **50**
Item: **AVRY-10100** - Bird House Kit

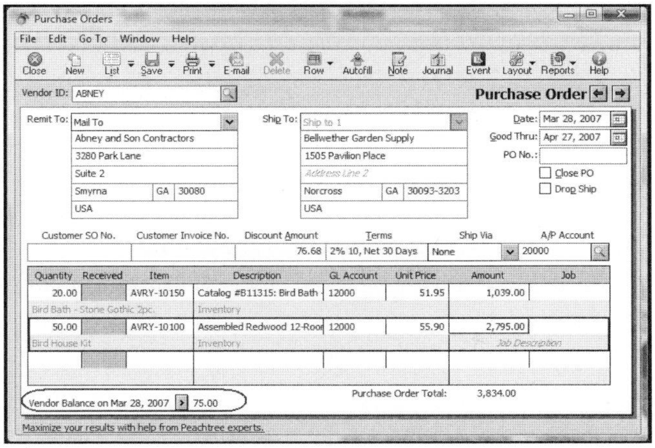

When you selected Abney and Son Contractors, the Vendor Account Balance as of March 28, 2007 also appears on the lower left side of the Purchase Orders window. You can drill down to Abney and Son Contractors vendor ledger by clicking on the right arrow () in the Vendor Balance area.

Observe that the icon bar also includes a Reports 

button. Click on the down-arrow next to the Reports button. You can also view these accounts payable reports from the Purchase Orders window.

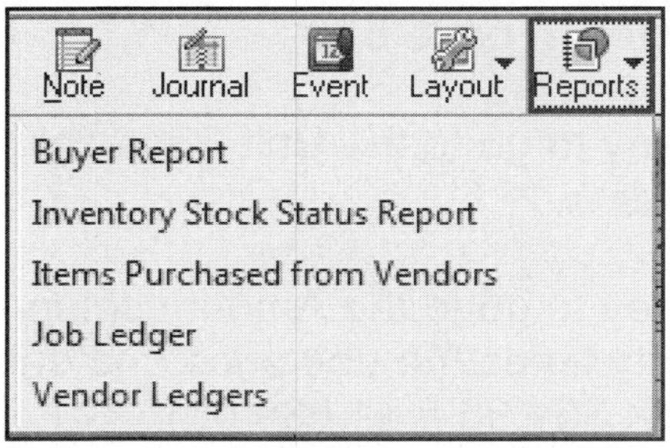

15. Click 

. The Accounting Behind the Screens, Purchase Order Journal window displays. Compare your Accounting Behind the Screens window to the one shown below. This window shows that Account No. 12000, Inventory, was debited for two items and that Accounts Payable was credited. (The vendor account, Abney and Sons, is also credited.)

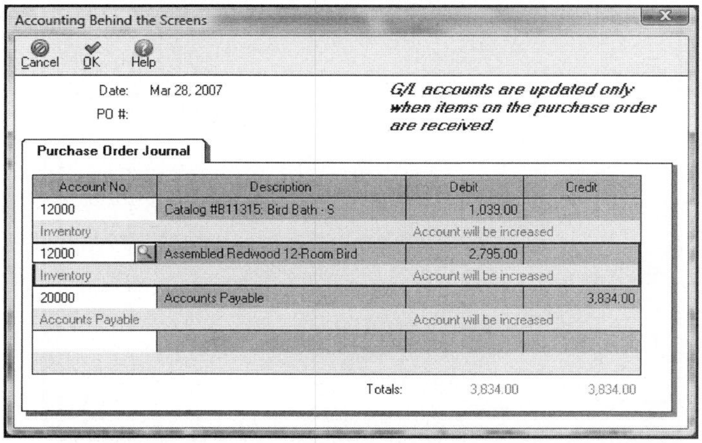

16. Click 

. You are returned to the Purchase Orders window. Since the vendor, ABNEY, is selected, this account is credited in the Vendor Ledger.

Printing Purchase Orders

When you select 

, PCA prints the purchase order and posts it to the purchase order journal. Follow these steps to print the purchase order:

1. Click 

. (*Or,* click on the down-arrow next to Print and select Print Preview to display the purchase order.)

2. The Print Forms: Purchase Orders window appears. Accept the default for First PO Number 101 by clicking 

. (If you selected Print Preview, instead of Print, you have a Print Preview button.) The purchase order starts to print. Compare your purchase order to the one shown on the next page.

ORDERED BY:

Bellwether Garden Supply
1505 Pavilion Place
Norcross, GA 30093-3203
USA

Voice: 770-724-4000
Fax: 770-555-1234

PURCHASE ORDER

Purchase Order No.: 101
Date Issued: 3/28/07

To:	Ship To:
Abney and Son Contractors 3280 Park Lane Suite 2 Smyrna, GA 30080 USA	Bellwether Garden Supply 1505 Pavilion Place Norcross, GA 30093-3203 USA

Good Thru	Ship Via	Account No.	Terms
4/27/07	None	BEL005	2% 10, Net 30 Days

Quantity	Item	Description	Unit Cost	Amount
20.00	AVRY-10150	Catalog #B11315: Bird Bath - Stone Gothic 2pc.	51.95	1,039.00
50.00	AVRY-10100	Assembled Redwood 12-Room Bird House on 14 ft. pole. Attracts Purple Martins, Bluebirds and Wrens	55.90	2,795.00
			TOTAL	$3,834.00

Authorized Signature ______________________

Comment

The purchase order form that printed is called Purchase Order. To print a different form, click [Change Form]. Then, select Purchase Preprinted as the form to print. When you select a different form, the information is the same but the look of the form changes.

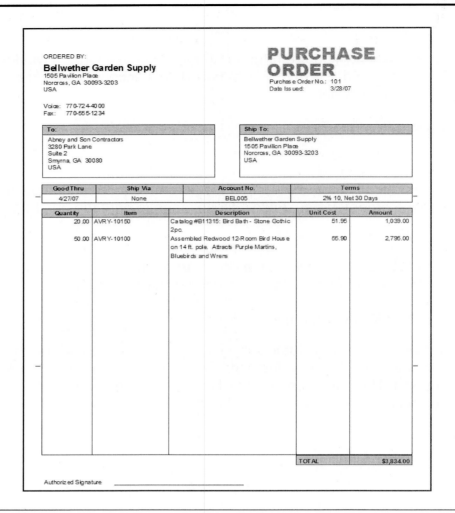

3. Click [Close] to return to the Vendors & Purchases page.

The Purchases/Receive Inventory Window

In PCA, the Purchases/Receive Inventory window is the Purchase Journal. The Apply to Purchases tab is the default. The lower half of the window shows columns for Quantity, Item (inventory items), Description, GL Account, Unit Price, Amount, and Job. Observe that the default for the A/P Account is 20000, Accounts Payable. The Purchases/Receive Inventory window looks like a purchase order. Similar to other PCA windows, the icon bar appears at the top of the window.

Follow these steps to learn how to process vendor transactions:

1. From the Vendors & Purchases page, select 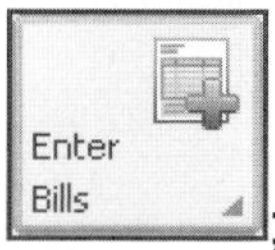

; New Bill. The Purchases/Receive Inventory window appears. Observe that the Apply to Purchases tab is selected. The cursor is in the Vendor ID field.

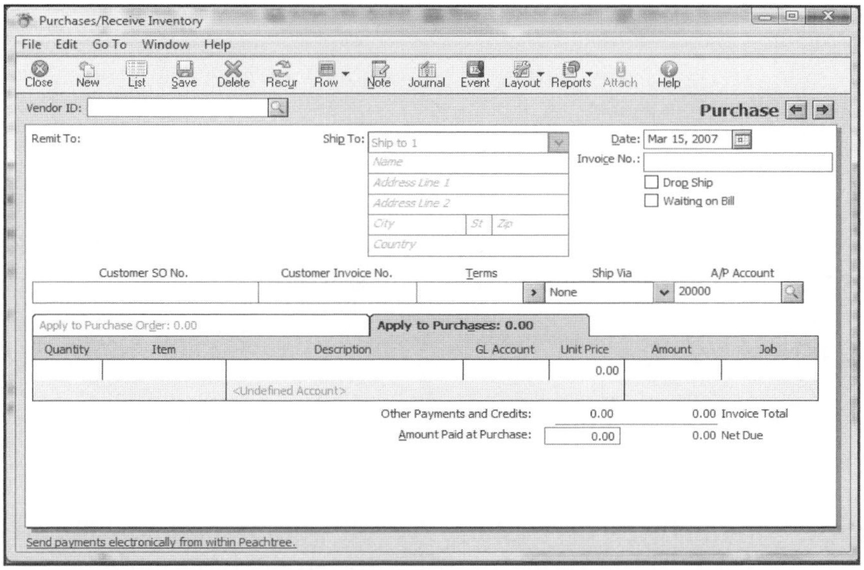

To see more lines in the Quantity/Item/Description table, make the Purchases/Receive Inventory window larger. You can do this by putting your mouse on the left border of the window. The mouse changes to a double-arrow [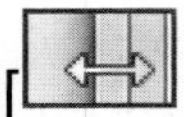]. With the cursor on the left border of the window, pull the window to the left to make it larger. If necessary, repeat this step on the bottom border.

2. With the cursor in the Vendor ID field, press the plus key **<+>** and the Maintain Vendors window appears.

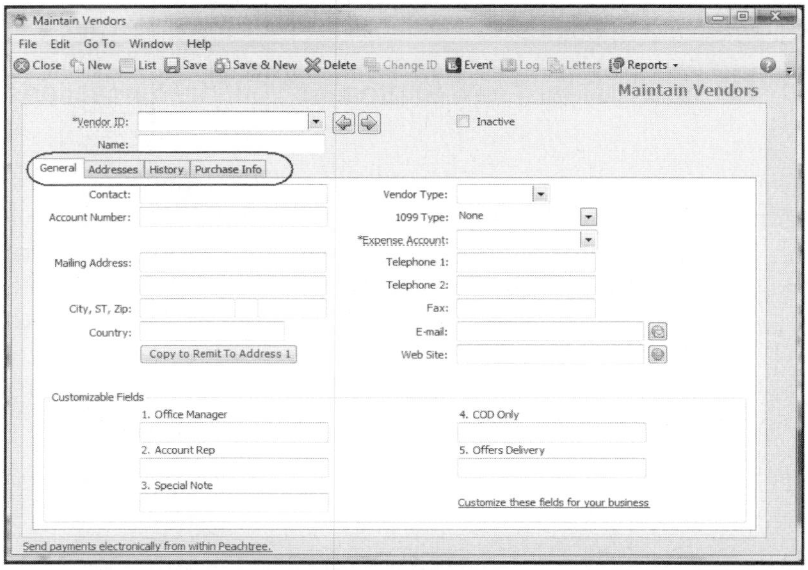

Observe that there are four tabs on the Maintain Vendors window: General, Addresses, History, Purchase Info.

Adding a New Vendor

You are going to enter a new vendor: Abbott's Landscaping. Since a ***coding system*** has already been established for Bellwether's vendors, you should continue to use the same one. The coding system used has uppercase letters. To be consistent, Abbott's Landscaping will use ABBOTT. Notice that the name of the company is typed in all capital letters. What if two companies have the same name, such as, Abbott's Landscaping and Abbott's Suppliers? They could be coded as ABBOTT and ABBSUPPL.

You should be consistent so that others working in your company can guess what a customer or vendor code is from the company's name. This is accomplished when you set up a logical, consistent coding system. Remember codes are ***case sensitive*** which means that you must type either upper or lowercase letters: ABBOTT is not the same as abbott.

You have choices for coding in PCA. Here are some other suggestions for coding Abbott's Landscaping:

ABB: the first three letters of the company's name.

ABBL the first three letters of a company's name, the first letter of the second name.

ABBOTT: an alphabetic code for a company name, using the first word. This is the Vendor ID used for Abbott's Landscaping and is consistent with Bellwether's other vendors.

Follow these steps to continue in the Maintain Vendors window:

1. Make sure the Maintain Vendors window is displayed. Type **ABBOTT** in the Vendor ID field and press **<Enter>**. Your cursor is in the Name field.

2. Type **Abbott's Landscaping** in the Name field.

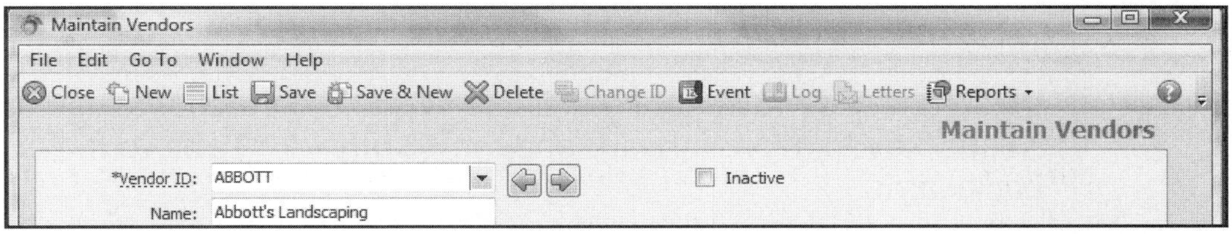

3. Press **<Enter>**. Your cursor is in the Contact field. The person who handles sales for Abbott's Landscaping is Lilio Chomette. Type **Lilio Chomette** and press **<Enter>**.

4. Your cursor is in the Account Number field. Click on the Vendor type filed. (Skip the Account Number and Address fields.) For now, you

are going to use only one more field in the Maintain Vendors window: Vendor Type. The Vendor Type field is used for classifying vendors. You could classify vendors as Service or Supply to indicate what type of goods you purchase from them.

5. Click on the down-arrow in the Vendor Type field. Select SUPPLY.

6. Click on the down-arrow in the Expense Account field. Scroll down the list. Double-click Account No. 57200, Materials Cost. Press **<Enter>**. When Abbott's Landscaping is selected as the vendor, Account No. 57200, Materials Cost, will be automatically debited.

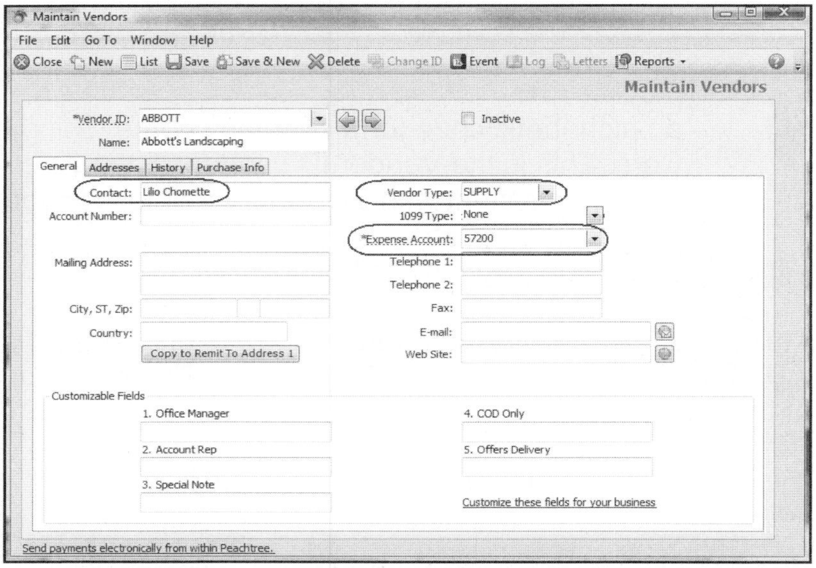

If you need to move between fields to make corrections, use the **<Tab>** key to move forward and the **<Shift> + <Tab>** to move backwards.

7. Click on the Purchase Info tab. Notice that the Vendor ID and Name fields stay the same: ABBOTT and Abbott's Landscaping.

8. Click 

, then 

return to the Purchases/Receive Inventory window.

Entering a Vendor Invoice

Make sure that the Purchases\Receive Inventory window is displayed and that the cursor is in the Vendor ID field. Follow the steps on the next page to enter the transaction.

Date	*Transaction Description*
03/15/2007	Invoice #ABB107 was received from Abbott's Landscaping for the purchase of Schultz Plant Food, $45. (*Hint:* Debit Account No. 57200, Materials Cost; Credit Account No. 20000, Accounts Payable/Abbott's Landscaping.)

1. In the Vendor ID field, type **A**. As soon as you type the letter **A**, the vendor list appears with ABBOTT, Abbott's Landscaping, highlighted. Press the **<Enter>** key.

2. Observe that the date is Mar 15, 2007. You are *not* going to change the date. Click on the Invoice No. field. In the Invoice # field, type **ABB107** and press **<Enter>**.

3. Click on the Quantity field and type **1** and press **<Enter>**.

4. Since you are not purchasing an inventory item, press the **<Enter>** key again.

5. The cursor moves to the Description field. In the Description field, type **Schultz Plant Food** and press **<Enter>**.

6. In the GL Account field press **<Enter>** to accept Account No. 57200, the Materials Cost account.

7. In the Unit Price field, type **45** and press **<Enter>**. Compare your Purchases/Receive Inventory window to the one shown on the next page.

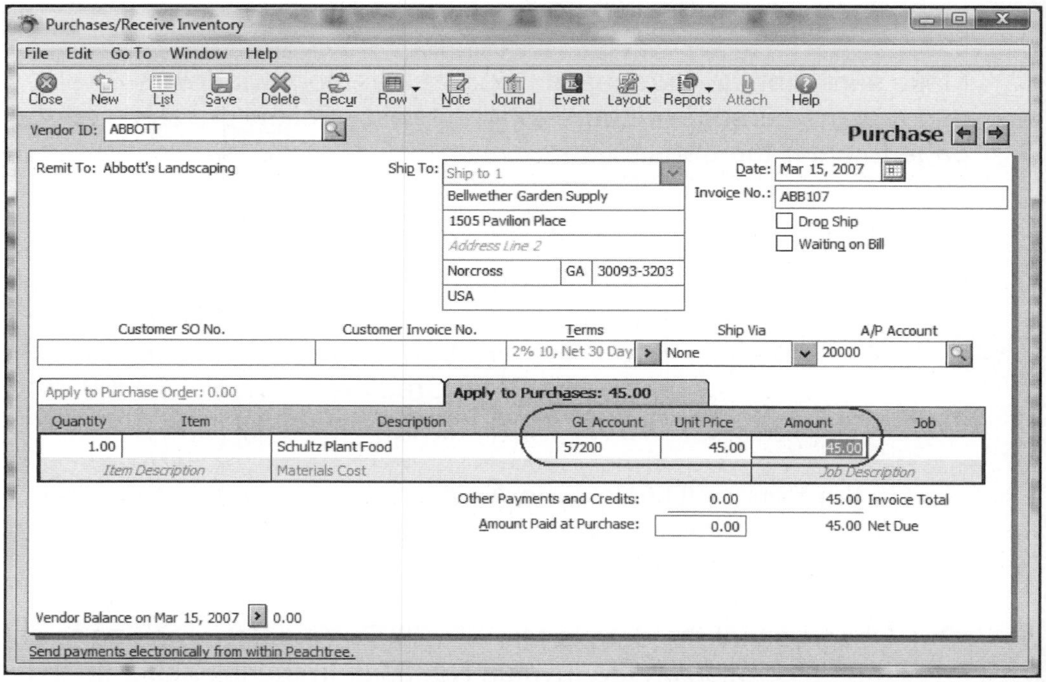

Comment: What if your Purchases/Receive Inventory window does *not* show an A/P Account field or GL Account column?

You should check your settings in the Options/Global selection. Make sure that the boxes in the Hide General Ledger Accounts section are unchecked. These steps were shown on pages 57-58, steps 1-4.

Editing a Journal Entry. Observe that the Purchases/Receive Inventory window includes a 

icon. Selecting List takes you the Purchase List window. From there you can drill down to an entry that you want to edit or change. The Purchases/Receive Inventory window is Peachtree's Purchase Journal. The List icon is included on journal-entry windows.

Posting a Purchase Transaction

When you made this entry in the Purchases/Receive Inventory window, you debited Account No. 57200, Material Costs, which is a General Ledger Cost of Sales account; and credited Accounts Payable/Abbott's Landscaping. ABBOTT is the vendor account.

Acct. #	Account Description	Debit	Credit
57200	Materials Cost	45.00	
20000/ ABBOTT	Accounts Payable/ Abbott's Landscaping		45.00

Follow these steps to post this transaction.

1. Make sure the Purchases/Receive Inventory window is displayed as shown on page 70.

2. Click 

to post the vendor invoice.

3. Click 

to return to the Vendors & Purchases page.

> **Read Me:**
>
> The Vendors area on the Vendors & Purchases page does *not* show the vendor that I added. How do I update the list?
>
> The toolbar (above Vendors & Purchases Tasks) includes a 
>
> button. Click it. Observe that the Vendors list now includes ABBOTT, Abbott's Landscaping with a $45.00 balance, which is the amount of the invoice added on pages 69 and 70.

PAYMENTS TO VENDORS

When you make a payment to a vendor, use the Payments window. The Payments window is the Cash Disbursements Journal. On pages 66-68, you added a new vendor; then entered and posted an invoice to that vendor on pages 69-70. *Both* the new vendor and invoice *must* be completed *before* a vendor payment can be made.

Date	*Transaction Description*
03/17/2007	Issued Check No. 10215 to Abbott's Landscaping in payment of Invoice No. ABB107.

Follow these steps to pay the Abbott's Landscaping invoice:

1. From the Vendors & Purchases page, select 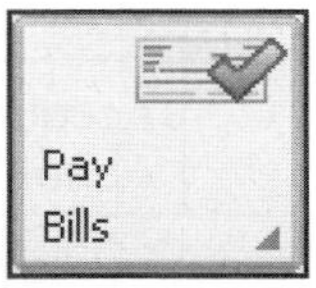

; Pay bill. Compare your Payments window to the one shown below. Remember, to enlarge the window use the cursor's double-arrow and pull the window to the left/right or top/bottom.

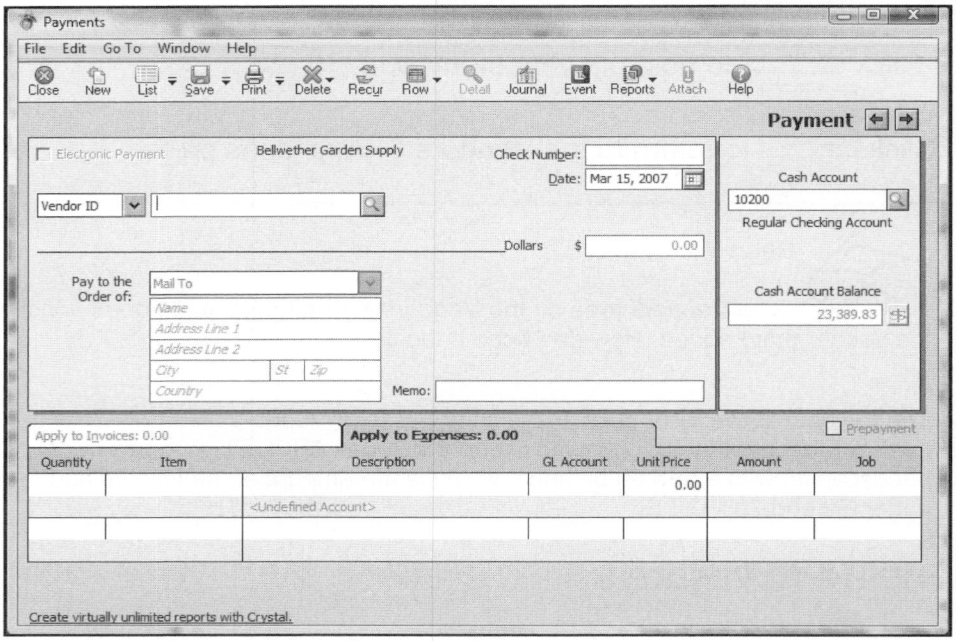

There are two parts to the Payments window: the check section at the top; and the invoice section at the bottom.

The cursor is in the Vendor ID field. Click on the magnifying-glass icon, then select ABBOTT, Abbott's Landscaping. Look at the invoice section. The invoice number ABB107 is shown with the amount that Bellwether owes to Abbott's Landscaping.

2. Click on the Date field. Type or select **17**.

3. Click on the Pay box for Invoice ABB107. Notice that the check portion of the window is completed. The amount to be paid is 44.10. This is the amount of the invoice less the 2% discount ($45 -.90 = $44.10).

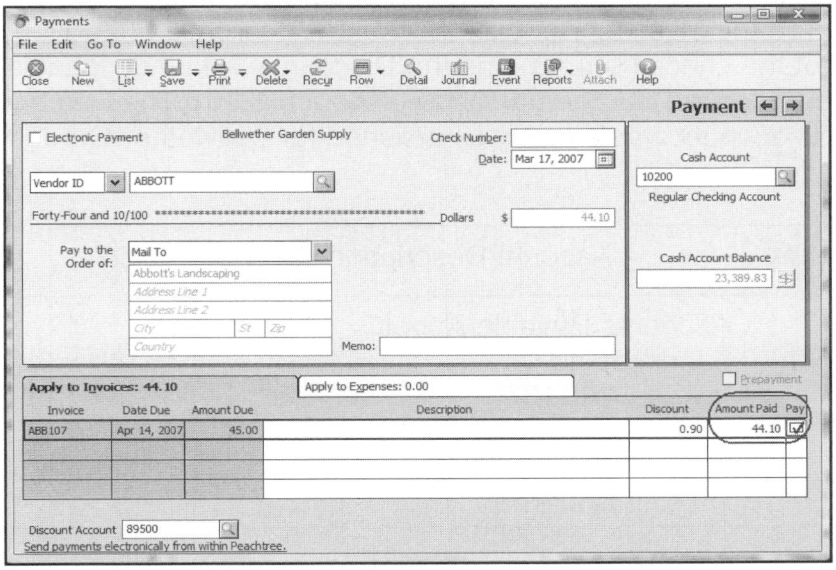

- **Troubleshooting Tip:** Observe that the Check Number field is blank. The check number is assigned when you print. You enter a check number if you are *not* going to print checks. You print checks on pages 74-77.

4. To see the Cash Disbursements Journal entry, click  . Observe the debits and credits (account distribution is shown on the next page). Click  to close Accounting Behind the Screens.

5. Click  to post the Payment window (cash disbursements journal).

6. Click  to return to the Vendors & Purchases page.

When you post this payment, the Accounts Payable account is debited for the full invoice amount ($45), which offsets the credit created when you entered the invoice. The cash account is decreased (credited) by the amount of the check ($44.10) and the Discounts Taken account is increased (credited) for the purchase discount ($.90). The Purchase Discounts account was already established for Bellwether Garden Supply.

Acct. #	Account Description	Debit	Credit
20000/ ABBOTT	Accounts Payable/Abbott's Landscaping Invoice ABB107	45.00	
10200	Regular Checking Account		44.10
89500	Discounts Taken		.90

PRINTING CHECKS

You can print a batch of checks or print one check at a time. Since we have only one check to print, you are going to print an individual check. PCA also has special check forms to use for printing checks. These may be purchased from Sage Software. Since you do not have check forms, print the check on a blank piece of paper.

Follow these steps to print a check:

1. From the menu bar, select Reports & Forms; Forms, Checks. The Select a Report or Form window appears.

2. Observe that the Forms tab is selected. If necessary, in the Forms Types list, click Checks. In the Forms list, OCR AP Laser Preprinted is automatically selected. (If not, select OCR AP Laser Preprinted.)

Comment

Step 2 instructs you to select OCR AP Laser Preprinted as the form to print. If this form does *not* print, select another one. The form you select is tied to the kind of printer you are using. Depending on your printer, you may need to make a different selection.

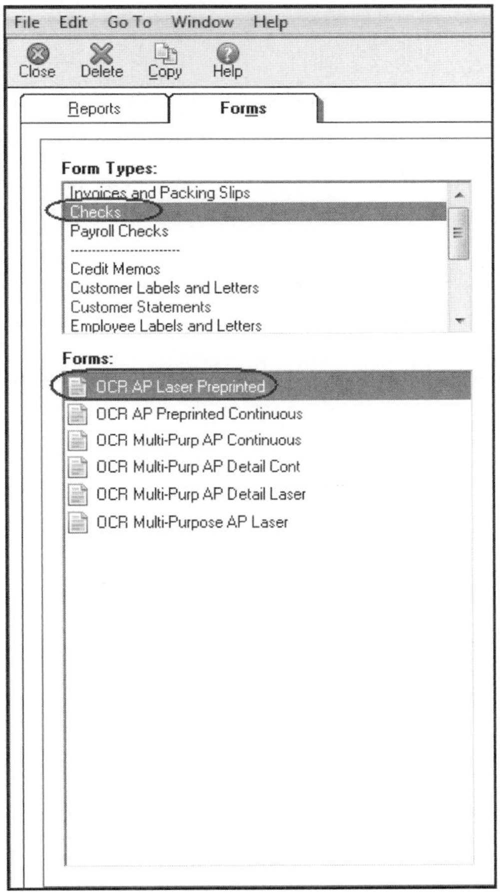

3. Double-click OCR AP Laser Preprinted.

4. In the Include checks through field, type or select March 17, 2007.

5. Type **10215** in the First check number field.

6. In the Filter vendor by fields, select ID, ABBOTT to ABBOTT.

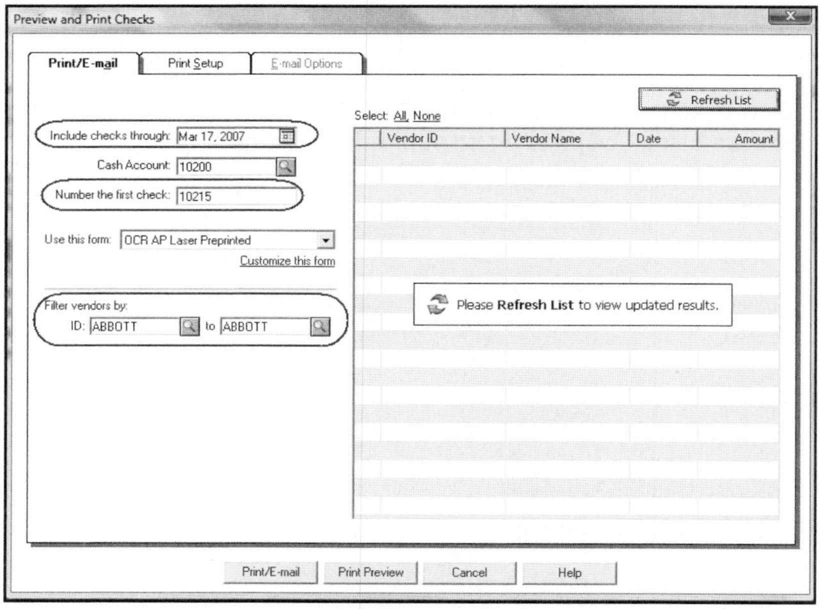

7. Click Print/E-mail or Print Preview. The check prints or displays.

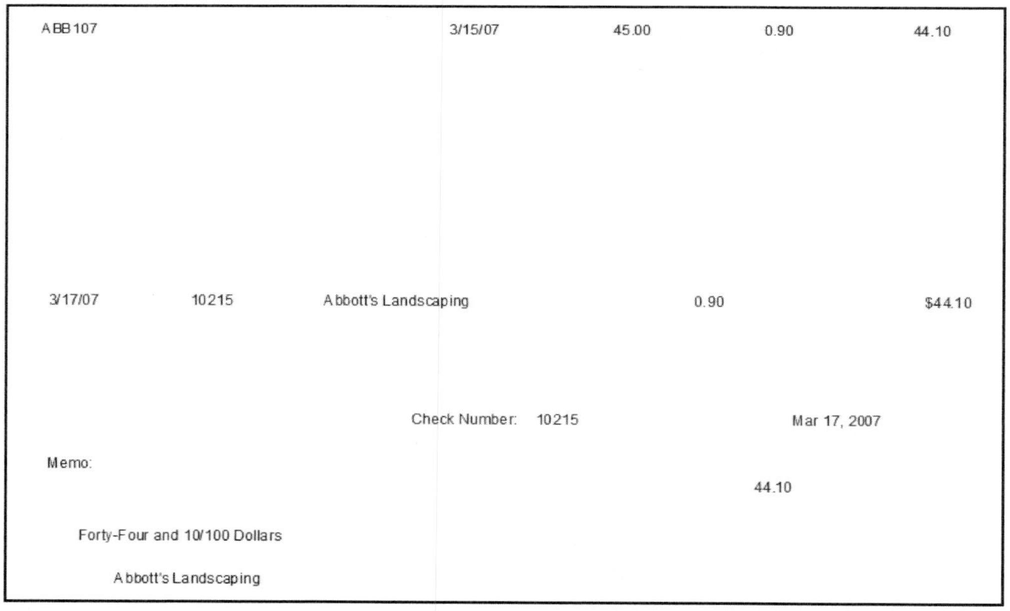

If you are printing the check, a window displays asking Did the Checks print properly, and is it OK to assign the check numbers to the checks? Make sure the check printed properly and the amount is correct. (See the Payments window on page 73.) The check illustrated above shows the check stub (top portion) and check portion. When you print Check No. 10215, there is also a bottom portion.

9. If needed, click Cancel and make the necessary corrections. If the check printed properly, click Yes.

10. Close the Select a Report or Form window.

DISPLAYING THE VENDOR LEDGERS

To display the Vendor Ledgers, follow these steps.

1. On the Vendors & Purchases page, Recently Used Vendor Reports area, link View All Vendor & Purchases Reports; select Vendor Ledgers, Display.

2. The Vendor Ledgers display. A partial Vendors Ledger is shown on the next page.

Bellwether Garden Supply
Vendor Ledgers
For the Period From Mar 1, 2007 to Mar 31, 2007

Filter Criteria includes: Report order is by ID.

Vendor ID Vendor	Date	Trans No	Type	Paid	Debit Amt	Credit Amt	Balance
ABBOTT	3/15/07	ABB107	PJ	*		45.00	45.00
Abbott's Landscaping	3/17/07	10215	CDJ		0.90	0.90	45.00
	3/17/07	10215	CDJ		45.00		0.00
ABNEY	3/1/07	B1000	PJ			75.00	75.00
Abney and Son Contracto	3/9/07	B1015	PJ	*		195.65	270.65
	3/12/07	VCM30001	PJ	*	195.65		75.00
	3/15/07		CDJ		50.00	50.00	75.00
AKERSON	3/1/07	Balance Fwd					9,398.75
Akerson Distribution	3/7/07	VCM30002	PJ	*	27.20		9,371.55
	3/8/07	4	PJ			5,179.20	14,550.75
	3/13/07		CDJ		1,000.00	1,000.00	14,550.75
	3/14/07	B1016	PJ	*		27.20	14,577.95
CALDWELL	3/1/07	Balance Fwd					21,214.10
Caldwell Tools Company	3/4/07	B1004	PJ			90.00	21,304.10
	3/6/07	B1017	PJ	*		45.90	21,350.00
	3/9/07	VCM30003	PJ	*	45.90		21,304.10
CLINE	3/6/07	B1023	PJ			55.65	55.65
Cline Construction, Inc.	3/15/07	B1006	PJ			400.00	455.65
	3/15/07	10213	CDJ		100.00		355.65
CLOONEY	3/1/07	Balance Fwd					124.68
Clooney Chemical Suppl	3/2/07	B1021	PJ			23.85	148.53
	3/12/07	116655	PJ			297.60	446.13
	3/12/07	10201	CDJ		124.68		321.45
CLOUDET							0.00
Cloudet Property Manage							
DANIEL	3/7/07	45541	PJ			75.00	75.00

The Vendor Ledger is the Accounts Payable subsidiary ledger. The Accounts Payable subsidiary ledger for Abbott's Landscaping was credited for $45 when you entered the vendor invoice in the Purchases/Receive Inventory window (pages 69-70). Once the invoice was entered, there was a balance of $45. When you posted the payment (see pages 71-74), PCA debited the vendor for the same amount. The balance after posting the payment is zero ($0.00).

VENDOR CREDIT MEMOS

Vendor credit memos are returns to vendors. You can apply vendor credit memos to any existing vendor invoice that has *not* been paid. All entries made on the Vendor Credit Memos window are posted to the general ledger, vendor records, and when applicable, inventory and job records.

You are going to use Peachtree's ***drill down*** feature to go to the original entry from the vendor ledger. Using the vendor ledger as an example, you use drill down to follow the path of an entry to its origin. In certain Peachtree reports, you can click transactions to drill down to the window that includes the original transaction information.

1. The vendor ledger should be displayed. Using the vendor, Abney and Son Contractors, put your cursor over the 3/9/07 vendor ledger entry. Your cursor changes to a magnifying-glass with a Z (for zoom) in it.

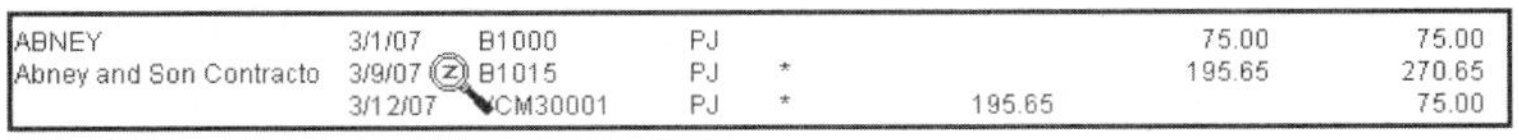

2. To drill down to 3/9/07 transaction window, double-click on it with your left mouse button. The Purchases/Receive Inventory window appears showing the original purchase of inventory items. The Purchases/Receive Inventory window appears.

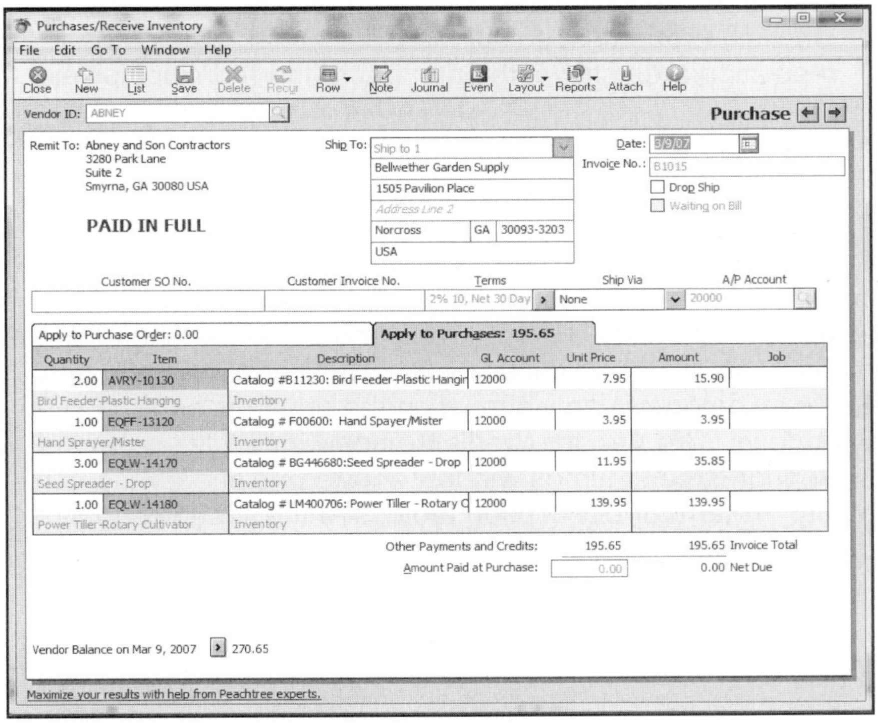

➢ **Troubleshooting Tip:** On my Purchases/Receive Inventory window, the Quantity, Item, Description, GL Account, Unit Price, and Amount table does *not* show multiple lines. If that is the case, you can use the arrows next to the Job column to scroll through the multiple lines. Try enlarging your screen with a cursor. If that doesn't work, read the next paragraph about screen resolution.

The number of lines on the Quantity, Item, Description, GL Account, Unit Price, and Amount table is determined by your screen resolution. On page iii of the Preface, the system requirements suggest screen resolution optimized for 1024X768.

If your Purchases/Receive Inventory window shows one line on the Quantity, Item table, then your computer is probably set up for 800 X 600 pixels. If your screen resolution is set at 1024 X 768 pixels, your Purchases/Receive Inventory window shows multiple lines in the Quantity/Item area. To check your screen resolution, go to the desktop and right click on an empty area; left click Properties, select the Settings tab. The screen resolution area shows the number of the monitor's pixels.

3. Click 

. You are returned to the Vendor Ledgers.

4. Drill down on the 3/12/07 vendor credit memo (VCM30001). The Vendor Credit Memos window appears. Observe that the Apply to Invoice No. tab shows B1015. This is the same merchandise that was purchased on 3/9/07, Invoice No. B1015. (See the Purchases/ Receive inventory window shown on the previous page.) Compare the two windows. The Vendor Credit Memos window is shown below. (If your Vendor Credit Memos window shows one line on the Item, Quantity, Returned, Description table, see the Troubleshooting Tip above.)

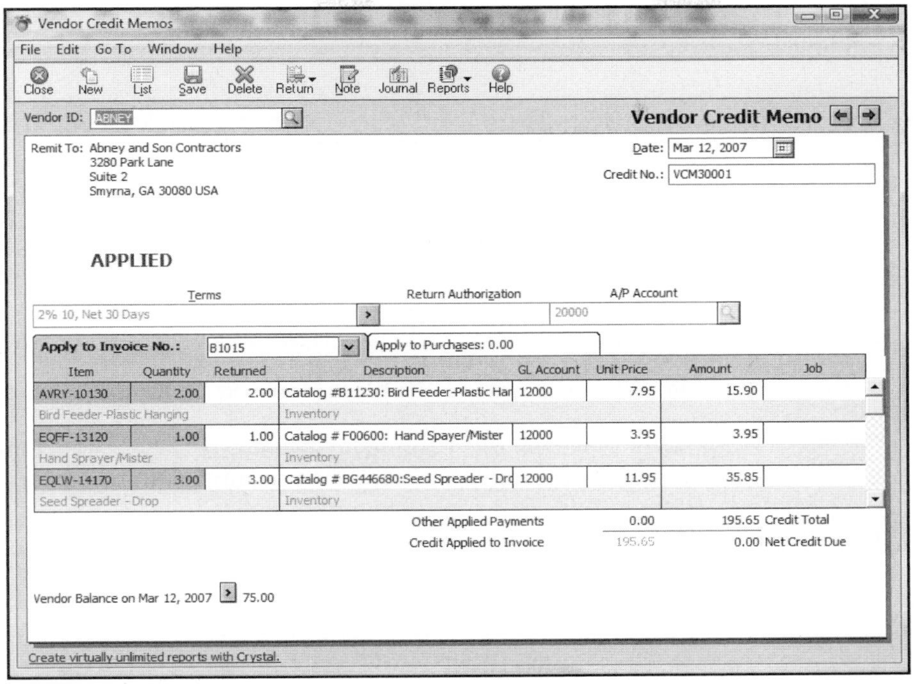

5. Click . You are returned to the Vendor Ledgers. Click  to return to the Vendors & Purchases page.

BACKING UP CHAPTER 2 DATA

Follow these steps to back up Chapter 2 data:

1. From the Navigation Bar, click ; link to <u>Back up</u>.

2. Click .

3. Accept the default for backing up to the hard drive or make the selections to back up to another location. Type **Chapter 2** in the File name field.

4. Click 

.

5. When the window prompts that This company backup will require approximately 5.57MB, click 

. When the Back Up Company scale is 100% complete, you have successfully backed up to the current point in Chapter 2. You are returned to the Company page.

Read Me: Windows Vista—Problem Backing Up to USB Drive

Because of Windows Vista operating system security features, you need to backup to your desktop first. Then copy the backup file from your desktop to the USB drive. Refer to Appendix A, Problem Backing Up to USB Drive or Other External Media, pages 700-702 for detailed steps.

6. Click File, Exit to exit Peachtree.

	INTERNET ACTIVITY
1.	From your Internet browser, go to the book's website at http://www.mhhe.com/yacht2008.
2.	Link to Student Edition.
3.	In the Course-wide Content list, link Internet Activities; then link to <u>Part 1 Internet Activities for Chapter 1-8</u>. Open or save. (You can also choose Chapter 2, then link to Internet Activities. (In the Choose a Chapter field, if you select Chapter 2 observe that other chapter-specific links are available; for example, Multiple Choice Quiz, True or False, PowerPoint Presentations and Going to the Net Exercises.) Also observe that Course-wide Content includes a Glossary link.
4.	If necessary, scroll down to ACCOUNTING STUDENTS – Chapter 2. Complete steps 1-3.
5.	Using a word processing program, write a summary about the site(s) you selected. Remember to include the website address of each link. Your summary should be no more than 75 words or less than 50 words.

SUMMARY AND REVIEW

SOFTWARE OBJECTIVES: In Chapter 2, you used the software to:

1. Restore data from Exercise 1-2. (Backup was made on page 49.)
2. Enter a purchase order.
3. Enter and post a vendor invoice in the Purchases/Receive Inventory window.

4. Go to the Payments window to pay a vendor.
5. Print a check in payment of the vendor invoice.
6. Analyze payments and vendor credit memos.
7. Make two backups: back up Chapter 2 data; and back up Exercise 2-2.

WEB OBJECTIVES: In Chapter 2, you did these Internet activities:

1. Used your Internet browser to go to the book's website at http://www.mhhe.com/yacht2008.
2. Completed the Internet activity for Accounting Students.
3. Used a word processing program to write a summary about the website(s) that you visited.

GOING TO THE NET

Access information about domain name statistics at http://www.zooknic.com/Domains/counts.html.

1. gTLD is an abbreviation for what word(s)? (*Hint:* Click gTLD to answer this question.)

2. What is the number of domain names worldwide?

3. How many .com names are there?

4. List the extensions that are used with domain names.

Multiple Choice Questions: In the space provided write the letter that best answers each question.

_____1. The default location for Bellwether backups is:

a. The location specified for external media.
b. C:\Peachtree\BCS\Company\[file name].
c. C:\Program Files\Company\BCS\[file name]\Exercise 2-2.
d. C:\Program Files\Sage Software\ Peachtree\Company\ BCS\[file name].
e. None of the above.

_____2. Cash discounts from vendors in return for early payment of an invoice are called:

a. Sales discounts.
b. Returns and allowances.
c. Purchase discounts.
d. Markdowns.
e. None of the above.

_____3. You can enter information within a lookup field by using one or more of the following keys:

a. Type the **<+>** symbol.
b. Double-click with the mouse.
c. a. or b.
d. Type the invoice number.
e. None of the above.

_____4. Why is it important that your coding system for vendors be consistent and logical?

a. All vendors and customers should be identified by 3 digits.
b. So that others working in your company can determine a vendor code from the company name.
c. All the vendors and customer numbers are already set up for Bellwether Garden Supply so you don't have to worry about it.
d. All customers and vendors should be identified by the first eight letters of a company's name.
e. None of the above.

______5. Which Navigation Bar selection do you use to record a vendor payment?

a. Reports/Accounts Payable/Disbursements Checks.
b. Maintain; Customers/Prospects.
c. Options; Global.
d. Vendors & Purchases; Pay Bills.
e. None of the above.

______6. It is important to use either upper or lowercase letters to identify a vendor because the program:

a. Is susceptible.
b. Doesn't recognize numbers.
c. Doesn't recognize symbols.
d. Is case sensitive.
e. None of the above.

______7, Which window do you use to add a new vendor?

a. Maintain Vendors.
b. Purchases/Receive Inventory.
c. Menu bar.
d. Select a Report.
e. None of the above.

______8. Going from the general ledger to the original entry window is called:

a. Drill down.
b. Coding.
c. Lookup.
d. None of the above.
e. All of the above.

_____9. When you make an entry in the Purchases/Receive Inventory window for Abbott's Landscaping you are debiting and crediting which accounts:

a. Dr. Accounts Payable/Abbott's Landscaping
   Cr. Cash in Checking
   Cr. Purchase Discounts
b. Dr. Cash
   Cr. Accounts Payable
c. Dr. Cash
   Cr. Sales
d. Dr. Materials Cost
   Cr. Accounts Payable/Abbott's Landscaping
e. None of the above.

_____10. Which of the following Navigation Bar; Vendor & Purchases selections do you use to issue a return of merchandise to a vendor?

a. Vendors & Purchases Tasks; Purchases/Receive Inventory.
b. Credits & Returns; New Vendor Credit Memo.
c. Sales/Invoicing.
d. Credit Memos.
e. None of the above.

Exercise 2-1: Follow the instructions below to complete Exercise 2-1.

1. Start PCA. Open Bellwether Garden Supply.
2. Follow these steps to restore your data from the end of Chapter 2:

   a. From the Navigation Bar, select 

; link to Restore. (The backup file was made on pages 81-82.)

   b. The Select Backup File window appears. If the Location field shows C:\Program Files\Sage Software\Peachtree\ Company\

BCS\Chapter 2.ptb, click **Next >**. If necessary, follow the steps in the Read Me box on the next page.

> **Read Me:**
>
> If your back up file is located on external media, *or* if the Location field does *not* show C:\Program Files\Sage Software\Peachtree\Company\BCS\Chapter 2.ptb in the Location field, click **Browse**, then follow these steps.
>
> a. The Open Backup File window appears. In the Look in field, select the appropriate location of your backup file.
> b. Highlight the Chapter 2.ptb file.
> c. Click **Open**, then **Next >**. Continue with step c below.

c. From the Select Company window make sure that the radio button next to An Existing Company is selected. The Company name field shows Bellwether Garden Supply; the Location field shows C:\ProgramFiles\Sage Software\Peachtree\Company\BCS (or the appropriate location on your computer). Click **Next >**.[2]

d. The Restore Options window appears. Make sure that the box next to Company Data is *checked*. Click **Next >**.

e. The Confirmation window appears. Check the From and To fields to make sure they are correct. Click **Finish**. When the Restore Company scale is 100% complete, your data is restored and you are returned to the menu bar.

f. If necessary, remove the external media.

3. Add the following vendor:

---

[2]If Bellwether Garden Supply is *not* shown in the Company Name field, refer to the steps shown in the Read Me box on page 27.

Vendor ID: LOZANOFC
Name: Lozano Office Supplies
Contact: Balt Lozano
Vendor Type: OFFICE
Expense Account: Account No. 75500, Supplies Expense

4. Enter the following transaction.

Date	*Transaction Description*
03/15/2007	Invoice No. H788 was received from Lozano Office Supplies for the purchase of five boxes of letter-size file folders, $10.95 each. (*Hint:* Account No. 75500, Supplies Expense, should be debited.)

5. Post this purchase.

6. Continue with Exercise 2-2.

Exercise 2-2: Follow the instructions below to complete Exercise 2-2.

1. Enter the following transaction.

Date	*Transaction Description*
03/17/07	Pay Lozano Office Supplies for Invoice H788, $53.65.

2. Post the Cash Disbursements Journal.

3. Print Check No. 10216. (*Hint: On the OCR AP Laser Preprinted Filter window, select the payment date and vendor.*)

4. Print the Vendor Ledgers.

5. Follow these steps to back up Exercise 2-2.

   a. Click 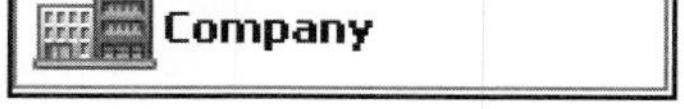

; link to Back up.

b. Click 

.

c. Accept the default for backing up to the hard drive; *or,* make the selections to back up to another location; *or* back up to external media. Type **Exercise 2-2** in the File name field.

d. Click 

.

e. When the window prompts that This company backup will require approximately 3.46MB, click 

. When the Back Up Company scale is 100% complete, you have successfully backed up to the current point in Chapter 2. You are returned to the menu bar.

f. If necessary, remove the external media.

Read Me: Windows Vista—Problem Backing Up to USB Drive

Because of Windows Vista operating system security features, you need to backup to your desktop first. Then copy the backup file from your desktop to the USB drive. Refer to Appendix A, Problem Backing Up to USB Drive or Other External Media, pages 700-702 for detailed steps.

6. Click File, Exit to exit Peachtree.

CHAPTER 2 INDEX

Chapter 3 Customers

SOFTWARE OBJECTIVES: In Chapter 3, you use the software to:

1. Restore data from Exercise 2-2. (This backup was made on pages 88-89.)
2. Go to the Customers & Sales page to enter quotes and sales orders.
3. Enter customer terms in the Maintain menu.
4. Record a sales invoice on the Sales/Invoicing window.
5. Print a sales invoice.
6. Analyze receipts and customer credit memos.
7. Post a receipt for previously invoiced amounts.
8. Make two backups: back up Chapter 3 data; and back up Exercise 3-2.[1]

WEB OBJECTIVES: In Chapter 3, you do these Internet activities:

1. Use your Internet browser to go to the book's website at http://www.mhhe.com/yacht2008.
2. Complete the Internet activity for the American Accounting Association.
3. Use a word processing program to write a summary about the website(s) that you visited.

Chapter 3 introduces you to the basics of how PCA works with customer transactions. First you learn about quotes and sales orders. Then, you learn how the information entered in customer maintenance is used when posting entries. For example, in the Maintain Customers/Prospects window, you set a range of days within which a customer can receive a discount and set the discount percentage. This information will print on the sales invoices you record. The discount is automatically applied when you enter a receipt within the allotted time. You can see an overview of all outstanding invoices via the Collection Manager in the Analysis menu.

---

[1]Refer to the chart on page 2 for the size of backup files.

GETTING STARTED

Follow these steps to start PCA:

1. Start Peachtree. Open the sample company, Bellwether Garden Supply. (If Bellwether Garden Supply is not shown, restore a New Company. Refer to the Read Me box on page 27.)

2. Restore your data from the Exercise 2-2 back up.

   a. From the Navigation Bar, select Company; link to <u>Restore</u>. (The Exercise 2-2 backup file was made pages 88-89.)

   b. The Select Backup File window appears. If the Location field shows C:\Program Files\Sage Software\Peachtree\ Company\ BCS\Exercise 2-2 .ptb, click Next >. (*Or,* click Browse, then select the appropriate location of the Exercise 2-2 backup file; click Next >.)

   c. The Select Company window appears. The radio button next to An Existing Company is selected. The Company name field shows Bellwether Garden Supply; the Location field shows C:\ProgramFiles\Sage Software\Peachtree\Company\BCS (or the appropriate location on your computer). Click Next >.

   d. The Restore Options window appears. Make sure that the box next to Company Data is *checked.* Click Next >.

   e. The Confirmation window appears. Check the From and To fields to make sure they are correct. Click Finish. When the Restore Company scale is 100% complete, your data is restored and you are returned to the menu bar.

   f. If necessary, remove the external media.

ACCOUNTS RECEIVABLE TASKS

The four basic tasks in Accounts Receivable are:

1. Quotes: Allows you to enter a quote for a customer.
2. Sales Orders: Sales orders provide you with a means of tracking backorders for your customers.
3. Sales/Invoicing: When you are ready to ship items, the sales/invoicing window is used.
4. Receipts: Used for recording receipts from customers. (PCA also includes credits and returns.)

Before you begin adding accounts receivable transactions, examine the Customers & Sales page. Follow these steps to do that.

1. From the Navigation Bar, select 

. The Customers & Sales Navigation Center appears.

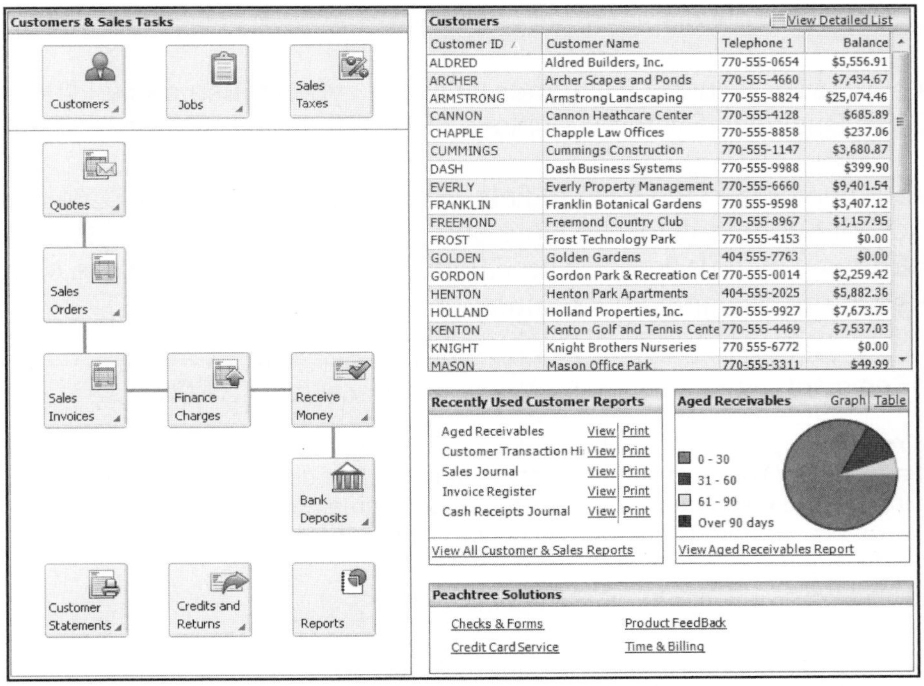

Peachtree's Customers & Sales Navigation Center displays information and access points related to customers. It includes a summary of customer information, access to recently used customer reports, and an overview of the company's aged receivables. In addition, the Navigation Center shows the flow of customer-related tasks. You can also link or drill down to various areas.

2. Link to a couple areas to explore the Customers & Sales page. Close any open windows, then continue with the next section.

Entering a Quote

When you enter a quote for a customer, you are *not* updating any accounting information or inventory amounts. PCA calculates what the total cost of the sale will be for a customer, including sales tax and freight. You can then print the quote for the customer. Follow these steps to enter a sales quote.

1. From the Customers & Sales page, click 

; New Quote. The Quotes window displays.

2. Your cursor is in the Customer ID field. Type **D** (use capital D). Dash Business Systems displays. Press the **<Enter>** key.

3. Your cursor is in the Ship to field (Ship to 1). Click on the Date field. Accept the default for the Date and Good thru dates by pressing the **<Enter>** key four times. The Quote No. field is blank. This is okay. Peachtree assigns a quote number automatically.

> **Comment**
>
> You can also enter a number that you want to print in the Quote # field. If you assign your own number, PCA sorts numbers one digit at a time. Therefore, it is a good idea to assign numbers with the same number of digits. For example, PCA sorts the following numbers in this order:
>
> 1
> 104
> 12
> 2
> 23

4. Your cursor should be in the Customer PO field. Observe that this field is blank. Since this customer does not have a purchase order number, you are going to leave this field blank. Click on Quantity column. Type **1** and press **<Enter>**. (If the Quantity column shows .01, refer to the steps 2 a. and b. on page 16 for setting two decimal places.)

5. In the Item column, select EQFF-13110 Fertilizer Compression Sprayer. (*Hint: Scroll down the Item list to make this selection.*) The Description, GL Account, Unit Price, Tax, and Amount columns are automatically completed.

> **Comment**
>
> If the GL Account column is not displayed on the Quotes window, you need to check your global settings. Refer to step 2d. on page 16 to make sure that the boxes in the Hide General Ledger Accounts section are unchecked (see Options/Global).

6. Click on the Quantity column. Type **4** then select EQWT-15120 Garden Hose - 75 ft. x 5/8 in. hose for the item. Compare your Quotes window to the one shown below.

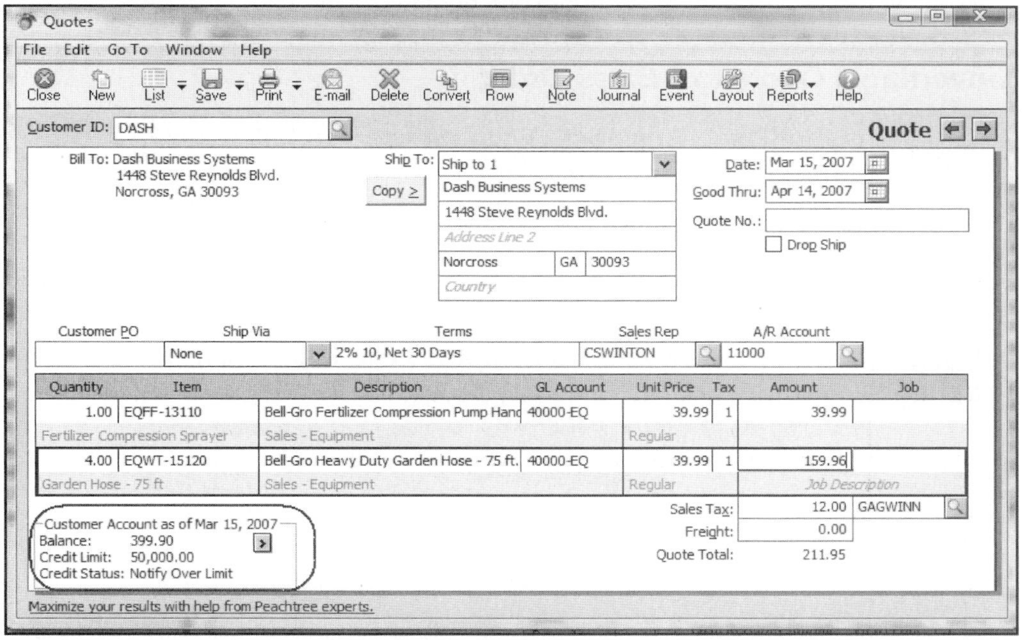

When you selected Dash Business Systems, the Customer Account balance as of March 15, 2007 also appears on the lower left side of the Quotes window, along with the Credit Limit and Credit Status. You can drill down to Dash Business Systems' customer ledger by clicking on the right arrow () in the Customer Account area.

7. To see the journal entry, click 

. The Quotes Journal lists the sales taxes that are paid for the transaction, the price for each item, and the amount that Bellwether will receive from the customer on this quote. Close the Accounting Behind the Screens window by clicking 

.

8. Click 

to post this sales quote, then click 

to return to the Customers & Sales page.

> **Comment**
>
> When a sales quote is saved, you are *not* updating any general ledger accounts. That is handled through the Sales/Invoicing window, which you work with after you convert the quote and print the sales order.

Converting a Quote to a Sales Order

Let's assume that Dash Business Systems accepts this sales quote. Let's convert the quote to a sales order.

1. Click 

; View and Edit Quotes. The Quote List window appears.

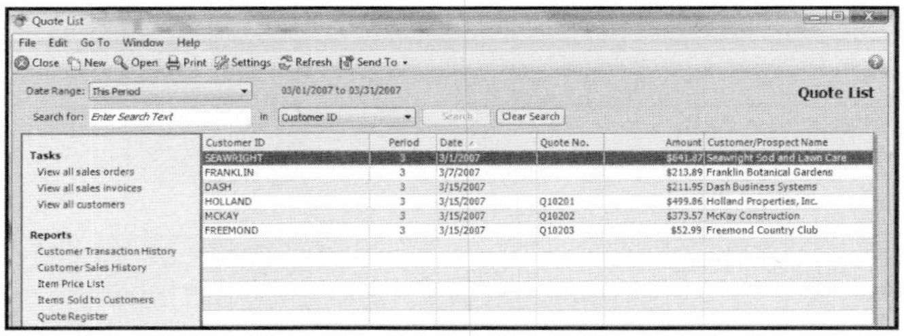

2. Double-click DASH. The Quotes window appears showing the March 15, 2007 quote. Compare this to the Quotes window shown on page 95.

3. Click 
Convert
. There are three options: Sales/Invoice; Sales/Invoice and Print Now; Sales Order. Click on the radio button next to Sales Order.

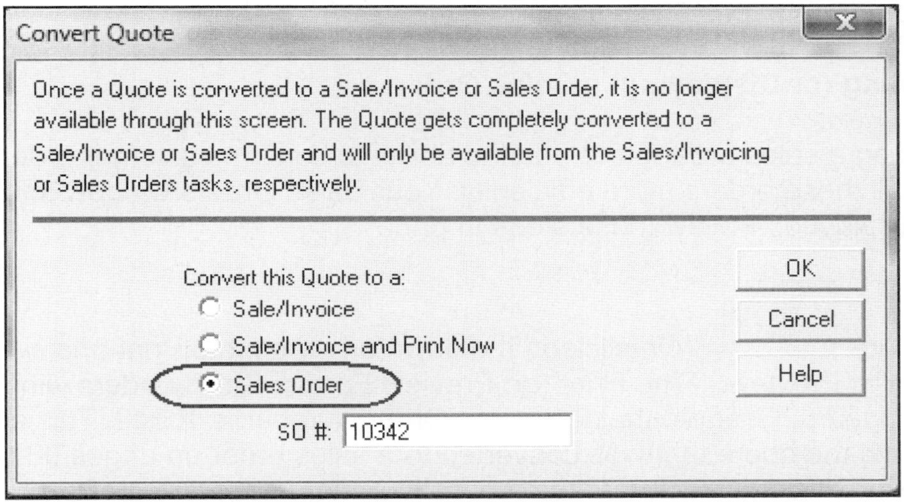
Convert Quote
Once a Quote is converted to a Sale/Invoice or Sales Order, it is no longer available through this screen. The Quote gets completely converted to a Sale/Invoice or Sales Order and will only be available from the Sales/Invoicing or Sales Orders tasks, respectively.
Convert this Quote to a:
Sale/Invoice
Sale/Invoice and Print Now
Sales Order
SO #: 10342
OK
Cancel
Help

4. Click 
OK
. You are returned to the Quotes window. Click 
Close
. You just converted the sales quote to a sales order. Now you can invoice the customer for shipment.

5. Close all windows. (*Hint:* Select Window; Close All.)

Sales Orders

The Sales Order window allows you to enter items ordered by your customer and track backorders. Sales orders also allow you to ship partial quantities of items, or quantities greater than the originally ordered quantity. In the steps that follow, use the Sales Quote converted to a Sales Order on pages 96-97.

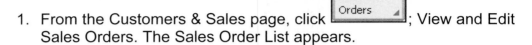

1. From the Customers & Sales page, click ; View and Edit Sales Orders. The Sales Order List appears.

2. Select the Dash Business Systems Sales Order, Reference number 10342. (*Hint:* Double click on Dash Business systems to open the Sales Orders window.) This sales order agrees with the Quotes window shown on page 95. (The Quote was converted to a sales order on pages 96-97.)

Printing (or Displaying) a Sales Order

Printing a sales order gives you the ability to confirm customer orders and fill these orders more efficiently. Your Sales Orders window should be displayed. Follow these steps to print.

1. Click . (*Or,* click on the down arrow next to Print and select Print Preview.) The Print (*or,* Preview Forms: Sales Orders window appears. Observe that the Sales Order Number is 10342. This agrees with the quote that was converted to a sales order on pages 96-97. Remember, Peachtree automatically assigned the sales order number. (*Hint:* If necessary, click anywhere on the Sales Orders window to activate the Print icon.)

2. Accept the Last used form – Sales Order w/Totals. Click  (*or,* ). The sales order starts to print or displays. Compare your sales order with the one shown on the next page.

Bellwether Garden Supply
1505 Pavilion Place
Norcross, GA 30093-3203
USA

Voice: 770-724-4000
Fax: 770-555-1234

SALES ORDER

Sales Order Number: 10342
Sales Order Date: Mar 15, 2007
Ship By: Mar 15, 2007
Page: 1

To:
Dash Business Systems
1448 Steve Reynolds Blvd.
Norcross, GA 30093

Ship To:
Dash Business Systems
1448 Steve Reynolds Blvd.
Norcross, GA 30093

Customer ID	PO Number	Sales Rep Name
DASH		Colista A. Swinton
Customer Contact	**Shipping Method**	**Payment Terms**
McKenzie Dash	None	2% 10, Net 30 Days

Quantity	Item	Description	Unit Price	Amount
1.00	EQFF-13110	Bell-Gro Fertilizer Compression Pump Hand Sprayer - 3 Gallon	39.99	39.99
4.00	EQWT-15120	Bell-Gro Heavy Duty Garden Hose - 75 ft. x 5/8 in. hose	39.99	159.96
		Subtotal		199.95
		Sales Tax		12.00
		Freight		0.00
		TOTAL ORDER AMOUNT		**211.95**

3. Close all windows. (*Hint:* From the menu bar, click Window, Close All.)

THE MAINTAIN CUSTOMERS/PROSPECTS WINDOW

The first step is to select the customer you are going to invoice and to change one item of information: the discount percentage offered for timely payment.

1. From the Customers & Sales page, click 

; New Customer. The Maintain Customers/Prospects window displays. The cursor is in the Customer ID field. Notice the down-arrow in this field.

2. Click on the down-arrow in the Customer ID field to open the customers/prospects list.[2]

3. The customer file you are going to use is Teesdale Real Estate. Scroll down the customer list, then click **TEESDALE** for **Teesdale Real Estate** to select it from the list. The Maintain Customers/Prospects window shows a completed record for Teesdale Real Estate.

---

[2]There are three ways to open the list in a lookup field. First, make sure that your cursor is in the Customer ID field: 1) Press the right mouse button; 2) type a question mark **<?>**; 3) left-click the down-arrow.

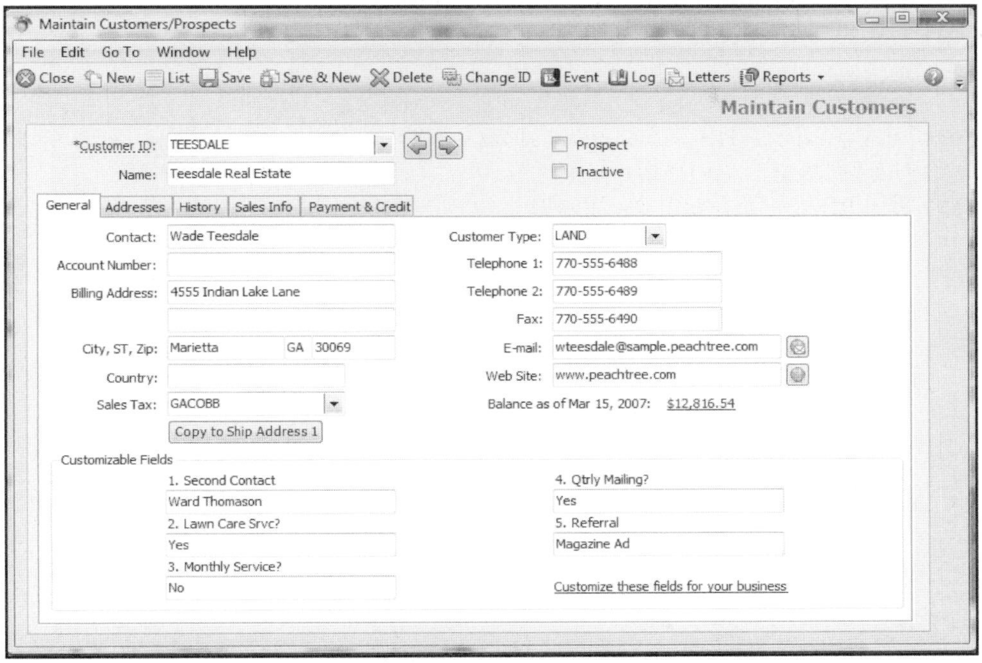

Entering a Discount for a Customer

Because Teesdale Real Estate is such a good customer, we're going to increase their discount from 2% to 5%. In accounting, this is called a ***sales discount***. The standard sales discount for Bellwether is 2% if paid within 10 days. Teesdale's new sales discount is 5% if paid within 15 days.

Follow these steps to enter a discount for a customer:

1. The Maintain Customers/Prospects window should be displayed. Click on the Payment & Credit tab.

2. In the Terms and Credit Area (right side of window), click on the down-arrow. Select Customize terms for this customer.

3. Click on the Discount in field. Type **15** and press **<Enter>**. The cursor moves to the Discount Percent field.

4. Type **5** and press **<Enter>**.[3]

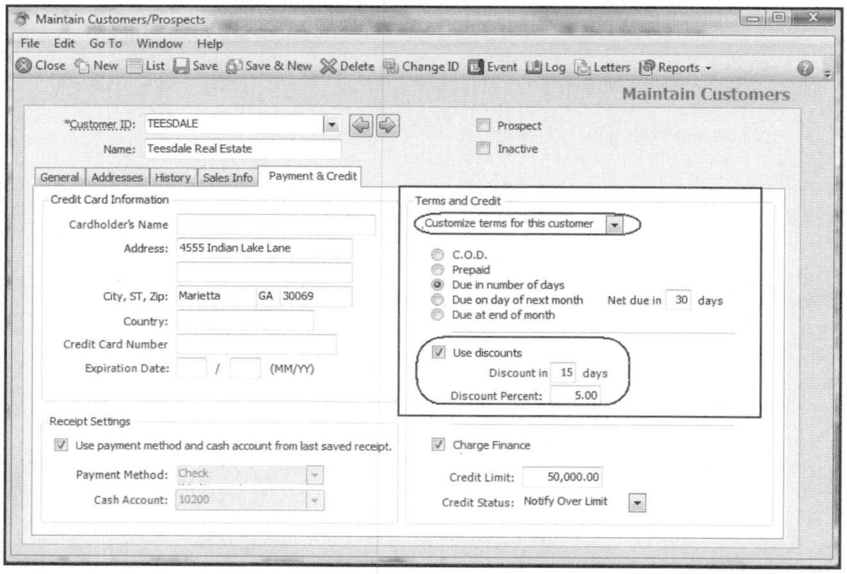

5. Click  .

6. Close the Maintain Customers/Prospects window to return to the Customers & Sales page.

Entering a Sale to a Customer

Let's learn how to invoice Teesdale Real Estate. When you want to print or record an invoice in PCA, you enter a sales invoice for a customer on the Sales/Invoicing window. Like a Sales Journal, the Sales/Invoicing window is reserved for sales from credit customers. The transaction you are going to enter is shown below.

Date	*Transaction Description*
03/01/07	Bellwether Garden Supply sold 5 hose-end sprayers to Teesdale Real Estate, Customer ID, TEESDALE.

---

[3]You should have set two decimal places in Chapter 1 (see page 16).

Follow these steps to learn how to use the Sales/Invoicing window:

1. From the Customers & Sales page, click 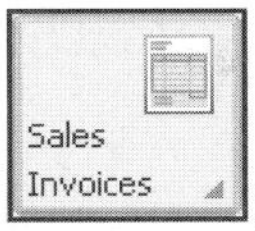; New Sales Invoice. The Sales/Invoicing window appears.

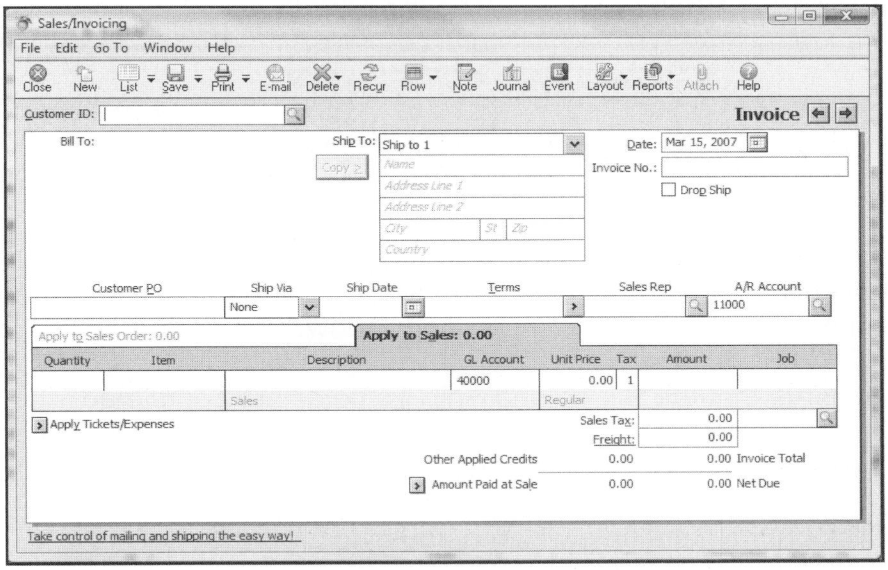

Use the Sales/Invoicing window for credit sales from customers. If you want to enter a cash sale, you would use the Receipts window, not the Sales/Invoicing window. The Sales/Invoicing window is for credit customers only. Here's a way to remember the difference between Receipts and Sales/Invoicing: if the transaction involves real money (cash or check), enter it in the Receipts window; if the transaction involves a credit sale, enter it in the Sales/Invoicing window. The Sales/Invoicing window posts to the Sales Journal. The Receipts window posts to the Cash Receipts Journal.

The Sales/Invoicing window should be displayed. The cursor is in the Customer ID field. Don't worry if you have forgotten Teesdale's customer ID number because PCA knows it. The Customer ID field has a lookup field.

2. With the cursor in the Customer ID field, click the right mouse button (or type a question mark, **<?>**). You may also click .

3. Highlight Teesdale Real Estate, TEESDALE.

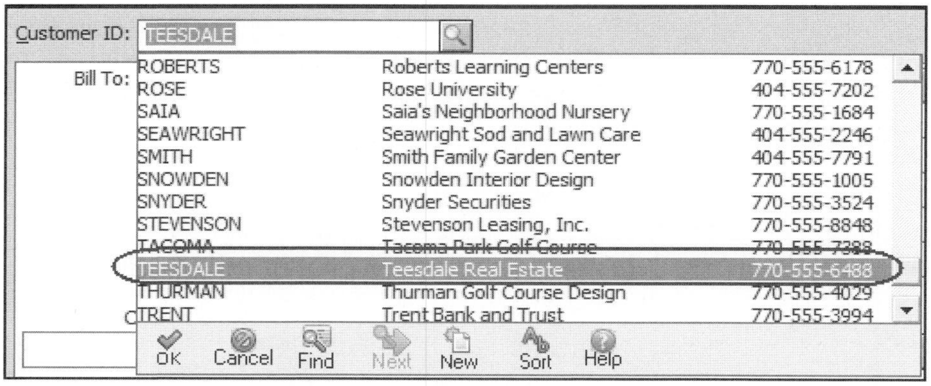

4. Click  . Information for Teesdale Real Estate is automatically completed on the Sales/Invoicing window.

   Observe that the Bill To and Ship To fields are completed automatically. PCA provides an invoice number when the sales invoice is printed so there is no need to enter an invoice number now.

5. Click on the Date field which defaults to 3/15/07.

   PCA offers flexibility when entering dates. For example, you can enter March 1, 2007 as 30107 and the program will format the date correctly. You can also enter just the day portion of the date and PCA formats the date in the current period. For example, if you're working in March of 2007, you can type 4 in the date field and the program formats the date as March 4, 2007. You can also use the pop-up calendar to click the date.

6. Type **1** (or select 1) for the date and press **<Enter>**. The cursor moves to the Invoice No. field, which you are going to leave blank. Peachtree will assign an invoice number when you print the sales invoice.

7. Click on the Apply to Sales tab.

8. Click on the Quantity column, type **5** and press **<Enter>**. Your cursor goes to the Item lookup field.

9. Click  to open the list of inventory items.

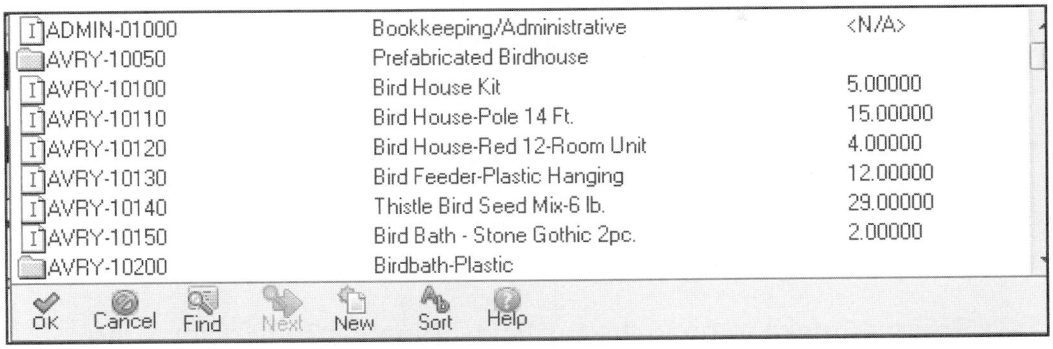

ADMIN-01000 Bookkeeping/Administrative <N/A>
AVRY-10050 Prefabricated Birdhouse
AVRY-10100 Bird House Kit 5.00000
AVRY-10110 Bird House-Pole 14 Ft. 15.00000
AVRY-10120 Bird House-Red 12-Room Unit 4.00000
AVRY-10130 Bird Feeder-Plastic Hanging 12.00000
AVRY-10140 Thistle Bird Seed Mix-6 lb. 29.00000
AVRY-10150 Bird Bath - Stone Gothic 2pc. 2.00000
AVRY-10200 Birdbath-Plastic
OK
Cancel
Find
Next
New
Sort
Help

There are two ways to enter transaction lines for an invoice:

- By Inventory Item: Because the price of each inventory item is stored in the Maintain Inventory Items file, you only have to enter the quantity supplied. The program will compute the credit amount.

- By Account Number: If there is no line item set up for a particular commodity you sell, or if you don't use the Inventory module, you can distribute directly against the proper General Ledger account.

10. The Inventory Item list should be open. Let's see what happens if the Sort icon is selected. Click  which is located at the bottom of the lookup list on the right side.

    What you have done by selecting Sort is to change the order of the list. The list was sorted by ID number; now the list is sorted alphabetically by name. This feature is available in all lookup lists.

11. Click Hand Sprayer/Mister as the item for this sale. EQFF-13120 displays in the Item field.

12. Your cursor should be in the Description field with the following description highlighted: Bell-Gro Plant All-Purpose Plastic Sprayer/Mister. Since we're not going to add a comment or explanation about this inventory item, press **<Enter>** to move to the GL Account field.

The default account is Account No. 40000-EQ, Sales – Equipment. The account name is shown below the transaction line. This account will be credited unless you change the account number in this GL Account field. The debit is automatically made to Accounts Receivable–Teesdale Real Estate.

13. Press **<Enter>** to accept Account No. 40000-EQ. The cursor moves to the Unit Price field and 9.99 is automatically completed. Since the price has been set up in the Maintain Inventory Item file, the unit price is automatically completed for you.

14. Press **<Enter>** to go to the tax field. Type a **<?>** to display the lookup list. Inventory Item tax types are set up in the Maintain Inventory Item file. This lookup list lets you specify certain items as exempt or having special tax situations. There is no need to specify any special tax situation.

15. Press **<Enter>** to go to the Amount field. PCA calculates the total, $49.95, and enters it in the field.

16. Press **<Enter>** to go to the Job field. The job field also has a lookup list. You'll learn about Jobs in more detail in Chapter 6.

17. Press **<Enter>** to go to a new transaction line.

➢ **Troubleshooting Tip:** Observe that the Invoice No. field is blank. The invoice number, similar to the check number, is assigned when you print. You enter an invoice number if you are *not* going to print invoices.

Compare the Sales/Invoice window to the one shown on the next page.

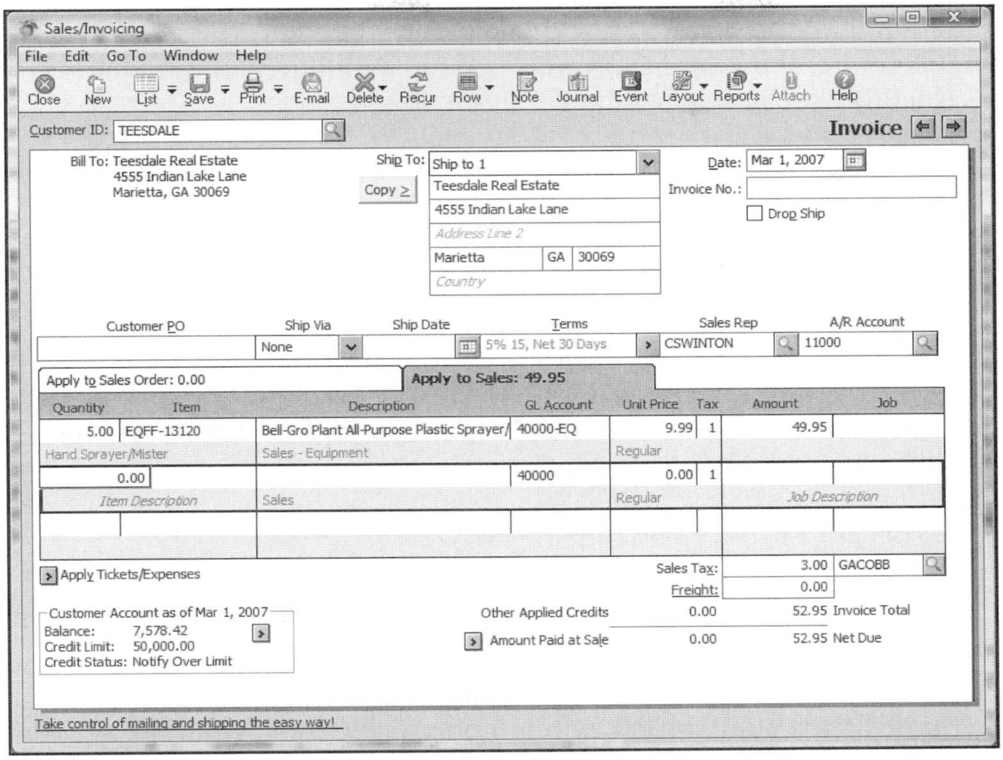

Notice that the Invoice Total and Net Due in the lower right of the window shows $52.95. The Invoice Total displays a running total of the amount by which the customer's account in the Accounts Receivable subsidiary ledger is increased (debited). When you add the next transaction line, this figure will increase. As you know from your study of accounting, two things happen when the Accounts Receivable subsidiary ledger is used:

a. The Accounts Receivable controlling account in the General Ledger is increased by the amount of the credit sale.

b. The credit to the applicable revenue account is offset by a debit to the Customer's account in the Accounts Receivable ledger.

Distributing Against a Specific Account

In this part of the transaction, Bellwether Garden Supply contracted with Teesdale Real Estate to clean up their back lot for $100. Because no Inventory Item is stored in the maintenance records, this transaction is different than the one you just completed (entering a sale to a customer). In this part of the transaction, you need to distribute the amount ($100.00) directly against the Other Income account.

1. Your cursor is in the Quantity field. Since you don't have a quantity number to enter with this transaction, press **<Enter>**. Your cursor should be in the Item field.

2. Press **<Enter>** to leave the Item field blank. Your cursor moves to the Description field.

3. Type **Cleaned parking lot** in the Description field and press **<Enter>**. Your cursor moves to the GL Account field. The default account displays, but it needs to be changed.

4. Type **41000** (for Other Income) and press **<Enter>**. Now the account description below the current transaction line reads Other Income and your cursor moves to the Unit Price field.

   The account number that automatically displayed, 40000, Sales, was the default account. Since we want to distribute this revenue to a specific account, 41000, Other Income, you must type this account number (41000); otherwise, the program will accept the default account number.

5. Press **<Enter>** to skip the Unit Price field because we don't need a unit price. Your cursor moves to the Tax field.

6. Press **<Enter>** to accept the default tax code. Your cursor moves to the Amount field.

7. Type **100** and press **<Enter>** two times. Notice the illustration shows the two amounts entered for this invoice. The Net Due is $158.95. Compare your Sales/Invoicing window to the one shown on the next page.

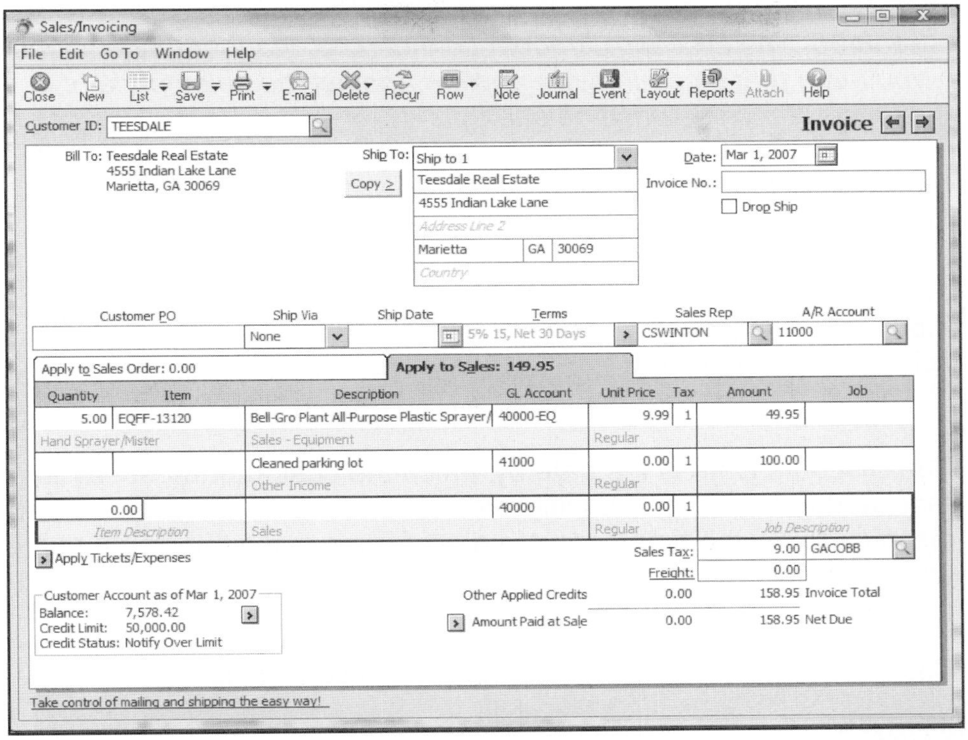

Discount Information

At the beginning of this chapter you changed the sales discount for Teesdale Real Estate. Let's check to make sure that the discount information is current for the invoice you just entered.

1. Click on the arrow  button to the right of Terms. This information is below the Ship To address. The Terms Information window displays.

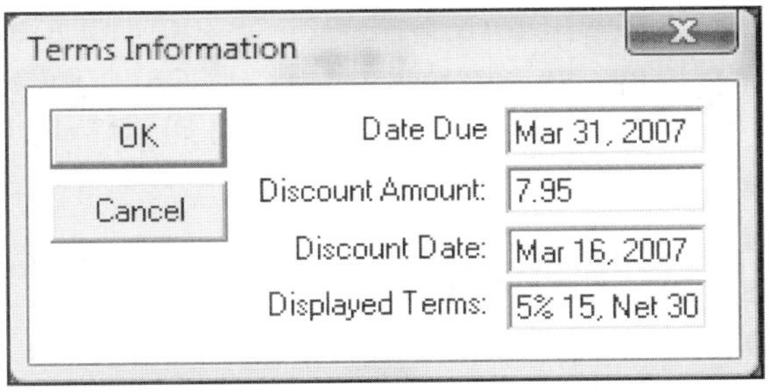

The Date Due, Mar 31, 2007, is the date by which the invoice should be paid. The Discount Amount is the invoice total multiplied by the discount percentage you entered in the Maintain Customer record ($158.95 x 5% = $7.95). (*Hint: Peachtree automatically calculates the Discount Amount on the full sales invoice amount,*

$158.95. The Discount Amount field can be changed. In accounting you learn that discounts are applied against the sales price of an item not *the sales price plus tax.*)

2. Since the taxable items add up to $149.95, the five-percent discount should be $7.50 ($149.95 x .05). Type **7.50** in the Discount Amount field, then press **<Enter>**.

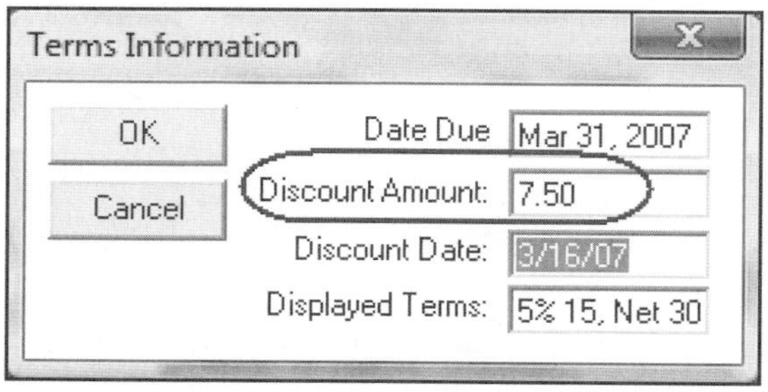

The Discount Date is the date by which the customer must pay to receive the discount. The Displayed Terms are the percentage of discount (5%), the time period in days for receiving the discount (15) and the number of days before the invoice is due (Net 30).

3. Click  to close the Terms Information window.

POSTING THE INVOICE

The sample company, Bellwether Garden Supply, uses ***real-time posting***. When real-time posting is used, the transactions that you enter are posted when you select the  icon.

There is another type of posting included in PCA. It is called ***batch posting***. When using batch posting, the transactions you enter are saved to a temporary holding area where you can review them before posting to the general ledger.

Follow these steps to save and post the invoice:

1. Click . The Sales/Invoicing window is ready for another transaction.
2. Close the Sales/Invoice window to return to the Customers & Sales page.

PRINTING (OR DISPLAYING) INVOICES

Follow these steps to print the invoice for Teesdale Real Estate:

1. From the menu bar, select Reports & Forms; Forms, Invoices and Packing Slips.
2. Observe that the Forms Types field shows Invoices and Packing Slips highlighted.

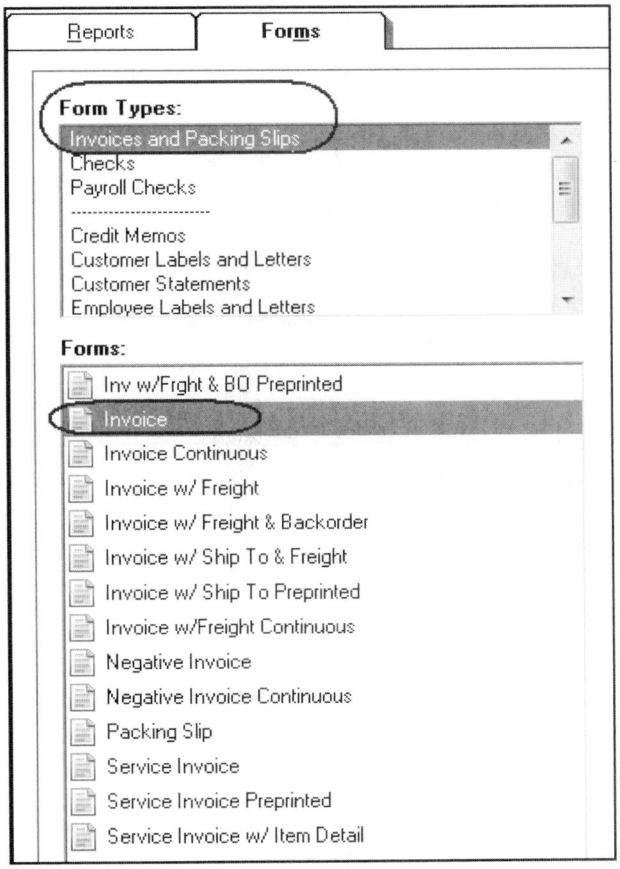

3. In the Forms list, double-click Invoice. The Preview and Print Invoices and Packing Slips window appears.
4. In the Filter customers by field select Teesdale in the ID and to fields.

5. In the Delivery method field, select Print.

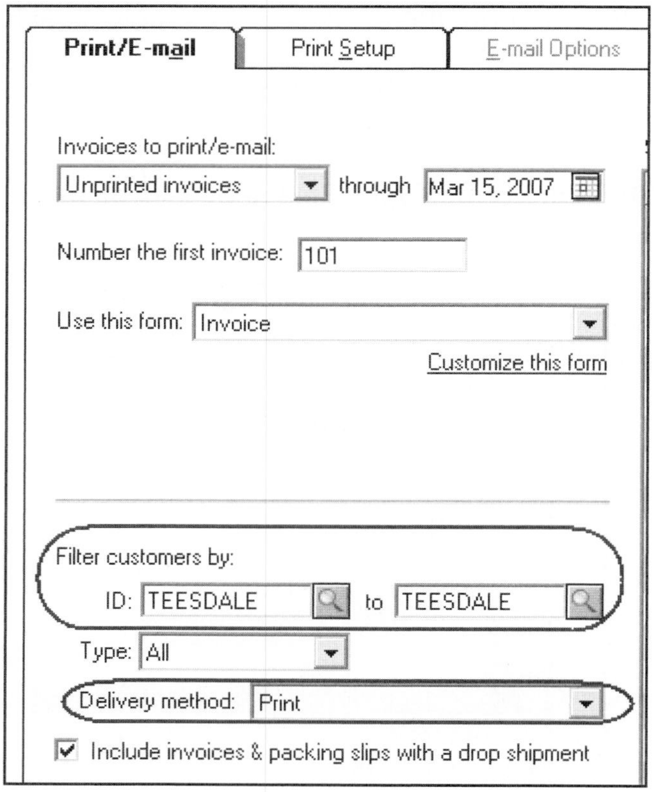

6. Click Print Preview. Compare Invoice 101 to the one shown on the next page.

Bellwether Garden Supply
1505 Pavilion Place
Norcross, GA 30093-3203
USA

Voice: 770-724-4000
Fax: 770-555-1234

INVOICE

Invoice Number: 101
Invoice Date: Mar 1, 2007
Page: 1

Bill To:	Ship to:
Teesdale Real Estate 4555 Indian Lake Lane Marietta, GA 30069	Teesdale Real Estate 4555 Indian Lake Lane Marietta, GA 30069

Customer ID	Customer PO	Payment Terms	
TEESDALE		5% 15, Net 30 Days	
Sales Rep ID	**Shipping Method**	**Ship Date**	**Due Date**
CSWINTON	None		3/31/07

Quantity	Item	Description	Unit Price	Amount
5.00	EQFF-13120	Bell-Gro Plant All-Purpose Plastic Sprayer/Mister	9.99	49.95
		Cleaned parking lot		100.00

	Subtotal	149.95
	Sales Tax	9.00
	Total Invoice Amount	158.95
Check/Credit Memo No:	Payment/Credit Applied	
	TOTAL	**158.95**

Read Me:

When I try to print Invoice 101, a Peachtree Accounting window appears that says There are no forms to preview. What should I do?

1. Click OK.
2. Close the Select a Report and Forms window.
3. On the Customers & Sales Tasks page, select Sales Invoices; View and Edit Sales Invoices.
4. Double-click Teesdale, Invoice 101, to go to the Sales/Invoicing window.
5. Make the selections to Print from the Sales/Invoicing window. Compare Invoice 101 to the one shown above.
6. Close all windows.

Notice the Payment Terms are 5% 15, Net 30 Days. This is the information you entered for Customer Terms on pages 101-102.

7. Click 

to print Invoice 101. If you printed the invoice, a message displays asking if the invoice printed properly. When you answer yes, PCA updates invoice numbers and flags the invoice as printed so that it will not print again. Click 

.

8. Close all windows.

ENTERING RECEIPTS

Teesdale Real Estate has sent a check in payment of their invoice. Follow these steps to enter the following transaction:

Date	*Transaction Description*
03/15/07	Received Check No. 8818 from Teesdale Real Estate in payment of Invoice No. 101, $151.45.

1. From the Customers & Sales page, click 

; Receive Money from Customer. The Receipts window appears.

   The Receipts window and Payments window look alike. There is a table in the lower half of the window that lists distribution lines for the current transaction. There is an icon bar at the top of the window. The item descriptions and account descriptions appear beneath each transaction line. The title bar identifies the window being used. In this case, the title bar says, Receipts.

2. Your cursor is in the Deposit ticket ID field. Type **03/15/07** (the receipt date). This Deposit Ticket ID field defaults to the current date (today's date) and is used to combine receipts for the bank reconciliation. Press **<Enter>**.

3. In the Customer ID field, type the Customer ID for Teesdale: **TEESDALE** and press **<Enter>**.

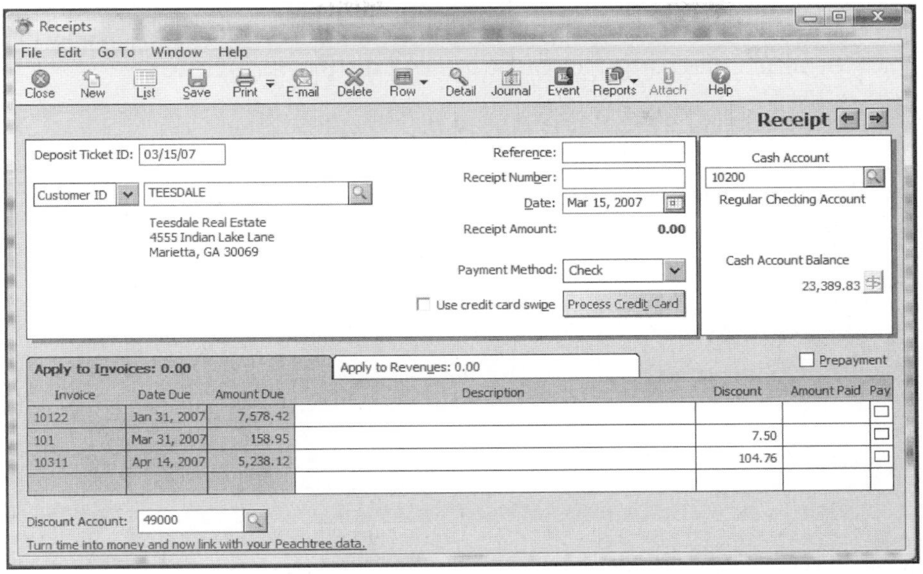

When you enter a Customer ID, the window shows a list of invoices. When the receipt is to pay for invoiced amounts, you can select an invoice(s) from the list. The invoice amounts, including discounts, complete the apply to invoices table.

4. Click on the Reference field. Type **8818** for the customer's check number (a Reference number must be entered). Press **<Enter>** key two times and the cursor moves to the Date field.

   On your window the Date field displays 3/15/07. This date is important because it is used by PCA to determine if a discount applies. For example, if the transaction date for the invoice was March 1, 2007, and the discount terms were 5% for 10 days, the receipt entered with a date of March 12, 2007 would miss qualifying for a discount. PCA automatically computes and displays the discount amount when one applies.

5. The terms for Teesdale are 5% 15 days, Net 30. Since March 15, 2007 is within the discount period, accept the March 15, 2007 date. Press **<Enter>**. If the Payment Method does *not* show Check, select it. Press **<Enter>**.

6. If the Cash Account field does *not* show Account No. 10200, Regular Checking Account, select it. Press **<Enter>**.

7. If necessary, select the Apply to Invoices tab.

8. Select Invoice 101 from the list by clicking on that line. Notice that a red line is placed around this selection.

9. Click on the Pay box. Compare your Receipts window to the one shown below.

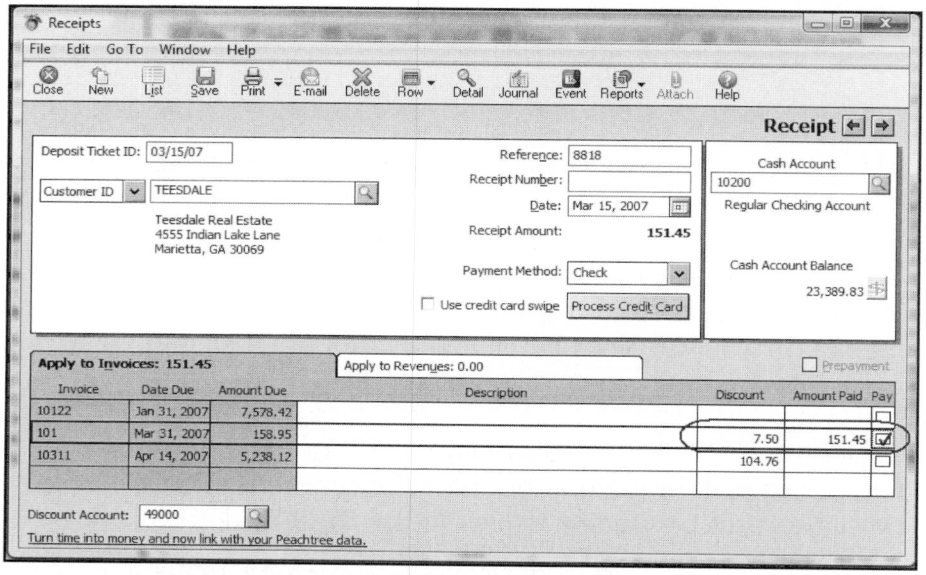

Notice that the Discount column displays the amount of the discount, $7.50. The discount displays because payment was received within the discount period (5%, 15 days). Therefore, the customer gets the 5% discount and the amount is automatically entered in the Discount field. Then, PCA automatically computes the check for the correct amount of the invoice: $151.45 (149.95 – 7.50 + 9.00 = $151.45). The Receipt Amount in the check portion of the Receipts window shows 151.45, Teesdale's invoice minus the 5% discount, plus sales tax.

10. Click 

and the receipt is posted.

11. Close the Receipts window to return to Customers & Sales page.

ANALYZING CUSTOMER PAYMENTS

How well does Bellwether Garden Supply manage its collections of payments from customers? To look at customers and aging amounts, use the Collection Manager. Follow these steps to learn how to use the Collection Manager:

1. From the menu bar, click Analysis; Collection Manager. The Collection Aging bar graph appears.

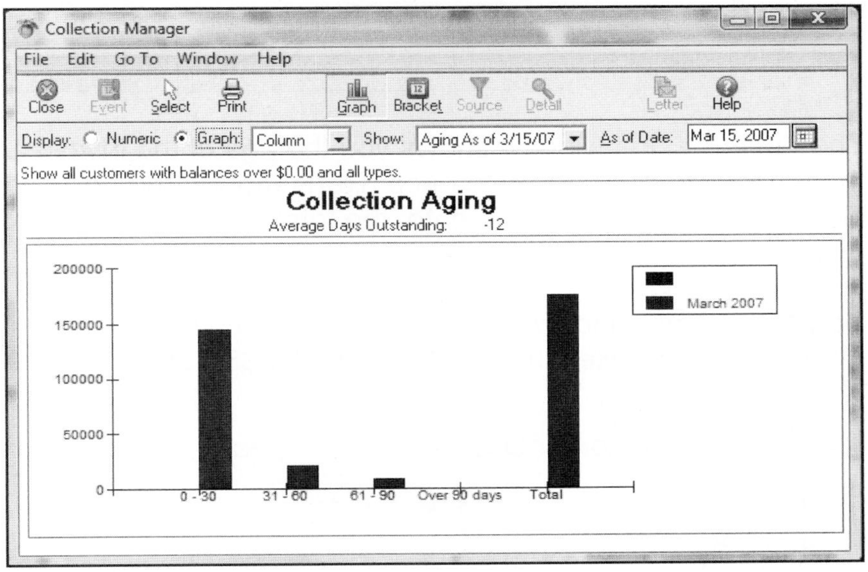

There are four aging brackets along the horizontal or X axis: 0 - 30 days, 31 - 60 days, 61 - 90 days, and over 90 days. The vertical or Y axis shows dollar amounts due.

2. Click  .

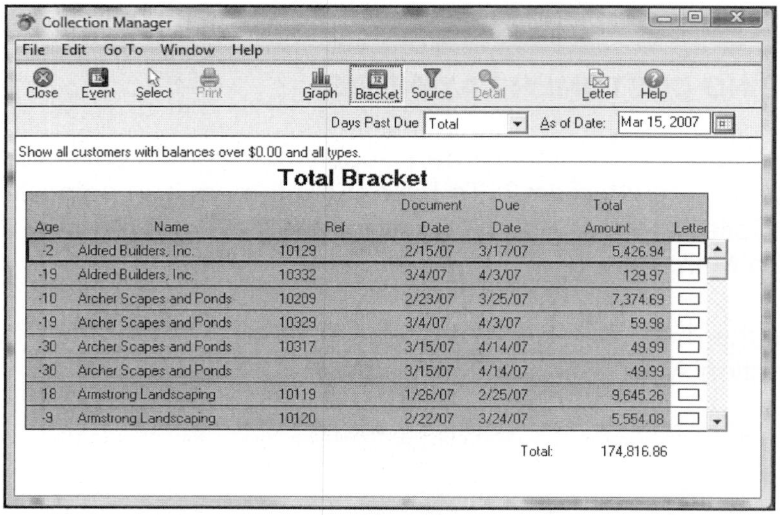

The Total Bracket window shows you the age of the invoice in days, the customer name, the reference (Ref) number, the document date or transaction date, the due date, the total amount due, and whether a letter was sent.

3. Scroll down the window to highlight the invoice for Teesdale Real Estate (Age, -30; Ref, 10311; Amt Due, 5,238.12). Then, click 

. The Customer Detail window appears.

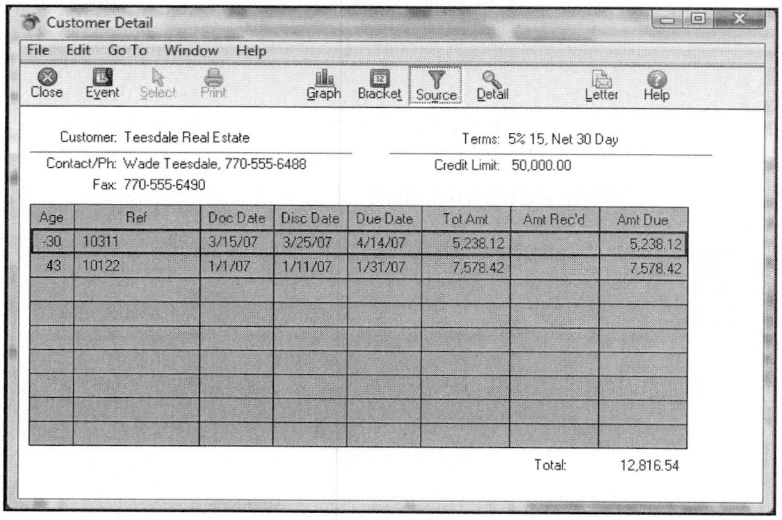

At this level you can see all of Teesdale Real Estate's invoices. If you want to send a collection letter you can do that from this window. By clicking 

on the icon bar you can send a collection letter to Teesdale Real Estate. (If you print a letter, Peachtree defaults to a letter addressed to Thurman Golf Course Design.)

4. Click 

to exit the Collection Manager.

DISPLAYING THE CUSTOMER LEDGERS

To display the Customer Ledgers, follow these steps:

1. From the Customers & Sales page, link to View All Customer & Sales Reports in the Recently Used Customer Reports area. The Select a Report window appear.

2. Highlight Customer Ledgers.

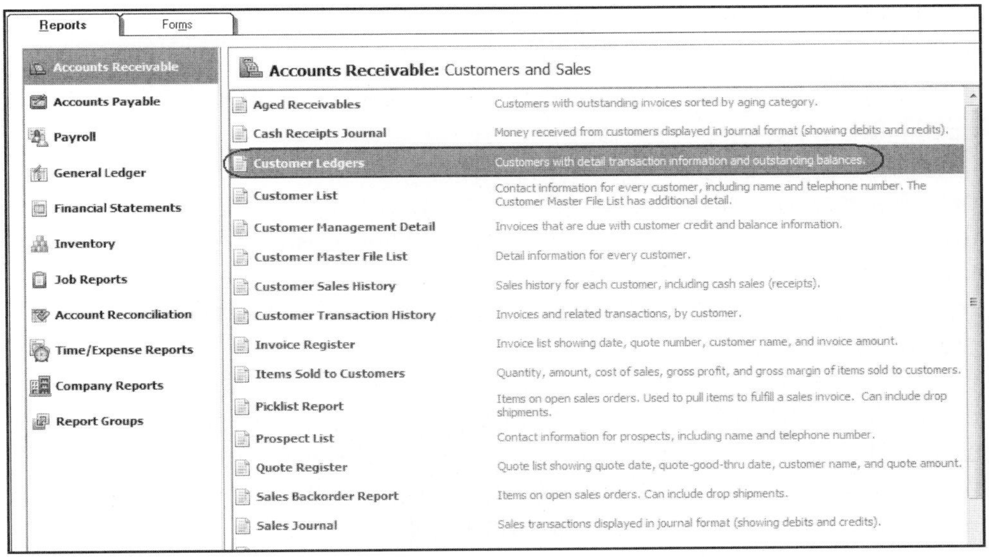

3. Click 

or 

.

4. The Customer Ledgers appear. Scroll down to TEESDALE. A partial customer ledger is shown below. Observe that the 3/15/07 entry shows the cash receipt of $158.95 minus the $7.50 discount.

Bellwether Garden Supply
Customer Ledgers
For the Period From Mar 1, 2007 to Mar 31, 2007
Filter Criteria includes: Report order is by ID. Report is printed in Detail Format.

Customer ID Customer	Date	Trans No	Type	Debit Amt	Credit Amt	Balance
SNYDER	3/1/07	Balance Fwd				2,981.04
Snyder Securities	3/4/07	10334	SJ	59.98		3,041.02
	3/13/07	CC0006	CRJ	99.98	99.98	3,041.02
STEVENSON	3/8/07	10318	SJ	49.99		49.99
Stevenson Leasing, Inc.	3/12/07	10118	SJ	7,790.42		7,840.41
TACOMA	3/1/07	Balance Fwd				4,675.57
Tacoma Park Golf Cours	3/14/07	10322	SJ	49.99		4,725.56
	3/15/07	10327	SJ	1,049.01		5,774.57
TEESDALE	3/1/07	Balance Fwd				7,578.42
Teesdale Real Estate	3/1/07	101	SJ	158.95		7,737.37
	3/15/07	10311	SJ	5,238.12		12,975.49
	3/15/07	8818	CRJ	7.50	7.50	12,975.49
	3/15/07	8818	CRJ		158.95	12,816.54
THURMAN	3/1/07	Balance Fwd				3,610.39
Thurman Golf Course De	3/15/07	10343	SJ	9,998.00		13,608.39
TRENT		No Activity				0.00
Trent Bank and Trust						
WILLIAMS	3/3/07	4452	CRJ	220.31	220.31	0.00
Williams Industries	3/5/07	10312V	SJ		939.72	-939.72
	3/15/07	10312	SJ	939.72		0.00
Report Total				90,818.51	80,942.32	174,816.86

CREDIT MEMOS

Credit Memos are returns to customers. Use the Credit Memos window to enter credit memos for customer returns and credits. You can apply credit memos to any existing customer invoice. All entries made on this window are posted to the General Ledger, customer records, if appropriate, and to inventory and job records.

The customer ledgers should be displayed on your screen. Scroll up the customer ledger to Armstrong Landscaping. Observe that Armstrong Landscaping has a customer credit memo (CCM4002) on 3/2/07. Follow these steps to see how the credit was applied.

1. The customer ledger should be displayed. Scroll up the Customer Ledgers window to Armstrong.

2. Double-click on the 3/2/07 CCM4002 transaction to drill down to Credit memos window.

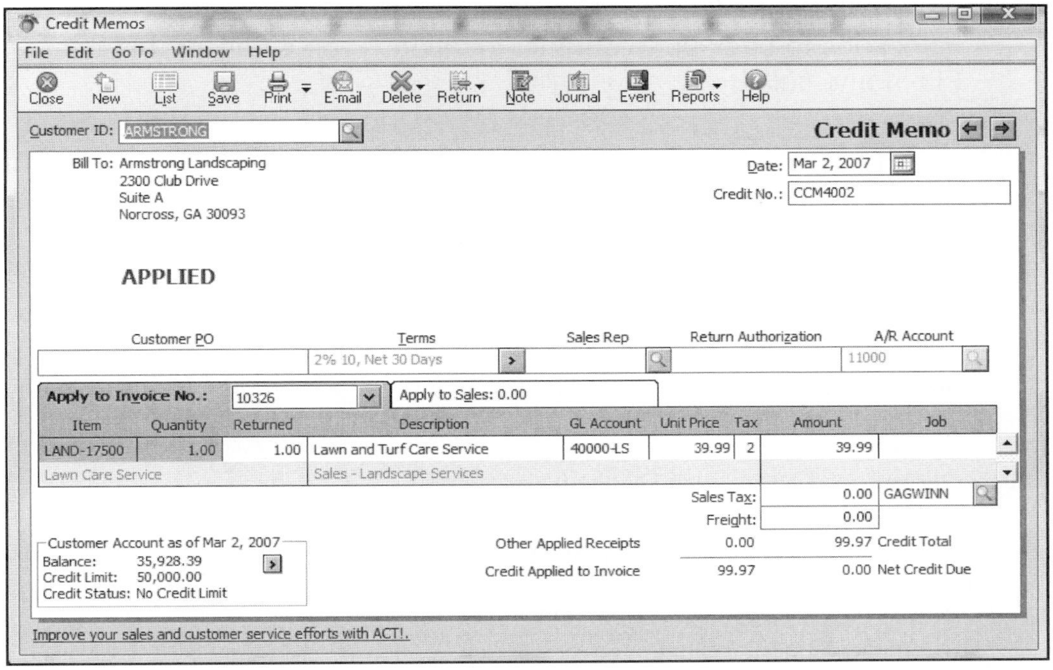

3. Observe that there is a $99.97 Credit Total. Close the Credit Memos window. You are returned to the Customer Ledgers. The amount of the credit memo is subtracted from the balance forward amount: $36,028.36 – 99.97 = $35,928.39.

4. Close the Credit Memos window; close the Customer Ledgers; close the Select a Report or Form window to return to the Customers & Sales page.

BACKING UP CHAPTER 3 DATA

Follow these steps to back up Chapter 3 data:

1. From the Navigation Bar, click 

; link to Back up.

2. Click 

.

3. Accept the default for backing up to the hard drive or make the selections to back up to another location. Type **Chapter 3** in the File name field.

4. Click 

.

5. When the window prompts that This company backup will require approximately 5.61MB, click 

. When the Back Up Company scale is 100% complete, you have successfully backed up to the current point in Chapter 3. You are returned to the menu bar.

6. Click File, Exit to exit Peachtree.

INTERNET ACTIVITY	
1.	From your Internet browser, go to the book's website at http://www.mhhe.com/yacht2008.
2.	Link to Student Edition.
3.	In the Course-wide Content list, link Internet Activities; then link to <u>Part 1 Internet Activities for Chapter 1-8</u>. Open or save. (You can also choose Chapter 3, then link to Internet Activities. (In the Choose a Chapter field, if you select Chapter 3 observe that other chapter-specific links are available; for example, Multiple Choice Quiz, True or False, PowerPoint Presentations and Going to the Net Exercises.) Also observe that Course-wide Content includes a Glossary link.
4.	If necessary, scroll down to the AMERICAN ACCOUNTING ASSOCIATION – Chapter 3. Complete steps 1-3.
5.	Using a word processing program, write a summary about the site(s) you selected. Remember to include the website address(es) of each link. Your summaries should be no more than 75 words or less than 50 words.

SUMMARY AND REVIEW

SOFTWARE OBJECTIVES: In Chapter 3, you used the software to:

1. Restore data from Exercise 2-2. (This backup was made on pages 88-89.)

2. Go to the Customers & Sales page to enter quotes and sales orders.

3. Enter customer terms in the Maintain menu.

4. Record a sales invoice on the Sales/Invoicing window.

5. Print a sales invoice.

6. Analyze receipts and customer credit memos.

7. Post a receipt for previously invoiced amounts.

8. Make two backups: back up Chapter 3 data; and back up Exercise 3-2

WEB OBJECTIVES: In Chapter 3, you did these Internet activities:

1. Used your Internet browser to go to the book's website at http://www.mhhe.com/yacht2008.

2. Completed the Internet activity for the American Accounting Association.

3. Used a word processing program to write a summary about the website(s) that you visited.

GOING TO THE NET

Access the Financial Accounting Standards Board website at http://raw.rutgers.edu. In the Quick links field, click on the down arrow. In the Accounting Organizations list, select Financial Acct Standards Board (FASB). Link to Facts about FASB; select FASB Board Members.

1. How many board members serve on the Financial Accounting Standards Board? Do they serve part time or full time?

2. What are the qualifications for the board members?

Short-Answer Questions: In the space provided write an answer to the question.

1. What icon(s) can be used to display lookup lists?

____

____

____

2. Describe three ways to open a lookup list.

____

____

____

____

3. If you want to look at a customer's account, what window do you open? Describe the selections.

____

____

____

4. What is the customer identification for Teesdale Real Estate?

____

____

5. What is the sales discount for Teesdale Real Estate?

____

____

6. What is the default discount for customers?

____

____

7. Describe what happens when you use the Accounts Receivable subsidiary ledger.

____

____

____

8. When you want to print an invoice in PCA, what are the steps?

____

____

9. What Internet site is used to go to sites related to the American Accounting Association?

____

____

10. If you receive payment from a customer, what window do you use?

____

____

____

Exercise 3-1: Follow the instructions below to complete Exercise 3-1.

1. Start PCA. Open Bellwether Garden Supply.
2. Restore data from the end of Chapter 3. This backup was made on pages 121-122.
3. Record the following transaction.

Date	*Transaction Description*
03/02/07	Bellwether Garden Supply sold one Rotary Mower – Riding 4P to Teesdale Real Estate, Invoice 102, $299.99; plus $18 sales tax; total, $317.99. (*Hint*: Do *not* enter an invoice number. Select the Apply to Sales tab. Type **1** in the Quantity field; select EQLW-14140; Bell-Gro Riding Lawn Mower - 4HP as the Item.)

4. Print or post. (*Hint:* If you print from the Sales/Invoicing window, the sales invoice prints and posts.)
5. Continue with Exercise 3-2.

Exercise 3-2: Follow the instructions below to complete Exercise 3-2.

1. Record the following transaction:

Date	*Transaction Description*
03/16/07	Received Check No. 9915 in the amount of $302.99 from Teesdale Real Estate in payment of Invoice 102. (*Hint: Type **3/16/07** in the Deposit ticket ID field. Remember to use the check number in the Reference field.* **Compute the discount and type the correct amount** *in the Discount field. Do* not *include sales tax in the sales discount computation.*)

2. Post the receipt.
3. Print the Customer Ledgers.
4. Back up Exercise 3-2. Use **Exercise 3-2** as the file name.
5. Exit PCA.

CHAPTER 3 INDEX

Chapter 4 Employees

SOFTWARE OBJECTIVES: In Chapter 4, you use the software to:

1. Restore data from Exercise 3-2. (This backup was made on page 127.)
2. Enter and store information using the Maintain Employees/Sales Rep window.
3. Set up default information for payroll.
4. Store constant information about payroll payment methods.
5. Transfer funds from the regular checking account to the payroll checking account.
6. Enter paychecks in the Payroll Entry window.
7. Print employee paychecks.
8. Make two backups: backup Chapter 4 data; and backup Exercise 4-2.[1]

WEB OBJECTIVES: In Chapter 4, you do these Internet activities:

1. Use your Internet browser to go to the book's website.
2. Complete the Internet activity for the American Institute of CPAs.
3. Use a word processing program to write a summary about the website(s) that you visited.

In Chapter 4 you learn how PCA processes payroll. Once default and maintain employee information is set up, payroll is a simple process.

The first step in setting up payroll is to go to the 

Navigation Center. Then, make the selections to set up payroll defaults. The flowchart on the next page describes PCA's payroll process.

---

[1]Refer to the chart on page 2 for the size of backup files.

These steps show you how payroll accounting is set up in PCA.

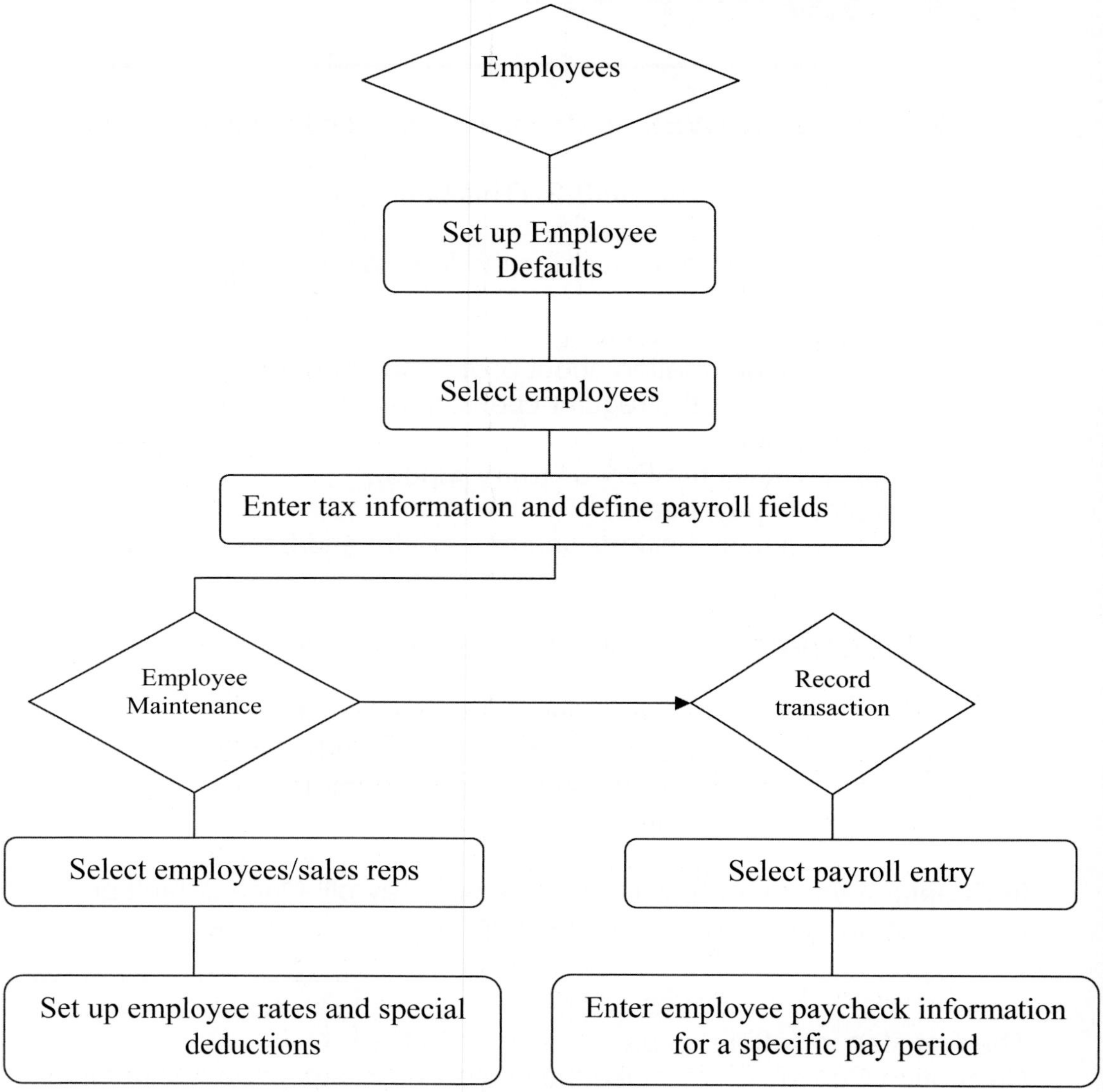

GETTING STARTED

Follow these steps to start PCA:

1. Start Peachtree. Open the sample company, Bellwether Garden Supply. (If Bellwether Garden Supply is not shown, restore a New Company. Refer to the Read Me box on page 27.)

2. Restore your data from the Exercise 3-2 back up.

   a. From the Navigation Bar, select Company; link to Restore. (The backup file was made on page 127.)

   b. The Select Backup File window appears. If the Location field shows C:\Program Files\Sage Software\Peachtree\ Company\ BCS\Exercise 3-2.ptb, click Next >. (*Or,* click Browse, then select the appropriate location of the Exercise 3-2 backup file; click Next >.)

   c. The Select Company window appears. The radio button next to An Existing Company is selected. The Company name field shows Bellwether Garden Supply; the Location field shows C:\ProgramFiles\Sage Software\Peachtree\Company\BCS (or the appropriate location on your computer). Click Next >.

   d. The Restore Options window appears. Make sure that the box next to Company Data is *checked.* Click Next >.

   e. The Confirmation window appears. Check the From and To fields to make sure they are correct. Click Finish. When the Restore Company scale is 100% complete, your data is restored and you are returned to the menu bar.

   f. If necessary, remove the external media.

DEFAULT INFORMATION

PCA allows you to set up default information for your business. This information is important for payroll, customer receivables, and vendor payables. Bellwether Garden Supply already has the receivable and payable default information set up. Defaults are not set up for payroll.

Follow these steps to set up payroll Default Information:

1. From the Navigation Bar, select 

; then click 

; Set Up Employee Defaults. Compare your Employee Defaults window with the one shown below.

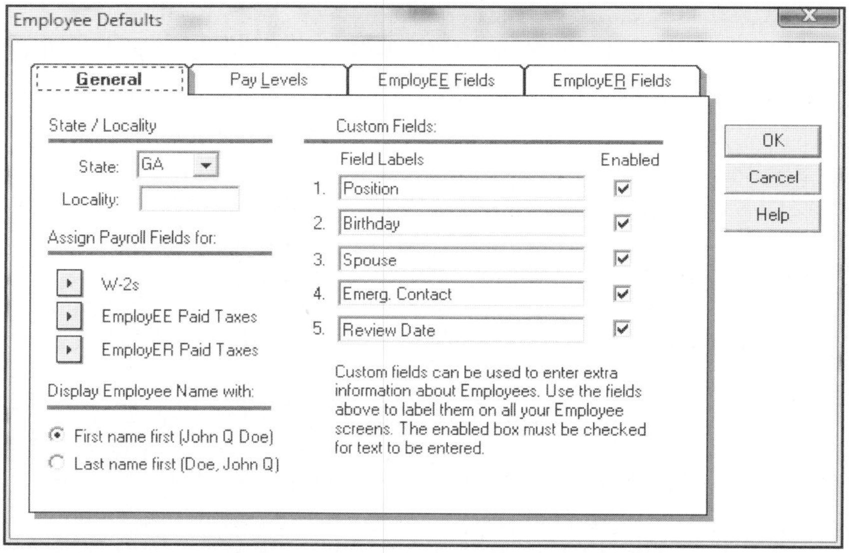

There are four tabs in the Employee Defaults window: General, Pay Levels, EmployEE Fields, and EmployER Fields. You can set up a great deal of information in these tabs. This will make your payroll processing almost automatic.

2. Click on the EmployEE Fields tab.

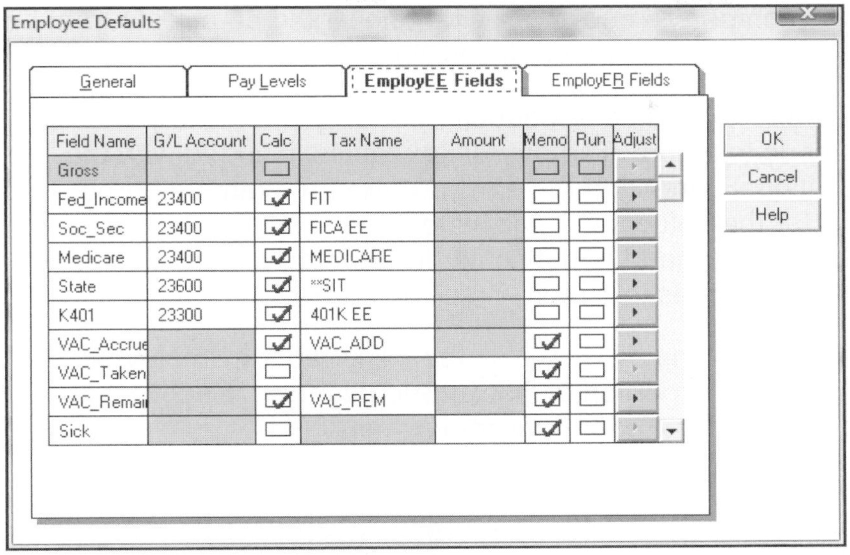

Notice that there are seven items checked in the Calc column: Fed_Income (FIT), Soc_Sec (FICA EE), Medicare (MEDICARE), State (**SIT), K401 (401K EE), VAC_Accrued (VAC_ADD), and VAC_Remaining (VAC_REM). These fields work together with the payroll tax tables to calculate common employee deductions.

The check marks in the Calc and Memo columns indicate common deductions. Bellwether Garden Supply computes Federal Income Tax, Social Security, Medicare, State Income Taxes, 401K, and vacation deductions. These deductions are calculated according to the appropriate tax tables and formulas entered for 401K's and vacation calculations.

The accounts affected by paychecks are liability accounts set up specifically to handle these kinds of deductions. Notice that the GL Account column shows the appropriate account numbers. All the accounts that are checked off are liability accounts. You can also set up voluntary deductions (called allowances in PCA). Voluntary allowances that are individually entered on the employee paycheck could include gas allowances, union dues, and savings bonds. There is a Memo column with a place to put check marks for amounts that should not be posted to the company's books. The Memo check box is used when you want the employee record to show amounts not on the company's books. An example would be a restaurant business that needed to show employees' tips.

Peachtree Complete Accounting 2008, Educational Version, includes a generic tax table. The payroll tax tables included with the educational version of the software are for example purposes only. In order for the software to calculate the correct payroll tax withholding amounts, you need to subscribe to Peachtree's tax service. Chapter 14, Payroll, goes into more detail about Peachtree's payroll system.

3. Click on the EmployER Fields tab. The tab for EmployER Fields is for the employer's portion of Social Security (Soc_Sec_ER), Medicare (Medicare_ER), Federal Unemployment (FUTA_ER), State Unemployment Insurance (SUI_ER), and 401K (K401_ER).

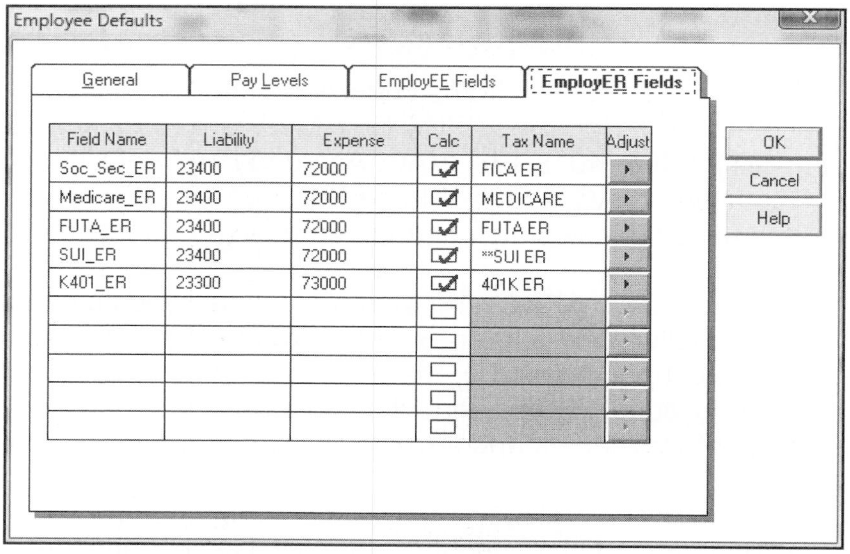

4. Select 

to return to the Employees and Payroll page.

EMPLOYEE MAINTENANCE

When default information is completed, PCA sets guidelines for processing the company's payroll. On the Maintain Employees/Sales Reps window, information is entered for each employee.

1. From the Employees & Tasks area, click 

; View and Edit Employees. The Employee List appears.

2. Double-click BNUNNLEY; Nunnley, Brandee. The Maintain Employees & Sales Reps window appears. You are going to look at this employees' record. (*Hint:* In Chapter 14, you learn about Peachtree's payroll features in more detail.)

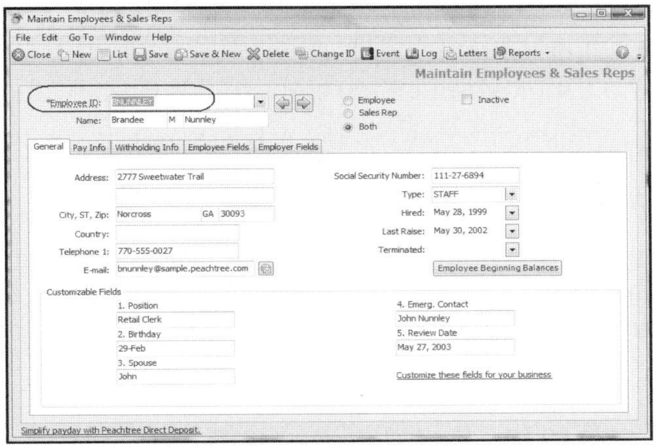

3. Click on the Pay Info tab.

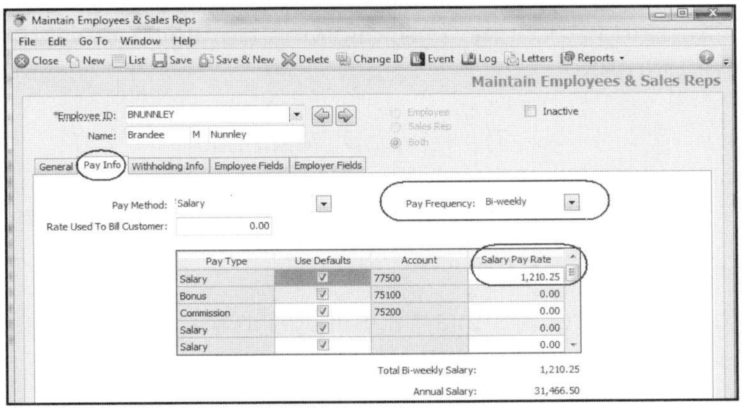

Notice the following about Ms. Nunnley.

a. She is paid a salary of $1,210.25.

b. She is paid bi-weekly (once every two weeks).

4. Click on the down-arrow in the Employee ID field.

5. Select employee **DCARTER**; **Drake V. Carter**. Notice that Mr. Carter is paid an hourly wage of $9.00; overtime pay of $13.50; and special rate of $18.00. Observe that Mr. Carter is paid bi-weekly.

6. Close the Maintain Employees & Sales Reps window to Employee List. Close the Employee List to return to the Employees & Payroll page.

PAYROLL TASKS

Once employee default information is set up, PCA automates the payroll process. Now that you have looked at Bellwether's payroll defaults, you can see how easily PCA computes and prints paychecks for hourly and salaried employees.

Transferring Cash to the Payroll Checking Account

Before you make a payroll entry, you need to transfer $8,000 from Account No. 10200, Regular Checking Account; to Account No. 10300, the Payroll Checking Account. The following transaction will be recorded in the general journal.

Date	*Transaction Description*
3/28/07	Transfer $8,000 from the regular checking account to the payroll checking account.

Follow these steps to record this transaction in the general journal.

1. From the Navigation Bar, click 

; link to General Journal Entry. The General Journal Entry window appears.

2. Select or type **28** as the date. Click on the Reference field. Type **Transfer** in the Reference field. Press the **<Enter>** key two times.

3. Your cursor is in the Account No. column. Select Account No. 10300, Payroll Checking Account (or you can type **10300**). Press **<Enter>**.

4. Your cursor should be in the Description column. Type **Payroll Checking Account** (or you can type a description) in the Description column. Press **<Enter>**.

5. Type **8000** in the Debit column. Press the **<Enter>** key three times to go to the Account No. column.

6. Your cursor should be in the Account No. column. Select Account No. 10200, Regular Checking Account.

7. Type **Regular Checking Account** in the Description column. Press the **<Enter>** key two times to go to the Credit column.

8. Your cursor is in the Credit column. Type **8000** in the Credit column. Press **<Enter>**. Observe that at the bottom of the General Journal Entry window, the Out of Balance column shows 0.00. This shows that debits equal credits, therefore, out of balance equals zero.

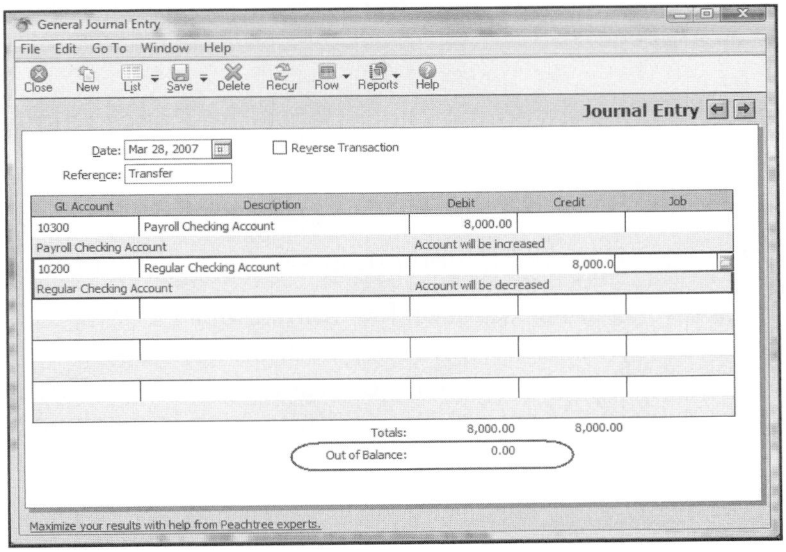

9. Click 

to post your entry to the general ledger.

10. Close the General Journal Entry window.

Payroll Entry for a Salaried Employee

In the next section you enter paychecks for these two employees: Brandee M. Nunnley and Drake V. Carter. When processing payroll checks, the information stored in Default Information and in the Maintain Employees file is important. Processing payroll is simple once you have set the defaults up correctly.

Follow these steps to see how a paycheck for a salaried employee is done.

1. From the Navigation Bar, select 

; 

, Enter Payroll For One Employee. The Payroll Entry window appears.

2. In the Employee ID field, type **BN** for Brandee M. Nunnley and press **<Enter>**.

3. To have the program print a check, leave the Check Number field blank by pressing **<Enter>**. If you type a check number, PCA prints Duplicate on the check.

4. Type **29** in the Date field, then press **<Enter>**. (*Remember you can also click on the Calendar icon*  *and select 29. If necessary, enlarge the Payroll Entry window.*) Your cursor goes to the Cash Account field. This check will be charged against the Payroll Checking Account (Account No. 10300) which is displayed in the Cash Account field.

5. Press **<Enter>**. Your cursor is in the Pay Period Ends field. Type **29** then press **<Enter>**. Your cursor goes to the Weeks in Pay Period box. The number 2 is displayed. Ms. Nunnley is on a bi-weekly pay period which means that Ms. Nunnley has two weeks in her pay period.

   Notice that Brandee M. Nunnley has a Salary Amounts table that includes Salary, Bonus, and Commission. If necessary, these amounts can be adjusted. All of the Taxes – Benefits – Liabilities fields you told the program to calculate for you–Fed_ Income, Soc_Sec, Medicare and State tax, etc. – have been calculated and display as negative amounts. They display as negative amounts because they decrease the check amount. The amounts shown as positive numbers are *not* deducted from the employee's check. Once everything is set up properly in Default Information and Maintain Employees, payroll processing is simple. Compare your Payroll Entry window for Brandee M. Nunnley to the one shown below.

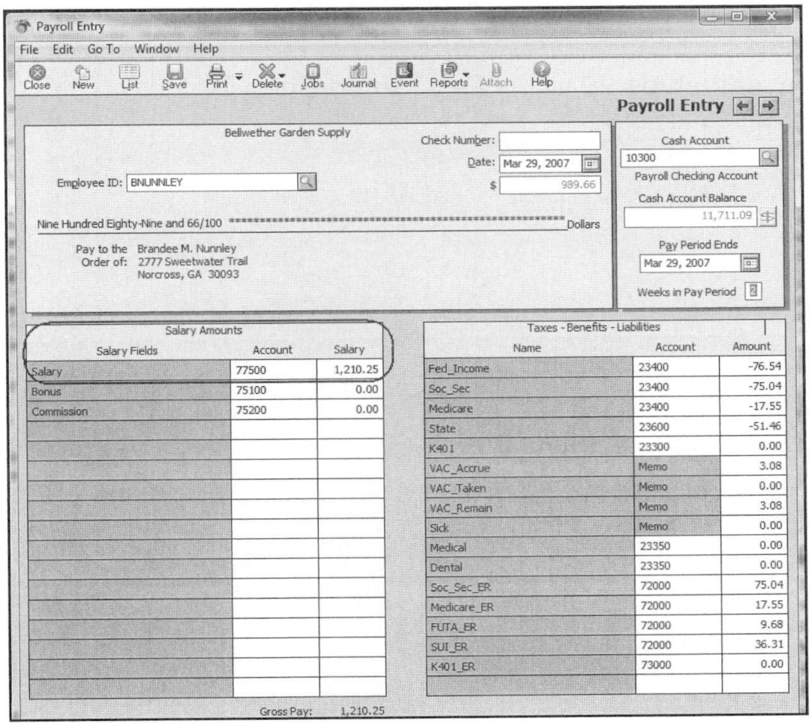

Observe that the Payroll Checking Account Balance in the upper right corner shows a balance of 11,711.09. This is because the default for Peachtree is to recalculate the cash balance automatically for receipts, payments, and payroll entries. From the menu bar, select Options, Global, and notice that a check mark **<✓>** is placed next to the Recalculate cash balance automatically in Receipts, Payments, and Payroll Entry field. If your balance field does *not* show an amount, then place a check mark in the recalculate cash balance automatically field. Also, notice that Ms. Nunnley's paycheck amount is $989.66.

6. Click  to post this payroll entry.

Payroll Entry for an Hourly Employee

1. In the Employee ID field, click . Select Drake V. Carter
2. If necessary, type **29** in the Date field and press **<Enter>** two times.
3. If necessary, type **29** in the Pay Period Ends field.

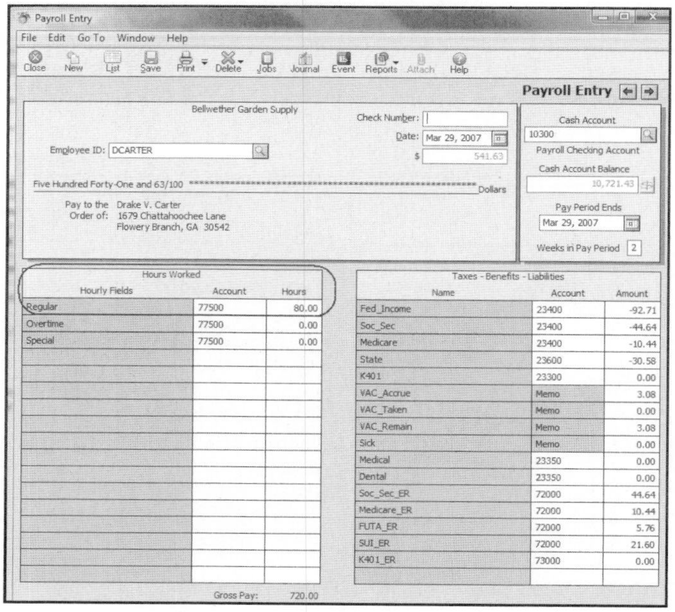

Since Drake V. Carter is an hourly employee, the Hours Worked table lists his regular and overtime hours. If necessary, these categories can be adjusted.

4. To see how to adjust the hours that he worked, do the following: in the Hours Worked table, click on Overtime. The Overtime row is highlighted. Make sure your cursor is in the Hours column. Type **3** and press **<Enter>**. Notice how the amounts in the Taxes - Benefits - Liabilities fields are automatically adjusted. The check amount also changed.

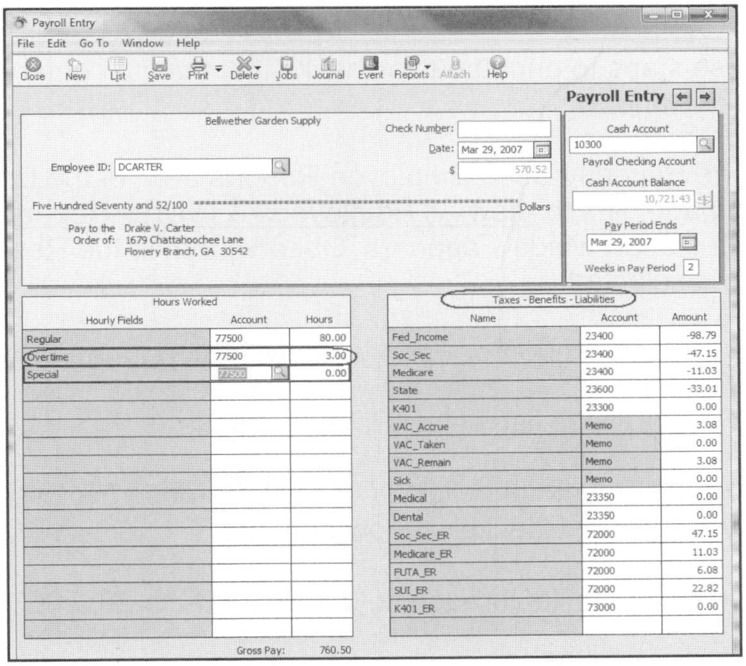

Observe that the Payroll Checking Account Balance in the Cash Account Balance field on the upper right side of the Payroll Entry window changed to 10,721.43. This is because the default for Peachtree is to recalculate the cash balance automatically for receipts, payments, and payroll entries. (If your Cash Account Balance did *not* automatically recalculate, see page 16, step 2d; Other Option selection, Recalculate cash balance automatically in Receipts, Payments, and Payroll Entry should be *checked*.)

5. Select  to post this paycheck. Close the Payroll Entry window

Printing Payroll Checks

Similar to vendor disbursements, you have a choice: you may print each check as you enter it in the Payroll Entry window or you may print all checks at once. If you use batch posting, you must print checks before you post. Since you are using real-time posting, you can print checks later. (You may also use the Preview icon to display checks instead of printing them.)

Follow these steps to print the two checks that you just entered in the Payroll Entry window:

1. From the Recently Used Employee Reports area of the Employees & Payroll page, link to View All Employees & Payroll Reports. The Select a Report window appears. Observe that in the Report Area list, Payroll is selected.

2. On the Select a Report or Form window, click on the Forms tab.

3. In the Forms Types list, select Payroll Checks.

4. In the Forms list, double-click OCR Multi-Purpose PR Laser. The Preview and Print Checks window appears.

5. In the Include checks through field, select March 29, 2007.

6. Type **1294** in the Number the first check field.

7. In the Filter employees by field, select ID, Brandee M. Nunnley; to Drake V. Carter.

8. Click  . The two employee names, both check marked, appear in the table on the right side of the window.

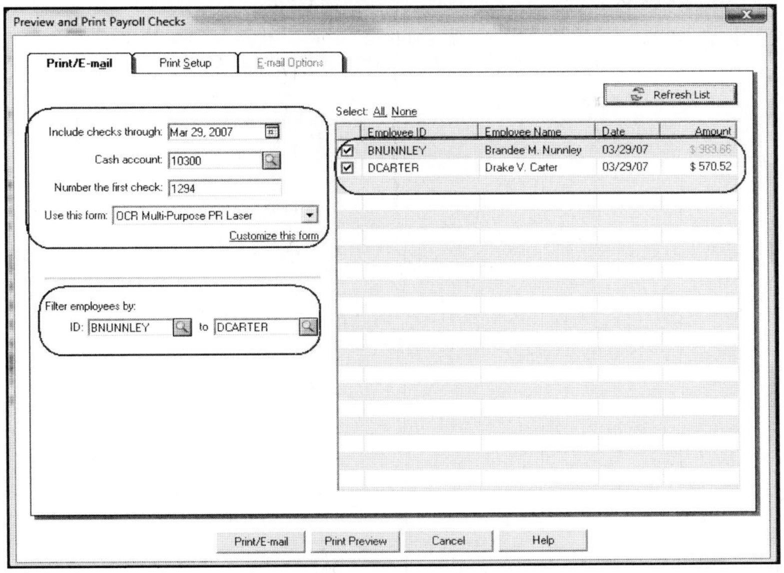

9. Click **Print Preview**. The Print Preview window appears. The top portion of Brandee M. Nunnley's check is shown below.

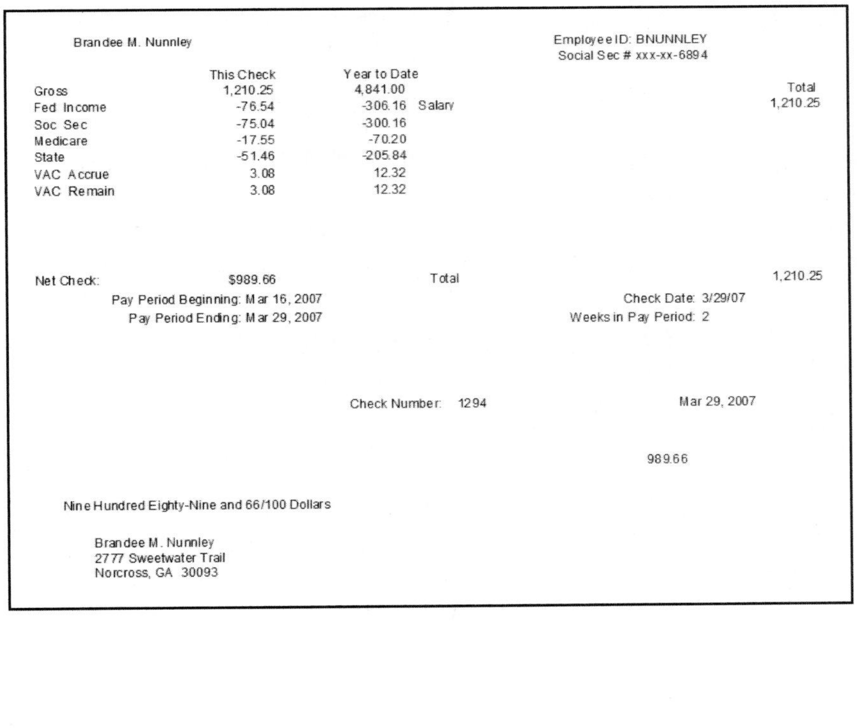

Brandee M. Nunnley

Employee ID: BNUNNLEY
Social Sec # xxx-xx-6894

	This Check	Year to Date		Total
Gross	1,210.25	4,841.00		
Fed Income	-76.54	-306.16	Salary	1,210.25
Soc Sec	-75.04	-300.16		
Medicare	-17.55	-70.20		
State	-51.46	-205.84		
VAC Accrue	3.08	12.32		
VAC Remain	3.08	12.32		

Net Check: $989.66 Total 1,210.25

Pay Period Beginning: Mar 16, 2007
Pay Period Ending: Mar 29, 2007

Check Date: 3/29/07
Weeks in Pay Period: 2

Check Number: 1294 Mar 29, 2007

989.66

Nine Hundred Eighty-Nine and 66/100 Dollars

Brandee M. Nunnley
2777 Sweetwater Trail
Norcross, GA 30093

10. Click Next to see Drake V. Carter's check.

Drake V. Carter

Employee ID: DCARTER
Social Sec # xxx-xx-8990

	This Check	Year to Date		Hours	Rate	Total
Gross	760.50	2,920.50				
Fed Income	-98.79	-376.92	Regular	80.00	9.00	720.00
Soc Sec	-47.15	-181.07	Overtime	3.00	13.50	40.50
Medicare	-11.03	-42.35				
State	-33.01	-124.75				
VAC Accrue	3.08	12.32				
VAC Remain	3.08	12.32				
Net Check:	$570.52		Total	83.00		760.50

Pay Period Beginning: Mar 16, 2007
Pay Period Ending: Mar 29, 2007

Check Date: 3/29/07
Weeks in Pay Period: 2

Check Number: 1295 Mar 29, 2007

570.52

Five Hundred Seventy and 52/100 Dollars

Drake V. Carter
1679 Chattahoochee Lane
Flowery Branch, GA 30542

11. Click Print to print the Check No. 1294 and 1295.

    Observe that the employee statement information (also known as the pay stub) is printed first, then the actual check is printed.

12. A window appears that says Did the checks print properly and is it is OK to assign the check numbers to the checks? If your checks are correct, click Yes.

13. Close the Select a Report or Form window to return to the Employees & Payroll page.

Comment

In Chapter 14, Payroll, you learn how to set the defaults for the payroll accounts. Each employee and employer deduction will be set for individual liability accounts and expense accounts. The sample company is used as an example of automatic payroll processing but does *not* reflect correct payroll accounting procedures.

JOURNAL ENTRY FOR PAYROLL

What happens when you post payroll? In the most common case, the Cash Account that you entered in the Payroll Default window is automatically credited for the net paycheck amount when you post payroll checks. The employee salary expense account is debited for the gross amount of the check and any deductions you use are credited. The following table shows the payroll journal entry for the hourly employee, Drake V. Carter.

Account Description	Debit	Credit
Wages Expense (Regular Hours)	720.00	
Wages Expense (Overtime Hours)	40.50	
Federal Payroll Taxes Payable (Fed_Income)		98.79
Social Security (Soc_Sec for the Employee)		47.15
Medicare (Medicare for the Employee)		11.03
State Payroll Taxes Payable		33.01
Payroll Checking Account		570.52

BACKING UP CHAPTER 4 DATA

Follow these steps to back up Chapter 4 data:

1. From the Navigation Bar, click 

; link to Back up.

2. Click 

.

3. Accept the default for backing up to the hard drive or make the selections to back up to another location. Type **Chapter 4** in the File name field.

4. Click 

.

5. When the window prompts that This company backup will require approximately 5.64MB, click 

. When the Back Up Company scale is 100% complete, you have successfully backed up to the current point in Chapter 4. You are returned to the menu bar.

6. Click File, Exit to exit Peachtree.

INTERNET ACTIVITY	
1.	From your Internet browser, go to the book's website at http://www.mhhe.com/yacht2008.
2.	Link to Student Edition.
3.	In the Course-wide Content list, link Internet Activities; then link to <u>Part 1 Internet Activities for Chapter 1-8</u>. Open or save. (You can also choose Chapter 4, then link to Internet Activities. (In the Choose a Chapter field, if you select Chapter 4 observe that other chapter-specific links are available; for example, Multiple Choice Quiz, True or False, PowerPoint Presentations and Going to the Net Exercises.) Also observe that Course-wide Content includes a Glossary link.
4.	If necessary, scroll down to the AMERICAN INSTITUTE OF CPAs – Chapter 4. Complete steps 1-3.
5.	Using a word processing program, write a summary about the site(s) you selected. Remember to include the website address(es) of each link. Your summary should be no more than 75 words or less than 50 words.

SUMMARY AND REVIEW

SOFTWARE OBJECTIVES: In Chapter 4, you used the software to:

1. Restore data from Exercise 3-2. (This backup was made on page 127.)

2. Enter and store information using the Maintain Employees/Sales Rep window.

3. Set up default information for payroll.

4. Store constant information about payroll payment methods.

5. Transfer funds from the regular checking account to the payroll checking account.

6. Enter paychecks in the Payroll Entry window.

7. Print employee paychecks.

8. Make two backups: backup Chapter 4 data; and backup Exercise 4-2.

WEB OBJECTIVES: In Chapter 4, you did these Internet activities:

1. Used your Internet browser to go to the book's website.
2. Completed the Internet activity for the American Institute of CPAs.
3. Used a word processing program to write a summary about the website(s) that you visited.

GOING TO THE NET

Access the SmartPros website at http://accounting.smartpros.com. Move your cursor over Career Center. From the Career Center list, select Career Resources, then link to "Effective Salary Negotiation (http://accounting.smartpros.com/x28536.xml)." Read the "Effective Salary Negotiation" article. Answer the following questions.

1. What skills should you objectively evaluate?

2. List three factors that affect starting salary.

Short-Answer Questions: In the space provided, write an answer to the question.

1. Draw the flowchart that shows how payroll accounting is done in PCA.

2. When setting up payroll defaults, what is the first step?

___

___

3. Identify the four tabs on the Employee Defaults window.

___

___

___

4. What is the Maintain Employees/Sales Reps window used for?

____

____

____

5. What do the check marks in the Calc column of the employee defaults indicate? Explain.

____

____

____

____

6. What is the difference in the appearance of the Payroll Entry window for an hourly employee and a salaried employee? Explain.

____

____

7. Why do the employee deductions display as negative amounts on the Payroll Entry window?

____

____

____

____

8. What are the gross pay amounts for Brandee M. Nunnley and for Drake V. Carter? Include Mr. Carter's overtime pay.

____

____

9. What is the net pay for Brandee M. Nunnley and for Drake V. Carter? Include Mr. Carter's overtime pay.

____

____

10. What is the fundamental purpose of the AICPA? (*Hint: Refer to the Internet Activity to answer this question.*)

____

____

____

Exercise 4-1: Follow the instructions below to complete Exercise 4-1:

1. Start PCA. Open Bellwether Garden Supply.
2. Restore data from the end of Chapter 4. This back up was made on pages 145-146.
3. Record the following transaction:

Date	*Transaction Description*
03/29/07	Record paycheck information for Brandon A. Hugley.

4. Post the payroll entry.
5. Continue with Exercise 4-2.

Exercise 4-2: Follow the instructions below to complete Exercise 4-2:

1. Record the following transaction:

Date	*Transaction Description*
03/29/07	Record paycheck information for Derrick P. Gross.

2. Post the payroll entry.
3. Print Check Nos. 1296 and 1297. (*Hint: The Include checks through field should show Mar 29, 2007; the Number the first check field should display 1296. If not, type 1296. Click* 

. *Remember to select From Brandon A. Hugley To Derrick P. Gross.*)
4. Print the Payroll Check Register. (*Hint*: In the Recently Used Employee Reports area of the Employees & Payroll page, link to Print the Payroll Check Register. Accept the default for This Period.)
5. Back up Exercise 4-2. Use **Exercise 4-2** as the file name. Exit PCA.

CHAPTER 4 INDEX

Chapter 5 General Ledger, Inventory, and Internal Control

SOFTWARE OBJECTIVES: In Chapter 5, you use the software to:

1. Restore data from Exercise 4-2. (This backup was made on page 151.)
2. Enter a new account in the Chart of Accounts.
3. Look at Peachtree's budget feature.
4. Make a General Journal entry to transfer funds.
5. Display the General Ledger Trial Balance.
6. Set up an Inventory Item.
7. Record an inventory adjustment.
8. Look at Peachtree's internal controls and audit trail.
9. Make two backups: backup Chapter 5 data; and backup Exercise 5-2.

WEB OBJECTIVES: In Chapter 5, you do these Internet activities:

1. Use your Internet browser to go to the book's website.
2. Complete the Internet activity for Ask Jeeves.
3. Complete the steps shown for this activity.

In Chapter 5, you learn how to use the General Ledger Chart of Accounts. When you set up a company, the following initial steps are performed: set up a chart of accounts and enter beginning balances or budget amounts. In this chapter, you continue to look at the sample company, Bellwether Garden Supply. In Parts 2 and 3 of the textbook (Chapters 9-17 and Projects 1 through 4A), you have an opportunity to set up 11 companies from scratch.

This chapter also shows you how to use PCA's Inventory system. PCA lets you track inventory items both at the purchasing and the sales level. When you set up an inventory item, you establish the General Ledger accounts that are updated by purchases and sales. PCA keeps track of cost of goods sold, stock levels, sales prices, and vendors. PCA uses a ***perpetual inventory*** system. In a perpetual inventory system, an up-to-date record of inventory is maintained, recording each purchase and each sale that occurs.

Another Peachtree feature is user security. On pages 175-182, Internal Control, you look at how Peachtree keeps company data secure.

CHART OF ACCOUNTS

In accounting you learn that a ***chart of accounts*** is a list of all the accounts used by a company showing the identifying number assigned to each account. PCA includes over 75 sample companies' Charts of Accounts. A Chart of Accounts can be set up from scratch or you can select an industry-specific simplified or extensive Chart of Accounts.

To see the sample companies and their Charts of Accounts, follow these steps:

1. Start PCA. Open Bellwether Garden Supply. (If Bellwether Garden Supply is not shown, restore a New Company. Refer to the Read Me box on page 27)

2. Click Help; Peachtree Accounting Help. The Peachtree Help window appears. Peachtree's help is also called online Help. Peachtree Help topics are displayed in the ***HTML*** (Hypertext Markup Language) Help Viewer.

3. If necessary, click on the Contents tab. Double-click References and Legal Notices; double-click Help about Your Specific Type of Business.

4. Click A-Z of Business Types.

5. Double-click List of Sample Charts of Accounts. Compare your Peachtree Help window to the one shown on the next page.

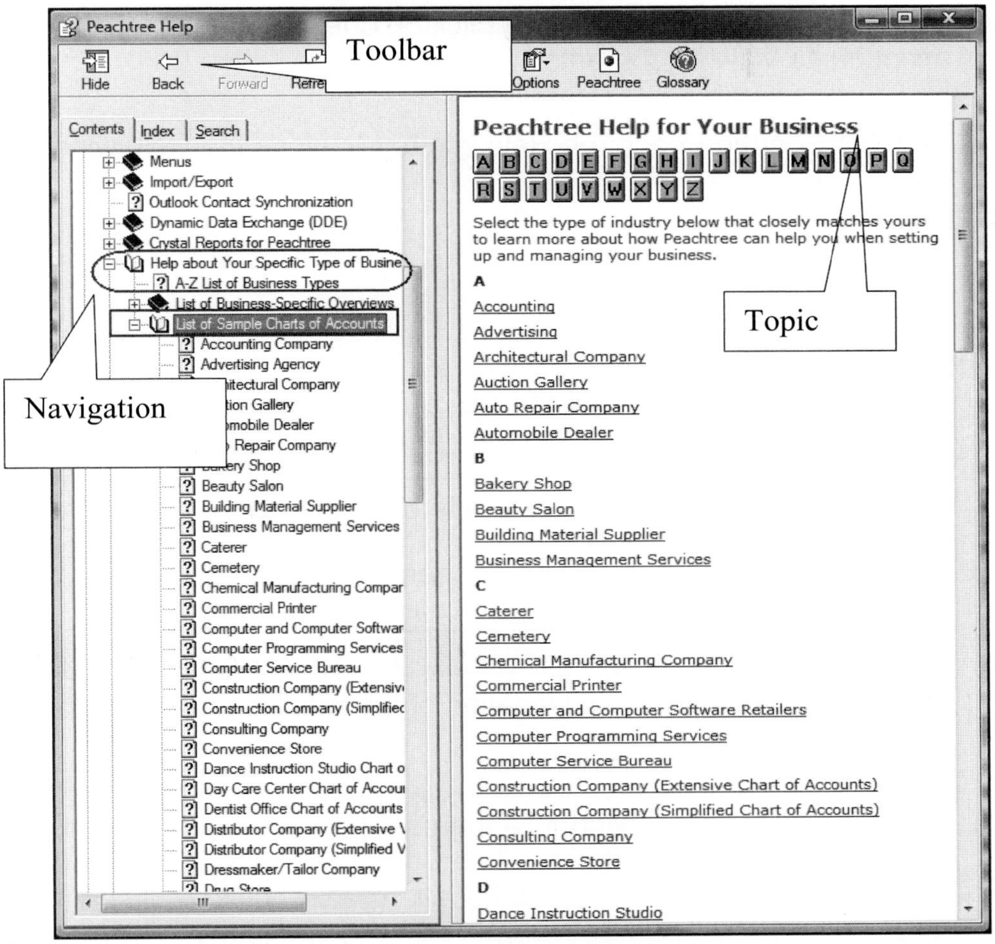

Observe that there are three panes on the Peachtree Help window:

- On the left side of the window is the Navigation pane. It contains three tabs: Contents, Index, and Search. Use the Navigation pane to browse or search for topics.
- On the right side of the window is the Topic pane. The topic pane displays each Help topic or Web page selected in the Navigation pane.
- The third pane is the toolbar, located below the Peachtree Help title bar. The toolbar is similar to Internet Explorer's toolbar.

6. On the Navigation pane (left side), click on one of the sample charts of accounts to view its contents.

7. Click X on the Peachtree Help title bar to close the Help window.

GETTING STARTED

1. PCA 's Navigation Bar should be displayed.

2. Restore your data from the Exercise 4-2 backup.

   a. From the Navigation Bar, select Company; link to <u>Restore</u>. (The backup file was made on page 151.)

   b. The Select Backup File window appears. If the Location field shows C:\Program Files\Sage Software\Peachtree\Company\BCS\Exercise 4-2.ptb, click Next >. (*Or,* click Browse, then select the appropriate location of the Exercise 4-2 backup file; click Next >.)

   c. The Select Company window appears. The radio button next to An Existing Company is selected. The Company name field shows Bellwether Garden Supply; the Location field shows C:\ProgramFiles\Sage Software\Peachtree\Company\BCS (or the appropriate location on your computer). Click Next >.

   d. The Restore Options window appears. Make sure that the box next to Company Data is *checked*. Click Next >.

   e. The Confirmation window appears. Check the From and To fields to make sure they are correct. Click Finish. When the Restore Company scale is 100% complete, your data is restored and you are returned to the menu bar.

   f. If necessary, remove the external media.

3. From the Navigation Bar, select 

; 

; New Account. The Maintain Chart of Accounts window appears.

4. To add a new Money Market account, follow these steps:

   a. In the Account ID field, type **10500** and press **<Enter>**

   b. Your cursor is in the Description field. Type the name of the account **Money Market Fund**, and press **<Enter>**.

   c. Your cursor is in the Account Type field. There is a drop-down list indicated by a down arrow. The default Account Type is Cash. 

. In the Account Type field you can specify the kind of account you are creating, such as, Cash, Cost of Sales, Equity-doesn't close, Equity-gets closed, etc. Select the drop-down list by clicking on the down arrow in the Account Type field to display the list of available account types. Make sure **Cash** is highlighted and press **<Enter>**. *The Account Type is important; it sorts each account on the financial statements.* Compare your Maintain Chart of Accounts window to the one shown below. (The top portion of the Maintain Chart of Accounts window is shown.)

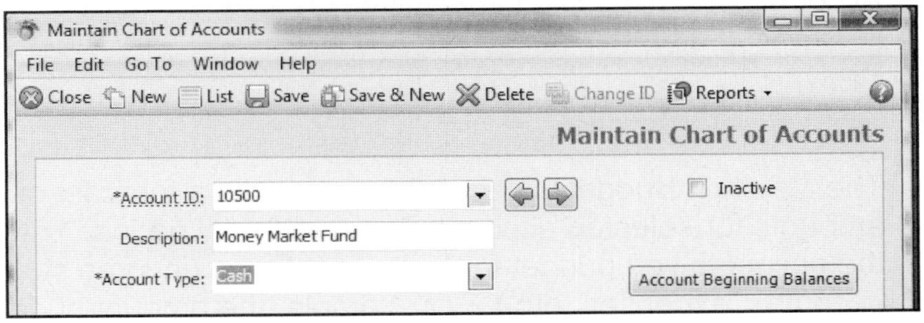

Remember to check the Account Type field. The selection made in the Account Type field classifies accounts on the financial statements.

5. Click 

then close to return to the Company page.

BUDGETS

Bellwether Garden Supply already has a budget set up. To see Bellwether's budget, follow these steps.

1. From the Company page, click 

; New Budget. The Maintain Budgets window appears. Let's examine what it shows. If necessary, enlarge the window.

   Observe that the Maintain Budgets window shows an icon bar

with an Excel selection. In later chapters, you convert Peachtree reports to Excel. The author recommends that if you are attaching Peachtree reports in an email for your instructor, that Excel attachments are used. See Chapter 17, Using PCA 2008 with Excel and Word, for more information.

The Maintain Budgets window defaults to Income Statement Accounts. This is shown in the Account Filters field –

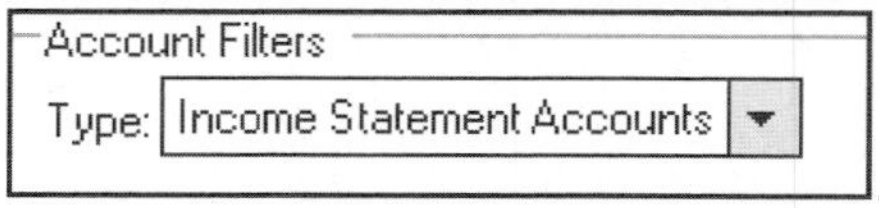

.

The Maintain Budgets window lets you build a forecast of dollar amounts for selected accounts for each fiscal period. You can filter the accounts you budget for by account type (income statement accounts, expenses, etc.). For example, the amount budgeted to Account No. 40000-AV, Sales Aviary for 3/31/07 was $7,000.00. Let's look at the Income Statement to see how close that amount was to the actual sales for Account No. 40000-AV, Sales Aviary. (*Hint:* The Total column shows the accumulated total for 1/31/07 through 12/31/07.)

Part of the Maintain Budgets window is shown below.

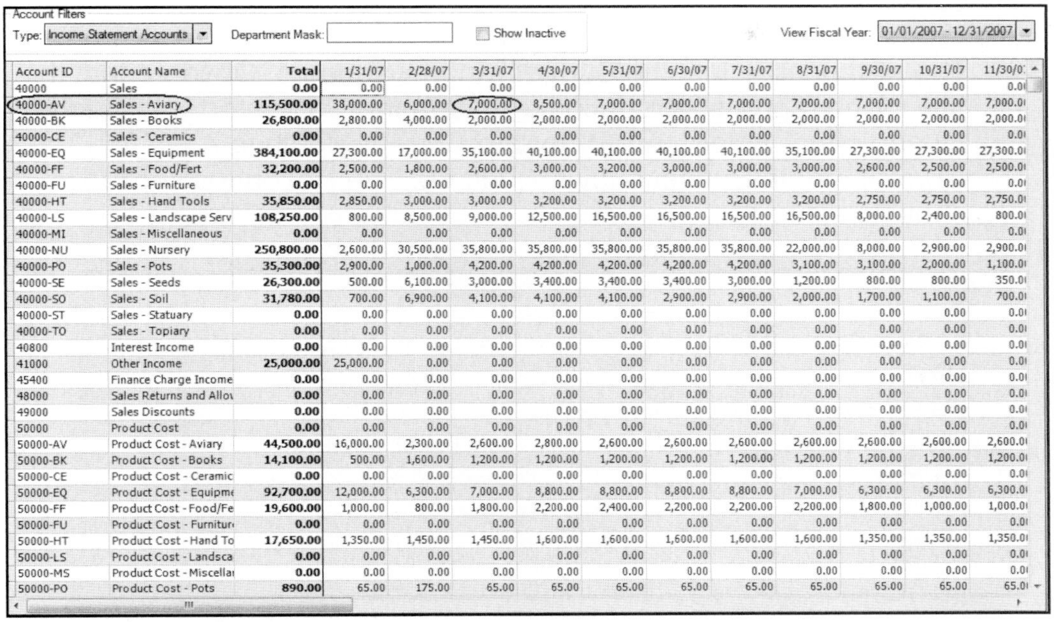

Account ID	Account Name	Total	1/31/07	2/28/07	3/31/07	4/30/07	5/31/07	6/30/07	7/31/07	8/31/07	9/30/07	10/31/07	11/30/0
40000	Sales	**0.00**	0.00	0.00	0.00	0.00	0.00	0.00	0.00	0.00	0.00	0.00	0.0
40000-AV	Sales - Aviary	**115,500.00**	38,000.00	6,000.00	7,000.00	8,500.00	7,000.00	7,000.00	7,000.00	7,000.00	7,000.00	7,000.00	7,000.0
40000-BK	Sales - Books	**26,800.00**	2,800.00	4,000.00	2,000.00	2,000.00	2,000.00	2,000.00	2,000.00	2,000.00	2,000.00	2,000.00	2,000.0
40000-CE	Sales - Ceramics	**0.00**	0.00	0.00	0.00	0.00	0.00	0.00	0.00	0.00	0.00	0.00	0.0
40000-EQ	Sales - Equipment	**384,100.00**	27,300.00	17,000.00	35,100.00	40,100.00	40,100.00	40,100.00	40,100.00	35,100.00	27,300.00	27,300.00	27,300.0
40000-FF	Sales - Food/Fert	**32,200.00**	2,500.00	1,800.00	2,600.00	3,000.00	3,200.00	3,000.00	3,000.00	3,000.00	2,600.00	2,500.00	2,500.0
40000-FU	Sales - Furniture	**0.00**	0.00	0.00	0.00	0.00	0.00	0.00	0.00	0.00	0.00	0.00	0.0
40000-HT	Sales - Hand Tools	**35,850.00**	2,850.00	3,000.00	3,000.00	3,200.00	3,200.00	3,200.00	3,200.00	3,200.00	2,750.00	2,750.00	2,750.0
40000-LS	Sales - Landscape Serv	**108,250.00**	800.00	8,500.00	9,000.00	12,500.00	16,500.00	16,500.00	16,500.00	16,500.00	8,000.00	2,400.00	800.0
40000-MI	Sales - Miscellaneous	**0.00**	0.00	0.00	0.00	0.00	0.00	0.00	0.00	0.00	0.00	0.00	0.0
40000-NU	Sales - Nursery	**250,800.00**	2,600.00	30,500.00	35,800.00	35,800.00	35,800.00	35,800.00	35,800.00	22,000.00	8,000.00	2,900.00	2,900.0
40000-PO	Sales - Pots	**35,300.00**	2,900.00	1,000.00	4,200.00	4,200.00	4,200.00	4,200.00	4,200.00	3,100.00	3,100.00	2,000.00	1,100.0
40000-SE	Sales - Seeds	**26,300.00**	500.00	6,100.00	3,000.00	3,400.00	3,400.00	3,400.00	3,000.00	1,200.00	800.00	800.00	350.0
40000-SO	Sales - Soil	**31,780.00**	700.00	6,900.00	4,100.00	4,100.00	4,100.00	2,900.00	2,900.00	2,000.00	1,700.00	1,100.00	700.0
40000-ST	Sales - Statuary	**0.00**	0.00	0.00	0.00	0.00	0.00	0.00	0.00	0.00	0.00	0.00	0.0
40000-TO	Sales - Topiary	**0.00**	0.00	0.00	0.00	0.00	0.00	0.00	0.00	0.00	0.00	0.00	0.0
40800	Interest Income	**0.00**	0.00	0.00	0.00	0.00	0.00	0.00	0.00	0.00	0.00	0.00	0.0
41000	Other Income	**25,000.00**	25,000.00	0.00	0.00	0.00	0.00	0.00	0.00	0.00	0.00	0.00	0.0
45400	Finance Charge Income	**0.00**	0.00	0.00	0.00	0.00	0.00	0.00	0.00	0.00	0.00	0.00	0.0
48000	Sales Returns and Allo	**0.00**	0.00	0.00	0.00	0.00	0.00	0.00	0.00	0.00	0.00	0.00	0.0
49000	Sales Discounts	**0.00**	0.00	0.00	0.00	0.00	0.00	0.00	0.00	0.00	0.00	0.00	0.0
50000	Product Cost	**0.00**	0.00	0.00	0.00	0.00	0.00	0.00	0.00	0.00	0.00	0.00	0.0
50000-AV	Product Cost - Aviary	**44,500.00**	16,000.00	2,300.00	2,600.00	2,800.00	2,600.00	2,600.00	2,600.00	2,600.00	2,600.00	2,600.00	2,600.0
50000-BK	Product Cost - Books	**14,100.00**	500.00	1,600.00	1,200.00	1,200.00	1,200.00	1,200.00	1,200.00	1,200.00	1,200.00	1,200.00	1,200.0
50000-CE	Product Cost - Ceramic	**0.00**	0.00	0.00	0.00	0.00	0.00	0.00	0.00	0.00	0.00	0.00	0.0
50000-EQ	Product Cost - Equipme	**92,700.00**	12,000.00	6,300.00	7,000.00	8,800.00	8,800.00	8,800.00	8,800.00	7,000.00	6,300.00	6,300.00	6,300.0
50000-FF	Product Cost - Food/Fe	**19,600.00**	1,000.00	800.00	1,800.00	2,200.00	2,400.00	2,200.00	2,200.00	2,200.00	1,800.00	1,000.00	1,000.0
50000-FU	Product Cost - Furnitur	**0.00**	0.00	0.00	0.00	0.00	0.00	0.00	0.00	0.00	0.00	0.00	0.0
50000-HT	Product Cost - Hand To	**17,650.00**	1,350.00	1,450.00	1,450.00	1,600.00	1,600.00	1,600.00	1,600.00	1,600.00	1,350.00	1,350.00	1,350.0
50000-LS	Product Cost - Landsca	**0.00**	0.00	0.00	0.00	0.00	0.00	0.00	0.00	0.00	0.00	0.00	0.0
50000-MS	Product Cost - Miscella	**0.00**	0.00	0.00	0.00	0.00	0.00	0.00	0.00	0.00	0.00	0.00	0.0
50000-PO	Product Cost - Pots	**890.00**	65.00	175.00	65.00	65.00	65.00	65.00	65.00	65.00	65.00	65.00	65.0

To compare the March 31, 2007 budgeted amount for Account No. 40000, Sales-Aviary to the actual amount, display the <Standard> Income/Budget report. Follow these steps to do that.

1. Minimize the Maintain Budgets window. The Company page is displayed.

2. From the menu bar, select Reports & Forms; Financial Statements. Select <Standard> Income/Budget.

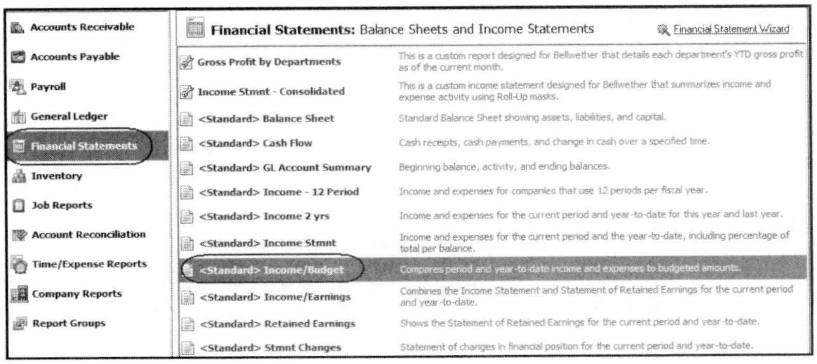

3. Click 

.

4. The <Standard> Income/Budget window appears. Observe that the title of the report shows Income Statement, Compared with Budget. Observe that Sales - Aviary for the Current Month is 7,127.71. The Current Month Budget shows 7,000.00. The Revenues section is shown below.

Bellwether Garden Supply
Income Statement
Compared with Budget
For the Three Months Ending March 31, 2007

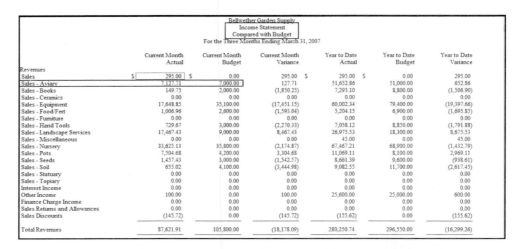

	Current Month Actual	Current Month Budget	Current Month Variance	Year to Date Actual	Year to Date Budget	Year to Date Variance
Revenues						
Sales	$ 295.00	$ 0.00	295.00	$ 295.00	$ 0.00	295.00
Sales - Aviary	7,127.71	7,000.00	127.71	51,652.86	51,000.00	652.86
Sales - Books	149.75	2,000.00	(1,850.25)	7,293.10	8,800.00	(1,506.90)
Sales - Ceramics	0.00	0.00	0.00	0.00	0.00	0.00
Sales - Equipment	17,648.85	35,100.00	(17,451.15)	60,002.34	79,400.00	(19,397.66)
Sales - Food/Fert	1,006.96	2,600.00	(1,593.04)	5,204.15	6,900.00	(1,695.85)
Sales - Furniture	0.00	0.00	0.00	0.00	0.00	0.00
Sales - Hand Tools	729.67	3,000.00	(2,270.33)	7,058.12	8,850.00	(1,791.88)
Sales - Landscape Services	17,467.43	9,000.00	8,467.43	26,975.53	18,300.00	8,675.53
Sales - Miscellaneous	0.00	0.00	0.00	45.00	0.00	45.00
Sales - Nursery	33,625.13	35,800.00	(2,174.87)	67,467.21	68,900.00	(1,432.79)
Sales - Pots	7,504.68	4,200.00	3,304.68	11,069.11	8,100.00	2,969.11
Sales - Seeds	1,457.43	3,000.00	(1,542.57)	8,661.39	9,600.00	(938.61)
Sales - Soil	655.02	4,100.00	(3,444.98)	9,082.55	11,700.00	(2,617.45)
Sales - Statuary	0.00	0.00	0.00	0.00	0.00	0.00
Sales - Topiary	0.00	0.00	0.00	0.00	0.00	0.00
Interest Income	0.00	0.00	0.00	0.00	0.00	0.00
Other Income	100.00	0.00	100.00	25,600.00	25,000.00	600.00
Finance Charge Income	0.00	0.00	0.00	0.00	0.00	0.00
Sales Returns and Allowances	0.00	0.00	0.00	0.00	0.00	0.00
Sales Discounts	(145.72)	0.00	(145.72)	(155.62)	0.00	(155.62)
Total Revenues	87,621.91	105,800.00	(18,178.09)	280,250.74	296,550.00	(16,299.26)

What does the Income/Budget report show? That for March 31, 2007 the budgeted amount of $7,000 was exceeded by the actual sales amount of $7,127.71 for Sales-Aviary. The current month variance is 127.71—sales exceeded the budgeted by that amount. Amounts shown in parentheses indicate that sales were lower than budgeted amounts.

5. Close the <Standard> Income/Budget report; and if necessary, close the Select a Report or Form window.

GENERAL JOURNAL

To open this Money Market Fund, you are taking $4,500 from Bellwether's regular checking account and putting $4,500 in the new account (10500, Money Market Fund). You also transfer $1,000 from Bellwether's regular checking account to their payroll checking account (10300, Payroll Checking Account). The transfer of funds is recorded in the General Journal, then posted to the General Ledger.

Date	*Transaction Description*
03/15/07	Transfer $4,500 to the Money Market Fund and $1,000 to the Payroll Checking Account from the Regular Checking Account.

Follow these steps to enter the transfer of funds:

1. From the Company page, link to General Journal Entry. The General Journal Entry window appears.

2. Press **<Enter>** to accept the displayed date (3/15/07) in the Date field.

3. Your cursor is in the Reference field. Type **Transfer** and press **<Enter>** two times.

4. Your cursor is in the GL Account field. Type the account number for the Money Market Fund account, **10500**, and press the **<Enter>** or **<Tab>**. Observe that Money Market Fund appears below the account number.

5. Type **Money Market Fund** in the Description field. In this textbook, the account name is used as the description. You may prefer to type a description instead; for example, Established money market account. When a description is typed, it will repeat automatically on each Description line. Press **<Enter>** or **<Tab>** to go to the Debit field.

6. You are going to increase this account by $4,500. Type a debit amount of **4500** and press **<Enter>** three times. (It doesn't matter whether you type the debit or credit part of the entry first.) Notice that the Totals field displays 4,500.00 below the Debit column. The Out of Balance amount beneath it totals 4,500.00.

7. Your cursor is in the Account No. field. Type **10300** and press **<Enter>**. Payroll Checking Account displays on the line below the account number. Type **Payroll Checking Account** in the Description field. Press **<Enter>** to go to the Debit field.

8. Type **1000** in the Debit field. Press **<Enter>** three times.

9. Your cursor is in the Account No. field. Type **10200**; press **<Enter>**. Type **Regular Checking Account** in the Description field. Press **<Enter>** two times to go to the Credit field.

10. Type **5500** in the Credit field. Notice that the Totals field now displays 5,500.00 beneath the Credit column. The Out of Balance amount equals zero (0.00). This means that the General Journal is in balance and can be posted. Compare your General Journal Entry window to the one shown below.

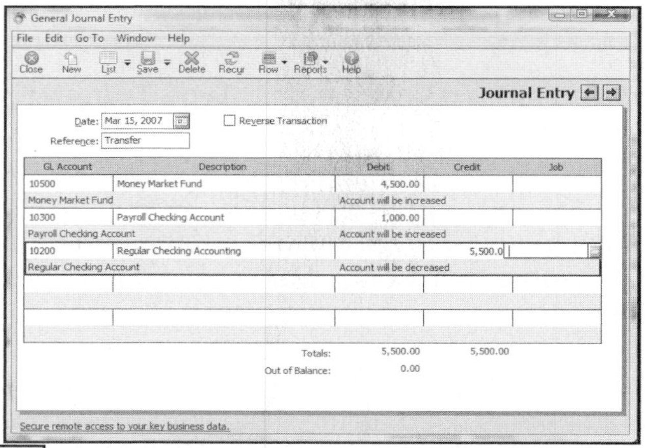

11. Click 

to post to the General Ledger. Close the General Journal Entry window to return to the Company page.

The General Journal entry that you just completed transferred $4,500 from Bellwether's Regular Checking Account (Account No. 10200) to their Money Market Fund (Account No. 10500) and $1,000 to their Payroll Checking Account (Account No. 10300). To check that the account transfers have been made, follow these steps:

1. From the menu bar, select Reports & Forms, then General Ledger. The Select a Report or Form window displays.

2. In the General Ledger: Account Information List, double-click General Ledger Trial Balance. The General Ledger Trial Balance is shown on the next two pages.

Bellwether Garden Supply
General Ledger Trial Balance
As of Mar 31, 2007

Filter Criteria includes: Report order is by ID. Report is printed in Detail Format.

Account ID	Account Description	Debit Amt	Credit Amt
10000	Petty Cash	327.55	
10100	Cash on Hand	1,850.45	
10200	Regular Checking Account	10,246.52	
10300	Payroll Checking Account	9,547.53	
10400	Savings Account	7,500.00	
10500	Money Market Fund	4,500.00	
11000	Accounts Receivable	174,689.31	
11400	Other Receivables	7,681.84	
11500	Allowance for Doubtful Account		5,000.00
12000	Inventory	12,182.06	
14000	Prepaid Expenses	14,221.30	
14100	Employee Advances	3,000.65	
14200	Notes Receivable-Current	11,000.00	
14700	Other Current Assets	120.00	
15000	Furniture and Fixtures	62,769.25	
15100	Equipment	38,738.33	
15200	Vehicles	86,273.40	
15300	Other Depreciable Property	6,200.96	
15500	Buildings	185,500.00	
15600	Building Improvements	26,500.00	
17000	Accum. Depreciation-Furniture		54,680.57
17100	Accum. Depreciation-Equipment		33,138.11
17200	Accum. Depreciation-Vehicles		51,585.26
17300	Accum. Depreciation-Other		3,788.84
17500	Accum. Depreciation-Buildings		34,483.97
17600	Accum. Depreciation-Bldg Imp		4,926.28
19000	Deposits	15,000.00	
19100	Organization Costs	4,995.10	
19150	Accum Amortiz - Organiz Costs		2,000.00
19200	Notes Receivable- Noncurrent	5,004.90	
19900	Other Noncurrent Assets	3,333.00	
20000	Accounts Payable		79,871.06
23000	Accrued Expenses		3,022.55
23100	Sales Tax Payable		18,005.62
23200	Wages Payable		2,320.30
23300	401 K Deductions Payable		2,490.32
23350	Health Insurance Payable	530.64	
23400	Federal Payroll Taxes Payable		41,942.04
23500	FUTA Tax Payable		258.20
23600	State Payroll Taxes Payable		6,885.21
23700	SUTA Tax Payable		658.67
23800	Local Payroll Taxes Payable		113.25
23900	Income Taxes Payable		11,045.75
24000	Other Taxes Payable		2,640.15
24100	Current Portion Long-Term Debt		5,167.00
24300	Contracts Payable- Current		2,000.00
24700	Other Current Liabilities		54.00
27000	Notes Payable-Noncurrent		4,000.00
39003	Common Stock		5,000.00
39004	Paid-in Capital		100,000.00
39005	Retained Earnings		189,037.60
40000	Sales		295.00
40000-AV	Sales - Aviary		51,652.86
40000-BK	Sales - Books		7,293.10
40000-EQ	Sales - Equipment		60,002.34
40000-FF	Sales - Food/Fert		5,204.15
40000-HT	Sales - Hand Tools		7,058.12
40000-LS	Sales - Landscape Services		26,975.53
40000-MI	Sales - Miscellaneous		45.00
40000-NU	Sales - Nursery		67,467.21
40000-PO	Sales - Pots		11,069.11
40000-SE	Sales - Seeds		8,661.39
40000-SO	Sales - Soil		9,082.55
41000	Other Income		25,600.00

Bellwether Garden Supply
General Ledger Trial Balance
As of Mar 31, 2007

Filter Criteria includes: Report order is by ID. Report is printed in Detail Format.

Account ID	Account Description	Debit Amt	Credit Amt
49000	Sales Discounts	155.62	
50000	Product Cost		68.50
50000-AV	Product Cost - Aviary	20,821.45	
50000-BK	Product Cost - Books	2,361.37	
50000-EQ	Product Cost - Equipment	24,075.20	
50000-FF	Product Cost - Food/Fert	2,060.04	
50000-HT	Product Cost - Hand Tools	2,813.85	
50000-PO	Product Cost - Pots	3,259.45	
50000-SE	Product Cost - Seeds	3,450.65	
50000-SO	Product Cost - Soil	4,048.47	
57000-NU	Direct Labor - Nursery	3,062.50	
57200	Materials Cost	1,397.45	
57200-NU	Materials Cost - Nursery	9,617.50	
57300-LS	Subcontractors - Landscaping	335.50	
57500	Freight	50.00	
60000	Advertising Expense	1,325.00	
61000	Auto Expenses	274.56	
61500	Bad Debt Expense	1,341.09	
62000	Bank Charges	18.00	
64000	Depreciation Expense	8,394.00	
68500	Legal and Professional Expense	510.00	
69000	Licenses Expense	150.00	
70000	Maintenance Expense	75.00	
71000	Office Expense	479.89	
72000	Payroll Tax Exp	15,854.36	
74000	Rent or Lease Expense	1,100.00	
74500	Repairs Expense	3,694.00	
75500	Supplies Expense	2,928.17	
77000	Utilities Expense	303.45	
77500	Wages Expense	138,465.46	
89000	Other Expense	464.90	
89500	Purchase Disc- Expense Items		10.11
	Total:	944,599.72	944,599.72

On page 163, Account No. 10200, Regular Checking Account, has a debit balance of $10,246.52; Account No. 10300, Payroll Checking Account, has a debit balance of $9,547.53; and Account No. 10500, Money Market Fund, has a debit balance of $4,500.00. This shows that the General Journal entry that you just completed is posted correctly. To see the rest of the General Ledger Trial Balance, scroll down the General Ledger Trial Balance window.

3. Close the General Ledger Trial Balance. You are returned to the Select a Report or Form window.

4. Close the Select a Report or Form window to return to the Company page.

SETTING UP AN INVENTORY ITEM

This part of Chapter 5 explains PCA 's Inventory system.

The sample company, Bellwether Garden Supply, has decided to track cleaning supplies as stock inventory items and to bill clients for supplies used. First, you need to enter the cleaning supplies they stock as Inventory Items. Follow these steps to set up an Inventory Item:

1. From the Navigation Bar, click 

; 

, New Inventory Item. The Maintain Inventory Items window displays.

2. In the Item ID field, type **AVRY-10300** (type a capital A because the ID code is case sensitive--the first four characters should in uppercase) and press **<Enter>**.

3. In the Description field, type **Oriole Feeder** and press **<Enter>**.

4. Your cursor is in the Item Class field. Stock Item displays as the default type.

Inventory Types

If you click on the down-arrow next to the Item Class field, observe that there are several types of Inventory Items:

- Stock item: This is the default in the Item Class list. It is the traditional inventory item where the program tracks descriptions, unit prices, stock quantities, and cost of goods sold. For stock items, you should complete the entire window. Once an item has been designated as a stock item, the type cannot be changed.

- Master Stock Item: A special item that does not represent inventory you stock rather contains information shared with a number of substock items generated from it.

- Non-stock item: PCA tracks the description and a unit price for sales. You can also track default accounts. You might use this type for service items such as hours where the unit price is set.

- Description only: PCA keeps track of the description of an Inventory Item. This saves time when entering purchases and sales because you don't have to retype the description. You might use this type for service items where the price fluctuates.

- Service: This is for services you can apply to your salary and wages account.

- Labor: This is for labor you can apply to your salary and wages account. You cannot purchase labor items but you can sell them.

- Assembly: You can specify items as assembly items and create a bill of materials for a unit made up of component stock or subassembly items.

- Activity item: To indicate how time is spent when performing services for a customer, for a job, or for internal administrative work, activity items are used with the Time & Billing feature.

- Charge item: Expenses recorded by an employee or vendor when company resources are used for a customer or job.

Follow these steps to continue setting up an Inventory Item:

1. Press the **<Enter>** key to accept the Item Class default as Stock item.

2. Your cursor is in the Description for Sales field. Press the **<Enter>** key to go to the description field. Type **Oriole Feeder** and press **<Enter>**.

3. Your cursor is in the Price Level 1 field. Click on the right arrow button 

in this field. The Multiple Price Levels window appears. In the Price Level 1 row, click on the Price column. Type **15** on the Price Level 1 row, then press **<Enter>**. You can set up ten different sales prices per item.

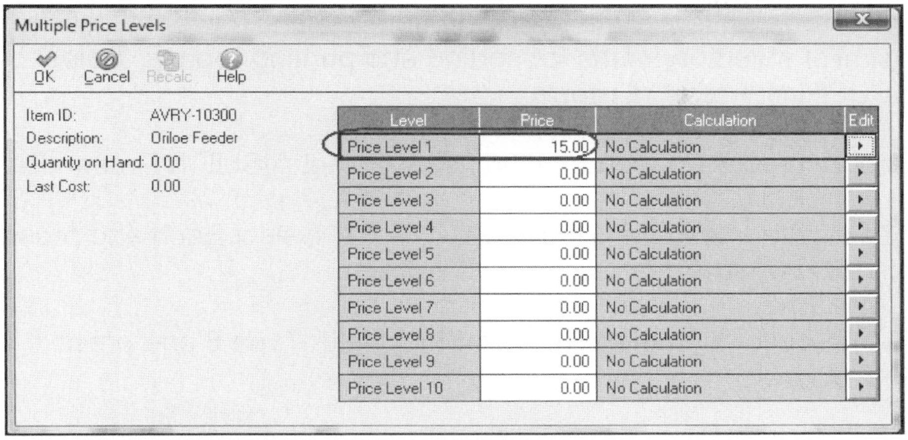

4. Click [OK] to close the Multiple Price Levels window. The Price Level 1 field shows 15.00.

5. Click on the Last Unit Cost field. Delete the 0.00. Type **7** and press **<Enter>**.

6. Observe that the Cost Method is FIFO. Peachtree includes three inventory cost methods: FIFO, LIFO and Average. Press **<Enter>**.

7. Your cursor is in the GL Sales Account field. Click [magnifier], then select Account No. 40000-AV, Sales – Aviary, as the sales account. Press **<Enter>**.

8. Accept the default for the GL Inventory Acct, Account No. 12000, Inventory, by pressing **<Enter>**.

9. Your cursor is in the GL Cost of Sales Acct field. Select Account No. 50000-AV, Product Cost – Aviary, as the product cost account. Press **<Enter>**.

10. Click [magnifier] in the Item Tax Type field. Observe that the default, 1, means that this is a regular, taxable item. Press **<Enter>**.

11. Click on the Item Type field. The Item Type is a way of classifying similar inventory items for sorting and printing reports. Select SUPPLY. Press **<Enter>**.

12. Your cursor is in the Location field. Select AISLE 1. Press **<Enter>**.

13. Your cursor is in the Stocking U/M field. Select Each and press **<Enter>** two times.

14. Your cursor is in the Minimum Stock field. Type **6** and press **<Enter>**.

15. Your cursor is in the Reorder Quantity field. Type **6** and press **<Enter>**

16. Select DEJULIA, DeJulia Wholesale Suppliers as the Preferred Vendor ID. Leave the Buyer ID field blank.

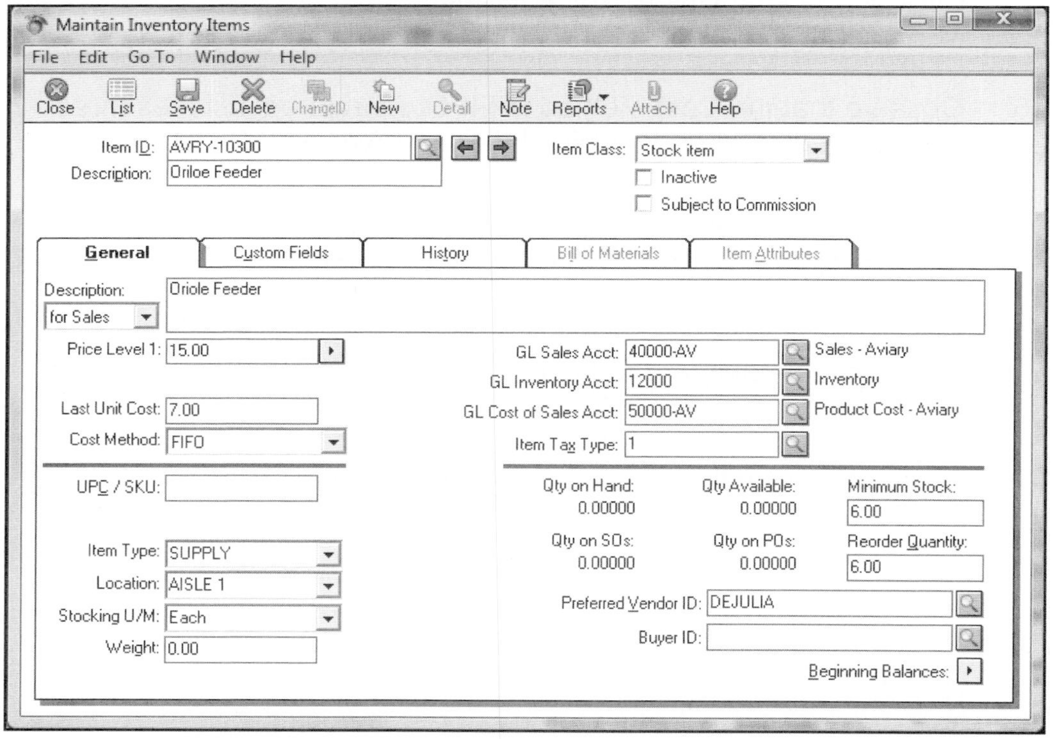

When you purchase inventory stock-type items, there is one journal entry: debit the Inventory account and credit Accounts Payable/Vendor account. When you sell Inventory stock-type items, there are two journal entries:

- Debit Accounts Receivable; Credit Revenue and Sales Tax Payable.
- Debit Costs of Goods Sold; Credit Inventory.

The Maintain Inventory Items window should be displayed.

Observe that you set the following account defaults for this stock item:

GL Sales Acct	40000-AV	Sales - Aviary
GL Inventory Acct	12000	Inventory
GL Cost of Sales Acct	50000-AV	Product Cost - Aviary

You also selected a preferred vendor. The Preferred Vendor ID field should display DEJULIA, which is the Vendor ID for DeJulia Wholesale Suppliers. Bellwether purchases oriole feeders from this vendor.

17. Click 

then close to return to the Inventory & Services page.

INVENTORY AND PURCHASES

In the following transaction, journalize and post a purchase of inventory.

Date	*Transaction Description*
03/17/07	Purchased 6 Oriole feeders from DeJulia Wholesale Suppliers, Invoice No. 55522, at a unit price of $7, for a total of $42.

Follow the steps shown on the next page to record this transaction.

1. From the Navigation Bar, click 

; 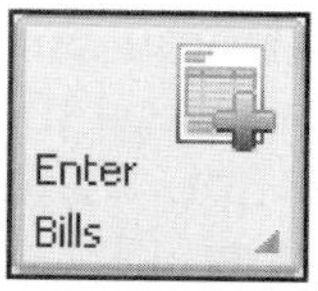

, New Bill. The Purchases/Receive Inventory window displays. If your GL Account column and A/P Account fields are *not* displayed on the Purchases/Receive Inventory window, see the instructions on page 16, Hide General Ledger Accounts area.

2. In the Vendor ID field, type **DEJULIA** and press **<Enter>** (or use the lookup icon to find DeJulia Wholesale Suppliers).

3. Type or select **17** as the date.

4. In the Invoice # field, type **55522** and press **<Enter>**. This is a required field.

5. If necessary, click on the Apply to Purchases tab.

6. Click on the Quantity field. Type **6** and press **<Enter>**.

7. Your cursor is in the Item field. Type or select the code you just created, **AVRY-10300** and press **<Enter>** three times. The description and the GL Account automatically default to the information you assigned in the Maintain Inventory Items window.

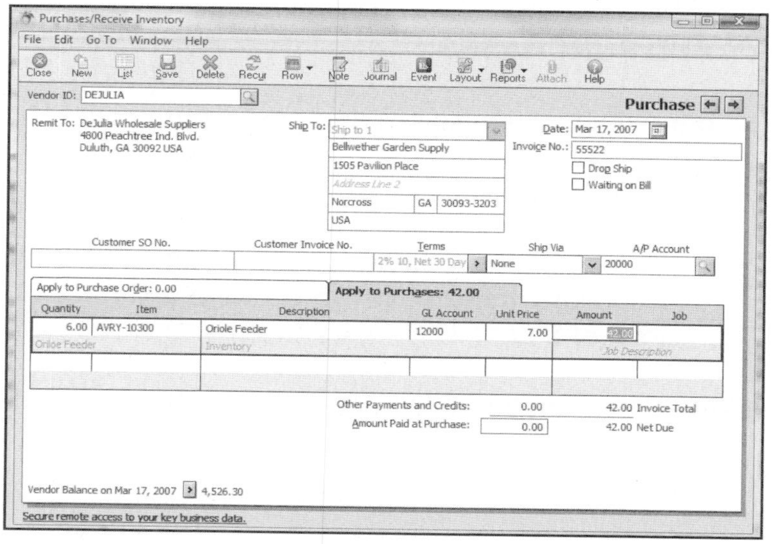

8. Click 

to post this purchase. Close the Purchases/Receive Inventory window.

INVENTORY AND SALES

When you sell a stock-type item, PCA updates Accounts Receivable and computes the Cost of Goods Sold (Product Cost), using one of three costing methods. In the General Ledger, a single entry encompassing all sales in the current period is made to the Product Cost account. This entry is dated the last day of the accounting period.

Henton Park Apartments wants three Oriole feeders. The following steps show you how to invoice Henton Park Apartments for three Oriole feeders.

Date	*Transaction Description*
03/17/07	Sold three Oriole feeders on account to Henton Park Apartments for $15 each plus sales tax.

1. From the Navigation Bar, click 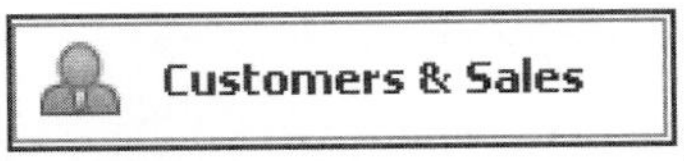

; 

, New Sales Invoice. The Sales/Invoicing window displays.

   If the GL Account column and A/R Account field are *not* displayed, refer to the instructions on page 16, Hide General Ledger Accounts area.

2. In the Customer ID field, click  and select **HENTON, Henton Park Apartments**.

3. Type or select **17** as the date. Do not complete the Invoice No. field.

4. If necessary, click on the Apply to Sales tab.

5. Click on the Quantity column. Type **3** and press **<Enter>**.

6. The cursor is in the Item column. Type **AVRY-10300** and press **<Enter>** five times.

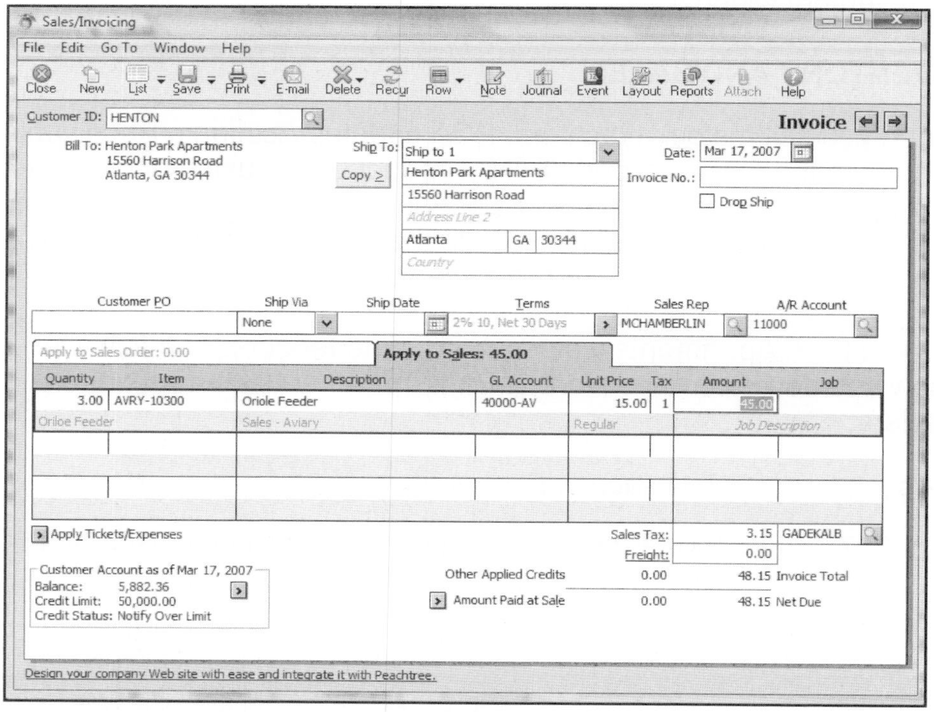

PCA computes the amount based on the quantity times the sales price that was established when setting up the inventory item. All the other lines for this invoice are automatically completed based on the inventory item information.

7. Click 

to see how Peachtree journalizes this entry in the Sales Journal. Scroll down the Accounting Behind the Screens, Sales Journal window, to see the entire entry. Observe that in a perpetual inventory system (Peachtree's default) the cost of sales accounts (50000-AV, Product Cost-Aviary; and 12000, Inventory) are "To be calculated." Once the sales invoice is paid, the cost of sales amounts will be calculated. Click 

to close the Accounting Behind the Screens window to return to the Sales/Invoicing window.

8. Click  to post this sales invoice. Close the Sales/Invoicing window to return to the Customer & Sales page.

Let's review the last two sections: Inventory and Purchases and Inventory and Sales. When Bellwether purchased six Oriole Feeders (an inventory stock item) on pages 169-171, the entry in the Purchase Journal was:

Account #	Account Description	Debit	Credit
12000/ AVRY-10300	Inventory	42.00	
20000/ DEJULIA	Accounts Payable/DeJulia Wholesale Suppliers		42.00

When three Oriole Feeders were sold on pages 171-173, the entry in the Sales Journal was:

Account #	Account Description	Debit	Credit
11000/ HENTON	Accts. Rec./Henton Park Apartments	48.15	
40000-AV	Sales-Aviary		45.00
23100	Sales Tax Payable		3.15
50000-AV	Product Cost-Aviary	21.00	
12000	Inventory		21.00

When three Oriole feeders were sold, they were sold for $15 each, plus sales tax. The total sale to Henton Park Apartments is $45 plus $3.15 in sales tax, for a total of $48.15. When Bellwether Garden Supply bought the Oriole Feeders from the vendor (DeJulia Wholesale Suppliers), they paid $7 each. The second journal entry reflects the product cost of the stock items, $7 X 3 = $21.

The journal entries shown above are examples of how purchases and sales are recorded in a perpetual inventory system.

INVENTORY ADJUSTMENTS

It may become necessary to adjust the amount of Inventory Items due to faulty records, pilferage or spoilage, or inventory changes. You use the Inventory Adjustment Journal to make inventory adjustment entries.

In the example that follows, one of Bellwether's employees dropped two bird house kits which damaged them beyond repair. Follow these steps to adjust inventory for this loss:

1. From the Navigation Bar, click 

; 

. The Inventory Adjustments window appears.

2. Type **AVRY-10100** (for Bird House Kit) in the Item ID field and the press **<Enter>** key six times. Your cursor is in the Adjust Quantity By.

3. Type **-2** in the Adjust Quantity By field to decrease the current inventory by two. Press the **<Enter>** key. The New Quantity field shows that you have 3.00 bird house kits.

4. Type **Damaged** as the Reason to Adjust.

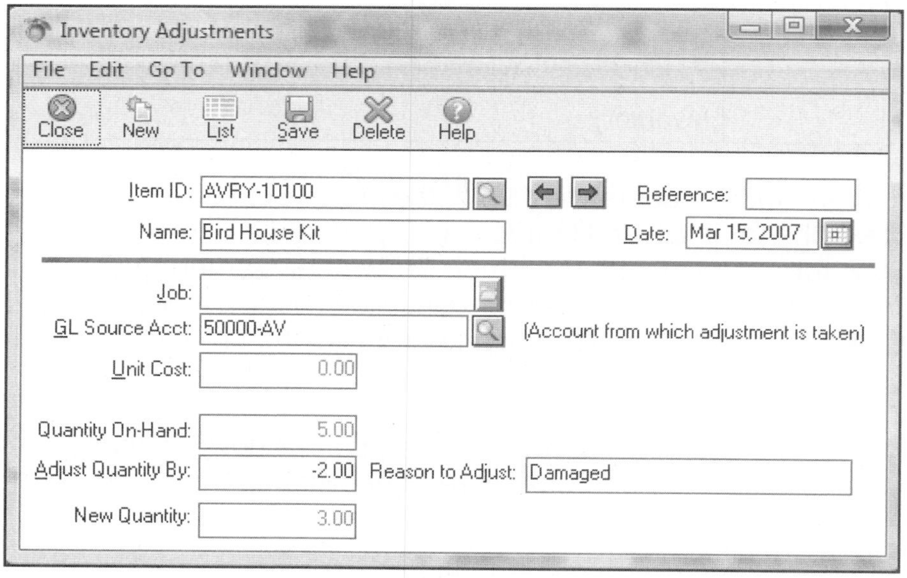

5. Click 

to post this adjustment, then close the Inventory Adjustments window.

   Adjustments to inventory, like the one you just made, only affect the average cost of the item. For example, let's say you purchased two bird house kits at $30 each and then damaged one. For accounting purposes you now have one bird house kit that costs $30.

INTERNAL CONTROL

Internal control is an integrated system of people, processes, and procedures that minimize or eliminate business risks, protect assets, facilitate reliable accounting, and promote efficient operations. If changes are made to company records, Peachtree's ***audit trail*** provides documentation. An audit trail records all entries and changes related to the company's data, including actions by specific users.

Peachtree has several methods to track information; for example, a combination of the general ledger, journals, reports, and financial statements can be used to trace transactions and balances. If you want to track when an action is performed, Peachtree's audit trail provides this information. The audit trail provides accountability of users, deters users from fraudulent activity or mistakes, and tracks transaction history. Three internal control methods are built into the software:

- Setting up user names, passwords, and access rights.
- The ability to associate the user currently logged into the Peachtree company with the data that is being entered.
- Audit Trail reports that show what each user entered.

In order to get the most use out of the audit trail feature, user records need to be set up. If User Security is set up, Peachtree can associate the user currently logged into the Peachtree company with the data being entered. For example, USER1 adds a customer record. USER2 then logs on and modifies the customer record. The Audit Trail report will show that USER2 was the last person who worked with the customer record, and it will display what was changed. This establishes user accountability.

Setting Up Company Users, Passwords, and Access Rights

In order to have data security and password protection, you need to set up user records. When user names and passwords are set up, Peachtree prompts you for a user name and password when you open a company. This is a two-step process:

- Set up the company administrator.
- Set up individual users.

The steps below are for example purposes only. Check with your instructor to see if he or she would like you to set up user access. *Remember, if you set up a user name and password you have to use it each time you start Peachtree.* To learn about setting up company users, passwords, and access rights, go to the following Help windows.

1. From Peachtree's menu bar select, Help; Peachtree Accounting Help. Select the Search tab.
2. Type **Set Up Company Users, Passwords, and Access Rights** in the Type in the keyword to find.
3. Click List Topics.
4. Scroll down the topics list' select Set Up Company Users, Passwords, and Access Rights to highlight it.
5. Click Display. The Set Up Company Users, Passwords, and Access Rights window appears. Enlarge the window. Link to Setting up the first users (administrator).
6. Link to Setting up additional company users. Read the information.
7. Link to Setting up users with selected access.
8. Read the information on this window. This Help window explains how to set up users, passwords and access rights.

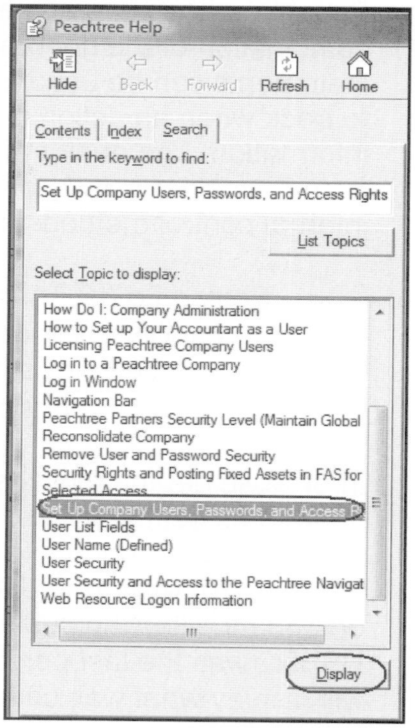

9. Check with your instructor to see if he or she would like you do this.

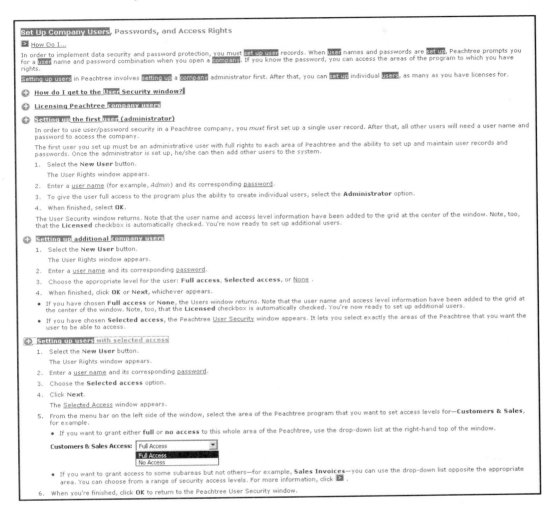

Set Up Company Users, Passwords, and Access Rights

How Do I...

In order to implement data security and password protection, you must set up user records. When user names and passwords are set up, Peachtree prompts you for a user name and password combination when you open a company. If you know the password, you can access the areas of the program to which you have rights.

Setting up users in Peachtree involves setting up a company administrator first. After that, you can set up individual users, as many as you have licenses for.

How do I get to the User Security window?

Licensing Peachtree company users

Setting up the first user (administrator)

In order to use user/password security in a Peachtree company, you *must* first set up a single user record. After that, all other users will need a user name and password to access the company.

The first user you set up must be an administrative user with full rights to each area of Peachtree and the ability to set up and maintain user records and passwords. Once the administrator is set up, he/she can then add other users to the system.

1. Select the **New User** button.

   The User Rights window appears.
2. Enter a user name (for example, *Admin*) and its corresponding password.
3. To give the user full access to the program plus the ability to create individual users, select the **Administrator** option.
4. When finished, select **OK**.

The User Security window returns. Note that the user name and access level information have been added to the grid at the center of the window. Note, too, that the **Licensed** checkbox is automatically checked. You're now ready to set up additional users.

Setting up additional company users

1. Select the **New User** button.

   The User Rights window appears.
2. Enter a user name and its corresponding password.
3. Choose the appropriate level for the user: **Full access**, **Selected access**, or None .
4. When finished, click **OK** or **Next**, whichever appears.

- If you have chosen **Full access** or **None**, the Users window returns. Note that the user name and access level information have been added to the grid at the center of the window. Note, too, that the **Licensed** checkbox is automatically checked. You're now ready to set up additional users.
- If you have chosen **Selected access**, the Peachtree User Security window appears. It lets you select exactly the areas of the Peachtree that you want the user to be able to access.

Setting up users with selected access

1. Select the **New User** button.

   The User Rights window appears.
2. Enter a user name and its corresponding password.
3. Choose the **Selected access** option.
4. Click **Next**.

   The Selected Access window appears.
5. From the menu bar on the left side of the window, select the area of the Peachtree program that you want to set access levels for—**Customers & Sales**, for example.
   - If you want to grant either **full** or **no access** to this whole area of the Peachtree, use the drop-down list at the right-hand top of the window.

   Customers & Sales Access: Full Access
   Full Access
   No Access

   - If you want to grant access to some subareas but not others—for example, **Sales Invoices**—you can use the drop-down list opposite the appropriate area. You can choose from a range of security access levels. For more information, click .
6. When you're finished, click **OK** to return to the Peachtree User Security window.

10. Click [X] on the Peachtree Help title bar to close Setting Up Company Users, Passwords, and Access Rights window.

Audit Trail Report

The Audit Trail report can trace fraudulent activity and other accounting adjustments you may not know were completed. Peachtree's default is to set the Audit Trail On. To see that, follow the steps shown on the next page.

1. From the Navigation Bar, click 

. The Company Information area shows that the Audit Trail is on. Compare your company information with the illustration below.

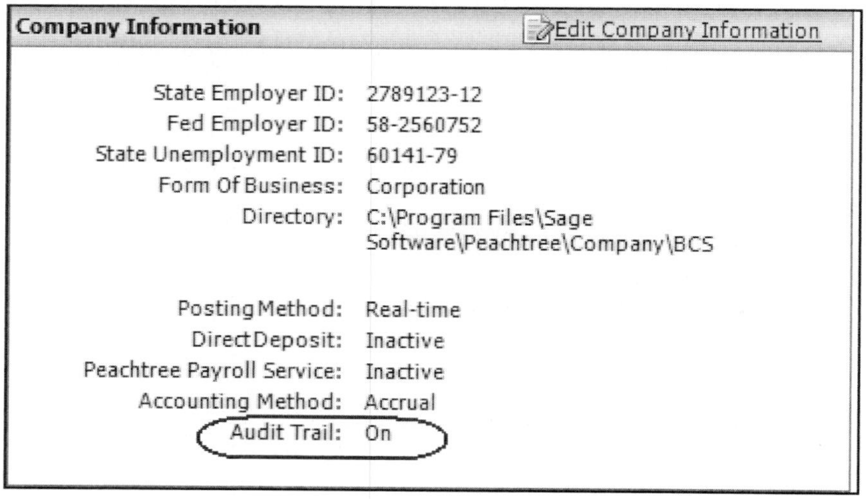

Company Information
Edit Company Information
State Employer ID: 2789123-12
Fed Employer ID: 58-2560752
State Unemployment ID: 60141-79
Form Of Business: Corporation
Directory: C:\Program Files\Sage Software\Peachtree\Company\BCS
Posting Method: Real-time
Direct Deposit: Inactive
Peachtree Payroll Service: Inactive
Accounting Method: Accrual
Audit Trail: On

The audit trail feature records the following items with each activity performed while operating in the Peachtree company:

2. Date: System (computer) date of action.
3. Time: System (computer) time of action.
4. User Name: User Name (if available); otherwise, Peachtree displays "Not Available."
5. Action: Add, Change, or Delete.
6. Window Name (or System Function): Name of window where action occurred (for example, Sales Orders) or name of system function implemented (for example, Unpost).
7. Transaction ID: For maintenance records, the ID associated with the record; for tasks, the ID associated with the transaction after change.
8. Transaction Reference: Reference number associated with the transaction after change.
9. Amount: Amount of transaction after change.
10. All the above items are recorded in the Audit Trail report.

Peachtree's audit trail tracks the following:

1. Records and Transactions

   Records include customers, vendors, employees, inventory items, and so on. Transactions include quotes, sales orders, invoices, payments, general journal entries, inventory adjustments, and so on.

   These include:

   - adding records or transactions (when Save is selected).
   - editing records or transactions (when Save is selected).
   - deleting records or transactions (when Delete is selected).
   - entering or maintaining record beginning balances (when OK or Save is selected).
   - voiding checks and paychecks.
   - making payments in Cash Manager and Payment Manager.

2. Miscellaneous Actions

   - reconciling accounts.
   - maintaining company information and options.
   - maintaining and loading user-maintained and Peachtree-maintained payroll tax tables.
   - importing data into the company.
   - adding transactions using Dynamic Data Exchange (DDE).

3. System Functions

   - posting and unposting journals (Batch mode only).
   - closing the fiscal year.
   - closing the payroll tax year.
   - backing up company data.

Displaying the Audit Trail Report & Find Transactions Report

Follow these steps to print an Audit Trail Report.

1. From the menu bar, select Reports & Forms; Company. The Select a Report or Form window appears. The Audit Trail Report is selected.
2. Click  .
3. In the Date field, select Range.
4. In the From field, click on the down-arrow and select January 1, 2006. (*Hint:* Use the left arrow to change the year and month.)
5. In the To field, select December 31, 2007. (*Hint:* Use the right arrow to go to 12/31/2007.

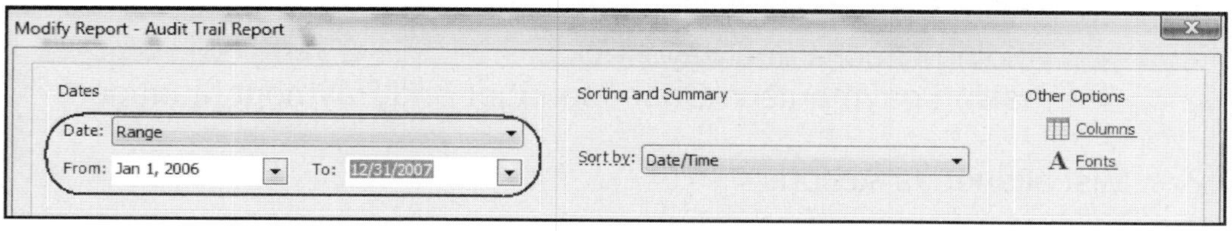

6. Click . The Audit Trail Report for the period from Jan 1, 2006 to Dec. 31, 2007 appears. Observe that each transaction shows the Date; Time; User Name, Action, Window Name, Transaction ID, Transaction Reference, and Amount. If users had been set up the User Name column would show that. Scroll down to see the whole report. A partial report is shown on the next page.

   Observe that the work completed in Chapters 1-5 is shown on the Audit Trail Report; for example, the employees added in Chapter 1 (CYACHT and BWOOD); the inventory items that applied to LOZANOOFFICE in Chapter in Chapter 2, etc. Scroll down the Audit Trail Report to see both pages.

Bellwether Garden Supply
Audit Trail Report
For the Period From Jan 1, 2006 to Dec 31, 2007

Filter Criteria includes: 1) All Actions.

Date	Time	User Name	Action	Window Name	Transaction ID	Transaction Reference	Amount
3/14/06	1:11 PM	Not Available	Change	Maintain Company	BCS	Bellwether Garden Supply	
3/14/06	1:38 PM	Not Available	Change	Maintain Budgets	Budget		
3/14/06	1:41 PM	Not Available	Change	Maintain Budgets	Budget		
3/14/06	1:43 PM	Not Available	Change	Maintain Budgets	Budget		
3/14/06	1:49 PM	Not Available	Change	Receipts	RETAIL	1679	358.02
3/14/06	1:49 PM	Not Available	Change	Receipts	RETAIL	654789	377.24
3/14/06	1:49 PM	Not Available	Change	Receipts	RETAIL	201	173.01
3/14/06	1:49 PM	Not Available	Change	Receipts	RETAIL	10386	77.22
3/14/06	1:50 PM	Not Available	Change	Receipts	DASH	10313	1,292.10
3/14/06	1:50 PM	Not Available	Change	Receipts	FROST	10314	48.99
3/14/06	1:50 PM	Not Available	Change	Receipts	RETAIL	5801	317.96
3/14/06	1:52 PM	Not Available	Change	Vendor Credit Memos	AKERSON	VCM30002	-27.20
3/14/06	1:56 PM	Not Available	Change	Backup Company Data			
3/14/06	1:57 PM	Not Available	Change	Data Verification	Data Reliability		
3/14/06	1:57 PM	Not Available	Change	Data Verification	Data Access		
3/14/06	1:59 PM	Not Available	Change	Backup Company Data			
3/14/06	4:34 PM	Not Available	Change	Maintain Budgets	Budget		
3/14/06	4:34 PM	Not Available	Change	Maintain Budgets	Budget		
3/14/06	4:35 PM	Not Available	Change	Maintain Budgets	Budget		
3/14/06	4:35 PM	Not Available	Change	Maintain Budgets	Budget		
3/14/06	4:36 PM	Not Available	Change	Maintain Budgets	Budget		
3/14/06	4:36 PM	Not Available	Change	Maintain Budgets	Budget		
3/14/06	4:37 PM	Not Available	Change	Backup Company Data			
3/14/06	4:38 PM	Not Available	Change	Data Verification	Data Reliability		
3/14/06	4:38 PM	Not Available	Change	Data Verification	Data Access		
3/14/06	4:46 PM	Not Available	Change	Backup Company Data			
5/22/06	9:50 AM	Not Available	Change	Payments	HAWKINS	10214	100.00
5/22/06	9:50 AM	Not Available	Change	Payments	CLINE	10213	100.00
4/17/07	2:00 PM	Conversion	Change	Data Integrity Check	File Tests	Reindex JRNLROW.DAT	
4/17/07	2:01 PM	Not Available	Change	Backup Company Data			
6/22/07	4:15 PM	Not Available	Change	Backup Company Data			
6/22/07	4:16 PM	Not Available	Change	Backup Company Data			
6/29/07	1:51 PM		Add	Maintain Employees &	CYACHT		
6/29/07	1:55 PM	Not Available	Change	Backup Company Data			
6/29/07	2:24 PM		Add	Maintain Employees &	BWOOD		
7/3/07	3:09 PM	Not Available	Add	Purchase Orders	ABNEY	101	3,834.00
7/3/07	3:33 PM		Add	Maintain Vendors	ABBOTT		
7/3/07	3:55 PM	Not Available	Add	Purchases/Receive Inve	ABBOTT	ABB107	45.00
7/6/07	12:10 PM	Not Available	Add	Payments	ABBOTT		44.10
7/6/07	1:07 PM	Not Available	Change	Backup Company Data			
7/6/07	1:07 PM	Not Available	Change	Backup Company Data			
7/6/07	1:50 PM		Add	Maintain Vendors	LOZANOFC		
7/6/07	1:53 PM	Not Available	Add	Purchases/Receive Inve	LOZANOFC	H788	54.75
7/6/07	1:54 PM	Not Available	Add	Payments	LOZANOFC		53.65
7/6/07	1:56 PM	Not Available	Change	Backup Company Data			

The Audit Trial Report provides a listing of the changes made to the maintenance items and transactions.

7. Close the Audit Trail Report. Then, display the Find Transactions Report from 3/15/07 to 3/15/07 (the default). A partial Find Transactions Report is shown on the next page.

Bellwether Garden Supply
Find Transactions Report
For the Period From Mar 15, 2007 to Mar 15, 2007
Filter Criteria includes: 1) All Transaction Types. Report order is by Date.

Date	Type	Reference	ID	Name	Amount
3/15/07	Credit Memo		ARCHER	Archer Scapes and Ponds	-49.99
3/15/07	Credit Memo		SAIA	Saia's Neighborhood Nursery	-49.99
3/15/07	General Journal Entry	ADJ0303103			0.11
3/15/07	General Journal Entry	Transfer			5,500.00
3/15/07	Inventory Adjustment		AVRY-10100	Bird House Kit	-2.00
3/15/07	Inventory Adjustment		AVRY-10050-SM-HTL	Prefabricated Birdhouse	8.00
3/15/07	Inventory Adjustment		AVRY-10050-SM-EFL	Prefabricated Birdhouse	8.00
3/15/07	Inventory Adjustment		AVRY-10050-SM-PYR	Prefabricated Birdhouse	4.00
3/15/07	Inventory Adjustment		AVRY-10050-LG-EFL	Prefabricated Birdhouse	4.00
3/15/07	Inventory Adjustment		AVRY-10050-SM-HTL	Prefabricated Birdhouse	6.00
3/15/07	Payment		ABNEY	Abney and Son Contractors	50.00
3/15/07	Payment	10210	SAFESTATE	Safe State Insurance Company	530.64
3/15/07	Payment	10212	PAYNE	Payne Enterprises	50.00
3/15/07	Payment	10213	CLINE	Cline Construction, Inc.	100.00
3/15/07	Payment	10214	HAWKINS	DPH Web Design	100.00
3/15/07	Payroll Entry	1250	ACHESTER	Amanda W. Chester	809.22

The Find Transactions Report provides a way to easily search for Peachtree Transactions. You can drill down to the original entry from each transaction.

8. Close the Find Transactions Report. Close the Select a Report or Form window.

BACKING UP CHAPTER 5 DATA

Follow these steps to back up Chapter 5 data:

1. From Company page, link to Back up.

2. Click Back Up.

3. Accept the default for backing up to the hard drive or make the selections to back up to another location. Type **Chapter 5** in the File name field.

4. Click Save.

5. When the window prompts that This company backup will require approximately 5.65MB, click  . When the Back Up Company scale is 100% complete, you have successfully backed up to the current point in Chapter 5. You are returned to the menu bar.

6. Click File, Exit to exit Peachtree.

INTERNET ACTIVITY	
1.	From your Internet browser, go to the book's website at http://www.mhhe.com/yacht2008
2.	Link to Student Edition.
3.	In the Course-wide Content list, link Internet Activities; then link to <u>Part 1 Internet Activities for Chapter 1-8</u>. Open or save. (You can also choose Chapter 5, then link to Internet Activities. (In the Choose a Chapter field, if you select Chapter 5 observe that other chapter-specific links are available; for example, Multiple Choice Quiz, True or False, PowerPoint Presentations and Going to the Net Exercises.) Also observe that Course-wide Content includes a Glossary link.
4.	Scroll down the window to the Internet Activity labeled ASK JEEVES – Chapter 5. Read steps 1-4.
5.	Follow the steps shown on the textbook's website to complete this Internet activity.
6.	Use a word processing program to answer the questions in steps 1-4.

SUMMARY AND REVIEW

SOFTWARE OBJECTIVES: In Chapter 5, you used the software to:

1. Restore data from Exercise 4-2. (This backup was made on page 151.)
2. Enter a new account in the Chart of Accounts.
3. Look at Peachtree's budget feature.
4. Make a General Journal entry to transfer funds.
5. Display the General Ledger Trial Balance.
6. Set up an Inventory Item.

7. Record an inventory adjustment.
8. Look at Peachtree's internal controls and audit trail.

9. Make two backups: backup Chapter 5 data; and backup Exercise 5-2.

WEB OBJECTIVES: In Chapter 5, you did these Internet activities:

1. Used your Internet browser to go to the book's website.

2. Completed the Internet activity for Ask Jeeves.

3. Completed the steps shown for this activity.

GOING TO THE NET

Access the Yahoo small business website at http://smallbusiness.yahoo.com/r-index; link to Ten Tips for New Small Businesses. The complete website address is http://smallbusiness.yahoo.com/r-article-a-41095-m-1-sc-12-ten_tips_for_new_small_businesses-i. (*Hint:* If this article is no longer available, link to another area from Yahoo's small business page and write a brief essay—no more than 125 words—describing the link.)

1. List the 10 tips for starting a new business.

2. Link to one additional site from this page.

Multiple Choice Questions: In the space provided, write the letter that best answers each question.

_____1. The inventory system used by PCA is called:

a. Sum-of-the-years digits.
b. Double-declining balance.
c. Straight-line.
d. Perpetual inventory.
e. None of the above.

_____2. A list of all the accounts used by a company showing an identifying number assigned to each account is called:

a. A chart of accounts.
b. Case-sensitive letters.
c. An account number.
d. A general ledger.
e. None of the above.

_____3. The account(s) added to Bellwether's Chart of Accounts in this chapter is:

a. Account No. 10200, Regular Checking Account.
b. Account No. 12000, Inventory.
c. Account No. 10500, Money Market Fund.
d. a. and c.
e. All of the above.

_____4. After the March 15, 2007 transfer of funds, the General Ledger Trial Balance shows the following amount in the Money Market Fund account:

a. $4,500.00.
b. $4,747.16.
c. $37,500.00.
d. $5,394.74.
e. None of the above.

_____5. In the Maintain Inventory Items window, the default in the Item Class list is:

a. Labor.
b. Description only.
c. Non stock.
d. Stock item.
e. None of the above.

_____6. For Stock-Type Inventory Items, PCA tracks the following:

a. Stock quantities.
b. Unit prices.
c. Descriptions.
d. Cost of goods sold.
e. All of the above.

_____7. The journal entry to purchase an inventory stock item is:

a. Debit Accounts Payable/Vendor
   Credit Inventory
b. Debit Inventory
   Credit Accounts Payable/Vendor
c. Debit Account Receivable/Customer
   Credit Sales Tax Payable
d. Debit Product Cost
   Credit Inventory
e. None of the above.

_____8. The journal entry or entries for the sale of an Inventory Item are:

a. Debit Accounts Receivable/Customer
   Credit Sales
b. Debit Accounts Receivable/Customer
   Credit Sales
   Credit Sales Tax Payable
   Debit Product Cost
   Credit Inventory
c. Debit Sales-Retail
   Debit Sales Tax Payable
   Credit Accounts Receivable/Customer
   Debit Product Cost
   Credit Inventory
d. Debit Inventory
   Credit Product Cost
e. None of the above.

_____9. Shows all entries and changes related to the company's data, including actions by specific users.

a. Find transactions.
b. Report groups.
c. Audit trail.
d. Internal control.
e. All of the above.

_____10. The integrated system of people, processes, and procedures that minimize or eliminate business risks, protect assets, ensure reliable accounting, and promote efficient operation is called:

a. Peachtree's find transactions capability.
b. Peachtree's audit trail reports.
c. Internal control.
d. Setting up the administrator for access to all records.
e. None of the above.

Exercise 5-1: Follow the instructions below to complete Exercise 5-1.

1. Start PCA. Open Bellwether Garden Supply.

2. Restore data from the end of Chapter 5. This back up was made on pages 182-183.

3. Journalize and post the following transactions:

Date	*Transaction Description*
03/18/07	Transfer $1,200 from the Regular Checking Account to the Payroll Checking Account.
03/19/07	Purchased two (2) Oriole Feeders from DeJulia Wholesale Suppliers, Invoice No. 94977, $14.

4. Continue with Exercise 5-2.

Exercise 5-2: Follow the instructions below to complete Exercise 5-2.

1. Print the General Ledger Trial Balance.

2. Back up Exercise 5-2. Use **Exercise 5-2** as the file name.

3. Exit PCA.

CHAPTER 5 INDEX

Chapter 6 Job Cost

SOFTWARE OBJECTIVES: In Chapter 6, you use the software to:

1. Restore data from Exercise 5-2. (This backup was made on page 188.)
2. Learn about PCA's Job Cost system.
3. Set up a job.
4. Coordinate job costs with purchases, sales, and payroll.
5. Display the Job Profitability Report.
6. Make two backups: Backup Chapter 6 data; and backup Exercise 6-2.

WEB OBJECTIVES: In Chapter 6, you do these Internet activities:

1. Use your Internet browser to go to the book's website.
2. Complete the Internet activity for Business Encyclopedia.
3. Complete the steps shown for this activity.

This chapter shows how to use PCA's Job Cost system. PCA lets you assign Job ID codes to purchases, sales, and employee hours. This way, you can track how each of these factors impacts costs for a specific job. The diagram that follows illustrates how this works:

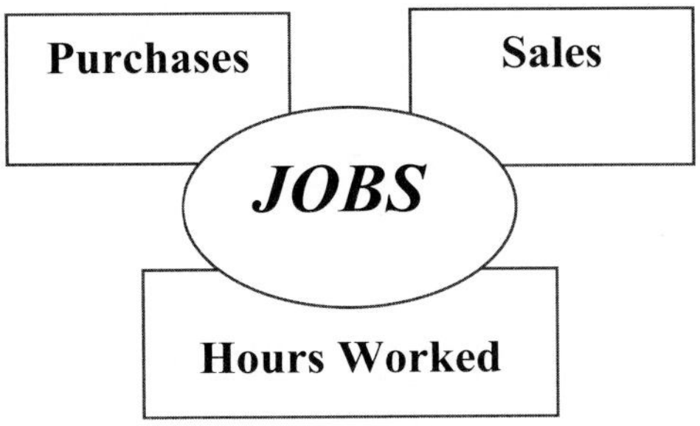

GETTING STARTED

Bellwether Garden Supply has a customer named Franklin Botanical Gardens. You need to set up a Job ID for Franklin Botanical Gardens so you can track supplies and employee hours charged to this customer.

1. Start PCA. Open Bellwether Garden Supply. (If Bellwether Garden Supply is not shown, restore A New Company. Refer to the Read me box on page 27.)

2. Restore your data from the Exercise 5-2.

   a. From the Navigation Bar, select Company; link to Restore. (The Exercise 5-2 backup file was made page 188.)

   b. The Select Backup File window appears. If the Location field shows C:\Program Files\Sage Software\Peachtree\ Company\ BCS\Exercise 5-2.ptb, click Next >. (*Or,* click Browse, then select the appropriate location of the Exercise 5-2 backup file; click Next >.)

   c. The Select Company window appears. The radio button next to An Existing Company is selected. The Company name field shows Bellwether Garden Supply; the Location field shows C:\ProgramFiles\Sage Software\Peachtree\company\BCS (or the appropriate location on your computer). Click Next >.

   d. The Restore Options window appears. Make sure that the box next to Company Data is *checked*. Click Next >.

   e. The Confirmation window appears. Check the From and To fields to make sure they are correct. Click Finish. When the Restore Company scale is 100% complete, your data is restored and you are returned to the menu bar.

   f. If necessary, remove the external media.

3. From the Navigation Bar, select 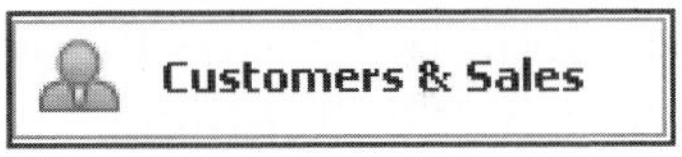

; 

, New Job. The Maintain Jobs window appears.

4. In the Job ID field, type **FRANKLIN** and press **<Enter>**. (*Hint: Peachtree is case sensitive: FRANKLIN is not the same as franklin.*)

5. In the Description field, type **Franklin Botanical Gardens** and press **<Enter>** two times.

6. Type **3/3/07** in the Start Date field. Press **<Enter>** four times.

7. Your cursor is in the For Customer field. Select FRANKLIN.

8. Click on the Job Type field. Select LAND. Compare your Maintain Jobs window to the one shown below.

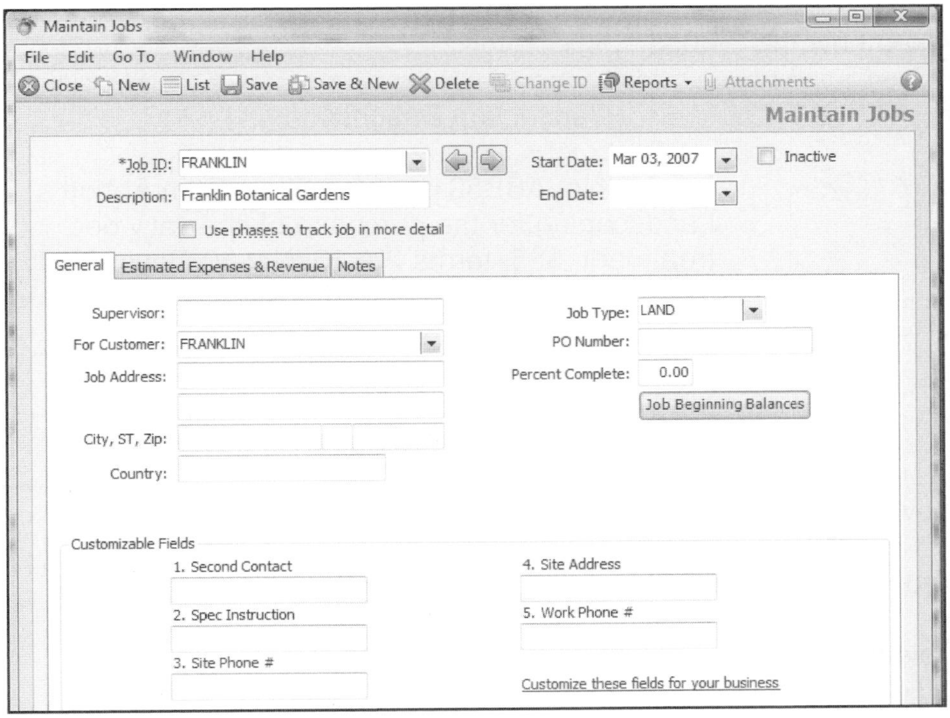

9. Save this job, then close the Maintain Jobs window to return to the Customers & Sales page.

JOB COSTING AND PURCHASING: Purchasing Inventory Items for Jobs

This new job has some special circumstances; namely, Franklin Botanical Gardens has a new building overlooking a park. In the park, there are several picnic tables. According to the terms of the contract with Franklin Botanical Gardens, you purchase and provide a special wood treatment to the picnic benches.

When inventory items are purchased for jobs, you need to do the following:

- Record the purchase directly as a job expense. You could indicate a Non-stock or a Description only Inventory Item but not a Stock Item.
- Record the purchase into Inventory without entering a Job. When you bill the customer, enter the Item and the Job. The system posts the price as Job revenue and the Cost of Goods Sold as Job Expense.

Let's see how this works:

Date	*Transaction Description*
3/20/07	Invoice No. ABB501 was received from Abbott's Landscaping for the purchase of special wood treatment, \$85; terms 2% 10, Net 30 Days. Apply this purchase to the Franklin Botanical Gardens job.

1. From the Navigation Bar, select 

; 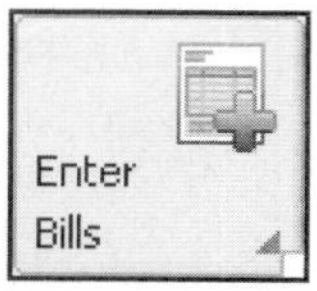

, New Bill. The Purchases/Receive Inventory window displays.

2. Type or select **ABB** (Abbott's Landscaping) for the Vendor ID.

3. Select or type **20** in the Date field. Press **<Enter>**.

4. Type **ABB501** for the Invoice #. (This is a *required* field.) Press **<Enter>**.

5. The Apply to Purchases tab is selected. Type **1** in the Quantity column and press **<Enter>** two times.

6. In the Description field, type **Special wood treatment for picnic tables** and press **<Enter>** two times.

7. Account No. 57200, Materials Cost, is the default account displayed in the GL Account column. Your cursor is in the Unit Price field. Type **85** and press **<Enter>** two times.

8. Type or select **FRANKLIN**, the new Job, in the Job column.

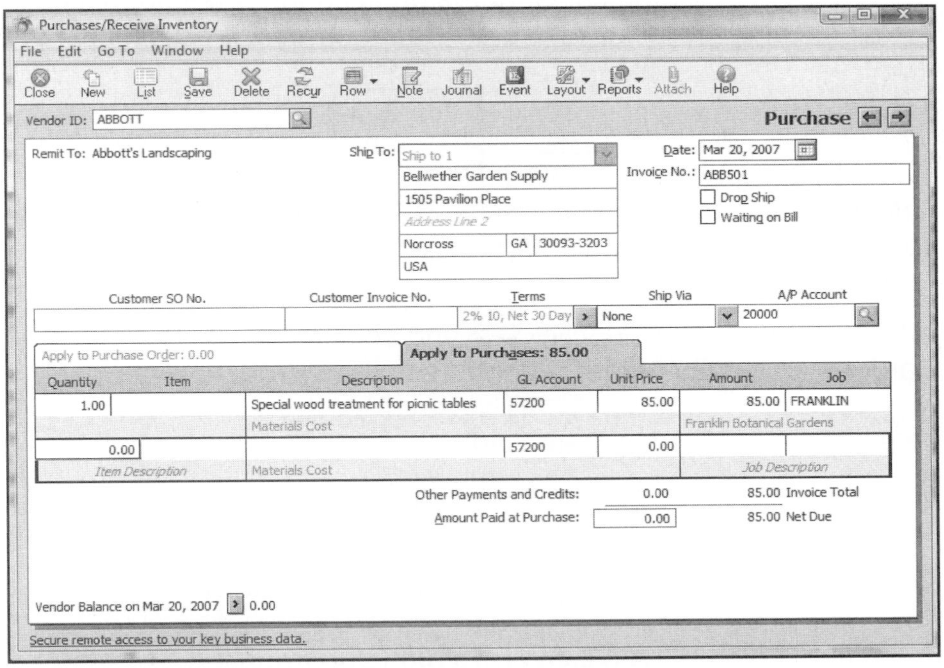

If your GL Account column and A/P Account field are *not* displayed on the Purchases/Receive Inventory window, see the instructions on page 16, Hide General Ledger Accounts area.

9. Click 

to post this purchase. Close the Purchases/Receive Inventory window to return to the Vendors & Purchases page.

JOB COSTING AND SALES

Follow these steps to invoice Franklin Botanical Gardens for a drip irrigation system and apply this sale to Franklin Botanical Gardens, Job ID, FRANKLIN.

Date	*Transaction Description*
3/21/07	Bellwether Garden Supply sold one Bell-Gro Home Irrigation System, Item No. EQWT-15100, to Franklin Botanical Gardens on account, $129.99, plus $9.10 sales tax, total $139.09; terms 2% 10, Net 30 Days.

1. Select 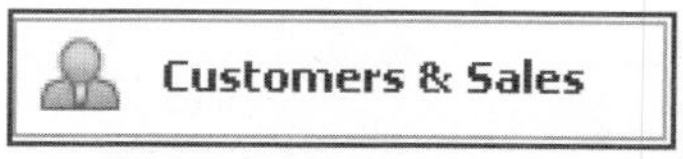

; 

, New Sales Invoice. The Sales/Invoicing window displays.

2. In the Customer ID field, click  and select Franklin Botanical Gardens as the Customer. Then, press the **<Enter>** key.

3. Select or type **21** in the Date field.

4. If necessary, click on the Apply to Sales tab.

5. Click on the Quantity column, type **1** and press **<Enter>**.

6. In the Item column, type **EQWT-15100** (Drip Irrigation System).

7. Press **<Enter>** until you are in the Job column. (You are accepting all of the displayed information when you do this.)

8. Type or select **FRANKLIN**, the Job ID for Franklin Botanical Gardens. Compare your Sales/Invoicing window to the one shown on the next page.

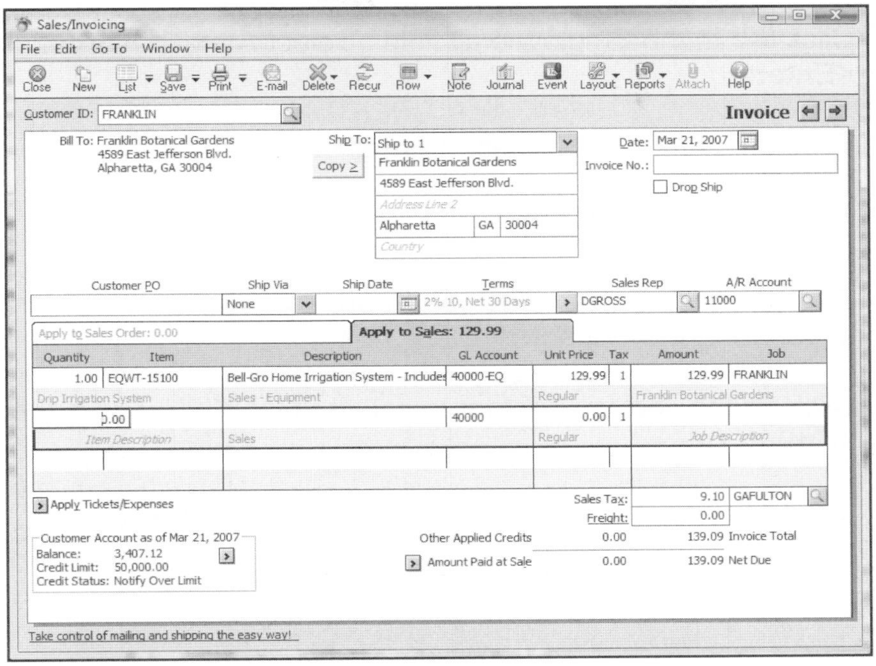

If your GL Account column and A/R Account field are *not* displayed on the Sales/Invoicing window, see the instructions on page 16, Hide General Ledger Accounts area.

9. Click 

to post this invoice. Close the Sales/Invoicing window to return to the Customers & Sales page.

JOB COST AND PAYROLL

In the example that follows, one employee applied the special wood treatment to the picnic tables at Franklin Botanical Gardens. The employee spent one hour applying the wood treatment.

1. From the Navigation Bar, select 

; 

, Enter Payroll for One Employee. The Payroll Entry window appears.

2. Click  in the Employee ID field. Select **Alex C. Kornel** and press **<Enter>**.

3. Type **29** as the Date. Press **<Enter>** two times.

4. Type **29** in the Pay Period End field.

5. On the icon bar, select the Jobs icon 

. The Labor Distribution to Jobs window appears.

6. Click on the Job row's folder to select FRANKLIN. Press the <**Enter**> key.

7. Type **1** in the Hours column. Press the <**Enter**> key.

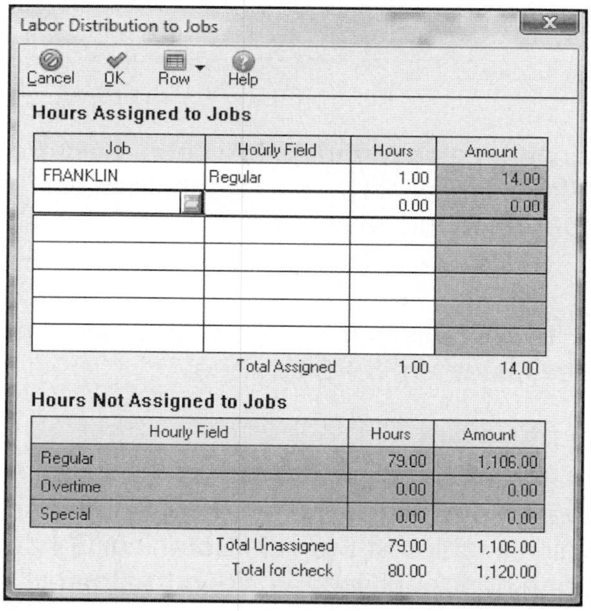

Labor Distribution to Jobs
Cancel
OK
Row
Help
Hours Assigned to Jobs
Job | Hourly Field | Hours | Amount
FRANKLIN | Regular | 1.00 | 14.00
0.00 | 0.00
Total Assigned 1.00 14.00
Hours Not Assigned to Jobs
Hourly Field | Hours | Amount
Regular | 79.00 | 1,106.00
Overtime | 0.00 | 0.00
Special | 0.00 | 0.00
Total Unassigned 79.00 1,106.00
Total for check 80.00 1,120.00

8. Click 

.

9. Click 

to post the paycheck. Close the Payroll Entry window to return to the Employees & Payroll window.

JOB COST REPORTS

Job cost reports tell you how jobs are progressing. Follow these steps to look at Job Cost Reports.

1. From the menu bar, select Reports & Forms; Jobs. The Select a Report or Form window displays.

2. In the Job Reports: Project Information list, double-click Job Profitability Report. The Job Profitability Report appears.

3. Scroll down to FRANKLIN.

FRANKLIN	40000-EQ	129.99			
	50000-EQ		59.95		
	57200		85.00		
	77500		14.00		
		129.99	**158.95**		
FRANKLIN Total		**129.99**	**158.95**	**-28.96**	**-22.28**

The report breaks down each job according to what was spent or earned for each affected general ledger account. It also shows the profit or loss for each job.

4. Close the Job Profitability Report window. Close the Select a report or Form window to return to the Employees & Payroll page.

BACKING UP CHAPTER 6 DATA

Follow these steps to back up Chapter 6 data:

1. From the Navigation Bar, select **Company**; link to Back up.

2. Click Back Up.

3. Accept the default for backing up to the hard drive or make the selections to back up to another location. Type **Chapter 6** in the File name field.

4. Click 

.

5. When the window prompts that This company backup will require approximately 5.68MB, click 

. When the Back Up Company scale is 100% complete, you have successfully backed up to the current point in Chapter 6. You are returned to the menu bar.

6. Click File, Exit to exit Peachtree.

	INTERNET ACTIVITY
1.	From your Internet browser, go to the book's website at http://www.mhhe.com/yacht2008.
2.	Link to Student Edition.
3.	In the Course-wide Content list, link Internet Activities; then link to <u>Part 1 Internet Activities for Chapter 1-8</u>. Open or save. (You can also choose Chapter 6, then link to Internet Activities. (In the Choose a Chapter field, if you select Chapter 6 observe that other chapter-specific links are available; for example, Multiple Choice Quiz, True or False, PowerPoint Presentations and Going to the Net Exercises.) Also observe that Course-wide Content includes a Glossary link.
4.	Scroll down the window to ENCYCLOPEDIA OF BUSINESS CASE TERMS – Chapter 6. Read steps 1-3.
5.	Use the Business Encyclopedia website to look up words related to accounting.
6.	Follow the steps shown on the book's website to complete this Internet Activity.

SUMMARY AND REVIEW

SOFTWARE OBJECTIVES: In Chapter 6, you used the software to:

1. Restore data from Exercise 5-2. (This backup was made on page 188.)

2. Learn about PCA's Job Cost system.

3. Set up a job.

4. Coordinate job costs with purchases, sales, and payroll.

5. Display the Job Profitability Report.

6. Make two backups: Backup Chapter 6 data; and backup Exercise 6-2.

WEB OBJECTIVES: In Chapter 6, you did these Internet activities:

1. Used your Internet browser to go to the book's website.

2. Completed the Internet activity for Business Encyclopedia.

3. Completed the steps shown for this activity.

GOING TO THE NET

Access the Sage website at www.sage.com. Choose your location; for example, select United States. Click Go. (*Or, select your location.*)

1. What two areas does Sage Software focus on for US operations?

2. List the products that Sage Software offers in their Small Business Division, US Operations. (Modify this answer if your location is different than the US.)

3. How many products are listed in Sage Software's Mid-Market Division?

Short-Answer Questions: Write a brief answer to each one of the questions.

1. Draw the diagram that shows how the job cost system works.

2. What is the description of the Franklin Botanical Gardens job?

___

___

3. What is the customer ID for Franklin Botanical Gardens?

___

___

4. How much does Franklin Botanical Gardens owe for the one Bel-Gro Drip Home Irrigation System (include the sales tax)?

___

___

5. What is the GL account (name and number) for the purchase of the wood treatment?

___

___

6. What is the name of the report that tells you about Bellwether's jobs?

___

___

7. What is the website address for the Encyclopedia of Business Case Terms?

____

____

8. How many hour(s) did Alex C. Kornel work on the Franklin Botanical Gardens job?

____

____

Exercise 6-1: Follow the instructions below to complete Exercise 6-1.

1. Start PCA. Open Bellwether Garden Supply.

2. Restore data from the end of Chapter 6.

3. Journalize and post the following transactions:

Date	*Transaction Description*
03/26/07	Sold two Bel-Gro Impulse Sprinklers (EQWT-15160) to Franklin Botanical Gardens, $64.18 (includes sales tax); terms 2% 10, Net 30 Days; Job ID Franklin Botanical Gardens.
03/26/07	Invoice No. ABB967 was received from Abbott's Landscaping for the purchase of one container of special wood treatment for $85; terms 2% 10, Net 30 Days; Job ID Franklin Botanical Gardens. (Debit Materials Cost.)
03/29/07	Amanda W. Chester worked one hour on the Franklin Botanical Gardens job. Apply her paycheck to this job.

4. Continue with Exercise 6-2.

Exercise 6-2: Follow the instructions below to complete Exercise 6-2.

1. Print a Job Profitability Report.

2. Back up Exercise 6-2. Use **Exercise 6-2** as the file name.

Read Me

This back up is important. If you are using external media; for example, a USB drive, do *not* delete the Exercise 6-2 back up. You restore the Exercise 6-2 file to complete work in Chapters 15, 16, and 17.

CHAPTER 6 INDEX

Chapter 7 Financial Statements

SOFTWARE OBJECTIVES: In Chapter 7, you use the software to:

1. Restore data from Exercise 6-2. This backup was made on page 204.
2. Explore Peachtree's Help feature.
3. Print the financial statements.
4. Use drill down to go from the income statement to the general ledger, then to the original entry window.
5. Make an optional backup of Chapter 7. The backups that were made in Chapter 6 include the data for this chapter.

WEB OBJECTIVES: In Chapter 7, you do these Internet activities:

1. Use your Internet browser to go to the book's website.
2. Complete the Internet activity for Peachtree Software.
3. Complete the steps shown for this activity.

FINANCIAL STATEMENTS

In Chapters 1 through 6, you have explored the sample company, Bellwether Garden Supply. You learned how PCA's graphical user interface works and how to navigate the software. In Chapters 1 through 6, you also journalized and posted various types of transactions. Beginning with Chapter 9, you learn how to use these features to set up service businesses from scratch.

In Chapter 7, you learn about PCA's financial statements. Once journal entries have been recorded and posted, Peachtree automatically calculates financial statements. Since business managers and owners have the primary responsibility for the organization, they depend on accounting information in the form of financial statements to understand what is happening.

All the financial statements printed by PCA reflect the current month and year-to-date amounts.

In this chapter, six financial statements are printed.

1. Balance Sheet.
2. Gross Profit by Departments.
3. Income Statement.
4. Statement of Cash Flow.
5. Statement of Retained Earnings.
6. Statement of Changes in Financial Position.

Balance Sheet

A balance sheet is a list of assets, liabilities, and capital of a business entity as of a specific date, such as the last day of an accounting period or the last day of the year.

Each financial statement may be modified to fit your needs. PCA includes a Design icon for that purpose. Later in this chapter, you learn more about how to use PCA's Help feature to design financial statements. In Chapter 15, Customize Forms, you learn more about modifying PCA's standard forms.

Gross Profit by Departments

A departmentalized accounting system provides information that management can use to evaluate the profitability or cost effectiveness of a department's activities. The Gross Profit by Departments financial statement is a custom report designed for Bellwether that details each department's year-to-date gross profit as of the current month.

Some of Bellwether's chart of account numbers have a dash, then an AV or a BK. For example, Account No. 40000-AV, Sales - Aviary; and Account No. 40000-BK, Sales - Books show the departmental designation.

PCA includes a feature called masking which allows you to organize your business by department. Then, you can design custom forms to accommodate your departmentalized accounting system. The red arrow to the left of some of Bellwether's financial statements indicates that those statements are custom-designed forms.

Income Statement

The income statement is a summary of the revenues and expenses a company accrues over a period of time, such as an accounting period or a year. Only revenue and expense accounts are displayed on the income statement. ***Net income*** is computed by subtracting total expenses from total revenues. Net income results when revenues exceed expenses. An excess of expenses over revenues results in a ***net loss***. Bellwether's net loss for the current month, March 1 through March 31, 2007, is $3,152.55. A net loss is indicated on the income statement with parenthesis ($3,152.55). Bellwether's year-to-date net income is $24,949.88. When you print the Income Statement on page 218 you see these amounts.

In addition to dollar figures, the income statement also includes percentage-of-revenue columns for the current month. The percentages shown for each expense, total expenses, and net income (or net loss) indicate the relationship of each item to total revenues.

Statement of Cash Flow

The cash flow from operations is roughly the same as income from operations plus depreciation, depletion, and adjusted for any other operating transactions that had no effect on cash during the period. The statement of cash flow also reports cash transactions associated with the purchase or sale of fixed assets (Investing Activities) and cash paid to or received from creditors and owners (Financing Activities).

The statement of cash flow provides the answers to three questions:

1. From where did cash receipts come?
2. For what were cash payments used?
3. What was the overall change in cash?

Statement of Retained Earnings

The Statement of Retained Earnings shows beginning and ending retained earnings amounts, adjustments made to retained earnings within the report period, and the detail for all Equity-gets closed accounts. The retained earnings balance is the cumulative, lifetime earnings of the company less its cumulative losses and dividends.

Statement of Changes in Financial Position

The statement of changes describes changes in a company's financial position that may not be obvious from other financial statements. The statement of changes shows the change in working capital, assets, and liabilities for a given period of time.

Interrelationship of Financial Statements

The financial statements work together. The net income (or net loss) from the income statement is on the balance sheet's capital section. The net income or net loss is used to update the capital amount: Capital Beginning of the Year - Net Loss (or + Net Income) = Total Capital.

On the statement of retained earnings, the Ending Retained Earnings balance is $213,987.48. On the balance sheet, if you add the net income $24,949.88 to the balance sheet's retained earnings amount, $189,037.60, the result is $213,987.48. This amount, $213,987.48, is the same as the Ending Retained Earnings balance on the Statement of Retained Earnings.

The total of all the cash accounts on the Balance Sheet (Petty Cash, Cash on Hand, Regular Checking Account, Payroll Checking Account, Savings Account, and Money-Market Fund) is shown as the Cash Balance at End of Period on the statement of cash flow, $32,317.77. The statement of cash flow uses information from both the balance sheet and income statement.

The statement of changes in financial position uses information from the income statement and balance sheet. The net income is shown on the income statement. Current assets and current liabilities are derived from the balance sheet.

No single financial statement tells the entire story. The income statement indicates how much revenue a business has earned during a specific period of time, but it says nothing about how much of that amount has or has not been received in cash. For information about cash and accounts receivable, we have to look at the balance sheet, statement of cash flow, and statement of changes in financial position.

GETTING STARTED

1. If necessary, start PCA. Open the sample company, Bellwether Garden Supply. (If Bellwether Garden Supply is not shown, restore A New Company. Refer to the Read me box on page 27.)

2. If necessary, follow steps a. through f. to restore your data from the Exercise 6-2 back up.

   a. From the Navigation Bar, select Company; link to Restore. (The Exercise 6-2 backup was made page 204.)

   b. The Select Backup File window appears. If the Location field shows C:\Program Files\Sage Software\Peachtree\Company\BCS\Exercise 6-2.ptb, click Next >. (*Or,* click Browse, then select the appropriate location of the Exercise 6-2 backup file; click Next >.)

   c. The Select Company window appears. The radio button next to An Existing Company is selected. The Company name field shows Bellwether Garden Supply; the Location field shows C:\ProgramFiles\Sage Software\Peachtree\Company\BCS (or the appropriate location on your computer). Click Next >.

   d. The Restore Options window appears. Make sure that the box next to Company Data is *checked*. Click Next >.

   e. The Confirmation window appears. Check the From and To fields to make sure they are correct. Click Finish. When the Restore Company scale is 100% complete, your data is restored and you are returned to the menu bar.

   f. If necessary, remove the external media.

USING PEACHTREE'S HELP FEATURE

In Chapter 5 on pages 154-156 you learned how to use PCA's Help feature to access the sample company's chart of accounts. Later in Chapter 5, on pages 175-182, you used Peachtree's Help feature to learn about internal controls. In this chapter, you learn how to access Peachtree's Help feature to learn more about financial statements.

Follow these steps to learn more about Help:

1. From the menu bar, click Help; Peachtree Accounting Help. The Peachtree Help window displays. If necessary, click on the Index tab.

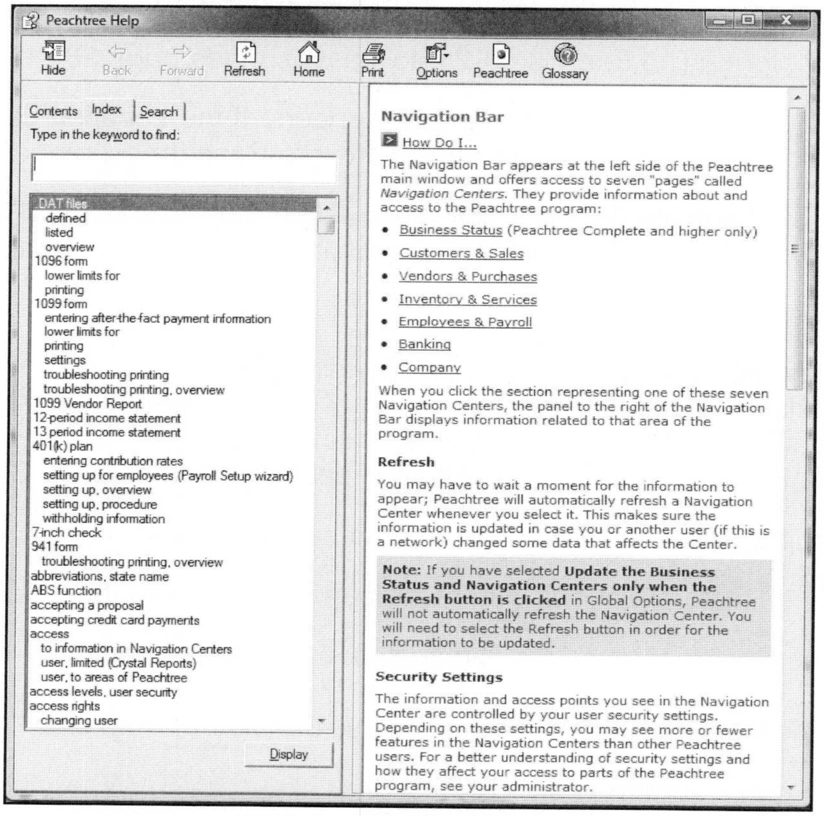

2. Type **balance sheet** in the Type in keyword to find field. Observe that Balance Sheet is highlighted.

3. Click 

. Read the information on the right pane.

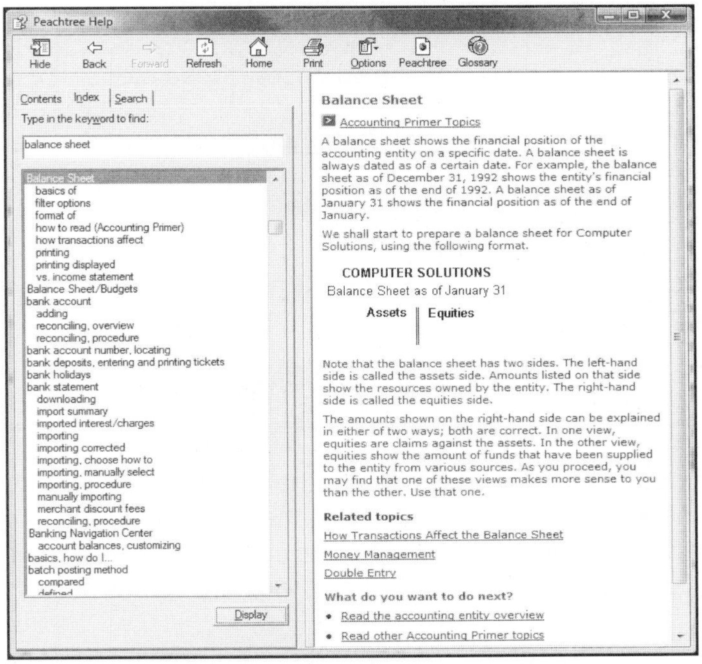

4. If necessary, on the Peachtree Help title bar click 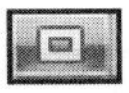 to enlarge the Peachtree Help window, *or* scroll down. Link to How Transactions Affect the Balance Sheet. Read the information on this page. From this page you can link to Accounting Primer Topics, or you can scroll down and link to other areas.

5. Click 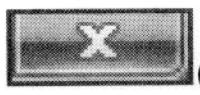 on the Peachtree Help title bar to close the window.

DISPLAYING THE FINANCIAL STATEMENTS

You have already used the Reports menu to print PCA reports. In the steps that follow you use the Company page to print financial statements.

1. From the Navigation Bar, click 

. The Recently Used Financial Stmnts area lists the reports that were viewed recently. Std Balance Sheet is shown.

2. Link to View or Print the Std Balance Sheet.

Read Me

If Std Balance Sheet is *not* shown, follow these steps:

1. Link to View All Financial Statements. The Select a Report window appears.
2. Select <Standard> Balance Sheet.
3. Click 

or 

. The <Standard> Balance Sheet window appears.
4. Click 

to print the Balance Sheet.

Standard (Std) refers to statements that PCA has already set up. As noted in the Help window, Peachtree has a feature that allows you to design financial statements to fit your company's needs. The financial statements with a red arrow next to them are customized forms.

Compare your balance sheet with the one shown on the next two pages.

Bellwether Garden Supply
Balance Sheet
March 31, 2007

ASSETS

Current Assets				
Petty Cash	$	327.55		
Cash on Hand		1,850.45		
Regular Checking Account		9,046.52		
Payroll Checking Account		9,093.25		
Savings Account		7,500.00		
Money Market Fund		4,500.00		
Accounts Receivable		174,940.73		
Other Receivables		7,681.84		
Allowance for Doubtful Account		(5,000.00)		
Inventory		12,021.41		
Prepaid Expenses		14,221.30		
Employee Advances		3,000.65		
Notes Receivable-Current		11,000.00		
Other Current Assets		120.00		
Total Current Assets				250,303.70
Property and Equipment				
Furniture and Fixtures		62,769.25		
Equipment		38,738.33		
Vehicles		86,273.40		
Other Depreciable Property		6,200.96		
Buildings		185,500.00		
Building Improvements		26,500.00		
Accum. Depreciation-Furniture		(54,680.57)		
Accum. Depreciation-Equipment		(33,138.11)		
Accum. Depreciation-Vehicles		(51,585.26)		
Accum. Depreciation-Other		(3,788.84)		
Accum. Depreciation-Buildings		(34,483.97)		
Accum. Depreciation-Bldg Imp		(4,926.28)		
Total Property and Equipment				223,378.91
Other Assets				
Deposits		15,000.00		
Organization Costs		4,995.10		
Accum Amortiz - Organiz Costs		(2,000.00)		
Notes Receivable- Noncurrent		5,004.90		
Other Noncurrent Assets		3,333.00		
Total Other Assets				26,333.00
Total Assets			$	500,015.61

LIABILITIES AND CAPITAL

Current Liabilities				
Accounts Payable	$	80,097.06		
Accrued Expenses		3,022.55		
Sales Tax Payable		18,022.07		
Wages Payable		2,320.30		
401 K Deductions Payable		2,579.92		
Health Insurance Payable		(530.64)		
Federal Payroll Taxes Payable		42,598.69		
FUTA Tax Payable		258.20		
State Payroll Taxes Payable		6,981.16		
SUTA Tax Payable		658.67		

Bellwether Garden Supply
Balance Sheet
March 31, 2007

Local Payroll Taxes Payable	113.25	
Income Taxes Payable	11,045.75	
Other Taxes Payable	2,640.15	
Current Portion Long-Term Debt	5,167.00	
Contracts Payable- Current	2,000.00	
Other Current Liabilities	54.00	
Total Current Liabilities		177,028.13
Long-Term Liabilities		
Notes Payable-Noncurrent	4,000.00	
Total Long-Term Liabilities		4,000.00
Total Liabilities		181,028.13
Capital		
Common Stock	5,000.00	
Paid-in Capital	100,000.00	
Retained Earnings	189,037.60	
Net Income	24,949.88	
Total Capital		318,987.48
Total Liabilities & Capital		$ 500,015.61

Follow these steps to display the Gross Profit by Departments financial statement for the current period.

1. Close the <Standard> Balance Sheet window. On the Company page, link to View All Financial Statements.

2. From the Select a Report or Form window, double-click Gross Profit by Departments.

3. If the Show Zero Amounts box is checked, click on it once to uncheck it. Click OK. The Departmental Gross Profit Totals report appears.

Bellwether Garden Supply
Departmental Gross Profit Totals
Year To Date Totals For the Month Ending March 31, 2007

	Aviary		Books		Equipment	
Revenues						
Sales	$ 51,697.86	100.00	$ 7,293.10	100.00	60,192.31	100.00
Total Revenues	51,697.86	100.00	7,293.10	100.00	60,192.31	100.00
Cost of Sales						
Product Cost - Aviary	20,954.25	40.53	0.00	0.00	0.00	0.00
Product Cost - Books	0.00	0.00	2,361.37	32.38	0.00	0.00
Product Cost - Equipment	0.00	0.00	0.00	0.00	24,159.05	40.14
Total Cost of Sales	20,954.25	40.53	2,361.37	32.38	24,159.05	40.14
Gross Profit	30,743.61	59.47	4,931.73	67.62	36,033.26	59.86

The Departmental Gross Profit Totals report lists the departmental gross profit totals for the following departments: Aviary, Books, and Equipment.

4. Close the Gross Profit by Departments window.

Departmental Masking

The Departmental Gross Profit report shown above is separated into three departments: Aviary, Books, and Equipment. A feature included in Peachtree called ***masking*** allows you to departmentalize financial statements. Masking is the ability to limit information on the report to a single division, department, location, or type code.

To take advantage of masking, you set up the chart of accounts with department codes. If you display Bellwether Garden Supply's chart of account, observe that a suffix is added to sales and cost of sales accounts for the Aviary, Books, and Equipment departments; for example, 40000-AV, Sales - Aviary; 40000-BK, Sales - Books; 40000-EQ, Sales - Equipment; 50000-AV, Product Cost - Aviary; 50000-BK, Product Cost - Books; 50000-EQ, Product Cost - Equipment. The last two characters of the account number (AV, BK, and EQ) identify the department.

You can filter or mask the information that appears on certain reports. In the example of masking shown to the right, you would type *****01 to mask all departments except 01. You would type ****M** to show only main branch numbers on the report.

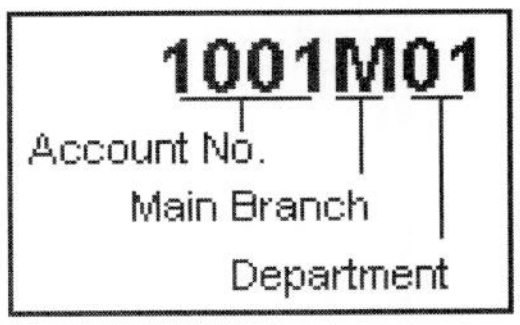

Bellwether Garden Supply masks departments by adding a suffix for the department name—AV for Aviary, BK for Books, etc.

Follow these steps to display the income statement:

1. From the Select a Report or Form window, double-click <Standard> Income Stmnt.

2. Uncheck the show Zero Amounts field. Click 

. The Income Statement appears.

Bellwether Garden Supply
Income Statement
For the Three Months Ending March 31, 2007

		Current Month			Year to Date	
Revenues						
Sales	$	295.00	0.34	$	295.00	0.11
Sales - Aviary		7,172.71	8.16		51,697.86	18.43
Sales - Books		149.75	0.17		7,293.10	2.60
Sales - Equipment		17,838.82	20.30		60,192.31	21.46
Sales - Food/Fert		1,006.96	1.15		5,204.15	1.86
Sales - Hand Tools		729.67	0.83		7,058.12	2.52
Sales - Landscape Services		17,467.43	19.88		26,975.53	9.62
Sales - Miscellaneous		0.00	0.00		45.00	0.02
Sales - Nursery		33,625.13	38.27		67,467.21	24.05
Sales - Pots		7,504.68	8.54		11,069.11	3.95
Sales - Seeds		1,457.43	1.66		8,661.39	3.09
Sales - Soil		655.02	0.75		9,082.55	3.24
Other Income		100.00	0.11		25,600.00	9.13
Sales Discounts		(145.72)	(0.17)		(155.62)	(0.06)
Total Revenues		87,856.88	100.00		280,485.71	100.00
Cost of Sales						
Product Cost		(68.50)	(0.08)		(68.50)	(0.02)
Product Cost - Aviary		2,210.60	2.52		20,954.25	7.47
Product Cost - Books		14.27	0.02		2,361.37	0.84
Product Cost - Equipment		7,402.55	8.43		24,159.05	8.61
Product Cost - Food/Fert		398.80	0.45		2,060.04	0.73
Product Cost - Hand Tools		287.15	0.33		2,813.85	1.00
Product Cost - Pots		2,984.45	3.40		3,259.45	1.16
Product Cost - Seeds		584.45	0.67		3,450.65	1.23
Product Cost - Soil		283.22	0.32		4,048.47	1.44
Direct Labor - Nursery		1,750.00	1.99		3,062.50	1.09
Materials Cost		1,567.45	1.78		1,567.45	0.56
Materials Cost - Nursery		5,387.40	6.13		9,617.50	3.43
Subcontractors - Landscaping		335.50	0.38		335.50	0.12
Total Cost of Sales		23,137.34	26.34		77,621.58	27.67
Gross Profit		64,719.54	73.66		202,864.13	72.33
Expenses						
Freight		0.00	0.00		50.00	0.02
Advertising Expense		1,325.00	1.51		1,325.00	0.47
Auto Expenses		274.56	0.31		274.56	0.10
Bad Debt Expense		1,341.09	1.53		1,341.09	0.48
Bank Charges		18.00	0.02		18.00	0.01
Depreciation Expense		2,761.30	3.14		8,394.00	2.99
Legal and Professional Expense		150.00	0.17		510.00	0.18
Licenses Expense		150.00	0.17		150.00	0.05
Maintenance Expense		75.00	0.09		75.00	0.03
Office Expense		479.89	0.55		479.89	0.17
Payroll Tax Exp		5,849.42	6.66		16,110.84	5.74
Rent or Lease Expense		550.00	0.63		1,100.00	0.39
Repairs Expense		125.00	0.14		3,694.00	1.32
Supplies Expense		2,928.17	3.33		2,928.17	1.04
Utilities Expense		303.45	0.35		303.45	0.11
Wages Expense		51,086.42	58.15		140,705.46	50.16
Other Expense		464.90	0.53		464.90	0.17
Purchase Disc- Expense Items		(10.11)	(0.01)		(10.11)	0.00
Total Expenses		67,872.09	77.25		177,914.25	63.43
Net Income	$	(3,152.55)	(3.59)	$	24,949.88	8.90

Drill Down from the Income Statement to Original Entry

Follow these steps to follow an account balance from the income statement, to the general ledger, then to the original entry window. This is called drill down.

1. The income statement should be displayed. Place your cursor over 7,172.71, Sales – Aviary. 

. Observe that the cursor becomes a magnifying glass icon with a Z in the middle. (Z is an abbreviation for zoom). Double-click with your left mouse button.

2. The General Ledger Account 40000-AV, Sales Aviary, appears. From the general ledger you can drill down to the Receipts window. For example, double click on the 3/5/07 Cash Receipts Journal (CRJ) entry for $79.96.

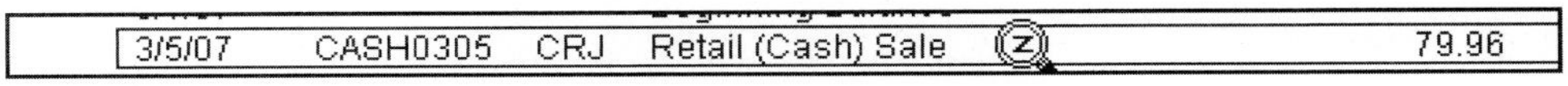

3. This takes you to the Receipts window. The original entry for 4 bags of thistle bird seed is shown for 79.96. Close the Receipts window to go back to the General Ledger Account No. 40000-AV.

4. Drill down from one of the Sales Journal (SJ) entries. The Sales/Invoicing window appears.

5. When you are through using drill down, close the Sales/Invoicing window, General Ledger, and Income Statement window to return to the Select a Report or Form window.

Follow these steps to display the Statement of Cash Flow.

1. From the Select a Report or Form window, double-click <Standard> Cash Flow.

2. The <Standard> Cash Flow Options window displays. Uncheck show Zero Amounts.

3. Click 

. The Statement of Cash Flow appears

Bellwether Garden Supply
Statement of Cash Flow
For the three Months Ended March 31, 2007

	Current Month	Year to Date
Cash Flows from operating activities		
Net Income	$ (3,152.55)	$ 24,949.88
Adjustments to reconcile net income to net cash provided by operating activities		
Accum. Depreciation-Furniture	420.80	1,262.40
Accum. Depreciation-Equipment	385.05	1,265.25
Accum. Depreciation-Vehicles	1,437.89	4,313.67
Accum. Depreciation-Other	64.57	193.71
Accum. Depreciation-Buildings	396.37	1,189.11
Accum. Depreciation-Bldg Imp	56.63	169.87
Accounts Receivable	(10,000.06)	(171,842.29)
Other Receivables	0.00	(3,672.24)
Inventory	14,015.42	6,576.78
Accounts Payable	9,742.43	76,194.31
Sales Tax Payable	4,324.70	15,561.52
401 K Deductions Payable	825.32	2,135.22
Health Insurance Payable	(530.64)	(530.64)
Federal Payroll Taxes Payable	14,834.00	41,011.84
State Payroll Taxes Payable	2,173.49	5,995.83
Other Taxes Payable	50.00	50.00
Other Current Liabilities	150.00	150.00
Total Adjustments	38,345.97	(19,975.66)
Net Cash provided by Operations	35,193.42	4,974.22
Cash Flows from investing activities		
Used For		
Net cash used in investing	0.00	0.00
Cash Flows from financing activities		
Proceeds From		
Used For		
Net cash used in financing	0.00	0.00
Net increase <decrease> in cash	$ 35,193.42	$ 4,974.22
Summary		
Cash Balance at End of Period	$ 32,317.77	$ 32,317.77
Cash Balance at Beg of Period	2,875.54	(27,343.66)
Net Increase <Decrease> in Cash	$ 35,193.31	$ 4,974.11

4. Close the Statement of Cash Flow.

Follow these steps to display the Statement of Retained Earnings:

1. From the Select a Report or Form window, double-click <Standard> Retained Earnings.

2. The <Standard> Retained Earnings Options window appears. Uncheck show Zero Amounts.

3. Click OK. The Statement of Retained Earnings appears.

Bellwether Garden Supply
Statement of Retained Earnings
For the Three Months Ending March 31, 2007

Beginning Retained Earnings	$	189,037.60
Adjustments To Date		0.00
Net Income		24,949.88
Subtotal		213,987.48
Ending Retained Earnings	$	213,987.48

4. Close the Statement of Retained Earnings.

Follow these steps to print the Statement of Changes in Financial Position:

1. From the Select a Report window or Form window, double-click <Standard> Stmnt Changes.

2. The <Standard> Stmnt Changes Options window displays. Uncheck Show Zero amounts.

3. Click OK. The Statement of Changes in Financial Position appears.

Bellwether Garden Supply
Statement of Changes in Financial Position
For the three months ended March 31, 2007

		Current Month		Year To Date
Sources of Working Capital				
Net Income	$	(3,152.55)	$	24,949.88
Add back items not requiring working capital				
Accum. Depreciation-Furniture		420.76		1,262.36
Accum. Depreciation-Equipment		384.99		1,265.19
Accum. Depreciation-Vehicles		1,437.89		4,313.67
Accum. Depreciation-Other		64.57		193.71
Accum. Depreciation-Buildings		396.36		1,189.10
Accum. Depreciation-Bldg Imp		56.63		169.87
Working capital from operations		(391.35)		33,343.78
Other sources				
Total sources		(391.35)		33,343.78
Uses of working capital				
Total uses		0.00		0.00
Net change	$	(391.35)	$	33,343.78
Analysis of componants of changes				
Increase <Decrease> in Current Assets				
Petty Cash	$	227.55	$	227.55
Regular Checking Account		(631.21)		(2,280.03)
Payroll Checking Account		31,096.97		2,526.59
Money Market Fund		4,500.00		4,500.00
Accounts Receivable		10,000.06		171,842.29
Other Receivables		0.00		3,672.24
Inventory		(14,015.42)		(6,576.78)
<Increase> Decrease in Current Liabilities				
Accounts Payable		(9,742.43)		(76,194.31)
Sales Tax Payable		(4,324.70)		(15,561.52)
401 K Deductions Payable		(825.32)		(2,135.22)
Health Insurance Payable		530.64		530.64
Federal Payroll Taxes Payable		(14,834.00)		(41,011.84)
State Payroll Taxes Payable		(2,173.49)		(5,995.83)
Other Taxes Payable		(50.00)		(50.00)
Other Current Liabilities		(150.00)		(150.00)
Net change	$	(391.35)	$	33,343.78

4. Close all windows to return to the Company page.

BACKING UP CHAPTER 7 DATA (Optional Backup)

You have not added any new data in Chapter 7. If you would prefer to have another backup disk, follow these steps to back up Chapter 7:

1. From the Company page, link to Back Up.

2. Click Back Up.

3. Accept the default for backing up to the hard drive or make the selections to back up to another location. Type **Chapter 7** in the File name field.

4. Click 

.

5. When the window prompts that This company backup will require approximately 5.69MB, click 

. When the Back Up Company scale is 100% complete, you have successfully backed up to the current point in Chapter 7. You are returned to the menu bar.

6. Click File, Exit to exit Peachtree.

	INTERNET ACTIVITY
1.	From your Internet browser, go to the book's website at http://www.mhhe.com/yacht2008.
2.	Link to Student Edition.
3.	In the Course-wide Content list, link Internet Activities; then link to Part 1 Internet Activities for Chapter 1-8. Open or save. (You can also choose Chapter 7, then link to Internet Activities. (In the Choose a Chapter field, if you select Chapter 7 observe that other chapter-specific links are available; for example, Multiple Choice Quiz, True or False, PowerPoint Presentations and Going to the Net Exercises.) Also observe that Course-wide Content includes a Glossary link.
4.	Scroll down the window to PEACHTREE SOFTWARE – Chapter 7. Read steps 1 and 2.
5.	Follow the steps shown on the textbook's website to complete this Internet activity.
6.	Use a word processing program to write a summary for each website visited. Your summaries should be no more than 75 words.

SUMMARY AND REVIEW

SOFTWARE OBJECTIVES: In Chapter 7, you used the software to:

1. Restore data from Exercise 6-2. This backup was on page 204.
2. Explore Peachtree's Help feature.
3. Print the financial statements.
4. Use drill down to go from the income statement to the general ledger, then to the original entry window.

5. Make an optional backup of Chapter 7. The backups that were made in Chapter 6 include the data for this chapter.

WEB OBJECTIVES: In Chapter 7, you did these Internet activities:

1. Used your Internet browser to go to the book's website
2. Completed the Internet activity for Peachtree Software.
3. Completed the steps shown for this activity.

GOING TO THE NET

Access the article How to Read a Balance Sheet: Introduction at http://www.fool.com/school/balancesheet/balancesheet01.htm. Read the article. Answer the following questions.

1. What are liquid assets?
2. What are the liquid assets called on the balance sheet?
3. In the How to Read a Balance Sheet: Introduction list, link to two other sites. Define each link; include the website address(es) in your answer.

True/Make True: Write the word True in the space provided if the statement is true. If the statement is not true, write the correct answer.

1. Peachtree automatically calculates financial statements once journal entries have been journalized and posted.

____

____

____

2. In Chapter 7, you printed three financial statements.

3. The statement of cash flow is roughly the same thing as a balance sheet.

4. The balance sheet lists the revenues and expenses of the business.

5. The income statement is a summary of the revenue and expenses of a company for a period of time, such as an accounting period or a year.

6. The financial statements printed by Peachtree reflect month-to-date amounts only.

____

____

7. The financial statements are interrelated.

____

____

8. The term standard refers to financial statements that are designed by the company.

____

____

9. Bellwether Garden Supply showed a net loss for the current month, March 31, 2007.

____

____

____

10. The statement of changes in financial position derives its information from the income statement.

____

____

Exercise 7-1: Answer the following questions about the balance sheet and income statement:

1. The total assets are: ____________
2. The total capital is: ____________
3. Indicate the amount of the net income or (net loss) for the month of March: ____________
4. The current month's gross profit is: ____________
5. The current month's total expenses are: ____________

Exercise 7-2: Answer the following questions about the statement of cash flow and the statement of retained earnings:

1. The current month's net cash provided by operations is: ____________
2. The year-to-date's net cash provided by operations is: ____________
3. The cash balance at end of period for the current month is: ____________
4. The beginning Retained Earnings balance is: ____________
5. The ending Retained Earnings balance is: ____________

CHAPTER 7 INDEX

Chapter 8 Stone Arbor Landscaping: Time & Billing

SOFTWARE OBJECTIVES: In Chapter 8, you use the software to:

1. Start the sample company, Stone Arbor Landscaping.
2. Explore Peachtree's time and billing feature.
3. Make one backup in Chapter 8.

WEB OBJECTIVES: In Chapter 8, you do these Internet activities:

1. Use your Internet browser to go to the book's website.
2. Complete the Internet activity for Search Engines.
3. Complete the steps shown for this activity.

STONE ARBOR LANDSCAPING

When you installed Peachtree Complete Accounting 2008, Release 15 Educational Version, two sample companies were included with the software: Bellwether Garden Supply and Stone Arbor Landscaping. In Chapters 1–7 you worked with Bellwether Garden Supply. This chapter focuses on how the second sample company, Stone Arbor Landscaping, uses PCA's time and billing feature.

TIME & BILLING

Time & Billing gives you a way to track expenses and time when working with customers. For example, Stone Arbor Landscaping has daily services that they perform for their customers like making copies, designing a proposal, and out-of-pocket expenses. These expenses can be tracked and documented using PCA's time and billing feature. The purpose of PCA's time and billing feature is to provide the tools to record customer-related work or expenses.

To track time and expenses, PCA uses two forms or tickets: the time ticket and the expense ticket. Each ticket type can be specific to a customer, job, or non-billable administrative tasks (miscellaneous items).

Each ticket has its own special type of inventory item: the activity item for time tickets and the charge item for expense tickets.

Time Tickets

Time tickets are used to record time-based activities such as research or consultations. They record the activities of either an employee or a vendor. The two methods of entering time ticket information are weekly or daily.

The billing rate used for a recorded activity can be based on the employee who records the ticket or one of the five billing rates assigned to the activity item. Or, you can record the billing at the time you enter the time ticket.

Expense Tickets

Expense tickets are used to track and aid in the recovery of customer-related expenses. These expenses are *not* based on time. Expenses can be based on the various charges related to the service being offered. For example, if you were an accountant, you might charge your client for copying fees or faxing fees.

Both time and expense tickets can be used in the Sales/Invoicing window to bill your customers. The Sales/Invoicing window includes a feature called Apply Tickets/Reimbursable Expenses which takes you to the time and billing feature. The rate for expense tickets is determined by the unit price of the charge item multiplied by the quantity.

The chart below shows how time and billing works:

Time & Billing Ticket Types			
Ticket Type	**Inventory Item Class**	**Examples**	**Billing Amount Equals**
Time Ticket	Activity Item	Research Consultants Writing Reports	Billing Rate Times Activity Divisions
Expense Ticket	Charge Item	Copying Faxing Court Fees	Unit Price of the Charge Item Times Quantity

GETTING STARTED

1. Start PCA. From the startup window, select Explore a sample company. (*Hint: Stone Arbor Landscaping will be listed in the Company Name list after the first time it is opened.*)

2. The Explore a Sample Company window appears. Select Stone Arbor Landscaping.

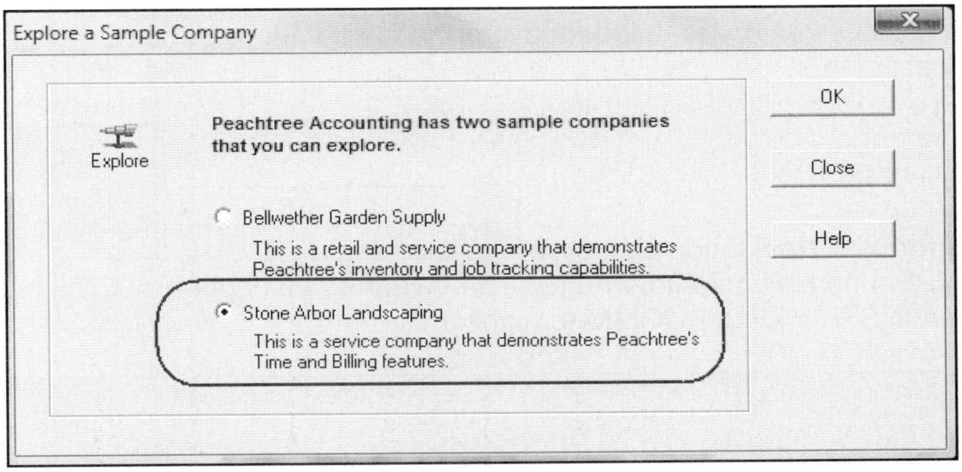

3. Click 

. The first time you start Stone Arbor Landscaping it takes a few moments. The title bar shows Peachtree Accounting: Stone Arbor Landscaping. The Customers & Sales page is shown.

USING TIME & BILLING

Let's look at how Stone Arbor Landscaping has set up time and billing. First, they set up how they are going to invoice for their services. There are two special inventory item classes for Time & Billing: ***activity items*** and ***charge items***. Activity items are used on time tickets. Charge items are used on expense tickets. These inventory items must be set up prior to entering a time or expense ticket.

There are four steps to complete PCA's Time & Billing:

Step 1: Set up the inventory item.

Step 2: Enter the time ticket.

Step 3: Record the sales invoice.

Step 4: Payroll.

Inventory Item Maintenance

You use maintenance windows to set up defaults. Follow these steps to look at the inventory maintenance information for Stone Arbor Landscaping.

1. From the Navigation Bar, click 

; 

, View and Edit Inventory Items. The Inventory List appears. Click once on INSTL HARD – COMM to highlight it.

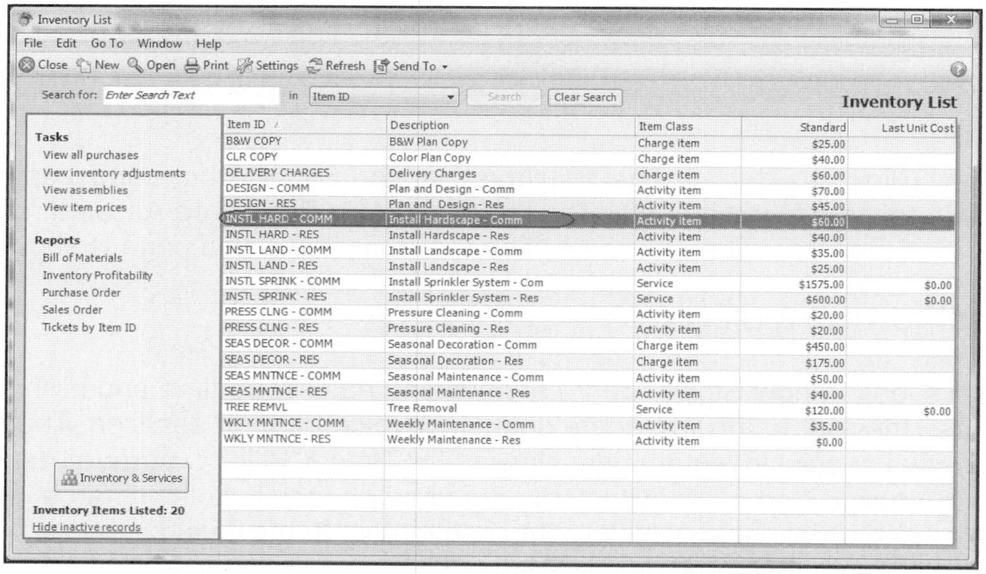

2. Double-click INSTL HARD – COMM. The Maintain Inventory Items window appears for INSTL HARD – COMM, Install Hardscape – Comm.

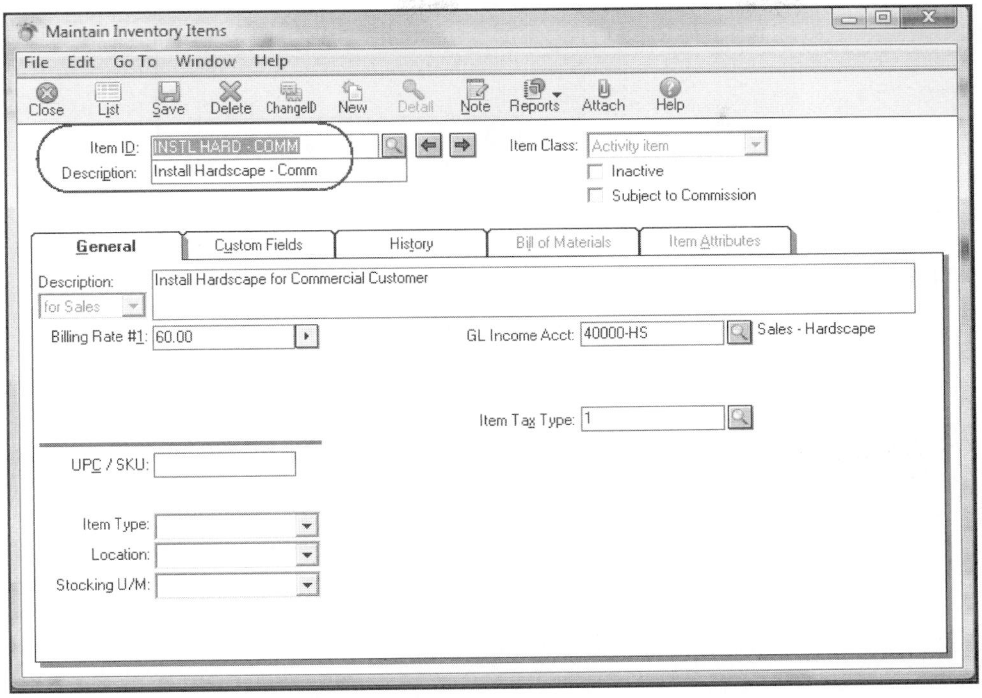

Review the information on the Maintain Inventory Items window. Observe that $60.00 is shown in the Billing Rate #1 field (click on the right-arrow to see other billing rates; then close the Multiple Price Levels window); the GL Income Acct is Account No. 40000-HS, Sales – Hardscape; and that the Item Tax Type is 1 (for Taxable). This maintenance window is similar to ones that you have set up before. *Remember, maintenance windows are where you set up defaults for PCA.*

3. Close all windows to return to the Inventory & Services page.

Time Ticket

The Time Ticket shows how much was billed to the customer. To see how time is billed, you are going to look at a job that Alan Hardman has already completed. This means you use the Open icon [
] to select one of the time ticket records.

Follow the steps on the next page to see time tickets.

1. From the Navigation Bar, click 

; 

, New Time Ticket.

2. The Time Tickets window appears. Make sure that the Daily tab is selected. Click 

.

3. Scroll down, or use your cursor to enlarge, the Select Time Ticket window. Select Reference 282 for Alan Hardman; Period/Date, 03-03/12/07.

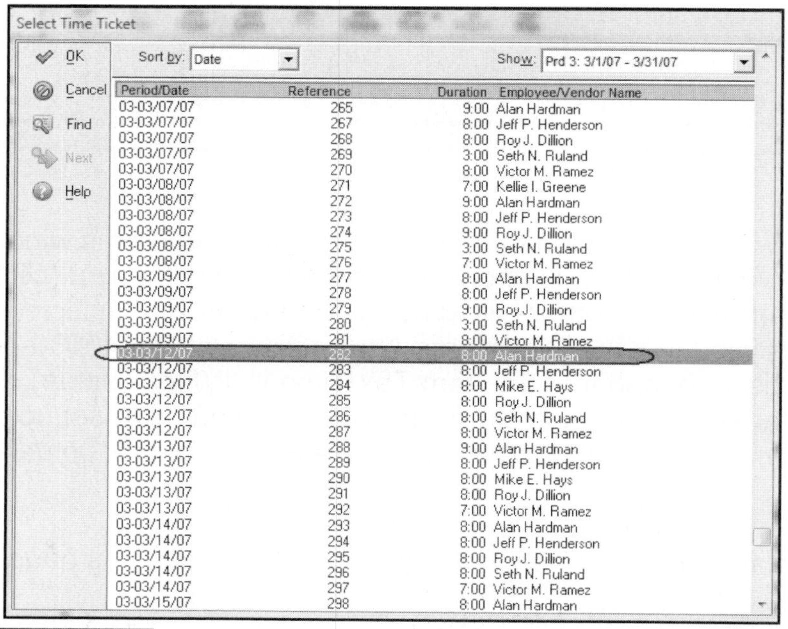

Period/Date	Reference	Duration	Employee/Vendor Name
03-03/07/07	265	9:00	Alan Hardman
03-03/07/07	267	8:00	Jeff P. Henderson
03-03/07/07	268	8:00	Roy J. Dillion
03-03/07/07	269	3:00	Seth N. Ruland
03-03/07/07	270	8:00	Victor M. Ramez
03-03/08/07	271	7:00	Kellie I. Greene
03-03/08/07	272	9:00	Alan Hardman
03-03/08/07	273	8:00	Jeff P. Henderson
03-03/08/07	274	9:00	Roy J. Dillion
03-03/08/07	275	3:00	Seth N. Ruland
03-03/08/07	276	7:00	Victor M. Ramez
03-03/09/07	277	8:00	Alan Hardman
03-03/09/07	278	8:00	Jeff P. Henderson
03-03/09/07	279	9:00	Roy J. Dillion
03-03/09/07	280	3:00	Seth N. Ruland
03-03/09/07	281	8:00	Victor M. Ramez
03-03/12/07	282	8:00	Alan Hardman
03-03/12/07	283	8:00	Jeff P. Henderson
03-03/12/07	284	8:00	Mike E. Hays
03-03/12/07	285	8:00	Roy J. Dillion
03-03/12/07	286	8:00	Seth N. Ruland
03-03/12/07	287	8:00	Victor M. Ramez
03-03/13/07	288	9:00	Alan Hardman
03-03/13/07	289	8:00	Jeff P. Henderson
03-03/13/07	290	8:00	Mike E. Hays
03-03/13/07	291	8:00	Roy J. Dillion
03-03/13/07	292	7:00	Victor M. Ramez
03-03/14/07	293	8:00	Alan Hardman
03-03/14/07	294	8:00	Jeff P. Henderson
03-03/14/07	295	8:00	Roy J. Dillion
03-03/14/07	296	8:00	Seth N. Ruland
03-03/14/07	297	7:00	Victor M. Ramez
03-03/15/07	298	8:00	Alan Hardman

4. Click 

. The Time Tickets window appears. The Daily tab should be selected. If it is not, select it. Notice that the Activity Item is for INSTL HARD – COMM, Install Hardscape, and that the customer is O'Hara Homes Contract. The Ticket Description for Invoicing is Installation of Decking/Patio. Mr. Hardman worked for eight hours on March 12, 2007; and O'Hara Homes was billed $480.00.

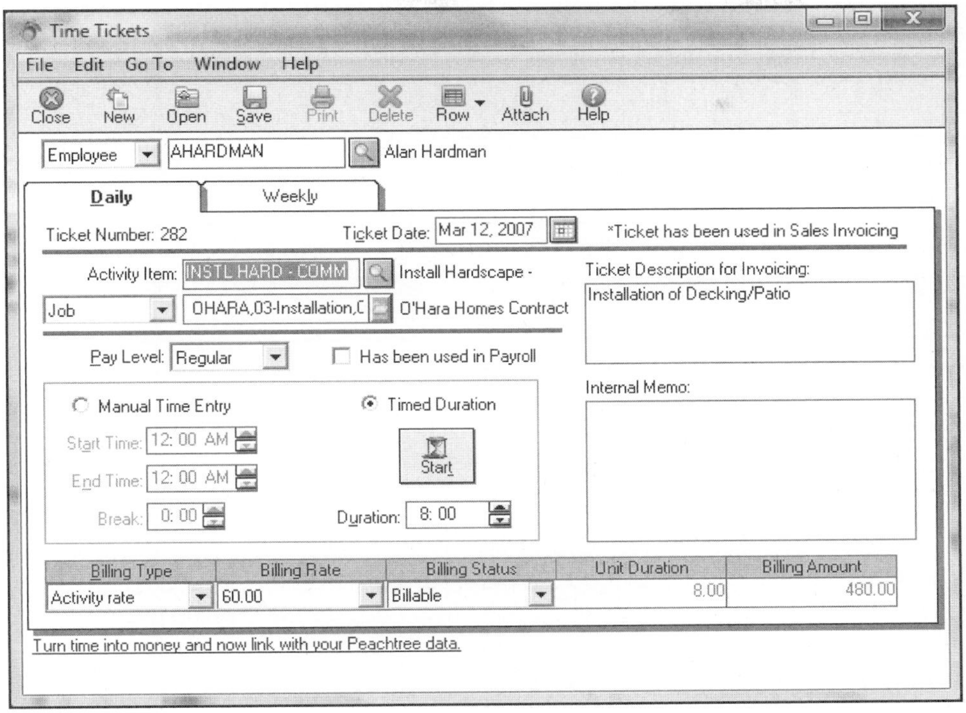

The Time Tickets window shows one instance, March 12, 2007 (refer to the Ticket Date field.) When the Weekly tab is selected, you see that Mr. Hardman worked from 3/12 through 3/15 on this job.

5. Click on the Weekly tab.

   The Time Tickets window; Weekly tab, shows the weekly time ticket for Stone Arbor Landscaping employee, Alan Hardman. Notice that the Activity item, INSTL is shown for Monday, 3/12; Tuesday, 3/13; Wednesday, 3/14; and Thursday, 3/15 for a total of 33 hours. Compare your Weekly Time Tickets window to the one shown on the next page.

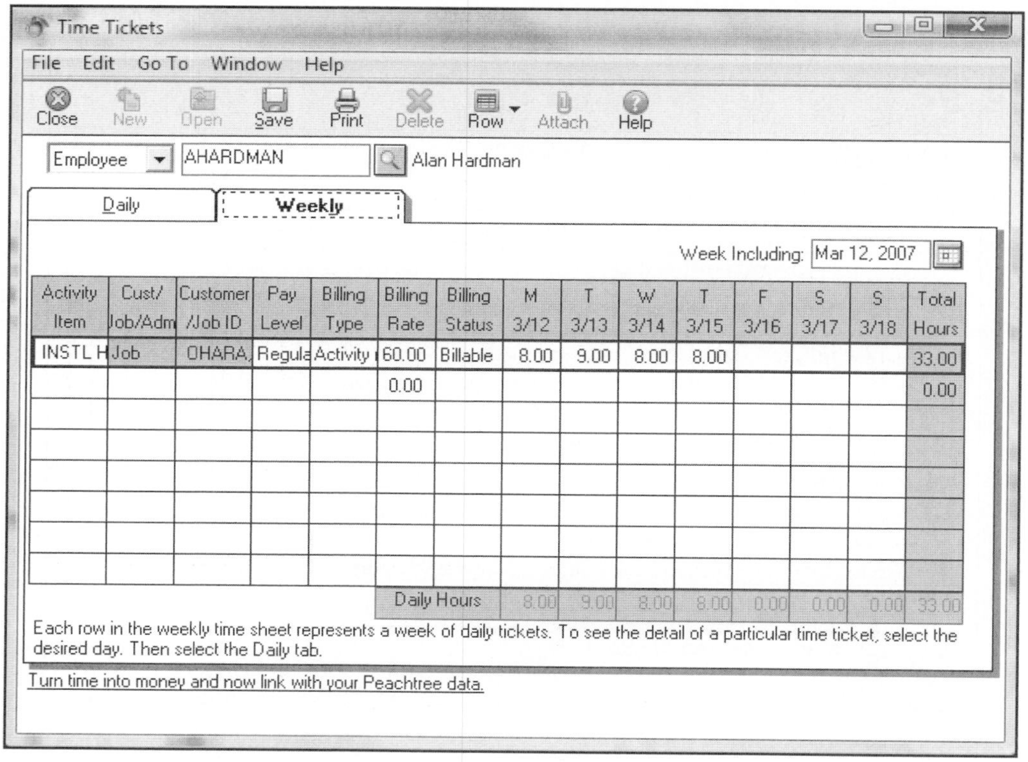

6. Close the Weekly Time Tickets window to return to Employees & Payroll page.

Sales Invoice

In order to see how Mr. Hardman charges were billed to the customer, O'Hara Homes, follow these steps.

1. From the Navigation Bar, click 

; 

, View and Edit Sales Invoices. The Sales/Invoice List Appears. Click on OHARA, Invoice No. 1008, 3/13/2007 to highlight it.

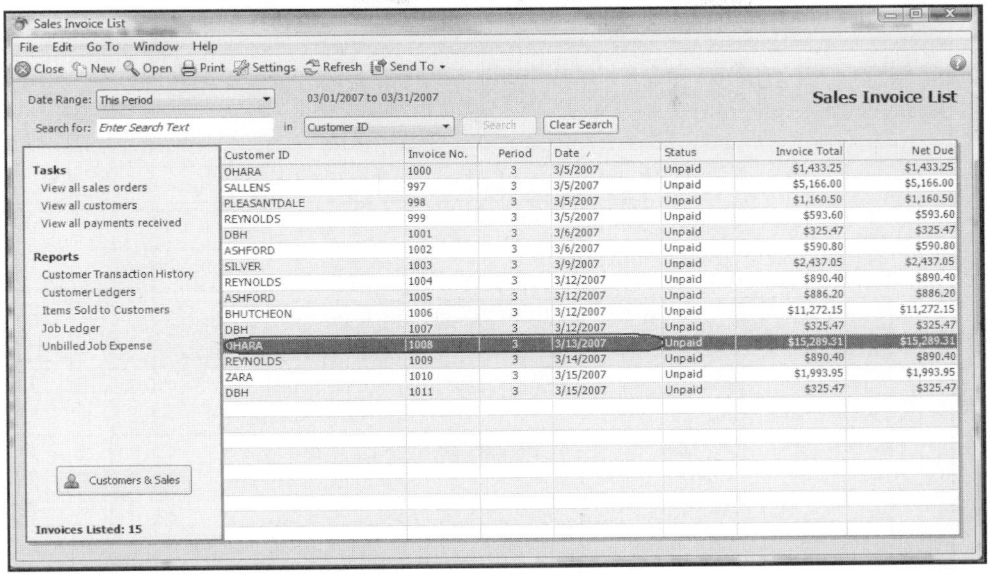

Customer ID	Invoice No.	Period	Date	Status	Invoice Total	Net Due
OHARA	1000	3	3/5/2007	Unpaid	$1,433.25	$1,433.25
SALLENS	997	3	3/5/2007	Unpaid	$5,166.00	$5,166.00
PLEASANTDALE	998	3	3/5/2007	Unpaid	$1,160.50	$1,160.50
REYNOLDS	999	3	3/5/2007	Unpaid	$593.60	$593.60
DBH	1001	3	3/6/2007	Unpaid	$325.47	$325.47
ASHFORD	1002	3	3/6/2007	Unpaid	$590.80	$590.80
SILVER	1003	3	3/9/2007	Unpaid	$2,437.05	$2,437.05
REYNOLDS	1004	3	3/12/2007	Unpaid	$890.40	$890.40
ASHFORD	1005	3	3/12/2007	Unpaid	$886.20	$886.20
BHUTCHEON	1006	3	3/12/2007	Unpaid	$11,272.15	$11,272.15
DBH	1007	3	3/12/2007	Unpaid	$325.47	$325.47
OHARA	1008	3	3/13/2007	Unpaid	$15,289.31	$15,289.31
REYNOLDS	1009	3	3/14/2007	Unpaid	$890.40	$890.40
ZARA	1010	3	3/15/2007	Unpaid	$1,993.95	$1,993.95
DBH	1011	3	3/15/2007	Unpaid	$325.47	$325.47

2. Double-click OHARA, Invoice 1008. The Sales/Invoicing window appears.

3. Click on the arrow next to Apply Tickets/Expenses [Apply Tickets/Expenses]. *(Hint: This is located in the lower left of the window.)*

4. The Apply Tickets/Reimbursable Expenses window appears. Observe that Alan Hardman's work on March 15 is billed, along with other employees that work on this customer's job. Compare your Apply Tickets/Reimbursable Expenses window to the one shown on the next page.

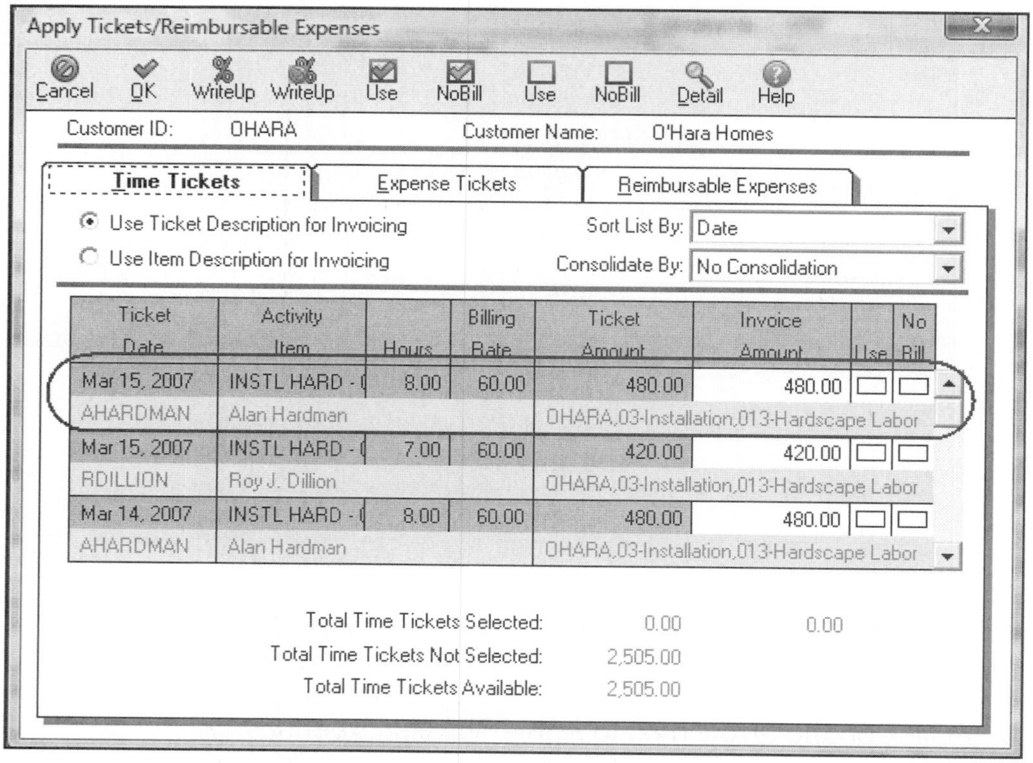

Observe that this time ticket shows that Alan Hardman's ticket amount is $480.00 for 8 hours at a billing rate of $60.00 ($60 x 8 = $480) on March 15, 2007. (Work by AHARDMAN is also shown for March 14, 2007.) This agrees with the weekly time ticket shown on page 236.

5. Click 

to close the Apply Tickets/Reimbursable Expenses window. You are returned to the O'Hara Homes Sales/Invoicing window.

6. Close all windows to return to the Customers & Sales page.

Payroll

You also need to set up information in Payroll. You do this by selecting Hourly-Time Ticket Hours for employees. Let's see how Stone Arbor Landscaping sets this up.

1. From the Navigation Bar click 

; 

View and Edit Employees. The Employee List appears. Double-click AHARDMAN, Alan Hardman. Click on the Pay Info tab.

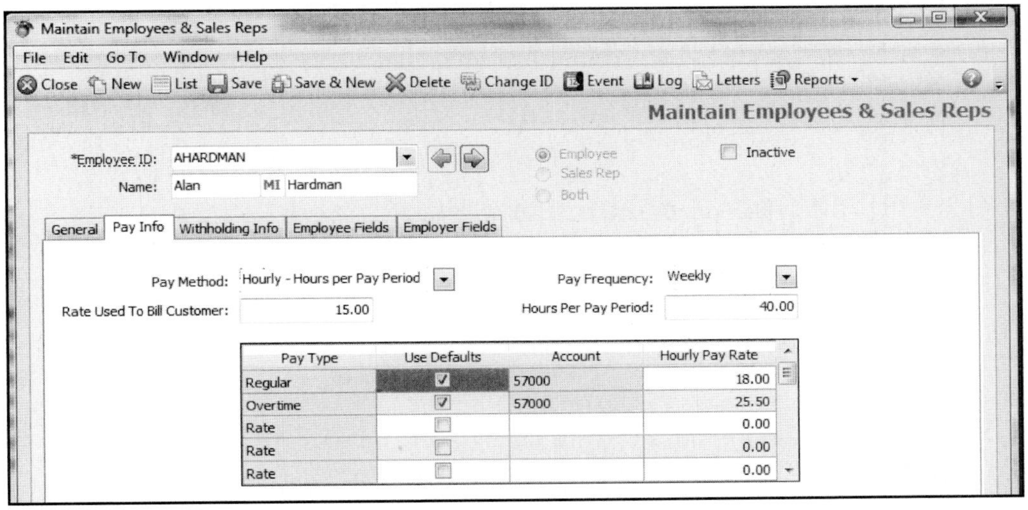

Observe that Mr. Hardman's Pay Method is Hourly – Hours per Pay Period. He is paid weekly.

2. Close all windows. Do not save this record. You are returned to the Employees & Payroll window.

You use the Payroll Entry window to issue Mr. Hardman a paycheck for the work completed for O'Hara Homes.

BACKING UP CHAPTER 8 DATA

Follow these steps to back up Chapter 8 data:

1. From the Navigation Bar, click 

; link to <u>Back up</u>.

2. If necessary, uncheck the box next to Include company name in the backup file name.

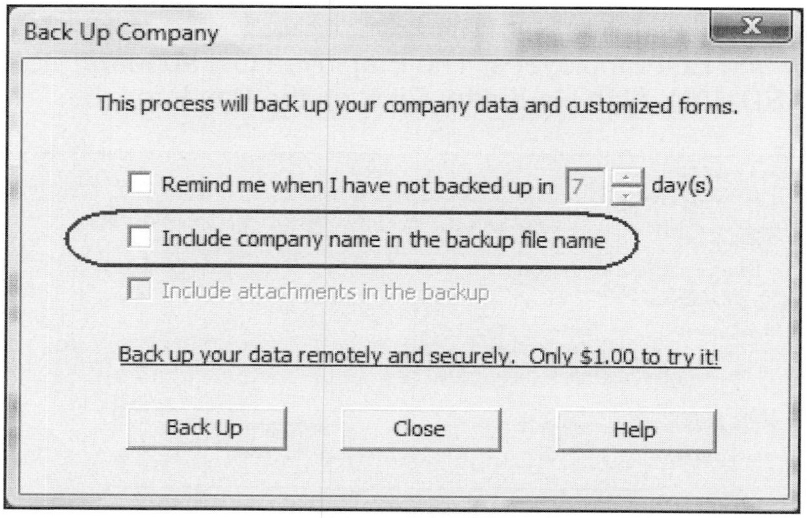

3. Click 

.

4. Accept the default for backing up to the hard drive or make the selections to back up to another location. Type **Chapter 8** in the File name field.

5. Click 

.

6. When the window prompts that This company backup will require approximately 4.01MB, click 

. When the Back Up Company scale is 100% complete, you have successfully backed up to the current point in Chapter 8. You are returned to the menu bar.

7. Click File, Exit to exit Peachtree.

INTERNET ACTIVITY	
1.	From your Internet browser, go to the book's website at http://www.mhhe.com/yacht2008.
2.	Link to Student Edition.
3.	In the Course-wide Content list, link Internet Activities; then link to <u>Part 1 Internet Activities for Chapter 1-8</u>. Open or save. (You can also choose Chapter 8, then link to Internet Activities. (In the Choose a Chapter field, if you select Chapter 8 observe that other chapter-specific links are available; for example, Multiple Choice Quiz, True or False, PowerPoint Presentations and Going to the Net Exercises.) Also observe that Course-wide Content includes a Glossary link.
4.	Scroll down the window to SEARCH ENGINES – Chapter 8. Read steps 1 and 2.
5.	Follow the steps shown on the textbook's website to complete this Internet activity.
6.	Use a word processing program to write a short summary of what you found. Your summary should be no more than 75 words.

SUMMARY AND REVIEW

SOFTWARE OBJECTIVES: In Chapter 8, you used the software to:

1. Start the sample company, Stone Arbor Landscaping.
2. Explore Peachtree's time and billing feature.
3. Make one backup in Chapter 8.

WEB OBJECTIVES: In Chapter 8, you did these Internet activities:

1. Used your Internet browser to go to the book's website.
2. Completed the Internet activity for Search Engines.
3. Completed the steps shown for this activity.

GOING TO THE NET

Access the Peachtree Complete Accounting 2008, Frequently Asked Questions and Answers website at http://www.peachtree.com/peachtreeaccountingline/complete/frequently_asked_questions.cfm. Answer the following questions.

1. What are the differences between the Peachtree 2008 products? Then link to <u>Compare Products</u>. Select three products, then click 

. Close the Comparison Results window. (If necessary, click  to go back to Frequently Asked Questions.)

2. What features are available in Peachtree 2008 to get me started quickly?

Multiple Choice Questions: In the space provided, write the letter that best answers each question.

_____1. The focus of Chapter 8 is to:

a. Complete a sales invoice.
b. Complete a payroll entry.
c. Complete defaults.
d. Look at PCA's time and billing features.
e. None of the above.

_____2. In Chapter 8, you work with the sample company called:

a. Bellwether Garden Supply.
b. Stone Arbor Graphic Design.
c. Franklin Botanical Gardens.
d. Abbott's Landscaping.
e. None of the above.

_____3. The purpose of PCA's time and billing feature is to:

a. Give you the tools to record customer-related work or expenses.
b. Track how much an employee earns.
c. Track how many sales invoices are completed in a month.
d. Record employee payroll.
e. None of the above.

_____4. You use maintenance windows to set up:

a. Payroll entries.
b. Sales/Invoicing.
c. Defaults.
d. Time tickets.
e. None of the above.

_____5. Time tickets are used to:

a. Record weekly or monthly information.
b. Record payroll.
c. Record time-based activities.
d. Track sales invoices.
e. None of the above.

_____6. Expense tickets are used to:

a. Track and aid in the recovery of customer-related expenses.
b. Record time-based activities such as research or consultants.
c. Track sales invoices.
d. Record payroll.
e. None of the above.

_____7. Examples of expense ticket charge items are:

a. Fixed asset accounts.
b. Inventory accounts.
c. Copying, faxing, court fees.
d. Research, consultants, writing reports.
e. None of the above.

_____8. How many hours did Mr. Hardman work on March 12, 2007 completing the installation of decking/patio for O'Hara Homes?

a. Three hours.
b. Four hours.
c. Five hours.
d. Six hours.
e. None of the above.

_____9. Examples of time ticket activity items are:

a. Copying, faxing, court fees.
b. Research, consultants, writing reports.
c. Inventory accounts.
d. Fixed asset accounts.
e. None of the above.

_____10. The time ticket shows:

a. How much was billed to a vendor.
b. How much was billed to a customer.
c. How much was billed to an employee.
d. Expenses minus revenue.
e. None of the above.

Exercise 8-1: Answer the following questions about time and billing.

1. Stone Arbor Landscaping's standard hourly billing rate for Installing hardscape for commercial customers is: ____________

2. The tax status for installing hardscape for commercial customers is: ____________

3. The general ledger account used for hardscape commercial is: ____________

4. The item identification for installing hardscape for a commercial customer is: ____________

Exercise 8-2: Answer the following questions.

1. O'Hara Homes 3/13/07 sales invoice is in the amount of? ____________

2. The sales tax on the O'Hara Homes sales invoice is? ____________

3. The G/L account number for Alan Hardman's regular pay is? ____________

4. How many hours did it take Alan Hardman to complete decking installation on 3/13/2007 on the O'Hara Homes job? ____________

CHAPTER 8 INDEX

Part 2 Peachtree Complete Accounting 2008 for Service Businesses

In Part 2 of *Computer Accounting with Peachtree Complete 2008, 12th Edition,* you are the owner of an accounting practice. Your accounting business does monthly record keeping for local service businesses. In Part 2, entries are recorded in the Cash Receipts Journal and Cash Disbursements Journal. Also adjusting entries are recorded in the General Journal. At the end of each month, you reconcile the bank statement and print the general ledger trial balance and financial statements. At the end of the fourth quarter, you use Peachtree to complete end-of-quarter adjusting entries, print the adjusted trial balance, print financial statements, close the fiscal year, and print a post-closing trial balance.

After recording journal entries, the next step is to post them to the general ledger. One of the best features of a computerized accounting system is how quickly ***posting*** is done. Once journal entries are recorded and checked for accuracy, posting is a click of the mouse. All entries are posted to the correct accounts in the ledger and account balances are calculated–fast, easy, and accurate. Think of it as a process where journalizing and posting is the first step, then ledgers and financial statements are next. The diagram below illustrates this process.

Remember that the accuracy of your ledger and financial statement reports depends on debiting and crediting journal entries correctly.

An added feature is that once entries are posted, account reconciliation can be completed.

Part 2 includes two chapters and two projects: Chapters 9 and 10 and Projects 1 and 1A. In Chapters 9 and 10, you maintain the accounting records for Jon Haney Design. You complete accounting tasks for the fourth quarter–October, November and December 2008. You also complete end-of-quarter adjusting entries for Mr. Haney. At the end of Chapter 9, you start an exercise for a new service business that is completed in Chapter 10.

In Project 1 you complete the Computer Accounting Cycle for Mary Albert, Accountant. This project gives you an opportunity to apply what you have learned in Chapters 9 and 10. At the end of Project 1, there is a Check Your Progress assessment.

Project 1A is an opportunity to design a service business of your own. You select a chart of accounts, write and journalize transactions, reconcile the bank statement, and complete the computer accounting cycle for your business.

The chart below and on the next page shows the size of the backups made in Part 2–Chapters 9, 10, and Project 1. The textbook steps explain how to back up to Peachtree's default hard drive location at C:\Program Files\Sage Software\Peachtree\ Company\[shortened company name]. *You can also specify a hard drive location; or, back up to external media, such as, a floppy disk (a blank, formatted disk holds 1,440,000 bytes; or about 1440 KB); CD-R; DVD-R; USB drive; or Zip disk.*

Chapter	Backup Name	Kilobytes	Page Nos.
9	Chapter 9 Begin	1,344 KB	277-279
	Chapter 9 Check Register October[1]	*1,367 KB*	*291*
	Chapter 9 October	1,376 KB	305
	Exercise 9-1	921 KB	313
	Exercise 9-2	936 KB	317
10	Chapter 10 November	1,386 KB	330-331
	Chapter 10 December UTB	1,392 KB	337-338
	Chapter 10 December	1,396 KB	347-348
	Chapter 10 EOY	1,394 KB	354-355
	Asset depreciation.xls	24 KB	356

[1]This is an optional back up.

Chapter	Backup Name	Kilobytes	Page Nos.
10	Exercise 10-1	964 KB	362
	Exercise 10-2 Unadjusted Trial Balance	978 KB	364
	Exercise 10-2 Financial Statements	978 KB	364
	Exercise 10-2 End of Year	977 KB	364
Project 1	Mary Albert Begin	921 KB	371
	Mary Albert UTB	943 KB	373
	Mary Albert December	948 KB	374
	Mary Albert EOY	954 KB	374

Read Me: Windows Vista—Problem Backing Up to USB Drive

Because of Windows Vista operating system security features, you need to backup to your desktop first. Then copy the backup file from your desktop to the USB drive. Refer to Appendix A, Problem Backing Up to USB Drive or Other External Media, pages 700-702 for detailed steps.

Chapter 9 Maintaining Accounting Records for Service Businesses

SOFTWARE OBJECTIVES: In Chapter 9, you use the software to:

1. Set up company information for Jon Haney Design.
2. Select a sample company.
3. Edit the chart of accounts.
4. Enter chart of accounts beginning balances.
5. Use Windows Explorer to see the company's file size.
6. Record and post transactions in the cash receipts and cash disbursements journals.
7. Complete account reconciliation.
8. Display the general ledger trial balance.
9. Display the cash account register.
10. Print financial statements.
11. Make four backups: 1) back up Chapter 9 beginning data; 2) back up October data; 3) back up Exercise 9-1; 4) back up Exercise 9-2.[1]

WEB OBJECTIVES: In Chapter 9, you do these Internet activities:

1. Use your Internet browser to go to the book's website. (Go online to www.mhhe.com/yacht2008).
2. Go to the Internet Activity link on the book's website. Then, select WEB EXERCISES, PART 2. Complete the first web exercise in Part 2, Starting a Business.
3. Use a word processing program to write summaries of the websites that you visited.

Chapter 9 begins Part 2 of the book–Peachtree Complete Accounting 2008 for Service Businesses. In this part of the book you are the owner of an accounting practice that does the monthly record keeping for several service businesses. In this chapter you maintain the accounting records for two service businesses—Jon Haney Design and the end-of-chapter exercise, Your Name, Designer. You set up a business using one of

[1]Refer to the chart on pages 248-249 for the size of backup files.

PCA's sample companies. Then, you complete the computer accounting cycle for the month of October using your client's checkbook register and bank statement as ***source documents***. In your study of accounting, you learned that source documents are used to show written evidence of a business transaction. For Jon Haney Design, the source documents used are his checkbook register and bank statement.

GETTING STARTED

Jon Haney is a designer and educator. His sources of income are: design work, book royalties, and part-time teaching at Madison Community College. He is single and has no dependents.

Follow these steps to select a sample chart of accounts for your client, Jon Haney:

1. Start Peachtree. (If a company opens, click File; Close Company.)

2. At the Peachtree Accounting startup window, click 

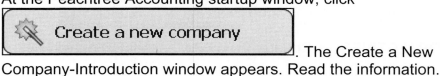

. The Create a New Company-Introduction window appears. Read the information.

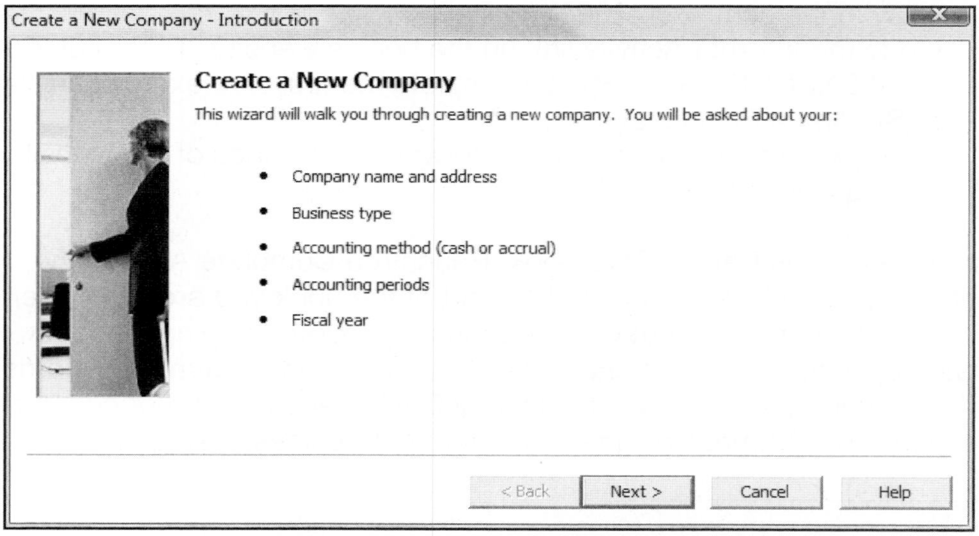

3. Click Next >. Type the company information shown below. Press the **<Tab>** key between each field.

Company Information

Company Name:	**Jon Haney Design (use your name)**[2]
Address Line 1:	**1967 West Park Street**
City, State, Zip:	**Madison, WI 53715**
Country:	**USA**
Telephone:	**608-555-2630**
Fax:	**608-555-2640**
Business Type:	Select Sole Proprietorship
Web Site:	www.jonhaney.com
E-Mail:	info@jonhaney.com

Compare your New Company Setup – Company Information window to the one below. *The company name field should show your first and last name Design. Do not complete the ID fields.* (*Hint: Observe that there is a red asterisk next to Company Name. The asterisk indicates a required field.*)

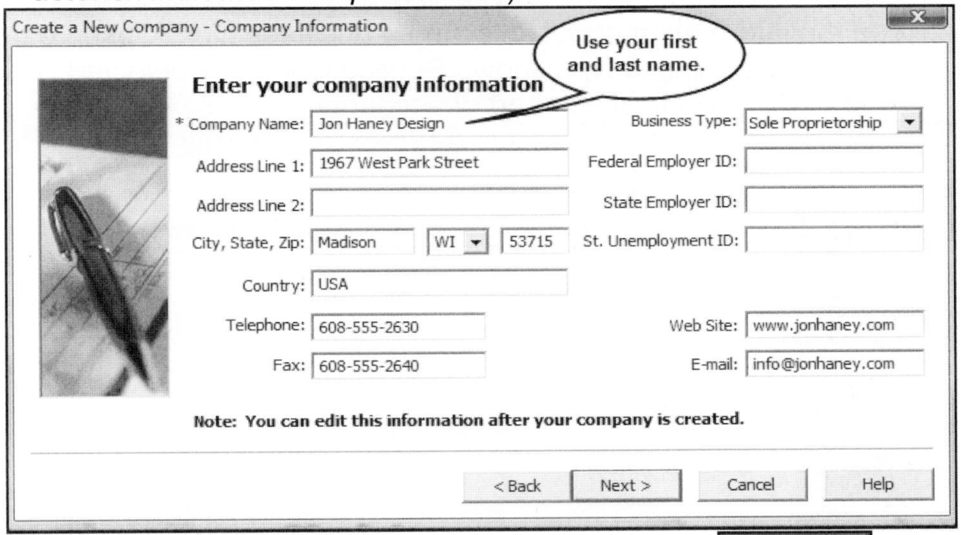

4. Check the information you just typed, then click Next >. The

[2]Boldface indicates information that you type. If you use your name as the company name then your Peachtree printouts will have your name on them.

Select a method to create your company window appears.

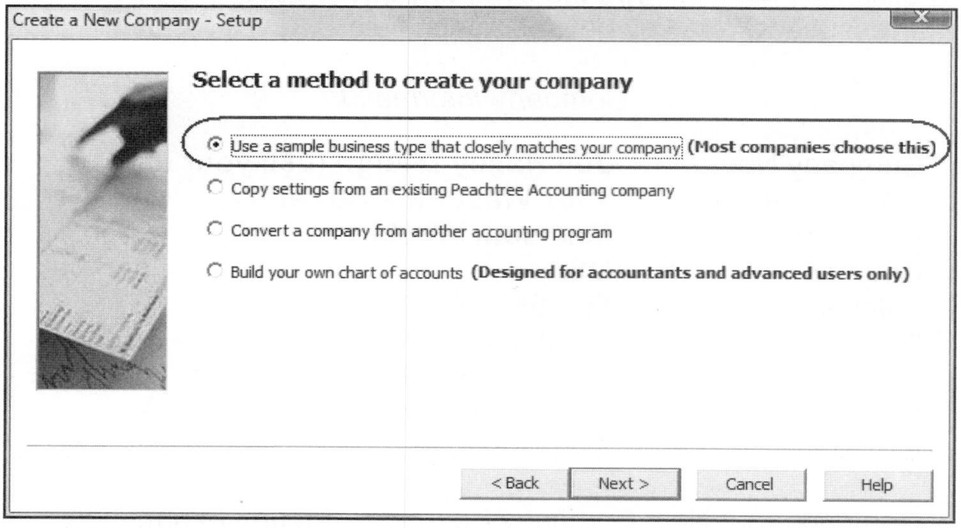

5. Accept the default to Use a sample business that closely matches your company **(Most companies choose this)**. Click Next >.

6. Read the information about selecting a business type. Observe that the Select a business type shows Service Company selected. This is one of PCA's simplified chart of accounts.

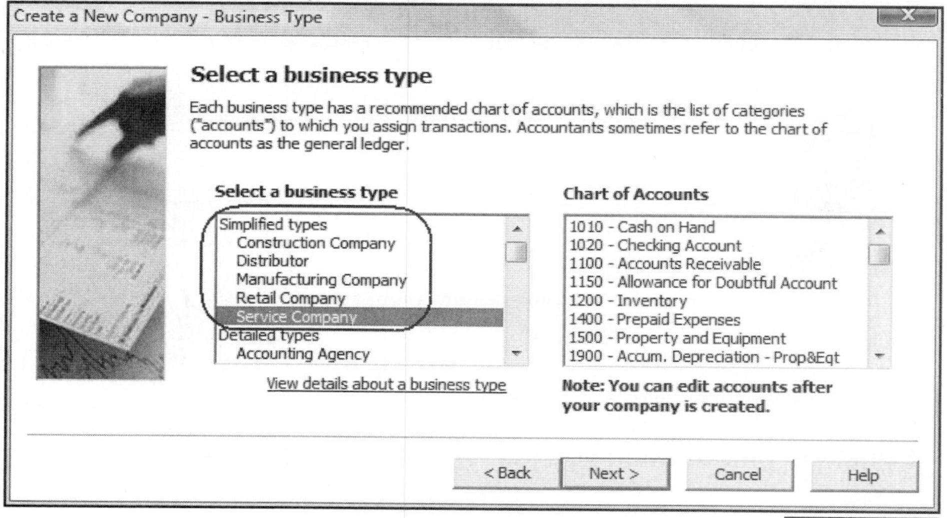

7. Make sure that Service Company is highlighted; click Next >. The Choose an accounting method window appears.

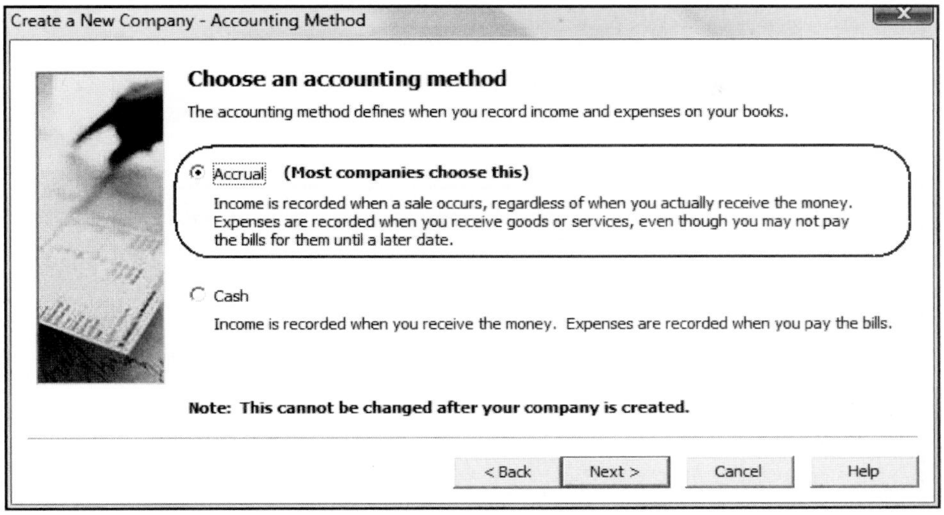

8. Accept the default for Accrual, by clicking Next >. The Choose a posting method window appears.

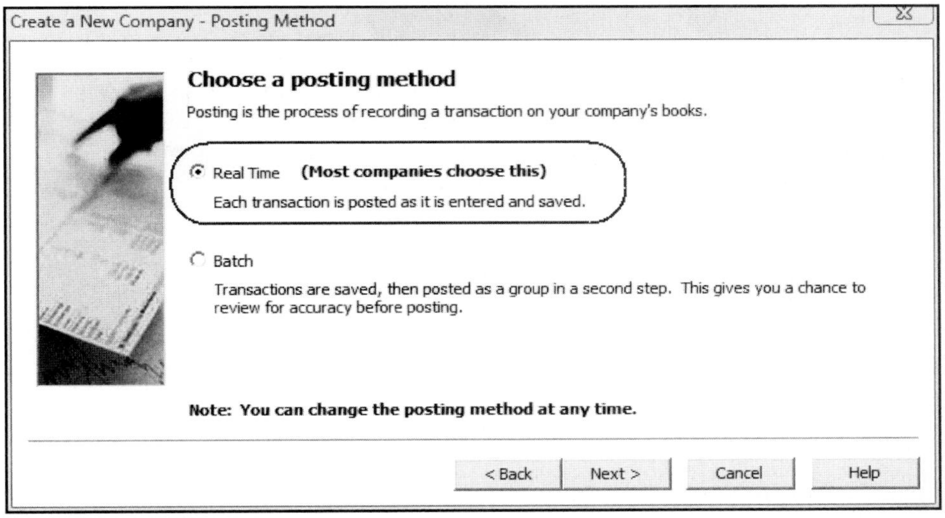

9. Accept the default for Real Time posting, by clicking Next >. The Choose an accounting period structure window appears.

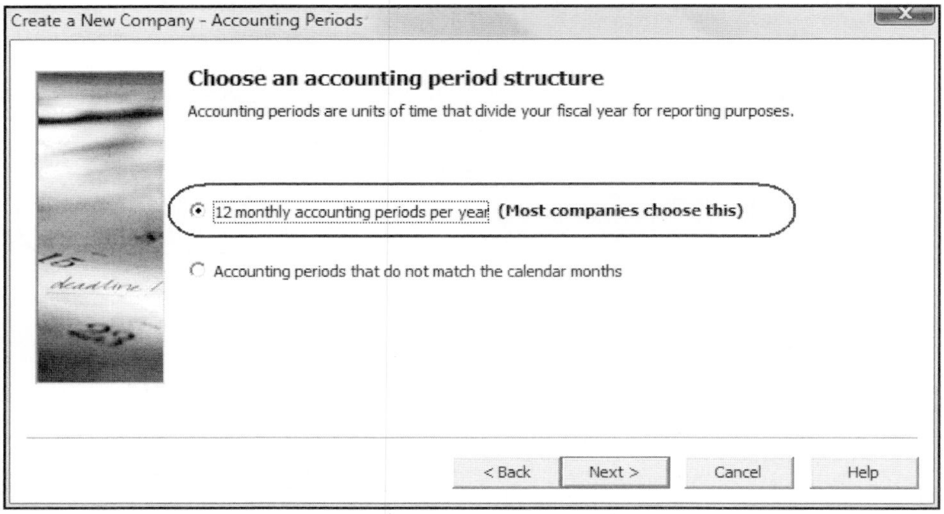

10. Accept the default for 12 monthly accounting periods per year by clicking 

. The Choose the first period of your fiscal year window appears. Select 2008.

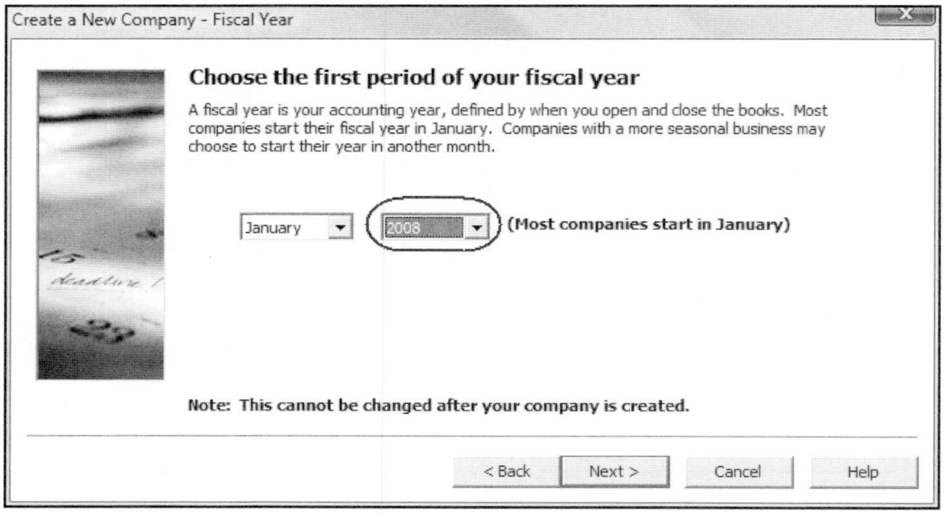

11. Make sure the Fiscal Year window shows January 2008. **This window is important. It cannot be changed after your company is created**. Click 

. The You are ready to create your company window appears.

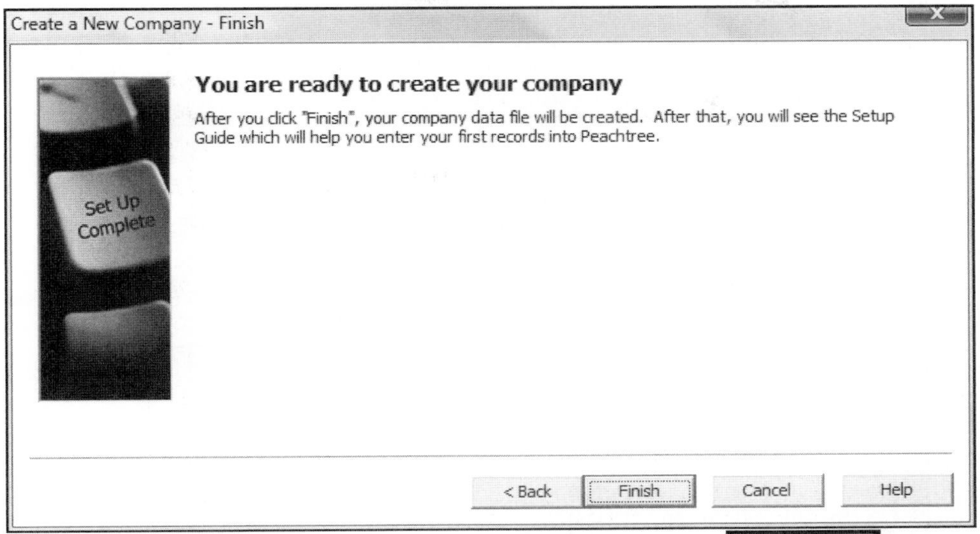

12. Read the information on the Finish window. Click [Finish]. After a few moments, the Have you started using credit cards for your Business? window appears, click [OK].

13. The Setup Guide window appears. Click on the box next to Don't show this screen at startup to put a checkmark in it– [☑ Don't show this screen at startup.]; click [Close]. The Peachtree Setup Guide window appears. Read what it says, then click [OK]. The title bar shows Peachtree Accounting: Jon Haney Design.

14. On the Navigation Bar, click [Business Status]. To set the Business Status page as your default page, from the toolbar select [Make this the default page]. When you open Jon Haney Design the Business Status page will open too.

15. On the toolbar (below the menu bar and Business Status), click on the Period button [Period]. The Change Accounting Period window appears. Click 10 – Oct 01, 2008 to Oct 31, 2008 to highlight it. Compare your Change Accounting Period window to the one shown on the next page.

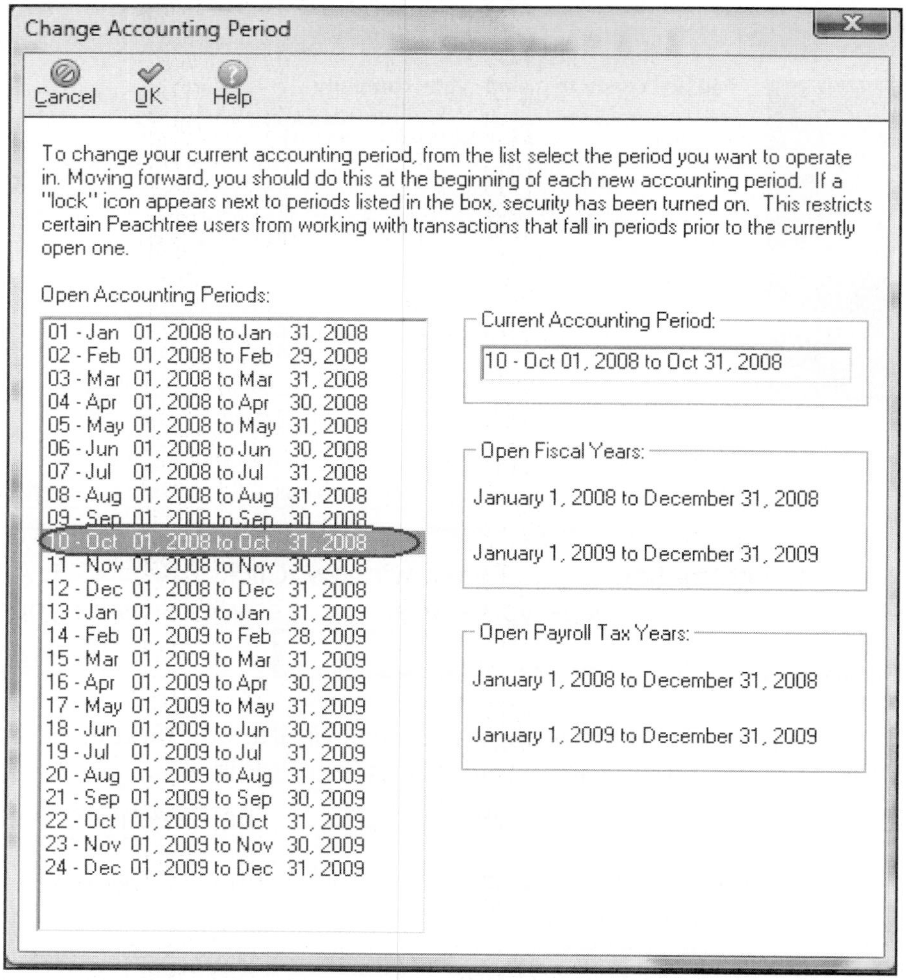

16. Make sure Period 10 is selected -- Period 10 - 10/01/08-10/31/08. October 2008 is the first month for recording transactions. Click OK.
17. If a window appears that says ask you to run an Internal Accounting Review, click No. Compare your Business Status window with the one shown on the next page. A partial window is shown. Scroll down to see all the information.

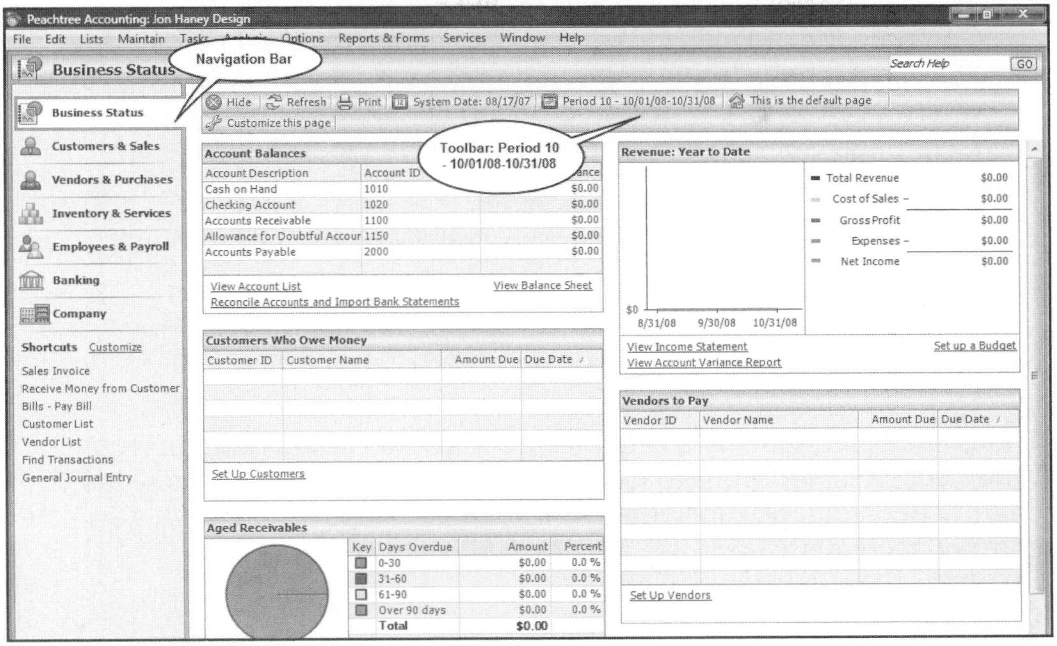

Read Me: *What is Peachtree's shortened name?*

To display information about your company, follow these steps:

1. From the menu bar, select Help; Customer Support and Service, File Statistics.

   Peachtree displays the company shortened name on the title bar. The Data File Statistics for XXXXXXXX window appears. (Substitute the Xs with your shortened name.) This represents the shortened name of the currently open company. Observe that there is also a Directory field at the bottom of the Data File Statistics window. The directory where Jon Haney Design resides is C:\Program Files\Sage Software\Peachtree\company\jonhande. (This assumes the default location was used. To go to the end of the Directory field, click on the field, then press <End>.)
2. Close the Data File Statistics window.
3. Click OK to close the Date File Statistics window.

Company Maintenance Information

Follow these steps to see information about your company.

1. From Peachtree's menu bar, select Maintain; Company Information.

2. Compare these fields to the company information set up on page 253. They should agree. Notice that the Directory field shows you where your company is stored on the computer: C:\Program Files\Sage Software\Peachtree\Company\jonhande. Make any needed corrections. Click to  return to the menu bar.

3. Continue with the next section, Chart of Accounts.

CHART OF ACCOUNTS

The chart of accounts is a list of all the accounts in the general ledger. When you selected Service Company from the list of business types, a chart of accounts was included. Follow these steps to edit PCA's sample chart of accounts.

Delete Accounts

1. From the Business Status page, link to View Account List. The Maintain Chart of Accounts window displays. The Account List appears. (*Or,* you can use the menu bar. Select Maintain; Chart of Accounts; in the Account ID field, click the down-arrow, continue with step 2.)

2. Double click Account ID, 1150, Allowance for Doubtful Account. The Maintain Chart of Accounts window appears.

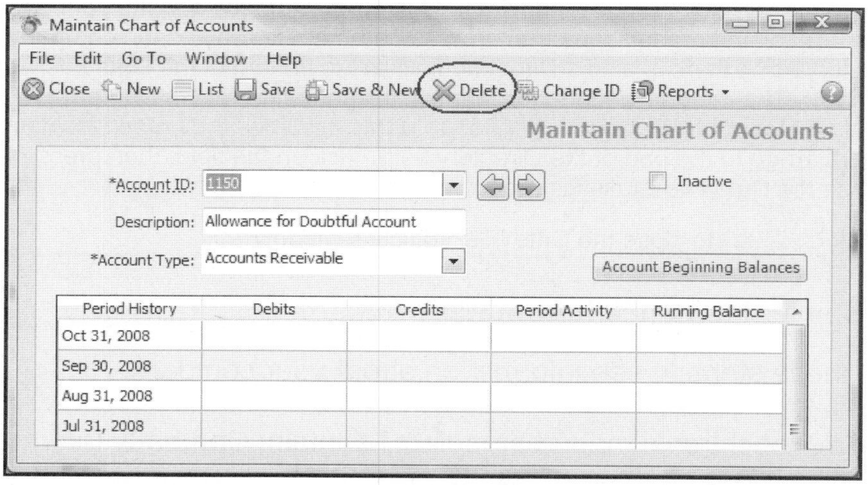

3. Click 

.

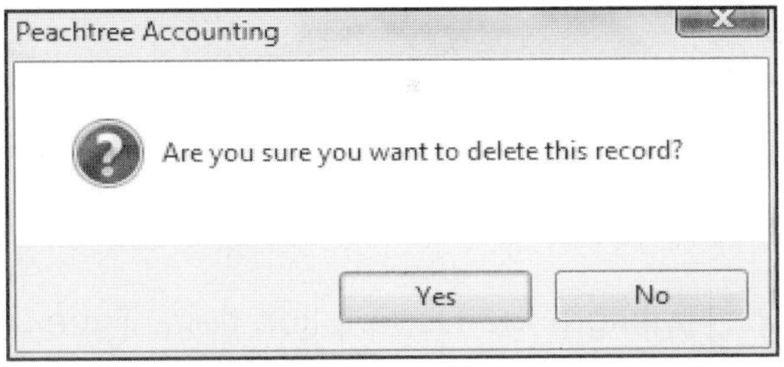

4. The Peachtree Accounting - Are you sure you want to delete this record? window appears.

5. Click 

.

6. Delete the following accounts. (*Hint:* On the Maintain Chart of Accounts window, type the account number in the Account ID field to expedite editing the chart of accounts.)

Acct. ID	**Account Description**
2310	Sales Tax Payable
2320	Deductions Payable
2330	Federal Payroll Taxes Payable
2340	FUTA Payable
2350	State Payroll Taxes Payable
2360	SUTA Payable
2370	Local Taxes Payable
2500	Current Portion Long-Term Debt
2700	Long-Term Debt - Noncurrent
4300	Other Income
5900	Inventory Adjustments
6050	Employee Benefit Programs Expense
6250	Other Taxes Expense
6650	Commissions and Fees Expense
7100	Gain/Loss on Sale of Assets Exp

Change Accounts

To change the name of an account, follow these steps:

1. On the Maintain Chart of Accounts window, type **3920**; Press <Tab> or <Enter>. Owner's Contribution appears in the Description field.

2. Highlight the Description field. Type **Jon Haney, Capital** (use your first and last name, Capital). Press <Tab> or <Enter>.

3. In the Account Type field, click on the down arrow. Select Equity-doesn't close. (When you change the Account Description of the accounts shown below step 5, you do *not* have to change the Account Type.)

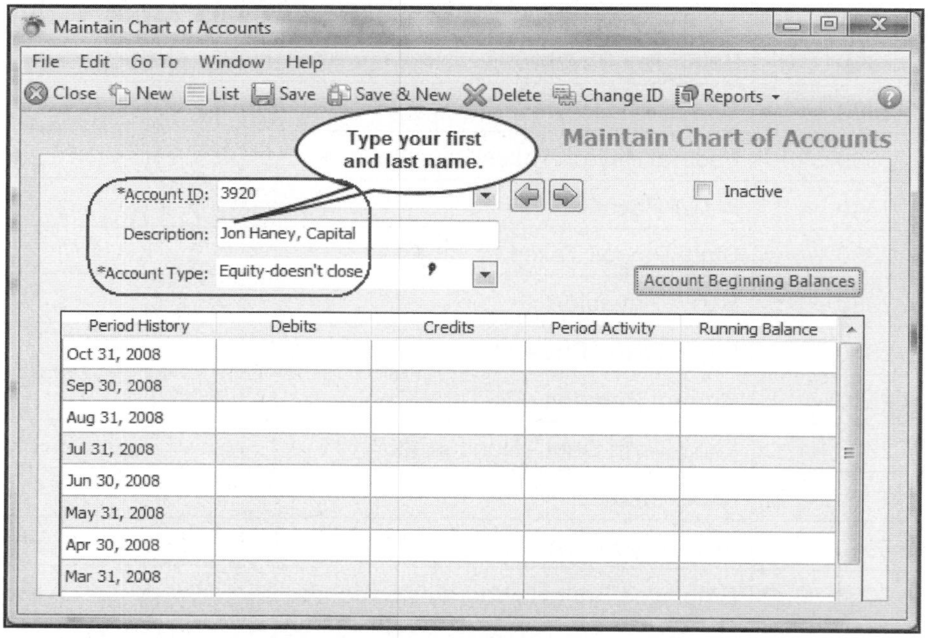

4. Click 

.

5. Change the names of the accounts shown on the next page.

Acct. ID	Account Description	New Account Description
1010	Cash on Hand	**Money Market Account**
1400	Prepaid Expenses	**Prepaid Rent**
1500	Property and Equipment	**Computer Equipment**
1900	Accum. Depreciation – Prop&Eqt	**Accum. Depreciation – Comp Eqt**
2000	Accounts Payable	**VISA Payable**
2400	Customer Deposits	**Publisher Advances**
3930	Owner's Draw	**Jon Haney, Draw** (your name, Draw)
4000	Professional Fees	**Teaching Income**
4050	Sales of Materials	**Royalty Income**
6100	Payroll Tax Expense	**Dues and Subscriptions**
6150	Bad Debt Expense	**Auto Registration**
6550	Other Office Expense	**Long Distance Co.**
6850	Service Charge Expense	**Bank Service Charge**
7050	Depreciation Expense	**Deprec. Exp. – Comp Eqt**

Add Accounts

To add an account to the Chart of Accounts, follow these steps:

1. On the Maintain Chart of Accounts window, click 

.

2. In the Account ID field, type **1040** and press **<Enter>**.

3. In the Description field, type **IRA Savings Account** and press **<Enter>**.

4. In the Account Type field, click on the down arrow. A list of account types drops down. Make sure that Cash is highlighted. If not, click once on Cash to select it.

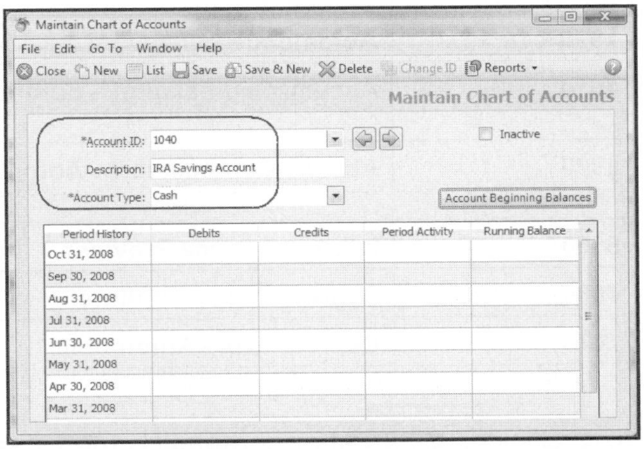

Read Me: *Why is the Account Type field important?*

Observe that the Account Type field shows Cash. This is an important field–the Account Type field classifies each account for the financial statements. For example, Account No. 1040, IRA Savings Account, is classified as Cash, which means this account will appear on the Balance Sheet, Statement of Cash Flow, and the Statement of Financial Position; but *not* on the Income Statement or Statement of Retained Earnings.

Always check that the Account Type field is correct so that accounts will be organized correctly on the financial statements.

5. Click Save & New. (*Hint:* What is the difference between Save & New and Save? If you click Save, the Account Type does not change. If you have a couple accounts with the same Account Type, click Save, then change the Account ID and Description. The Account Type stays the same.)

Add the following accounts:

Acct. ID	Account Description	Account Type
1045	**WI State Retirement**	Cash
1300	**Prepaid Insurance**	Other Current Assets
1450	**Supplies**	Other Current Assets
1510	**Furniture**	Fixed Assets
1520	**Automobile**	Fixed Assets
1910	**Accum. Depreciation – Furnitur**	Accumulated Depreciation
1920	**Accum. Depreciation – Automobi**	Accumulated Depreciation
6560	**Internet Service Provider**	Expenses
7060	**Deprec. Exp. - Furniture**	Expenses
7070	**Deprec. Exp. - Automobile**	Expenses

6. Click Close after completing the Chart of Accounts. You are returned to the Business Status page.

Displaying the Chart of Accounts

1. From the menu bar, click Reports & Forms; General Ledger.

2. At the Select a Report or Form window, click on the Chart of Accounts to highlight it.

3. Select 

.

> **Comment**
>
> Move the mouse to the blue arrows 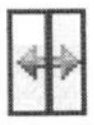 between columns. The cursor becomes a crossbar. Left click on the crossbar and drag the mouse to the right. After you have adjusted the Account Description column, click on the Print icon to print the chart of accounts. When you click on the Close icon, a window prompts that The report has been modified. Do you want to save it? Click No.

4. Compare your chart of accounts to the one on the next page.

Jon Haney Design
Chart of Accounts
As of Oct 31, 2008

Filter Criteria includes: Report order is by ID. Report is printed with Accounts having Zero Amounts and in Detail Format.

Account ID	Account Description	Active?	Account Type
1010	Money Market Account	Yes	Cash
1020	Checking Account	Yes	Cash
1040	IRA Savings Account	Yes	Cash
1045	WI State Retirement	Yes	Cash
1100	Accounts Receivable	Yes	Accounts Receivable
1200	Inventory	Yes	Inventory
1300	Prepaid Insurance	Yes	Other Current Assets
1400	Prepaid Rent	Yes	Other Current Assets
1450	Supplies	Yes	Other Current Assets
1500	Computer Equipment	Yes	Fixed Assets
1510	Furniture	Yes	Fixed Assets
1520	Automobile	Yes	Fixed Assets
1900	Accum. Depreciation - Comp Eqt	Yes	Accumulated Depreciation
1910	Accum. Depreciation - Furnitur	Yes	Accumulated Depreciation
1920	Accum. Depreciation - Automobi	Yes	Accumulated Depreciation
2000	VISA Payable	Yes	Accounts Payable
2380	Income Taxes Payable	Yes	Other Current Liabilities
2400	Publisher Advances	Yes	Other Current Liabilities
3910	Retained Earnings	Yes	Equity-Retained Earnings
3920	Jon Haney, Capital	Yes	Equity-doesn't close
3930	Jon Haney, Draw	Yes	Equity-gets closed
4000	Teaching Income	Yes	Income
4050	Royalty Income	Yes	Income
4100	Interest Income	Yes	Income
4200	Finance Charge Income	Yes	Income
4900	Sales/Fees Discounts	Yes	Income
5000	Cost of Sales	Yes	Cost of Sales
5400	Cost of Sales-Salary & Wage	Yes	Cost of Sales
6000	Wages Expense	Yes	Expenses
6100	Dues and Subscriptions	Yes	Expenses
6150	Auto Registration	Yes	Expenses
6200	Income Tax Expense	Yes	Expenses
6300	Rent or Lease Expense	Yes	Expenses
6350	Maintenance & Repairs Expense	Yes	Expenses
6400	Utilities Expense	Yes	Expenses
6450	Office Supplies Expense	Yes	Expenses
6500	Telephone Expense	Yes	Expenses
6550	Long Distance Co.	Yes	Expenses
6560	Internet Service Provider	Yes	Expenses
6600	Advertising Expense	Yes	Expenses
6800	Freight Expense	Yes	Expenses
6850	Bank Service Charge	Yes	Expenses
6900	Purchase Disc-Expense Items	Yes	Expenses
6950	Insurance Expense	Yes	Expenses
7050	Deprec. Exp. - Comp Eqt	Yes	Expenses
7060	Deprec. Exp. - Furniture	Yes	Expenses
7070	Deprec. Exp. - Automobile	Yes	Expenses

Observe that the chart of accounts is dated As of Oct 31, 2008. Since Peachtree posts on the last day of the month, your reports will show October 31, 2008 as the date.

Notice that Jon Haney's chart of accounts includes Account No. 3910, Retained Earnings. At the end of every fiscal year, the temporary owner's equity accounts (revenues, expenses, and drawing) are closed to a permanent owner's equity account. In PCA, there are two permanent owner's equity accounts: the owner's capital account and the Retained Earnings account. PCA closes the temporary accounts to the Retained Earnings account. This will be discussed in more detail in Chapter 10 when you close the fiscal year. In order to post transactions to the general ledger, Peachtree requires a Retained Earnings account.

5. To print the Chart of Accounts, click 

. When the Print window appears, make the selections to print. Check your Chart of Accounts to make sure that you have deleted accounts and made the necessary changes and additions.

6. Click 

two times to return to the Business Status page. If you need to edit your Chart, select Maintain, then Chart of Accounts, *or* from the Business Status page, link to View Account List.

The next section describes how to enter the chart of accounts beginning balances. After entering the beginning balances and using Windows Explorer (pages 275 and 276) to see the size of Jon Haney's company file, you back up the company's data.

ENTERING CHART OF ACCOUNTS BEGINNING BALANCES

Mr. Haney has hired you to do his monthly record keeping. In order to begin accounting tasks for Mr. Haney, you asked him for a ***Balance Sheet***. A Balance Sheet lists the types and amounts of assets, liabilities, and equity as of a specific date. A balance sheet is also called a ***statement of financial position***.

The October 1, 2008 balance sheet is shown on the next page.

Jon Haney Design Balance Sheet **October 1, 2008**		
ASSETS		
Current Assets		
1010 - Money Market Account	$ 6,700.00	
1020 - Checking Account	7,750.75	
1040 - IRA Savings Account	27,730.35	
1045 - WI State Retirement	35,612.00	
1300 - Prepaid Insurance	2,100.00	
1400 - Prepaid Rent	600.00	
1450 - Supplies	1,771.83	
Total Current Assets		$ 82,264.93
Property and Equipment		
1500 - Computer Equipment	$ 6,800.00	
1510 - Furniture	5,000.00	
1520 - Automobile	19,000.00	
Total Property and Equipment		30,800.00
Total Assets		$ 113,064.93
LIABILITIES AND CAPITAL		
Current Liabilities		
2000 - VISA Payable	$ 5,250.65	
Total Current Liabilities		$ 5,250.65
Capital		
3920 - Jon Haney, Capital		107,814.28
Total Liabilities and Capital		$ 113,064.93

The information in this Balance Sheet will be the basis for recording Mr. Haney's beginning balances.

Follow these steps to record Jon Haney's beginning balances.

1. Click Maintain, then Chart of Accounts.

2. Click Account Beginning Balances.

   Observe that the balance sheet on page 268 is for October 1, 2008. **Beginning balances must be set for the preceding month–September 1 through 30, 2008**. You select September 1 through 30, 2008, because Peachtree posts on the last day of the month (September 30). When you select September 1 through 30, 2008, as your chart of accounts beginning balance period, your journals will start on October 1, 2008, and your reports will be dated October 31, 2008. **The September 30 ending balance is the October 1 beginning balance.**

   In Chapter 10, you print end-of-year financial statements. In order for your end-of-year financial statements to show the correct current month and year-to-date amounts, you *must* set your beginning balances for the preceding month. *Remember, you must select September 1 through 30, 2008, as the period for setting beginning balances. The beginning balance period cannot be changed later.*

3. Scroll down the Select Period list. Click From 9/1/08 through 9/30/08 to highlight it.

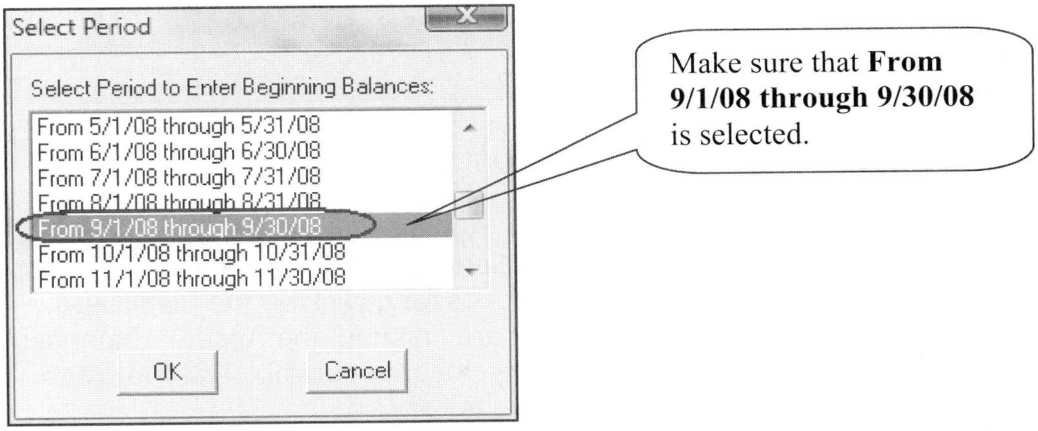

Check this window. The period you select should be From 9/1/08 through 9/30/08.

4. Make sure that you have selected **From 9/1/08 through 9/30/08** on the Select Period window. You cannot change this period later. *Make sure the period is correct*, then click OK .

5. The Chart of Accounts Beginning Balances window appears. Below the icon bar, make sure it shows **Beginning Balances as of September 30, 2008**. The Assets, Expenses column is highlighted. Account No. 1010, Money Market Account is selected. A magenta line is placed around the row. Type **6700** in the Assets, Expenses column. Press **<Enter>**.

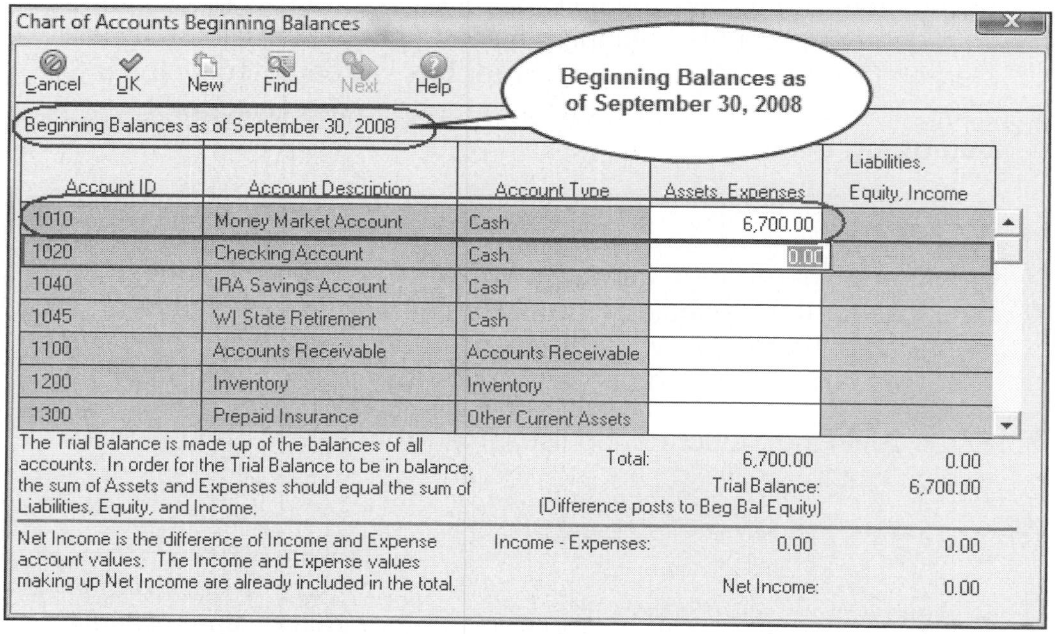

6. Account No. 1020, Checking Account is selected. Type **7750.75** and press **<Enter>**.

   Continue entering the beginning balances using the Balance Sheet on page 268. For credit balances, if necessary, click on the Liabilities, Equity, Income column. When you are finished, the Assets, Expenses column equals the Liabilities, Equity, Income column. This indicates that there are equal debits and credits.

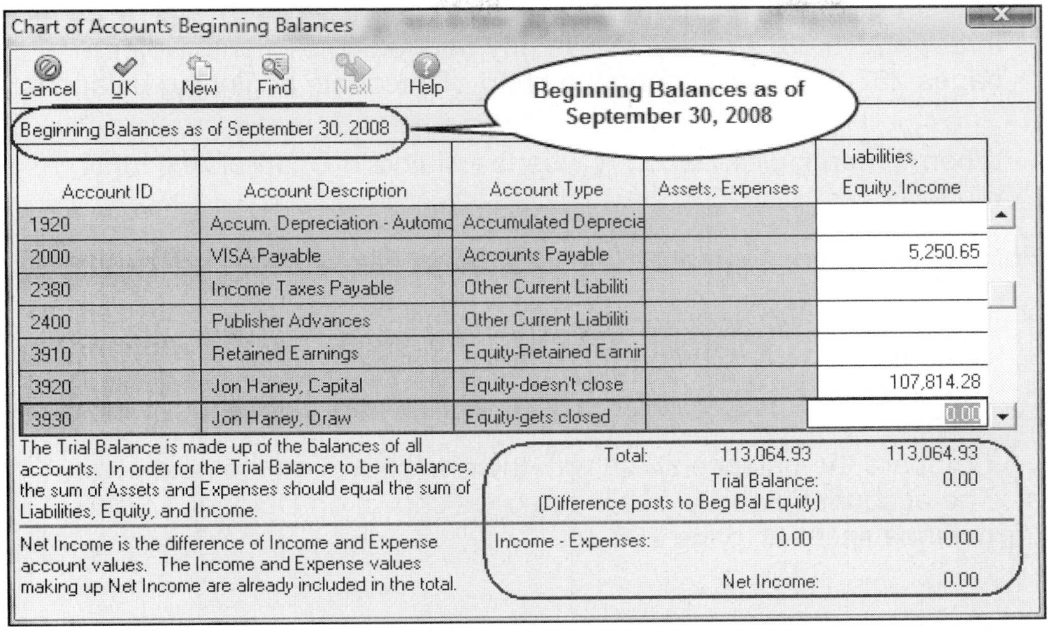
Chart of Accounts Beginning Balances
Cancel
OK
New
Find
Next
Help
Beginning Balances as of September 30, 2008
Beginning Balances as of September 30, 2008
Account ID
Account Description
Account Type
Assets, Expenses
Liabilities, Equity, Income
1920 Accum. Depreciation - Automo Accumulated Deprecia
2000 VISA Payable Accounts Payable 5,250.65
2380 Income Taxes Payable Other Current Liabiliti
2400 Publisher Advances Other Current Liabiliti
3910 Retained Earnings Equity-Retained Earnir
3920 Jon Haney, Capital Equity-doesn't close 107,814.28
3930 Jon Haney, Draw Equity-gets closed 0.00
The Trial Balance is made up of the balances of all accounts. In order for the Trial Balance to be in balance, the sum of Assets and Expenses should equal the sum of Liabilities, Equity, and Income.
Total: 113,064.93 113,064.93
Trial Balance: 0.00
(Difference posts to Beg Bal Equity)
Net Income is the difference of Income and Expense account values. The Income and Expense values making up Net Income are already included in the total.
Income - Expenses: 0.00 0.00
Net Income: 0.00

Comment
What if your Trial Balance does *not* show 0.00? Make sure that debit balances for assets and credit balances for liabilities and capital accounts were entered correctly.

Make sure that your beginning balances are as of September 30, 2008. If you enter your balances for the wrong month (period), your financial statements will not show the current month and year-to-date amounts correctly. Remember, Chapters 9 and 10 work together. If beginning balances are incorrect in Chapter 9, Chapter 10's financial statements will be incorrect.

7. Click [OK]. A window appears briefly that says Creating Journal Entries.

8. At the Maintain Chart of Accounts window, click [Close].

   To check your chart of accounts beginning balances, select Maintain, Chart of Accounts, [Account Beginning Balances]; then select the From 9/1/08 through 9/30/08, 

. Make any needed corrections. Refer to pages 267-272 for entering the chart of accounts beginning balances.

When through, click 

. Close the Maintain Chart of Accounts window.

Follow these steps to print a Balance Sheet:

1. From the menu bar, select Reports & Forms, then Financial Statements. The <Standard> Balance Sheet is highlighted. Make the selections to display or print.

   Compare the balance sheet with the one shown on the next page. The account balances match the ones shown on October 1, 2008 balance sheet on page 268.

Jon Haney Design
Balance Sheet
October 31, 2008

ASSETS

Current Assets				
Money Market Account	$	6,700.00		
Checking Account		7,750.75		
IRA Savings Account		27,730.35		
WI State Retirement		35,612.00		
Prepaid Insurance		2,100.00		
Prepaid Rent		600.00		
Supplies		1,771.83		
Total Current Assets				82,264.93
Property and Equipment				
Computer Equipment		6,800.00		
Furniture		5,000.00		
Automobile		19,000.00		
Total Property and Equipment				30,800.00
Other Assets				
Total Other Assets				0.00
Total Assets			$	113,064.93

LIABILITIES AND CAPITAL

Current Liabilities				
VISA Payable	$	5,250.65		
Total Current Liabilities				5,250.65
Long-Term Liabilities				
Total Long-Term Liabilities				0.00
Total Liabilities				5,250.65
Capital				
Jon Haney, Capital		107,814.28		
Net Income		0.00		
Total Capital				107,814.28
Total Liabilities & Capital			$	113,064.93

2. Close the Balance Sheet and Select a Report or Form window.

3. On the Business Status page's toolbar, click Refresh. Notice that the account balances are updated. Balances shown in red are credit balances.

Account Balances — Customize

Account Description	Account ID	Balance
Money Market Account	1010	$6,700.00
Checking Account	1020	$7,750.75
IRA Savings Account	1040	$27,730.35
WI State Retirement	1045	$35,612.00
Accounts Receivable	1100	$0.00
VISA Payable	2000	($5,250.65)

View Account List — View Balance Sheet
Reconcile Accounts and Import Bank Statements

4. Observe that there are links to View Account List and View Balance Sheet. Link to View Account List to see all the accounts and their Running Balance. A partial Account List is shown below. (*Hint:* Accounts shown in red with a parenthesis are credit balances.) These account balances agree with the Balance Sheet shown on page 273.

Account ID	Description	Type	Running Balance
1010	Money Market Account	Cash	$6,700.00
1020	Checking Account	Cash	$7,750.75
1040	IRA Savings Account	Cash	$27,730.35
1045	WI State Retirement	Cash	$35,612.00
1100	Accounts Receivable	Accounts Receivable	$0.00
1200	Inventory	Inventory	$0.00
1300	Prepaid Insurance	Other Current Assets	$2,100.00
1400	Prepaid Rent	Other Current Assets	$600.00
1450	Supplies	Other Current Assets	$1,771.83
1500	Computer Equipment	Fixed Assets	$6,800.00
1510	Furniture	Fixed Assets	$5,000.00
1520	Automobile	Fixed Assets	$19,000.00
1900	Accum. Depreciation - Comp Eqt	Accumulated Depreciation	$0.00
1910	Accum. Depreciation - Furnitur	Accumulated Depreciation	$0.00
1920	Accum. Depreciation - Automobi	Accumulated Depreciation	$0.00
2000	VISA Payable	Accounts Payable	($5,250.65)
2380	Income Taxes Payable	Other Current Liabilities	$0.00
2400	Publisher Advances	Other Current Liabilities	$0.00
3910	Retained Earnings	Equity-Retained Earnings	$0.00
3920	Jon Haney, Capital	Equity-does not close	($107,814.28)

5. Close the Account List.

USING WINDOWS EXPLORER TO SEE THE FILE SIZE

To see the size of the Jon Haney Design file, following these steps.

1. Right-click  [start button]; left-click Explore.

2. Go to the location of the company data. The default program and data path is C:\Program Files\Sage Software\Peachtree\ Company. Click on the Company folder.

3. Right-click on the jonhande folder (or the one with your shortened name).

4. Left-click Properties. The default location is drive C. The xxxxxxxx Properties window is shown below. (Substitute the X's for your shortened name.)

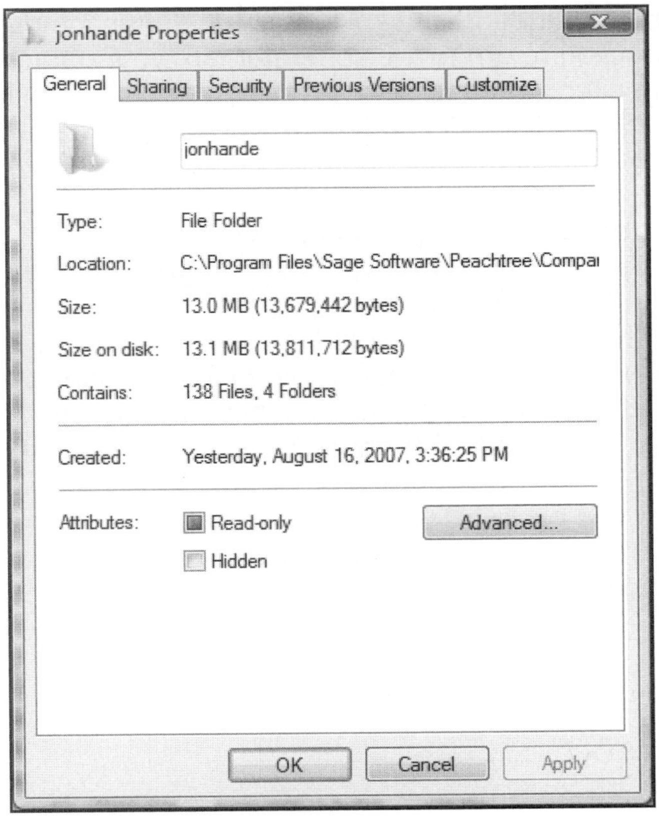

Observe that the size of the file is 13.0 MB (13,679,442 bytes). That means if you want to save all the data contained in Jon Haney folder, you should use Windows Explorer to copy, then paste the jonhande subfolder from drive C to a USB drive, Zip disk, CD, or DVD. The jonhande folder is too large for a floppy disk. If you use Windows Explorer to copy/paste, you need a USB drive, Zip disk, CD, or DVD because of the size of the Jon Haney Design subfolder. (Your file size may differ from the jonhande Properties window shown on page 275. This is okay.)

When you are finished comparing your properties window, click 

, then  on the Windows Explorer title bar.

BACKING UP COMPANY DATA

At this point you should back up your data. When using PCA, information is automatically saved to the hard drive of the computer. In a classroom setting, a number of students may be using the same computer. This means that when you return to the computer lab, your data will be gone. Backing up data simply means saving it to a hard drive location or external media. Saving (backing up) your data means that it will be available when you want to work again.

In this textbook, detailed steps are shown for backing up to Peachtree's default hard drive location: C:\Program Files\Sage Software\Peachtree\Company\jonhande [or, your shortened name]. The chart on pages 248-249 shows you the size of the backup files. If you want to backup to external media, you can check the file size before backing up. A blank, formatted floppy disk holds 1,440,000 bytes of data (about 1440 KB), CD-Rs, DVD-Rs, Zip disks, and USB drives have larger capacities.

When you make this back up, you are saving the new company set up information, the revised chart of accounts, and the chart of accounts beginning balances.

Comment

When you back up, you are saving to the current point in Peachtree. Each backup made should have a different backup name (file name) to distinguish one backup from another. In this way, if you need to restore to an earlier backup, you have the data for that purpose.

Remember, you can Restore if you need to go back to an earlier point in the company's data. Without a backup file, you cannot go back to an earlier point in the data. Since Chapters 9 and 10 work together, your backup files are important.

In the business world, backups are unique to each business: daily, weekly, monthly. *Remember, back up before you leave the computer lab!*

Follow these steps to back up Jon Haney's company:

1. From the Navigation Bar, click 

. In the Data Maintenance list, link to Back up. The Back Up Company window appears. Read the information on this window. (Make sure to Include company name in the backup file name field is *unchecked*.)

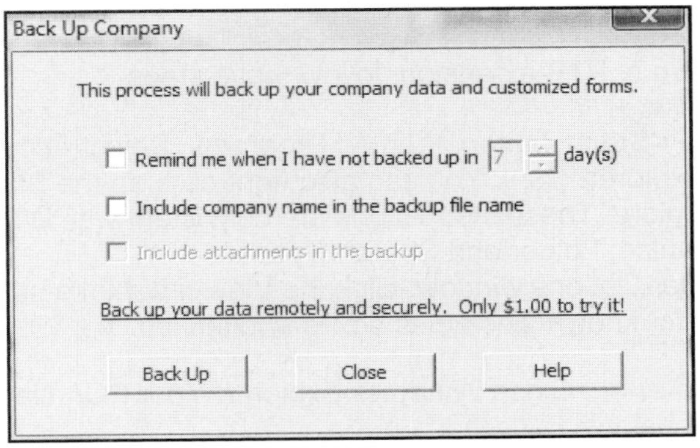

2. Click 

.

3. The Save Backup for Jon Haney Design [*or, your name]* as window appears. The instructions that follow assume the default location is used for backing up. *If you are backing up to a specific hard drive location or to external media, select the appropriate location in the Save in field.*

4. Type **Chapter 9 Begin** in the File name field.

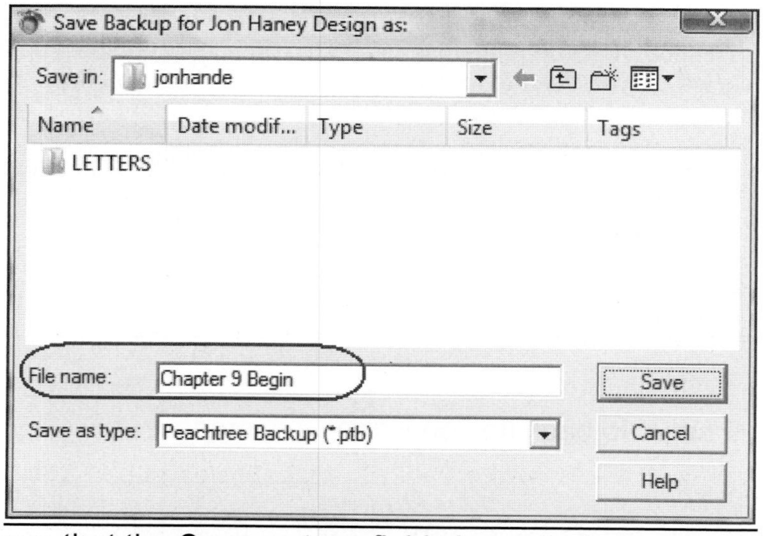

Observe that the Save as type field shows that you are making a Peachtree Backup (*.ptb), which is abbreviated ptb. This is the standard default for Peachtree backups.

Comment

If you do *not* have a .PTB extension, follow these steps:

1. Click on the **<Start>** button, then All Programs. Select Accessories, then Windows Explorer. (*Hint:* You can also right-click on the Start button; left-click Explore. These instructions are consistent with Windows Vista.)
2. Select Organize; Folder and Search Options.
3. On the Folder Options window, click the View tab. Make sure the Hide extensions for known files types box is *unchecked*.
4. Click 

. Close Windows Explorer. Your PCA files will now have file extensions.

5. Click 

.

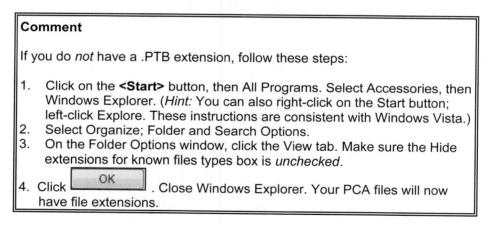

6. A window appears that says This company backup will require approximately 3.31MB.

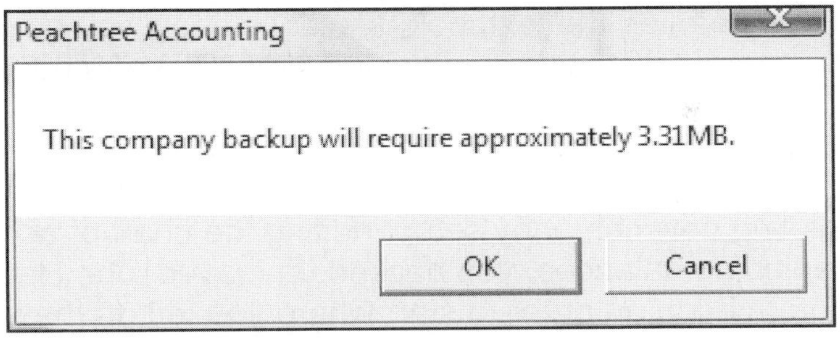

7. Click OK. When the Back Up Company scale is 100% complete, you have successfully backed up to the current point in your company's data.

> **Read Me: Windows Vista–Problem Backing Up to USB Drive**
>
> Because of Windows Vista operating system security features, you need to backup to your desktop first. Then copy the backup file from your desktop to the USB drive. Refer to Appendix A, Problem Backing Up to USB Drive or Other External Media, pages 700-702 for detailed steps.

8. Click File; Exit to exit Peachtree.

Follow these steps to see the size of the backup file.

1. Right-click [start button]; left-click Explore.
2. Go to the location of your backup file. If you backed up to the default location it is C:\Program Files\Sage Software\Peachtree\company\jonhande [*or,* your directory name]. Compare your file size to the one shown below.

Name	Date modified	Type	Size	Tags
Chapter 9 Begin.ptb	8/17/2007 1:17 PM	PTB File	1,344 KB	

The Name of the file is Chapter 9 Begin.ptb; the Size of the file is 1,344 KB; the Type is PTB File. The Date Modified will differ. Since the backup file is 1,344 KB, and a disk holds 1.44MB of data, you can save this backup file on a blank, formatted disk. *(Your file size may differ slightly.)* Other external media may also be used. As mentioned earlier, the textbook directions show you how to back up to Peachtree's default hard drive location. Close Windows Explorer.

RESTORING COMPANY DATA

After completing new company setup, editing the chart of accounts, and entering beginning balances, you backed up (saved) Jon Haney Design company information. In order to start where you left off the last time you backed up, you use Peachtree's Restore Wizard.

In the steps that follow you are shown how to restore the Peachtree backup file (.ptb extension). You made this backup on pages 276-279. Peachtree backups are compressed files which means that the file is made smaller.

1. Start Peachtree. Each time you exit Peachtree, then start the program, a Setup Guide window may appear. Since you are *not* going to use the Setup Guide, click Close. When the Peachtree Setup Guide window appears, click OK.
2. These instructions assume that the Peachtree Accounting: Jon Haney [your name] Design window appears. If *not*, click File; Open Previous Company, then select Jon Haney Design.

   ➢ **Troubleshooting: What if Jon Haney Design (or another name Design) is not shown?**

   a. Click File; Close Company.

   b. From Peachtree's startup window, select Open an existing company.

   c. Click Browse. The Open Company window appears.

   d. If Jon Haney Design (or, other name Design) is shown select it, and then click OK. Go to page 281, step 3, and follow the steps to restore your data.

   e. If *no Design company is shown*, click Close.

f. There are three menu bar options--

. Click File; Restore.

g. The Select Backup File window appears. Click 

. In the Look in field, select the appropriate location of your backup file. If necessary, put external media in the drive and open the backup file from that location.

h. Select the file you backed up, Chapter 9 Begin.ptb; click 

.

i. Make sure the Location field shows the correct place for the Chapter 9 Begin.ptb file. Click 

.

j. The Select Company window appears. Click on the radio button next to A New Company.

Read Me

Observe that there are two options on the Select Company window: An Existing Company *and* A New Company. If you select A New Company, then the company will be named exactly as the backup file you selected. You can restore to an existing company—one that is previously set up—*or* you can restore to a new company, bypassing the process of setting up a new company.

Let's say you wanted to restore a backup file for a company that was *not* set up in Peachtree. Some computer labs delete directories from the hard drive; for example, you have a back up file but the company, in this case Jon Haney Design, is *not* listed as a Peachtree company. If you start Peachtree and you *cannot* select the appropriate company, use the Restore Wizard to select A New Company. Using your backup file, and the selection for A New Company, you are able to start where you left off the last time you used Peachtree.

k. The Company Name field shows Jon Haney Design. The Location field shows C:\Program Files\Sage Software\Peachtree\Company\jonhande. (Or your shortened company name; the last two letters of the location field shows "de.") Click 

. Continue with step 5 on page 282.

3. From the Navigation Bar, click 

; link to Restore. The Select Backup File window appears. If the location field shows the correct location for the Chapter 9 Begin.ptb back up file, click Next >. (*Or, click* Browse, *then select the appropriate location of the Chapter 9.ptb backup file; click* Next >.)

4. The Select Company window appears. The radio button next to An Existing Company is selected. The Company name field shows Jon Haney Design [or your name Design]; the Location field shows C:\Program Files\Sage Software\Peachtree\Company\ jonhande (or the appropriate shortened company name). Click Next >.[3]
5. The Restore Options window appears. Make sure that the box next to Company Data is *checked*. Click Next >.
6. The Confirmation window appears. Check the From and To fields to make sure they are correct. Click Finish. When the Restore Company scale is 100% complete, your data is restored.

Now that you have restored Jon Haney's data, you are ready to continue. *Remember before you exit PCA, make a backup of your work.*

Comment

In the Preface on page xix, you were instructed to select manual and 2 decimal places in the Decimal Entry and Number of December Places fields. If you did *not* do this, follow these steps:

1. From the menu bar, click Options; Global.
2. In the Decimal Entry field, click Manual. When Manual is selected, a black circle is placed within a circle (radio button).
3. In the Quantity fields, Standard fields, and Unit Price fields make sure **2** is selected.
4. Click OK.

Check the Global Settings shown on pages xix-xx. In order for your windows to look like the ones shown in this textbook, you need to have the *same* global settings as the ones shown on pages xix-xx (Preface). When global options are selected, this feature is in effect for all companies.

[3]If Jon Haney Design is *not* shown in the Company Name field, refer to Troubleshooting, steps a. – j., pages 280-281. (*Hint:* Cancel the Restore Wizard, then browse to the location of your Chapter 9 Begin.ptb backup file.)

You just learned how to use information from a Balance Sheet for an opening entry and then you saved your beginning or starting data. Now you are going to see how Mr. Haney's check register can provide information for Cash Receipts Journal entries and Cash Disbursements Journal entries for the month of October 2008.

RECORDING ENTRIES IN THE CASH RECEIPTS JOURNAL AND CASH DISBURSEMENTS JOURNAL

In PCA, the Receipts window is used to record deposits. When you save a receipt, PCA automatically journalizes the entry in the Cash Receipts Journal. When Mr. Haney writes a check, this disbursement is recorded in the Write Checks window. When you save the recorded check, PCA automatically journalizes the entry in the Cash Disbursements Journal.

Peachtree's write checks task is a simplified version of the Payments window. In this chapter, use the Write Checks window to issue a check for expenses, assets, or owner's draw.

Mr. Haney's check register has the information necessary to record entries for the month of October. Since Mr. Haney is a new client, information from his Balance Sheet was used for an opening entry. Now his check register has the financial information for the rest of the month.

Follow these steps to show the cash balance on the Receipts window and Payments window.

1. From the menu bar, click Options, Global.

2. Make sure the box next to Recalculate cash balance automatically in Receipts, Payments, and Payroll Entry has a check mark next to it.

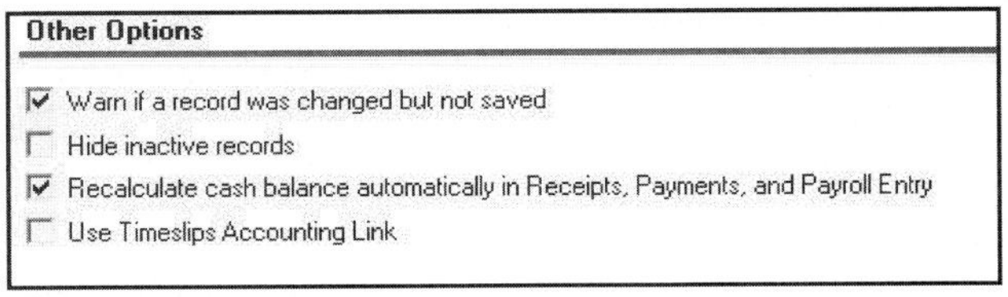

3. Click 

. When you use the Receipts window or Write Checks window, the check register balance agrees with the Cash Account balance shown on these windows.

Mr. Haney's check register shows an October 1 deposit of $10,000. A section of Mr. Haney's check register is shown.

Check Number	Date	Description of Transaction	Payment	Deposit	Balance
	9/30				*7,750.75*
	10/1	**Deposit (publisher's advance)**		**10,000.00**	**17,750.75**

Follow these steps to record the October 1 deposit from Mr. Haney's check register:

1. From the menu bar, select Tasks; Receipts. The Select a Cash Account window displays. If necessary click on the down arrow to select Checking Account.

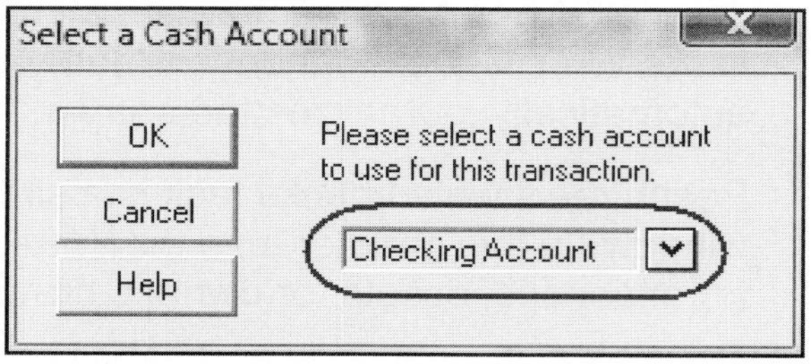

2. Click  . The Receipts window displays.

3. Your cursor is in the Deposit ticket ID field. Type **10/01/08**. (*Hint: Use the date of the deposit for the Deposit ticket ID field.*)

4. Click on the Name field. Type **Deposit** in the Name field.

5. Click on the Reference field. Type **Advance** in the Reference field. Press **<Enter>** two times.

6. Accept the default for Oct 1, 2008 in the Date field by pressing **<Enter>**.

7. Verify that the Payment Method is Check and that Account No. 1020, Checking Account, is displayed in the Cash Account.

8. The Cash Account Balance field displays $7,750.75. This agrees with the partial check register balance shown above.

9. Make sure that the Apply to Revenues tab is selected. Click once on the Quantity column. Type **1** in the Quantity column. Press the **<Enter>** key two times.

10. Type **Publisher's advance** in the Description column. Press **<Enter>**.

11. Click  in the GL Account column. Select Account No. 2400, Publisher Advances.

12. Type **10000** in the Unit Price column.

Comment

When you enter **10000** does 100.00 display in the Unit Price field rather than 10,000.00? To change the global settings for two decimal places, follow these steps. (These steps are also shown in the Preface, pages xix, step 3.)

1. From the menu bar, click Options; Global.
2. In the Decimal Entry field, click Manual. When Manual is selected, a black circle is placed within a circle (radio button).
3. The Quantity fields, Standard fields, and Unit Price fields, make sure that **2** is selected.
4. Click 

.

When global options are selected, this feature is in effect for all companies.

13. Press the **<Enter>** key two times. Compare your Receipts window to the one shown on the next page. If your window looks different, refer to the global settings, Preface, pages xix-xx.

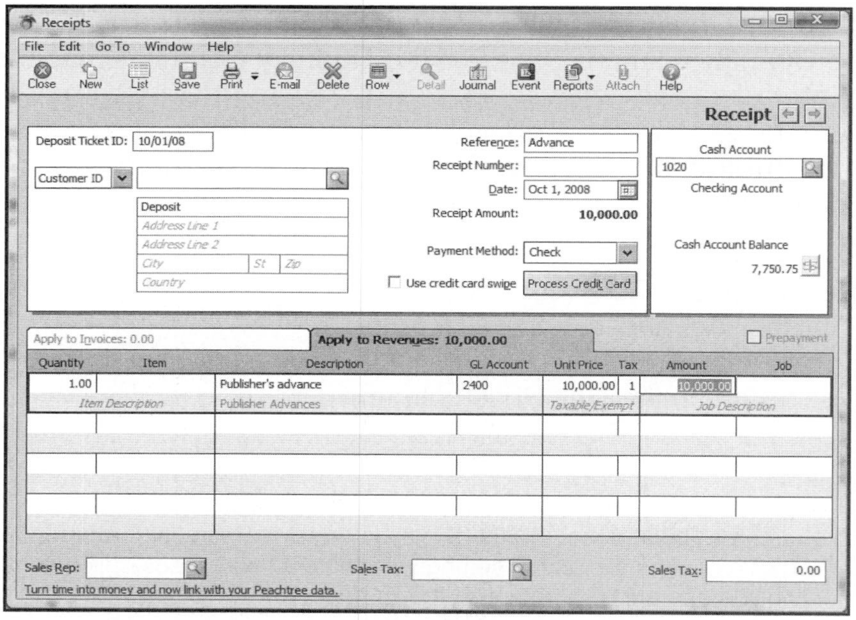

14. Click 

to post this entry. After you post, the Cash Account Balance field shows the same balance, $17,750.75, as the partial check register shown below. The Receipts window is ready for another transaction and the transaction is posted to the Cash Receipts Journal.

15. Click 

to close the Receipts window. Or, you can minimize the Receipts window by clicking on the minimize button  on the Receipts window title bar.

You use Write Checks for Check No. 4001. A section of the check register is shown below.

Ck. No.	Date	Description of Transaction	Payment	Deposit	Balance
					7,750.75
	10/1	*Deposit (publisher's advance)*		*10,000.00*	*17,750.75*
4001	**10/2**	**Transfer to Money Market Account**	**6,000.00**		**11,750.75**

From the Navigation Bar, click 

. Observe that the Banking Tasks diagram appears. In this chapter you focus on banking; in Part 3 (Chapters 11-14), you work with customers and vendors to receive money and enter bills.

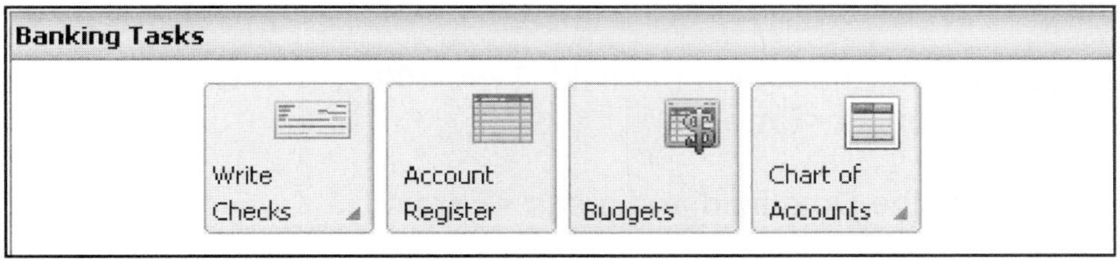

Read Me: Navigation Bar or Menu Bar

In this textbook, you are going to use *both* menu bar selections and the Navigation Bar. In PCA 2008, there are two ways to access features. You can make selections from the menu bar *or* the Navigation Bar. Throughout the textbook, these two methods are shown.

Use these steps to enter Check No. 4001 and post it to the Cash Disbursements Journal.

1. From the Banking page, click 

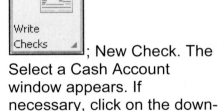

; New Check. The Select a Cash Account window appears. If necessary, click on the down-arrow to select the Checking Account.

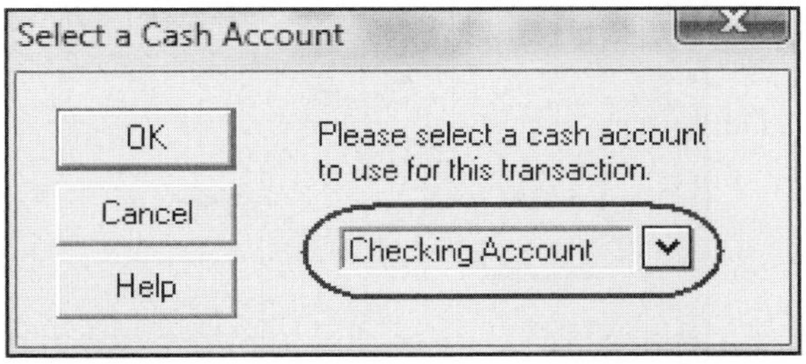

2. Click 

.

3. The Write Checks window displays. Click on the Pay to the Order of, Name field. Type **Money Market Account**.

4. Click [icon] in the Expense Account field. The Chart of Accounts list is displayed. Even though you are *not* charging Check No. 4001 against an expense account, you use the Expense Account field to select the appropriate account. Select Account No.1010, Money Market Account. The Description field is automatically completed with Money Market Account.

5. Click on the Check Number field. Type **4001** in the Check Number field and press **<Enter>**.

6. Type **2** in the Date field and press **<Enter>**.

7. Verify that the Cash Account Balance field shows $17,750.75. This agrees with the partial check register on page 286 (beginning balance plus publisher's advance). If the Cash Account Balance field does not agree with your check register, see the instructions on page 283, steps 1-3, for setting the global options for recalculating the cash balance for receipts, payments, and payroll.

8. Type **6000** in the $ field. Press **<Enter>**. Observe that the check is completed.

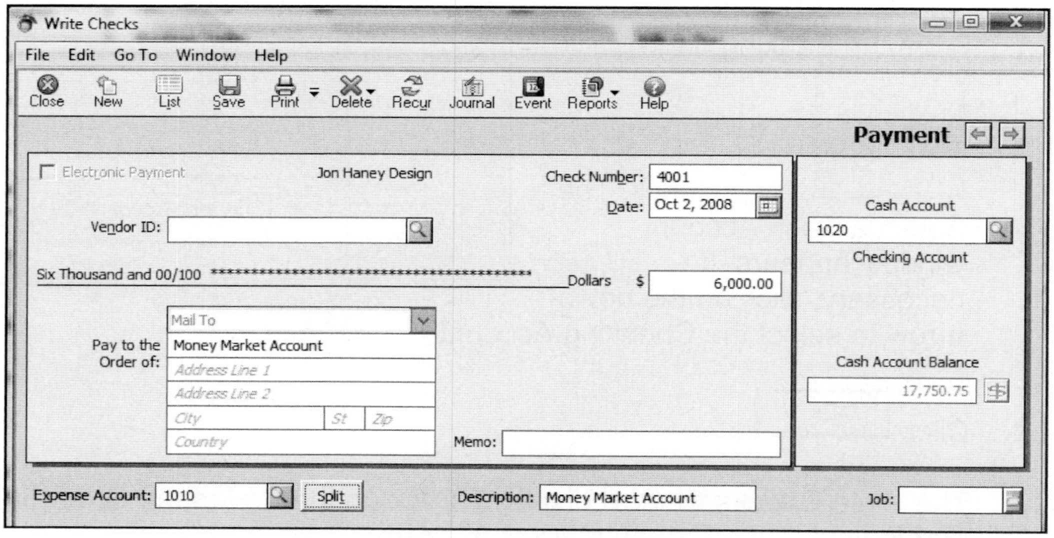

9. Click 

to post your entry to the Cash Disbursements Journal. Verify that the Cash Account Balance field displays the October 2 balance (this is the same balance, $11,750.75, as the partial check register on page 286). You are ready for your next transaction. (*Hint: you may need to change the date to 10/2/08 to see the correct cash balance.*)

10. Click 

to return to the Banking Tasks page. Or, minimize the Write Checks window.

Comment
PCA automatically completes the Check Number field once the first number is typed. After you type another reference in the Check Number field (for example, ATM), then you need to type the appropriate check number.

In accounting, you learn that source documents are used to show written evidence of a business transaction or events. Examples of source documents are sales invoices, purchase invoices, and in this case, Mr. Haney's check register for his checking account. Starting with the ATM withdrawal on October 3 for $200, record the transactions shown in the check register on pages 290 and 291 in the Cash Disbursements Journal (Banking; Write Checks, New Checks) or Cash Receipts Journal (Tasks; Receipts). Assign each transaction in the check register an appropriate account number from Mr. Haney's Chart of Accounts. Some of the transactions listed in Mr. Haney's check register are for the same date. Record individual journal entries for each check number, deposit, or ATM transaction.

Each deposit (cash or check received) is a debit to Account No. 1020, Checking Account, and is recorded in the Cash Receipts Journal using the Receipts task. On the Receipts window, you select the appropriate general ledger account for the credit part of the entry. The debit part of the entry is automatically entered for Account No. 1020, Checking Account.

Each payment (check issued and ATM withdrawal) listed on the check register is a credit to Account No. 1020, Checking Account, and is recorded in the Cash Disbursements Journal using the Write Checks window. On the Write Checks window, you select the appropriate general ledger account for the debit part of the entry. The credit part of the entry is automatically entered for Account No. 1020, Checking Account.

After recording each check, deposit, or ATM, you should verify that the Balance field on the Write Checks and Receipts window agrees with the check register balances below and on page 291. You have already entered the first two transactions for October 1 and October 2. Continue recording entries with the October 3 ATM transaction.

Remember to click Save *to post each transaction in the check register. Each saved entry in the check register is a transaction.*

Read Me: *Why should I use Write Checks instead of the Payments window?*

The Write Checks window is a simplified version of the Payments window. Both Write Checks and Payments post to the Cash Disbursements Journal. In Chapters 9 and 10, you use the Write Checks window for checks and ATM withdrawals. You could use the Payments window for checks and ATMs but it is quicker to use Write Checks.

Ck. No.	Date	Description of Transaction	Payment	Deposit	Balance
	9/30				*7,750.75*
	10/1	*Deposit (publisher's advance)*		*10,000.00*	*17,750.75*
4001	*10/2*	*Transfer to Money Market Fund*	*6,000.00*		*11,750.75*
	10/3	**ATM**[4]	**200.00**		**11,550.75**
	10/4	Deposit (book royalty)		3,965.05	15,515.80
4002	10/4	CTS Office Supplies (computer equipment)	1,105.68		14,410.12
4003	10/9	U.S. Post Office (stamps)[5]	41.00		14,369.12
					continued

[4]For each ATM transaction use Account No. 3930, Jon Haney, Draw [*or,* your name, Draw]. Type **ATM** in the Check Number field and Pay to the Order of field. For the next check, you need to type the check number in the Check Number field.

[5]Add account No. 7400, Postage Expense on the fly. (*Hint: In the Expense Account field, click* [search]; New. In the Account Type field, select Expenses.)

4004	10/9	Independent News (newspaper subscription)[6]	45.00		14,324.12
4005	10/9	Unisource Gas (utilities)	39.64		14,284.48
4006	10/10	Midwest Water and Power[7]	98.59		14,185.89
4007	10/10	Madison Bell (telephone expense)	35.00		14,150.89
4008	10/10	Long Distance Co.	46.20		14,104.69
	10/13	Deposit (Madison Community College)		2,716.19	16,820.88
	10/14	ATM[8]	400.00		16,420.88
4009	10/15	Auto Parts (car headlight - auto expenses)[9]	201.00		16,219.88
4010	10/16	Matthew Wood (install headlight)	110.00		16,109.88
4011	10/29	Motor Vehicles Dept. (auto registration)	210.00		15,899.88
4012	10/29	Office Supplies & More (letterhead and envelopes)[10]	215.98		15,683.90
4013	10/30	Internet Service Provider	29.99		15,653.91

You may want to back up your data before you do account reconciliation. A suggested file name for this optional back up is Chapter 9 Check Register October.

Read Me: Company Back up

Another way to back up is to use the menu bar selections, File; Back Up. Follow steps 2-8 on pages 277-279.

---

[6]Debit Account No. 6100, Dues and Subscriptions.

[7]Add Account No. 6420, Water & Power Expense.

[8]If you typed ATM in the Check Number field for the October 3 withdrawal, a WARNING! That reference number has already been entered for this Cash Account displays. Click OK.

[9]Add Account No. 6180, Automobile Expense.

[10]Debit, Account No. 1450, Supplies.

ACCOUNT RECONCILIATION

Jon Haney receives a bank statement every month for his checking account (Account No. 1020) from First Interstate Bank. The bank statement shows which checks and deposits cleared the bank. PCA's Account Reconciliation feature allows you to reconcile his bank statement. Mr. Haney's bank statement for his Checking Account is shown below.

Statement of Account First Interstate Bank October 1 to October 31, 2008		Account No. 213381-17	Jon Haney Design 1967 West Park Street Madison, WI 53715
	REGULAR CHECKING		
Previous Balance		$ 7,750.75	
3 Deposits (+)		16,681.24	
9 checks (-)		7,682.47	
2 Other Deductions (-)		600.00	
Service Charges (-)	10/31/08	10.00	
Ending Balance	10/31/08	**$16,139.52**	
	DEPOSITS		
	10/4/08	10,000.00	
	10/7/08	3,965.05	
	10/17/08	2,716.19	
CHECKS (Asterisk * indicates break in check number sequence)			
10/2/08	4001	6,000.00	
10/6/08	4002	1,105.68	
10/15/08	4003	41.00	
10/16/08	4004	45.00	
10/16/08	4006*	98.59	
10/17/08	4007	35.00	
10/20/08	4008	46.20	
10/23/08	4009	201.00	
10/30/08	4010	110.00	
	OTHER DEDUCTIONS (ATM's)		
10/3/08	ATM	200.00	
10/14/08	ATM	400.00	

Follow the steps on the next page to reconcile Mr. Haney's bank statement balance to Account No. 1020, Checking Account.

1. From the Navigation Bar, select 

; 

. (*Hint:* You may also use the menu bar selections; Tasks, Account Reconciliation.) The Account Reconciliation window appears.

2. In the Account to Reconcile field, select Account No. 1020, Checking Account. If necessary, enlarge the window.

3. Did you notice that the bank statement shows a service charge of $10? In the Service charges field type **10** on the Account Reconciliation window. The Date defaults to October 31, 2008. In the Account field, select Account No. 6850, Bank Service Charge.

4. In the Statement Ending Balance field (at the bottom of the window), type **16139.52**. (This is the ending balance on Mr. Haney's bank statement.)

5. In the Deposit/Bank Credit; Check/Bank Debit table, place a check mark **<✓>** in the Status column for each deposit, check, and ATM transaction that is listed on the bank statement. Observe that the Clear window appears with a checkmark in it for each deposit, check, and ATM transaction. Do not check off the outstanding checks: 4005, 4011, 4012, 4013.

Comment

Observe that the Unreconciled Difference is zero (0.00). This zero balance is proof that Account No. 1020, Checking Account, is reconciled.

The GL (System) Balance is $15,643.91. The check register on page 291 shows an October 30 balance of $15,653.91. When you subtract the service charge of $10, the check register balance (15,653.91 – 10 = 15,643.91) agrees with the GL (System) Balance.

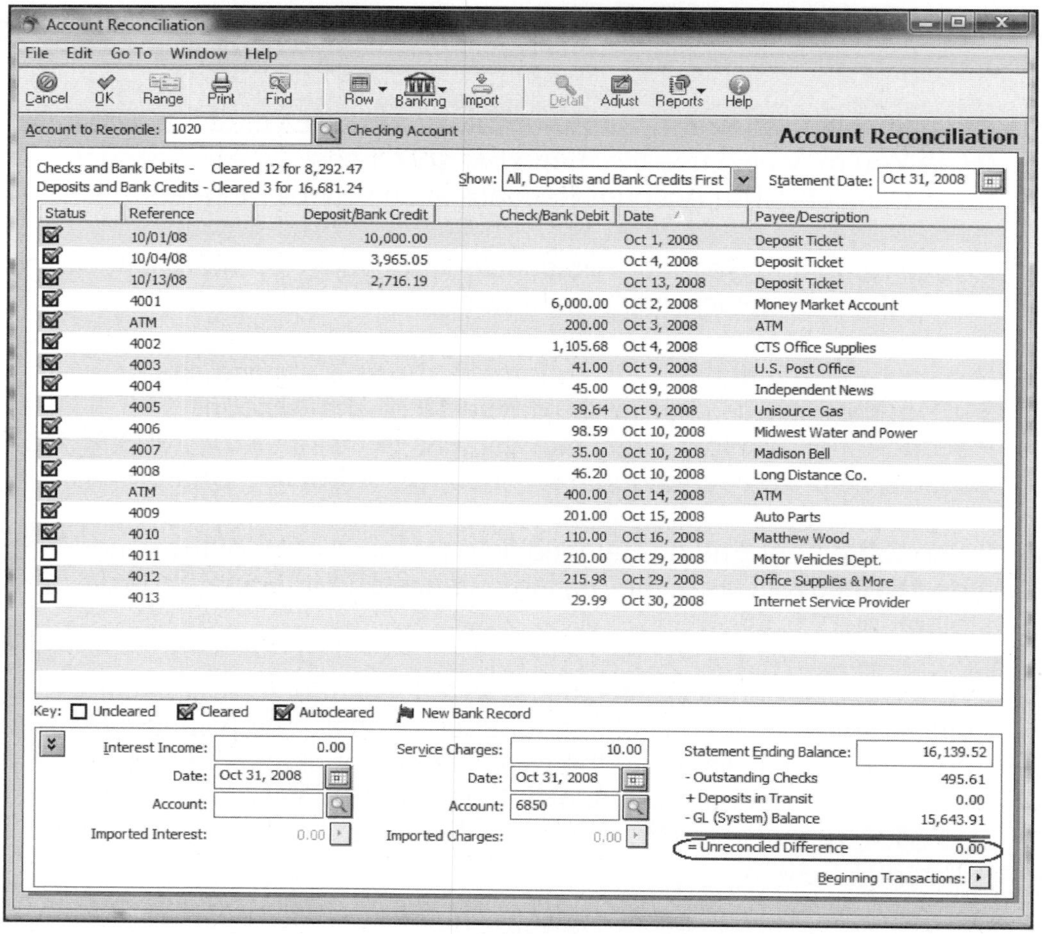

6. When you are finished, click 

The Account Reconciliation feature allows you to adjust Mr. Haney's bank statement. Another name for this is ***bank reconciliation*** – the process of bringing the balance of the bank statement and the balance of the cash account into agreement. The Account Reconciliation feature applies to other accounts, too.

DISPLAYING THE CASH ACCOUNT REGISTER

Entries for Write Checks and Receipts, are also placed in PCA's Account Register.

1. From the Banking page, select 

.

2. Compare your Account Register window to the check register on pages 290 and 291. Click  to enlarge your window. If necessary, scroll up (or down) the Account Register window to see all of the entries. A partial Account Register is shown below.

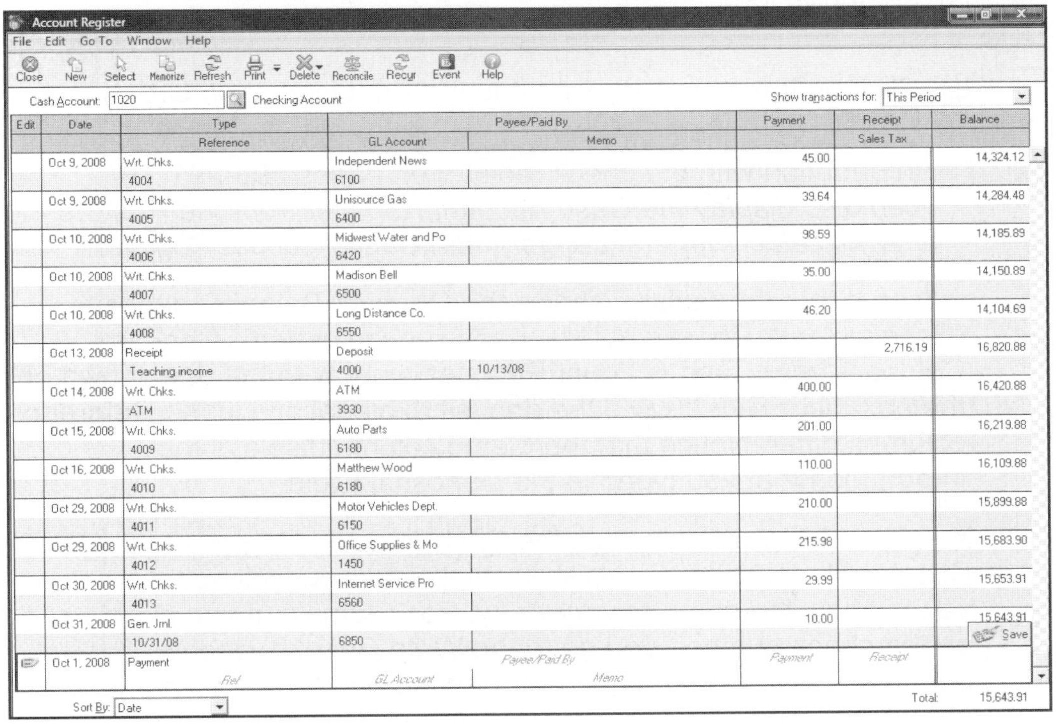

Edit	Date	Type / Reference	Payee/Paid By / GL Account	Memo	Payment	Receipt / Sales Tax	Balance
	Oct 9, 2008	Wrt. Chks. 4004	Independent News 6100		45.00		14,324.12
	Oct 9, 2008	Wrt. Chks. 4005	Unisource Gas 6400		39.64		14,284.48
	Oct 10, 2008	Wrt. Chks. 4006	Midwest Water and Po 6420		98.59		14,185.89
	Oct 10, 2008	Wrt. Chks. 4007	Madison Bell 6500		35.00		14,150.89
	Oct 10, 2008	Wrt. Chks. 4008	Long Distance Co. 6550		46.20		14,104.69
	Oct 13, 2008	Receipt Teaching income	Deposit 4000	10/13/08		2,716.19	16,820.88
	Oct 14, 2008	Wrt. Chks. ATM	ATM 3930		400.00		16,420.88
	Oct 15, 2008	Wrt. Chks. 4009	Auto Parts 6180		201.00		16,219.88
	Oct 16, 2008	Wrt. Chks. 4010	Matthew Wood 6180		110.00		16,109.88
	Oct 29, 2008	Wrt. Chks. 4011	Motor Vehicles Dept. 6150		210.00		15,899.88
	Oct 29, 2008	Wrt. Chks. 4012	Office Supplies & Mo 1450		215.98		15,683.90
	Oct 30, 2008	Wrt. Chks. 4013	Internet Service Pro 6560		29.99		15,653.91
	Oct 31, 2008	Gen. Jrnl. 10/31/08	6850		10.00		15,643.91
	Oct 1, 2008	Payment Ref	Payee/Paid By GL Account	Memo	Payment	Receipt	

3. PCA's Account Register lists payments and receipts similarly to the check register on pages 290-291. If you notice a discrepancy use drill down to follow the path of the transaction's origin. Follow these steps to use drill down.

a. Double-click on the first Oct. 4, 2008 transaction (Receipt for $3,965.05). Notice that your cursor turns into a magnifying glass with a Z in the center 

.

b. The Receipts window appears with the October 4, 2008 deposit shown.

c. If there is no need to make a correction, close the Receipts window. You are returned to the Account Register window. Notice that the Account Register window includes a Reconcile icon 

. This is another way to perform account reconciliation.

d. Click on the down arrow next to the Print icon; then click 

; 

. The Cash Account Register appears. Compare this information with the check register on pages 290-291. (*Hint: You can also display the Cash Account Register from the Reports menu; select General Ledger, then Cash Account Register.*)

Observe that the register shows the Opening Balance; deposits (Receipt Amt); Checks, ATMs, bank service charge (Gen. Jrnl.). Compare your Cash Account Register window to the one shown on the next page. It is okay if the deposit explanations in the Reference columns differ. Notice that the Memo column displays the information that you typed in the Deposit ID field.

You can also drill down from the Cash Account Register to the Write Checks, Receipts, or General Journal windows. Drill down allows you to show the origin of your entry. For example, if you double-click on the check number, you go to the Write Checks window; if you double-click on the 10/31/08 entry for the bank service charge (10.00) you go to the General Journal Entry window.

Jon Haney Design
Cash Account Register
For the Period From Oct 1, 2008 to Oct 31, 2008
1020 - Checking Account

Filter Criteria includes: Report order is by Transaction Date.

Date	Reference	Type	Payee/Paid By	Memo	Payment Am	Receipt Amt	Balance
			Opening Balance			7,750.75	7,750.75
10/1/08	Advance	Receipt	Deposit	10/01/08		10,000.00	17,750.75
10/2/08	4001	Wrt. Chks.			6,000.00		11,750.75
10/3/08	ATM	Wrt. Chks.			200.00		11,550.75
10/4/08	Book royalty	Receipt	Deposit	10/04/08		3,965.05	15,515.80
10/4/08	4002	Wrt. Chks.			1,105.68		14,410.12
10/9/08	4003	Wrt. Chks.			41.00		14,369.12
10/9/08	4004	Wrt. Chks.			45.00		14,324.12
10/9/08	4005	Wrt. Chks.			39.64		14,284.48
10/10/08	4006	Wrt. Chks.			98.59		14,185.89
10/10/08	4007	Wrt. Chks.			35.00		14,150.89
10/10/08	4008	Wrt. Chks.			46.20		14,104.69
10/13/08	Teaching in	Receipt	Deposit	10/13/08		2,716.19	16,820.88
10/14/08	ATM	Wrt. Chks.			400.00		16,420.88
10/15/08	4009	Wrt. Chks.			201.00		16,219.88
10/16/08	4010	Wrt. Chks.			110.00		16,109.88
10/29/08	4011	Wrt. Chks.			210.00		15,899.88
10/29/08	4012	Wrt. Chks.			215.98		15,683.90
10/30/08	4013	Wrt. Chks.			29.99		15,653.91
10/31/08	10/31/08	Gen. Jrnl.			10.00		15,643.91
		Total			8,788.08	16,681.24	

4. Close the Cash Account Register window. Close the Account Register.

5. Follow these steps to display the General Journal.

   a. From the menu bar, click Reports & Forms, and then select General Ledger.

   b. Click General Journal; then click , 

.

Jon Haney Design
General Journal
For the Period From Oct 1, 2008 to Oct 31, 2008

Filter Criteria includes: Report order is by Date. Report is printed with Accounts having Zero Amounts and with shortened descriptions and in Detail Format.

Date	Account ID	Reference	Trans Description	Debit Amt	Credit Amt
10/31/08	1020	10/31/08	Service Charge		10.00
	6850		Service Charge	10.00	
		Total		10.00	10.00

c. Close the General Journal report.

PRINTING THE CASH RECEIPTS JOURNAL

Follow these steps to print the Cash Receipts Journal:

1. From the Select a Report or Form window, select Accounts Receivable in the Reports area. (*Hint:* If you are at the menu bar, select Reports & Forms; Accounts Receivable.)

2. Double-click Cash Receipts Journal. The Cash Receipts Journal appears.

Jon Haney Design
Cash Receipts Journal
For the Period From Oct 1, 2008 to Oct 31, 2008
Filter Criteria includes: Report order is by Check Date. Report is printed in Detail Format.

Date	Account ID	Transaction Ref	Line Description	Debit Amnt	Credit Amnt
10/1/08	2400	Advance	Publisher's advance		10,000.00
	1020		Deposit	10,000.00	
10/4/08	4050	Book royalty			3,965.05
	1020		Deposit	3,965.05	
10/13/08	4000	Teaching income	Madison Community College		2,716.19
	1020		Deposit	2,716.19	
				16,681.24	16,681.24

Comment

The information in the Transaction Ref column may differ. The information in this column is the same as what you typed in the Reference column of the Receipts window (Cash Receipts Journal).

3. Close the Cash Receipts Journal.

PRINTING THE CASH DISBURSEMENTS JOURNAL

1. The Select a Report or Form window should be displayed. In the Reports area, highlight Accounts Payable.

2. Double-click the Cash Disbursements Journal.

Jon Haney Design
Cash Disbursements Journal
For the Period From Oct 1, 2008 to Oct 31, 2008
Filter Criteria includes: Report order is by Date. Report is printed in Detail Format.

Date	Check #	Account ID	Line Description	Debit Amount	Credit Amount
10/2/08	4001	1010	Money Market Account	6,000.00	
		1020	Money Market Account		6,000.00
10/3/08	ATM	3930	Jon Haney, Draw	200.00	
		1020	ATM		200.00
10/4/08	4002	1500	Computer Equipment	1,105.68	
		1020	CTS Office Supplies		1,105.68
10/9/08	4003	7400	Postage Expense	41.00	
		1020	U.S. Post Office		41.00
10/9/08	4004	6100	Dues and Subscriptions	45.00	
		1020	Independent News		45.00
10/9/08	4005	6400	Utilities Expense	39.64	
		1020	Unisource Gas		39.64
10/10/08	4006	6420	Water & Power Expense	98.59	
		1020	Midwest Water and Power		98.59
10/10/08	4007	6500	Telephone Expense	35.00	
		1020	Madison Bell		35.00
10/10/08	4008	6550	Long Distance Co.	46.20	
		1020	Long Distance Co.		46.20
10/14/08	ATM	3930	Jon Haney, Draw	400.00	
		1020	ATM		400.00
10/15/08	4009	6180	Automobile Expense	201.00	
		1020	Auto Parts		201.00
10/16/08	4010	6180	Automobile Expense	110.00	
		1020	Matthew Wood		110.00
10/29/08	4011	6150	Auto Registration	210.00	
		1020	Motor Vehicles Dept.		210.00
10/29/08	4012	1450	Supplies	215.98	
		1020	Office Supplies & More		215.98
10/30/08	4013	6560	Internet Service Provider	29.99	
		1020	Internet Service Provider		29.99
	Total			**8,778.08**	**8,778.08**

3. Close the Cash Disbursements Journal; close the Select a Report or Form window.

EDITING JOURNAL TRANSACTIONS

Compare your journal entries to the ones shown on pages 297–299. Some of the Line Descriptions may vary. If your dates, check numbers, or account numbers are different, you should edit the journal entry. Follow these steps to edit the Cash Receipts Journal:

1. From the menu bar, click Tasks, Receipts. The Receipts window displays.

2. Click 

. The Receipt List window appears showing the three deposits.

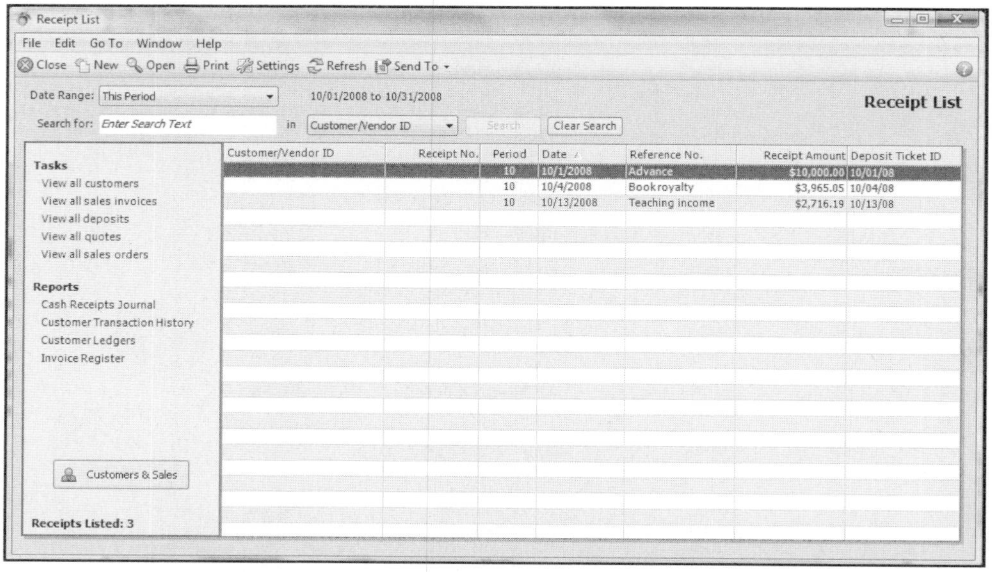

3. If you need to edit a deposit, double-click on it. This takes you to the original entry on the Receipts window. (This is called ***drill down***.)

   Make any necessary corrections, then click 

 to post.

4. Click 

 to return to the Receipt List. Close the Receipt List.

5. Editing the Cash Disbursements Journal is similar. Go to 

; select View and Edit Checks. The Write Checks List appears. Drill down to the check or ATM that needs to be edited.

6. If necessary, close the Write Checks and Write Checks List windows.

DISPLAYING THE GENERAL LEDGER TRIAL BALANCE

Follow these steps to display the General Ledger Trial Balance:

1. From the menu bar, click Reports; General Ledger, General Ledger Trial Balance.

2. Click 

. Compare your General Ledger Trial Balance with the one shown below.

Jon Haney Design
General Ledger Trial Balance
As of Oct 31, 2008

Filter Criteria includes: Report order is by ID. Report is printed in Detail Format.

Account ID	Account Description	Debit Amt	Credit Amt
1010	Money Market Account	12,700.00	
1020	Checking Account	15,643.91	
1040	IRA Savings Account	27,730.35	
1045	WI State Retirement	35,612.00	
1300	Prepaid Insurance	2,100.00	
1400	Prepaid Rent	600.00	
1450	Supplies	1,987.81	
1500	Computer Equipment	7,905.68	
1510	Furniture	5,000.00	
1520	Automobile	19,000.00	
2000	VISA Payable		5,250.65
2400	Publisher Advances		10,000.00
3920	Jon Haney, Capital		107,814.28
3930	Jon Haney, Draw	600.00	
4000	Teaching Income		2,716.19
4050	Royalty Income		3,965.05
6100	Dues and Subscriptions	45.00	
6150	Auto Registration	210.00	
6180	Automobile Expense	311.00	
6400	Utilities Expense	39.64	
6420	Water & Power Expense	98.59	
6500	Telephone Expense	35.00	
6550	Long Distance Co.	46.20	
6560	Internet Service Provider	29.99	
6850	Bank Service Charge	10.00	
7400	Postage Expense	41.00	
	Total:	**129,746.17**	**129,746.17**

3. To print the general ledger trial balance, select , then make the selections to print.

   Notice that the Checking Account (Account No. 1020) balance on the General Ledger Trial Balance and the GL (System) Balance on the Account Reconciliation window on page 294 are the same: 15,643.91.

PRINTING FINANCIAL STATEMENTS

The Computer Accounting Cycle shows that adjusting entries are needed at this point. (See the Computer Accounting Cycle on page 43.) There is no need to complete adjusting entries at the end of October since quarterly adjusting entries are done on December 31, 2008. Instead, you print Mr. Haney's financial statements.

Print the following financial statements:

1. <Standard> Balance Sheet. (*Hint:* Reports & Forms; Financial Statements. *Or,* from the Company page's Recently Used Financial Statements, link to Std Balance Sheet, View, *or* Print.) The October 31, 2008 balance sheet is shown on the next page.

Jon Haney Design
Balance Sheet
October 31, 2008

ASSETS

Current Assets		
Money Market Account	$ 12,700.00	
Checking Account	15,643.91	
IRA Savings Account	27,730.35	
WI State Retirement	35,612.00	
Prepaid Insurance	2,100.00	
Prepaid Rent	600.00	
Supplies	1,987.81	
Total Current Assets		96,374.07
Property and Equipment		
Computer Equipment	7,905.68	
Furniture	5,000.00	
Automobile	19,000.00	
Total Property and Equipment		31,905.68
Other Assets		
Total Other Assets		0.00
Total Assets		$ 128,279.75

LIABILITIES AND CAPITAL

Current Liabilities		
VISA Payable	$ 5,250.65	
Publisher Advances	10,000.00	
Total Current Liabilities		15,250.65
Long-Term Liabilities		
Total Long-Term Liabilities		0.00
Total Liabilities		15,250.65
Capital		
Jon Haney, Capital	107,814.28	
Jon Haney, Draw	(600.00)	
Net Income	5,814.82	
Total Capital		113,029.10
Total Liabilities & Capital		$ 128,279.75

2. Display or print the <Standard> Income Stmnt.

Comment

To print an Income Statement without zero balances, uncheck the Show Zero Amounts box on the <Standard> Income Statement Options window.

Jon Haney Design
Income Statement
For the Ten Months Ending October 31, 2008

	Current Month		Year to Date	
Revenues				
Teaching Income	$ 2,716.19	40.65	$ 2,716.19	40.65
Royalty Income	3,965.05	59.35	3,965.05	59.35
Total Revenues	6,681.24	100.00	6,681.24	100.00
Cost of Sales				
Total Cost of Sales	0.00	0.00	0.00	0.00
Gross Profit	6,681.24	100.00	6,681.24	100.00
Expenses				
Dues and Subscriptions	45.00	0.67	45.00	0.67
Auto Registration	210.00	3.14	210.00	3.14
Automobile Expense	311.00	4.65	311.00	4.65
Utilities Expense	39.64	0.59	39.64	0.59
Water & Power Expense	98.59	1.48	98.59	1.48
Telephone Expense	35.00	0.52	35.00	0.52
Long Distance Co.	46.20	0.69	46.20	0.69
Internet Service Provider	29.99	0.45	29.99	0.45
Bank Service Charge	10.00	0.15	10.00	0.15
Postage Expense	41.00	0.61	41.00	0.61
Total Expenses	866.42	12.97	866.42	12.97
Net Income	$ 5,814.82	87.03	$ 5,814.82	87.03

In addition to dollar figures, observe that the income statement also includes percentage of revenue columns for both the current month and the year to date. The percentages shown for each expense, total expenses, and net income indicate the relationship of each item to total revenues.

You print the additional financial statements at the end of the quarter.

BACKING UP CHAPTER 9 DATA

Follow these steps to back up Chapter 9 data.

1. If necessary, close all windows. From the Company page, link to Back up. (*Or,* from the menu bar, select File, then Back Up.)

2. If necessary, uncheck the box next to Include company name in the backup file name. Click Back Up.

3. Accept the default for backing up to the hard drive or make the selections to back up to another location. Type **Chapter 9 October** in the File name field.

4. Click Save.

5. When the window prompts that This company backup will require approximately 3.33MB, click OK. When the Back Up Company scale is 100% complete, you have successfully backed up to the current point in Chapter 9.

6. Click File; Exit to exit Peachtree.

INTERNET ACTIVITY	
1.	From your Internet browser, go to the book's website at http://www.mhhe.com/yacht2008
2.	Link to Student Edition.
3.	In the Course-wide Content list, link Internet Activities; then link to Part 2 Internet Activities for Chapter 9-10. Open or save. (You can also choose Chapter 9, then link to Internet Activities. (In the Choose a Chapter field, if you select Chapter 9 observe that other chapter-specific links are available; for example, Multiple Choice Quiz, True or False, PowerPoint Presentations and Going to the Net Exercises.) Also observe that Course-wide Content includes a Glossary link.
4.	If necessary, scroll down to STARTING A BUSINESS – Chapter 9. Read steps 1, 2, and 3.
5.	Follow the steps shown on the textbook's website to complete this Internet activity.
6.	Use a word processing program to write a summary for each website visited. Your summaries should be no more than 75 words.

SUMMARY AND REVIEW

SOFTWARE OBJECTIVES: In Chapter 9, you used the software to:

1. Set up company information for Jon Haney Design.
2. Select a sample company.
3. Edit the chart of accounts.
4. Enter chart of accounts beginning balances.
5. Use Windows Explorer to see the company's file size.
6. Record and post transactions in the cash receipts and cash disbursements journals.
7. Complete account reconciliation.
8. Display the general ledger trial balance.
9. Display the cash account register.
10. Print financial statements.
11. Make four backups: 1) back up Chapter 9 beginning data; 2) back up October data; 3) back up Exercise 9-1; 4) back up Exercise 9-2.

WEB OBJECTIVES: In Chapter 9, you did these Internet activities:

1. Used your Internet browser to go to the book's website. (Go online to www.mhhe.com/yacht2008.)
2. Went to the Internet Activity link on the book's website. Then, selected WEB EXERCISES, PART 2. Completed the first web exercise in Part 2, Starting a Business.
3. Used a word processing program to write summaries of the websites that you visited.

GOING TO THE NET

Comment

The textbook website at www.mhhe.com/yacht2008 has a link to Textbook Updates. Check this link for updated Going to the Net exercises.

Access the information about the chart of accounts at http://www.allianceonline.org. In the Search field, type **chart of accounts**; click ⊙. Link to What should our chart of accounts include?, and then link to What are the Features of a Simple Chart of Accounts?. The URL for this website is www.allianceonline.org/FAQ/financial_management/what_should_our_chart.faq/#features

1. List the standard order that accounts are presented on the balance sheet and income statement.

2. How are account numbers organized? Why are they organized that way?

Multiple Choice Questions: In the space provided, write the letter that best answers each question.

_____1. In Part 2 of the book, you complete monthly accounting for which type of business?

a. Corporate form of business.
b. Merchandising business.
c. Manufacturing business.
d. Service business.
e. None of the above.

_____2. Which type of accounting method does Jon Haney Design use?

a. Cash basis accounting.
b. Accrual accounting.
c. PCA does not require you to make a choice.
d. There is no difference between cash basis and accrual accounting.
e. None of the above.

_____3. Jon Haney' s business type is a:

a. Corporation.
b. Partnership.
c. Sole proprietorship.
d. Non-profit.
e. None of the above.

_____4. What chart of accounts did you pick for Mr. Haney's chart of accounts?

a. Accounting firm.
b. Merchandising Company.
c. Non-profit business.
d. Service Company.
e. None of the above.

_____5. Mr. Haney uses which type of posting method?

a. Batch posting.
b. Real-time posting.
c. There is no need to post his books.
d. PCA does not require you to make a posting choice.
e. None of the above.

_____6. You can restore data by making which menu bar selection?

a. File; Restore
b. Tasks; Backup
c. Maintain; Restore
d. Maintain; Backup
e. None of the above.

_____7. The correct file name for backing up Chapter 9 data for the month of October is:

a. Chapter 9 October
b. Chapter 9 Begin
c. chap6
d. chap7
e. None of the above.

_____8. Another term for the Balance Sheet is:

a. Income statement.
b. Assets and liabilities.
c. Statement of financial position.
d. Statement of cash flow.
e. None of the above.

_____9. Jon Haney's Balance Sheet at the end of October 2008 shows the following total assets:

a. $88,327.16
b. $99,763.33
c. $128,279.75
d. $104,482.19
e. None of the above.

_____10. Jon Haney's net income for the month of October is:

a. $6,691.05
b. $5,814.82
c. $3,955.15
d. $2,735.90
e. None of the above.

Exercise 9-1: Follow the instructions below to complete Exercise 9-1:

1. Start Peachtree. If Jon Haney [your name] Design opens, select File; New Company. When the window prompts, This will close the current company, click 

. The Create a New Company – Introduction window appears. Click 

.

2. Type the following company information:

Company Name:	Your Name, Designer (*Use your own name)*
Address Line 1:	Your address
City, State, Zip	Your city, Your State, Your Zip code
Country:	USA
Telephone:	Your telephone number

Fax:	Your fax number (if any)
Business Type:	Sole Proprietorship
E-mail:	Type your email address

Leave the Tax ID Numbers fields blank. Click Next > to go to the next window.

3. At the Create a New Company – Setup; Select a method to create your company window, select Copy settings from an existing Peachtree Accounting company.

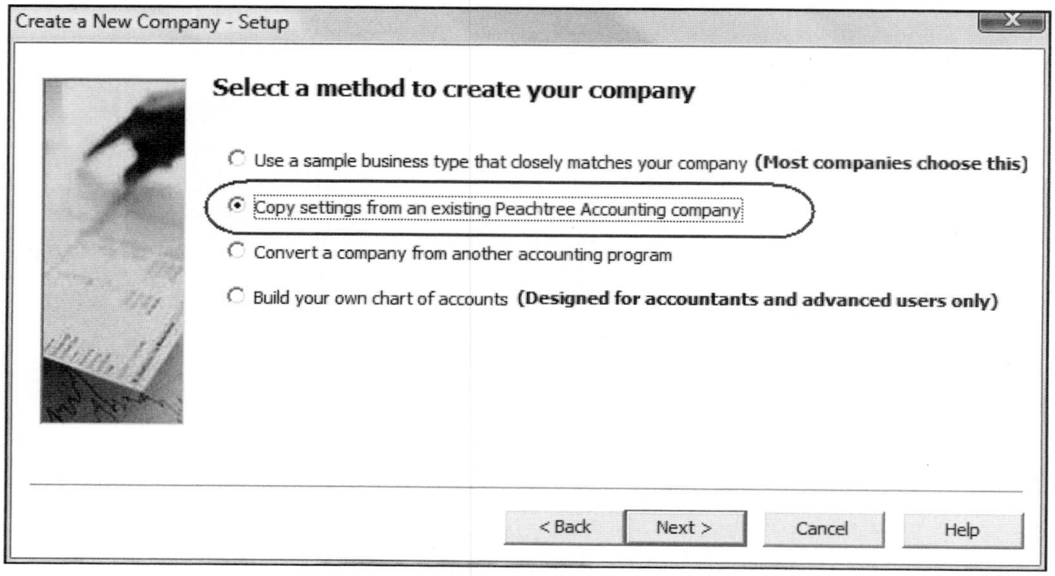

4. Click Next >.

5. Highlight Jon Haney Design, then click Next >.

6. At the Copy Company Information window click Next >.

7. Accept the default for accrual accounting by clicking Next >.

8. Accept the default for Real Time posting by clicking Next >.

9. At the You are ready to create your company window, click Finish.

10. When the Sign Up for Peachtree Payments Solutions window appears, click OK.

11. The Peachtree Accounting: Student Name, Designer window appears. Make sure the period is Period 10 for October 1-31, 2008—Period 10 - 10/01/08-10/31/08. (*Hint:* If a Setup Guide window appears, click on the box next to Don't show this screen at startup. Then click Close.)

12. Make the following changes to the Chart of Accounts:

    a. Change the name of the following accounts:

    - Account No. 1020, Checking Account to Stockmen's Bank
    - Account No. 2000, VISA Payable to Accounts Payable
    - Account No. 3920, Jon Haney, Capital to Your Name, Capital
    - Account No. 3930, Jon Haney, Draw to Your Name, Draw
    - Account No. 4050, Royalty Income to Designer Income
    - Account No. 6800 Freight Expense to Conference Fees

    b. Delete the following accounts:

    - Account No. 1010, Money Market Fund
    - Account No. 1040, IRA Savings Account
    - Account No. 1045, WI State Retirement
    - Account No. 2400, Publisher Advances

13. Print the chart of accounts.

14. Use the Balance Sheet on the next page to record the Chart of Accounts Beginning Balances. (Hint: Remember to select **9/1/08 through 9/30/08** as the period for entering chart of accounts beginning balances. Enter beginning balances of September 30, 2008.)

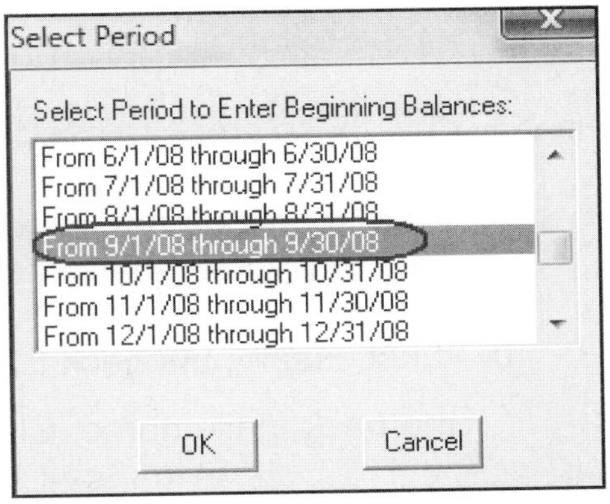

Your Name, Designer Balance Sheet October 1, 2008		
ASSETS		
Current Assets		
Stockmen's Bank	$10,500.00	
Prepaid Insurance	1,000.00	
Prepaid Rent	700.00	
Supplies	850.00	
Total Current Assets		$13,050.00
Property and Equipment		
Computer Equipment	6,500.00	
Furniture	3,500.00	
Automobile	19,000.00	
Total Property and Equipment		29,000.00
Total Assets		$ 42,050.00
LIABILITIES AND CAPITAL		
Current Liabilities		
Accounts Payable	$1,050.00	
Total Current Liabilities		$1,050.00
Capital		
Your Name, Capital		41,000.00
Total Liabilities and Capital		$ 42,050.00

15. Print the balance sheet.

16. Follow these steps to back up Exercise 9-1.

    a. From the Company page, link to Back up. (*Or,* from the menu bar, select File, then Back Up.)

    b. If necessary, uncheck the box next to Include company name in the backup file name. Click [Back Up].

c. Accept the default for backing up to the hard drive or make the selections to back up to another location. Type **Exercise 9-1** in the File name field.

d. Click Save.

e. When the window prompts that This company backup will require approximately 3.14MB, click OK. When the Back Up Company scale is 100% complete, you have successfully backed up to the current point in Chapter 9.

17. Click File; Exit to exit Peachtree.

Exercise 9-2: Follow the instructions below to complete Exercise 9-2. Exercise 9-1 *must* be completed before starting Exercise 9-2.

1. Start PCA. Open the company that you set up in Exercise 9-1, Student Name, Designer. (*Hint:* If a different company opens, select File; Open Previous Company.)

2. Follow these steps to restore Exercise 9-1.[11]

   a. From the Navigation Bar, select Company; link to Restore. (If necessary, put external media into the appropriate drive.)

   b. The Select Backup File window appears. (If necessary, click Browse. In the Look in field, select the appropriate location of the Exercise 9-1.ptb back file.) Make sure the Location field on the Select Backup File window shows Exercise 9-1.ptb. Click Next >.

---

[11]You can restore from your back up file even if *no* Peachtree company exists. From the menu bar, click File; Close Company. Peachtree's startup window appears with three menu bar options--File Options Help. Select File; Restore. Browse to the location of the Exercise 9-1.ptb backup file. On the Restore Wizard's Select Company window, select A New Company. The *A New Company* selection allows you to restore backup data *and* set up the company. For more information, refer to Troubleshooting on pages 280 and 281.

c. The Select Company window appears. The radio button next to An Existing Company is selected. Check that the Company Name and Location fields are correct. Click Next >.

d. The Restore Options window appears. Make sure that the box next to Company Data is *checked*. Click Next >.

e. The Confirmation window appears. Check the From and To fields to make sure they are correct. Click Finish. When the Restore Company scale is 100% complete, your data is restored.

f. If necessary, remove the external media.

3. Use the check register on the next page to journalize and post cash receipts journal and cash disbursement journal transactions. (*Hint: From the Banking Page, use Write Checks for checks and ATMs. From the menu bar, use Tasks; Receipts for deposits.*)

Check Number	Date	Description of Transaction	Payment/ Dr (-)	Deposit/ Cr. (+)	Balance
	9/30/08	*Balance brought forward*			10,500.00
	10/2/08	ATM	100.00		10,400.00
	10/3/08	Deposit (Designer Income)		2,300.00	12,700.00
1001	10/3/08	Accounts Payable	1,050.00		11,650.00
	10/8/08	Deposit (Teaching Income)		2,105.00	13,755.00
1002	10/9/08	Utilities Co.	45.80		13,709.20
1003	10/10/08	Vincent Advertising, Inc.	115.00		13,594.20
1004	10/13/08	U.S. Post Office	41.00		13,553.20
1005	10/13/08	Designer's Workshop (conference)[12]	195.00		13,358.20
1006	10/15/08	Eastern Telephone	55.15		13,303.05
1007	10/16/08	DSL Service[13]	29.95		13,273.10
	10/20/08	ATM	100.00		13,173.10
1008	10/28/08	The Office Store[14]	137.80		13,035.30
	10/30/08	ATM	200.00		12,835.30

4. Use the Bank Statement on the next page to complete Account Reconciliation. *Record the bank service charge on the Account Reconciliation window.*

[12]Debit Account No. 6800, Conference Fees.

[13]Debit Account No. 6560, Internet Service Provider.

[14]Debit Account No. 1450, Supplies.

Statement of Account Stockmen's Bank October 1 to October 31, 2008	Account No. 2178992-30		Your Name Your Address Your City, State, Zip	
		REGULAR CHECKING		
Previous Balance	9/30/08	10,500.00		
2 Deposits(+)		4,405.00		
6 Checks (-)		1,476.75		
2 Other Deductions (-)		400.00		
Service Charges (-)	10/31/08	12.00		
Ending Balance	10/31/08	**13,016.25**		
		DEPOSITS		
	10/6/08	2,300.00		
	10/8/08	2,105.00		
		CHECKS (Asterisk * indicates break in check number sequence)		
	10/10/08	1001	1,050.00	
	10/10/08	1002	45.80	
	10/24/08	1003	115.00	
	10/24/08	1004	41.00	
	10/27/08	1005	195.00	
	10/30/08	1007*	29.95	
		OTHER DEDUCTIONS (ATM's)		
	10/2/08	100.00		
	10/20/08	100.00		
	10/30/08	200.00		

5. Print an Account Reconciliation report.
6. Print the Cash Account Register.
7. Print the General Journal.
8. Print the Cash Receipts Journal.
9. Print the Cash Disbursements Journal.
10. Print the General Ledger Trial Balance.

11. Print the Balance Sheet and Income Statement.

12. Follow these steps to back up Exercise 9-2

a. From the Navigation Bar, select 

; link to <u>Back up</u>. (*Or*, from the menu bar, select File, then Back up.

b. If necessary, uncheck the box next to Include company name in the backup file name. Click 

.

c. Accept the default for backing up to the hard drive or make the selections to back up to another location. Type **Exercise 9-2** in the File name field.

d. Click 

.

e. When the window prompts that This company backup will require approximately 3.18MB, click on 

. When the Back Up Company scale is 100% complete, you have successfully backed up to the current point in Chapter 9.

Read Me: Windows Vista--Problem Backing Up to USB Drive

Because of Windows Vista operating system security features, you need to backup to your desktop first. Then copy the backup file from your desktop to the USB drive. Refer to Appendix A, Problem Backing Up to USB Drive or Other External Media, pages 700-702 for detailed steps.

13. Exit Peachtree.

CHAPTER 9 INDEX

Chapter 10 Completing Quarterly Activities and Closing the Fiscal Year

SOFTWARE OBJECTIVES: In Chapter 10, you use the software to:

1. Restore data from Chapter 9.[1] (This backup was made on page 305.)
2. Change accounting periods.
3. Journalize and post transactions for November and December.
4. Complete account reconciliation.
5. Print a General Ledger Trial Balance (unadjusted).
6. Journalize and post quarterly adjusting entries in the General Journal.
7. Print adjusted trial balance and financial statements.
8. Close the fiscal year.
9. Print a Post-Closing Trial Balance.
10. Make eight backups: four backups of Jon Haney Design data; one backup of Exercise 10-1; three backups of Exercise 10-2.[2]

WEB OBJECTIVES: In Chapter 10, you do these Internet activities:

1. Use your Internet browser to go to the book's website.
2. Go to the Internet Activity link on the book's website. Then, select WEB EXERCISES PART 2. Complete the second web exercise in Part 2, Understanding Accounting Terms.
3. Use a word processing program to write summaries of the websites that you visited.

Chapters 9 and 10 work together. In Chapter 10 you continue recording financial information for Jon Haney Design. You complete the Computer Accounting Cycle for November and December. Mr. Haney's checkbook registers and bank statements are used as source documents. At the end of December, which is also the end of the fourth quarter, you complete adjusting entries for Mr. Haney, print financial statements, and close the fiscal year.

---

[1]All activities in Chapter 9 must be completed before starting Chapter 10.

[2]For the size of backup files, refer to the chart on pages 248-249.

The steps of the Computer Accounting Cycle that will be completed in Chapter 10 are:

PCA's Computer Accounting Cycle	
1.	Change accounting periods.
2.	Journalize entries.
3.	Post entries to the General Ledger.
4.	Account Reconciliation.
5.	Print the General Ledger Trial Balance (unadjusted).
6.	Journalize and post adjusting entries.
7.	Print the General Ledger Trial Balance (adjusted).
8.	Print the financial statements: Balance Sheet, Income Statement, Statement of Cash Flow, Statement of Retained Earnings, and Statement of Changes in Financial Position.
9.	Close the fiscal year.
10.	Interpret accounting information.

GETTING STARTED

Follow these steps to continue using Jon Haney's company data.

1. Start Peachtree. Open an existing company, Jon Haney Design (or your name Design).[3] (*Hint:* If a different company opens, select File; Open a Previous Company. Select Jon Haney Design; click 

.)

2. To restore Jon Haney's data from Chapter 9, do the following. The Chapter 9 October.ptb backup was made on page 305.

   a. From the Company page, link to Restore. (*Or,* from the menu bar, click File, Restore. If necessary, put external media into the appropriate drive.)

[3]You can restore from your back up file even if *no* design company exists. From Peachtree's start up window, select File; Restore. Select the location of your backup file. On the Restore Wizard's Select Company window, select A New Company. The *A New Company* selection allows you to restore your backup data, bypassing the process of new company set up. For more information, refer to Troubleshooting on pages 280-281.

b. The Select Backup File window appears. (If necessary, click Browse. In the Look in field, select the appropriate location of your Chapter 9 October.ptb file.) Make sure the Location field on the Select Backup File window shows the Chapter 9 October.ptb file. Click Next >.

c. The Select Company window appears. The radio button next to An Existing Company is selected. Check that the Company Name and Location fields are correct. Click Next >.

d. The Restore Options window appears. Make sure that the box next to Company Data is *checked*. Click Next >.

e. The Confirmation window appears. Check the From and To fields to make sure they are correct. Click Finish. When the Restore Company scale is 100% complete, your data is restored.

f. If necessary, remove the external media.

3. To make sure you are starting in the right place, display the general ledger trial balance and compare it to the one shown on page 301. Close all windows.

4. Follow these steps to change accounting periods:

a. From the menu bar, select Tasks, then System.

b. From the System menu, select Change Accounting Period.

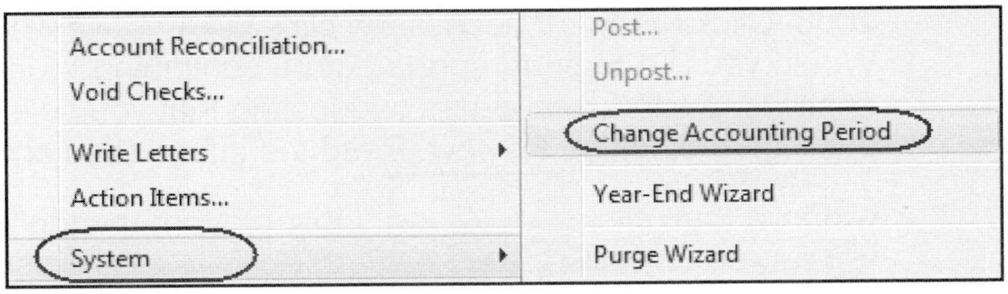

c. From the Open Accounting Periods list, select 11-Nov 01, 2008 to Nov 30, 2008. Compare your Change Accounting Period window to the one shown below.

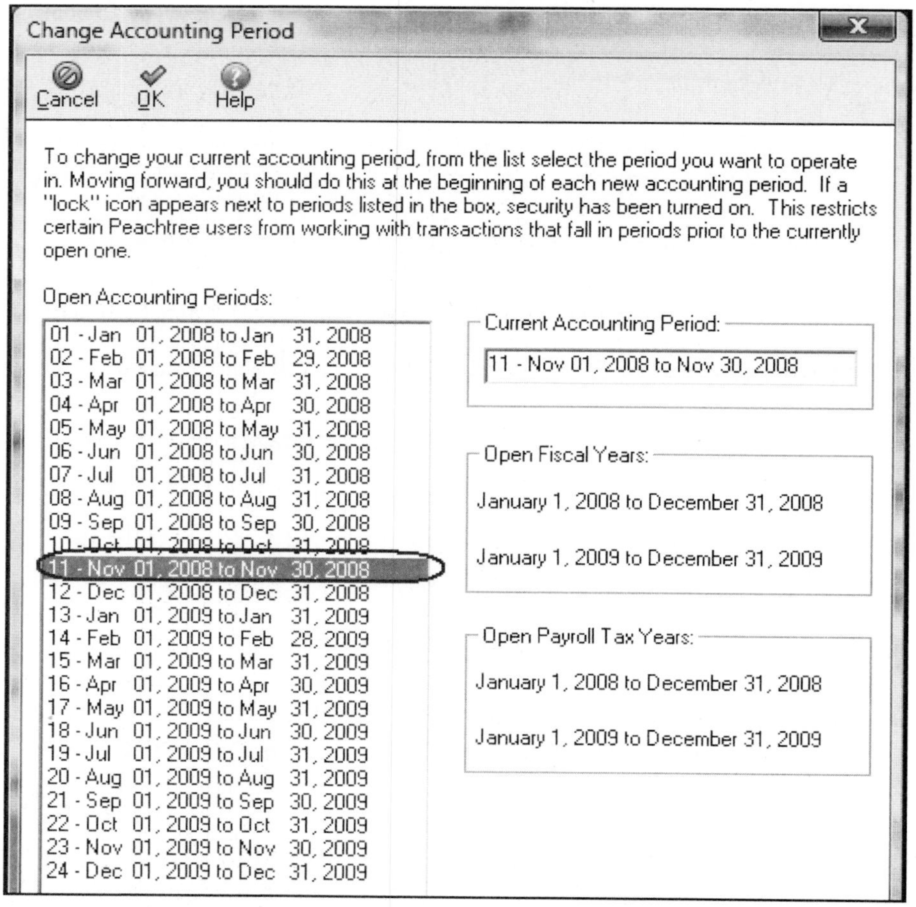

d. Make sure you selected period 11 - Nov 01, 2008 to Nov 30, 2008. Click 

. If necessary, click 

when the Would you like to print reports before continuing? window appears. A window appears suggesting that you select the Internal Accounting Review. Read the information on this window, then click 

. Observe that the toolbar shows 

.

When you changed accounting periods, you prepared Peachtree to record November's journal entries.

CHECKBOOK REGISTER AND BANK STATEMENT: NOVEMBER 2008

Use Mr. Haney's checkbook register to journalize and post transactions for the month of November. (*Hint: Use Write Checks* from the Banking page *for recording checks and ATMs; use Receipts from the Tasks menu for recording deposits. Remember to Save after each transaction.*)

> **Comment**
>
> Before journalizing entries, make sure that you are starting with correct data. To do that, display the General Ledger Trial Balance and compare it to the one shown on page 301 in Chapter 9. Since you changed accounting periods on pages 321 and 322, your trial balance will be dated November 30, 2008.
>
> Verify that Account No. 1020, Checking Account, shows a balance of $15,643.91 which is the same as the starting balance on the check register below.

Check Number	Date	Description of Transaction	Payment	Deposit	Balance
	10/31	*Bank Service Charge*	*10.00*		*15,643.91*
	11/3	Deposit (book royalty)		2,455.85	18,099.76
	11/5	ATM	200.00		17,899.76
	11/6	Deposit (Madison CC)		2,716.19	20,615.95
4014	11/10	Midwest Water and Power	90.50		20,525.45
4015	11/10	Unisource Gas	53.90		20,471.55
4016	11/12	Madison Bell	45.08		20,426.47
4017	11/14	Long Distance Co.	81.50		20,344.97
	11/16	ATM	200.00		20,144.97
4018	11/27	VISA card payment	5,250.65		14,894.32
4019	11/28	Internet Service Provider	29.99		14,864.33
	11/28	ATM	200.00		14,664.33

Follow the steps below to complete the Computer Accounting Cycle.

1. Journalize and post the Cash Receipts and Cash Disbursements Journals. (*Hint: Start your journal entries with the November 3*

deposit. Remember to record each transaction--checks, deposits, ATM withdrawals--as a separate journal entry. Post after each transaction).

2. Use Mr. Haney's bank statement to complete account reconciliation for Account No. 1020, Checking Account.

   Remember to record the bank service charge (Account No. 6850) on the Account Reconciliation window.

Statement of Account First Interstate Bank November 1 to November 30, 2008		Account No. 213381-17	Jon Haney Design 1967 West Park Street Madison, WI 53715	
REGULAR CHECKING				
Previous Balance	10/31/08	16,139.52		
2 Deposits(+)		5,172.04		
8 checks (-)		766.59		
3 Other deduction (-)		600.00		
Service Charges (-)	11/30/08	10.00		
Ending Balance	11/30/08	**19,934.97**		
DEPOSITS				
	11/3/08	2,455.85		
	11/8/08	2,716.19		
CHECKS (Asterisk * indicates break in check number sequence)				
	11/3/08	4005*	39.64	
	11/3/08	4011	210.00	
	11/3/08	4012	215.98	
	11/5/08	4013	29.99	
	11/17/08	4014	90.50	
	11/27/08	4015	53.90	
	11/28/08	4016	45.08	
	11/28/08	4017	81.50	
OTHER DEDUCTIONS (ATM's)				
	11/5/08	200.00		
	11/14/08	200.00		
	11/28/08	200.00		

3. Follow these steps to display the Cash Account Register.

   a. From the menu bar, select Tasks; Account Register. Click  to enlarge your window. (*Hint: You can access the Cash Account Register two ways: from the Tasks menu or from the Reports & Forms menu; General Ledger, Cash Account Register selections.*)

   b. Click on the down arrow next to the Print icon (); then click , .

   c. Compare your Cash Account Register to the one shown below and to the check register on page 323. If necessary, drill down to make corrections.

Jon Haney Design
Cash Account Register
For the Period From Nov 1, 2008 to Nov 30, 2008
1020 - Checking Account

Filter Criteria includes: Report order is by Transaction Date.

Date	Reference	Type	Payee/Paid By	Memo	Payment Am	Receipt Amt	Balance
			Opening Balance			15,643.91	15,643.91
11/3/08	Book royalty	Receipt	Deposit	11/03/08		2,455.85	18,099.76
11/5/08	ATM	Wrt. Chks.			200.00		17,899.76
11/6/08	Teaching in	Receipt	Deposit	11/06/08		2,716.19	20,615.95
11/10/08	4014	Wrt. Chks.			90.50		20,525.45
11/10/08	4015	Wrt. Chks.			53.90		20,471.55
11/12/08	4016	Wrt. Chks.			45.08		20,426.47
11/14/08	4017	Wrt. Chks.			81.50		20,344.97
11/16/08	ATM	Wrt. Chks.			200.00		20,144.97
11/27/08	4018	Wrt. Chks.			5,250.65		14,894.32
11/28/08	4019	Wrt. Chks.			29.99		14,864.33
11/28/08	ATM	Wrt. Chks.			200.00		14,664.33
11/30/08	11/30/08	Gen. Jrnl.			10.00		14,654.33
		Total			**6,161.62**	**5,172.04**	

4. Close all windows.

5. Follow these steps to print an Account Reconciliation report:

   a. From the menu bar, click Reports & Forms; Account Reconciliation.

   b. At the Select a Report window, highlight Account Reconciliation.

c. Click 

. The Modify Report – Account Reconciliation window appears. Observe that the As of field shows Current Period. Click 

. Make the selections to print.

d. At the Print window, click 

.

Jon Haney Design
Account Reconciliation
As of Nov 30, 2008
1020 - Checking Account
Bank Statement Date: November 30, 2008

Filter Criteria includes: Report is printed in Detail Format.

Beginning GL Balance				15,643.91
Add: Cash Receipts				5,172.04
Less: Cash Disbursements				(6,151.62)
Add (Less) Other				(10.00)
Ending GL Balance				14,654.33
Ending Bank Balance				19,934.97
Add back deposits in transi				
Total deposits in transit				
(Less) outstanding checks				
	Nov 27, 2008	4018	(5,250.65)	
	Nov 28, 2008	4019	(29.99)	
Total outstanding checks				(5,280.64)
Add (Less) Other				
Total other				
Unreconciled difference				0.00
Ending GL Balance				14,654.33

6. Close the account reconciliation report.

7. Print or display the Cash Receipts Journal. Compare it to the one shown on the next page.

Jon Haney Design
Cash Receipts Journal
For the Period From Nov 1, 2008 to Nov 30, 2008
Filter Criteria includes: Report order is by Check Date. Report is printed in Detail Format.

Date	Account ID	Transaction Ref	Line Description	Debit Amnt	Credit Amnt
11/3/08	4050	Book royalty	Royalty Income		2,455.85
	1020		Deposit	2,455.85	
11/6/08	4000	Teaching income	Madison Community College		2,716.19
	1020		Deposit	2,716.19	
				5,172.04	**5,172.04**

8. Print or display your Cash Disbursements Journal and compare it to the one shown.

Jon Haney Design
Cash Disbursements Journal
For the Period From Nov 1, 2008 to Nov 30, 2008
Filter Criteria includes: Report order is by Date. Report is printed in Detail Format.

Date	Check #	Account ID	Line Description	Debit Amount	Credit Amount
11/5/08	ATM	3930	Jon Haney, Draw	200.00	
		1020	ATM		200.00
11/10/08	4014	6420	Water & Power Expense	90.50	
		1020	Midwest Water and Power		90.50
11/10/08	4015	6400	Utilities Expense	53.90	
		1020	Unisource Gas		53.90
11/12/08	4016	6500	Telephone Expense	45.08	
		1020	Madison Bell		45.08
11/14/08	4017	6550	Long Distance Co.	81.50	
		1020	Long Distance Co.		81.50
11/16/08	ATM	3930	Jon Haney, Draw	200.00	
		1020	ATM		200.00
11/27/08	4018	2000	VISA Payable	5,250.65	
		1020	VISA card payment		5,250.65
11/28/08	4019	6560	Internet Service Provider	29.99	
		1020	Internet Service Provider		29.99
11/28/08	ATM	3930	Jon Haney, Draw	200.00	
		1020	ATM		200.00
	Total			**6,151.62**	**6,151.62**

9. Print or display the general journal to see the bank service charge.

Jon Haney Design
General Journal
For the Period From Nov 1, 2008 to Nov 30, 2008
Filter Criteria includes: Report order is by Date. Report is printed with Accounts having Zero Amounts and with shortened descriptions and in Detail Format.

Date	Account ID	Reference	Trans Description	Debit Amt	Credit Amt
11/30/08	1020	11/30/08	Service Charge		10.00
	6850		Service Charge	10.00	
		Total		**10.00**	**10.00**

If your journals do not agree with the ones shown, edit the journals and post again. (Refer to page 300 Editing Journal Transactions.)

10. Print or display the General Ledger Trial Balance.

Jon Haney Design
General Ledger Trial Balance
As of Nov 30, 2008
Filter Criteria includes: Report order is by ID. Report is printed in Detail Format.

Account ID	Account Description	Debit Amt	Credit Amt
1010	Money Market Account	12,700.00	
1020	Checking Account	14,654.33	
1040	IRA Savings Account	27,730.35	
1045	WI State Retirement	35,612.00	
1300	Prepaid Insurance	2,100.00	
1400	Prepaid Rent	600.00	
1450	Supplies	1,987.81	
1500	Computer Equipment	7,905.68	
1510	Furniture	5,000.00	
1520	Automobile	19,000.00	
2400	Publisher Advances		10,000.00
3920	Jon Haney, Capital		107,814.28
3930	Jon Haney, Draw	1,200.00	
4000	Teaching Income		5,432.38
4050	Royalty Income		6,420.90
6100	Dues and Subscriptions	45.00	
6150	Auto Registration	210.00	
6180	Automobile Expense	311.00	
6400	Utilities Expense	93.54	
6420	Water & Power Expense	189.09	
6500	Telephone Expense	80.08	
6550	Long Distance Co.	127.70	
6560	Internet Service Provider	59.98	
6850	Bank Service Charge	20.00	
7400	Postage Expense	41.00	
	Total:	**129,667.56**	**129,667.56**

11. Print or display the Balance Sheet.

Jon Haney Design
Balance Sheet
November 30, 2008

ASSETS

Current Assets				
Money Market Account	$	12,700.00		
Checking Account		14,654.33		
IRA Savings Account		27,730.35		
WI State Retirement		35,612.00		
Prepaid Insurance		2,100.00		
Prepaid Rent		600.00		
Supplies		1,987.81		
Total Current Assets				95,384.49
Property and Equipment				
Computer Equipment		7,905.68		
Furniture		5,000.00		
Automobile		19,000.00		
Total Property and Equipment				31,905.68
Other Assets				
Total Other Assets				0.00
Total Assets			$	127,290.17

LIABILITIES AND CAPITAL

Current Liabilities				
Publisher Advances	$	10,000.00		
Total Current Liabilities				10,000.00
Long-Term Liabilities				
Total Long-Term Liabilities				0.00
Total Liabilities				10,000.00
Capital				
Jon Haney, Capital		107,814.28		
Jon Haney, Draw		(1,200.00)		
Net Income		10,675.89		
Total Capital				117,290.17
Total Liabilities & Capital			$	127,290.17

12. Print or display the Income Statement.

Jon Haney Design
Income Statement
For the Eleven Months Ending November 30, 2008

		Current Month			Year to Date	
Revenues						
Teaching Income	$	2,716.19	52.52	$	5,432.38	45.83
Royalty Income		2,455.85	47.48		6,420.90	54.17
Total Revenues		5,172.04	100.00		11,853.28	100.00
Cost of Sales						
Total Cost of Sales		0.00	0.00		0.00	0.00
Gross Profit		5,172.04	100.00		11,853.28	100.00
Expenses						
Dues and Subscriptions		0.00	0.00		45.00	0.38
Auto Registration		0.00	0.00		210.00	1.77
Automobile Expense		0.00	0.00		311.00	2.62
Utilities Expense		53.90	1.04		93.54	0.79
Water & Power Expense		90.50	1.75		189.09	1.60
Telephone Expense		45.08	0.87		80.08	0.68
Long Distance Co.		81.50	1.58		127.70	1.08
Internet Service Provider		29.99	0.58		59.98	0.51
Bank Service Charge		10.00	0.19		20.00	0.17
Postage Expense		0.00	0.00		41.00	0.35
Total Expenses		310.97	6.01		1,177.39	9.93
Net Income	$	4,861.07	93.99	$	10,675.89	90.07

BACKING UP NOVEMBER DATA

Follow these steps to back up Chapter 10 data:

1. From the Company page, link to Back up. (*Or*, from the menu bar, select File, then Back up.)
2. If necessary, uncheck the box next to Include company name in the backup file name. Click Back Up.
3. Accept the default for backing up to the hard drive or make the selections to back up to another location. Type **Chapter 10 November** in the File name field.
4. Click Save.

5. When the window prompts that This company backup will require approximately 3.39MB, click 

. When the Back Up Company scale is 100% complete, you have successfully backed up to the current point in Chapter 10.

6. Click File, Exit to exit Peachtree. Or, continue with the next section.

DATA FILE STATISTICS

To display information about your company data files, follow these steps.

1. From the menu bar, click Help; Customer Support and Service, File Statistics.

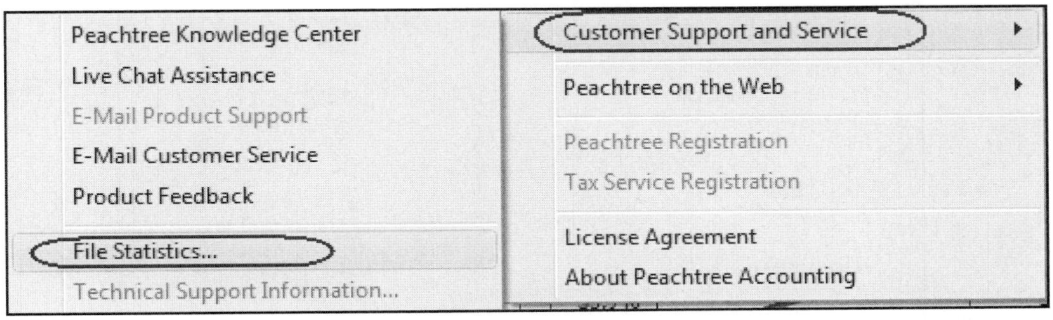

2. The Data File Statistics window lists the number of records and sizes in kilobytes for each data file for the company that is open. It also provides a grand total (scroll down).

   Peachtree displays the company's shortened name (jonhande) on the title bar.[4] This represents the name of the folder where the opened company resides. Observe that the Directory field shows where the company resides on your hard drive: C:\Program Files\Sage Software\Peachtree\ company\jonhande [*or, your shortened name*]. (*Hint:* The author's directory shows drive F.)

   Compare your Data File Statistics window to the one shown on the next page.

[4]If you used your name, the company's shortened name will differ.

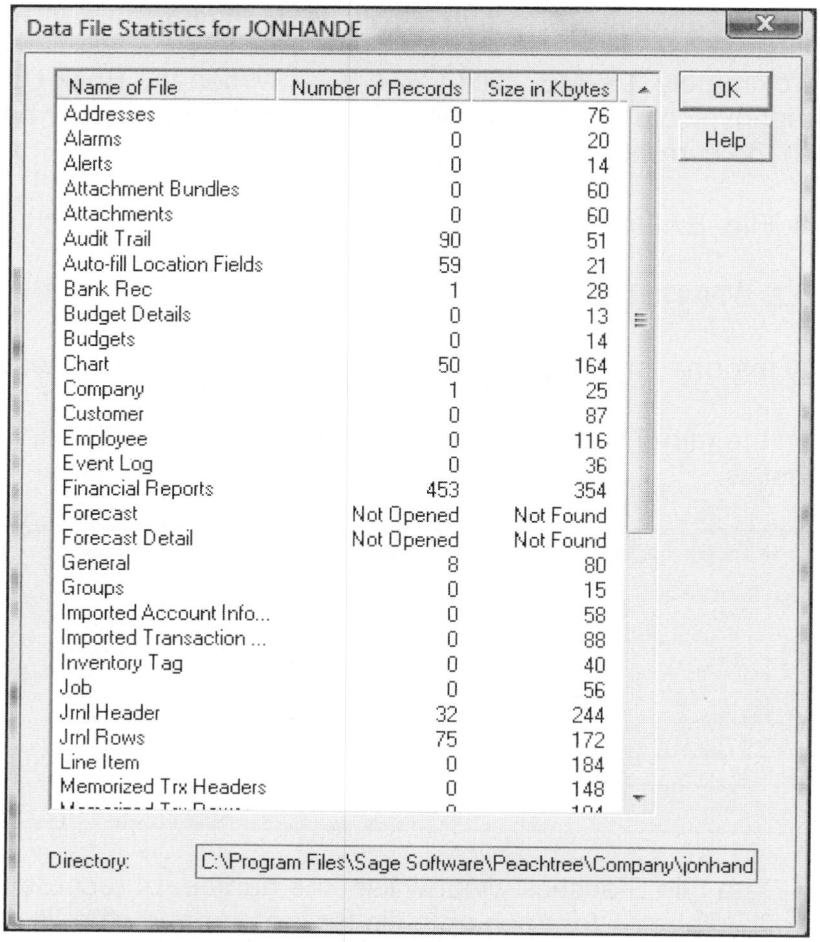
Data File Statistics for JONHANDE
Name of File | Number of Records | Size in Kbytes
Addresses 0 76
Alarms 0 20
Alerts 0 14
Attachment Bundles 0 60
Attachments 0 60
Audit Trail 90 51
Auto-fill Location Fields 59 21
Bank Rec 1 28
Budget Details 0 13
Budgets 0 14
Chart 50 164
Company 1 25
Customer 0 87
Employee 0 116
Event Log 0 36
Financial Reports 453 354
Forecast Not Opened Not Found
Forecast Detail Not Opened Not Found
General 8 80
Groups 0 15
Imported Account Info... 0 58
Imported Transaction ... 0 88
Inventory Tag 0 40
Job 0 56
Jrnl Header 32 244
Jrnl Rows 75 172
Line Item 0 184
Memorized Trx Headers 0 148
OK
Help
Directory:
C:\Program Files\Sage Software\Peachtree\Company\jonhand

3. To close the Data File Statistics window, click OK.

CHANGING ACCOUNTING PERIODS

Follow these steps to change accounting periods:

1. From the menu bar, select Tasks, then System.
2. From the System menu, select Change Accounting Period.
   a. From the drop-down list, select period 12 - Dec 01, 2008 to Dec 31, 2008.

b. Click OK. If necessary, at the Would you like to print your reports before continuing? window, click No. A window appears suggesting that you select the Internal Accounting Review. Read the information on this window, then click No. Observe that your toolbar shows Period 12 - 12/01/08-12/31/08.

CHECKBOOK REGISTER AND BANK STATEMENT: DECEMBER 2008

1. Use Mr. Haney's checkbook register to journalize and post transactions for the month of December. His checkbook register is shown below.

> **Comment**
>
> Before you start journalizing entries, make sure that you are starting with correct data. To do that, display the General Ledger Trial Balance and compare it to the one shown on page 328.

Check Number	Date	Description of Transaction	Payment	Deposit	Balance
	11/30	*Bank Service Charge*	*10.00*		*14,654.33*
	12/3[5]	ATM	400.00		14,254.33
	12/8	Deposit (Madison CC)		2,716.19	16,970.52
4020	12/10	Midwest Water and Power	75.45		16,895.07
4021	12/11	Unisource Gas (utilities)	102.92		16,792.15
4022	12/12	Madison Bell	45.95		16,746.20
4023	12/15	Gallery (business cards - debit, Supplies)	115.25		16,630.95
4024	12/18	Long Distance Co.	75.49		16,555.46
4025	12/18	Internet Service Provider	29.99		16,525.47
	12/19	ATM	400.00		16,125.47
	12/29	ATM	400.00		15,725.47

[5] Start your journal transactions with the December 3 ATM transaction.

2. Use Mr. Haney's bank statement to complete account reconciliation. (*Remember to record the bank service charge on the Account Reconciliation window.*)

Statement of Account First Interstate Bank December 1 to December 31, 2008		Account No. 213381-17	Jon Haney Design 1967 West Park Street Madison, WI 53715	
REGULAR CHECKING				
Previous Balance	11/30/08	19,934.97		
1 Deposit(+)		2,716.19		
7 Checks (-)		5,695.70		
3 Other Deduction (-)		1,200.00		
Service Charges (-)	12/31/08	10.00		
Ending Balance	12/31/08	**15,745.46**		
DEPOSITS				
	12/8/08	2,716.19		
CHECKS (Asterisk * indicates break in check number sequence)				
	12/8/08	4018	5,250.65	
	12/8/08	4019	29.99	
	12/22/08	4020	75.45	
	12/29/08	4021	102.92	
	12/29/08	4022	45.95	
	12/31/08	4023	115.25	
	12/31/08	4024	75.49	
OTHER DEDUCTIONS (ATM's)				
	12/3/08	400.00		
	12/19/08	400.00		
	12/29/08	400.00		

3. Display the Cash Account Register (Reports & Forms; General Ledger, Cash Account Register; Preview). Compare the Cash Account Register on the next page to the check register on page 333. Use drill down to make any needed corrections.

Jon Haney Design
Cash Account Register
For the Period From Dec 1, 2008 to Dec 31, 2008
1020 - Checking Account

Filter Criteria includes: Report order is by Transaction Date.

Date	Reference	Type	Payee/Paid By	Memo	Payment Am	Receipt Amt	Balance
			Opening Balance			14,654.33	14,654.33
12/5/08	ATM	Wrt. Chks.			400.00		14,254.33
12/8/08	Teaching in	Receipt	Deposit	12/08/07		2,716.19	16,970.52
12/10/08	4020	Wrt. Chks.			75.45		16,895.07
12/11/08	4021	Wrt. Chks.			102.92		16,792.15
12/12/08	4022	Wrt. Chks.			45.95		16,746.20
12/15/08	4023	Wrt. Chks.			115.25		16,630.95
12/18/08	4024	Wrt. Chks.			75.49		16,555.46
12/18/08	4025	Wrt. Chks.			29.99		16,525.47
12/19/08	ATM	Wrt. Chks.			400.00		16,125.47
12/29/08	ATM	Wrt. Chks.			400.00		15,725.47
12/31/08	12/31/08	Gen. Jrnl.			10.00		15,715.47
		Total			1,655.05	2,716.19	

4. Print or display the Account Reconciliation report.

Jon Haney Design
Account Reconciliation
As of Dec 31, 2008
1020 - Checking Account
Bank Statement Date: December 31, 2008

Filter Criteria includes: Report is printed in Detail Format.

Beginning GL Balance				14,654.33
Add: Cash Receipts				2,716.19
Less: Cash Disbursements				(1,645.05)
Add (Less) Other				(10.00)
Ending GL Balance				15,715.47
Ending Bank Balance				15,745.46
Add back deposits in transi				
Total deposits in transit				
(Less) outstanding checks	Dec 18, 2008	4025	(29.99)	
Total outstanding checks				(29.99)
Add (Less) Other				
Total other				
Unreconciled difference				0.00
Ending GL Balance				15,715.47

5. Print or display the General Journal.

Jon Haney Design
General Journal
For the Period From Dec 1, 2008 to Dec 31, 2008
Filter Criteria includes: Report order is by Date. Report is printed with Accounts having Zero Amounts and with shortened descriptions and in Detail Format.

Date	Account ID	Reference	Trans Description	Debit Amt	Credit Amt
12/31/08	1020	12/31/08	Service Charge		10.00
	6850		Service Charge	10.00	
		Total		10.00	10.00

6. Print or display the Cash Receipts Journal.

Jon Haney Design
Cash Receipts Journal
For the Period From Dec 1, 2008 to Dec 31, 2008
Filter Criteria includes: Report order is by Check Date. Report is printed in Detail Format.

Date	Account ID	Transaction Ref	Line Description	Debit Amnt	Credit Amnt
12/8/08	4000	Teaching income	Madison Community College		2,716.19
	1020		Deposit	2,716.19	
				2,716.19	2,716.19

7. Print or display the Cash Disbursements Journal.

Jon Haney Design
Cash Disbursements Journal
For the Period From Dec 1, 2008 to Dec 31, 2008
Filter Criteria includes: Report order is by Date. Report is printed in Detail Format.

Date	Check #	Account ID	Line Description	Debit Amount	Credit Amount
12/5/08	ATM	3930	Jon Haney, Draw	400.00	
		1020	ATM		400.00
12/10/08	4020	6420	Water & Power Expense	75.45	
		1020	Midwest Water and Power		75.45
12/11/08	4021	6400	Utilities Expense	102.92	
		1020	Unisource Gas		102.92
12/12/08	4022	6500	Telephone Expense	45.95	
		1020	Madison Bell		45.95
12/15/08	4023	1450	Supplies	115.25	
		1020	Gallery		115.25
12/18/08	4024	6550	Long Distance Co.	75.49	
		1020	Long Distance Co.		75.49
12/18/08	4025	6560	Internet Service Provider	29.99	
		1020	Internet Service Provider		29.99
12/19/08	ATM	3930	Jon Haney, Draw	400.00	
		1020	ATM		400.00
12/29/08	ATM	3930	Jon Haney, Draw	400.00	
		1020	ATM		400.00
	Total			1,645.05	1,645.05

If your journals do not agree with the ones shown, edit your records and post again.

8. Display or print a General Ledger Trial Balance (unadjusted).

Jon Haney Design
General Ledger Trial Balance
As of Dec 31, 2008

Filter Criteria includes: Report order is by ID. Report is printed in Detail Format.

Account ID	Account Description	Debit Amt	Credit Amt
1010	Money Market Account	12,700.00	
1020	Checking Account	15,715.47	
1040	IRA Savings Account	27,730.35	
1045	WI State Retirement	35,612.00	
1300	Prepaid Insurance	2,100.00	
1400	Prepaid Rent	600.00	
1450	Supplies	2,103.06	
1500	Computer Equipment	7,905.68	
1510	Furniture	5,000.00	
1520	Automobile	19,000.00	
2400	Publisher Advances		10,000.00
3920	Jon Haney, Capital		107,814.28
3930	Jon Haney, Draw	2,400.00	
4000	Teaching Income		8,148.57
4050	Royalty Income		6,420.90
6100	Dues and Subscriptions	45.00	
6150	Auto Registration	210.00	
6180	Automobile Expense	311.00	
6400	Utilities Expense	196.46	
6420	Water & Power Expense	264.54	
6500	Telephone Expense	126.03	
6550	Long Distance Co.	203.19	
6560	Internet Service Provider	89.97	
6850	Bank Service Charge	30.00	
7400	Postage Expense	41.00	
	Total:	**132,383.75**	**132,383.75**

BACK UP THE UNADJUSTED TRIAL BALANCE

Follow these steps to back up Chapter 10 data:

1. From the Company page, link to Back up. (*Or,* from the menu bar, select File, then Back up.)

2. If necessary, uncheck the box next to Include company name in the backup file name. Click Back Up.

3. Accept the default for backing up to the hard drive or make the selections to back up to another location. Type **Chapter 10 December UTB** in the File name field. (UTB is an abbreviation of unadjusted trail balance.)

4. Click 

.

5. When the window prompts that This company backup will require approximately 3.40MB, click 

. When the Back Up Company scale is 100% complete, you have successfully backed up to the current point in Chapter 10.

6. Click File, Exit to exit Peachtree. Or, continue with the next section.

You print the financial statements after you journalize and post the end-of-quarter adjusting entries.

END-OF-QUARTER ADJUSTING ENTRIES

It is the policy of your accounting firm to record adjusting entries at the end of the quarter. Mr. Haney's accounting records are complete through December 31, 2008. The following adjusting entries need to be recorded in the General Journal.

Follow these steps to journalize and post the adjusting entries in the general journal.

1. From the Company page, link to General Journal Entry. (*Or,* from the menu bar, click Tasks, then General Journal Entry.
2. Type **31** in the Date field. Press **<Enter>** three times.
3. In the GL Account No. column, select the appropriate account to debit. Type the account name in the Description column. Press the **<Enter>** key once to go to the Debit column. Type the debit amount, then press the **<Enter>** key three times.
4. In the Account No. column, select the appropriate account to credit. Type the account name in the Description column. Press the

<Enter> key two times to go to the Credit column. Type the credit amount. Press the **<Enter>** key.

5. Click 

to post each adjusting entry.

Journalize and post the following December 31, 2008 adjusting entries:

1. Office supplies on hand are $1,700.00

Acct. #	Account Name	Debit	Credit
6450	Office Supplies Expense	403.06	
1450	Supplies		403.06

Computation:		
	Supplies	$2,103.06
	Office supplies on hand	- 1,700.00
	Adjustment	$ 403.06

Hint: To post your transaction to the general ledger, click 

after each general journal entry.

2. Adjust three months of prepaid insurance ($2,100 X 3/12 = $525). Mr. Haneys paid a one year insurance premium on 10/1/08.

Acct. #	Account Name	Debit	Credit
6950	Insurance Expense	525.00	
1300	Prepaid Insurance		525.00

3. Adjust three months of prepaid rent ($200 X 3 = $600.)

Acct. #	Account Name	Debit	Credit
6300	Rent or Lease Expense	600.00	
1400	Prepaid Rent		600.00

4. Use straight-line depreciation for Mr. Haney's computer equipment. His computer equipment has a three-year service life and a $1,000 salvage value. To depreciate computer equipment for the fourth quarter, use this calculation:

   $7,905.68 - $1,000 ÷ 3 years X 3/12 = $575.47

Computer Equipment, 10/1/08	$6,800.00
Hardware Upgrade, 10/4/08	1,105.68
Total computer equipment, 12/31/08	$7,905.68

Acct. #	Account Name	Debit	Credit
7050	Deprec. Exp.- Comp Eqt	575.47	
1900	Accum. Depreciation - Comp Eqt		575.47

5. Use straight-line depreciation to depreciate Mr. Haney's furniture. His furniture has a 5-year service life and a $500 salvage value. To depreciate furniture for the fourth quarter, use this calculation:

   $5,000 - $500 ÷ 5 X 3/12 = $225.00

Acct. #	Account Name	Debit	Credit
7060	Deprec. Exp.- Furniture	225.00	
1910	Accum. Depreciation - Furniture		225.00

6. Mr. Haney's purchased his automobile on October 1, 2008. Use the following adjusting entry. The computation is:

   $19,000 X 20% X 3/12 = $950.00

Acct. #	Account Name	Debit	Credit
7070	Deprec. Exp. - Automobile	950.00	
1920	Accum. Depreciation - Automobile		950.00

7. Mr. Haney's received a $10,000 advance from his publisher. This was recorded as ***unearned revenue*** on October 2, 2008. Unearned revenue is a liability account used to report advance collections from customers or clients. The amount of this adjusting entry is based on Mr. Haney's royalty statement.

Acct. #	Account Name	Debit	Credit
2400	Publisher Advances	3,500.00	
4050	Royalty Income		3,500.00

8. After journalizing and posting the end-of-quarter adjusting entries, print the General Journal for December 31, 2008. Follow these steps to print your December 31, 2008 General Journal:

   a. From the menu bar, click Reports & Forms; General Ledger.

   b. Highlight General Journal.

   c. Click 

.

   d. In the From field, click on the down arrow. A December appears. Select 31. Press <Enter>.

   e. From the Print window, make the selections to print. (Since the bank service charge posts to the general journal, December's service charge is also shown.)

Jon Haney Design
General Journal
For the Period From Dec 1, 2008 to Dec 31, 2008
Filter Criteria includes: Report order is by Date. Report is printed with Accounts having Zero Amounts and with shortened descriptions and in Detail Format.

Date	Account ID	Reference	Trans Description	Debit Amt	Credit Amt
12/31/08	6450		Office Supplies Expense	403.06	
	1450		Supplies		403.06
	6950		Insurance Expense	525.00	
	1300		Prepaid Insurance		525.00
	6300		Rent or Lease Expense	600.00	
	1400		Prepaid Rent		600.00
	7050		Deprec. Exp.-Comp Eqt	575.47	
	1900		Accum. Depreciation - Comp Eqt		575.47
	7060		Deprec. Exp.-Furniture	225.00	
	1910		Accum. Depreciation-Furniture		225.00
	7070		Deprec. Exp.-Automobile	950.00	
	1920		Accum. Depreciation-Automobile		950.00
	2400		Publisher Advances	3,500.00	
	4050		Royalty Income		3,500.00
12/31/08	1020	12/31/08	Service Charge		10.00
	6850		Service Charge	10.00	
		Total		6,788.53	6,788.53

If any of your general journal entries are incorrect, click  to drill down to the General Journal Entry window. Make the appropriate corrections, and then post your revised general journal entry. Display or print the general journal report.

9. Print the General Ledger Trial Balance (adjusted).

Jon Haney Design
General Ledger Trial Balance
As of Dec 31, 2008

Filter Criteria includes: Report order is by ID. Report is printed in Detail Format.

Account ID	Account Description	Debit Amt	Credit Amt
1010	Money Market Account	12,700.00	
1020	Checking Account	15,715.47	
1040	IRA Savings Account	27,730.35	
1045	WI State Retirement	35,612.00	
1300	Prepaid Insurance	1,575.00	
1450	Supplies	1,700.00	
1500	Computer Equipment	7,905.68	
1510	Furniture	5,000.00	
1520	Automobile	19,000.00	
1900	Accum. Depreciation - Co		575.47
1910	Accum. Depreciation - Furn		225.00
1920	Accum. Depreciation - Auto		950.00
2400	Publisher Advances		6,500.00
3920	Jon Haney, Capital		107,814.28
3930	Jon Haney, Draw	2,400.00	
4000	Teaching Income		8,148.57
4050	Royalty Income		9,920.90
6100	Dues and Subscriptions	45.00	
6150	Auto Registration	210.00	
6180	Automobile Expense	311.00	
6300	Rent or Lease Expense	600.00	
6400	Utilities Expense	196.46	
6420	Water & Power Expense	264.54	
6450	Office Supplies Expense	403.06	
6500	Telephone Expense	126.03	
6550	Long Distance Co.	203.19	
6560	Internet Service Provider	89.97	
6850	Bank Service Charge	30.00	
6950	Insurance Expense	525.00	
7050	Deprec. Exp. - Comp Eqt	575.47	
7060	Deprec. Exp. - Furniture	225.00	
7070	Deprec. Exp. - Automobile	950.00	
7400	Postage Expense	41.00	
	Total:	**134,134.22**	**134,134.22**

10. Print the Balance Sheet.

Jon Haney Design
Balance Sheet
December 31, 2008

ASSETS

Current Assets			
Money Market Account	$ 12,700.00		
Checking Account	15,715.47		
IRA Savings Account	27,730.35		
WI State Retirement	35,612.00		
Prepaid Insurance	1,575.00		
Supplies	1,700.00		
Total Current Assets			95,032.82
Property and Equipment			
Computer Equipment	7,905.68		
Furniture	5,000.00		
Automobile	19,000.00		
Accum. Depreciation - Comp Eqt	(575.47)		
Accum. Depreciation - Furnitur	(225.00)		
Accum. Depreciation - Automobi	(950.00)		
Total Property and Equipment			30,155.21
Other Assets			
Total Other Assets			0.00
Total Assets		$	125,188.03

LIABILITIES AND CAPITAL

Current Liabilities			
Publisher Advances	$ 6,500.00		
Total Current Liabilities			6,500.00
Long-Term Liabilities			
Total Long-Term Liabilities			0.00
Total Liabilities			6,500.00
Capital			
Jon Haney, Capital	107,814.28		
Jon Haney, Draw	(2,400.00)		
Net Income	13,273.75		
Total Capital			118,688.03
Total Liabilities & Capital		$	125,188.03

11. Print the Income Statement.

Jon Haney Design
Income Statement
For the Twelve Months Ending December 31, 2008

		Current Month			Year to Date	
Revenues						
Teaching Income	$	2,716.19	43.70	$	8,148.57	45.10
Royalty Income		3,500.00	56.30		9,920.90	54.90
Total Revenues		6,216.19	100.00		18,069.47	100.00
Cost of Sales						
Total Cost of Sales		0.00	0.00		0.00	0.00
Gross Profit		6,216.19	100.00		18,069.47	100.00
Expenses						
Dues and Subscriptions		0.00	0.00		45.00	0.25
Auto Registration		0.00	0.00		210.00	1.16
Automobile Expense		0.00	0.00		311.00	1.72
Rent or Lease Expense		600.00	9.65		600.00	3.32
Utilities Expense		102.92	1.66		196.46	1.09
Water & Power Expense		75.45	1.21		264.54	1.46
Office Supplies Expense		403.06	6.48		403.06	2.23
Telephone Expense		45.95	0.74		126.03	0.70
Long Distance Co.		75.49	1.21		203.19	1.12
Internet Service Provider		29.99	0.48		89.97	0.50
Bank Service Charge		10.00	0.16		30.00	0.17
Insurance Expense		525.00	8.45		525.00	2.91
Deprec. Exp. - Comp Eqt		575.47	9.26		575.47	3.18
Deprec. Exp. - Furniture		225.00	3.62		225.00	1.25
Deprec. Exp. - Automobile		950.00	15.28		950.00	5.26
Postage Expense		0.00	0.00		41.00	0.23
Total Expenses		3,618.33	58.21		4,795.72	26.54
Net Income	$	2,597.86	41.79	$	13,273.75	73.46

Comment

If your income statement or the other financial statements shown on pages 343 through 347 *do not agree* with the textbook illustrations, edit your journals, post, then reprint your reports. If the Year to Date column *does not agree* with what is shown on the Income Statement, Statement of Cash Flow (p. 346) and the Statement of Changes in Financial Position (p. 347), refer to Entering Chart of Accounts Beginning Balances in Chapter 9 on pages 267-272. Correct year-to-date balances depend on setting the beginning balances correctly for 9/1/08 through 9/30/08 (see the Select Period window on p. 269, below step 3).

12. Follow these steps to print the Statement of Retained Earnings.

    a. In the Financial Statement list, click <Standard> Retained Earnings to highlight it.

    b. Click 

    c. Uncheck Show Zero Amounts. Make the selections to print. Compare your Statement of Retained Earnings to the one shown below.

Jon Haney Design
Statement of Retained Earnings
For the Twelve Months Ending December 31, 2008

Beginning Retained Earnings	$	0.00
Adjustments To Date		0.00
Net Income		13,273.75
Subtotal		13,273.75
Jon Haney, Draw		(2,400.00)
Ending Retained Earnings	$	10,873.75

The Statement of Retained Earnings shows the net income at the end of the Quarter, $13,273.75, minus Mr. Haney's drawing, $2,400. When you close the fiscal year, the Ending Retained Earnings amount, $10,873.75, will be shown on the post-closing trial balance, page 354.

13. Print the Statement of Cash Flow. Compare it to the one shown on the next page.

Jon Haney Design
Statement of Cash Flow
For the twelve Months Ended December 31, 2008

		Current Month		Year to Date
Cash Flows from operating activities				
Net Income	$	2,597.86	$	13,273.75
Adjustments to reconcile net income to net cash provided by operating activities				
Accum. Depreciation - Comp Eqt		575.47		575.47
Accum. Depreciation - Furnitur		225.00		225.00
Accum. Depreciation - Automobi		950.00		950.00
Prepaid Insurance		525.00		(1,575.00)
Prepaid Rent		600.00		0.00
Supplies		287.81		(1,700.00)
Publisher Advances		(3,500.00)		6,500.00
Total Adjustments		(336.72)		4,975.47
Net Cash provided by Operations		2,261.14		18,249.22
Cash Flows from investing activities				
Used For				
Computer Equipment		0.00		(7,905.68)
Furniture		0.00		(5,000.00)
Automobile		0.00		(19,000.00)
Net cash used in investing		0.00		(31,905.68)
Cash Flows from financing activities				
Proceeds From				
Jon Haney, Capital		0.00		107,814.28
Used For				
Jon Haney, Draw		(1,200.00)		(2,400.00)
Net cash used in financing		(1,200.00)		105,414.28
Net increase <decrease> in cash	$	1,061.14	$	91,757.82
Summary				
Cash Balance at End of Period	$	91,757.82	$	91,757.82
Cash Balance at Beg of Period		(90,696.68)		0.00
Net Increase <Decrease> in Cash	$	1,061.14	$	91,757.82

14. Print the Statement of Changes in Financial Position (<Standard> Stmnt Changes). This is a Peachtree report that describes changes in a company's financial position that may not be obvious from the balance sheet, income statement, or other financial statements. Peachtree's financial statements are meant for management purposes. Financial statements can also be customized to reflect the specific needs of the company.

Jon Haney Design
Statement of Changes in Financial Position
For the twelve months ended December 31, 2008

		Current Month		Year To Date
Sources of Working Capital				
Net Income	$	2,597.86	$	13,273.75
Add back items not requiring working capital				
Accum. Depreciation - Comp Eqt		575.47		575.47
Accum. Depreciation - Furnitur		225.00		225.00
Accum. Depreciation - Automobi		950.00		950.00
Working capital from operations		4,348.33		15,024.22
Other sources				
Jon Haney, Capital		0.00		107,814.28
Total sources		4,348.33		122,838.50
Uses of working capital				
Computer Equipment		0.00		(7,905.68)
Furniture		0.00		(5,000.00)
Automobile		0.00		(19,000.00)
Total uses		0.00		(31,905.68)
Net change	$	4,348.33	$	90,932.82
Analysis of componants of changes				
Increase <Decrease> in Current Assets				
Money Market Account	$	0.00	$	12,700.00
Checking Account		1,061.14		15,715.47
IRA Savings Account		0.00		27,730.35
WI State Retirement		0.00		35,612.00
Prepaid Insurance		(525.00)		1,575.00
Prepaid Rent		(600.00)		0.00
Supplies		(287.81)		1,700.00
<Increase> Decrease in Current Liabilities				
Publisher Advances		3,500.00		(6,500.00)
Net change	$	3,148.33	$	88,532.82

BACKING UP DECEMBER DATA

Follow these steps to back up Jon Haney's December data:

1. From the Company page, link to <u>Back up</u>. (*Or,* from the menu bar, select File, then Back up.)

2. If necessary, uncheck the box next to Include company name in the backup file name. Click 
.

3. Accept the default for backing up to the hard drive or make the selections to back up to another location. Type **Chapter 10 December** in the File name field.

4. Click 
.

5. When the window prompts that This company backup will require approximately 3.40MB, click 
. When the Back Up Company scale is 100% complete, you have successfully backed up to the current point in Chapter 10.

6. Click File, Exit to exit Peachtree. Or, continue with the next section.

CLOSING THE FISCAL YEAR

At the end of the year, PCA automatically completes the closing procedure. Follow these steps to close Jon Haney's fiscal year:

1. If necessary, start Peachtree, then open Jon Haney Design. From the menu bar, select Tasks, System, Year-End Wizard.[6]

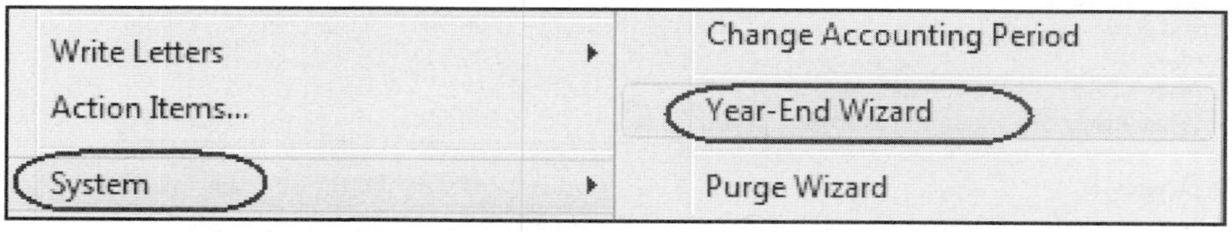

---

[6]If a Peachtree Accounting window appears that asks if you still want to open the Year-End Wizard, click Yes.

2. The Year-End Wizard - Welcome window appears. Read the information on the Welcome to the Peachtree Year-End Wizard window.

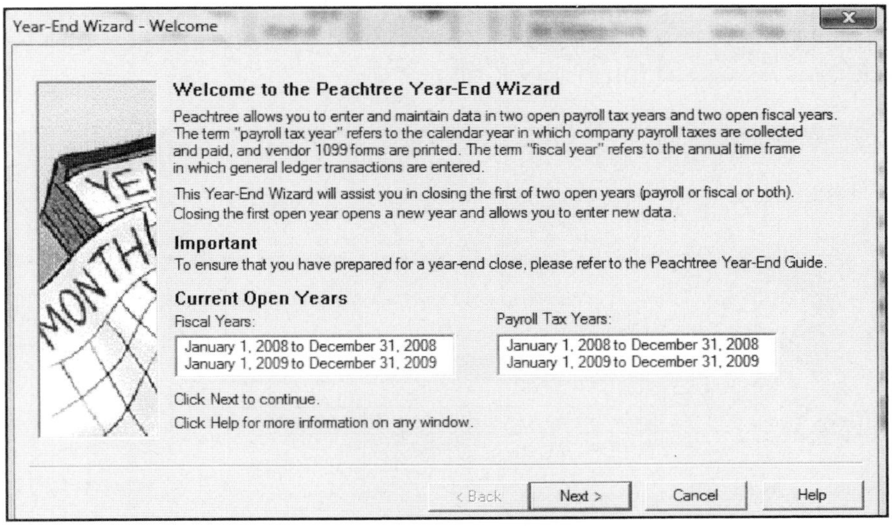

3. Click  .

4. The Close Options window appears. In the Years to Close list, Fiscal and Payroll Tax Years is the default. Read the information on this window.

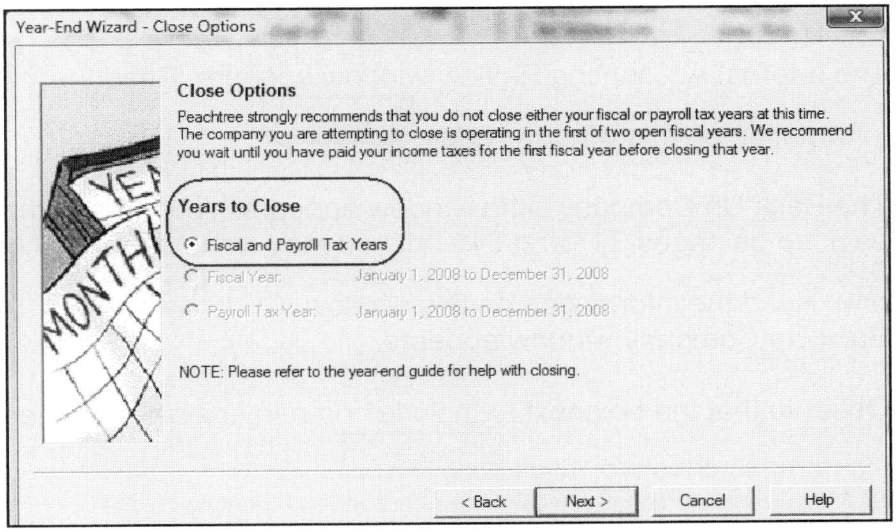

5. Click Next >.

6. The Print Fiscal Year-End Reports window appears. Read the information on this window. Since you have already printed reports, click Check None to uncheck all.

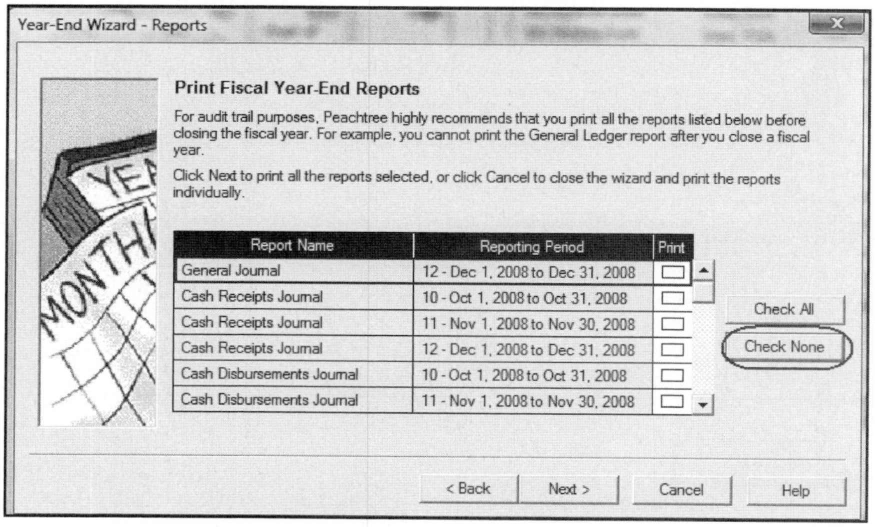

Hint: If you do not *uncheck the boxes, the general ledger prints.*

7. Click Next >.

8. The Internal Accounting Review window appears. Read the information on this window. Click Next >.

9. The Back Up Company Data window appears. You already made a back up on pages 347 and 348 but you may want to make another one. Read the information on this window. Click Back Up. The Back Up Company window appears.

10. Observe that the box next to Include company name in the backup file name is checked. Click Back Up.

11. The Save Backup for Jon Haney Design as window appears. Observe that the File name field includes the name of the company and today's date.

12. Click Save. Make the selections to back up.

13. After the backup is made, you are returned to the Back Up Company Data window. Click Next >.

14. The New Open Fiscal Years window appears. Read the information on this window.

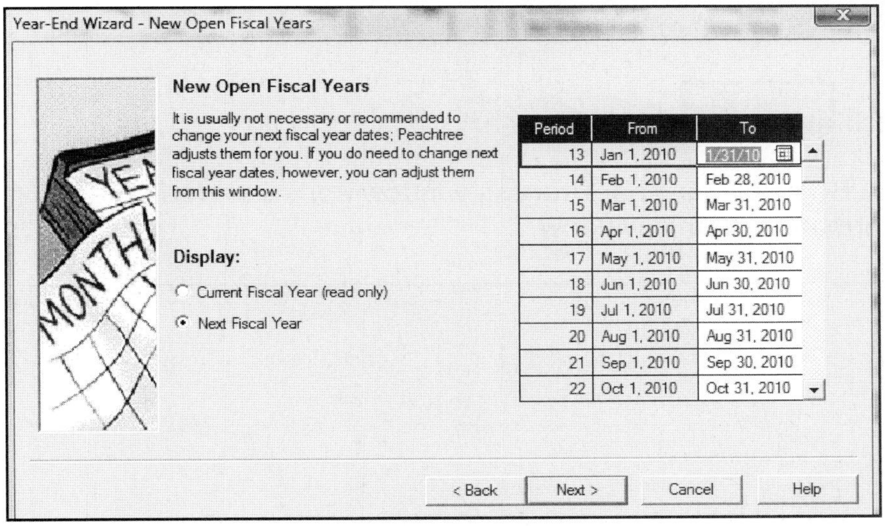

15. Accept the default for Next Fiscal Year by clicking on Next >.

16. The Important - Confirm Year-End Close window appears. Read the information on this window.

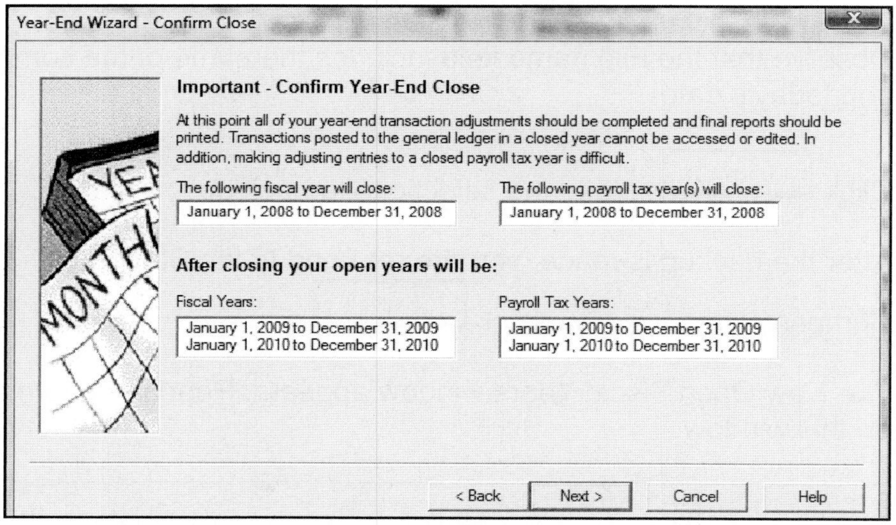

17. Click 

.

18. The Begin Close-Year Process window appears. Read the information on this window.

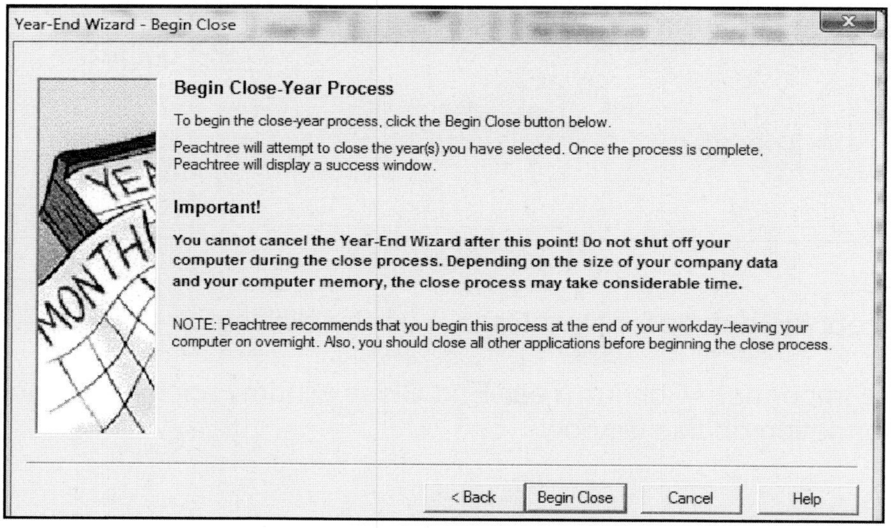

19. Click 

.

20. After a few moments the scale shows 100%. The Congratulations! window appears. Read the information on this window.

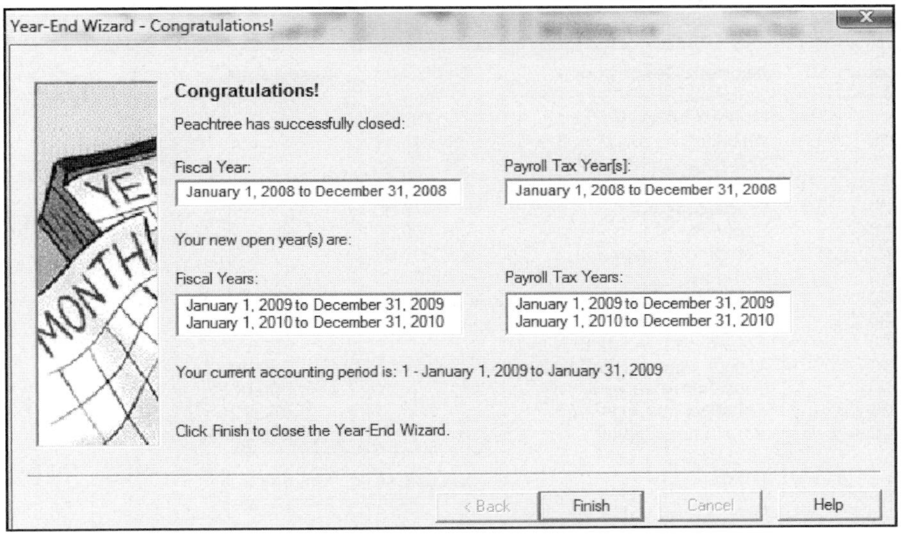

21. Click 

.

PRINTING THE POST-CLOSING TRIAL BALANCE

After the fiscal year is closed, a post-closing trial balance is printed. Only permanent accounts appear on the post-closing trial balance. All temporary accounts (revenues and expenses) have been closed. This completes the computer accounting cycle.

Follow these steps to print Jon Haney's post-closing trial balance:

1. From the menu bar, select Reports & Forms, General Ledger, General Ledger Trial Balance.

2. Make the selections to print the post-closing trial balance. Compare your general ledger trial balance (post-closing) to the one shown on the next page.

Jon Haney Design
General Ledger Trial Balance
As of Jan 31, 2009

Filter Criteria includes: Report order is by ID. Report is printed in Detail Format.

Account ID	Account Description	Debit Amt	Credit Amt
1010	Money Market Account	12,700.00	
1020	Checking Account	15,715.47	
1040	IRA Savings Account	27,730.35	
1045	WI State Retirement	35,612.00	
1300	Prepaid Insurance	1,575.00	
1450	Supplies	1,700.00	
1500	Computer Equipment	7,905.68	
1510	Furniture	5,000.00	
1520	Automobile	19,000.00	
1900	Accum. Depreciation - Co		575.47
1910	Accum. Depreciation - Furn		225.00
1920	Accum. Depreciation - Auto		950.00
2400	Publisher Advances		6,500.00
3910	Retained Earnings		10,873.75
3920	Jon Haney, Capital		107,814.28
	Total:	**126,938.50**	**126,938.50**

Observe that the post-closing trial balance is dated January 31, 2009. The balance in retained earnings (Account No. 3910) is Mr. Haney's year-to-date net income minus the total of his drawing accounts (13,273.75 – 2,400 = 10,873.75). The Retained Earnings balance was also shown on page 345, Statement of Retained Earnings.

BACKING UP YEAR-END DATA

Follow these steps to back up Jon Haney's year-end data:

1. From the Company page, link to Back up. (*Or,* from the menu bar, select File, then Back up.)
2. If necessary, uncheck the box next to Include company name in the backup file name. Click Back Up.
3. Accept the default for backing up to the hard drive or make the selections to back up to another location. Type **Chapter 10 EOY** in the File name field.
4. Click Save.

5. When the window prompts that This company backup will require approximately 3.40MB, click OK. When the Back Up Company scale is 100% complete, you have successfully backed up to the current point in Chapter 10.

6. Click File, Exit to exit Peachtree.

	INTERNET ACTIVITY
1.	From your Internet browser, go to the book's website at http://www.mhhe.com/yacht2008.
2.	Link to Student Edition.
3.	In the Course-wide Content list, link Internet Activities; then link to Part 2 Internet Activities for Chapter 9-10. Open or save. (You can also choose Chapter 10, then link to Internet Activities. (In the Choose a Chapter field, if you select Chapter 10 observe that other chapter-specific links are available; for example, Multiple Choice Quiz, True or False, PowerPoint Presentations and Going to the Net Exercises.) Also observe that Course-wide Content includes a Glossary link.
4.	If necessary, scroll down the window to UNDERSTANDING ACCOUNTING TERMS – Chapter 10. Read steps 1 – 3.
5.	Follow the steps shown on the book's website to complete this Internet activity.

SUMMARY AND REVIEW

SOFTWARE OBJECTIVES: In Chapter 10, you used the software to:

1. Restore data from Chapter 9. (This backup was made on page 305.)
2. Change accounting periods.
3. Journalize and post transactions for Jon Haney Design, for the months of November and December.
4. Complete account reconciliation.
5. Print a General Ledger Trial Balance (unadjusted).
6. Journalize and post quarterly adjusting entries in the General Journal.
7. Print adjusted trial balance and financial statements.
8. Close the fiscal year.

9. Print a Post-Closing Trial Balance.

10. Make eight backups: four backups of Jon Haney Design data; one backup of Exercise 10-1; three backups of Exercise 10-2.

WEB OBJECTIVES: In Chapter 10, you did these Internet activities:

1. Used your Internet browser to go to the book's website.

2. Went to the Internet Activity link on the book's website. Then, selected WEB EXERCISES PART 2. Completed the second web exercise in Part 2, Understanding Accounting Terms.

3. Used a word processing program to write summaries of the websites that you visited.

GOING TO THE NET[7]

Access the asset depreciation schedule at http://office.microsoft.com/en-us/templates/TC010460991033.aspx. (*Hint:* Excel 2000 or later is required.) Click Download. Save the asset depreciation schedule. An Asset Depreciation worksheet appears.

Complete the following fields. Press <Enter> to move between fields.

Date:	1/1/2004
Initial cost:	7000
Salvage value:	0
Useful life (years)	7

1. Click on Asset Depreciation. Type **Furniture** to replace it.
2. From Excel's menu bar, make the selections to Print.
3. Make the selections to save. The suggested file name is **Asset depreciation.xls**. (*Hint:* If using Excel 2007, the file extension is .xlsx.)
4. What depreciation methods are shown?
5. Close Excel; close Internet Explorer.

[7]The file used to complete this exercise is included on the textbook website at www.mhhe.com/yacht2008; link to the Student Edition, then link to Text Updates.

True/Make True: Write the word True in the space provided if the statement is true. If the statement is not true, write the correct answer.

1. You can complete the activities in Chapter 10 without completing Chapter 9.

____

____

2. Step 4 of PCA's Computer Accounting Cycle is reconciling the bank statement.

____

____

3. To change an accounting period, use the Maintain menu.

____

____

4. Jon Haney's checkbook register and bank statement are used as source documents for recording journal entries.

____

____

5. The account reconciliation feature can reconcile the cash account only.

____

____

____

6. The accounting periods used in Chapter 10 are November 1 - 30 and December 1 - 31, 2008.

____

____

7. PCA includes an editing feature so that records can be corrected.

____

____

____

8. For the two months ending November 30, 2008, Mr. Haney's net income is $4,861.07.

____

____

9. At the end of the quarter, Mr. Haney's total assets are $95,032.82.

____

____

10. The statement of retained earnings and the post-closing trial balance show the same balance for retained earnings.

____

____

____

Exercise 10-1: Follow the instructions below to complete Exercise 10-1. You must complete Exercises 9-1 and 9-2 *before* you can do Exercise 10-1.

1. Start Peachtree. Open the company that you started in Exercise 9-1. The company name is Your Name, Designer.

2. Restore your data from Exercise 9-2.[8] The suggested file name was Exercise 9-2.ptb. This back up was made on page 317. (Hint: To make sure you are starting in the right place, display the general ledger trial balance and compare it to the one printed for Exercise 9-2, step 10, page 316. Compare the Stockmen's Bank account

---

[8]You can restore from your back up file even if *no* Peachtree company exists. From Peachtree's start up window, select File; Restore. Select the location of your backup file. On the Restore Wizard's Select Company window, select A New Company. The *A New Company* selection allows you to restore your backup data, bypassing the process of new company set up. For more information, refer to Troubleshooting on pages 280-281.

balance on the general ledger trial balance with the 10/31/08 balance on the check register below.)

3. Change accounting periods to November 1 through November 30, 2008.

4. Use the check register below to journalize and post cash receipts journal and cash disbursement journal transactions. (*Hint: Use Write Checks for checks and ATMs; use Receipts for deposits.*)

Check Number	Date	Description of Transaction	Payment/ Dr (-)	Deposit/ Cr. (+)	Balance
	10/31/08	Bank Service Charge	12.00		12,823.30
	11/2/08	ATM	100.00		12,723.30
	11/3/08	Deposit (Designer income)		2,200.00	14,923.30
1009	11/3/08	Vince's Maintenance and Repairs	75.00		14,848.30
	11/8/08	Deposit (Teaching income)		2,105.00	16,953.30
1010	11/9/08	Utilities Co.	55.75		16,897.55
1011	11/10/08	Vincent Advertising, Inc.	175.00		16,722.55
1012	11/13/08	U.S. Post Office	41.00		16,681.55
1013	11/15/08	Eastern Telephone	41.97		16,639.58
1014	11/16/08	DSL Service	29.95		16,609.63
	11/20/08	ATM	100.00		16,509.63
1015	11/28/08	Office Shoppe[9]	47.80		16,461.83
	11/29/08	ATM	200.00		16,261.83

5. Use the Bank Statement on the next page to complete Account Reconciliation. (*Hint: Remember to record the bank service charge on the Account Reconciliation window.*)

[9]Debit Account No. 1450, Supplies.

Statement of Account Stockmen's Bank November 1 to November 30, 2008		Account No. 2178992-30	Your Name Your Address Your city, state, Zip	
REGULAR CHECKING				
Previous Balance	10/31/08	13,016.25		
2 Deposits(+)		4,305.00		
6 Checks (-)		539.70		
2 Other Deductions (-)		400.00		
Service Charges (-)	11/30/08	12.00		
Ending Balance	11/30/08	**16,369.55**		
DEPOSITS				
	11/6/08	2,200.00		
	11/8/08	2,105.00		
CHECKS (Asterisk * indicates break in check number sequence)				
	11/10/08	1006*	55.15	
	11/10/08	1008	137.80	
	11/24/08	1009	75.00	
	11/24/08	1010	55.75	
	11/27/08	1011	175.00	
	11/30/08	1012	41.00	
OTHER DEDUCTIONS (ATM's)				
	11/2/08	100.00		
	11/20/08	100.00		
	11/29/08	200.00		

6. Print an Account Reconciliation report.
7. Print the Cash Account Register.
8. Print the General Journal.
9. Print the Cash Receipts Journal.
10. Print the Cash Disbursements Journal.
11. Print the General Ledger Trial Balance.

12. Print a Balance Sheet and Income Statement.

13. Backup your data. The suggested file name is Exercise 10-1.

Exercise 10-2: Follow the instructions below to complete Exercise 10-2. Exercise 10-1 *must* be completed before starting Exercise 10-2.

1. Start PCA. Open the company that you set up in Exercise 9-1 (Student Name, Designer).

2. Restore Exercise 10-1.[10]

3. Change accounting periods to December 1 through December 31, 2008.

4. Use the check register below and on the next page to journalize and post cash receipts journal and cash disbursement journal transactions. (*Hint:* The balance, $16,249.83, should match Account No. 1020 for Stockmen's Bank. On the Business Status toolbar, click 

. The balance shows $16,249.83.)

Check Number	Date	Description of Transaction	Payment/ Dr (-)	Deposit/ Cr. (+)	Balance
	11/30/08	Bank Service Charge	12.00		16,249.83
	12/2/08	ATM	100.00		16,149.83
	12/3/08	Deposit (Designer income)		2,850.00	18,999.83
1016	12/3/08	Vincent Advertising	100.00		18,899.83
	12/3/08	Deposit (Teaching income)		2,105.00	21,004.83
1017	12/8/08	Vince's Maintenance and Repairs	75.00		20,929.83
1018	12/9/08	Utilities Co.	95.75		20,834.08
1019	12/13/08	U.S. Post Office	41.00		20,793.08
1020	12/15/08	Eastern Telephone	45.05		20,748.03

[10]You can restore from your backup file even if *no* Peachtree company exists. From Peachtree's start up window, select File; Restore. Select the location of your backup file. On the Restore Wizard's Select Company window, select A New Company. The *A New Company* selection allows you to restore your backup data, bypassing the process of new company set up. For more information, refer to Troubleshooting on pages 280-281.

1021	12/16/08	DSL Service	29.95		20,718.08
	12/20/08	ATM	100.00		20,618.08
1022	12/28/08	Office Shoppe[11]	137.80		20,480.28
	12/30/08	ATM	200.00		20,280.28

5. Use the following Bank Statement to complete Account Reconciliation. *Record the bank service charge on the Account Reconciliation window*. (*Hint:* Two deposits were made on 12/3/08 for a total of $4,955.00.)

Statement of Account Stockmen's Bank December 1 to December 31, 2008		Account No. 2178992-30	Your Name Your Address Your City, State, Zip	
		REGULAR CHECKING		
Previous Balance	11/30/08	16,369.55		
2 Deposits(+)		4,955.00		
6 Checks (-)		390.47		
3 Other Deductions (-)		400.00		
Service Charges (-)	12/31/08	12.00		
Ending Balance	12/31/08	**20,522.08**		
		DEPOSITS		
	12/6/08	2,850.00		
	12/6/08	2,105.00		
		CHECKS (Asterisk * indicates break in check number sequence)		
	12/10/08	1013	41.97	
	12/10/08	1014	29.95	
	12/24/08	1015	47.80	
	12/24/08	1016	100.00	
	12/27/08	1017	75.00	
	12/30/08	1018	95.75	
		OTHER DEDUCTIONS (ATM's)		
	12/2/08	100.00	12/30/08	~~100.00~~ 200
	12/20/08	100.00		

[11] Debit Account No. 1450, Supplies.

6. Print an Account Reconciliation report.
7. Print the Cash Account Register.
8. Print the General Journal.
9. Print the Cash Receipts Journal.
10. Print the Cash Disbursements Journal.
11. Print the General Ledger Trial Balance (unadjusted).
12. Back up your data. The suggested file name is Exercise 10-2 Unadjusted Trial Balance.
13. Complete the following end-of-quarter adjusting entries.

    a. Supplies on hand: $850.00.
    b. Depreciation for Computer Equipment: $458.33.
    c. Depreciation for Furniture: $150.00.
    d. Depreciation for the Automobile: $950.00.
    e. Adjust three months prepaid rent: $700.00.
    f. Adjust three months prepaid insurance: $250.00.

14. Print the December 31, 2008 general journal.
15. Print the General Ledger Trial Balance (adjusted).
16. Print the financial statements: Balance Sheet, Income Statement, Statement of Cash Flow, Statement of Retained Earnings and Statement of Changes in Financial Position.
17. Back up your data. The suggested filename is Exercise 10-2 Financial Statements.
18. Close the fiscal year.
19. Print the General Ledger Trial Balance (post-closing).
20. Back up your data. The suggested filename is Exercise 10-2 End of Year.
21. Exit Peachtree.

CHAPTER 10 INDEX

Project 1 Mary Albert, Accountant

In Project 1, you will complete the Computer Accounting Cycle for Mary Albert, Accountant. Ms. Albert started her accounting practice on December 1, 2008 in Mesa, AZ. Ms. Albert employs two accounting technicians and one administrative assistant. Ms. Albert's employees are independent contractors. Further study of payroll accounting will be done in Chapter 14.

In this project you will complete the accounting cycle for the month of December 2008. Mary Albert's balance sheet, checkbook register, and bank statement are provided as source documents.

At the end of this project, a checklist is shown listing the printed reports you should have. The step-by-step instructions remind you to print reports at certain intervals. Your instructor may require these printouts for grading purposes. Remember to make backups at periodic intervals.

Follow these steps to complete Project 1:

Step 1: Start Peachtree. If a company opens, select File; New Company. When the window prompts, This will close the current company, click 

. The Create a New Company – Introduction window appears. Click 

.

Step 2: Type the following company information:

Company Name:	**Mary Albert, Accountant** (*use your name*)
Address Line 1:	**7760 Camelback Road**
City, State, Zip	**Mesa, AZ 85012**
Country:	**USA**
Telephone:	**480-555-3602**
Fax:	**480-555-3604**
Business Type:	Select Sole Proprietorship

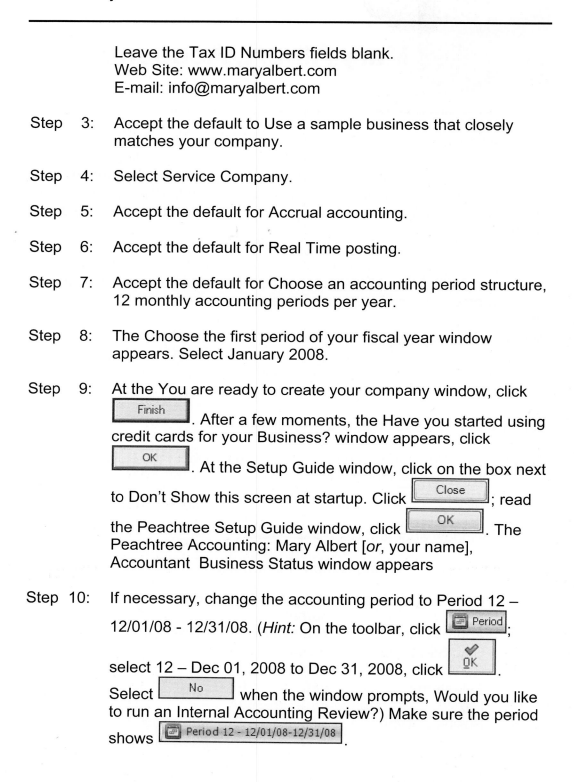

Leave the Tax ID Numbers fields blank.
Web Site: www.maryalbert.com
E-mail: info@maryalbert.com

Step 3: Accept the default to Use a sample business that closely matches your company.

Step 4: Select Service Company.

Step 5: Accept the default for Accrual accounting.

Step 6: Accept the default for Real Time posting.

Step 7: Accept the default for Choose an accounting period structure, 12 monthly accounting periods per year.

Step 8: The Choose the first period of your fiscal year window appears. Select January 2008.

Step 9: At the You are ready to create your company window, click Finish. After a few moments, the Have you started using credit cards for your Business? window appears, click OK. At the Setup Guide window, click on the box next to Don't Show this screen at startup. Click Close; read the Peachtree Setup Guide window, click OK. The Peachtree Accounting: Mary Albert [*or*, your name], Accountant Business Status window appears

Step 10: If necessary, change the accounting period to Period 12 – 12/01/08 - 12/31/08. (*Hint:* On the toolbar, click Period; select 12 – Dec 01, 2008 to Dec 31, 2008, click OK. Select No when the window prompts, Would you like to run an Internal Accounting Review?) Make sure the period shows Period 12 - 12/01/08-12/31/08.

Step 11: Make the following changes to the Chart of Accounts:

Delete these accounts:

1010	Cash on Hand
1150	Allowance for Doubtful Account
2310	Sales Tax Payable
2320	Deductions Payable
2330	Federal Payroll Taxes Payable
2340	FUTA Payable
2350	State Payroll Taxes Payable
2360	SUTA Payable
2370	Local Taxes Payable
2400	Customer Deposits
2700	Long-Term Debt–Noncurrent
4300	Other Income
5900	Inventory Adjustments
6250	Other Taxes Expense
6650	Commissions and Fees Expense
7100	Gain/Loss – Sale of Assets Exp

Change these accounts:[1]

1020	Checking Account	**Mesa Bank**
1400	Prepaid Expenses	**Prepaid Rent**
1500	Property and Equipment	**Computer Equipment**
1900	Accum. Depreciation-Prop&Eqt	**Accum. Depreciation-Comp Eqt**
2500	Current Portion Long-Term Debt	**Notes Payable**
3920	Owner's Contribution	**Mary Albert, Capital** (Use your name; *Account Type*: *Equity-doesn't close*)
3930	Owner's Draw	**Mary Albert, Draw** (Use your name)
4000	Professional Fees	**Accounting Fees**
6000	Wages Expense	**Wages Expense – Adm Asst**

[1]New account names are shown in boldface. Click Save & New between accounts.

6050	Employee Benefit Programs Exp.	**Wages Expense - Acctg Tech**
6150	Bad Debts Expense	**Subscriptions Expense**
6450	Office Supplies Expense	**Supplies Expense**
6550	Other Office Expense	**DSL Internet Service**
7050	Depreciation Expense	**Deprec Exp – Comp Eqt**

Add these accounts:

1450	**Supplies**	Other Current Assets
1510	**Furniture and Fixtures**	Fixed Assets
1520	**Automobile**	Fixed Assets
1910	**Accum. Depreciation – Furn&Fix**	Accum. Depreciation
1920	**Accum. Depreciation – Automobi**	Accum. Depreciation
7060	**Deprec Exp - Furn&Fix**	Expenses
7070	**Deprec Exp - Automobile**	Expenses
7400	**Postage Expense**	Expenses

Step 12: Print the Chart of Accounts.

Step 13: Use Mary Albert's Balance Sheet to enter the beginning balances. Remember when selecting the beginning balance period, use 11/1/08 through 11/30/08—Beginning Balances as of November 30, 2008.

Mary Albert, Accountant, Balance Sheet December 1, 2008		
ASSETS		
Current Assets		
Mesa Bank	$28,500.00	
Accounts Receivable	15,400.00	
Prepaid Rent	4,000.00	
Supplies	3,300.00	
Total Current Assets		$51,200.00
Property and Equipment		
Computer Equipment	12,600.00	
Furniture and Fixtures	15,000.00	
		continued

Automobile	21,500.00	
Total Property and Equipment		49,100.00
Total Assets		$100,300.00
LIABILITIES AND CAPITAL		
Current Liabilities		
Accounts Payable	$11,200.00	
Notes Payable	8,400.00	
Total Current Liabilities		19,600.00
Capital		
Mary Albert, Capital		80,700.00
Total Liabilities and Capital		$ 100,300.00

Step 14: Back up Ms. Albert's beginning data. The suggested file name is Mary Albert Begin.

Step 15: The checkbook register below provides the information necessary for December's journal entries. Remember to post between each transaction.

Check Number	Date	Transaction Description	Payment/ Dr. (-)	Deposit/ Cr. (+)	Balance
					28,500.00
	12/1	Deposit (accounting fees)		3,500.00	32,000.00
9001	12/1	Mesa Bank (Notes Payable)	2,700.00		29,300.00
9002	12/1	Mesa Office Equipment - laser printer (computer equipment)	625.87		28,674.13
9003	12/5	Administrative Asst.	1,250.00		27,424.13
9004	12/5	Acctg. Technician	690.00		26,734.13
9005	12/11	Office Supplies, etc. (letterhead - supplies)	105.65		26,628.48
9006	12/12	Administrative Asst.	1,250.00		25,378.48
9007	12/12	Acctg. Technician	690.00		24,688.48
	12/16	Deposit (accounting fees)		3,500.00	28,188.48
9008	12/17	Southwest Telephone (telephone bill)	70.47		28,118.01
					continued

9009	12/19	U.S. Post Office (stamps)	41.00		28,077.01
9010	12/19	Journal of Accounting (subscription)	545.00		27,532.01
9011	12/19	Administrative Asst.	1,250.00		26,282.01
9012	12/19	Acctg. Technician	620.00		25,662.01
	12/23	Deposit (accounting fees)		4,000.00	29,662.01
9013	12/24	Maricopa Electric Co. (utilities bill)	105.20		29,556.81
	12/26	Deposit (accounting fees)		4,000.00	33,556.81
9014	12/26	Administrative Asst.	1,250.00		32,306.81
9015	12/26	Acctg. Technician	750.00		31,556.81
	12/30	Deposit (payment received from client on account)		1,500.00	33,056.81
9016	12/30	DSL Internet Service	29.99		33,026.82

Step 16: Mary Albert's bank statement is shown below. (*Hint:* Remember to record the bank service charge.)

Statement of Account
Mesa Bank
December 1 to December 31, 2008 Account No. 4733-620512

Mary Albert, Accountant
7760 Camelback Road
Mesa, AZ 85012

REGULAR CHECKING				
Previous Balance	11/30/08	28,500.00		
4 Deposits(+)		15,000.00		
12 Checks (-)		10,607.19		
Service Charges (-)	12/31/08	25.00		
Ending Balance	12/31/08	**32,867.81**		
DEPOSITS				
	12/3/08	3,500.00	12/26/08	4,000.00
	12/17/08	3,500.00	12/30/08	4,000.00
CHECKS (Asterisk * indicates break in check number sequence)				
	12/10/08	9001	2,700.00	
	12/11/08	9002	625.87	
	12/15/08	9003	1,250.00	
	12/15/08	9004	690.00	
	12/15/08	9005	105.65	
	12/15/08	9006	1,250.00	

continued

	12/15/08	9007	690.00	
	12/22/08	9008	70.47	
	12/22/08	9011*	1,250.00	
	12/22/08	9012	620.00	
	12/29/08	9013	105.20	
	12/30/08	9014	1,250.00	

Step 17: Print an Account Reconciliation report.

Step 18: Print a Cash Account Register.

Step 19: Print a General Ledger Trial Balance (unadjusted).

Step 20: Back up. The suggested file name is Mary Albert UTB. (UTB is an abbreviation for unadjusted trial balance.)

Step 21: Complete these adjusting entries:

a. Supplies on hand: $3,250.00.
b. Depreciation for Computer Equipment: $353.50.
c. Depreciation for Furniture and Fixtures: $166.67.
d. Depreciation for the Automobile: $358.33.
e. Rent was paid for two months on November 30, 2008. Adjust one month's rent.[2]

Step 22: Print the December 31, 2008 General Journal, Cash Receipts Journal, and Cash Disbursements Journal.

Step 23: Print the General Ledger Trial Balance (adjusted).

Step 24: Print the General Ledger. (*Hint: Select Reports & Forms; General Ledger, highlight General Ledger, make the selections to print.*)

Step 25: Print the financial statements: balance sheet, income statement, statement of retained earnings, statement of cash flow, statement of changes in financial position.

---

[2]Refer to the December 1, 2008, Balance Sheet for the account balance in the Prepaid Rent account.

Step 26: Back up December data. The suggested file name is Mary Albert December.

Step 27: Close the fiscal year. (If a window appears saying that The current Peachtree system date falls within the first of two open fiscal years. Do you still want to open the Year-End Wizard? Click Yes. Continue closing the fiscal year.)

Step 28: Print the Post-Closing Trial Balance.

Step 29: Back up year-end data. The suggested file name is Mary Albert EOY.

Your instructor may want to collect this project. A Checklist of Printouts is shown below.

Checklist of Printouts, Project 1: Mary Albert, Accountant	
	Chart of Accounts
	Account Reconciliation
	Cash Account Register
	General Ledger Trial Balance (unadjusted)
	December 31, 2008 General Journal
	Cash Receipts Journal
	Cash Disbursements Journal
	General Ledger Trial Balance (adjusted)
	General Ledger
	Balance Sheet
	Income Statement
	Statement of Retained Earnings
	Statement of Cash Flow
	Statement of Changes in Financial Position
	Post-Closing Trial Balance

Student Name______________________________ **Date**____________

CHECK YOUR PROGRESS: PROJECT 1, Mary Albert, Accountant

1. What are the total debit and credit balances on your unadjusted trial balance? __________

2. What are the total debit and credit balances on your adjusted trial balance? __________

3. According to your account reconciliation report, what is the Ending GL Balance? __________

4. What is the depreciation expense for furniture and fixtures on December 31? __________

5. What is the depreciation expense for computer equipment on December 31? __________

6. What is the amount of total revenues as of December 31? __________

7. How much net income <or net loss> is reported on December 31? __________

8. What is the account balance in the Supplies account on December 31? __________

9. What is the account balance in the Accounts Payable account on December 31? __________

10. What is the total capital balance on December 31? __________

11. Is there an Increase or Decrease in cash for the the month of December? __________

12. Were any Accounts Payable incurred during the month of December? (Circle your answer). YES NO

Project 1A Student-Designed Service Business

In Chapters 9, 10 and Project 1, you learned how to complete the Computer Accounting Cycle for a service business. Project 1A gives you a chance to design a service business of your own.

You create a service business, edit your business's Chart of Accounts, create source documents, and complete PCA's Computer Accounting Cycle. Project 1A also gives you an opportunity to review the software features learned so far.

You should think about the kind of business to create. Since you have been working on sole proprietorship service businesses in Part 2, you might want to design a business similar to these. Service businesses include: accountants, beauty salons, architects, hotels, airlines, cleaning stores, doctors, artists, etc. If you have a checking account and receive a monthly bank statement, you could use your own records for this project.

Before you begin you should design your business. You will need the following:

1. Company information that includes business name, address, and telephone number. (*Hint: Set your company up for Period 12, December 1 - 31, so that you can close the fiscal year.)*
2. One of PCA's sample companies.
3. A Chart of Accounts: 25 accounts minimum; 30 maximum.
4. One month's transactions for your business. You will need a Balance Sheet, checkbook register, and bank statement. Your checkbook register should include a minimum of 15 transactions and a maximum of 25. You should have at least four adjusting entries.

If you don't want to use a checkbook register and bank statement, you could write 15 to 25 narrative transactions.

After you have designed your business, you should follow the steps of PCA's Computer Accounting Cycle to complete Project 1A.

For grading purposes, Project 1A should include the following printouts:

Checklist of Printouts Project 1A Student-Designed Project	
	Chart of Accounts
	Account Reconciliation
	Cash Account Register
	General Ledger Trial Balance (unadjusted)
	Cash Receipts Journal
	Cash Disbursements Journal
	December 31, 200X General Journal
	General Ledger
	General Ledger Trial Balance (adjusted)
	Balance Sheet
	Income Statement
	Statement of Retained Earnings
	Statement of Cash Flow
	Statement of Changes in Financial Position
	Post-Closing Trial Balance

Part 3 Peachtree Complete Accounting 2008 for Merchandising Businesses

In Part 3 of *Computer Accounting with Peachtree Complete 2008*, 12th Edition, your accounting business is hired to do the monthly record keeping for three merchandising businesses: Susan's Service Merchandise; the end-of-chapter exercise, Student Name Sales & Service; and Stanley's Sports.

Part 3 includes four chapters and two projects.

Chapter 11: Vendors & Purchases

Chapter 12: Customers & Sales

Chapter 13: Inventory & Services

Chapter 14: Employees, Payroll and Account Reconciliation

Project 2: Stanley's Sports

Project 2A: Student-Designed Merchandising Business

Merchandising businesses purchase products ready-made from a vendor and then resell these products to their customers. (Merchandising businesses are also called retail businesses.) Items purchased by a retail business for resale are referred to as merchandise. A merchandising business earns revenue from buying and selling goods. Items purchased for use by the business are *not* merchandise; for example, supplies or computer equipment are *not* sold to customers.

In Part 1 you were shown how the sample company, Bellwether Garden Supply, used Peachtree's customer, vendor, payroll, and inventory features. The chapters that follow illustrate these features in detail.

Chapters 11 through 14 are cumulative. This means that the businesses you set up in Chapter 11, Susan's Service Merchandise; and Exercise 11-1, Student Name Sales & Service, are continued in Chapters 12, 13, and 14.

At the end of Part 3, you complete Project 2, Stanley's Sports, which reviews PCA's merchandising business features. At the end of Project 2, there is a Check Your Progress assessment that your instructor may want you to turn in. Project 2A, Student-Designed Merchandising Business, gives you an opportunity to create a merchandising business from scratch.

The chart below shows the size of the backups made in Part 3–Chapters 11, 12, 13, 14, and Project 2. The textbook steps show you how to back up to Peachtree's default location at C:\Program Files\Sage Software\ Peachtree\ Company\[shortened company name]. *You can also specify a hard drive location; or, backup to external media, such as, a USB drive (in Windows Vista backup to desktop, then copy to external media).*

Chapter	Backup Name	Kilobytes	Page Nos.
11	*Chapter 11 Starting Balance Sheet (optional backup)*	932 KB	393
	Chapter 11 Begin	940 KB	405
	Chapter 11	986 KB	429-430
	Exercise 11-1	932 KB	440
	Exercise 11-2	955 KB	443
12	Chapter 12 Begin	990 KB	457
	Chapter 12	1,013 KB	486-487
	Exercise 12-1	958 KB	493
	Exercise 12-2	965 KB	494
13	Chapter 13 Begin	1,014 KB	506
	Chapter 13	1,033 KB	516-517
	Exercise 13-1	970 KB	521
14	Chapter 14 Begin	1,050 KB	539-540
	Chapter 14	1,089 KB	561
	Exercise 14-1	984 KB	568
	Exercise 14-2	1,012 KB	571
Project 2	*Stanley's Sports Starting Balance Sheet (optional backup)*	*932 KB*	577
	Stanley's Sports Begin	947 KB	585
	Stanley's Sports January	1,026 KB	589

The size of your backups may differ from those shown above.

Chapter 11 Vendors & Purchases

SOFTWARE OBJECTIVES: In Chapter 11, you use the software to:

1. Set up company information for Susan's Service Merchandise.
2. Enter the following general ledger information: chart of accounts and beginning balances.
3. Enter the following accounts payable information: vendor defaults and vendor records.
4. Enter the following inventory information: inventory defaults, inventory items, and inventory beginning balances.
5. Record accounts payable transactions: merchandise purchases, purchase orders, cash purchases, and purchase returns.
6. Make four backups: 1) back up Chapter 11 beginning data; 2) back up Chapter 11 data; 3) back up Exercise 11-1; 4) back up Exercise 11-2.[1]

WEB OBJECTIVES: In Chapter 11, you do these Internet activities:

1. Use your Internet browser to go to the book's website. (Go online to www.mhhe.com/yacht2008.)
2. Go to the Internet Activity link on the book's website. Then, select WEB EXERCISES PART 3. Complete the first web exercise in Part 3—Accounting List.
3. Use a word processing program to write summaries of the websites that you visited.

Chapter 11 begins Part 3 of the book: Peachtree Complete Accounting 2008 for Merchandising Businesses. Merchandising businesses are retail stores that resell goods and services. In this chapter, you set up a merchandising business called Susan's Service Merchandise. Susan's Service Merchandise is a partnership owned by Joe Greene and Susan Currier. Mr. Greene and Ms. Currier divide their income equally.

---

[1]The chart on page 380 shows the size of each backup file. An optional backup for Chapter 11 Starting Balance Sheet.ptb is also listed.

Merchandising businesses purchase the merchandise they sell from suppliers known as ***vendors***. Vendors are the businesses that offer Susan's Service Merchandise credit to buy merchandise and/or assets, or credit for expenses incurred. When Susan's Service Merchandise makes purchases on account from vendors, the transactions are known as ***accounts payable transactions***.

PCA organizes and monitors Susan's Service Merchandise's ***accounts payable***. Accounts Payable is the amount of money the business owes to suppliers or vendors.

When entering a purchase, you first enter the vendor's code. The vendor's name and address information, the standard payment terms, and the general ledger purchase account are automatically entered in the appropriate places. This information can be edited if any changes are needed. This works similarly for accounts receivable.

Once you have entered purchase information, printing a check to pay for a purchase is simple. When you enter the vendor's code, a list of purchases displays. You simply select the ones you want to pay and click on the Pay box. You can print the check or wait to print a batch of checks later. You can also pay a whole batch of vendors at one time, using the Select for Payment option.

The diagram below illustrates how vendors are paid.

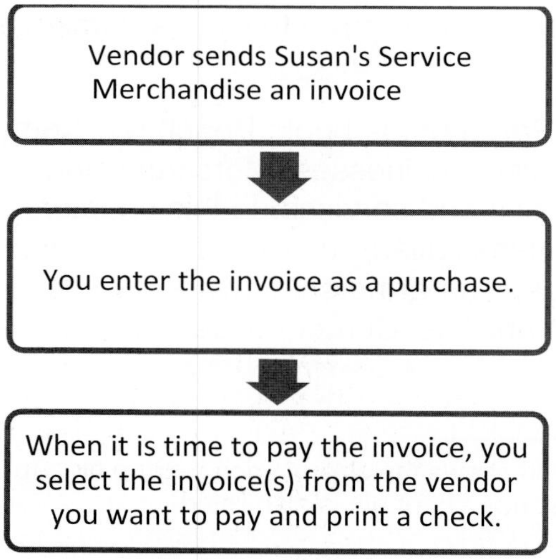

In Chapter 11, the businesses that you set up are continued in Chapters 12, 13, and 14.

GETTING STARTED

Susan's Service Merchandise started operations on January 1, 2008. Susan's Service Merchandise is a partnership owned by Joe Greene and Susan Currier and is located in Los Angeles, CA. Follow these steps to set up a Sales & Service company.

1. Start Peachtree. If a company opens, select File; New Company, click OK.

2. The Create a New Company – Introduction window appears. Click Next >.

3. The Enter your company information window appears. (Observe that a red asterisk (*) indicates a required field.) Complete the following fields. Press the **<Tab>** key between each field.

Company Information

Company Name:	**Susan's Service Merchandise** *(use your first name then Service Merchandise)*
Address Line 1:	**7709 Wilshire Boulevard**
City, State, Zip:	**Los Angeles, CA 90060**
Country:	**USA**
Telephone:	**213-555-9800**
Fax:	**213-555-8804**
Business Type:	Partnership

Tax ID Information

Federal Employer ID:	**82-9831432**
State Employer ID:	**27-8170062**
State Unemployment ID:	**275382-7**
Web Site:	**www.susanservmdse.biz**
E-mail:	**info@susanservmdse.biz**

> **Comment**
>
> If you use your name in the Company Name field, the name of your company will appear on all printouts.

4. Check the information you just typed, then click 

. The Select a method to create your Company window appears.

5. Accept the default for Use a sample business type that closely matches your company.

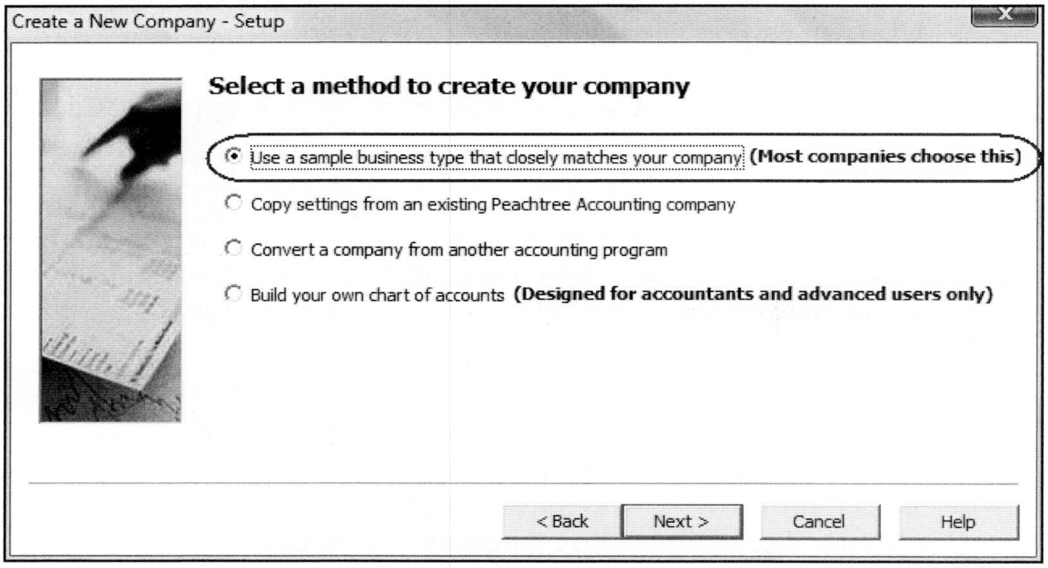

6. Click 

.

7. Read the information about selecting a business type. Numerous business types are available. Scroll down. In the Detailed types list, select Retail Company. Compare your selection to the one shown on the next page.

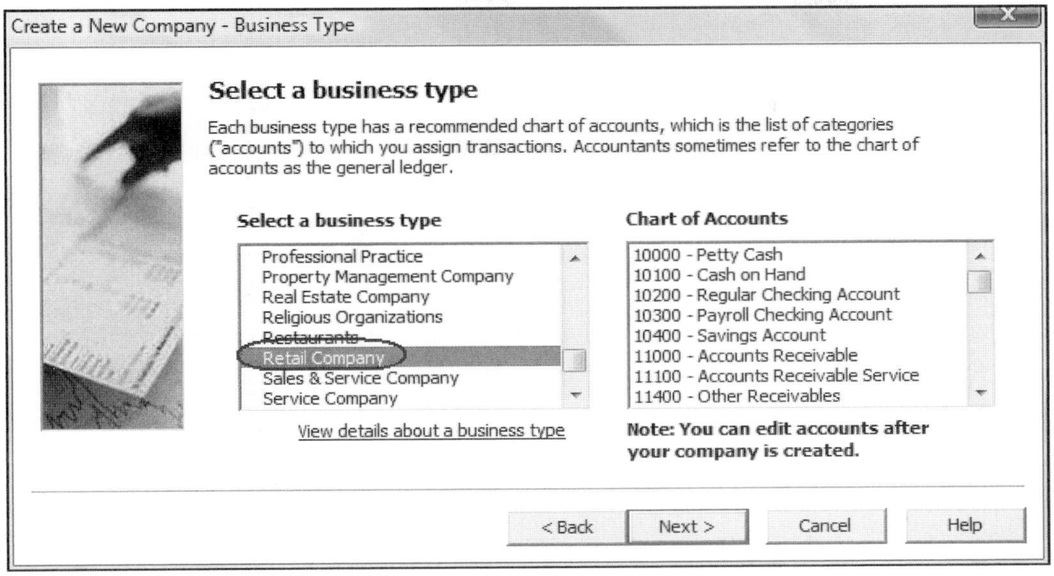

8. Make sure that Retail Company is selected from the Detailed types list. Click Next >.

9. Read the information about the Accounting Method. Accept the default for Accrual by clicking Next >.

10. Read the information about Posting Method. Peachtree Software recommends real-time posting for networked computers. Accept the default for real-time posting by clicking Next >.

11. At the Choose an accounting period structure window, accept the default for 12 monthly accounting periods per year by clicking Next >.

12. The Choose the first period of your fiscal year window appears. Select **2008** as the year. Compare your Fiscal Year window to the one shown on the next page.

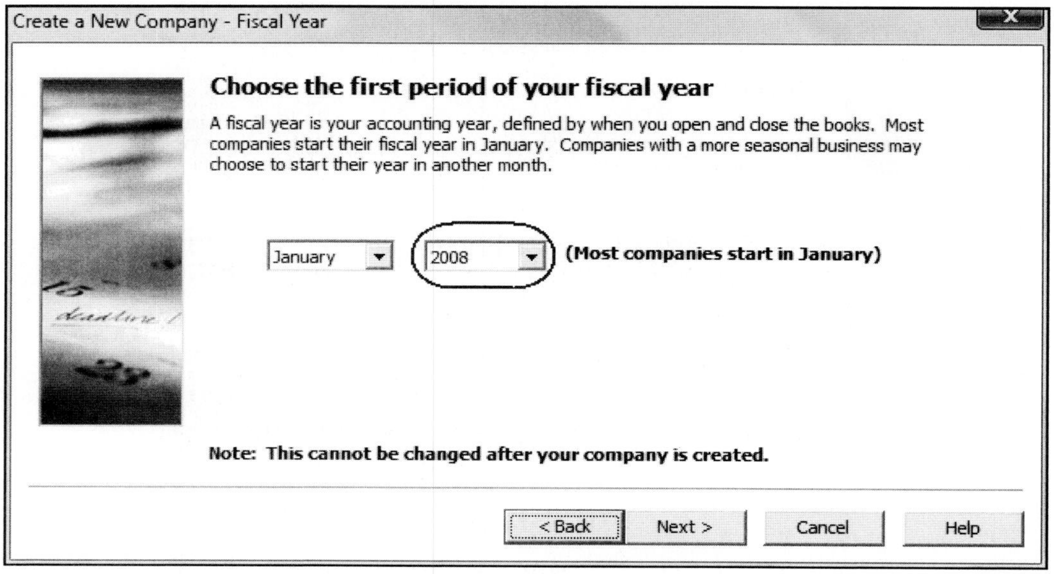

Check this window carefully. You cannot change it later.

13. Click Next >.

14. The You are ready to create your company window appears. Click Finish. When the Have you started using credit cards for your Business? window appears, click OK.

15. The Setup Guide window appears. Click on the box next to Don't show this screen at startup to place a checkmark in it-- ☑ Don't show this screen at startup. Click Close. The window prompts to Click OK to exist the Peachtree Setup Guide; click OK. Peachtree Accounting: Susan's (your name) Service Merchandise appears on the title bar (above the menu bar).

16. The Period shown on the toolbar defaults to the current period (month). If necessary, change the accounting period to 01 – Jan 01,2008 to Jan 31,2008; Period 1 - 01/01/08-01/31/08. (*Hint:* Click on the Period shown on the toolbar to change accounting periods.)

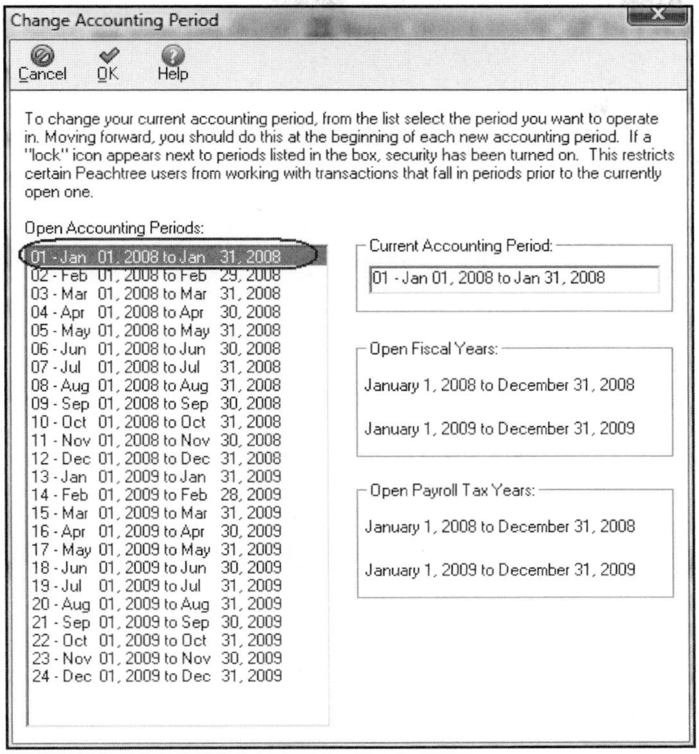

17. Click 

. The Business Status page shows the following sections:

- Account Balances
- Customers Who Owe Money
- Aged Receivables
- Find a Report
- Revenue: Year to Date
- Vendors to Pay
- Aged Payables

In Chapters 11-14, you use links from the Business Status page and the Navigation Bar to record transactions. Observe that the Navigation Bar's selections include:

These selections provide ways to navigate the software for the retail business, Susan's Service Merchandise.

GENERAL LEDGER

Follow these steps to record general ledger information.

1. From the Navigation Bar, click 

; 

; View and Edit Accounts.

   Delete the following accounts:

> **Comment**
>
> Double-click on the account you want to delete. Then, click 
>
> . You can also type the account number into the Account ID field, then delete.

10000 Petty Cash
10100 Cash on Hand
11400 Other Receivables
14100 Employee Advances
14200 Notes Receivable-Current
14700 Other Current Assets
15200 Automobiles
15300 Other Depreciable Property

15400 Leasehold Improvements
15600 Building Improvements
16900 Land
17200 Accum. Depreciation-Automobi
17300 Accum. Depreciation-Other
17400 Accum. Depreciation-Leasehol
17600 Accum. Depreciation-Bldg Imp
19000 Deposits
19100 Organization Costs
19150 Accum. Amortiz -Org. Costs
19200 Notes Receivable-Noncurrent
19900 Other Noncurrent Assets
23300 Deductions Payable
23800 Local Payroll Taxes Payable
24800 Other Current Liabilities
24900 Suspense-Clearing Account
58000 Cost of Sales-Other
60500 Amortization Expense
61000 Auto Expenses
62500 Cash Over and Short
63000 Charitable Contributions Exp
63500 Commissions and Fees Exp
65000 Employee Benefit Programs Exp
68000 Laundry and Cleaning Exp
73000 Other Taxes
74000 Rent or Lease Expense
76500 Travel Expense
77000 Salaries Expense

Change the following accounts:

10200	Regular Checking Account	**La Brea Bank**
10400	Savings Account	**Worldwide Savings & Loan**
12000	Product Inventory	**Merchandise Inventory**
14000	Prepaid Expenses	**Prepaid Insurance**
15100	Equipment	**Computers & Equipment**
17000	Accum. Depreciation-Furniture	**Accum. Depreciation - Furn&Fix**
17100	Accum. Depreciation-Equipment	**Accum. Depreciation - Comp&Eqt**
24000	Other Taxes Payable	**FICA Employee Taxes Payable**
24100	Employee Benefits Payable	**FICA Employer Taxes Payable**

24200	Current Portion Long-Term Debt	**Medicare Employee Taxes Payabl**
24400	Customer Deposits	**Medicare Employer Taxes Payabl**
27000	Notes Payable-Noncurrent	**Long-Term Notes Payable**
27400	Other Long Term-Liabilities	**Mortgage Payable**
39006	Partner's Contribution	**Joe Greene, Capital** *(Note: Account Type, Equity-doesn't close)*
39007	Partner's Draw	**Joe Greene, Drawing**
40000	Sales-Merchandise	**Sales-Hardware**
40200	Sales-Services	**Sales-Wall**
40400	Sales-Clearance	**Sales-Floor**
40600	Interest Income	**Service Fees**
50000	Cost of Goods Sold	**Cost of Sales-Hardware**
50500	Cost of Sales-Service	**Cost of Sales-Wall**
57000	Cost of Sales-Salaries and Wag	**Cost of Sales-Floor**
64000	Depreciation Expense	**Deprec Exp-Furn & Fixtures**
64500	Dues and Subscription Exp	**Deprec Exp-Computers & Equip**

Add the following accounts:		*Account Type:*
13000	**Supplies**	Other Current Assets
39008	**Susan Currier, Capital**	Equity-doesn't close
39009	**Susan Currier, Drawing**	Equity- gets closed
64600	**Deprec Exp-Building**	Expenses
72510	**FICA Expense**	Expenses
72530	**FUTA Expense**	Expenses
72540	**SUTA Expense**	Expenses
77600	**Overtime Expense**	Expenses

2. If necessary, close the Account List. Select Maintain; Chart of Accounts. Click Account Beginning Balances.

3. The Select Period window appears. Highlight From 12/1/07 through 12/31/07. Beginning balances *must* be set for the preceding month. The starting balance sheet on pages 392 is dated January 1, 2008. This means that the period for entering beginning balances must be from December 1 through December 31, 2007 the month *before* the starting balances.

Comment
Select December 1 - 31, 2007 as your Chart of Accounts Beginning Balance period so that your journals will start on January 1, 2008. Your reports will be dated January 31, 2008. Remember, Peachtree posts on the last day of the month. The December 31, 2007 balances are the January 1, 2008 starting balances.

Compare your Select Period window to the one shown below.

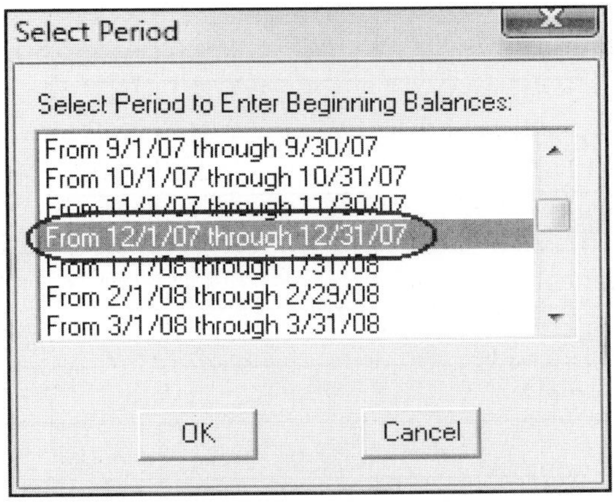

Check this window carefully. You cannot change the period for entering beginning balances.

4. Click 

. The Chart of Accounts Beginning Balances window appears. Observe that this window shows that you are going to enter Beginning Balances as of December 31, 2007.

5. Joe Greene and Susan Currier purchased Susan's Service Merchandise in December 2007. Use the Balance Sheet shown on the next page to record the Chart of Accounts Beginning Balances. If you need to review how to record beginning balances, see Chapter 9 pages 267-272.

Susan's Service Merchandise Balance Sheet January 1, 2008		
ASSETS		
Current Assets:		
La Brea Bank	$71,500.00	
Worldwide Savings & Loan	20,000.00	
Merchandise Inventory	27,740.00	
Supplies	1,750.00	
Prepaid Insurance	2,400.00	
Total Current Assets		$123,390.00
Property and Equipment:		
Furniture and Fixtures	5,000.00	
Computers & Equipment	7,500.00	
Building	100,000.00	
Total Property and Equipment		112,500.00
Total Assets		$235,890.00
LIABILITIES AND CAPITAL		
Long-Term Liabilities:		
Long-Term Notes Payable	20,500.00	
Mortgage Payable	75,000.00	
Total Long-Term Liabilities		$95,500.00
Capital:		
Joe Greene, Capital	70,195.00	
Susan Currier, Capital	70,195.00	
Total Capital		140,390.00
Total Liabilities and Capital		$235,890.00

6. When you are finished entering the beginning balances, click 

.

7. Close the Maintain Chart of Accounts window. You may want to backup the January 1, 2008 starting balances. *This is an optional backup*. The suggested filename is Chapter 11 Starting Balance Sheet.ptb. (For detailed backup steps, refer to page 405.)

ACCOUNTS PAYABLE

The next section shows you how to set up Accounts Payable defaults. This is where you set up information about the vendors who offer credit to Susan's Service Merchandise. Vendors offer Susan's Service Merchandise a 2 percent discount for invoices paid within 10 days (2% 10, Net 30 Days).

Follow these steps to enter vendor default information.

1. From the Navigation Bar, select 

; 

, Set Up Vendor Defaults. The Vendor Defaults window appears.

2. Due in number of days is selected in the Standard Terms list. Type **10** in the Discount in field. Press <Tab>.

3. Type **2** in the Discount % field, then press the **<Tab>** key two times.

4. In the Expense Account field, click . Select Account No. 12000, Merchandise Inventory.

5. In the Discount GL Account field, click . Select Account No. 59500, Purchase Discounts.

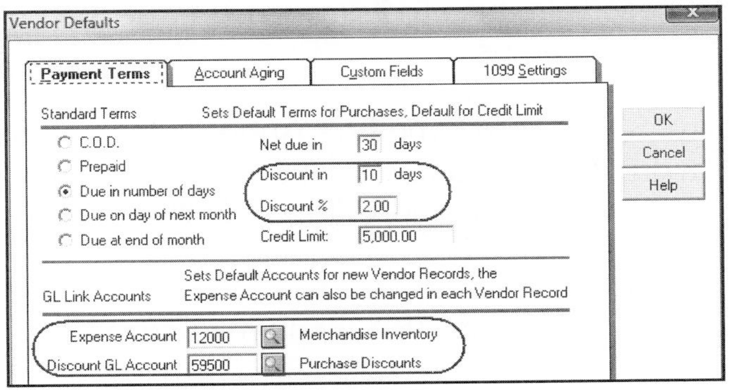

Make sure that the Expense Account field shows Account No. 12000, Merchandise Inventory; and that the Discount GL Account field shows Account No. 59500, Purchase Discounts. This sets up the default accounts for merchandise purchases and vendor discounts.

In PCA, the Merchandise Inventory account contains summary information about the total cost of the merchandise on hand and available for sale. In addition, PCA tracks vendor discounts in Account No. 59500, Purchase Discounts. PCA also keeps a detailed inventory record for each item of merchandise in stock. PCA automatically updates subsidiary records every time there is a change in the Merchandise Inventory account caused by a purchase, sale, or return of merchandise.

6. Click 

. When the screen prompts that The default terms for vendors have been changed, click 

. You are returned to the Vendors & Payables page.

7. Click 

; New Vendor. The Maintain Vendors window displays. Follow these steps to enter vendor information:

    a. In the Vendor ID field, type **JJH06** (use a zero) then press the **<Enter>** key.

    b. In the Name field, type **Jesse Jensen Hardware** then press the **<Enter>** key four times.

    c. In the Address field, type **612 Clover Avenue** then press the **<Enter>** key two times.

    d. In the City, ST Zip field, type **Los Angeles** then press the **<Enter>** key. Click on the down arrow  then select CA from the list of states. Press the **<Enter>** key. Type **90006** as the Zip code, press **<Enter>**.

    e. In the Country field, type **USA** then press **<Enter>**.

f. In the Vendor Type field, type **hardware** then press **<Enter>**.

g. In the 1099 Type field, click on the down arrow ▼ and select Independent Contractor. Press the **<Enter>** key. Observe that the Expense Account automatically displays 12000. This is the default Expense Account entered on page 393.

h. In the Telephone 1 field, type **213-555-3081** then press **<Enter>** two times.

i. In the Fax field, type **213-555-2392** then press **<Enter>**.

j. In the E-mail field, type **jesse@jensenhardware.com** and then press <Enter>.

k. Type **www.jensenhardware.com** in the Web Site field.

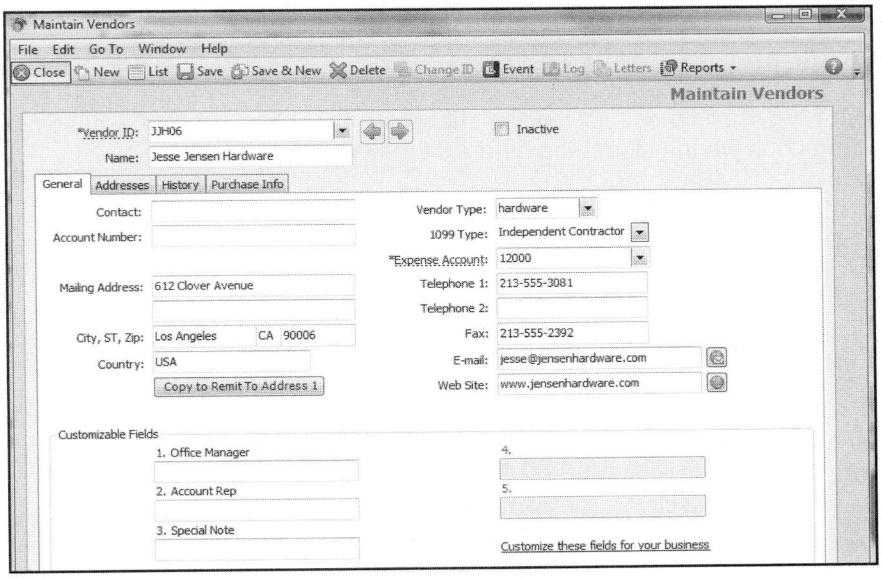

8. Click on the Purchase Info tab. Follow these steps to complete the fields:

   a. Type **27-3215289** in the Tax ID Number field. Observe that the credit terms entered on page 393 are shown.

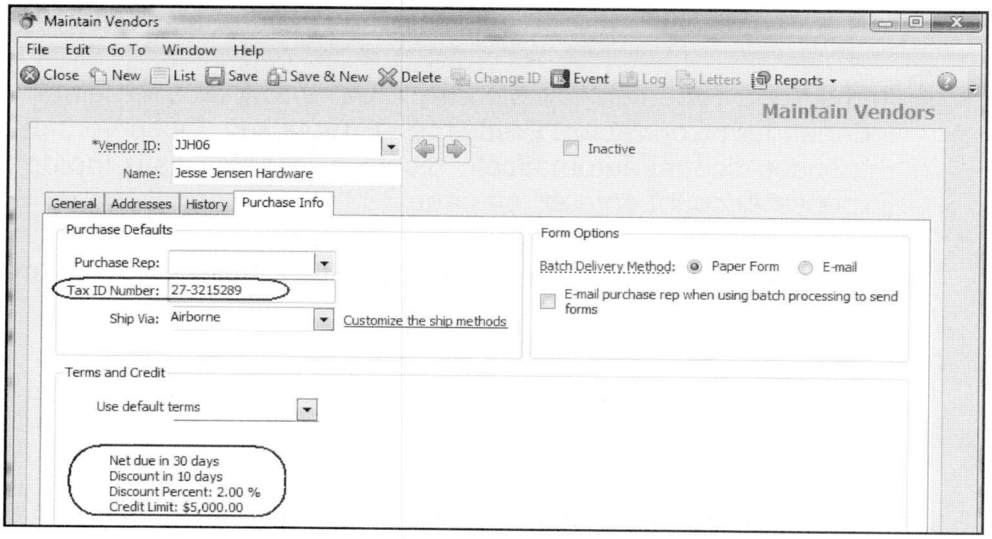

> **Comment**
>
> The Ship Via field on this window shows Airborne. You complete shipping information when you set the defaults for inventory.

b. Click 

.

c. Click on the General tab. Add the next vendor.

1) | | |
|---|---|
| Vendor ID: | **LLP07** |
| Name: | **Lyle Lewis Products** |
| Address: | **20 North Broadway** |
| City, ST Zip | **San Diego, CA 97311** |
| Country: | **USA** |
| Vendor Type: | **floor** |
| 1099 Type: | **Independent Contractor** |
| Telephone 1: | **619-555-4211** |
| Fax: | **619-555-4213** |
| E-mail: | **lyle@lewisproducts.com** |
| Web Site: | **www.lewisproducts.com** |

Purchase Info:

Tax ID Number: **27-9250881**

2) Vendor ID: **RBF08**
   Name: **Ronald Baker Fabrics**
   Address: **915 Motor Avenue**
   City, ST Zip **Los Angeles, CA 90069**
   Country: **USA**
   Vendor Type: **wall**
   1099 Type: **Independent Contractor**
   Telephone 1: **310-555-1399**
   Fax: **310-555-1400**
   E-mail: **ron@bakerfabrics.biz**
   Web Site: **www.bakerfabrics.biz**

Purchase Info:

Tax ID Number: **27-7899504**

9. Check your vendor information carefully. When you are finished entering vendor information, close the Maintain Vendors window.

   How does vendor information work in PCA? The diagram below shows how vendor maintenance information, vendor default information and purchases and payments work together.

Vendor Maintenance Information	*Vendor Default Information*
Terms: 2% 10, Net 30 Days *Purchase Account*: Merchandise Inventory	*Accounts*: Accounts Payable; Merchandise Inventory (purchase account); Purchase Discounts (discount GL account); La Brea Bank (cash disbursed).

↓

Purchases/Receive Inventory and Payments
Purchase Order ↓ Check to Vendor

On the Vendors & Purchases Navigation Center, Peachtree illustrates its accounts payable system. In Chapter 11, you work with vendors, writing checks for expenses and owners' withdrawals, entering bills, credits and returns, and paying vendor bills. (*Hint:* To see Vendors, click 

.)

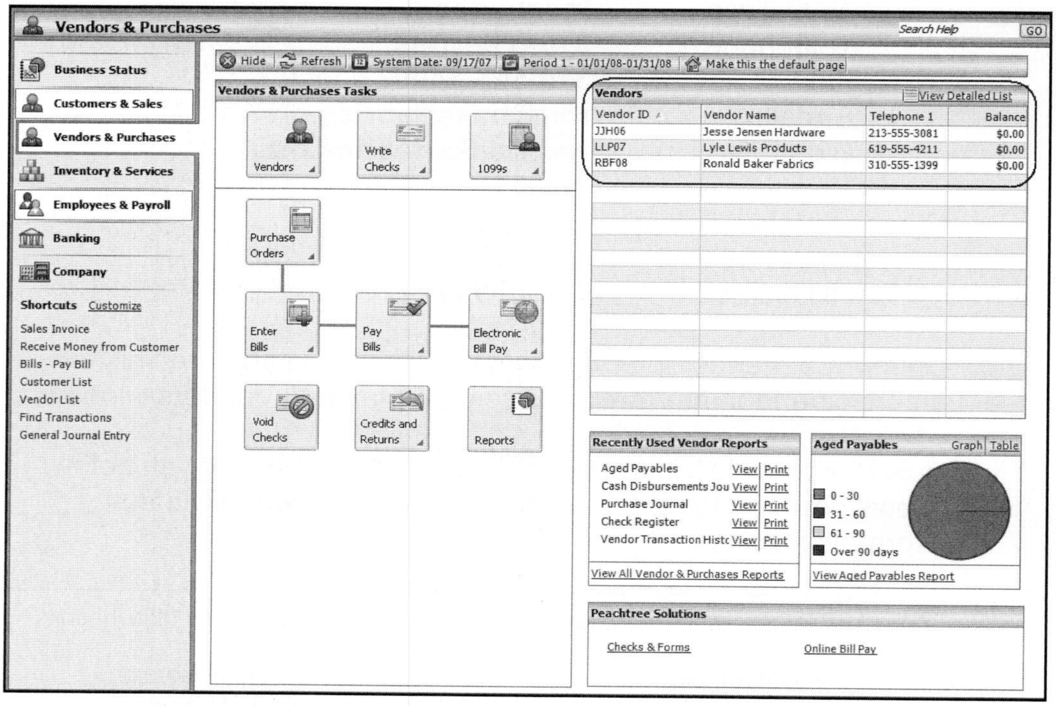

INVENTORY ITEMS

In the next section default information for inventory items is completed. Because the Merchandise Inventory account is increased or decreased for every purchase, sale or return, its balance in the general ledger is current.

1. From the Navigation Bar, select 

. Observe how the Inventory & Services Tasks are organized. This illustration show how Peachtree's inventory system works.

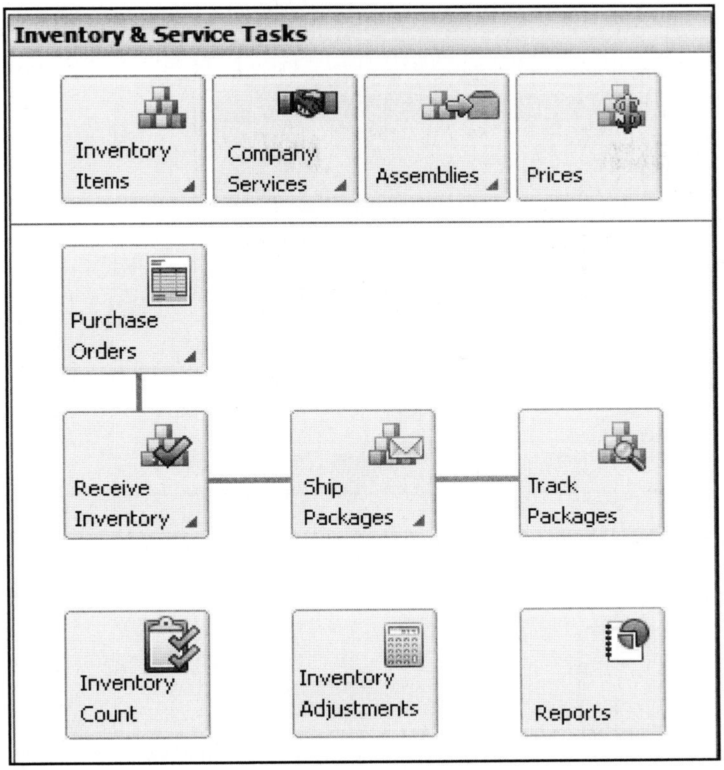

2. Click 

; Set Up Inventory Defaults. The Inventory Item Defaults window appears.

3. Click on the GL Accts/Costing tab. In the Stock item row, click on the down arrow next to FIFO in the Costing column. Select Average.

> **Comment**
>
> Further study of inventory costing methods will be done in Chapter 13, Merchandise Inventory.

4. On the Master Stock item row, change FIFO to Average.

5. On the Assembly row, change FIFO to Average.

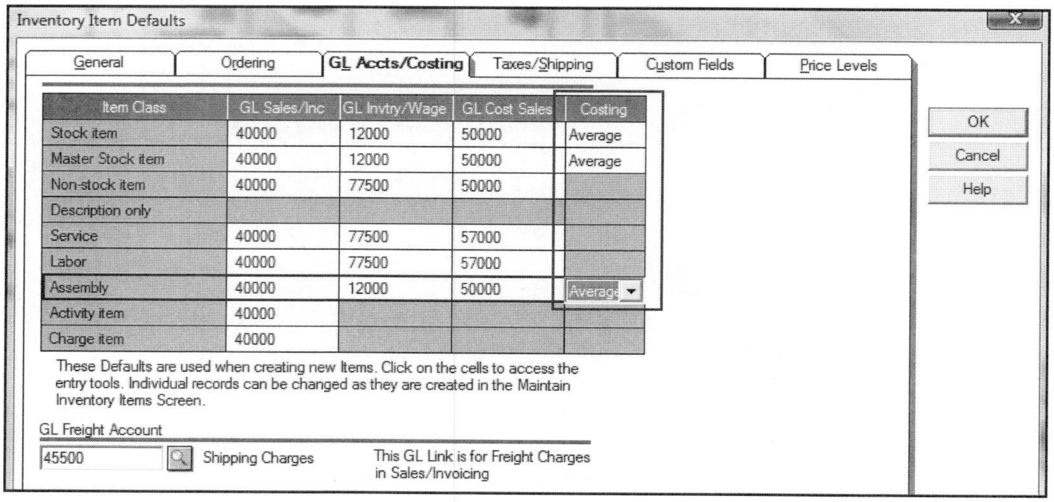

6. Make sure Average is selected in the Costing column. Click 

.

7. Click 

; New Inventory item. Follow these steps to add inventory items.

   a. In the Item ID field, type **001hardware**, then press the **<Enter>** key.

   b. In the Description field, type **hardware** then press **<Enter>**.

   c. Accept the default for Stock item by pressing the **<Enter>** key two times.

   d. In the Description: for Sales field, type **restoration hardware** then press **<Enter>**.

   e. Click on the right arrow  in the Price Level 1 field. The Multiple Price Levels window appears. Type **150** in the Price column of Price Level 1, then press **<Enter>**.

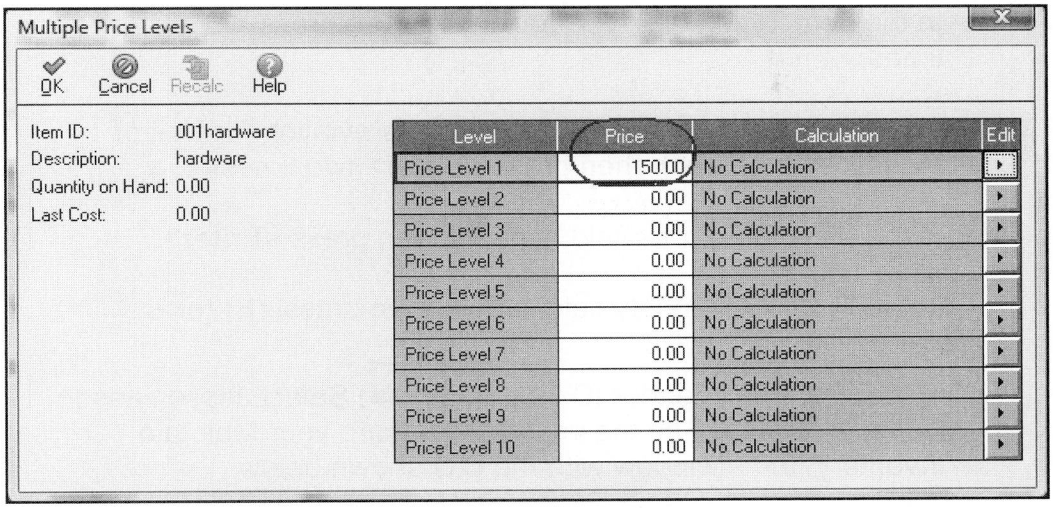

f. Click 

.

> **Comment:** What if your Price Level 1 field does not display 150.00 but 1.50? Follow these steps to set the decimal point:
>
> 1. From the menu bar, click Options, then Global. If necessary, select the Accounting tab.
> 2. In the Decimal Entry field, click Manual. Make sure that the number 2 is shown in the Number of decimal places field.
> 3. Click 
>
> . This sets your decimal place globally. That means from now on all numbers with decimal places will be set automatically; for example, 150 will display as 150.00.

g. Type **50** in the Last Unit Cost field. Press **<Enter>**.

h. Accept the default for Account No. 40000, Sales-Hardware as the GL Sales Acct.

i. Accept the default for Account No. 12000, Merchandise Inventory, as the GL Inventory Acct by pressing **<Enter**>

j. Accept the default for Account No. 50000, Cost of Sales-Hardware as the GL Cost of Sales Acct by pressing **<Enter>** three times.

k. In the Item Type field, type **hardware** then press **<Enter>** two times.

l. In the Stocking U/M field (U/M is an abbreviation for Unit of Measure), type **each** then press **<Enter>** two times.

m. In the Minimum Stock field, type **10** then press **<Enter>**.

n. In the Reorder Quantity field, type **4** then press **<Enter>**.

o. In the Preferred Vendor ID field, click . Select Jesse Jensen Hardware, JJH06, as the vendor. Compare your Maintain Inventory Items window with the one shown below.

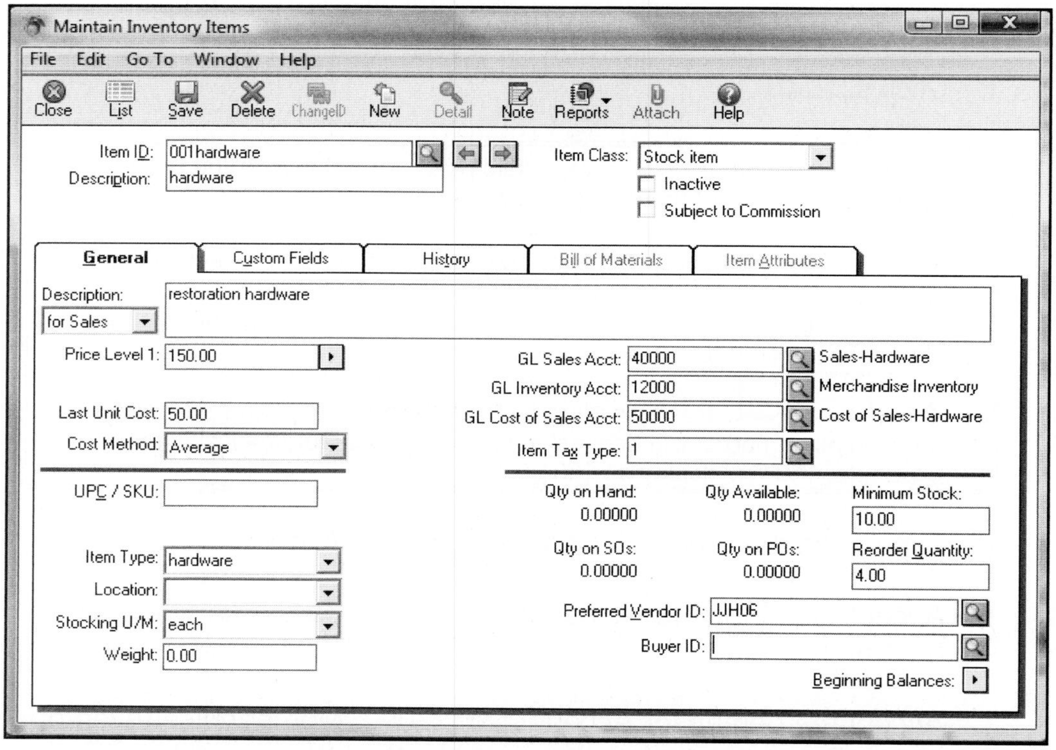

p. Click .

q. Click 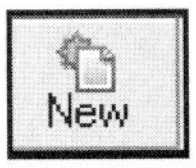.

Enter the following stock items:

1)

Item ID:	**002wall**
Description:	**wall**
Description for Sales:	**wall coverings**
Price Level 1:	**100**
Last Unit Cost:	**30**
GL Sales Acct:	**40200 Sales-Wall**
GL Inventory Acct:	**12000 Merchandise Inventory**
GL Cost of Sales Acct:	**50500 Cost of Sales-Wall**
Item Type:	**wall**
Stocking U/M:	**each**
Minimum Stock:	**10**
Reorder Quantity:	**4**
Preferred Vendor ID:	**RBF08**

2)

Item ID:	**003floor**
Description:	**floor**
Description for Sales:	**flooring**
Price Level 1:	**160**
Last Unit Cost:	**54**
GL Sales Acct:	**40400 Sales-Floor**
GL Inventory Acct:	**12000 Merchandise Inventory**
GL Cost of Sales Acct:	**57000 Cost of Sales-Floor**
Item Type:	**floor**
Stocking U/M:	**each**
Minimum Stock:	**25**
Reorder Quantity:	**10**
Preferred Vendor ID:	**LLP07**

8. Save then click Beginning Balances. The Inventory Beginning Balances window displays. Follow these steps to record beginning balances.

   a. In the Item ID table, click on 001hardware. Press the **<Tab>** key.

   b. In the Quantity field, type **90** then press **<Enter>**.

c. In the Unit Cost field, type **50** then press **<Enter>**.

d. The Total Cost field displays 4,500.00. Press the **<Enter>** key.

e. Enter the beginning balances for walls and floors:

Item ID	*Description*	*Quantity*	*Unit Cost*	*Total Cost*
002wall	wall	148	30	4,440.00
003floor	floor	200	54	10,800.00

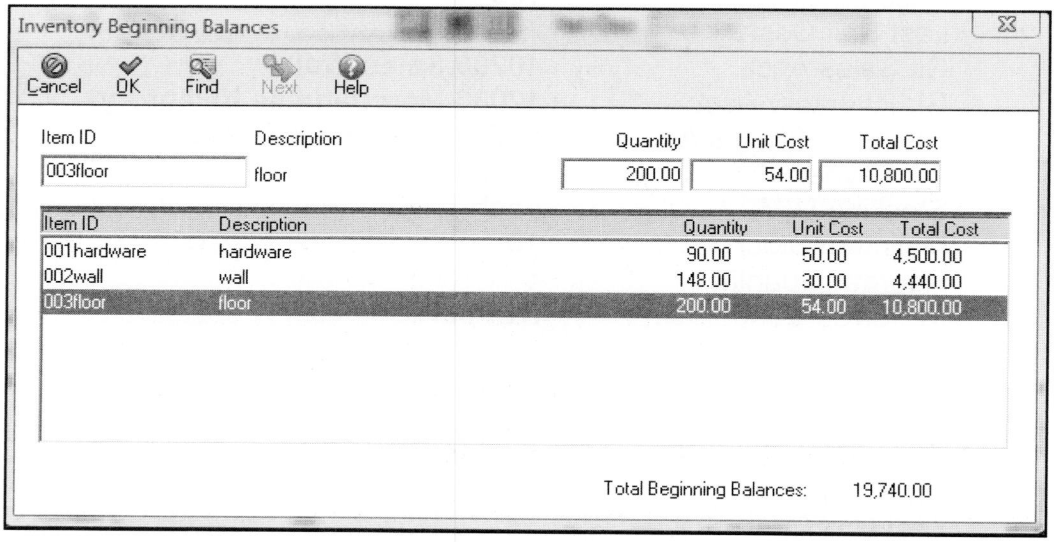

f. Observe that the Total Beginning Balance is 19,740. You add additional inventory in Chapter 13, Merchandise Inventory.[2] Click 

.

g. Close the Maintain Inventory Items window.

---

[2] If you compare the total beginning balance in inventory, $19,740, to the balance sheet on page 392, observe that the Merchandise Inventory account has a $27,740 balance. Additional inventory valued at $8,000 is added in Chapter 13.

BACKING UP YOUR DATA

Follow these steps to back up Chapter 11 data.

1. Select Company; link to Back up.
2. Click Back Up.
3. Accept the default for backing up to the hard drive or make the selections to back up to another location. Type **Chapter 11 Begin** in the File name field.
4. Click Save.
5. When the window prompts that This company backup will require approximately 3.25MB, click OK. When the Back Up Company scale is 100% complete, you have successfully backed up to the current point in Chapter 11. .
6. Continue or click File; Exit to exit Peachtree.

VENDORS & PURCHASES: PURCHASES/RECEIVE INVENTORY

The Vendors & Purchases Tasks flowchart includes a selection for Enter Bills; New Bill. This selection takes you to the Purchases/Receive Inventory window. In PCA, all information about a purchase is recorded in the Purchases/Receive Inventory window. Then, PCA takes the necessary information from the window and automatically journalizes the transaction in the Purchase Journal.

In Peachtree, the Purchases/Receive Inventory window is the ***Purchase Journal***. In the Purchases/Receive Inventory window, you enter invoices received from vendors. In the study of accounting, you learn that purchase orders are the business forms used by the purchasing department to place orders with vendors. Purchase Orders authorize the vendor to ship the ordered merchandise at the stated price and terms.

After recording vendor purchases in the Purchases/Receive Inventory window, you can display or print the Purchase Journal by selecting Reports, then Accounts Payable and highlighting the Purchase Journal. These steps are included in this chapter. Just remember, each time you use the Purchases/Receive Inventory window you are also journalizing in the Purchase Journal.

Purchases are posted both to the General Ledger and to the ***Vendor Ledger*** or ***Accounts Payable Ledger***. You can also apply purchases to Inventory Items or Jobs.

Purchases work hand in hand with paying bills. On the Vendors & Purchases Tasks flowchart, Pay Bills is one of the selections. Once you have entered and posted a purchase (vendor invoice), that invoice is available when you enter the Vendor's ID code in Payments. You can select the invoice, then save (post) the payment; PCA distributes the appropriate amounts.

Using the Purchase Journal: Purchases/Receive Inventory Window

1. If you exited Peachtree, start Peachtree. Then, open Susan's Service Merchandise and restore the Chapter 11 Begin.ptb backup file.

2. From the Navigation Bar, select 

; 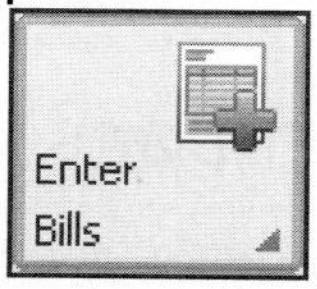

, New Bill. The Purchases/Receive Inventory window displays. Check that *both* the A/P Account lookup field and GL Account column are shown on your Purchases/Receive Inventory window. If *not*, read the paragraph below the Purchases/Receive Inventory window on the next page. (*Hint:* To see multiple lines in the Apply to Purchases table, use your cursor to enlarge the Purchases/Receive Inventory window.)

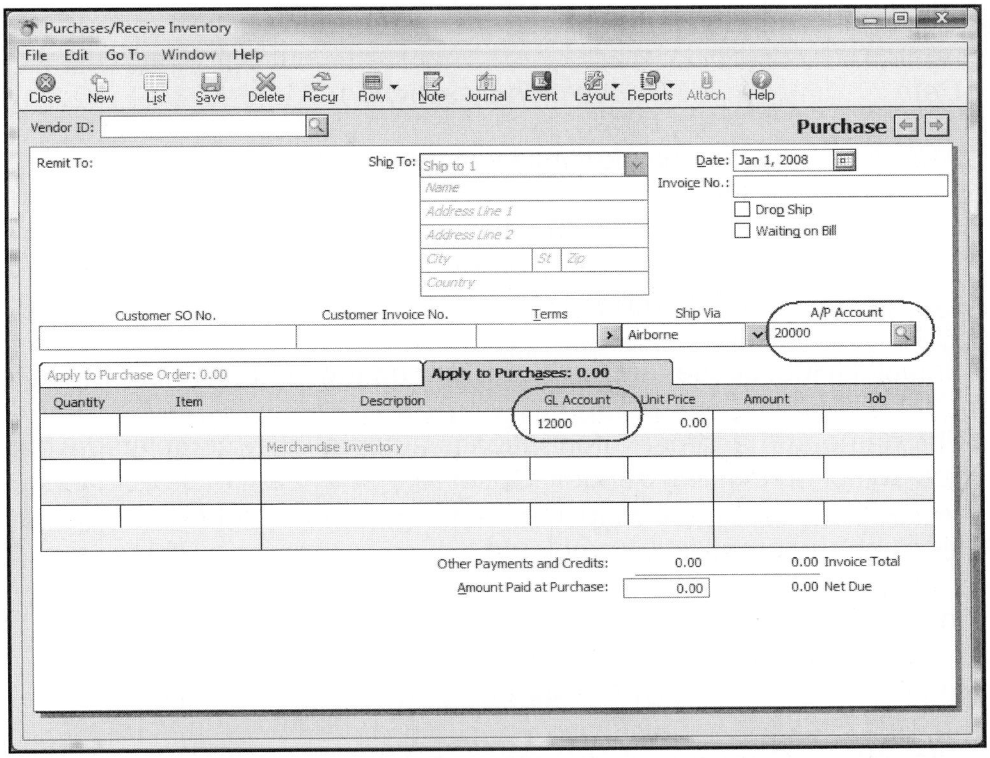

If the A/P Account lookup field and GL Account column are *not* shown, check your global settings. To do that, click Options, Global. If necessary, select the Accounting tab. The boxes in the Hide General Ledger Accounts section *must* be unchecked. (See pages xix-xx, Peachtree's Global Options.)

On the Purchases/Receive Inventory window, your cursor is in the Vendor ID field. There are three ways to select a vendor or add a new vendor:

- In the Vendor ID field, type a question mark **<?>** in the field and the vendor list displays.
- With the mouse pointer in the Vendor ID field, click on the right mouse button. The vendor list displays.
- In the Vendor ID field, click  and the vendor list displays.

The transaction that you are going to work with is:

Date	*Transaction Description*
01/02/08	Invoice No. 56JJ was received from Jesse Jensen Hardware for the purchase of six curtain rods for a unit cost of $50.00 each, and a total of $300.00. (Susan's Service Merchandise classifies curtain rods as hardware.)

3. Select JJH06, Jesse Jensen Hardware as the vendor.

   The name and address information is automatically completed when you select an existing vendor. Observe that when you select Jesse Jensen Hardware, the Ship To, Ship Via, Terms, and A/P Account[3] fields are automatically completed.

4. In the Date field type **2** (or select 2).

5. In the Invoice # field, type **56JJ** and press the **<Enter>** key.

6. Click on the Quantity column and type **6** then press the **<Enter>** key.

7. In the Item column, click  and select 001hardware. Accept the description. Press the **<Tab>** key. Observe that the following purchase information is automatically completed:

   a. Description column, restoration hardware.

   b. GL Account 12000, Merchandise Inventory. (If the account name, Merchandise Inventory does *not* show, go to Options; Global, General tab. In the Line Item Entry Display area, make sure 2 Line is selected; click OK. Click on the Purchases/Receive Inventory button on the taskbar to enlarge the window.)

   c. Unit Price 50.00.

---

[3] If the A/P Account lookup field does not display, click Options, Global. The boxes in the Hide General Ledger Accounts section *must* be unchecked. (See Preface pages xix-xx, Peachtree's Global Settings.)

d. Amount 300.00.

e. Invoice Total and Net Due, 300.00

f. Vendor Balance on Jan 2, 2008: 0.00.

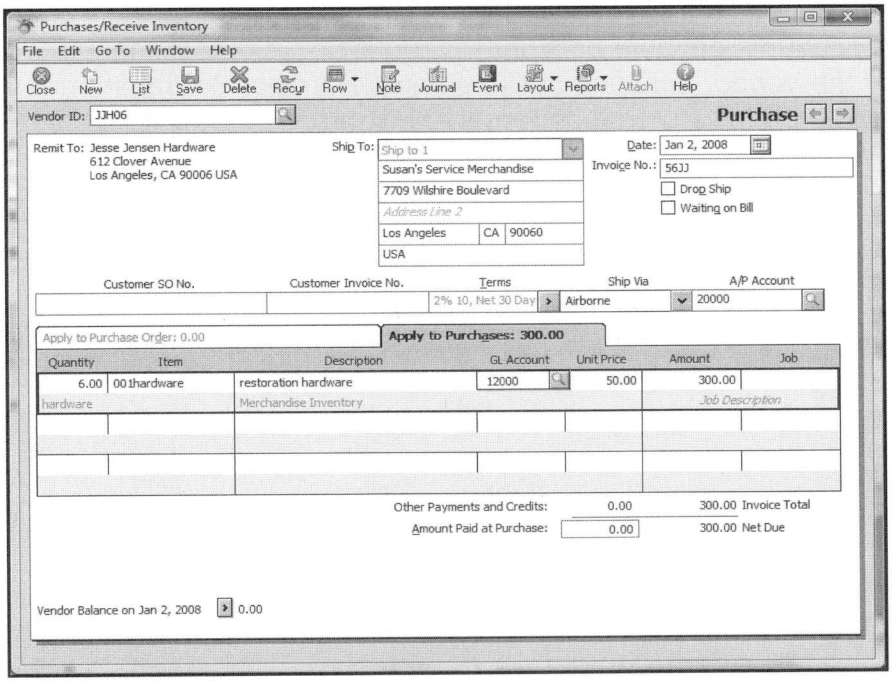

Read Me

On the Purchases/Receive Inventory window, if the Quantity, Item, Description, GL Account, Unit Price, and Amount table does *not* show multiple lines you can use the arrows next to the Job column to scroll through the multiple lines. *Or,* try using the cursor to enlarge the window.

The number of lines on the Quantity, Item/Description table is determined by how the screen resolution is set. If your Purchases/Receive Inventory window shows one line on the Quantity, Item table, then your computer is probably set up for 800 X 600 pixels. If your screen resolution is set at 1024 X 768 pixels, your Purchases/Receive Inventory window shows multiple lines in the Quantity/Item area. To check your screen resolution, go to the desktop and right click; left click Properties, select the Settings tab. The screen resolution area shows the number of the monitor's pixels.

Invoice Total: The Invoice Total keeps a running total of the entry lines you have added to the Purchase Journal. Before you post a Purchase Journal entry, you should check to see that the amount column is the same as the total invoice amount (Net Due) on the vendor invoice.

The total that shows in the Amount column is automatically credited to the accounts payable account (Account No. 20000, Accounts Payable and the vendor account, Jesse Jensen Hardware). The information entered on the Purchases/Receive Inventory window will be recorded in the Purchase Journal.

8. Click 

to see this entry in the Purchases Journal.

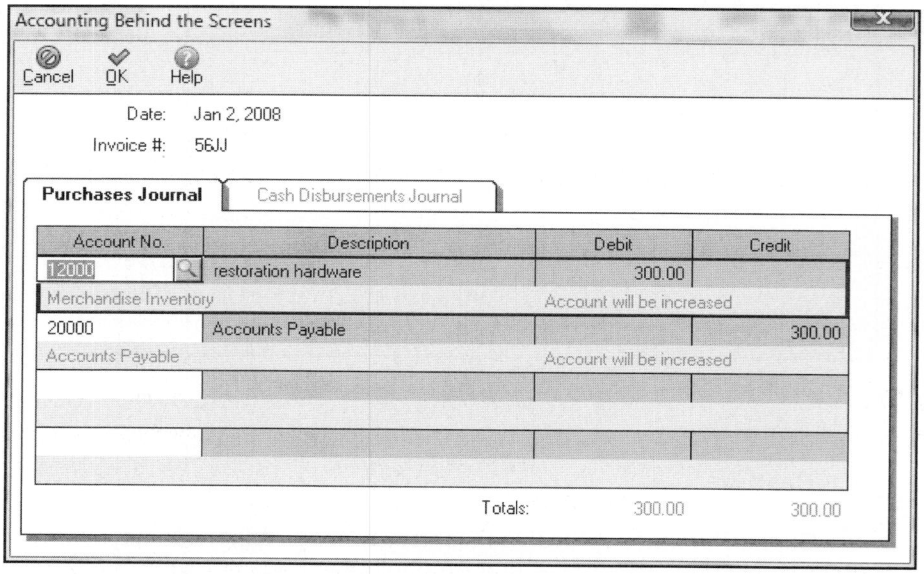

Inventory Items and Purchases: Since you entered an Inventory Item (hardware), the debit amount is shown in the merchandise inventory account (Account No. 12000). (On page 393, step 5, you set up the Expense Account default for Account No. 12000, Merchandise Inventory.)

9. Click 

to return to the Purchases/Receive Inventory window.

10. Click Save to post this entry. The Purchases/Receive Inventory window is ready for another entry. When you enter and post purchases of inventory items, three things happen:

    a. The amount or stock level of the item is updated.

    b. The ***Average Cost*** is updated based on the Unit Price entered. Average cost is computed using the ***weighted-average method*** for inventory. The Average Cost is used by PCA to compute Cost of Goods Sold when these Inventory Items are entered as Sales.

    c. For Stock-Type items, the Inventory account is debited and Accounts Payable is credited (debit, Account No. 12000, Merchandise Inventory; credit, Account No. 20000, Accounts Payable/Vendor.)

Additional Purchases

The following transactions need to be entered in the Purchases Journal.

Remember to click Save after each transaction to post.

Date	*Transaction Description*
01/20/08	Invoice 90 was received from Lyle Lewis Products for the purchase of eight rolls of vinyl flooring at $54 each, for a total of $432. (*Hint: Select 003floor as the inventory item.*)
01/20/08	Invoice 210 was received from Ronald Baker Fabrics for four pairs of curtains at $30 each, for a total vendor invoice of $120. (*Hint: Select 002wall as the inventory item.*)
01/20/08	Invoice 78JJ was received from Jesse Jensen Hardware for the purchase of 10 curtain rods at $50 each, for a total of $500. (*Hint: Select 001hardware as the inventory item.*)

CASH PURCHASES: Write Checks Window

Susan's Service Merchandise pays cash for some purchases. Usually these cash disbursements are for expenses. All payments of cash are recorded in the ***cash disbursements journal***. Follow these steps to see how cash purchases are entered.

Read Me:

The Write Checks window is a simplified version of the Payments window. Both the Write Checks window and the Payments window post to the Cash Disbursements Journal.

1. From the Vendors & Purchases page, click 

, New Check. When the Select a Cash Account window appears, make sure La Brea Bank is selected. Then, click 

. The Write Checks window displays.

Date	*Transaction Description*
01/23/08	Susan's Service Merchandise issued check 3030 in the amount of $160 to Dave Heinrich for cleaning (debit Account No. 70000, Maintenance Expense). Print Check No. 3030.

Comment

Your Write Checks window will show a cash account balance in the Balance field. Your Cash Account Balance field shows the same amount as the January 1, 2008 balance sheet, page 392, La Brea Bank.

2. Click on the Pay to the Order of Name field and type **Dave Heinrich**.

3. Type **3030** in the Check Number field. Press **<Enter>**.

4. Type **23** in the Date field and press **<Enter>**.

5. Type **160** in the $ field.

6. In the Expense Account field, select Account No. 70000, Maintenance Expense.

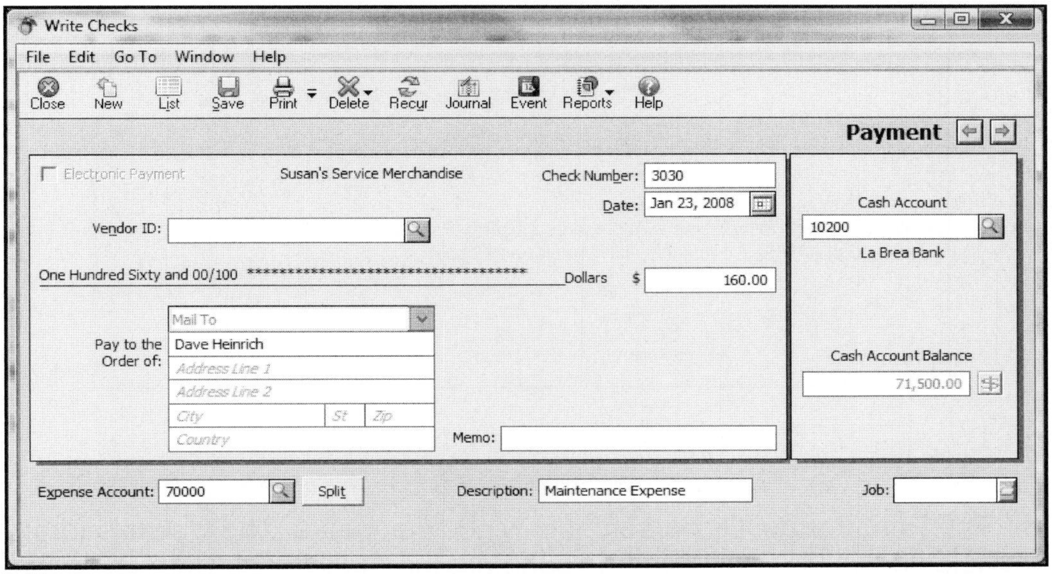

Printing the Check

Follow these steps to print the check:

1. The Write Checks window with Dave Heinrich's check should be displayed.

2. Click 

.

> **Comment**
>
> Step 3 instructs you to select OCR AP Laser Preprinted as the form to print. If this form does *not* print, select another one. The form you select is tied to the kind of printer you are using. Depending on your printer, you may need to make a different selection.

3. The Print Forms: Disbursement Checks window appears. Click . 

Then click OCR AP Laser Preprinted to highlight it.

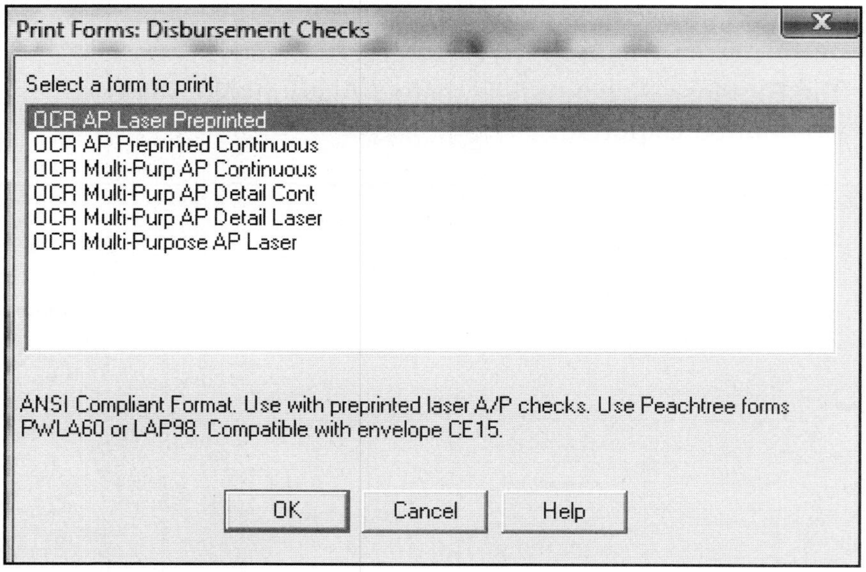

4. Click 

.

5. The Print Forms: Disbursements window appears. The Use this form field shows OCR AP Laser Preprinted; the First Check Number shows 3030.

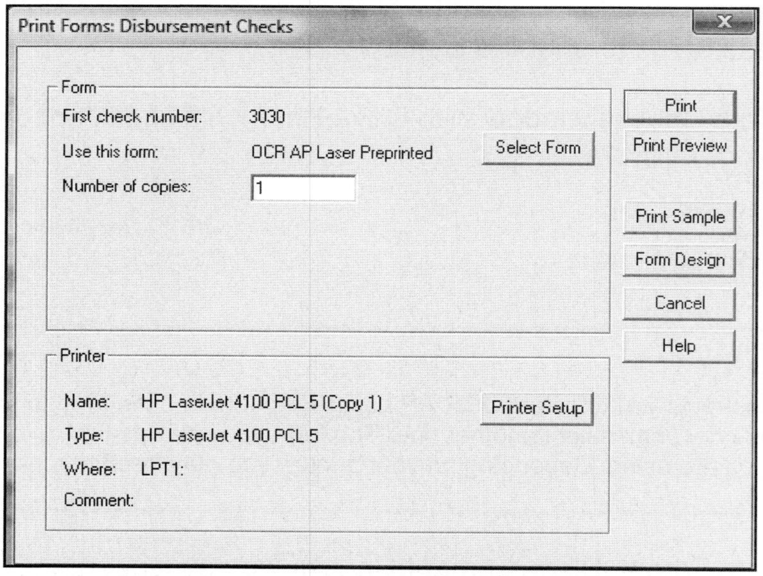

6. Peachtree automatically sequences check numbers after the first one is entered. Click [Print]. The check starts to print.

	Maintenance Expense		160.00
1/23/08	3030	Dave Heinrich	$160.00

Check Number: 3030 Jan 23, 2008

Memo:

160.00

One Hundred Sixty and 00/100 Dollars

Dave Heinrich

Comment

If your check does not show the same amount, go back to the Write Checks window and click [List]. Double-click Check No. 3030, 1/23/2008; the Write Checks window appears. Make the necessary corrections. When you reprint Check No. 3030, Duplicate will be shown on the printout.

After you print a check, the Write Checks window is ready for another payment. Remember, the check form that you select is tied to the kind of printer you are using. If necessary, select a different form to print.

7. Record the additional payments shown below. Since you are *not* going to print Check Nos. 3031-3035, type the appropriate check number in the Check Number field on the Write Checks window.

Date	*Transaction Description*
01/23/08	Susan's Service Merchandise issued Check No. 3031 in the amount of $41.00 to the U.S. Post Office for stamps. (*Hint: Since your are not going to print checks, type Check No.* **3031** *in the Check Number field. Click*  *after each entry.*)
01/23/08	Issued Check No. 3032 in the amount of $107.65 to Century City Office Supplies for letterhead paper, envelopes, and note pads. (Debit Account No. 75500, Supplies Expense.)
01/23/08	Issued Check No. 3033 in the amount of $72.14 to RCT Phone Co.
01/24/08	Issued Check No. 3034 to Joe Greene for $500.
01/24/08	Issued Check No. 3035 to Susan Currier for $500.

8. Click  to see if you have issued Check Nos. 3030 through 3035.

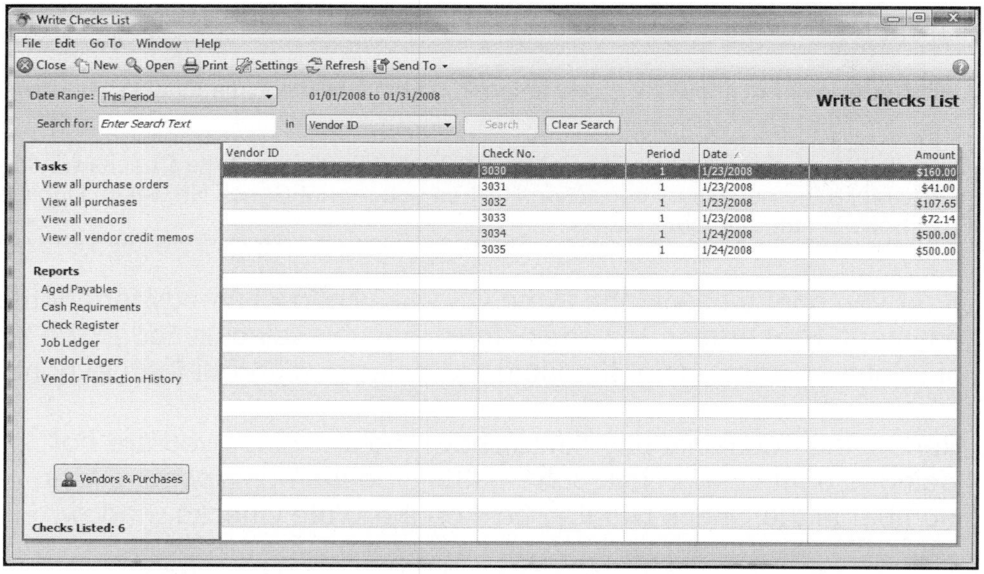

9. If you have any transactions to edit, highlight the line. Double-click. When the Write Checks window appears, make the necessary corrections. Remember to click 

for any revised transactions. If no corrections are needed, close the Write Checks List window.

10. Close the Write Checks window and the Write Checks List window.

PURCHASE RETURNS: CREDITS & RETURNS

Sometimes it is necessary to return merchandise that has been purchased from a vendor. When entering a purchase return, you need to record it as a vendor credit memo.

The following transaction is for merchandise returned to a vendor:

Date	*Transaction Description*
01/24/08	Returned one roll of vinyl flooring to Lyle Lewis Products, Invoice 90 and paid the invoice on the same day.

Follow these steps to enter a purchase return:

1. From the Vendors & Purchases page, click 

. New Vendor Credit Memo. The Vendor Credit Memos window appears.

2. In the Vendor ID field, select Lyle Lewis Products.

3. Type **24** in the Date field.

4. Type **VCM90** in the Credit No field. For the credit number you are using the abbreviation VCM for Vendor Credit Memo, then the invoice number.

5. The Apply to Invoice No. tab is selected. Click on the down-arrow to select 90.

Observe that the Item, Quantity, Description, GL Account, and Unit Price columns are completed.

6. Type **1** in the Returned column; Press <Enter>. After you type 1 in the Returned column, the Amount column shows 54.00. Also, notice that the Credit Applied to Invoice shows 54.00. This agrees with the Credit Total.

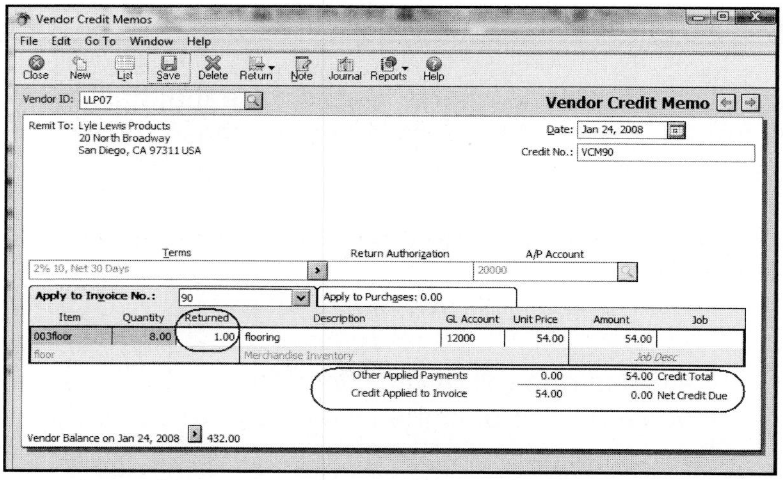

7. To see how the vendor credit memo is journalized, click . Notice that Account No. 12000, Merchandise Inventory, is credited for $54.00 and Account No. 20000, Account Payable, is debited for $54.00.

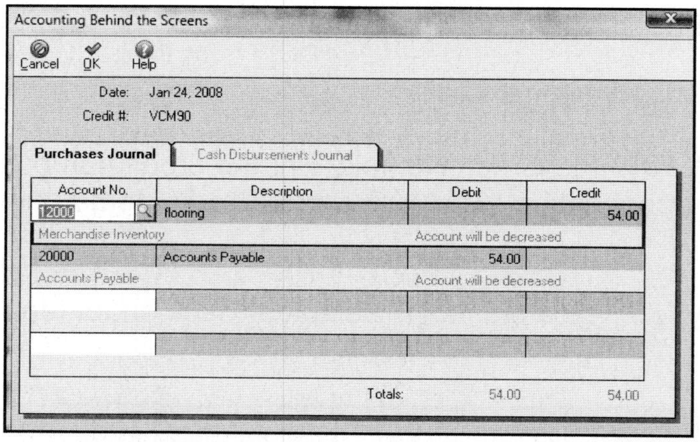

8. Click 

to close the Accounting Behind the Screens window.

9. Click 

to post, then 

the Vendor Credit Memos window.

Paying a Vendor, Minus a Return of Merchandise

How does the return of merchandise affect the payment to the vendor? Follow these steps to pay Invoice No. 90 less the return.

1. From the Vendors & Purchases page, select 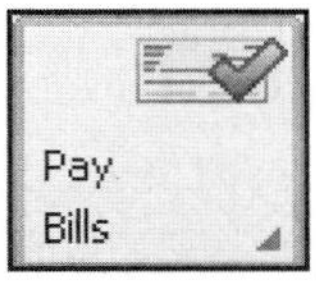

, Pay Bill. The Payments window appears.

Date	*Transaction Description*
01/24/08	Susan's Service Merchandise issued Check No. 3036 to Lyle Lewis Products in payment of Invoice No. 90 (less the return of merchandise). Print Check No. 3036.

2. In the Vendor ID field, select Lyle Lewis Products.

3. Type **24** in the Date field. Observe that the Apply to Invoices tab is selected and that the Invoice, 90; Date Due (Feb 19, 2008) and Amount Due 378.00 columns are completed. Susan's Service Merchandise owes Lyle Lewis Products $378 ($432, original invoice amount, less the $54 return). Lyle Lewis Products extends a 2% vendor discount to Susan's Service Merchandise. Type **7.56** in the Discount column (.02 x 378 = 7.56). Press <Enter>. Observe that the Pay box is checked. The payment was calculated as follows:

Jan. 20	Invoice 90	$432.00
Jan. 24	Less, VCM90	54.00
Jan. 24	Less, Purchase discount	7.56
Total Paid		$370.44

Compare your Payments window to the one shown below. Make sure that Discount column is shows 7.56 and that the Discount Account field shows Account No. 59500, Purchase Discounts.

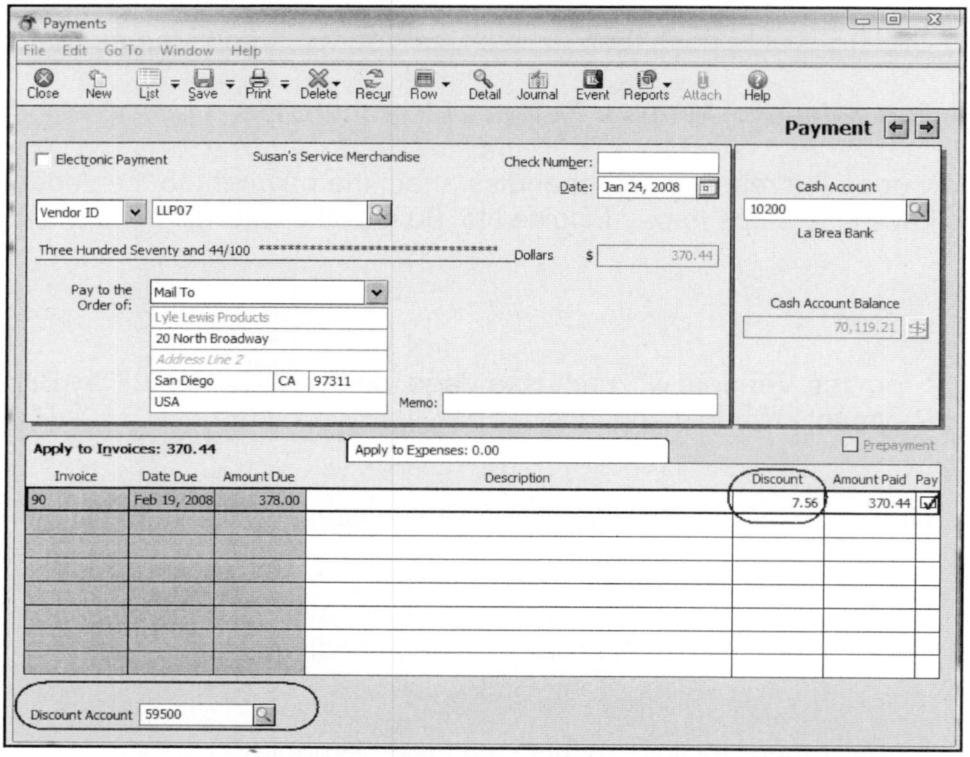

➢ **Troubleshooting Tip:** What if your Cash Account Balance field does not show an amount? Close the Payments window without saving. Then, from the menu bar, go to Options; Global. A checkmark should be placed next to Recalculate cash balance automatically in Receipts, Payments, and Payroll Entry. If necessary, click on the appropriate field, then OK. Go back to step 1, on page 419.

4. Click Print.

5. The Print Forms: Disbursement Checks window displays. Type **3036** in the First Check Number field.

6. The Use this form field shows OCR AP Laser Preprinted. If this selection is *not* made, click Select Form, then select OCR AP Laser Printed. Click Print. Check No. 3036 starts to print. Make sure the check amount is $370.44.

7. Close the Payments window.

8. Record the following purchase return and payment:

Date	*Transaction Description*
01/28/08	Returned two curtain rods (001hardware) to Jesse Jensen Hardware, Invoice No. 78JJ; VCM78JJ. Susan's Service Merchandise paid $50 each for the two curtain rods; credit total, $100.00.
01/28/08	Issued Check No. 3037 to pay Jesse Jensen Hardware for Invoice No. 78JJ (minus returned merchandise). (*Hint: Type the check number in the Check Number field instead of printing it. The discount is 8.00*)

PAYING SPECIFIC VENDOR INVOICES

Once you have entered a vendor invoice in the Purchases/Receive Inventory window, you can apply payments to specific invoices. You enter the vendor invoice using the Purchases/Receive Inventory window; then when you post, the purchase journal is updated. To pay for the merchandise purchased, you select the specific invoice from the vendor's transaction list. When you print a check, you are also posting to the cash disbursements journal. The journal entry below shows a specific vendor payment.

Account Name	Debit	Credit
Accounts Payable/Ronald Baker Fabrics	$120.00	
Purchase Discounts		$2.40
La Brea Bank		$117.60

You should take advantage of both the Purchases/Receive Inventory and Payments features. Because amounts are disbursed and discounts are tracked automatically, your job is made easier. This also provides a detailed and complete audit trail. An audit trail is the path from the source document to the accounts. (Refer to pages 175-182 for more information about Peachtree's internal controls and audit trail.)

The diagram below shows how Purchases/Receive Inventory works together with Payments.

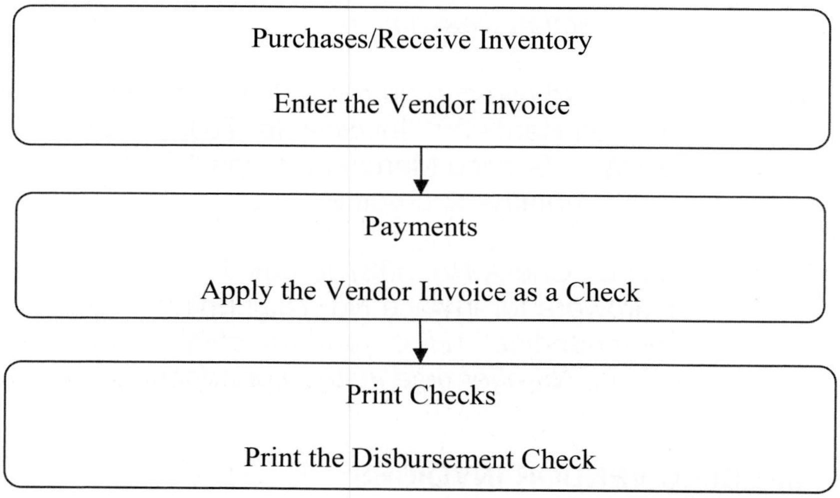

Date	*Transaction Description*
01/28/08	Issued Check No. 3038 to Ronald Baker Fabrics in payment of Invoice No. 210.

Follow these steps to pay vendor invoice 210:

1. From the Payments window, select Ronald Baker Fabrics as the vendor.

2. If necessary, type **3038** in the Check Number field.

3. Type **28** in the Date field.

4. The Apply to Invoices tab should already be selected. For Invoice No. 210, click on the Pay box.

5 Click 

to post.

Editing Payments

If you have already paid a vendor, you can edit payments. Follow these steps to see what vendors have been paid:

1. Display the Payments window.

2. Click 

. The Payment List window appears.

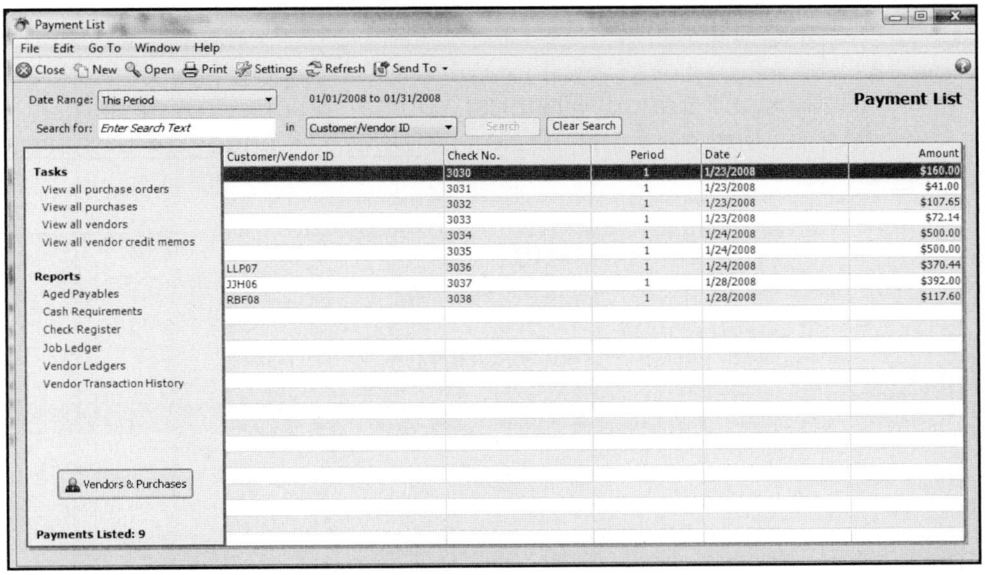

3. If you need to edit a payment, double-click on the appropriate one. Or, if no corrections are needed, close the Payment List window.

4. Make any necessary changes, then post.

5. When you are finished close the Payments window.

PRINTING THE PURCHASE JOURNAL AND CASH DISBURSEMENTS JOURNAL

Observe that the Vendors & Purchases Navigation Center shows the following sections.

- Vendors & Purchases Tasks: The flowchart that shows the Peachtree's accounts payable system.
- Vendors: Each vendor balance is shown. Observe that each vendor has a zero balance. You can link to individual vendors or View Detailed List.

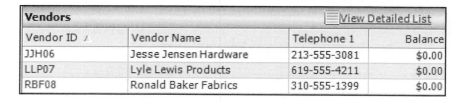

Vendors View Detailed List

Vendor ID	Vendor Name	Telephone 1	Balance
JJH06	Jesse Jensen Hardware	213-555-3081	$0.00
LLP07	Lyle Lewis Products	619-555-4211	$0.00
RBF08	Ronald Baker Fabrics	310-555-1399	$0.00

- Recently Used Vendor Reports: You can link to view or print vendor reports from this section or View All Vendor & Purchases Reports.

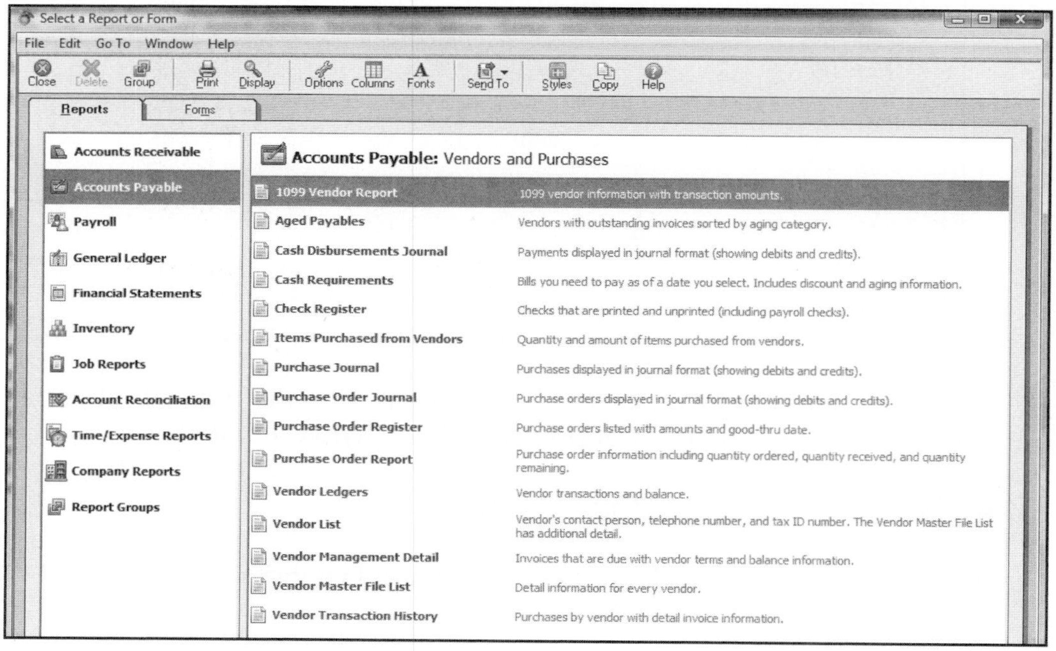

- Aged Payables: From this section, graphs or tables may be viewed.

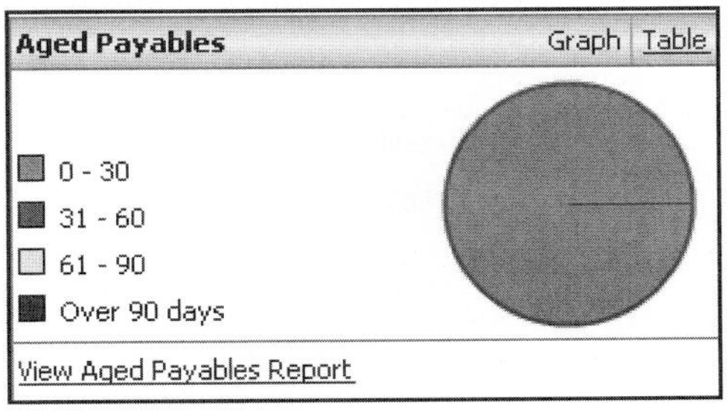

- Peachtree Solutions: Checks and Forms and Online Bill Pay are available through third party vendors who supply checks and online services to Peachtree.

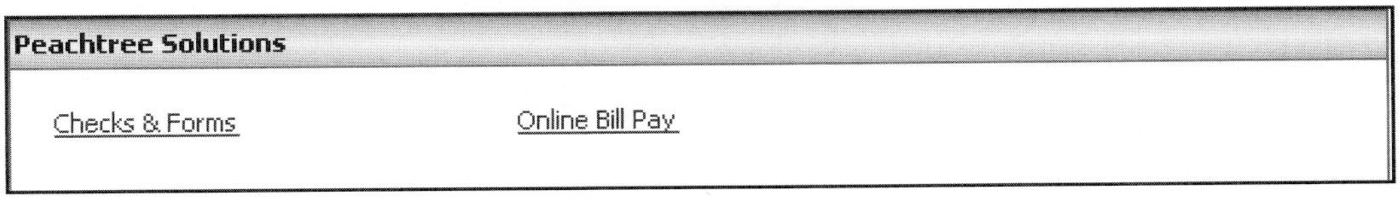

1. From the Recently Used Vendor Reports area, go to the Purchase Journal Print link.

2. The Modify Report - Purchase Journal window appears. Click 

.

3. The Print window appears. Click 

. Compare your purchase journal to the one shown on the next page.

Susan's Service Merchandise
Purchase Journal
For the Period From Jan 1, 2008 to Jan 31, 2008
Filter Criteria includes: 1) Includes Drop Shipments. Report order is by Date. Report is printed in Detail Format.

Date	Account ID Account Description	Invoice/CM #	Line Description	Debit Amount	Credit Amount
1/2/08	12000 Merchandise Inventory	56JJ	restoration hardware	300.00	
	20000 Accounts Payable		Jesse Jensen Hardware		300.00
1/20/08	12000 Merchandise Inventory	210	wall coverings	120.00	
	20000 Accounts Payable		Ronald Baker Fabrics		120.00
1/20/08	12000 Merchandise Inventory	78JJ	restoration hardware	500.00	
	20000 Accounts Payable		Jesse Jensen Hardware		500.00
1/20/08	12000 Merchandise Inventory	90	flooring	432.00	
	20000 Accounts Payable		Lyle Lewis Products		432.00
1/24/08	12000 Merchandise Inventory	VCM90	flooring		54.00
	20000 Accounts Payable		Lyle Lewis Products	54.00	
1/28/08	12000 Merchandise Inventory	VCM78JJ	restoration hardware		100.00
	20000 Accounts Payable		Jesse Jensen Hardware	100.00	
				1,506.00	**1,506.00**

4. To print the Cash Disbursements Journal, close the Purchase Journal. Link to Print for the Cash Disbursements Journal then make the selections to print.

Susan's Service Merchandise
Cash Disbursements Journal
For the Period From Jan 1, 2008 to Jan 31, 2008
Filter Criteria includes: Report order is by Date. Report is printed in Detail Format.

Date	Check #	Account ID	Line Description	Debit Amount	Credit Amount
1/23/08	3030	70000	Maintenance Expense	160.00	
		10200	Dave Heinrich		160.00
1/23/08	3031	73500	Postage Expense	41.00	
		10200	U.S. Post Office		41.00
1/23/08	3032	75500	Supplies Expense	107.65	
		10200	Century City Office Supplies		107.65
1/23/08	3033	76000	Telephone Expense	72.14	
		10200	RCT Phone Co.		72.14
1/24/08	3034	39007	Joe Greene, Drawing	500.00	
		10200	Joe Greene		500.00
1/24/08	3035	39009	Susan Currier, Drawing	500.00	
		10200	Susan Currier		500.00
1/24/08	3036	59500	Discounts Taken		7.56
		20000	Invoice: 90	378.00	
		10200	Lyle Lewis Products		370.44
1/28/08	3037	59500	Discounts Taken		8.00
		20000	Invoice: 78JJ	400.00	
		10200	Jesse Jensen Hardware		392.00
1/28/08	3038	59500	Discounts Taken		2.40
		20000	Invoice: 210	120.00	
		10200	Ronald Baker Fabrics		117.60
	Total			**2,278.79**	**2,278.79**

Comment

Observe that the Line Description on the Cash Disbursements Journal shows the account name (e.g. Account No. 70000, Maintenance Expense) for the debit amount. The person to whom the check was written (e.g. Dave Heinrich) is shown for the amount credited.

VENDOR LEDGERS

Follow these steps to print a Vendor Ledger for Susan's Service Merchandise:

1. From the Recently Used Vendor Reports area, link to <u>View All Vendor & Purchases Reports</u>. The Select a Report or Form window appears.

2. Double-click Vendor Ledgers then make the selections to print.

Susan's Service Merchandise
Vendor Ledgers
For the Period From Jan 1, 2008 to Jan 31, 2008
Filter Criteria includes: Report order is by ID.

Vendor ID Vendor	Date	Trans No	Type	Paid	Debit Amt	Credit Amt	Balance
JJH06	1/2/08	56JJ	PJ			300.00	300.00
Jesse Jensen Hardware	1/20/08	78JJ	PJ	*		500.00	800.00
	1/28/08	VCM78JJ	PJ	*	100.00		700.00
	1/28/08	3037	CDJ		8.00	8.00	700.00
	1/28/08	3037	CDJ		400.00		300.00
LLP07	1/20/08	90	PJ	*		432.00	432.00
Lyle Lewis Products	1/24/08	VCM90	PJ	*	54.00		378.00
	1/24/08	3036	CDJ		7.56	7.56	378.00
	1/24/08	3036	CDJ		378.00		0.00
RBF08	1/20/08	210	PJ	*		120.00	120.00
Ronald Baker Fabrics	1/28/08	3038	CDJ		2.40	2.40	120.00
	1/28/08	3038	CDJ		120.00		0.00
Report Total					**1,069.96**	**1,369.96**	**300.00**

3. Close the Vendor Ledgers.

PRINTING THE GENERAL LEDGER TRIAL BALANCE

1. In the Reports list, highlight General Ledger. Then, select General Ledger Trial Balance.

2. Make the selections to print. Compare your printout with the one shown on the next page.

Susan's Service Merchandise
General Ledger Trial Balance
As of Jan 31, 2008

Filter Criteria includes: Report order is by ID. Report is printed in Detail Format.

Account ID	Account Description	Debit Amt	Credit Amt
10200	La Brea Bank	69,239.17	
10400	Worldwide Savings & Loan	20,000.00	
12000	Merchandise Inventory	28,938.00	
13000	Supplies	1,750.00	
14000	Prepaid Insurance	2,400.00	
15000	Furniture and Fixtures	5,000.00	
15100	Computers & Equipment	7,500.00	
15500	Building	100,000.00	
20000	Accounts Payable		300.00
27000	Long-Term Notes Payable		20,500.00
27400	Mortgage Payable		75,000.00
39006	Joe Greene, Capital		70,195.00
39007	Joe Greene, Drawing	500.00	
39008	Susan Currier, Capital		70,195.00
39009	Susan Currier, Drawing	500.00	
59500	Purchase Discounts		17.96
70000	Maintenance Expense	160.00	
73500	Postage Expense	41.00	
75500	Supplies Expense	107.65	
76000	Telephone Expense	72.14	
	Total:	**236,207.96**	**236,207.96**

3. Close all windows.

BACKING UP CHAPTER 11 DATA

Follow these steps to back up Chapter 11 data.

1. From the Navigation Bar, select **Company**; link to Back up.

2. Click Back Up.

3. Accept the default for backing up to the hard drive or make the selections to back up to another location. Type **Chapter 11** in the File name field.

4. Click Save.

5. When the window prompts that This company backup will require approximately 3.30MB, click OK. When the Back Up Company scale is 100% complete, you have successfully backed up to the current point in Chapter 11.

6. Continue or click File; Exit to exit Peachtree.

INTERNET ACTIVITY	
1.	From your Internet browser, go to the book's website at http://www.mhhe.com/yacht2008.
2.	Link to Student Edition.
3.	In the Course-wide Content list, link to Part 3 Internet Activities for Chapters 11-14. Open or Save. (You can also choose Chapter 11, then link to Internet Activities. If you Choose a Chapter, observe that other chapter-specific links are available; for example, Quizzes, PowerPoints, and Going to the Net Exercises.)
4.	Complete the ACCOUNTING LIST – Chapter 11 exercise. Read steps 1 – 4.
5.	Follow the steps shown on the book's website to complete this Internet activity.
6.	Using a word processing program write a brief summary of what you find. Include all appropriate website addresses.

SUMMARY AND REVIEW

SOFTWARE OBJECTIVES: In Chapter 11, you used the software to:

1. Set up company information for Susan's Service Merchandise.
2. Enter the following general ledger information: chart of accounts and beginning balances.
3. Enter the following accounts payable information: vendor defaults and vendor records.
4. Enter the following inventory information: inventory defaults, inventory items, inventory beginning balances.

5. Record accounts payable transactions: merchandise purchases, purchase orders, cash purchases, and purchase returns.

6. Make four backups: 1) back up Chapter 11 beginning data; 2) back up Chapter 11 data; 3) back up Exercise 11-1; 4) back up Exercise 11-2.

WEB OBJECTIVES: In Chapter 11, you did these Internet activities:

1. Used your Internet browser to go to the book's website. (Go online to www.mhhe.com/yacht2008.)

2. Went to the Internet Activity link on the book's website. Then, select WEB EXERCISES PART 3. Complete the first web exercise in Part 3—Accounting List.

3. Used a word processing program to write summaries of the websites that you visited.

GOING TO THE NET

Access information about Peachtree's Easy Startup, Easy to Learn features at www.peachtree.com/PeachtreeAccountingLine/Complete/features_easy_startup.cfm.

Answer the following questions.

1. List four features that make Peachtree easy to learn.

2. What are the Navigation Centers?

3. How many sample company chart of accounts can you choose from?

True/Make True: Write the word True in the space provided if the statement is true. If the statement is not true, write the correct answer.

1. Accounts Payable is money you pay to customers.

 ____

 ____

2. Vendor default information needs to be set up to establish the criteria used when computing vendor discounts.

 ____

 ____

3. Susan's Service Merchandise is organized as a partnership.

 ____

 ____

4. The purchase discount offered to Susan's Service Merchandise from their vendors is 2% 10, Net 30 Days

 ____

 ____

5. Each time you use the Purchases/Receive Inventory window, you are journalizing in the Cash Disbursements Journal.

 ____

 ____

6. The merchandise that Susan's Service Merchandise buys from Ronald Baker Fabrics is classified as wall coverings.

____

____

7. Each time you use the Payments window, you are journalizing in the Purchase Journal.

____

____

8. The Maintain Vendors window is used to enter information about vendors from whom you purchase merchandise.

____

____

9. The purchase discount amount is debited to Account No. 50000, Purchase Discounts.

____

____

10. Vendor Credit Memos post to the Purchases Journal.

____

____

Exercise 11-1: Follow the instructions below to complete Exercise 11-1.

1. Start Peachtree. From the menu bar, select File; New Company. Set up a retail business using *your first and last name*; for example, *Your Name Sales & Service.* For the address, use 207 East Elm Street; Eugene, OR 97401; telephone, 541-555-4003; Fax, 541-555-9123. Your company is a Sole Proprietorship. For the Tax ID information, use the following:

Federal Employer ID:	75-3189922
State Employer ID:	62-5192278
State Unemployment ID:	625429-7

   Leave the Web Site and E-mail address fields blank.

2. At the New Company – Setup; Chart of Accounts window, select Copy settings from an existing Peachtree Accounting company.

3. Highlight Susan's Service Merchandise (*or,* your name Sales & Service), then click Next >.

4. Observe that the information on the Copy Company Information window includes a selection for Accounting Periods. Since this company is using the same accounting period (January 1 - 31, 2008) as Susan's Service Merchandise, leave that box checked. To enter a different accounting period, click on the Accounting Periods field to uncheck it. For purposes of Exercise 11-1 accept all the defaults on the Copy Company Information window by clicking on Next >.

5. Read the information about the Accounting Method. Accept the default for accrual accounting by clicking on Next >.

6. Accept the default for Real Time posting by clicking on Next >.

7. At the Create a New Company – Finish window, click Finish.

8. Click OK when the Have you started using credit cards window appears. Close the Setup Guide. (*Hint:* Click on the box next to Don't show this screen at startup to place a checkmark in it.) Close the Setup Guide window.

General Ledger

1. Delete the following accounts:

   3900A Owner's Draw
   40400 Sales-Floors

   Change the following accounts:

10200	La Brea Bank	**Eugene Bank**
10400	Worldwide Savings & Loan	**Oregon Savings & Loan**
39009	Owner's Contribution	**Student Name, Capital** (Equity–doesn't close)
40200	Sales-Wall	**Sales-Tools**
50500	Cost of Sales-Wall	**Cost of Sales-Tools**
57000	Cost of Sales-Floor	**Cost of Sales**

   Add the following account:

   39010 Student Name, Drawing Equity-gets closed

2. Use the Balance Sheet on the next page to record chart of accounts beginning balances. You purchased your retail business in December 2007. Remember to select the period From 12/1/07 through 12/31/07

Student Name Sales & Service Balance Sheet January 1, 2008		
ASSETS		
Current Assets		
Eugene Bank	$60,500.00	
Oregon Savings & Loan	12,300.00	
Merchandise Inventory	14,750.00	
Supplies	1,000.00	
Prepaid Insurance	2,400.00	
Total Current Assets		$90,950.00
Property and Equipment		
Furniture and Fixtures	$3,500.00	
Computers & Equipment	5,500.00	
Building	85,000.00	
Total Property and Equipment		$94,000.00
Total Assets		$184,950.00
LIABILITIES AND CAPITAL		
Long Term Liabilities		
Long-Term Notes Payable	10,000.00	
Mortgage Payable	60,000.00	
Total Long-Term Liabilities		$70,000.00
Capital		
Student Name, Capital		114,950.00
Total Liabilities and Capital		$184,950.00

Accounts Payable

Follow the instructions below to set up vendor information.

1. Click 

; Set up Vendor Defaults. Set up the following vendor defaults:

Standard Terms:	Due in number of days
Net due in:	30 days
Discount in:	10 days
Discount %:	2.00
Credit Limit:	5,000.00

GL Link Accounts:

Expense Account:	12000 Merchandise Inventory
Discount GL Account:	59500 Purchase Discounts

2. Click 

; New Vendor. Set up the following vendors:

a. Vendor ID:	**CPT12**
Name:	**Charles Perkins Tools**
Contact:	**Sandra Perkins**
Address:	**1035 Melrose Ave.**
City, ST Zip	**Los Angeles, CA 90046**
Country:	**USA**
Vendor Type:	**tools**
1099 Type:	**Independent Contractor**
Expense Account:	12000 Merchandise Inventory
Telephone 1:	**213-555-4280**
Fax:	**213-555-4284**
E-mail:	**info@charlesperkins.com**
Web Site:	**www.charlesperkins.com**

Purchase Info:

Tax ID Number:	**27-1238977**

b.

Vendor ID:	**SJH14**
Name:	**Sherry Jackson Hardware**
Contact:	**Sherry Jackson**
Address:	**160 Spaulding Drive**
City, ST Zip	**Beverly Hills, CA 90212**
Country:	**USA**
Vendor Type:	**hardware**
1099 Type:	**Independent Contractor**
Expense Account:	12000 Merchandise Inventory
Telephone 1:	**310-555-9820**
Fax:	**310-555-2065**
E-mail:	**info@jacksonhardware.net**
Web Site:	**www.jacksonhardware.net**

Purchase Info:

Tax ID Number:	**27-2539852**

Inventory

Follow these steps to set up inventory defaults:

1. Click 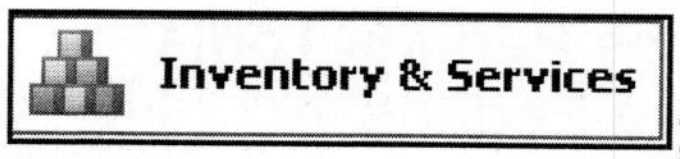

; 

, Set Up Inventory Defaults.

2. Select the GL Accts/Costing tab. If necessary, set up Average as the inventory costing method (Stock item, Master Stock item, Assembly).

3. If necessary, select Account No. 45500, Shipping Charges. This GL Link is for Freight Charges in Sales/Invoicing.

4. Click 

; New Inventory Item. Set up the following inventory stock items:

a.

Item ID:	**002tools**
Description:	**tools**
Description for Sales:	**tools**
Price Level 1:	**85**
Last Unit Cost:	**30**
Cost Method:	Average
GL Sales Acct:	**40200 Sales-Tools**
GL Inventory Acct:	**12000 Merchandise Inventory**
GL Cost of Sales Acct:	**50500 Cost of Sales-Tools**
Item Type:	**tools**
Stocking U/M:	**each**
Minimum Stock:	**10**
Reorder Quantity:	**4**
Vendor ID:	**CPT12, Charles Perkins Tools**

b.

Item ID:	**003hardware**
Description:	**hardware**
Description for Sales:	**copper hardware**
Price Level 1:	**150**
Last Unit Cost:	**50**
Cost Method:	Average
GL Sales Acct:	**40000 Sales-Hardware**
GL Inventory Acct:	**12000 Merchandise Inventory**
Cost of Sales Acct:	**50000 Cost of Sales-Hardware**
Item Type:	**hardware**
Stocking U/M:	**each**
Minimum Stock:	**10**
Reorder Quantity:	**4**
Vendor ID:	**SJH14, Sherry Jackson Hardware**

5. Click on Inventory Beginning Balances. Record the following beginning balances shown on the next page.

Item ID	*Description*	*Quantity*	*Unit Cost*	*Total Cost*
002tools	tools	175	30	5,250.00
003hardware	hardware	190	50	9,500.00

6. Click 

.

7. Print the chart of accounts.

8. Print the balance sheet.

9. Follow these steps to back up Exercise 11-1.

   a. From the Company page, link to <u>Back up</u>.

   b. If necessary, uncheck the box next to Include company name in the backup file name. Click 

.

   c. Accept the default for backing up to the hard drive or make the selections to back up to another location. Type **Exercise 11-1** in the File name field.

   d. Click 

.

   e. When the window prompts that This company backup will require approximately 3.23MB, click 

. When the Back Up Company scale is 100% complete, you have successfully backed up to the current point in Chapter 11.

   f. Continue or exit.

Exercise 11-2: Follow the instructions below to complete Exercise 11-2. Exercise 11-1 *must* be completed before starting Exercise 11-2.

1. Follow these steps to restore the data that you backed up in Exercise 11-1.[4]

   a. If necessary, start Peachtree and open the company that you created in Exercise 11-1. (*Hint:* Make sure the Student Name Sales & Service company is opened *before* you restore.)

   b. From the Company page, link to <u>Restore</u>. (If necessary, put external media in the drive.)

   c. The Select Backup File window appears. (If necessary, click

. In the Look in field, select the appropriate location of your Exercise 11-1.ptb backup file.) Make sure the Location field on the Select Backup File window shows the Exercise 11-1.ptb file. Click

.

   d. The Select Company window appears. The radio button next to An Existing Company is selected. Check that the Company Name and Location fields are correct. Click

.

   e. The Restore Options window appears. Make sure that the box next to Company Data is *checked*. Click

.

   f. The Confirmation window appears. Check the From and To fields to make sure they are correct. Click

. When the Restore Company scale is 100% complete, your data is restored.

[4]You can restore from your back up file even if *no* Peachtree company exists. From Peachtree's start up window, select File; Restore. Select the location of your backup file. On the Restore Wizard's Select Company window, select A New Company. The *A New Company* selection allows you to restore your backup data, bypassing the process of new company set up. For more information, refer to Troubleshooting on pages 280 and 281.

2. Journalize and post the following transactions and print each check.

01/2/08	Invoice No. 480CP was received from Charles Perkins Tools for the purchase of 10 tool kits for a unit cost of $30.
01/5/08	Invoice No. SJH52 was received from Sherry Jackson Hardware for the purchase of 8 hardware sets at a unit cost of $50.
01/6/08	Returned two tool kits to Charles Perkins Tools, Invoice No. 480CP. Paid $30 for each tool kit; VCM480CP.
01/9/08	Issued Check No. 2020 to pay Sherry Jackson Hardware for Invoice No. SJH52. (*Hint: Type the check number, 2020, in the Check Number field.*)
01/9/08	Issued Check No. 2021 to pay Charles Perkins Tools for merchandise purchased on January 2, less the January 6 return, Invoice No. 480CP. (*Hint: Remember to calculate, then type the correct discount amount in the Discount column.*)
01/13/08	Issued Check No. 2022 to Sam Carson for $125 for cleaning and maintenance.
01/15/08	Issued Check No. 2023 to the U.S. Post Office for $41 for postage stamps.
01/16/08	Issued Check No. 2024 to Eugene Office Supplies for $145.72 for cell phone. (Debit Account No. 71000, Office Expense.)
01/16/08	Issued Check No. 2025 to West Telephone for $46.65 to pay the telephone bill.
01/26/08	Issued Check No. 2026 to the owner of the business for $400.

3. Print the Purchase Journal.

4. Print the Cash Disbursements Journal.

5. Print the Vendor Ledgers.

6. Print the General Ledger Trial Balance.

7. Follow these steps to back up Exercise 11-2:

    a. From the Company page, link to <u>Back up</u>.

    b. If necessary, uncheck the box next to Include company name in the backup file name. Click Back Up.

    c. Accept the default for backing up to the hard drive or make the selections to back up to another location. Type **Exercise 11-2** in the File name field.

    d. Click Save.

    e. When the window prompts that This company backup will require approximately 3.25MB, click OK. When the Back Up Company scale is 100% complete, you have successfully backed up to the current point in Chapter 11.

    f. Exit.

CHAPTER 11 INDEX

Chapter 12 Customers & Sales

SOFTWARE OBJECTIVES: In Chapter 12, you will use the software to:

1. Set up customer default information.
2. Set up sales tax information.
3. Set up customer maintenance information.
4. Record credit sales, cash sales, and sales returns.
5. Record customer receipts, partial payments, and edit invoices.
6. Make four backups: 1) back up Chapter 12 beginning data; 2) back up Chapter 12 data; 3) back up Exercise 12-1; 4) back up Exercise 12-2.[1]

WEB OBJECTIVES: In Chapter 12, you will do these Internet activities:

1. Use your Internet browser to go to the book's website.
2. Go to the Internet Activity link on the book's website. Then, select WEB EXERCISES PART 3. Complete the second web exercise in Part 3–WebCPA: Tools and Resources for the Electronic Accountant.
3. Use a word processing program to write summaries of the websites that you visited.

In Chapter 11, you learned how to use PCA's Purchases/Receive Inventory and Payments features. Now that you have purchased merchandise from vendors, you are ready to sell that merchandise. To do that, you need to learn how to use PCA's Customers & Sales Navigation Center.

In Chapter 3, Customer Transactions, when you entered a sales invoice for Bellwether Garden Supply, the unit price, description, account number, and sales taxes were automatically calculated for you. (See pages 103-107.)

---

[1]The chart on page 380 shows you the size of each backup file. Refer to this chart for backing up data.

Before using the Sales/Invoicing window, you need to set up customer defaults, sales tax information, and customer maintenance information. After you set up these defaults, PCA will use this information when you record a sale.

Chapter 12 explains how PCA's accounts receivable system works. ***Accounts receivable*** are what customers owe your business. Credit transactions from customers are called ***accounts receivable transactions***.

Customer receipts work similarly to paying vendor invoices. When a customer pays an existing ***invoice*** there are two steps:

1. Enter the customer's ID code so that a list of existing invoices for the customer displays.

2. Select the invoice that applies to the customer's check, then select the Pay box.

This diagram illustrates PCA's accounts receivable system.

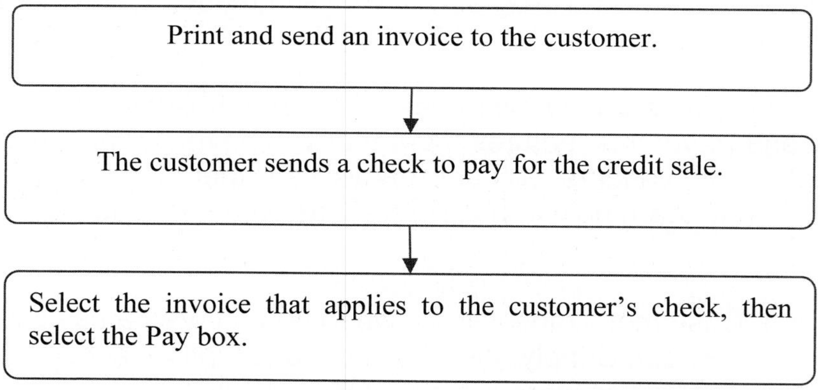

On the Customers & Sales Navigation Center, Peachtree illustrates the accounts receivable system. In Chapter 12, you work with customers, sales invoices, credits and returns, and receipts from customers. The Customers & Sales Navigation Center is shown on the next page.

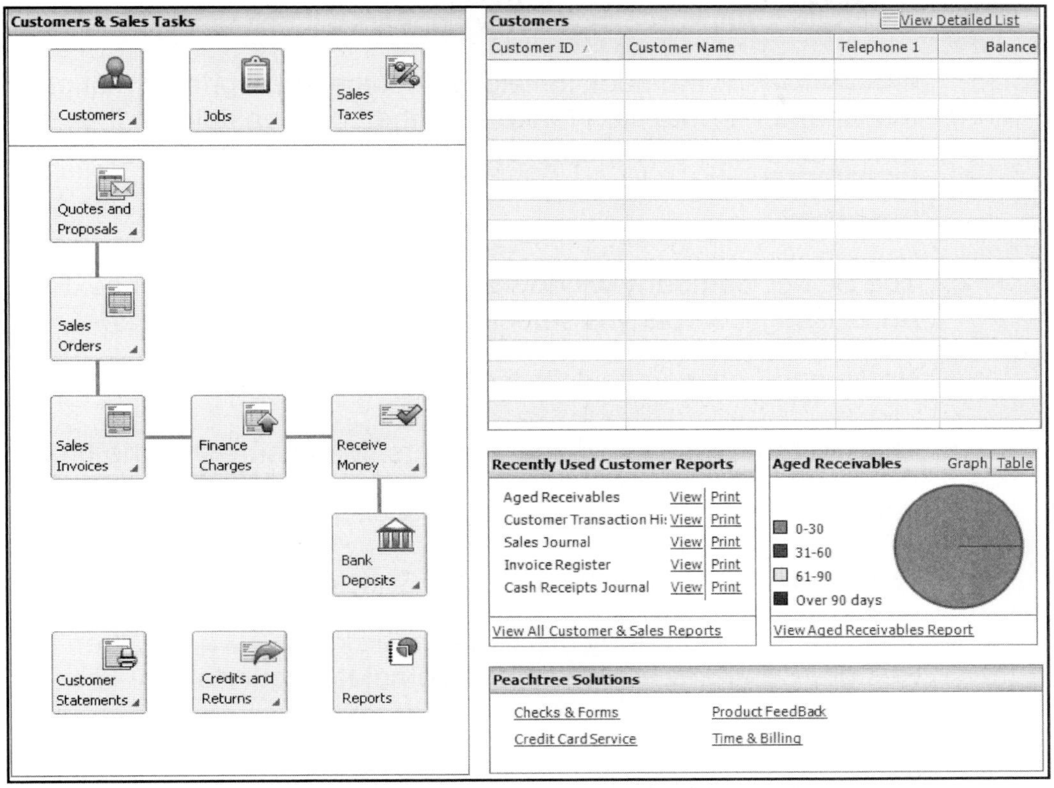

GETTING STARTED

1. Start Peachtree. Open Susan's Service Merchandise, or if you used a unique name, select it. This company was set up in Chapter 11 on pages 383–388. (*Hint:* If another company opens, click File; Open Previous Company, select Susan's [your name] Service Merchandise.)

2. Follow these steps to restore data from Chapter 11. This file was backed up on pages 429-430.

   a. From the Company page, link to Restore. (If necessary, put external media in the appropriate drive.)

b. The Select Backup File window appears. (If necessary, click Browse. In the Look in field, select the appropriate location of the Chapter 11.ptb file.) Make sure the Location field on the Select Backup File window shows the Chapter 11.ptb file. Click Next >.

c. The Select Company window appears. The radio button next to An Existing Company is selected. Check that the Company Name and Location fields are correct. Click Next >.

d. The Restore Options window appears. Make sure that the box next to Company Data is *checked*. Click Next >.

e. The Confirmation window appears. Check the From and To fields to make sure they are correct. Click Finish. When the Restore Company scale is 100% complete, your data is restored.

f. If necessary, remove the external media.

g. To verify your data, display the General Ledger Trial Balance. Compare your trial balance to the one shown on page 429 in Chapter 11.

Setting Up Customer Defaults

In Chapter 11, you entered General Ledger, Accounts Payable, and Inventory Item defaults. The directions that follow show you how to enter customer defaults.

1. From the Navigation Bar, select Customers & Sales; Customers, Set Up Customer Defaults. The Customer Defaults window appears.

2. If necessary, click on the Discount % field. Type **0** (zero) in the Discount % field, then press **<Enter>**. Susan's Service Merchandise does *not* offer a discount to its credit customers.

3. If necessary, type **2500** in the Credit Limit field, press **<Enter>**.

4. Accept the default for GL Sales Account 40000, Sales-Hardware by pressing **<Enter>**. (When you set up individual customers, you will select a GL Sales Account for that customer.)

5. Accept the default for Discount GL Account 49000, Sales Discounts by pressing **<Enter>**.

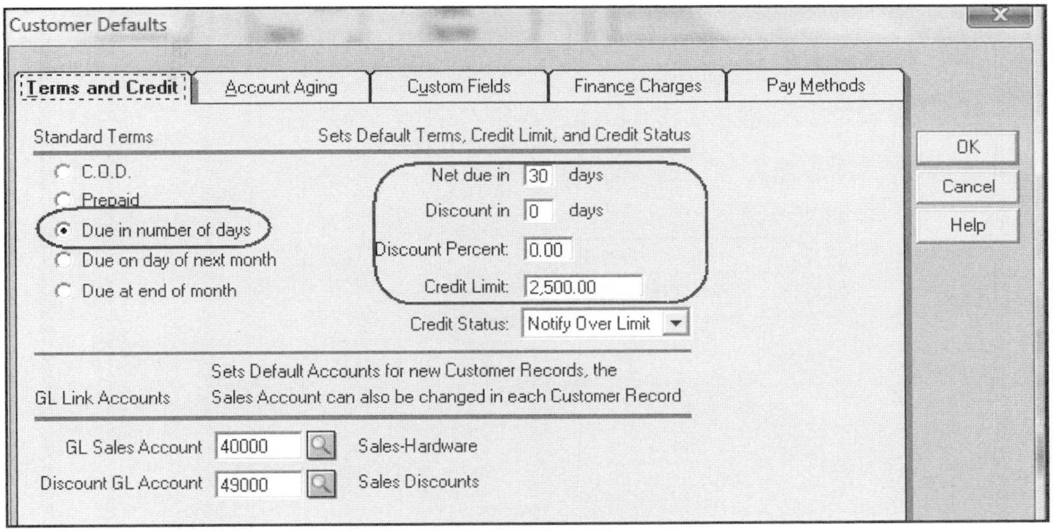

Observe that the default for Standard Terms is Due in number of days.

6. Click 

.

Setting Up Sales Tax Defaults

You can enter sales tax default information for these areas:

➢ Sales Tax Authorities: codes for governments or other tax authorities and their tax rates. These are used to assemble the sales tax codes.

➢ Sales Tax Codes: the overall rate applied to taxable items on invoices to customers. This is composed of rates entered as Sales Tax Authorities.

Follow these steps to set up sales tax defaults:

1. From the Customers & Sales page, click 

; Set up a new sales tax.

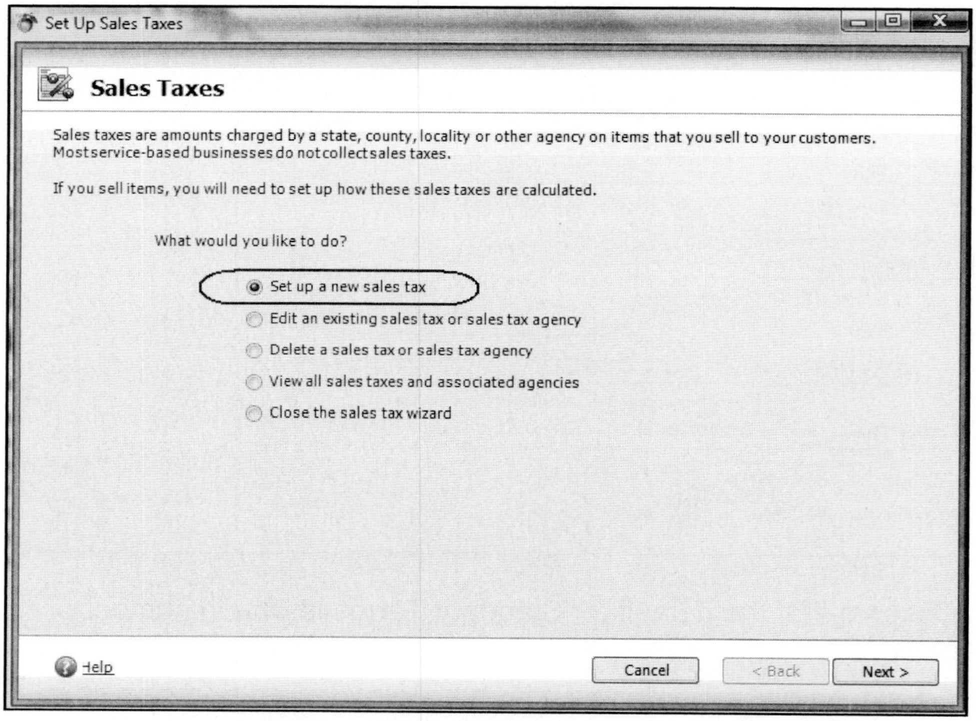

2. Click 

. The Set Up New Sales Tax window appears.

3. Type **8.00**% in the What is the total rate that you will charge?

4. Accept the default for 1 in the How many individual rates make up this total rate? field.

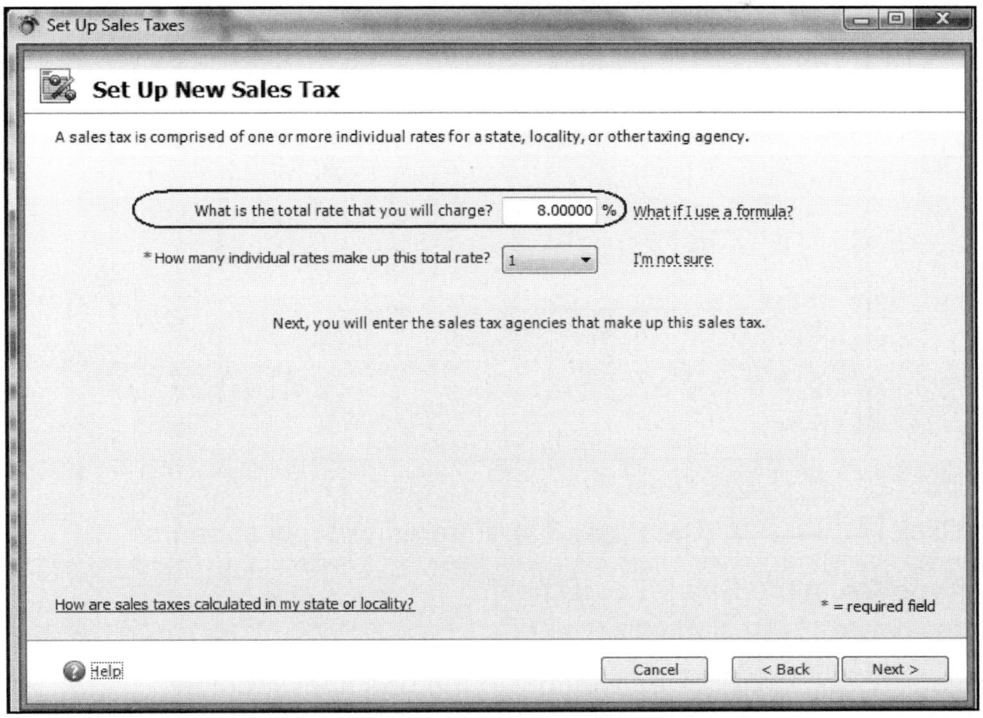

5. Click [Next >]. The Add Sales Tax Agency window appears.

6. Type **CA** in the Sales tax agency ID field.

7. Type **California Dept. of Revenue** in the Sales tax agency name field.

8. Accept the default by single rate in the How are sales taxes calculated for this agency? field.

9. Type **8.00**% in the Rate field. Press **<Enter>**.

10. Select Account No. 23100, Sales Tax Payable in the Select an account to track sales taxes field. Press **<Enter>**.

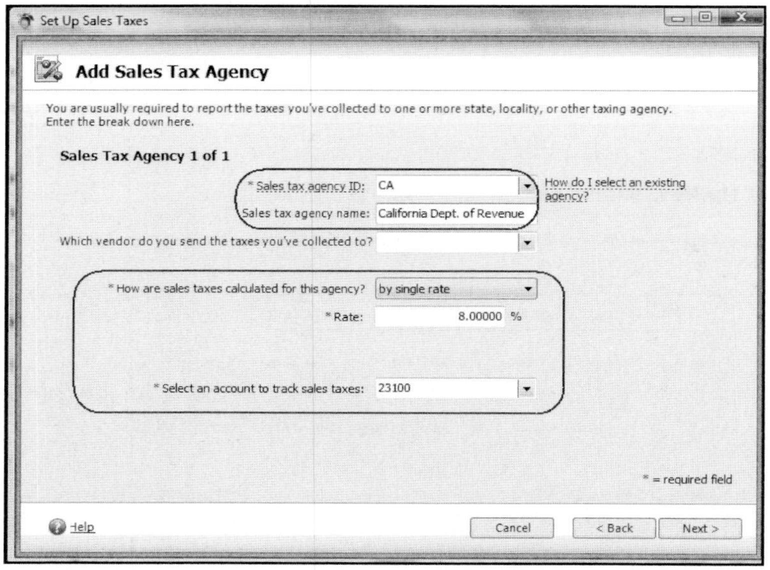

11. Click Next >. The Sales Tax Entered window appears.
12. Type **CA** in the Sales Tax ID field.
13. Type **California sales taxes** in the Sales tax name field. Compare your Sales Tax Entered window to the one shown below.

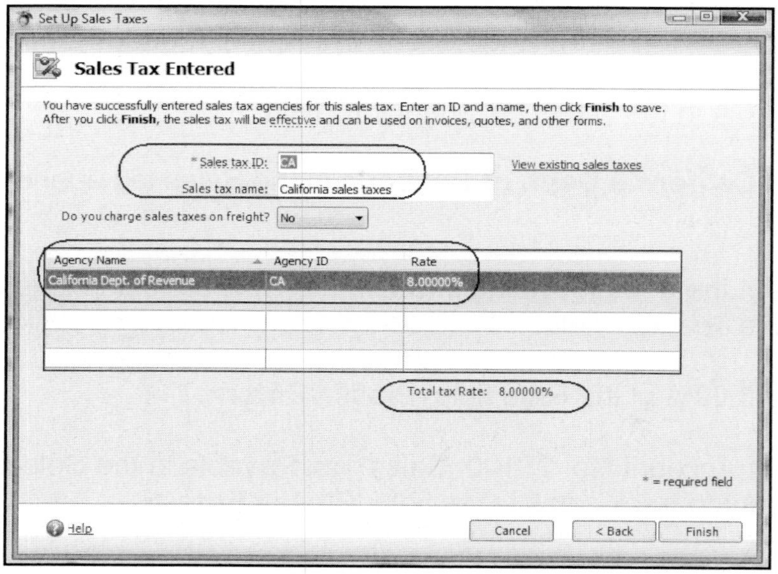

14. Click Finish. The Sales Taxes window appears. Select Close the sales tax wizard -- Close the sales tax wizard. Click Finish. You are returned to the Customers & Sales Tasks page.

To make sure you have set up sales taxes for Susan's Service Merchandise, follow these steps:;

1. From the Customers & Sales page, click Sales Taxes; View all sales taxes and associated agencies.

2. The Sales Taxes window appears. Click Next >. The View All Sales Taxes window appears and shows the sales tax that were set up on pages 449-453. Compare your View All Sales Taxes window with the one shown below.

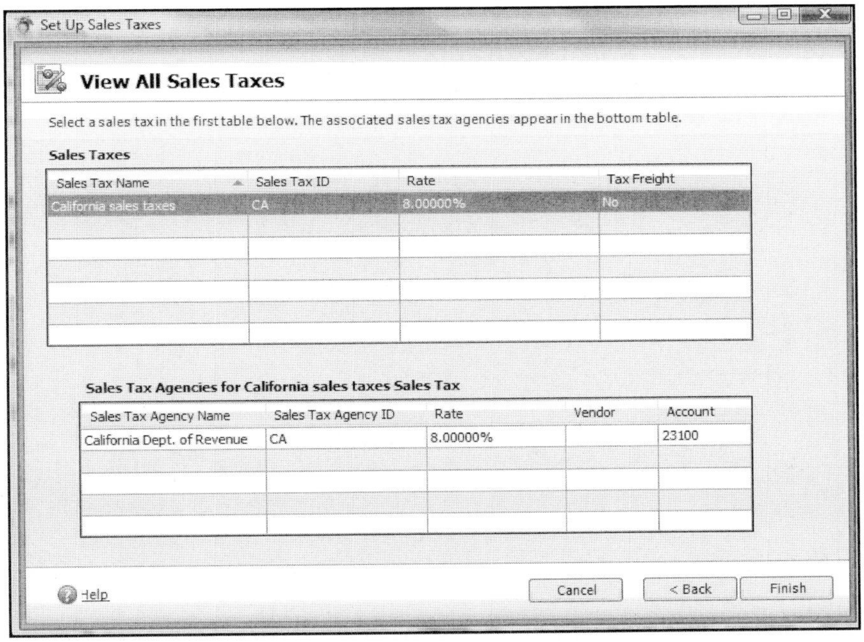

3. Click Finish. Click X on the title bar to close the Sales Taxes window.

Setting Up Customer Maintenance Information

To enter default information about your customers, follow these steps:

1. Select 

; New Customer. The Maintain Customers/Prospects window appears.

2. Complete the following fields.

Customer ID:	**ap001** (Use lowercase letters and zeroes)
Name:	**Alice Peters**
Billing Address:	**709 Poinsettia Avenue**
City, ST Zip:	**Los Angeles, CA 90046**
Country:	**USA**
Sales Tax:	Select **CA** (for California sales taxes)
Customer Type:	**LA**[2]
Telephone 1:	**323-555-8612**
Fax:	**323-555-8614**
E-mail:	**ap@losangeles.com**
Web Site:	**www.losangeles.com/Alice**

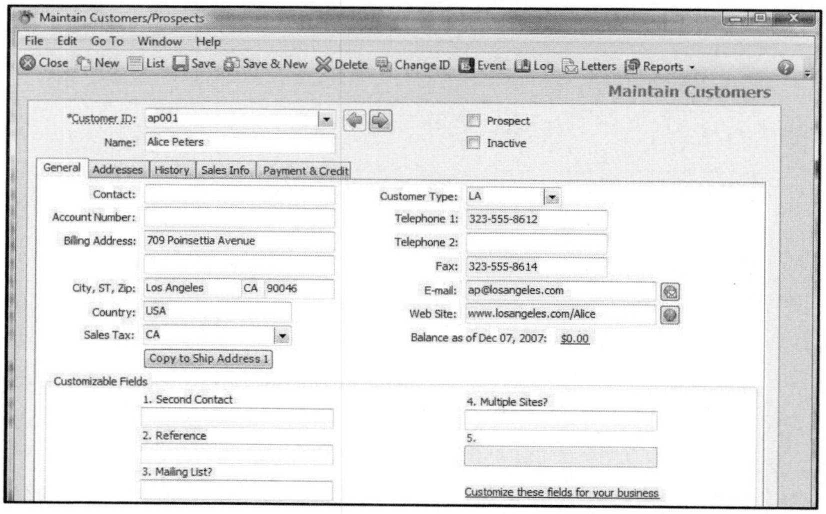

[2]It is important to indicate Customer Type. This groups similar customers together. In this case, customers from Los Angeles (LA) are grouped together.

3. Click on the Sales Info tab.

4. In the GL Sales Acct field, if necessary, select Account No. 40000, Sales-Hardware.

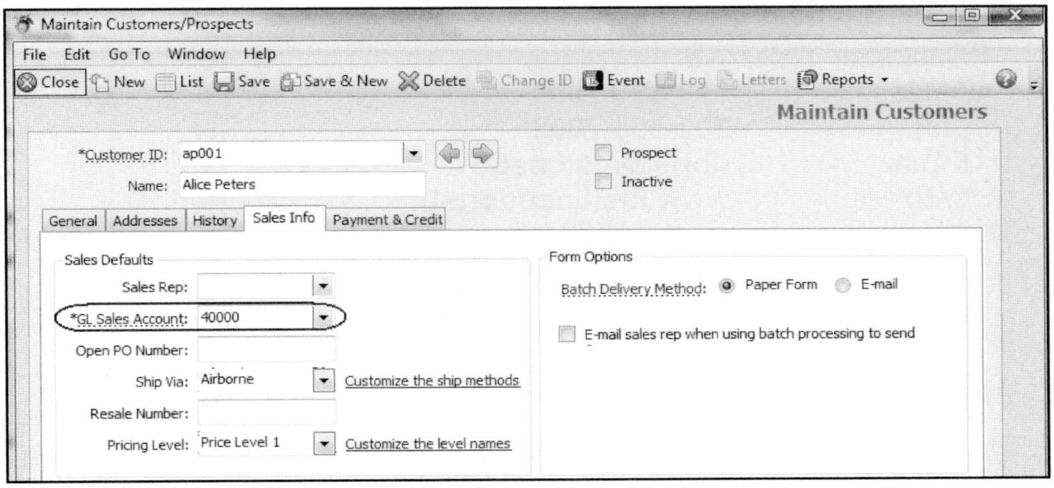

5. Click 

.

6. Click on the General tab. Add in the following customers:

Customer ID:	**bb002**
Name:	**Betty Barton**
Billing Address:	**110 Washington Street**
City, ST Zip:	**Los Angeles, CA 92011**
Country:	**USA**
Sales Tax:	**CA**
Customer Type:	**LA**
Telephone 1:	**310-555-3211**
Fax:	**310-555-3245**
E-mail:	**betty@mail.com**
Web Site:	**www.mail.com/barton**

In the Sales Info tab, select the GL Sales Acct 40200, Sales-Wall for Betty Barton.

Customer ID:	**dc003**
Name:	**Doris Conlin**
Billing Address:	**660 Clark Street**
City, ST Zip:	**Phoenix, AZ 85213**
Country:	**USA**
Sales Tax:	Skip this field--see footnote.[3]
Customer Type:	**AZ**
Telephone 1:	**602-555-7500**
Fax:	**602-555-7502**
E-mail:	**doris@mail.net**
Web Site:	**www.mail.net/dorisC**

In the Sales Info tab, select the GL Sales Acct 40400, Sales-Floor for Doris Conlin.

Customer ID:	**jp004**
Name:	**Judy Prince**
Billing Address:	**7109 Orange Grove Avenue**
City, ST Zip:	**Los Angeles, CA 90036**
Country:	**USA**
Sales Tax:	**CA**
Customer Type:	**LA**
Telephone 1:	**323-555-7764**
Fax:	**323-555-7774**
E-mail:	**prince@lamail.com**
Web Site:	**www.lamail.com/judy**

In the Sales Info tab, select the GL Sales Acct 40000, Sales-Hardware for Judy Prince.

Customer ID:	**pm005**
Name:	**Phil Merchant**
Billing Address:	**17340 West Moreno Drive**
City, ST Zip:	**Los Angeles, CA 90068**
Country:	**USA**
Sales Tax:	**CA**
Customer Type:	**LA**
Telephone 1:	**310-555-5343**

[3]Since this customer is out of state, there is no Sales Tax.

Fa<u>x</u>:	**310-555-7791**
E-mail:	**PhilpM@mymail.com**
Web Site:	**www.mymail.com/phil**

In the Sales Info tab, select the GL Sales Acct 40200, Sales-Wall for Phil Merchant. Close the Maintain Customers/Prospects window.

BACKING UP YOUR DATA

Follow these steps to back up Chapter 12 data:

1. From the Company page, link to <u>Back up</u>.

2. Click 

.

3. Accept the default for backing up to the hard drive or make the selections to back up to another location. Type **Chapter 12 Begin** in the File name field.

4. Click 

.

5. When the window prompts that This company backup will require approximately 3.31MB, click on 

. When the Back Up Company scale is 100% complete, you have successfully backed up to the current point in Chapter 12.

6. Continue or click on File, Exit to exit Peachtree.

RECORDING SALES

Two types of sales are entered in PCA:

- Credit sales or invoiced sales—sales where you enter an invoice.

- Cash sales—sales where you do not enter an invoice.

In PCA, all the information about a sale is recorded on the Sales/ Invoicing window. Then, PCA takes the necessary information from the window and automatically journalizes the transaction in the ***sales***

journal. Only sales on account are recorded in this special journal. You can also print sales invoices.

Cash sales are entered on the Receipts window. Then, PCA takes the necessary information from the window and automatically journalizes the transaction in the ***cash receipts journal***.

On the Sales/Invoicing window, enter invoices for the customers stored in PCA's customer file. You entered five credit customers for Susan's Service Merchandise. (Click Refresh on the Customers & Tasks page to see the customer list.)

Customers — View Detailed List

Customer ID	Customer Name	Telephone 1	Balance
ap001	Alice Peters	323-555-8612	$0.00
bb002	Betty Barton	310-555-3211	$0.00
dc003	Doris Conlin	602-555-7500	$0.00
jp004	Judy Prince	323-555-7764	$0.00
pm005	Phil Merchant	310-555-5343	$0.00

All journal entries made to the Sales Journal (Sales/Invoicing window) are posted both to the General Ledger and to the ***Customer Ledger*** or ***Accounts Receivable Ledger***. You can apply transactions to inventory items and jobs.

Entering sales works hand in hand with entering receipts. Once an invoice is posted it is simple to show that a customer has paid. Just display the appropriate invoice and click on the Pay box. PCA takes care of all the correct accounting distributions for you.

Entering Invoices for Credit Sales

In the steps that follow, you record the following transaction:

Date	*Transaction Description*
01/06/08	Alice Peters purchased two doorknobs on account; $324 ($300 plus $24, sales tax). (*Hint: Doorknobs are classified as hardware.)*

1. From the Customers & Sales page, select 

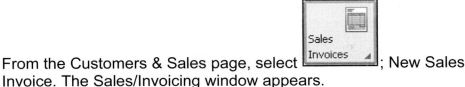

; New Sales Invoice. The Sales/Invoicing window appears.

2. Your cursor is in the Customer ID field. Click  and select **Alice Peters**. PCA supplies the customer default information: billing address, payment terms, GL account default, A/R Account default, and the sales tax code. (*Hint: If the GL Account column and A/R Account field does* not *display Account Nos. 40000 and 11000, refer to pages xix-xx, Peachtree's Global Options.*)

3. Type **6** in the Date field and press **<Enter>**. Since you want to print an invoice, you will skip the Invoice # field. PCA automatically numbers the invoices for you.

4. Click on the Quantity column, type **2** and press **<Enter>**.

5. In the Item column, click . Select **001hardware** for hardware.

6. In the Description field, type **Two doorknobs** and press **<Enter>**. Notice that the GL Account,[4] Unit Price, Amount column, A/R Account, and Sales Tax Code are automatically completed. Compare your Sales/Invoicing window to the one shown on the next page.

---

[4] If the G/L Account column and A/R Account fields are *not* displayed on your Sales/Invoicing window, click on Options, Global. Make sure the boxes in the Hide General Ledger Accounts section are unchecked.

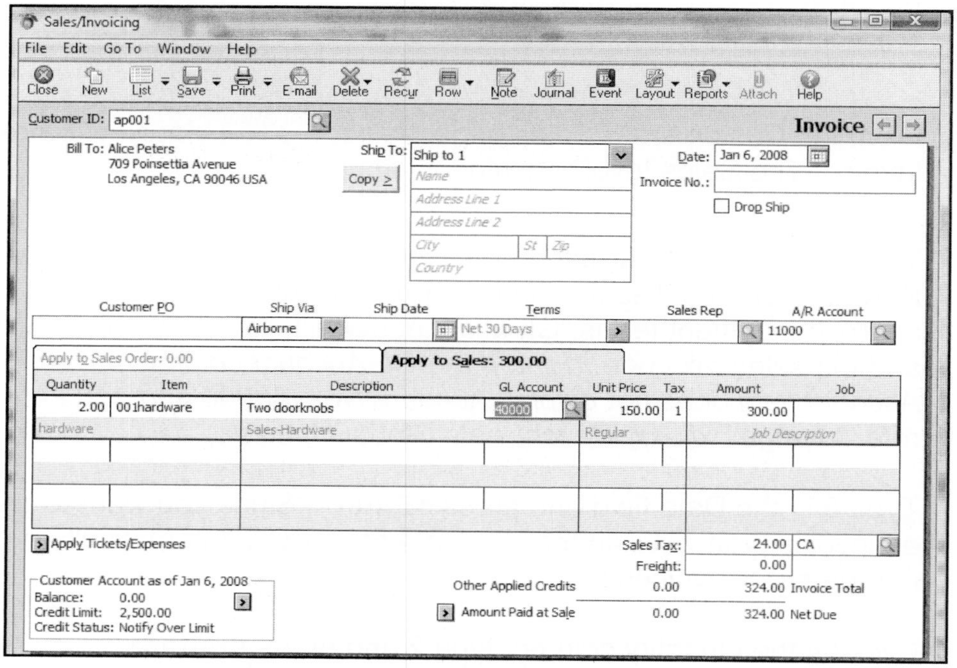

Printing the Sales Invoice

When you print the sales invoice, it also posts the transaction to the Sales Journal. To print this sales invoice, follow these steps:

1. Click 

.

2. The Print Forms: Invoices window appears. Click 

.

3. The Print Forms: Invoices/Pkg. Slips window appears. If necessary, select Invoice.

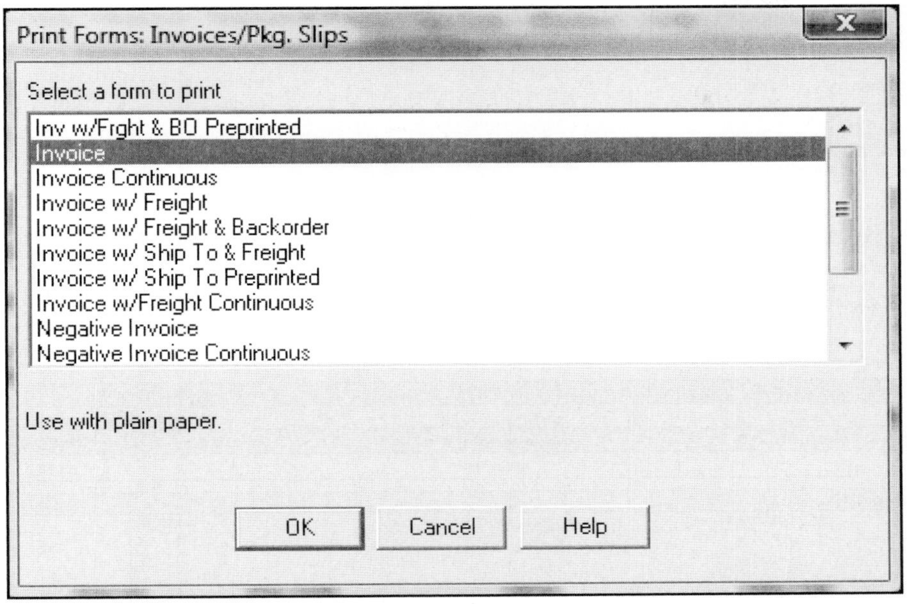

4. Click .

5. The Print Forms: Invoices window appears. The First Invoice Number field displays 101. PCA numbers subsequent invoices consecutively. The Last used form shows Invoice.

6. Click . The invoice starts to print. Compare your invoice to the one shown on the next page.

Comment

The form you select is tied to the kind of printer you are using. If your invoice does not print, you should select a different form to print. Refer to step 3 above to change the form for printing invoices.

Susan's Service Merchandise
7709 Wilshire Boulevard
Los Angeles, CA 90060
USA

Voice: 213-555-9800
Fax: 213-555-8804

INVOICE

Invoice Number: 101
Invoice Date: Jan 6, 2008
Page: 1

Bill To:	Ship to:
Alice Peters 709 Poinsettia Avenue Los Angeles, CA 90046 USA	

Customer ID	Customer PO	Payment Terms	
ap001		Net 30 Days	
Sales Rep ID	**Shipping Method**	**Ship Date**	**Due Date**
	Airborne		2/5/08

Quantity	Item	Description	Unit Price	Amount
2.00	001hardware	Two doorknobs	150.00	300.00

	Subtotal	300.00
	Sales Tax	24.00
	Total Invoice Amount	324.00
Check/Credit Memo No:	Payment/Credit Applied	
	TOTAL	324.00

7. The Sales/Invoicing window is ready for the next sales invoice. (*Hint:* When you printed the invoice, the transaction was posted to the sales journal, accounts receivable account in the general ledger, and customer account in the customer ledger. Once the transaction is posted, cost of sales is also calculated.)

8. Record the following credit sales in the Sales/Invoicing window:

Date *Transaction Description*

01/06/08 Doris Conlin purchased four rolls of vinyl flooring on account. Print Invoice No. 102. (*Hint: Since Ms. Carson is an out-of-state customer, on the Sales/Invoicing window click* [Copy >] *to place address information in the Ship To fields. Vinyl flooring is classified as floor. Ms. Carson's sales invoice shows no tax because this sale is made to an out-of-state customer.*)

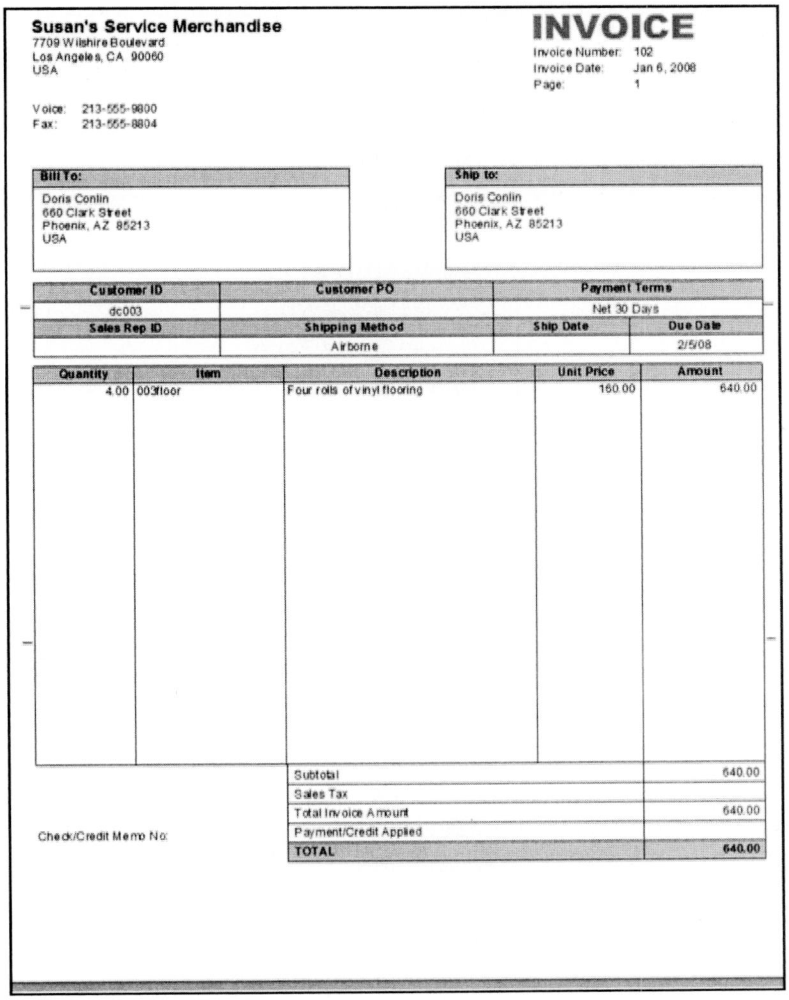

Susan's Service Merchandise
7709 Wilshire Boulevard
Los Angeles, CA 90060
USA

Voice: 213-555-9800
Fax: 213-555-8804

INVOICE
Invoice Number: 102
Invoice Date: Jan 6, 2008
Page: 1

Bill To:	Ship to:
Doris Conlin 660 Clark Street Phoenix, AZ 85213 USA	Doris Conlin 660 Clark Street Phoenix, AZ 85213 USA

Customer ID	Customer PO	Payment Terms	
dc003		Net 30 Days	
Sales Rep ID	**Shipping Method**	**Ship Date**	**Due Date**
	Airborne		2/5/08

Quantity	Item	Description	Unit Price	Amount
4.00	003floor	Four rolls of vinyl flooring	160.00	640.00

	Subtotal	640.00
	Sales Tax	
	Total Invoice Amount	640.00
Check/Credit Memo No:	Payment/Credit Applied	
	TOTAL	640.00

Date	*Transaction Description*
01/06/08	Phil Merchant purchased four pairs of curtains on account. Print Invoice No. 103. (*Hint: Curtains are classified as wall.*)

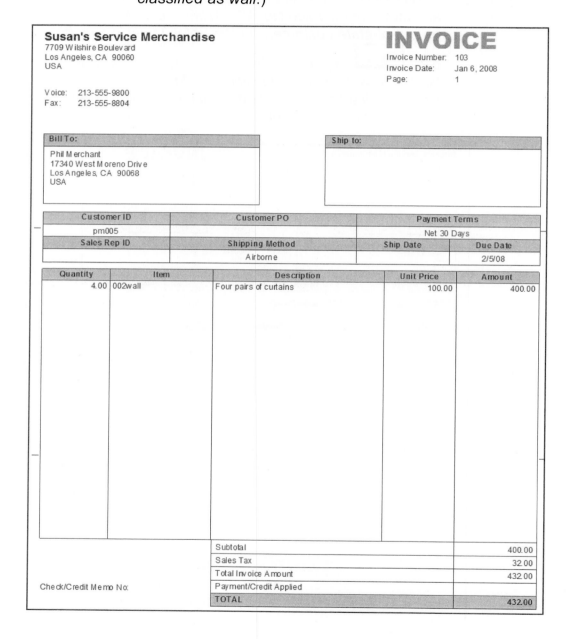

Susan's Service Merchandise
7709 Wilshire Boulevard
Los Angeles, CA 90060
USA

Voice: 213-555-9800
Fax: 213-555-8804

INVOICE

Invoice Number: 103
Invoice Date: Jan 6, 2008
Page: 1

Bill To:	Ship to:
Phil Merchant 17340 West Moreno Drive Los Angeles, CA 90068 USA	

Customer ID	Customer PO	Payment Terms	
pm005		Net 30 Days	
Sales Rep ID	**Shipping Method**	**Ship Date**	**Due Date**
	Airborne		2/5/08

Quantity	Item	Description	Unit Price	Amount
4.00	002wall	Four pairs of curtains	100.00	400.00

Subtotal	400.00
Sales Tax	32.00
Total Invoice Amount	432.00
Payment/Credit Applied	
TOTAL	432.00

Check/Credit Memo No:

Date	*Transaction Description*
01/06/08	Judy Prince purchased three curtain rods on account. Print Invoice No. 104. (*Hint: Curtain rods are classified as hardware.*)

Susan's Service Merchandise
7709 Wilshire Boulevard
Los Angeles, CA 90060
USA

Voice: 213-555-9800
Fax: 213-555-8804

INVOICE

Invoice Number: 104
Invoice Date: Jan 6, 2008
Page: 1

Bill To:	Ship to:
Judy Prince 7109 Orange Grove Avenue Los Angeles, CA 90036 USA	

Customer ID	Customer PO	Payment Terms	
jp004		Net 30 Days	
Sales Rep ID	**Shipping Method**	**Ship Date**	**Due Date**
	Airborne		2/5/08

Quantity	Item	Description	Unit Price	Amount
3.00	001hardware	Three curtain rods	150.00	450.00

	Subtotal	450.00
	Sales Tax	36.00
	Total Invoice Amount	486.00
Check/Credit Memo No:	Payment/Credit Applied	
	TOTAL	486.00

Entering a Service Invoice

Susan's Service Merchandise sells and repairs household items. When repairs are done, a ***service invoice*** is used. A service invoice is an alternative to the standard invoice. It is used when you want to create an invoice without inventory items.

Follow these steps to enter a service invoice:

Date	*Transaction Description*
01/09/08	Repaired curtains for Betty Barton, $49.89, plus sales tax of $3.99, for a total of $53.88.

1. From the Sales/Invoicing window, click 

. Then select <Predefined> Service.

   The Sales/Invoicing window changes to include only the information necessary for a service invoice. This means that you no longer can select inventory items. When you complete the service transaction, you click 

 again. Then, you are ready to enter an inventory sale on the Sales/Invoicing window.

2. In the Customer ID field, select Betty Barton.
3. Type **9** in the Date field, then press **<Enter>**.
4. Click on the Description field. Type **Repair** and press **<Enter>**.
5. In the GL Account column, select Account No. 40600, Service Fees.
6. Type **49.89** in the Amount column. Compare your Sales/Invoicing window to the one shown on the next page.

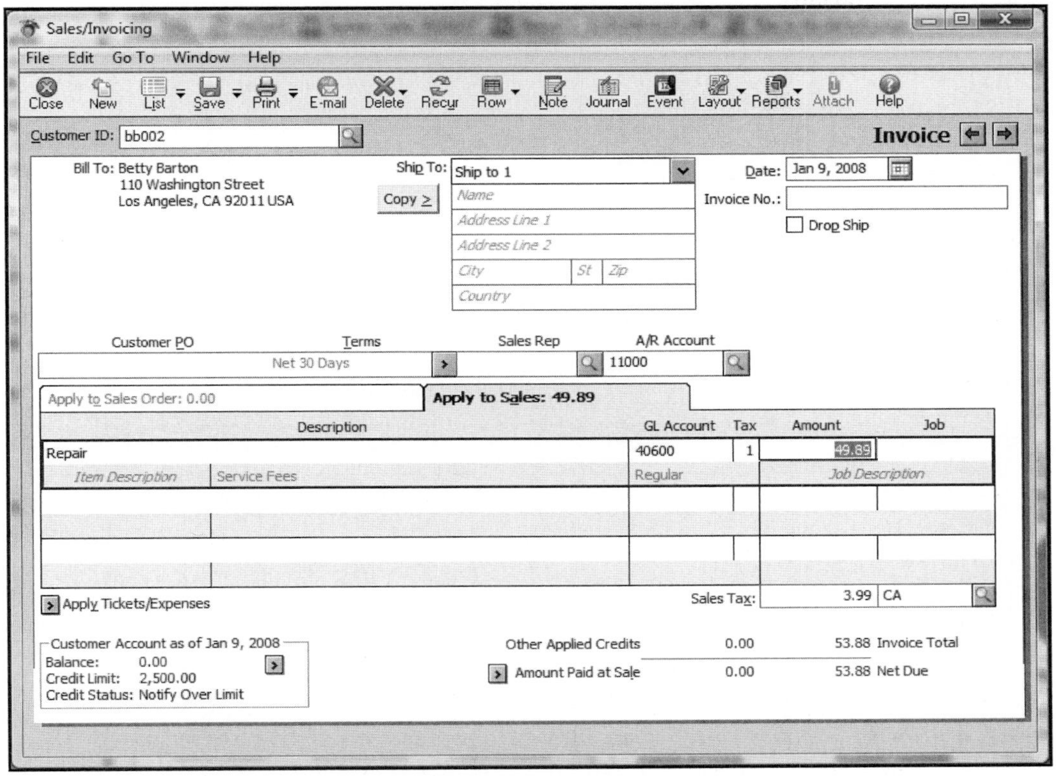

7. Print Invoice No. 105 and compare it to the one shown on the next page.

Susan's Service Merchandise
7709 Wilshire Boulevard
Los Angeles, CA 90060
USA

Voice: 213-555-9800
Fax: 213-555-8804

INVOICE

Invoice Number: 105
Invoice Date: 1/9/08
Page: 1

Bill To:
Betty Barton
110 Washington Street
Los Angeles, CA 92011
USA

Customer ID: bb002

Customer PO	Payment Terms	Sales Rep ID	Due Date
	Net 30 Days		2/8/08

Description	Amount
Repair	49.89

Check/Credit Memo No:

Subtotal	49.89
Sales Tax	3.99
Total Invoice Amount	53.88
Payment/Credit Applied	
TOTAL	53.88

8. Click Layout, then <Predefined> Product. Click Close.

Sales Returns: Credits & Returns

A sales return, or credit memo, is used when merchandise is returned by a customer. Credit memos for sales returns are entered similarly to vendor credit memos.

Before you can apply a credit, you must post the invoice. Invoice Nos. 101–105 were posted to the sales journal when you printed the sales invoices (see pages 462-468). This work must be completed *before* you can apply a sales return. When a credit memo is entered, select the customer's ID code and the appropriate invoice number. Then, the return will be applied to that invoice and the customer's account balance will be adjusted.

In the steps that follow, you will record the following transaction:

Date	*Transaction Description*
01/14/08	Phil Merchant returned one pair of curtains that he purchased on January 6, Invoice No. 103. He also paid the balance of that invoice.

1. From the Customers & Sales page, select 

; New Credit Memo.

2. In the Customer ID field, select Phil Merchant.

3. In the Date field, type **14** and press **<Enter>**.

4. Type **CM103** in the Credit No. field. (CM is an abbreviation for Credit Memo; use the sales invoice number to identify the credit memo.) Press **<Enter>**.

5. The Apply to Invoice No. tab is selected. Click on the down-arrow and select 103.

6. Type **1** in the Returned column. Press **<Enter>**

7. Type **Returned one pair of curtains** in the Description column.

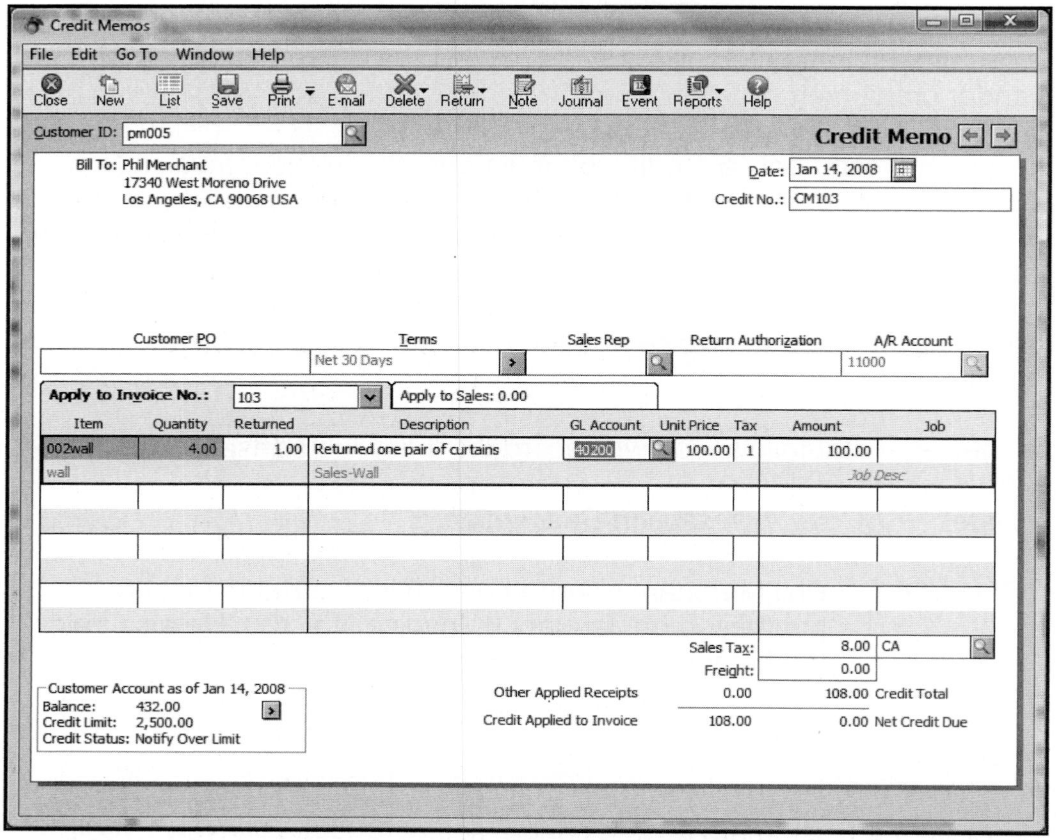

8. Click 

to post, then click 

.

Apply a sales return: Follow these steps:

1. From the Customers & Sales page, select 

; Receive Money From Customer. At the Select a Cash Account window, accept the default for La Brea Bank by clicking 

.

2. Type **01/14/08** in the Deposit ticket ID field. Press **<Enter>**.

3. In the Customer ID field, select Phil Merchant.

4. In the Reference field, type **Invoice 103** then press the **<Enter>** key two times.

5. In the Date field, type **14**, then press the **<Enter>** key two times.

6. Observe that the Payment Method field displays Check; and that the Cash Account field displays Account No. 10200, La Brea Bank. In the Apply to Invoices list, click on the Pay box. Observe that the Receipt Amount shown is 324.00 ($432 original invoice - $108, return).

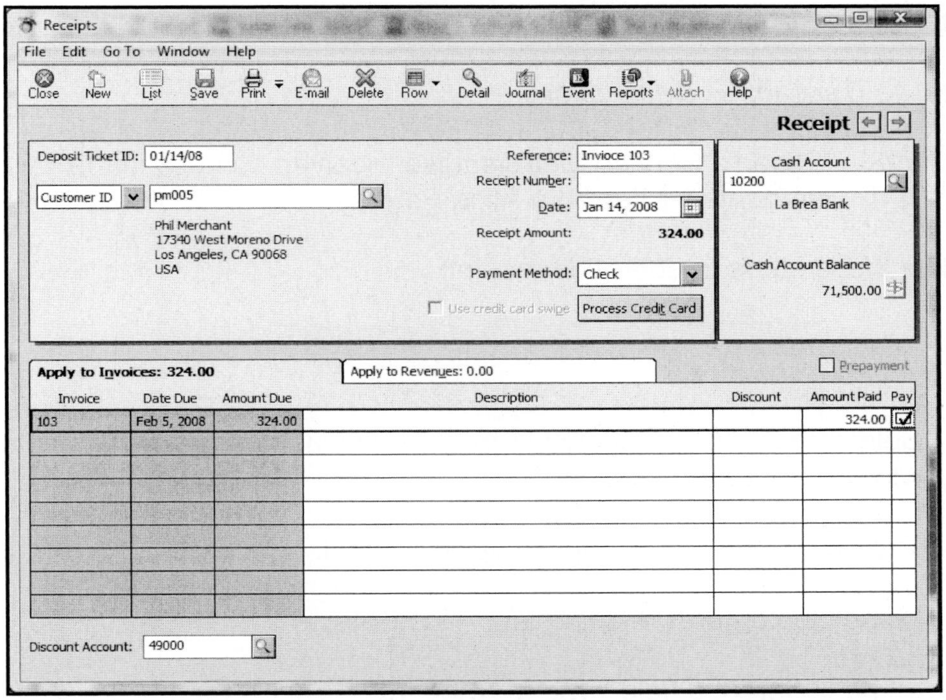

7. Click 

to post, then click 

.

RECORDING RECEIPTS AND CASH SALES

The Receipts window is used for recording checks, cash, and credit card sales that are received and deposited in the checking account. Then, PCA takes the necessary information from the Receipts window and automatically journalizes the transactions in the Cash Receipts Journal. If the receipt is from a credit customer, then the receipt is posted to the customer's subsidiary ledger as well.

There are two categories for receipts that result from sales:

- Receipts for which an invoice was entered in the Sales/Invoicing window.

- Direct sales receipts for which no invoice was entered in the Sales/Invoicing window.

Entering A Receipt

Date *Transaction Description*

01/21/08 Susan's Service Merchandise received a check in the amount of $324 from Alice Peters in payment of Invoice 101.

Follow these steps to enter this receipt:

1. Select 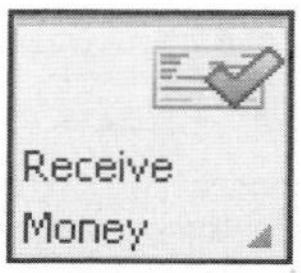

; Receive Money From Customer. The Receipts window appears.

2. Type **01/21/08** in the Deposit ticket ID field.

3. In the Customer ID field, select Alice Peters.

4. In the Reference field, type **Invoice 101**. (This is the Invoice that is being paid.) Press the **<Enter>** key two times.

5. Type **21** in the Date field.

6. Verify that Account No. 10200, La Brea Bank, is displayed in the Cash Account field. The Apply to Invoices tab is selected. Click on the Pay box for Invoice 101. Compare your Receipts window to the one shown on the next page.

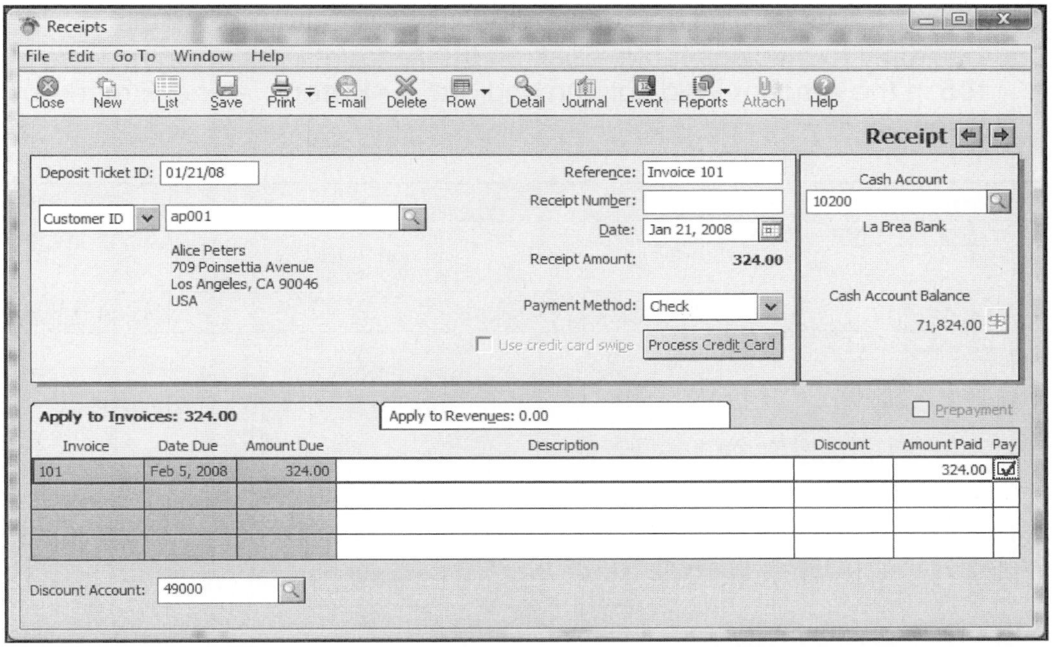

7. Click  to post this receipt. The Receipts window is ready for another transaction.

In the preceding steps, each customer paid the invoice in full. What if a customer made a partial payment on an invoice?

Date	*Transaction Description*
01/22/08	Judy Prince paid $105 on account, Invoice No. 104.

Follow these steps for partial payment:

1. The Receipts window should be displayed. Type **01/22/08** in the Deposit ticket ID field.
2. Select Judy Prince as the customer.
3. Type **Invoice 104** in the Reference field. Press the **<Enter>** key two times.
4. Type **22** in the Date field.

5. Judy Prince's Invoice number, Date Due, and Amount Due display in the Apply to Invoices table. Click on the Amount Paid column. Type **105** in the Amount Paid column and press **<Enter>**. A check mark is automatically placed in the Pay box.

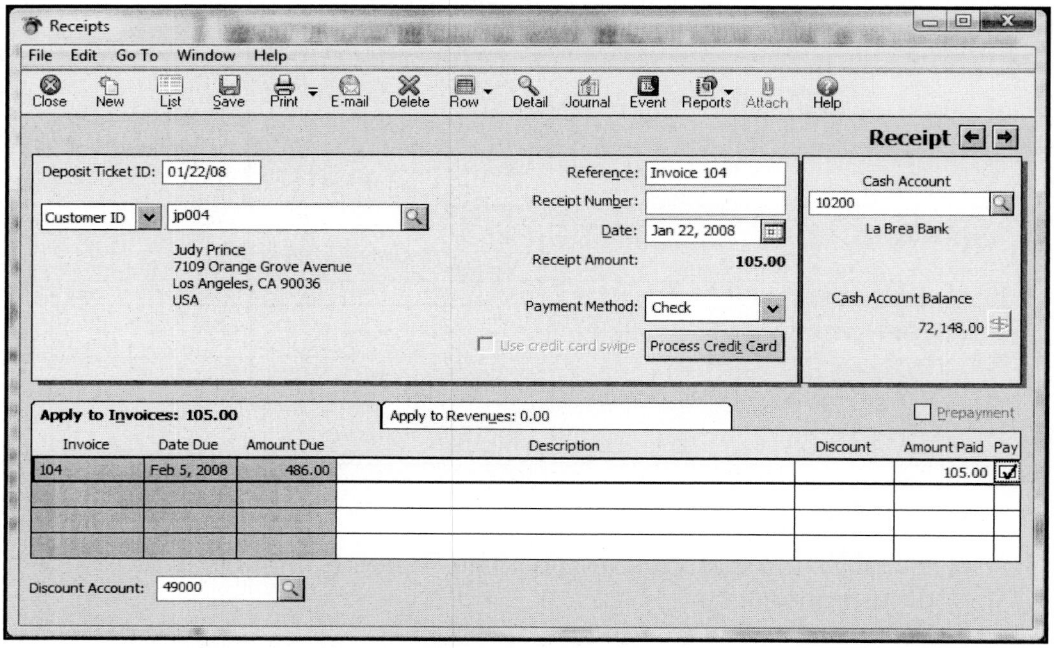

6. Click  to post.

Enter the following receipts:

Date	*Transaction Description*
01/28/08	Received a check in the amount of $53.88 from Betty Barton in full payment of Invoice No. 105.
01/28/08	Received a check in the amount of $640 from Doris Conlin in full payment of Invoice No. 102.

Cash Sales

Follow these steps to record a cash sale.

Date *Transaction Description*

01/29/08 Harriet Wilson bought two pairs of curtains for cash, $200.

1. On the Receipts window, type **01/29/08** in the Deposit ticket ID field.
2. Click on the Name field, then type **Harriet Wilson**. You do not enter address information for a cash sale.
3. Since this is a cash sale, type **Cash** in the Reference field. Press **<Enter>** two times.
4. Type **29** as the date.
5. Verify that account 10200, La Brea Bank, is displayed in the Cash Account field.
6. Make sure that the Apply to Revenues tab is selected.

   PCA assumes you are going to apply the receipt to revenue unless you select a customer with open invoices.

   You can also apply a portion of the receipt to both invoices and revenue. You do this by selecting each heading, then entering the distribution information for that portion of the receipt. A running subtotal is kept to show how much of the receipt has been applied.
7. Type **2** in the Quantity column.
8. Select 002wall as the inventory item.
9. Type **Two pairs of curtains** as the Description and press the **<Enter>** key.
10. Observe that the GL Account field, shows Account No. 40200, Sales-Wall (this is the default account). (*Hint:* Make sure the correct sales account is selected.)

11. Make sure the Sales Tax Code field shows California sales taxes. (If not, select CA.) Observe that 16.00 is automatically calculated in the Sales Tax field.

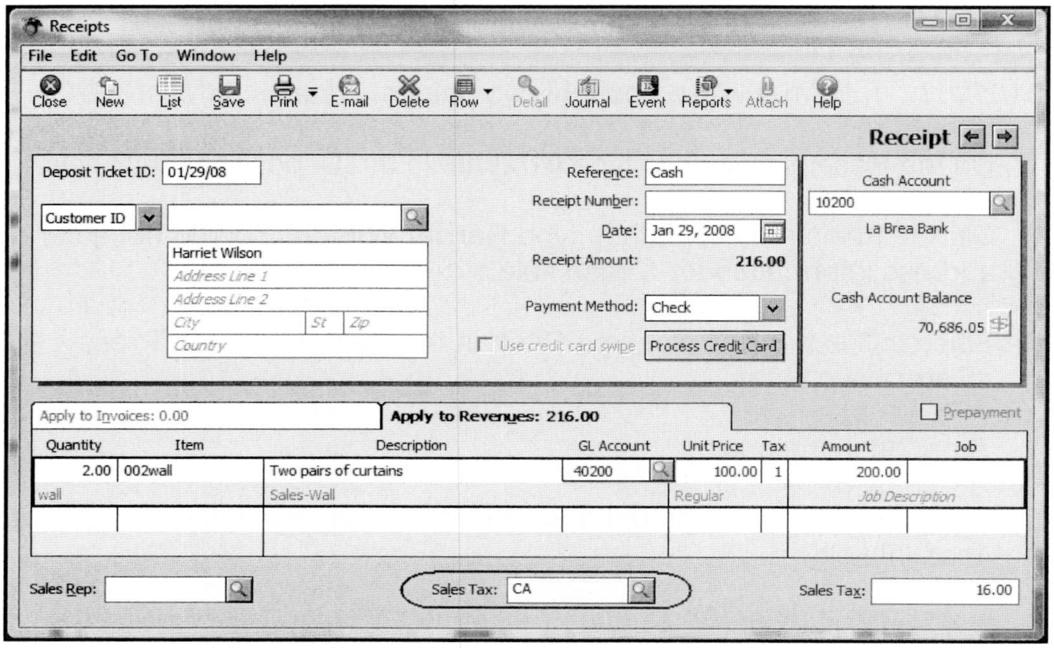

12. Click 

, then close the Receipts window.

Finance Charges

PCA includes a feature in the Tasks menu for computing finance or interest charges. This option computes and applies finance charges for customers and/or prints a report listing all finance charges.

You use this feature by selecting the Finance Charge option. You may want to try this out on your own. Use the Tasks menu and select Finance Charge to see how this feature works.

PRINTING CUSTOMER FORMS

PCA provides forms for the following types of customer correspondence:

- Invoices.
- Statements.
- Mailing labels.
- Collection letters.

These reports can be accessed by selecting Reports, then Accounts Receivable. Select a predefined form to print customer information or design your own form. In Part 4 of this book you will learn more about Custom Forms.

Printing Invoices

You can print a single invoice from the Sales/Invoicing window by selecting 

. This saves and prints the invoice.

You can also print a batch of invoices from the Reports menu by selecting Accounts Receivable and then selecting Invoices/Pkg. Slips. There are several types of predefined invoices available for printing customer information or you can design your own form.

Printing Statements

The information that is printed on customer statements is defined in the Statement/Invoices Defaults which are set up from the Maintain menu. You can set up collection letters and also select from these print options.

- Whether to print your company name, address, phone, and fax on the statement.
- Whether to print zero and credit balance statements.
- The minimum balance necessary to print a statement.
- The number of grace days before printing a statement.
- Whether to print statements for accounts with no activity.

You can print or display statements. Or, if you want to display customer information before printing, you can display or print the customer ledger.

You print statements from the Reports menu by selecting Accounts Receivable and then Invoices/Pkg. Slips. There are several types of predefined statements available for printing customer account balances. Select the form that best suits your needs. As mentioned before, you can also design your own statement.

When the statements stop printing, a message box displays, asking if the statements printed okay and if you want to update the customer file. Look at your printed statements carefully before you answer Yes to this question. When you answer Yes, PCA records the statement date in the customer record. This is used as the balance brought forward date the next time you print a statement. This way the ending balance on one statement is the same as the beginning balance on the next statement.

You should enter, print, and post all invoices prior to printing statements. In this way the Balance Forward amounts are correct from month to month.

Printing Mailing Labels

From the Reports menu you can print labels. If you want to try this out, select the Reports menu, Accounts Receivable, then Labels - Customers, select one of the types of labels, and print. There are several predefined labels available for printing. You can elect to use these forms or design your own.

When printing labels you can do the following.

- Select a range of customers.
- Enter all or part of a Zip code to limit the mailing labels to customers in a certain area.
- Print labels for customers, prospects, or both.
- Enter a Status for customers so that you print labels for all, active, or inactive customers.

- Enter a Type Code for customers so that only customers of a specific Type Code will print.

Preparing Collection Letters

What if credit customers are slow to pay their bills? Collection letters can play an important role in generating revenue from customers who are slow to pay off their balances. Sometimes just a friendly reminder is all that is needed.

The table below shows how important it is to get paid on time because the longer a bill remains unpaid, the less chance there is of collecting.

Number of Days Overdue	Percent Uncollectible
1 to 30 days	2%
31 to 60 days	10%
61 to 90 days	20%
91 to 180 days	30%
181 to 365 days	50%
over 365 days	90%

Collection letters are an effective way to remind customers to pay their unpaid balances. Most customers will pay after they receive a friendly reminder of a past-due account. It is worthwhile to send these letters because past-due amounts can be a burden on a company's cash flow.

Depending on how late the payment is, collection letters vary in tone and urgency. For example, a friendly reminder may be all that's needed for someone who is 30 days past due, but a different letter may be needed for someone who is more than 90 days past due. Remember that while it is important to collect past-due amounts, you would also like to keep the customer.

PCA's letters are grouped by lateness of payment and severity of tone. The less than 30 days overdue letter is soft while the 61-90 days overdue letter is much firmer. You may edit all of these letters to suit your needs.

To print a collection letter you use the analysis menu. Follow these steps to do that:

1. From the menu bar, click on Analysis, then Collection Manager.

2. Type **01/31/08** in the As of Date field. Press **<Enter>**. The Collection Aging bar graph appears.

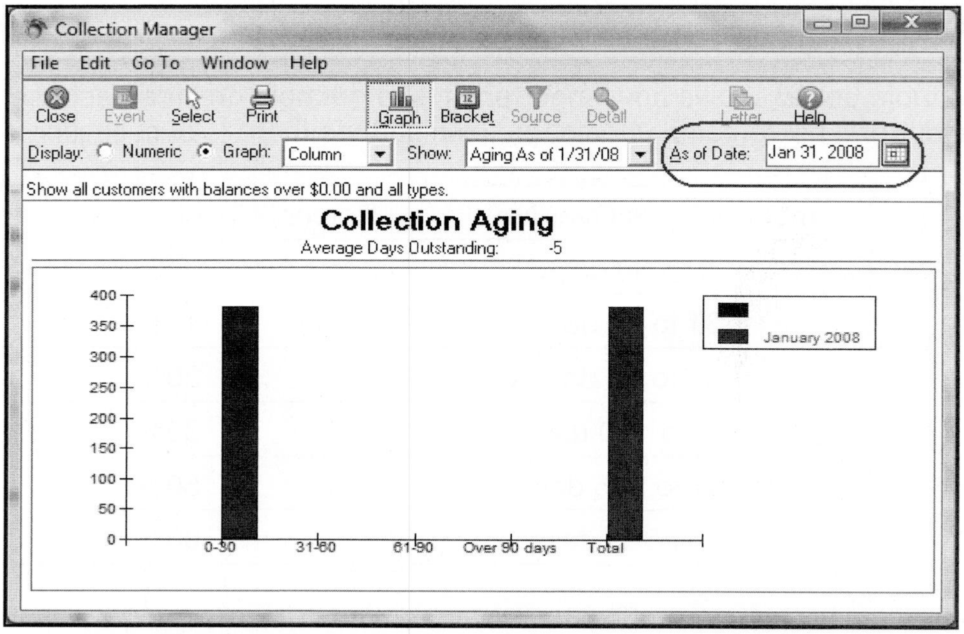

3. Click 

. The Total Bracket table lists an invoice for Judy Prince.

4. Click on the Letter box on the Total Bracket table to place a check mark in it. Then, click 

.

5. The Print Forms: Collection Letters window appears. Click 

. You may want to try one of these selections and see what Peachtree's collection letters look like. The sample letters are sorted as follows.

- Overdue < 30 Days - Soft
- Overdue >90 Days
- Overdue >90 Days – Coll Agency
- Overdue 31-60 Days - Medium
- Overdue 61-90 Days - Firm

6. Select a form to print, then click 

.

7. Click 

. A collection letter prints. Read the letter that you printed. The collection letter that prints is an example. Since Ms. Prince does *not* have an overdue bill, no amount shows in the letter's Amount Overdue field.

8. Close the Collection Manager.

PRINTING THE SALES JOURNAL

The Sales/Invoicing window is the Sales Journal in PCA. Like a Sales Journal, credit sales are recorded in the Sales/Invoicing window. Follow these steps to print the Sales Journal:

1. From the Recently Used Customer Reports area on the Customers & Sales page, link to <u>Print</u> the Sales Journal.

2. The Modify Report – Sales Journal window appears. Click 

. Make the selections to print. Compare your sales journal report to the one shown on the next page.

Susan's Service Merchandise
Sales Journal
For the Period From Jan 1, 2008 to Jan 31, 2008
Filter Criteria includes: Report order is by Invoice/CM Date. Report is printed in Detail Format.

Date	Account ID	Invoice/CM #	Line Description	Debit Amnt	Credit Amnt
1/6/08	23100	101	CA: California Dept. of Revenue		24.00
	40000		Two doorknobs		300.00
	50000		Cost of sales	100.00	
	12000		Cost of sales		100.00
	11000		Alice Peters	324.00	
1/6/08	40400	102	Four rolls of vinyl flooring		640.00
	57000		Cost of sales	216.00	
	12000		Cost of sales		216.00
	11000		Doris Conlin	640.00	
1/6/08	23100	103	CA: California Dept. of Revenue		32.00
	40200		Four pairs of curtains		400.00
	50500		Cost of sales	120.00	
	12000		Cost of sales		120.00
	11000		Phil Merchant	432.00	
1/6/08	23100	104	CA: California Dept. of Revenue		36.00
	40000		Three curtain rods		450.00
	50000		Cost of sales	150.00	
	12000		Cost of sales		150.00
	11000		Judy Prince	486.00	
1/9/08	23100	105	CA: California Dept. of Revenue		3.99
	40600		Repair		49.89
	11000		Betty Barton	53.88	
1/14/08	23100	CM103	CA: California Dept. of Revenue	8.00	
	40200		Returned one pair of curtains	100.00	
	50500		Cost of sales		30.00
	12000		Cost of sales	30.00	
	11000		Phil Merchant		108.00
		Total		**2,659.88**	**2,659.88**

PRINTING THE CASH RECEIPTS JOURNAL

The Receipts window is the Cash Receipts Journal in PCA. Like the Cash Receipts Journal, payments from customers and cash sales are recorded in the Receipts window. Follow these steps to print the Cash Receipts Journal.

1. From the Recently Used Customer Reports area on the Customers & Sales page, link to <u>Print</u> the Cash Receipts Journal. (Or, from the menu bar select Reports, then Accounts Receivable, then highlight Cash Receipts Journal.)

2. The Modify Report - Cash Receipts Journal window displays. Click OK. Make the selections to print.

Susan's Service Merchandise
Cash Receipts Journal
For the Period From Jan 1, 2008 to Jan 31, 2008
Filter Criteria includes: Report order is by Check Date. Report is printed in Detail Format.

Date	Account ID	Transaction Ref	Line Description	Debit Amnt	Credit Amnt
1/14/08	11000	Invoice 103	Invoice: 103		324.00
	10200		Phil Merchant	324.00	
1/21/08	11000	Invoice 101	Invoice: 101		324.00
	10200		Alice Peters	324.00	
1/22/08	11000	Invoice 104	Invoice: 104		105.00
	10200		Judy Prince	105.00	
1/28/08	11000	Invoice 105	Invoice: 105		53.88
	10200		Betty Barton	53.88	
1/28/08	11000	Invoice 102	Invoice: 102		640.00
	10200		Doris Conlin	640.00	
1/29/08	23100	Cash	CA: California Dept. of Revenue		16.00
	40200		Two pairs of curtains		200.00
	50500		Cost of sales	60.00	
	12000		Cost of sales		60.00
	10200		Harriet Wilson	216.00	
				1,722.88	1,722.88

PRINTING THE CUSTOMER LEDGERS

Follow these steps to print the Customer Ledgers for Susan's Service Merchandise:

1. From the Recently Used Customer Reports area on the Customers & Sales page, link to View All Customer & Sales Reports. The Select a Report or Form window appears.

2. In the Accounts Receivable: Customers and Sales list, select Customer Ledger. Then, make the selections to print.

Susan's Service Merchandise
Customer Ledgers
For the Period From Jan 1, 2008 to Jan 31, 2008
Filter Criteria includes: Report order is by ID. Report is printed in Detail Format.

Customer ID Customer	Date	Trans No	Type	Debit Amt	Credit Amt	Balance
ap001	1/6/08	101	SJ	324.00		324.00
Alice Peters	1/21/08	Invoice 101	CRJ		324.00	0.00
bb002	1/9/08	105	SJ	53.88		53.88
Betty Barton	1/28/08	Invoice 105	CRJ		53.88	0.00
dc003	1/6/08	102	SJ	640.00		640.00
Doris Conlin	1/28/08	Invoice 102	CRJ		640.00	0.00
jp004	1/6/08	104	SJ	486.00		486.00
Judy Prince	1/22/08	Invoice 104	CRJ		105.00	381.00
pm005	1/6/08	103	SJ	432.00		432.00
Phil Merchant	1/14/08	CM103	SJ		108.00	324.00
	1/14/08	Invoice 103	CRJ		324.00	0.00
Report Total				**1,935.88**	**1,554.88**	**381.00**

PRINTING THE GENERAL LEDGER TRIAL BALANCE

1. In the Reports list, highlight General Ledger. Then, in the General Ledger: Account Information list highlight General Ledger Trial Balance.

2. Make the selections to print. Compare your general ledger trial balance to the one shown on the next page.

Susan's Service Merchandise
General Ledger Trial Balance
As of Jan 31, 2008

Filter Criteria includes: Report order is by ID. Report is printed in Detail Format.

Account ID	Account Description	Debit Amt	Credit Amt
10200	La Brea Bank	70,902.05	
10400	Worldwide Savings & Loan	20,000.00	
11000	Accounts Receivable	381.00	
12000	Merchandise Inventory	28,322.00	
13000	Supplies	1,750.00	
14000	Prepaid Insurance	2,400.00	
15000	Furniture and Fixtures	5,000.00	
15100	Computers & Equipment	7,500.00	
15500	Building	100,000.00	
20000	Accounts Payable		300.00
23100	Sales Tax Payable		103.99
27000	Long-Term Notes Payable		20,500.00
27400	Mortgage Payable		75,000.00
39006	Joe Greene, Capital		70,195.00
39007	Joe Greene, Drawing	500.00	
39008	Susan Currier, Capital		70,195.00
39009	Susan Currier, Drawing	500.00	
40000	Sales-Hardware		750.00
40200	Sales-Wall		500.00
40400	Sales-Floor		640.00
40600	Service Fees		49.89
50000	Cost of Sales-Hardware	250.00	
50500	Cost of Sales-Wall	150.00	
57000	Cost of Sales-Floor	216.00	
59500	Purchase Discounts		17.96
70000	Maintenance Expense	160.00	
73500	Postage Expense	41.00	
75500	Supplies Expense	107.65	
76000	Telephone Expense	72.14	
	Total:	**238,251.84**	**238,251.84**

EDITING RECEIPTS

Is your Customer Ledger correct? Judy Prince's account is used to show how to edit the Customer Ledger. Follow these steps to see how the editing feature works:

1. From the Customers & Sales page, select 

; View and Edit Payments Received.

2. The Receipt List appears. Click on Invoice 104, $105.00 to highlight it.

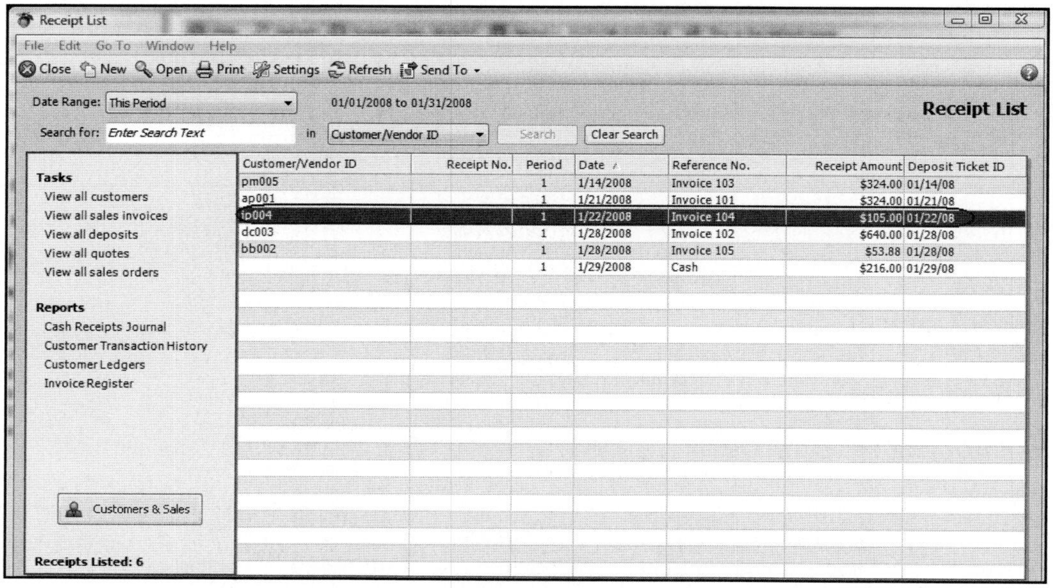

3. Click **Open**. The original Receipts window with Judy Prince's partial payment appears. Make any necessary corrections, then Save.

4. Close the Receipts window and Receipts List window.

BACKING UP CHAPTER 12 DATA

Follow these steps to back up Chapter 12 data:

1. From the Company page, link to Back up.

2. Click **Back Up**.

3. Accept the default for backing up to the hard drive or make the selections to back up to another location. Type **Chapter 12** in the File name field.

4. Click **Save**.

5. When the window prompts that This company backup will require approximately 3.32MB, click on OK. When the Back Up Company scale is 100% complete, you have successfully backed up to the current point in Chapter 12.

6. Continue or click on File, Exit to exit Peachtree.

INTERNET ACTIVITY	
1.	From your Internet browser, go to the book's website at http://www.mhhe.com/yacht2008.
2.	Link to Student Edition.
3.	In the Course-wide Content list, link to Part 3 Internet Activities for Chapters 11-14. Open or Save. (You can also choose Chapter 12, then link to Internet Activities. If you Choose a Chapter, observe that other chapter-specific links are available; for example, Quizzes, PowerPoints, and Going to the Net Exercises.)
4.	Complete the WebCPA–Tools and Resources for the Electronic Accountant exercise. Read steps 1–3.
5.	Follow the steps shown on the book's website to complete this Internet activity.
6.	Using a word processing program write a brief summary of what you find. Include all appropriate website addresses.

SUMMARY AND REVIEW

SOFTWARE OBJECTIVES: In Chapter 12, you have used the software to:

1. Set up customer default information.
2. Set up sales tax information.
3. Set up customer maintenance information.
4. Record credit sales, cash sales, and sales returns.
5. Record customer receipts, partial payments, and edit invoices.
6. Make four backups: 1) back up Chapter 12 beginning data; 2) back up Chapter 12 data; 3) back up Exercise 12-1; 4) back up Exercise 12-2.

WEB OBJECTIVES: In Chapter 12, you did these Internet activities:

1. Used your Internet browser to go to the book's website.
2. Went to the Internet Activity link on the book's website. Then, select WEB EXERCISES PART 3. Complete the second web exercise in Part 3—Tools and Resources for the Electronic Accountant.
3. Used a word processing program to write summaries of the websites that you visited.

GOING TO THE NET

Access the Business Owner's Toolkit website at http://www.toolkit.cch.com/text/P06_1430.asp. Read the accounts receivable page, and then answer the following questions.

1. What is the common abbreviation for accounts receivable?
2. What is the control account for customer sales on account?
3. How is the ending accounts receivable total computed?

Multiple-Choice Questions: In the space provided, write the letter that best answers each question.

_____1. Susan's Service Merchandise charges sales tax to all sales made in:

a. Arizona.
b. Oregon.
c. Washington.
d. California.
e. None of the above.

_____2. The money that your customers owe to the business is known as:

a. Accounts payable.
b. Revenue.
c. Accounts receivable.
d. Cash in bank.
e. None of the above.

______3. Use the following Navigation Bar options to record entries in the Cash Receipts Journal:

a. Customers & Sales; Receive Money, Receive Money from Customer.
b. Customers & Sales; Customers, Receive Money, View and Edit Payment Received.
c. Vendor & Payments; Customers, Receive Money, Receive Money from Customer.
d. Tasks; Sales/Invoicing.
e. None of the above.

______4. Use the following Navigation Bar options to record entries in the Sales Journal:

a. Maintain/Customers Prospects.
b. Customers & Sales; Customers, Set Up Customer Defaults.
c. Customers & Sales; Sales Invoices, New Sales Invoice.
d. Maintain; Default Information, Customers.
e. None of the above.

______5. The owner(s) of Susan's Service Merchandise are:

a. Joe Greene.
b. Susan Currier.
c. both a. and b.
d. Judy Prince.
e. None of the above.

______6. The sales tax rate is:

a. 6%.
b. 7%.
c. 8%.
d. 9%.
e. None of the above.

_____7. PCA's accounts receivable system allows you to set up all of the following, EXCEPT:

a. Customers.
b. Inventory items.
c. Finance charges.
d. Vendors.
e. None of the above.

_____8. All journal entries made to the Sales Journal are posted to the General ledger and to the:

a. Accounts payable ledger.
b. Customer ledger.
c. Job cost ledger.
d. Payroll register.
e. None of the above.

_____9. The sales tax payable account is:

a. Account No. 52000.
b. Account No. 53000.
c. Account No. 23100.
d. Account No. 12000.
e. None of the above.

_____10. The Customer ID for Alice Peters is:

a. AAP001.
b. ap001.
c. ap002.
d. AP002.
e. None of the above.

_____11. The Cash Account number is shown on which of the following windows:

a. Sales/Invoicing.
b. Purchases/Receive Inventory.
c. Receipts.
d. General Journal Entry.
e. None of the above.

_____12. The account used for hardware sales is:

a. Account No. 40000.
b. Account No. 40800.
c. Account No. 40200.
d. Account No. 40400.
e. None of the above.

_____13. A sales return is also called a/an:

a. Credit memo.
b. Debit memo.
c. Invoice.
d. Receipt.
e. None of the above.

_____14. To back up all of Chapter 12's data, the following file name is typed:

a. Chapter 12 Begin.
b. Chapter 12b.
c. Backup.
d. Chapter 12.
e. None of the above.

_____15. The GL Sales Account for wall is:

a. Account No. 44200.
b. Account No. 44300.
c. Account No. 44400.
d. Account No. 40200.
e. None of the above.

Exercise 12-1: You must complete Exercises 11-1 and 11-2 before starting Exercise 12-1.

1. Start PCA. Open the company that you set up in Exercise 11-1 on page 434, Your Name Sales & Service.

2. Restore your data from Exercise 11-2. (*Hint: This backup was made on page 443.*) To make sure you are starting in the right place, display Exercise 11-2's general ledger trial balance (step 6, page 443).

3. If necessary, enter the following customer defaults:

a. Standard Terms:	Due in number of days
b. Net due in:	30 days
Discount in:	0 days
Discount %:	0.00
Credit Limit:	2,500.00
GL Sales Account:	40000 Sales Hardware
Discount GL Account:	49000 Sales Discounts

4. Enter the following customer maintenance information:

a. Customer ID:	**ac001**
Name:	**Allen Canto**
Billing Address:	**143 North Third Avenue**
City, ST Zip:	**Eugene, OR 97401**
Country:	**USA**
Sales Tax:	Skip this field. There are no sales taxes in Oregon.
Customer Type:	**LANE** (for Lane County)
Telephone 1:	**541-555-4321**
Fax:	**541-555-5328**
E-mail:	**allen@allencanto.com**
Web Site:	**www.allencanto.com**

In the Sales Info tab, select the GL Sales Acct 40200, Sales-Tools for Allen Canto.

b. Customer ID: **bb002**
Name: **Benjamin Bermudez**
Billing Address: **3125 Sycamore Avenue**
City, ST Zip: **Eugene, OR 97404**
Country: **USA**
Sales Tax: n/a
Customer Type: **LANE**
Telephone 1: **541-555-3489**
Fax: **541-555-3490**
E-mail: **info@benbermudez.net**
Web Site: **www.benbermudez.net**

In the Sales Info tab, select the GL Sales Acct 40000, Sales-Hardware for Benjamin Bermudez.

c. Customer ID: **rn003**
Name: **Rita Nicholson**
Billing Address: **2558 North Fourth Street**
City, ST Zip: **Eugene, OR 97402**
Country: **USA**
Sales Tax: n/a
Customer Type: **LANE**
Telephone 1: **541-555-3289**
Fax: **541-555-9006**
E-mail: **rita@ritanicholson.com**
Web Site: **www.ritanicholson.com**

In the Sales Info tab, select the GL Sales Acct 40000, Sales-Hardware for Rita Nicholson.

5. Make a backup of your work. (Use **Exercise 12-1** as the file name.)

Exercise 12-2: Exercise 12-1 must be completed before Exercise 12-2.

1. Start PCA. Open your service merchandise company.

2. Restore data from Exercise 12-1.

3. Record the following transactions:

01/06/08	Sold five tool kits on account to Allen Canto, Customer ac001. Type **101** in the Invoice No. field. Subsequent invoices will be numbered automatically.
01/06/08	Sold three hardware sets on account to Benjamin Bermudez, Customer bb002.
01/06/08	Sold six hardware sets on account to Rita Nicholson, Customer rn003.
01/09/08	Allen Canto returned one of the tool kits that he purchased on January 6, Invoice No. 101, CM101. Mr. Canto also paid the balance of Invoice 101. (*Hint: This transaction requires two entries.*)
01/13/08	Received a check in full payment of Invoice No. 102 from Benjamin Bermudez.
01/16/08	Made a cash sale to Mary Sable for two hardware sets *and* two tool kits. (*Hint:* Remember to select the appropriate sales account.)
01/17/08	Made a cash sale to Jamie Moffet for three tool kits.

4. Print the Sales Journal.

5. Print the Cash Receipts Journal.

6. Print the Customer Ledgers.

7. Print the General Ledger Trial Balance.

8. Make a backup. Use **Exercise 12-2** as the file name.

CHAPTER 12 INDEX

Chapter 13 Inventory & Services

SOFTWARE OBJECTIVES: In Chapter 13, you use the software to:

1. Enter inventory maintenance and default information.
2. Enter inventory item information, including Sales account, Merchandise Inventory account, and Cost of Sales account.
3. Enter item codes when recording purchases and sales.
4. Enter inventory adjustments.
5. Make three backups: two for Susan's Service Merchandise; one for the end-of-chapter exercises.

WEB OBJECTIVES: In Chapter 13, you do these Internet activities:

1. Use your Internet browser to go to the book's website.
2. Go to the Internet Activity link on the book's website. Then, select WEB EXERCISES PART 3. Complete the third web exercise in Part 3— Accountant's World.
3. Use a word processing program to write summaries of the websites that you visited.

Merchandise inventory includes all goods owned by the business and held for sale. The account used for Susan's Service Merchandise's merchandise inventory is Account No. 12000, Merchandise Inventory.

PCA uses a perpetual inventory system. In a perpetual inventory system a ***merchandising business*** continuously updates inventory each time an item is purchased or sold.

Inventory calculations include FIFO, LIFO, and average cost methods. The ***FIFO*** (first in, first out) method assumes that the items in the beginning inventory are sold first. The ***LIFO*** (last in, first out) method assumes that the goods received last are sold first. The average cost method (also known as weighted average method) is the default that PCA uses for inventory items sold. The formula used is: Average Cost x Quantity Sold = Cost of Sales.

PCA tracks the inventory items you buy and sell. After you post, PCA automatically updates the cost and quantity of each inventory item. Generally, all of your inventory should use the same costing method.

Tracking inventory is a three-step process:

- Enter item information, including Sales account, Merchandise Inventory account, and Cost of Sales account.

- Use item codes when entering purchases and sales. PCA automatically calculates and tracks average cost, which is the default, using this to calculate and enter the Cost of Sales. You can change the cost method to LIFO (last in, first out) or FIFO (first in, first out). This chapter will explain these inventory cost methods in detail.

- If necessary, enter inventory adjustments.

PCA does the rest automatically: adjusts inventory levels each time you post a purchase or sale of an inventory item, tracks the cost of each item, and makes a Cost of Goods Sold journal entry at the end of the accounting period.

COST METHODS

PCA includes three types of cost methods for inventory: average cost, LIFO, and FIFO. Once you select the costing method for an inventory item, you cannot change it if transactions have been posted. Therefore, if you want to change the cost method for an item with posted transactions, you must enter the item again.

Average Cost

When you set up inventory items for Susan's Service Merchandise, you selected the Average cost method. In Chapter 11, Susan's Service Merchandise purchased four pairs of curtains from Ronald Baker Fabrics for $30 each (Invoice 210, page 411). What happens when these curtains are sold?

The journal entries would look like this:

Purchased four pairs of curtains from Ronald Baker Fabrics at $30 each.

Account ID	Account Description, Purchase Invoice 210	Debit	Credit
12000	Merchandise Inventory	120.00	
20000/RBF08	Accounts Payable/Ronald Baker Fabrics		120.00

Sold four pairs of curtains to Phil Merchant for $100 each (Invoice 103, page 464).

Account ID	Account Description, Sales Invoice 103	Debit	Credit
50500	Cost of Sales-Wall	120.00	
11000/pm005	Accounts Receivable/Phil Merchant	432.00	
12000	Merchandise Inventory		120.00
40200	Sales-Wall		400.00
23100	Sales Tax Payable		32.00

You can see from these journal entries that the Merchandise Inventory account is updated with each purchase and sale. After these transactions, the balance in Merchandise Inventory looks like this:

Merchandise Inventory, Account No. 12000

Purchased inventory	120.00	Sold Inventory	120.00
Balance	0.00		

LIFO (Last In, First Out)

The LIFO (last in, first out) method of inventory pricing assumes that the last goods received are sold first. LIFO assumes that cost is based on replacement and that the last price paid for merchandise is more accurate.

Accountants recommend that you select LIFO when you desire to charge the most recent inventory costs against revenue. LIFO yields the lowest amount of net income in periods of rising costs because the cost of the most recently acquired inventory more closely approximates the replacement cost.

FIFO (First In, First Out)

The FIFO (first in, first out) method of inventory pricing assumes that the items in the beginning inventory are sold first. FIFO costs your sales and values your inventory as if the items you sell are the ones that you have had in stock for the longest time.

Accountants recommend that you select FIFO when you desire to charge costs against revenue in the order in which costs occur. FIFO yields a higher amount of profit during periods of rising costs. This happens because merchandise was acquired prior to the increase in cost.

TYPES OF INVENTORY ITEMS

There are nine types of inventory items in PCA:

- Stock item: This is the default in the Item Class list. It is the traditional inventory item where the program tracks descriptions, unit prices, stock quantities, and cost of sales. For stock items, you should complete the entire window. Once an item has been designated as a stock item, the type cannot be changed.
- Master Stock Item: PCA uses this item class as a special item that does not represent inventory stocked but contains information (item attributes) shared with a number of substock items.
- Non-stock item: PCA tracks the description and a unit price for sales. You can also track default accounts. You might use this type for service items such as hours where the unit price is set.
- Description only: PCA keeps track of the description of an Inventory Item. This saves time when entering purchases and sales because you don't have to retype the description. You might use this type for service items where the price fluctuates.
- Service: This is for services you can apply to your salary and wages account.
- Labor: This is for labor you can apply to your salary and wages account. You cannot purchase labor items but you can sell them.

- Assembly: You can specify items as assembly items and create a bill of materials for a unit made up of component stock or subassembly items.
- Activity item: To indicate how time is spent when performing services for a customer, for a job, or for internal administrative work. Activity items are used with the Time & Billing feature.
- Charge item: Expenses recorded by an employee or vendor when company resources are used for a customer or job.

GETTING STARTED

In the preceding chapters, you set up inventory items. The instructions that follow show you how to add inventory items to Susan's Service Merchandise.

1. Start Peachtree. Open Susan's Service Merchandise. If you used a unique name, select it.
2. Follow these steps to restore data from Chapter 12.

   a. Start Peachtree. Open Susan's Service Merchandise.[1] This company was set up in Chapter 11 on pages 383-388. (*Hint:* If another company opens, click File; Open Previous Company, select Susan's [your name] Service Merchandise.)

   b. From the Company page, link to Restore.

   c. The Select Backup File window appears. (If necessary, click [Browse]. In the Look in field, select the appropriate location of the Chapter 12.ptb file.) Make sure the Location field on the Select Backup File window shows the Chapter 12.ptb file. You made this backup on pages 486-487. Click [Next >].

---

[1]You can restore from your back up file even if *no* Peachtree company exists. From Peachtree's start up window, select File; Restore. Select the location of your backup file. On the Restore Wizard's Select Company window, select A New Company. The *A New Company* selection allows you to restore your backup data, bypassing the process of new company set up. For more information, refer to Troubleshooting on page 280-281.

d. The Select Company window appears. The radio button next to An Existing Company is selected. Check that the Company Name and Location fields are correct. Click Next >.

e. The Restore Options window appears. Make sure that the box next to Company Data is *checked*. Click Next >.

f. The Confirmation window appears. Check the From and To fields to make sure they are correct. Click Finish. When the Restore Company scale is 100% complete, your data is restored.

g. If necessary, remove the external media.

h. To verify your data, display the General Ledger Trial Balance. Compare it to the one shown on page 485 in Chapter 12.

3. From the Navigation Bar, select Inventory & Services; Inventory Items, Set Up Inventory Defaults. The Inventory Item Defaults window displays. Click on the GL Accts/Costing tab. The default for inventory costing is the Average method. Since this is what Susan's Service Merchandise uses, there is no need to make any changes to this window.

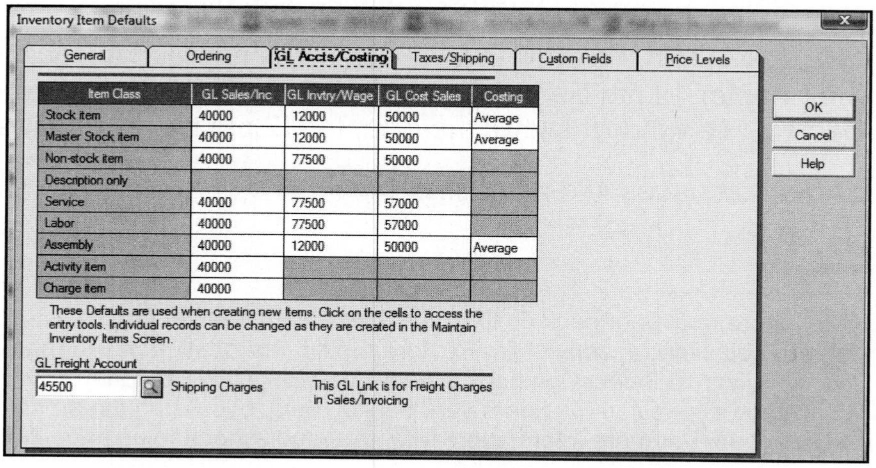

Item Class	GL Sales/Inc	GL Invtry/Wage	GL Cost Sales	Costing
Stock item	40000	12000	50000	Average
Master Stock item	40000	12000	50000	Average
Non-stock item	40000	77500	50000	
Description only				
Service	40000	77500	57000	
Labor	40000	77500	57000	
Assembly	40000	12000	50000	Average
Activity item	40000			
Charge item	40000			

4. Click on the Taxes/Shipping tab.

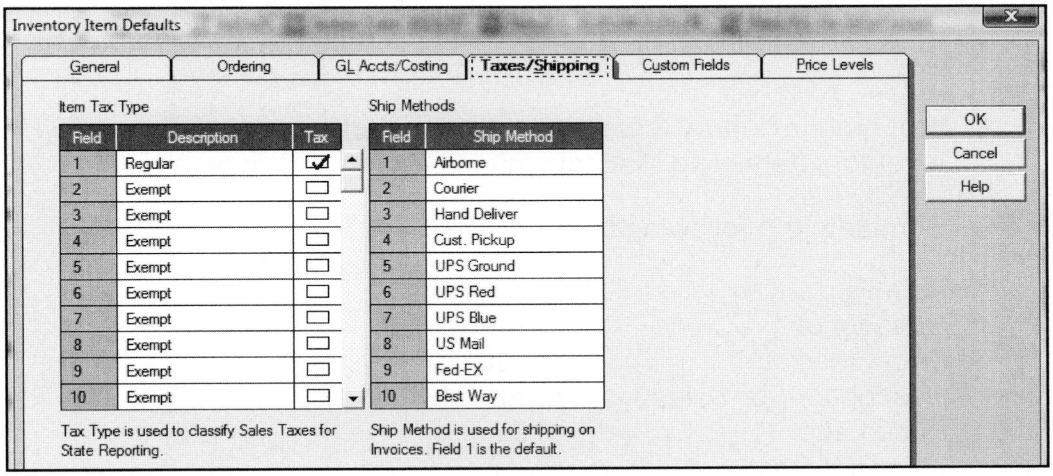

The Regular tax type is selected with a check mark. This is correct because there is an 8% sales tax in California. (Remember: If you click 

, you close the window without saving any changes.)

The Ship Methods that appear on this tab are also shown on the Sales/Invoicing and Purchases/Receive Inventory windows. You can also use these ship methods to set up defaults for customers and vendors.

5. Click 

to close this window.

ENTERING INVENTORY ITEM MAINTENANCE INFORMATION

Inventory items are set up on the Maintain Inventory Items window. You can establish general ledger accounts, vendors, tax exemptions, sales prices and reorder quantities. The information on the Maintain Inventory Items window is displayed as five tabs: General, Custom Fields, History, Bill of Materials, and Item Attributes. The fields are visible on one tab at a time, but you can view others by selecting a tab.

Follow these steps to enter inventory maintenance information:

1. From the Inventory & Services page, select , New Inventory Item. The Maintain Inventory Items window appears.

2. Complete the following information:

Item ID:	**004lights**
Description:	**lighting**
Item Class:	**Stock item**
Description(for Sales):	**light fixtures**
Price Level 1:	**175**
Last Unit Cost:	**64**
Cost Method:	Average
GL Sales Acct:	Add Account No. **40500 Sales-Lights** (Income)
GL Inventory Acct:	**12000 Merchandise Inventory**
GL Cost of Sales Acct:	Add Account No. **57050 Cost of Sales-Lights** (Cost of Sales)
Item Tax Type:	1
Item Type:	**lights**
Stocking U/M:	**each**
Minimum Stock:	**8**
Reorder Quantity:	**4**

Preferred Vendor ID:

You need to add a new vendor. To add a vendor, click  in the Preferred Vendor ID field, then click . The Maintain Vendors window displays.

Vendor ID:	**TSS09**
Name:	**Taylor Sales and Service**
Contact:	**Joann Taylor**
Mailing Address:	**1342 North Tenth Street.**
City, ST Zip:	**Los Angeles, CA 90010**
Country:	**USA**

Vendor Type:	**lights**
1099 Type:	**Independent Contractor**
Expense Accounting:	12000 Merchandise Inventory
Telephone 1:	**213-555-6032**
Fax:	**213-555-6034**
E-Mail:	**joann@taylor.com**
Web Address:	**www.taylor.com/joannT**

Purchase Info:

Tax ID Number:	**36-4390241**

a. Click , then close the Maintain Vendors window. You are returned to the Maintain Inventory Items window. In the Preferred Vendor ID field, select Taylor Sales and Service as the vendor. Click .

b. Click on the Beginning Balances arrow (lower right corner of the Maintain Inventory Items window.) The Inventory Beginning Balances window displays. Select lighting. Complete the following:

Quantity:	125
Unit Cost:	64.00
Total Cost:	8,000.00 (completed automatically)

3. Observe that the Total Beginning Balances field shows 27,740.00. This amount agrees with the Merchandise Inventory balance on page 392 (January 1, 2008 balance sheet).

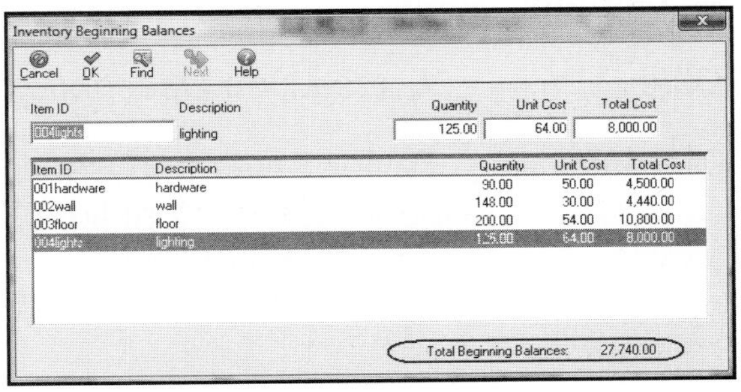

4. Click  to close the Inventory Beginning Balances window.

5. Make sure TSS09, Taylor Sales and Service is shown in the Preferred Vendor ID field. Save, then close the Maintain Inventory Items window.

BACKING UP YOUR DATA

Follow these steps to back up Chapter 13 data:

1. From the Company page, link to Back up.

2. Click 

.

3. Accept the default for backing up to the hard drive or make the selections to back up to another location. Type **Chapter 13 Begin** in the File name field.

4. Click 

.

5. When the window prompts that This company backup will require approximately 3.32MB, click 

. When the Back Up Company scale is 100% complete, you have successfully backed up to the current point in Chapter 13.

6. Continue or click File; Exit to exit Peachtree.

INVENTORY ADJUSTMENTS

Follow these steps to record the following purchase and inventory adjustment.

Date	*Transaction Description*
01/14/08	Taylor Sales and Service sent Invoice No. 112 for the purchase of eight light fixtures for a unit cost of $64 each, and a total of $512.

1. From the Vendors & Purchases page, select 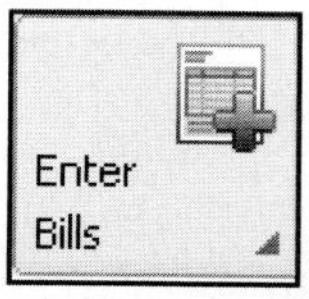

; New Bill. The Purchases/Receive Inventory window appears. Record the January 14, 2008, transaction. Compare your Purchases/Receive Inventory window with the one shown on the next page.

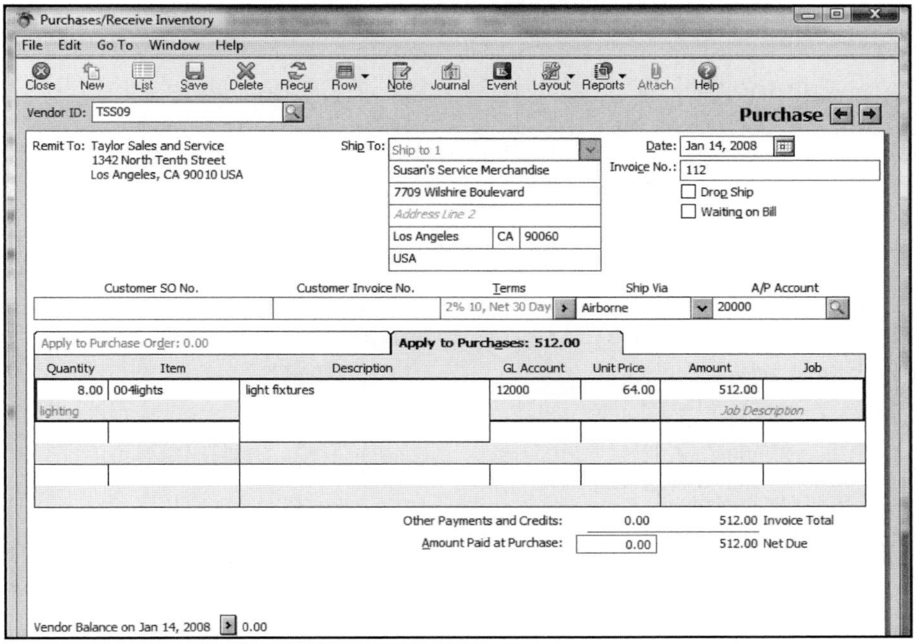

2. Post, then close.

The transaction that follows needs to be recorded.

Date	*Transaction Description*
01/15/08	Two light fixtures were damaged when they were dropped on the floor by the owner, Joe Greene.

Follow the steps on the next page to make an inventory adjustment.

1. From the Inventory & Services page, select 

. The Inventory Adjustments window appears.

2. In the Item ID field, select lighting.

3. In the Reference field, type **JG** (Joe Greene' initials).

4. Type **15** in the Date field.

5. Type **-2** in the Adjust Quantity By field. (PCA calculates the New Quantity after you enter the adjustment.)

6. In the Reason to Adjust field, type **Two damaged light fixtures**.

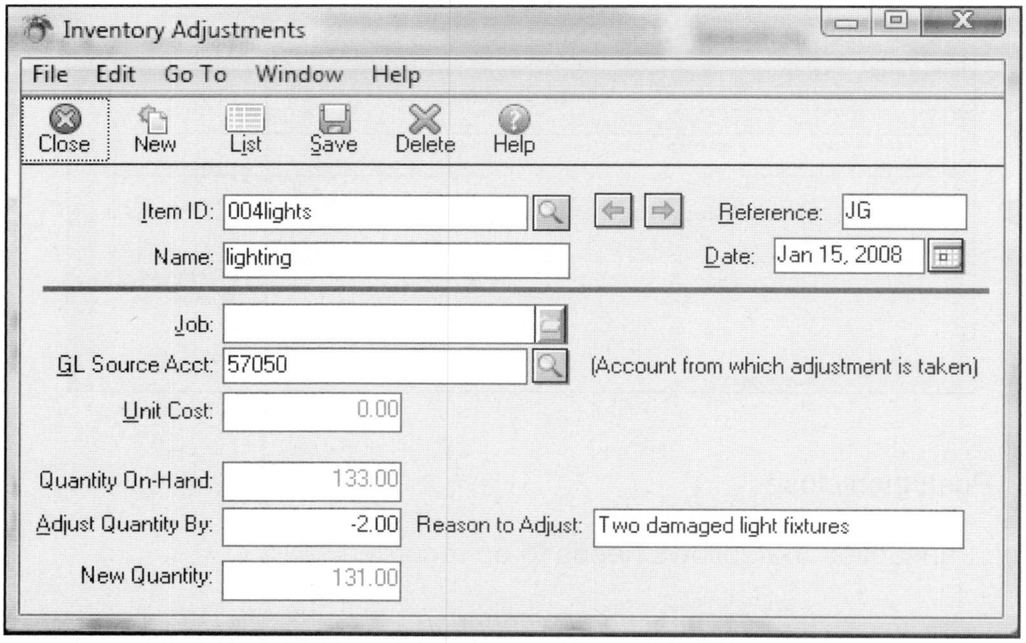

7. Click  to post, then close the Inventory Adjustments window.

ADDITIONAL TRANSACTIONS

Record the following transactions for Susan's Service Merchandise.

Date	*Transaction Description*
01/19/08	Sold two doorknobs on account to Alice Peters. Type Invoice **106** in the Invoice No. field. Subsequent invoices will be numbered automatically. (*Hint: Select hardware as the inventory item for doorknobs.*)

01/19/08 Sold two rolls of vinyl flooring on account to Doris Conlin, Invoice No. 107. There is no sales tax because merchandise is being shipped out of state.

01/19/08 Sold two pairs of curtains on account to Phil Merchant, Invoice No. 108. (*Hint: Select wall as the inventory item for curtains.*)

01/20/08 Susan's Service Merchandise completed repair work for Betty Barton at a cost of $75, Invoice No. 109. (*Hint: Remember to credit Account No. 40600, Service Fees.*)

01/23/08 Cash sales in the amount of $1,404 ($1,300 plus $104, CA sales taxes) were deposited at La Brea Bank: 10 pairs of curtains, $1,000; 2 doorknobs, $300. (*Hint: If a window appears saying that reference has been used before, click OK.*)

01/24/08 Received a check in the amount of $324 from Alice Peters in full payment of Invoice 106.

01/26/08 Received a check in the amount of $216 from Phil Merchant in full payment of Invoice No. 108.

01/30/08 Issued Check No. 3039 to TMI Mortgage Co. in the amount of $685.80. To distribute this amount between the principal amount of $587.95 and Interest Expense of $97.85, click 

. Click 

to accept the split transaction.

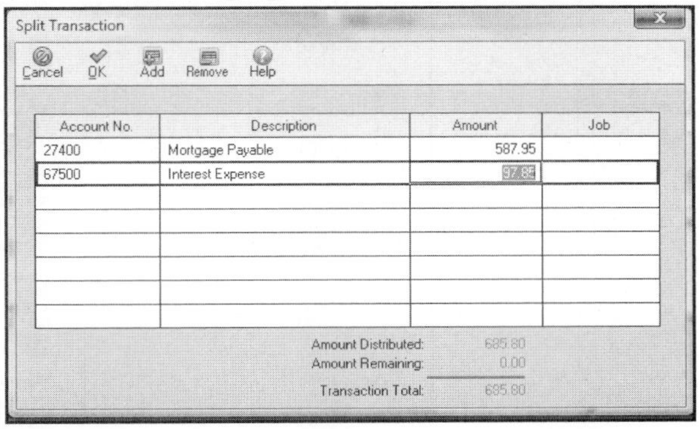

These steps assume you are using the Write Checks window.

(*Hint: On the Write Checks window, type **3039** in the Check number field.*)

01/30/08 Issued Check No. 3040 in the amount of $500 to Joe Greene.

01/30/08 Issued Check No. 3041 in the amount of $500 to Susan Currier.

01/30/08 Cash sales in the amount of $2,376 ($2,200 plus $176, CA sales taxes) were deposited at La Brea Bank: 8 doorknobs, $1,200; 10 pairs of curtains, $1,000.

PRINTING REPORTS

1. Print the Sales Journal.

Susan's Service Merchandise
Sales Journal
For the Period From Jan 1, 2008 to Jan 31, 2008
Filter Criteria includes: Report order is by Invoice/CM Date. Report is printed in Detail Format.

Date	Account ID	Invoice/CM #	Line Description	Debit Amnt	Credit Amnt
1/6/08	23100	101	CA: California Dept. of Revenue		24.00
	40000		Two doorknobs		300.00
	50000		Cost of sales	100.00	
	12000		Cost of sales		100.00
	11000		Alice Peters	324.00	
1/6/08	40400	102	Four rolls of vinyl flooring		640.00
	57000		Cost of sales	216.00	
	12000		Cost of sales		216.00
	11000		Doris Conlin	640.00	
1/6/08	23100	103	CA: California Dept. of Revenue		32.00
	40200		Four pairs of curtains		400.00
	50500		Cost of sales	120.00	
	12000		Cost of sales		120.00
	11000		Phil Merchant	432.00	
1/6/08	23100	104	CA: California Dept. of Revenue		36.00
	40000		Three curtain rods		450.00
	50000		Cost of sales	150.00	
	12000		Cost of sales		150.00
	11000		Judy Prince	486.00	
1/9/08	23100	105	CA: California Dept. of Revenue		3.99
	40600		Repair		49.89
	11000		Betty Barton	53.88	
1/14/08	23100	CM103	CA: California Dept. of Revenue	8.00	
	40200		Returned one pair of curtains	100.00	
	50500		Cost of sales		30.00
	12000		Cost of sales	30.00	
	11000		Phil Merchant		108.00
1/19/08	23100	106	CA: California Dept. of Revenue		24.00
	40000		Two doorknobs		300.00
	50000		Cost of sales	100.00	
	12000		Cost of sales		100.00
	11000		Alice Peters	324.00	
1/19/08	40400	107	Two rolls of vinyl flooring		320.00
	57000		Cost of sales	108.00	
	12000		Cost of sales		108.00
	11000		Doris Conlin	320.00	
1/19/08	23100	108	CA: California Dept. of Revenue		16.00
	40200		Two pairs of curtains		200.00
	50500		Cost of sales	60.00	
	12000		Cost of sales		60.00
	11000		Phil Merchant	216.00	
1/20/08	23100	109	CA: California Dept. of Revenue		6.00
	40600		Repair		75.00
	11000		Betty Barton	81.00	
		Total		**3,868.88**	**3,868.88**

If any of your transactions do *not* agree with the Sales Journal, you can drill-down () to the original entry, make any needed corrections, then save and reprint.

2. Print the Cash Receipts Journal.

Susan's Service Merchandise
Cash Receipts Journal
For the Period From Jan 1, 2008 to Jan 31, 2008

Filter Criteria includes: Report order is by Check Date. Report is printed in Detail Format.

Date	Account ID	Transaction Ref	Line Description	Debit Amnt	Credit Amnt
1/14/08	11000	Invoice 103	Invoice: 103		324.00
	10200		Phil Merchant	324.00	
1/21/08	11000	Invoice 101	Invoice: 101		324.00
	10200		Alice Peters	324.00	
1/22/08	11000	Invoice 104	Invoice: 104		105.00
	10200		Judy Prince	105.00	
1/23/08	23100	Cash	CA: California Dept. of Revenue		104.00
	40200		Ten pairs of curtains		1,000.00
	50500		Cost of sales	300.00	
	12000		Cost of sales		300.00
	40000		Two doorknobs		300.00
	50000		Cost of sales	100.00	
	12000		Cost of sales		100.00
	10200		Cash	1,404.00	
1/24/08	11000	Invoice 106	Invoice: 106		324.00
	10200		Alice Peters	324.00	
1/26/08	11000	Invoice 108	Invoice: 108		216.00
	10200		Phil Merchant	216.00	
1/28/08	11000	Invoice 105	Invoice: 105		53.88
	10200		Betty Barton	53.88	
1/28/08	11000	Invoice 102	Invoice: 102		640.00
	10200		Doris Conlin	640.00	
1/29/08	23100	Cash	CA: California Dept. of Revenue		16.00
	40200		Two pairs of curtains		200.00
	50500		Cost of sales	60.00	
	12000		Cost of sales		60.00
	10200		Harriet Wilson	216.00	
1/30/08	23100	Cash	CA: California Dept. of Revenue		176.00
	40000		Eight doorknobs		1,200.00
	50000		Cost of sales	400.00	
	12000		Cost of sales		400.00
	40200		Ten pairs of curtains		1,000.00
	50500		Cost of sales	300.00	
	12000		Cost of sales		300.00
	10200		Cash	2,376.00	
				7,142.88	**7,142.88**

3. Print the Customer Ledgers.

Susan's Service Merchandise
Customer Ledgers
For the Period From Jan 1, 2008 to Jan 31, 2008
Filter Criteria includes: Report order is by ID. Report is printed in Detail Format.

Customer ID Customer	Date	Trans No	Type	Debit Amt	Credit Amt	Balance
ap001	1/6/08	101	SJ	324.00		324.00
Alice Peters	1/19/08	106	SJ	324.00		648.00
	1/21/08	Invoice 101	CRJ		324.00	324.00
	1/24/08	Invoice 106	CRJ		324.00	0.00
bb002	1/9/08	105	SJ	53.88		53.88
Betty Barton	1/20/08	109	SJ	81.00		134.88
	1/28/08	Invoice 105	CRJ		53.88	81.00
dc003	1/6/08	102	SJ	640.00		640.00
Doris Conlin	1/19/08	107	SJ	320.00		960.00
	1/28/08	Invoice 102	CRJ		640.00	320.00
jp004	1/6/08	104	SJ	486.00		486.00
Judy Prince	1/22/08	Invoice 104	CRJ		105.00	381.00
pm005	1/6/08	103	SJ	432.00		432.00
Phil Merchant	1/14/08	CM103	SJ		108.00	324.00
	1/14/08	Invoice 103	CRJ		324.00	0.00
	1/19/08	108	SJ	216.00		216.00
	1/26/08	Invoice 108	CRJ		216.00	0.00
Report Total				**2,876.88**	**2,094.88**	**782.00**

4. Print the Purchase Journal.

Susan's Service Merchandise
Purchase Journal
For the Period From Jan 1, 2008 to Jan 31, 2008
Filter Criteria includes: 1) Includes Drop Shipments. Report order is by Date. Report is printed in Detail Format.

Date	Account ID Account Description	Invoice/CM #	Line Description	Debit Amount	Credit Amount
1/2/08	12000 Merchandise Inventory	56JJ	restoration hardware	300.00	
	20000 Accounts Payable		Jesse Jensen Hardware		300.00
1/14/08	12000 Merchandise Inventory	112	light fixtures	512.00	
	20000 Accounts Payable		Taylor Sales and Service		512.00
1/20/08	12000 Merchandise Inventory	210	wall coverings	120.00	
	20000 Accounts Payable		Ronald Baker Fabrics		120.00
1/20/08	12000 Merchandise Inventory	78JJ	restoration hardware	500.00	
	20000 Accounts Payable		Jesse Jensen Hardware		500.00
1/20/08	12000 Merchandise Inventory	90	flooring	432.00	
	20000 Accounts Payable		Lyle Lewis Products		432.00
1/24/08	12000 Merchandise Inventory	VCM90	flooring		54.00
	20000 Accounts Payable		Lyle Lewis Products	54.00	
1/28/08	12000 Merchandise Inventory	VCM78JJ	restoration hardware		100.00
	20000 Accounts Payable		Jesse Jensen Hardware	100.00	
				2,018.00	**2,018.00**

5. Print the Cash Disbursements Journal.

Susan's Service Merchandise
Cash Disbursements Journal
For the Period From Jan 1, 2008 to Jan 31, 2008

Filter Criteria includes: Report order is by Date. Report is printed in Detail Format.

Date	Check #	Account ID	Line Description	Debit Amount	Credit Amount
1/23/08	3030	70000	Maintenance Expense	160.00	
		10200	Dave Heinrich		160.00
1/23/08	3031	73500	Postage Expense	41.00	
		10200	U.S. Post Office		41.00
1/23/08	3032	75500	Supplies Expense	107.65	
		10200	Century City Office Supplies		107.65
1/23/08	3033	76000	Telephone Expense	72.14	
		10200	RCT Phone Co.		72.14
1/24/08	3034	39007	Joe Greene, Drawing	500.00	
		10200	Joe Greene		500.00
1/24/08	3035	39009	Susan Currier, Drawing	500.00	
		10200	Susan Currier		500.00
1/24/08	3036	59500	Discounts Taken		7.56
		20000	Invoice: 90	378.00	
		10200	Lyle Lewis Products		370.44
1/28/08	3037	59500	Discounts Taken		8.00
		20000	Invoice: 78JJ	400.00	
		10200	Jesse Jensen Hardware		392.00
1/28/08	3038	59500	Discounts Taken		2.40
		20000	Invoice: 210	120.00	
		10200	Ronald Baker Fabrics		117.60
1/30/08	3039	27400	Mortgage Payable	587.95	
		67500	Interest Expense	97.85	
		10200	TMI Mortgage Co.		685.80
1/30/08	3040	39007	Joe Greene, Drawing	500.00	
		10200	Joe Greene		500.00
1/30/08	3041	39009	Susan Currier, Drawing	500.00	
		10200	Susan Currier		500.00
	Total			**3,964.59**	**3,964.59**

6. Print the Vendor Ledgers.

Susan's Service Merchandise
Vendor Ledgers
For the Period From Jan 1, 2008 to Jan 31, 2008

Filter Criteria includes: Report order is by ID.

Vendor ID Vendor	Date	Trans No	Type	Paid	Debit Amt	Credit Amt	Balance
JJH06	1/2/08	56JJ	PJ			300.00	300.00
Jesse Jensen Hardware	1/20/08	78JJ	PJ	*		500.00	800.00
	1/28/08	VCM78JJ	PJ	*	100.00		700.00
	1/28/08	3037	CDJ		8.00	8.00	700.00
	1/28/08	3037	CDJ		400.00		300.00
LLP07	1/20/08	90	PJ	*		432.00	432.00
Lyle Lewis Products	1/24/08	VCM90	PJ	*	54.00		378.00
	1/24/08	3036	CDJ		7.56	7.56	378.00
	1/24/08	3036	CDJ		378.00		0.00
RBF08	1/20/08	210	PJ	*		120.00	120.00
Ronald Baker Fabrics	1/28/08	3038	CDJ		2.40	2.40	120.00
	1/28/08	3038	CDJ		120.00		0.00
TSS09	1/14/08	112	PJ			512.00	512.00
Taylor Sales and Service							
Report Total					**1,069.96**	**1,881.96**	**812.00**

7. Follow these steps to print the Cost of Goods Sold Journal and the Inventory Adjustment Journal:

   a. From the Reports area of the Select a Report for Form window, select Inventory.

   b. Highlight Cost of Goods Sold Journal, then make the selections to print. Compare your printout to the one shown on the next page.

Susan's Service Merchandise
Cost of Goods Sold Journal
For the Period From Jan 1, 2008 to Jan 31, 2008
Filter Criteria includes: Report order is by Date. Report is printed in Detail Format and with shortened descriptions.

Date	GL Acct ID	Reference	Qty	Line Description	Debit Amount	Credit Amount
1/6/08	12000	101	2.00	Two doorknobs		100.00
	50000		2.00	Two doorknobs	100.00	
1/6/08	12000	102	4.00	Four rolls of vinyl floorin		216.00
	57000		4.00	Four rolls of vinyl floorin	216.00	
1/6/08	12000	103	4.00	Four pairs of curtains		120.00
	50500		4.00	Four pairs of curtains	120.00	
1/6/08	12000	104	3.00	Three curtain rods		150.00
	50000		3.00	Three curtain rods	150.00	
1/14/08	12000	CM103	-1.00	Returned one pair of curt	30.00	
	50500		-1.00	Returned one pair of curt		30.00
1/19/08	12000	106	2.00	Two doorknobs		100.00
	50000		2.00	Two doorknobs	100.00	
1/19/08	12000	107	2.00	Two rolls of vinyl flooring		108.00
	57000		2.00	Two rolls of vinyl flooring	108.00	
1/19/08	12000	108	2.00	Two pairs of curtains		60.00
	50500		2.00	Two pairs of curtains	60.00	
1/23/08	12000	Cash	10.00	Ten pairs of curtains		300.00
	50500		10.00	Ten pairs of curtains	300.00	
	12000		2.00	Two doorknobs		100.00
	50000		2.00	Two doorknobs	100.00	
1/29/08	12000	Cash	2.00	Two pairs of curtains		60.00
	50500		2.00	Two pairs of curtains	60.00	
1/30/08	12000	Cash	8.00	Eight doorknobs		400.00
	50000		8.00	Eight doorknobs	400.00	
	12000		10.00	Ten pairs of curtains		300.00
	50500		10.00	Ten pairs of curtains	300.00	
		Total			**2,044.00**	**2,044.00**

c. Highlight the Inventory Adjustment Journal, then make the selections to print.

Susan's Service Merchandise
Inventory Adjustment Journal
For the Period From Jan 1, 2008 to Jan 31, 2008
Filter Criteria includes: Report order is by Date. Report is printed in Detail Format and with shortened descriptions.

Date	GL Acct ID	Reference	Qty	Line Description	Debit Amount	Credit Amount
1/15/08	12000	JG	-2.00	lighting		128.00
	57050		-2.00	Two damaged light fixtures	128.00	
		Total			**128.00**	**128.00**

8. Print the General Ledger Trial Balance.

Susan's Service Merchandise
General Ledger Trial Balance
As of Jan 31, 2008

Filter Criteria includes: Report order is by ID. Report is printed in Detail Format.

Account ID	Account Description	Debit Amt	Credit Amt
10200	La Brea Bank	73,536.25	
10400	Worldwide Savings & Loan	20,000.00	
11000	Accounts Receivable	782.00	
12000	Merchandise Inventory	27,338.00	
13000	Supplies	1,750.00	
14000	Prepaid Insurance	2,400.00	
15000	Furniture and Fixtures	5,000.00	
15100	Computers & Equipment	7,500.00	
15500	Building	100,000.00	
20000	Accounts Payable		812.00
23100	Sales Tax Payable		429.99
27000	Long-Term Notes Payable		20,500.00
27400	Mortgage Payable		74,412.05
39006	Joe Greene, Capital		70,195.00
39007	Joe Greene, Drawing	1,000.00	
39008	Susan Currier, Capital		70,195.00
39009	Susan Currier, Drawing	1,000.00	
40000	Sales-Hardware		2,550.00
40200	Sales-Wall		2,700.00
40400	Sales-Floor		960.00
40600	Service Fees		124.89
50000	Cost of Sales-Hardware	850.00	
50500	Cost of Sales-Wall	810.00	
57000	Cost of Sales-Floor	324.00	
57050	Cost of Sales-Lights	128.00	
59500	Purchase Discounts		17.96
67500	Interest Expense	97.85	
70000	Maintenance Expense	160.00	
73500	Postage Expense	41.00	
75500	Supplies Expense	107.65	
76000	Telephone Expense	72.14	
	Total:	**242,896.89**	**242,896.89**

BACKING UP CHAPTER 13 DATA

If your reports agree with the ones shown, make a backup of Chapter 13 data. If your printouts do not agree with the ones shown, make the necessary corrections.

Follow the steps on the next page to back up Chapter 13 data.

1. From the Company page, link to Back up.
2. Click Back Up.
3. Accept the default for backing up to the hard drive or make the selections to back up to another location. Type **Chapter 13** in the File name field.
4. Click Save.
5. When the window prompts that This company backup will require approximately 3.33MB, click OK. When the Back Up Company scale is 100% complete, you have successfully backed up to the current point in Chapter 13.
6. Continue or click File; Exit to exit Peachtree.
7. Exit PCA or continue.

INTERNET ACTIVITY	
1.	From your Internet browser, go to the book's website at http://www.mhhe.com/yacht2008.
2.	Link to Student Edition.
3.	In the Course-wide Content list, link to Part 3 Internet Activities for Chapters 11-14. Open or Save. (You can also choose Chapter 13, then link to Internet Activities. If you Choose a Chapter, observe that other chapter-specific links are available; for example, Quizzes, PowerPoints, and Going to the Net Exercises.)
4.	Complete the Accountant's World-Chapter 13 exercise. Read steps 1 and 2.
5.	Follow the steps shown on the book's website to complete this Internet activity.
6.	Using a word processing program write a brief summary of what you find. Include all appropriate website addresses.

SUMMARY AND REVIEW

SOFTWARE OBJECTIVES: In Chapter 13, you have used the software to:

1. Enter inventory maintenance and default information.
2. Enter inventory item information, including Sales account, Merchandise Inventory account, and Cost of Sales account.
3. Enter item codes when recording purchases and sales.
4. Enter inventory adjustments.
5. Make three backups: two for Susan's Service Merchandise; one for the end-of-chapter exercises.

WEB OBJECTIVES: In Chapter 13, you did these Internet activities:

1. Used your Internet browser to go to the book's website.
2. Went to the Internet Activity link on the book's website. Then, selected WEB EXERCISES PART 3. Completed the third web exercise in Part 3–Accountant's World.
3. Used a word processing program to write summaries of the websites that you visited.

GOING TO THE NET

Access the Small Business Knowledge Base website at http://www.bizmove.com/finance/m3d3.htm. Scroll down the window to Merchandise Inventories: Perpetual Inventory. Answer these questions about perpetual inventory.

1. What is a perpetual inventory at retail?
2. When is a physical count of inventory necessary?

Short-Answer Questions: Write an answer to each question in the space provided.

1. Identify and explain the three-step process for tracking inventory.

____

____

____

____

2. Explain how PCA uses a perpetual inventory system.

____

____

3. Define the term merchandise inventory.

____

____

4. Explain the terms Average Cost, LIFO and FIFO.

____

____

____

5. What do Invoice Nos. 106, 107, and 108 show? Identify to whom the merchandise was sold, what was purchased, and the amount of the invoice.

6. What are the journal entries for the following transactions when a perpetual inventory system is used: Purchased four pairs of curtains from Ronald Baker Fabrics at $30 each? Sold four pairs of curtains to Phil Merchant for $400?

7. What kind of invoice is 109? Identify this transaction and the amount.

Exercise 13-1: Follow the instructions on the next page to complete Exercise 13-1. Exercises 11-1, 11-2, 12-1, and 12-2 must be completed before starting Exercise 13-1.

1. Start PCA. Open the company that you set up in Exercise 11-1, Your Name Sales & Service.

2. Restore the data that you backed up in Exercise 12-2. This back up was made on page 494. To verify your data, display the general ledger trial balance and compare it to the one printed for Exercise 12-2, step 7, page 494.

3. Make the following inventory purchase.

   01/27/08 Charles Perkins Tools sent Invoice No. 732CP for the purchase of 8 tool kits for a unit cost of $30.

4. Make the following inventory adjustment:

   01/28/08 Two tool kits ordered by Charles Perkins Tools on 1/27/08 were accidentally damaged by the owner, Susan Currier.

5. Complete the following additional transactions:

   01/29/08 Received check in the amount of $900 from Rita Nicholson in payment of Invoice No. 103.

   01/30/08 Cash Sales in the amount of $4,400 were deposited at Eugene Bank: 20 tool kits, $1,700; 18 hardware sets, $2,700.

6. Make a backup of Exercise 13-1. (Use **Exercise 13-1** as the file name.)

Exercise 13-2: Follow the instructions below to complete Exercise 13-2.

1. Print the Cash Receipts Journal.

2. Print the Purchase Journal.

3. Print the Cost of Goods Sold Journal.

4. Print the Inventory Adjustment Journal.

5. Print the General Ledger Trial Balance.

CHAPTER 13 INDEX

Chapter 14 Employees, Payroll, and Account Reconciliation

SOFTWARE OBJECTIVES: In Chapter 14, you use the software to:

1. Explore the Payroll Setup Wizard.
2. Enter initial payroll fields.
3. Enter employee and employer default information.
4. Journalize and post Payroll Journal entries.
5. Print paychecks.
6. Reconcile La Brea Bank Account and the Payroll Checking Account.
7. Compare the vendor ledgers, customer ledgers, and inventory valuation report to the associated general ledger accounts.
8. Print the financial statements.
9. Make four backups: two for Susan's Service Merchandise; two for the end-of-chapter exercises.

WEB OBJECTIVES: In Chapter 14, you do these Internet activities:

1. Use your Internet browser to go to the book's website.
2. Go to the Internet Activity link on the book's website. Then, select WEB EXERCISES PART 3. Complete the fourth web exercise in Part 3–Salary Calculator.
3. Use a word processing program to write a summary of the websites that you visited.

In accounting you learn that employees and employers are required to pay local, state, and federal payroll taxes. Employers must withhold taxes from each employee's paycheck. The amount withheld for federal taxes is determined from tax tables published by the Internal Revenue Service (IRS). Circular E, Employer's Tax Guide, is available from the IRS. It shows the applicable tax tables and forms that are necessary for filing employee payroll information. PCA has payroll tax tables built into the software. In this chapter you learn how to access and use the payroll tax tables.

The amount withheld also depends on the employee's earnings and the number of ***exemptions*** *or* ***withholding allowances*** claimed by the employee. The number of withholding allowances usually includes one for the employee, one for the employee's spouse, and one for each dependent. PCA will automatically calculate the amounts withheld from employees' paychecks.

Also deducted from employees' paychecks are ***FICA taxes*** or social security taxes. This deduction from wages provides qualified workers who retire at age 62 or older with monthly payments from the federal government. The retiree also receives medical benefits called ***Medicare*** after reaching age 65. In addition to these retirement benefits, social security also provides payments to the surviving family of a qualified deceased worker. PCA will automatically compute FICA and Medicare taxes.

By January 31 of each year employers are required to issue ***W-2 Forms*** to employees and to the Internal Revenue Service. The W-2 Form is an annual report of the employee's wages subject to FICA and federal income tax and shows the amounts that were withheld.

In PCA, the employee's W-2 Form shows the Federal Income Tax, State Income Tax, Social Security, and Medicare withheld. In 2008, yearly income up to $102,600 (wage ceiling estimate) is subject to FICA tax. FICA is actually two taxes—the Social Security portion and the Medicare portion.

Congress usually adjusts the Social Security portion of the FICA tax annually; for example, in 2007 the wage ceiling on Social Security was $97,500. There is no income limit on amounts subject to the Medicare tax. The FICA tax percentage for social security in 2008 is 6.20%; the percentage for Medicare, 1.45%, for a total of 7.65%. These percentages are only half of the total tax. The employee pays 7.65% and the employer pays 7.65% for a total of 15.3%.

Employees may also voluntarily deduct other amounts from wages. These voluntary deductions include: charitable contributions, medical insurance premiums, U.S. savings bonds, or union dues.

It is the purpose of this chapter to show you how to use PCA to enter payroll default information, add employees, make the correct journal entries for payroll, and to print the various payroll reports. Once you set up the default information and employee information, PCA automates the payroll process.

You establish the following default information for processing payroll:

1. The cash account to credit when disbursing paychecks. Susan's Service Merchandise credits Account No. 10300, Payroll Checking Account.

2. The accounts that comprise the employee's fields.

3. The accounts that comprise the employer's fields.

4. The payroll fields that go on the W-2 form.

5. The employee-paid taxes.

6. The employer-paid taxes.

At the Maintain Employees level, you enter the following types of information:

1. The employee name, address, telephone number, and information from the Employee's Withholding Allowance Certificate, Form W-4.

2. Information about employee pay: hourly, salaried, and amount.

3. The tax filing status of the employee for federal, state, and local purposes, including withholding allowances.

On the Payroll Entry window, payroll tax withholdings are calculated automatically. All you need to do is select the employee you want to pay, date the paycheck and pay period, and post the paycheck. For a yearly fee, Peachtree's payroll tax service offers the appropriate state's payroll tax amounts. For more information, go online to Peachtree's website at www.peachtree.com, then link to Services, Payroll Tax.

The diagram on the next page shows you the steps for setting up and using PCA's payroll system.

Default and Setup Information

Deductions:	*Cash Account*:
FICA, Federal Payroll Tax, State Payroll Tax	10300, Payroll Checking Account

↓

Maintain Employees

Rate of Pay:	*Frequency:*
$12.50 per hour, regular rate $18.75 per hour, overtime rate	Weekly

↓

Payroll Journal

Paycheck, net pay: $424.94

Wages Expense	537.50	
FICA: Soc. Sec.		33.33
FICA: Medicare		7.79
Federal Payroll Tax		56.39
State Payroll Tax		10.75
SDI		4.30
Payroll Checking Account		424.94

GETTING STARTED

Follow these steps to start PCA:

1. Start Peachtree. Open Susan's Service Merchandise. If you used a unique name, select it. (*Hint:* If a different company opens, select File; Open Previous Company.)

2. Follow the steps on the next page to restore data from Chapter 13.

a. From the Company page, link to Restore. (If necessary put external media in the appropriate drive.)[1]

b. The Select Backup File window appears. (If necessary, click Browse. In the Look in field, select the appropriate location of the Chapter 13.ptb file. This backup was made on pages 516-517.) Make sure the Location field on the Select Backup File window shows the Chapter 13.ptb file. Click Next >.

c. The Select Company window appears. The radio button next to An Existing Company is selected. Check that the Company Name and Location fields are correct. Click Next >.

d. The Restore Options window appears. Make sure that the box next to Company Data is *checked*. Click Next >.

e. The Confirmation window appears. Check the From and To fields to make sure they are correct. Click Finish. When the Restore Company scale is 100% complete, your data is restored.

f. If necessary, remove the external media.

g. To verify your data, display the General Ledger Trial Balance. Compare it to the one shown on page 516 in Chapter 13.

Checking Your Global Tax Table Version

In this chapter, you record payroll transactions for the month of January 2008. Follow the steps on the next page to see what payroll tax table is included with the software you are using.

---

[1] You can restore from your back up file even if *no* Peachtree company exists. From Peachtree's start up window, select File; Restore. Select the location of your backup file. On the Restore Wizard's Select Company window, select A New Company. The *A New Company* selection allows you to restore your backup data, bypassing the process of new company set up. For more information, refer to Chapter 9, Troubleshooting on page 280-281.

1. From the menu bar, click Help; About Peachtree Accounting. The illustration for the educational version is shown below. If you are using the commercial release of Peachtree, your window will differ.

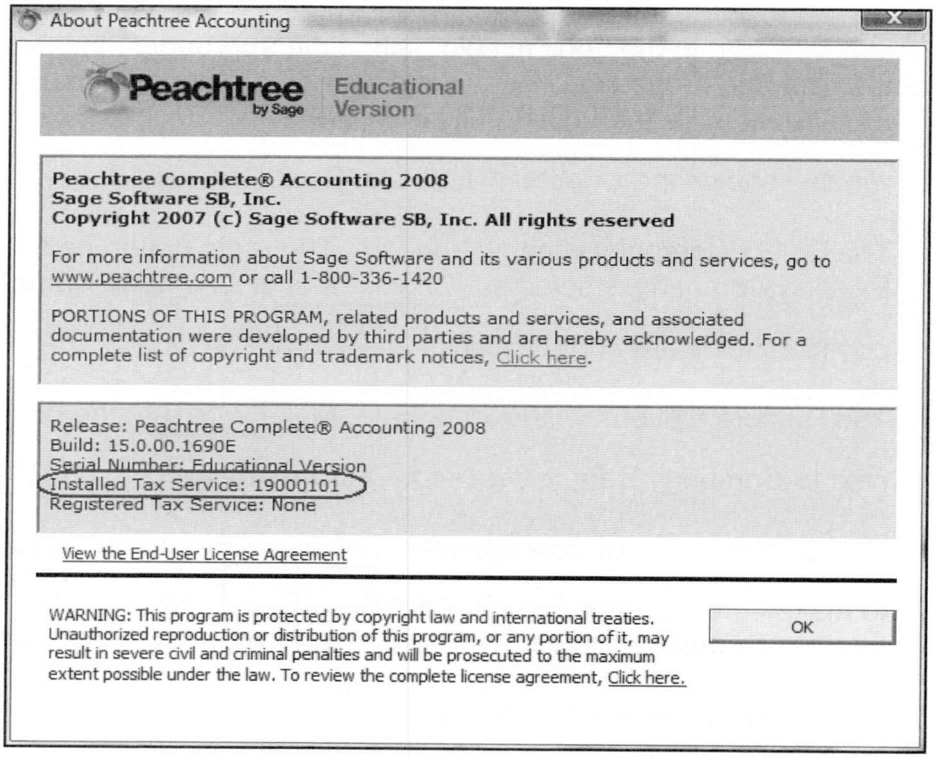

If your Tax Table Version is 19000101, a generic tax table is installed on your computer. The tax table supplied with the educational version of the software is provided for example purposes only and should not be relied upon for accurate withholding amounts. For purposes of this chapter and subsequent payroll work in the textbook, you use the tax tables supplied with the PCA 2008, Educational Version.

For an additional fee, Peachtree Software has a payroll tax service. To learn more about the Peachtree Payroll Tax Service, access their website at http://www.peachtree.com/payroll.

2. After reading the information on the window, click 

.

Establishing the Payroll Account

In order to establish the payroll checking account, transfer funds from La Brea Bank (Account No. 10200) to the Payroll Checking Account (Account No. 10300). Journalize and post the following General Journal transaction:

Date	*Transaction Description*
01/04/08	Susan's Service Merchandise transferred $6,500 from Account No. 10200, La Brea Bank, to Account No. 10300, Payroll Checking Account.

After posting this general journal entry, display the general journal. (*Hint: Click on Reports & Forms; General Leger, General Journal, Display, OK.*)

Susan's Service Merchandise
General Journal
For the Period From Jan 1, 2008 to Jan 31, 2008
Filter Criteria includes: Report order is by Date. Report is printed with Accounts having Zero Amounts and with shortened descriptions and in Detail Format.

Date	Account ID	Reference	Trans Description	Debit Amt	Credit Amt
1/4/08	10300		Payroll Checking Accounting	6,500.00	
	10200		La Brea Bank		6,500.00
		Total		6,500.00	6,500.00

Close the General Journal window and the Select a Report or Form window.

INITIAL PAYROLL FIELDS

1. From the Navigation Bar, select 

; 

, Set Up Employee Defaults. The Payroll Setup Wizard – Initial Payroll Setup window appears. Read the information on this window.

2. Type **3.4** in the Unemployment Percent for Your Company field.[2]

---

[2] All states support their unemployment insurance programs by placing a payroll tax on employers. In most states, the basic rate is 5.4% of the first $7,000 paid each employee. The employer's experience in creating or avoiding unemployment allows the employer to pay more or less than the basic 5.4% rate.

Press the **<Enter>** key to accept the default No for Do you want to record employee meals and tips? Observe that the Default Accounts for payroll are shown. You make changes to these accounts later in the chapter.

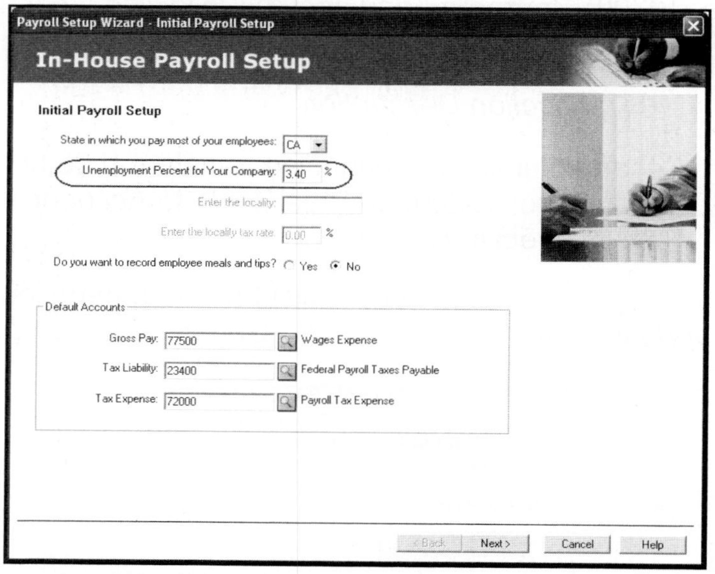

3. Review the information on the Initial Payroll Setup window. Make sure that 3.40% is shown in the unemployment percent field. Accept the default accounts by clicking Next > . The 401 (k) Setup window appears. Compare yours to the one shown below.

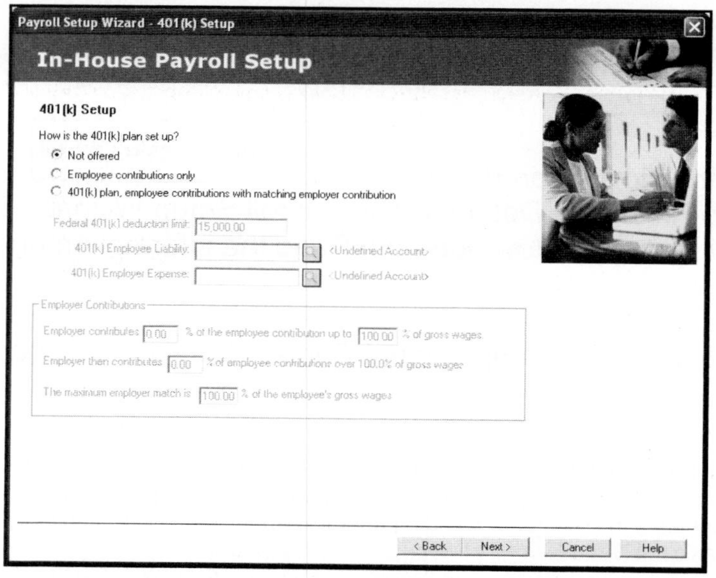

4. Since you are *not* going to make any changes, click Next >.

5. The Vacation Time Tracking and Sick Time Tracking window appears.

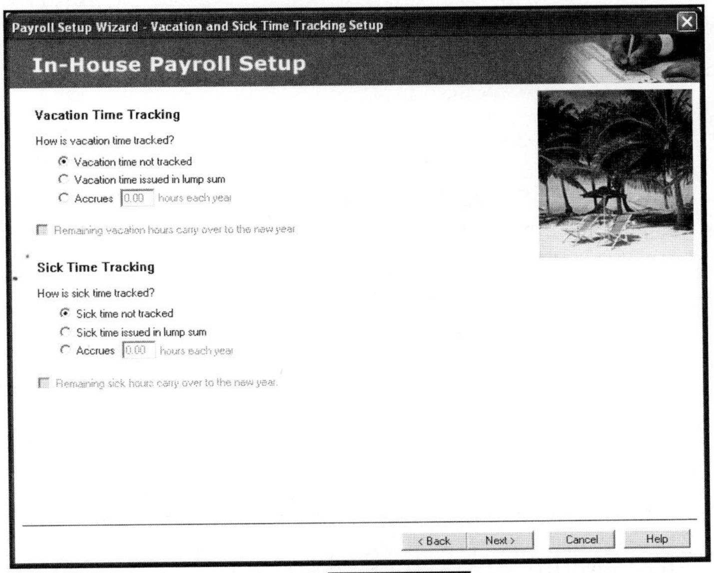

6. Accept the defaults by clicking Next >.

7. The Payroll Setup Complete window appears.

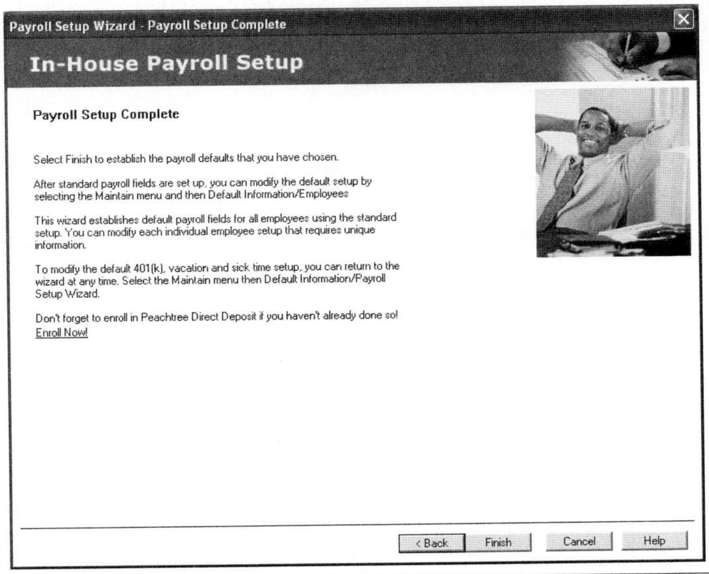

8. Read the information on the Payroll Setup Complete window. Click 

.

ENTERING EMPLOYEE AND EMPLOYER DEFAULT INFORMATION

Follow these steps to enter employee and employer default information:

1. Select 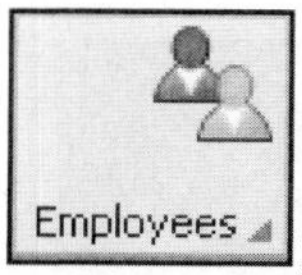

; Set Up Employee Defaults. The Employee Defaults window displays. In the Employee Defaults window, you enter constant information that serves as the basis for payroll processing.

   There are four tabs:

   - General
   - Pay Levels
   - EmployEE Fields
   - EmployER Fields

   There are three other areas on this window: Assign Payroll Fields for, Display Employee Name with, and Custom Fields. The Custom Fields can be used for specific information, such as employees' birthdays.

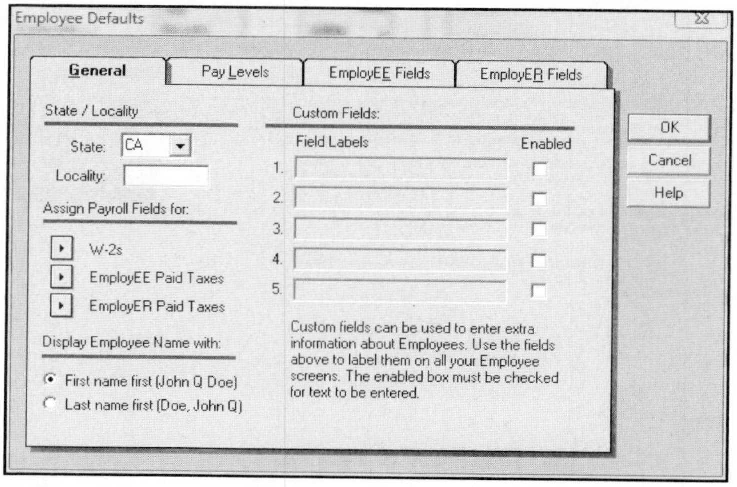

Follow these steps to enter General information in the Employee Defaults window:

1. The General tab should be selected. Notice that CA is already entered in the State field.

2. Under Assign Payroll Fields for: click on the arrow for W-2s.

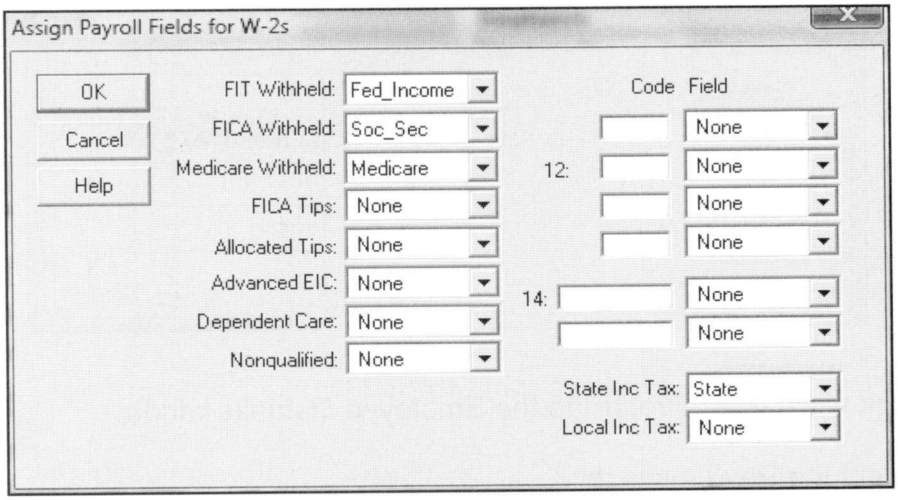

Each line on the Assign Payroll Fields for W-2s window is identified by its field number on the 2008 Form W-2 Wage and Tax Statement.

3. Click 

.

4. Click on the arrow next to EmployeEE Paid Taxes.

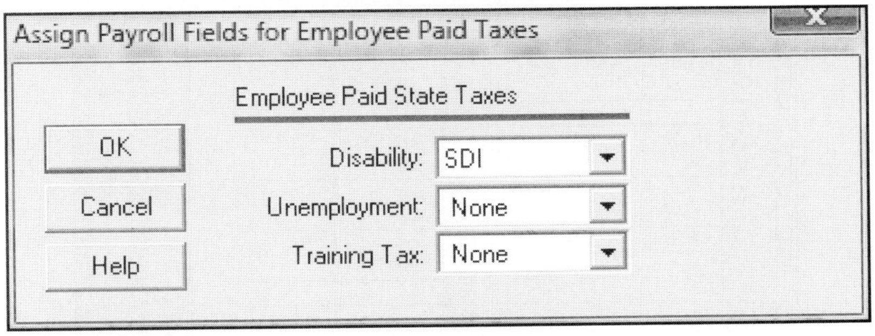

5. Click 

.

6. Click on the arrow next to EmployER Paid Taxes.

7. Click on the down-arrow in the State Disability (SDI) field. Select SDI. Compare your window to the one below.

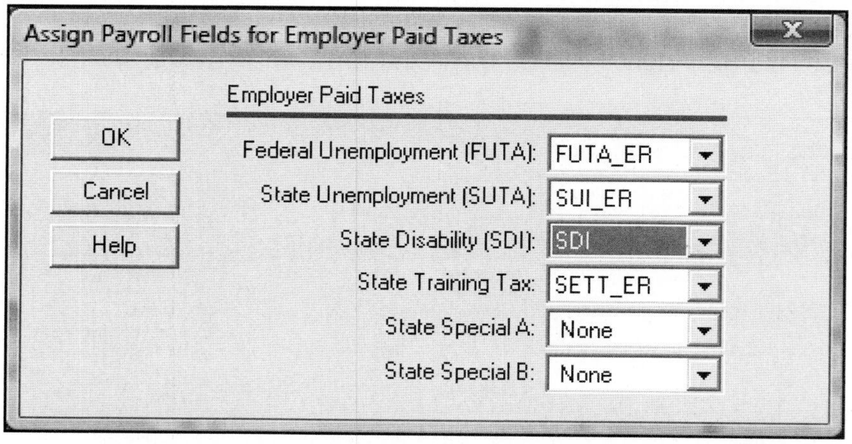

8. Click  to return to the Employee Defaults window.

9. Select the Pay Levels tab.

10. Susan's Service Merchandise employees are paid $12.50/hour and $18.75/hour for overtime. Click on the G/L Account column for Overtime. The magnifying-glass icon displays. Type or select Account No. **77600** for Overtime Expense. Press **<Enter>**.

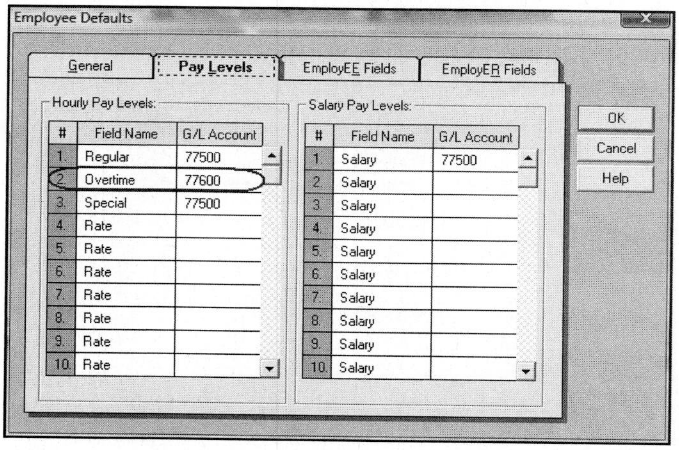

11. Click on the EmployEE Fields tab.

12. The Fed_Income line shows the default G/L Account as 23400 (Federal Payroll Taxes Payable) for FIT. This was also shown as the Tax Liability Acct: on pages 529-530, step 2. Account No. 23400, Federal Payroll Taxes Payable, is the correct account for the Fed Income line.

13. Click on the G/L Account field for Soc_Sec and select Account No. 24000, FICA Employee Taxes Payable.

14. Click on the G/L Account field for Medicare and select Account No. 24200, Medicare Employee Taxes Payable.

15. Click on the G/L Account field for State and select Account No. 23600, State Payroll Taxes Payable.

16. Click on the Tax Name field for State and select CASIT. (CASIT stands for California State Income Tax.)

17. In the G/L Account field on the SDI row, add Account No. 23650, State Disability Insurance (Other Current Liabilities) to the Chart of Accounts. (*Hint: Be sure this account is selected for SDI.)*

18. In the Tax Name field for SDI, select CASDI. (CASDI stands for California State Disability Insurance.)

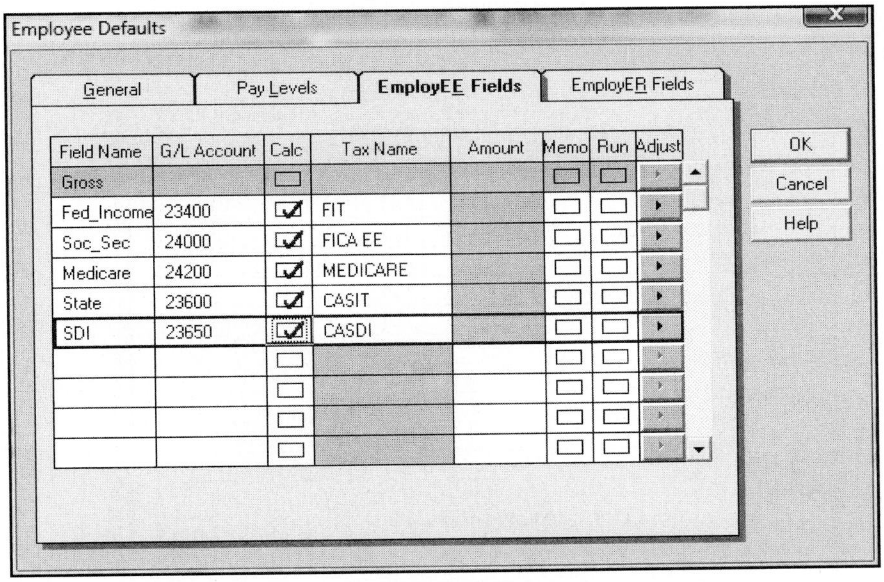

19. Click on the EmployER Fields tab. Change the following account numbers:

	Liability Column	*Expense Column*
Soc_Sec_ER	24100, FICA Employer Taxes Payable	72510, FICA Expense
Medicare_ER	24400, Medicare Employer Taxes Payable	Add Account No. 72520, Medicare Expense
FUTA_ER	23500, FUTA Tax Payable	72530, FUTA Expense
SUI_ER	23700, SUTA Payable	72540, SUTA Expense
SETT_ER	Add Account No. 23800, SETT Payable	Add Account No. 72550, SETT Expense

There is a third column to change for SUI_ER. Click on the Tax Name column for **SUI ER, then select CASUI ER. (CASUI ER stands for California State Unemployment Insurance, Employer.)

There is a third column to change for SETT_ER. Click on the Tax Name column for **SETT ER, then select CASETT ER. (CASETT ER stands for California State Training Tax, Employer.)

Compare your Employee Defaults window, EmployER Fields tab, to the one shown below.

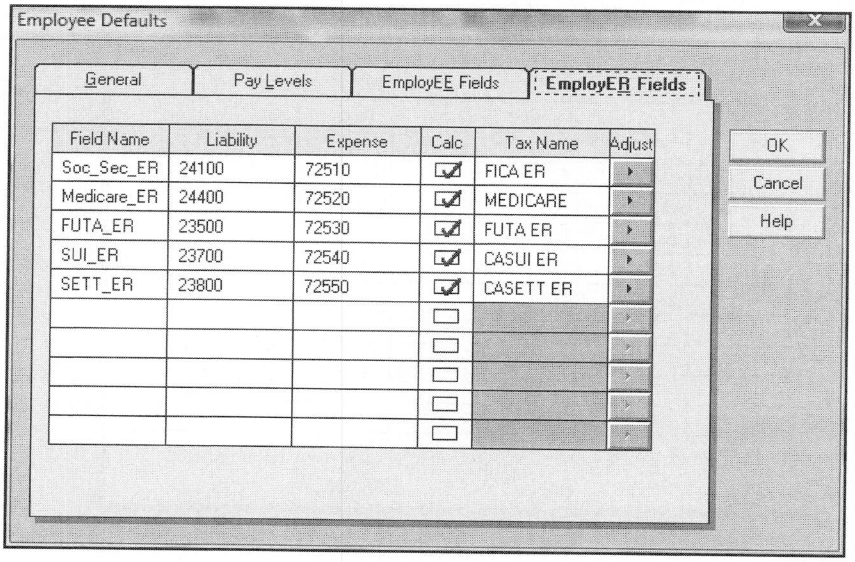

20. Make sure the EmployER Fields are selected correctly. Click 

to save your changes and return to the menu bar.

ENTERING EMPLOYEE MAINTENANCE INFORMATION

The Maintain Employees/Sales Reps window includes information about your employees or sales representatives. The information is displayed as five tabbed folders: General, Pay Info, Withholding Info, Employee Fields, and Employer Fields.

Follow these steps to set up employee maintenance information.

1. Select 

, New Employee. The Maintain Employees & Sales Reps window appears.

2. Complete the following fields.

Employee ID:	**A001**
Name:	**Terry Allen**
Accept the default for Employee	
Address:	**771 Sycamore Avenue**
City, ST Zip:	**Los Angeles, CA 90068**
Telephone 1:	**323-555-2911**
E-mail:	**terry@mail.com**
Social Security #:	**219-00-4113**
Type:	**FULL**
Hired:	**1/2/08**

3. Click on the Withholding Info tab. Complete the following fields.

Filing Status:	Single for Federal, State, and Local
Allowances:	**1** for Federal, State, and Local

Compare your Withholding Info to the Maintain Employees &Sales Reps window shown on the next page.

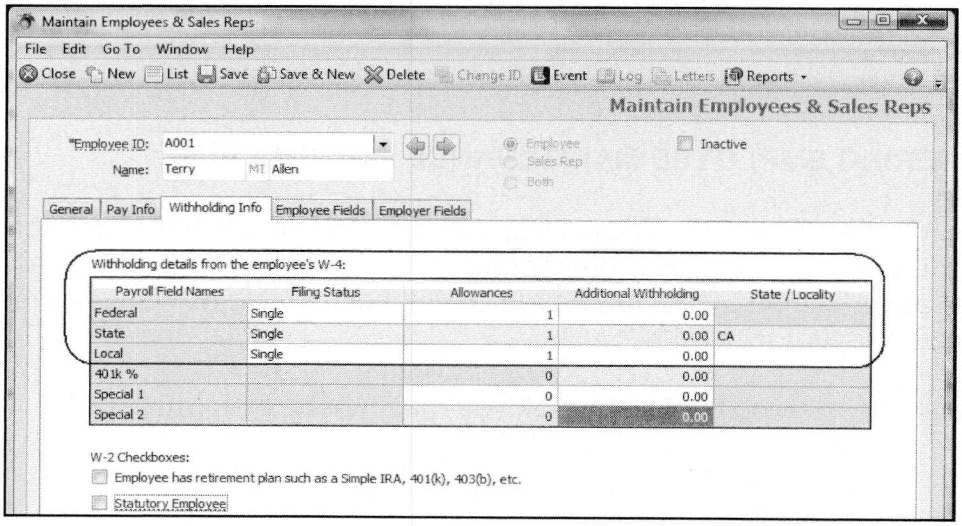

4. Click on the Pay Info tab.

5. Type **12.50** in the Hourly Rate column. Press the **<Enter>** key two times.

6. Type **18.75** in the Hourly Rate column for Overtime. Press the **<Enter>** key. Make sure that the Pay Method field displays Hourly - Hours per Pay Period, and that the Pay Frequency field displays Weekly.

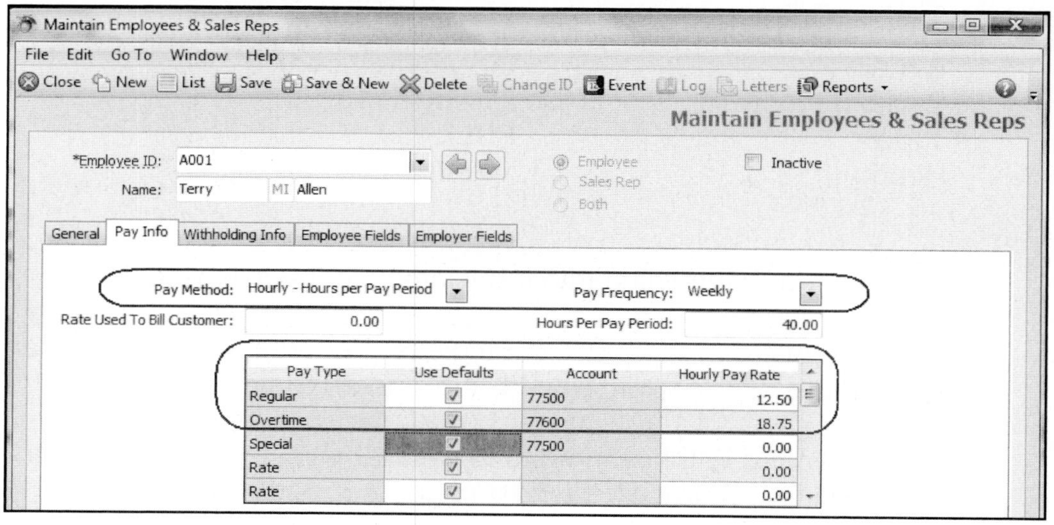

7. Select the Employee Fields tab. Notice that the Employee Default information matches the illustration on page 535, step 18.

8. Click on the Employer Fields tab. Notice that the Employer Default information matches the illustration on page 536, step 19.

9. Click 

.

10. Click on the General tab. Enter another employee.

Employee ID:	**G001**
Name:	**Lynn Goode**
Accept the default for	Employee.
Address:	**123 Highland Avenue**
City, ST Zip:	**Los Angeles, CA 90026**
Telephone 1:	**323-555-1416**
E-mail:	**lynn@mail.com**
Social Security #:	**467-00-8900**
Type:	**FULL**
Hired:	**1/2/08**

Withholding Info:

Filing Status:	**Married** for Federal, State, and Local
Allow:	**2** for Federal, State, and Local

11. Ms. Goode is paid hourly. Her regular pay is $12.50 per hour and her overtime pay is $18.75. Select the Pay Info tab and record this information.

12. Save, then close the Maintain Employee & Sales Reps window.

BACKING UP YOUR DATA

Follow these steps to back up Chapter 14 data:

1. From the Company page, link to Back up.

2. Click 

.

3. Accept the default for backing up to the hard drive or make the selections to back up to another location. Type **Chapter 14 Begin** in the File name field.

4. Click 

.

5. When the window prompts that This company backup will require approximately 3.37MB, click on 

. When the Back Up Company scale is 100% complete, you have successfully backed up to the current point in Chapter 14.

6. Continue or click on File, Exit to exit Peachtree.

PAYROLL ENTRY

Once the defaults for payroll are set up, you have very little work to do. In Chapter 4, Employees, Bellwether Garden Supply already had the default information set up. Since the payroll tax tables were included for the sample company, all you needed to do for payroll was:

- Enter or select the Employee ID.
- Specify the pay period (period-ending date).
- Verify the information the window displays (name and address of employee, amount of hours, and employee/employer fields.)
- Print or post the paycheck.

In Chapter 14, you use the payroll tax tables included with the software. The payroll tax tables provided with PCA 2008, Educational Version, are for example purposes only.

In Peachtree, the Payroll Entry window is also the ***payroll journal***. All entries made in the Payroll Entry window show up in the payroll journal, and then are posted to both the General Ledger and to the Employee file.

Payroll entry is a simple process after completing the Payroll Setup Wizard and employee/employer default and maintenance information. When you set up employee and employer defaults, you set up the liability and expense accounts for payroll. When you set up the employee maintenance information, you set up the employee's name; address; social security number; Federal, State, and Local withholding allowances; and pay levels.

All journal entries made to the Payroll Journal are posted both to the General Ledger and to the Employee file. Once an Employee ID is selected, the rest of the employee information is completed automatically. Enough information is entered in the Maintain Employees record, Default Information, and the payroll tax tables included with the software to determine what the paycheck amount should be. If the information is correct, you print or post the paycheck and proceed to the next employee.

The check amount (or net pay) is automatically credited to Account No. 10300, Payroll Checking Account. The withholding amounts are calculated based on the Payroll Fields which were also defined in the Default Information that you previously entered. The rate and frequency of pay were set up in the Employee/Sales Rep record. For Susan's Service Merchandise, employees are paid weekly.

To issue a payroll check, follow these steps:

1. From the Navigation Bar, select 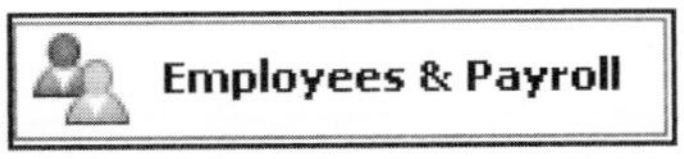

; 

, Enter Payroll For One Employee.

2. The Select a Cash Account window displays. Select the Payroll Checking Account.

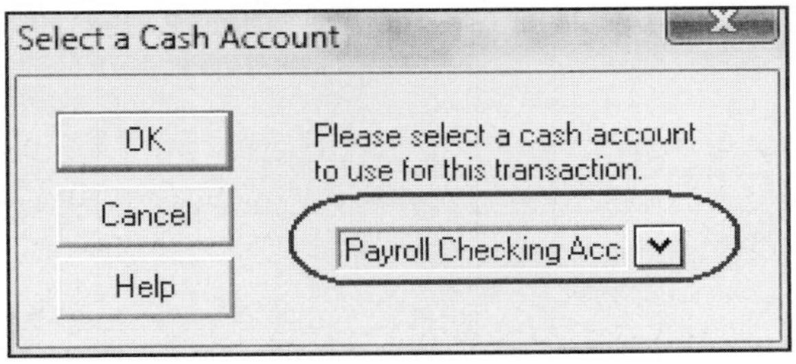

3. Click 

.

4. In the Employee ID field, select Terry Allen.

5. Leave the Check Number field blank. Type or select **4** as the Date.

6. Make sure that Account No. 10300, Payroll Checking Account, is displayed in the Cash Account field.

7. In the Pay Period End field, type **4** and press **<Enter>**.

8. Accept the default for Weeks in Pay Period which is 1 week.[3]

9. In the Hours Worked table go to the Overtime Hours field. Type **2** and press **<Enter>**.

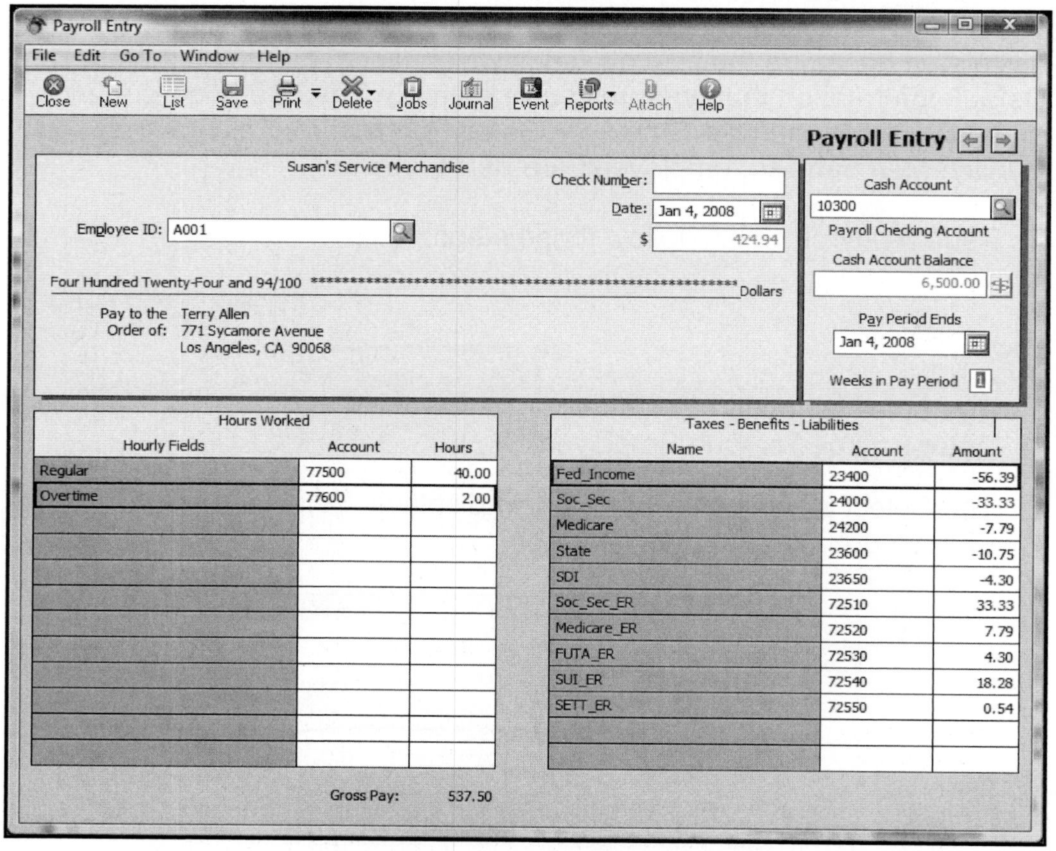

[3] Susan's Service Merchandise paid each employee a full week of wages plus overtime, when appropriate. The new employees helped set up merchandise prior to the January 2 grand opening.

Comment

Observe that the Taxes- Benefits - Liabilities table on the Payroll Entry window includes withholding amounts. These amounts are for example purposes only and do not reflect accurate payroll taxes.

A separate service provided by Peachtree Software at an additional cost includes payroll tax tables. More information about Peachtree's Payroll Tax Service is included on their website at www.peachtree.com/payroll.

10. Click 

.

11. The Print Forms: Payroll Checks window appears. Click 

. Select OCR Multi-Purpose PR Laser.

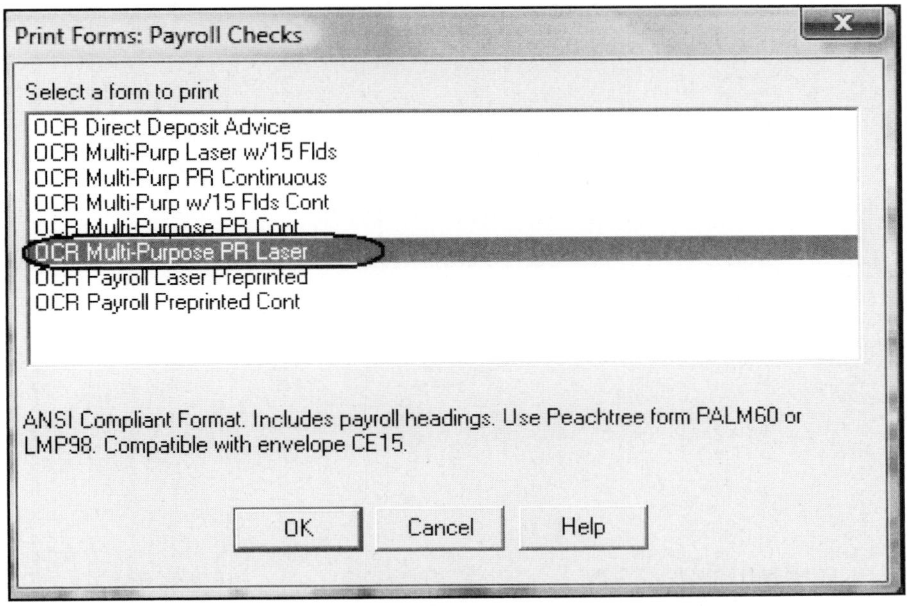

Comment

The form you select is tied to the kind of printer you are using. You may need to make a different selection depending on your printer.

12. Click 

.

13. The Print Forms: Payroll Checks window appears. Make sure that the form you chose is shown in the Last used form field.

14. Type **101** as the First check number.

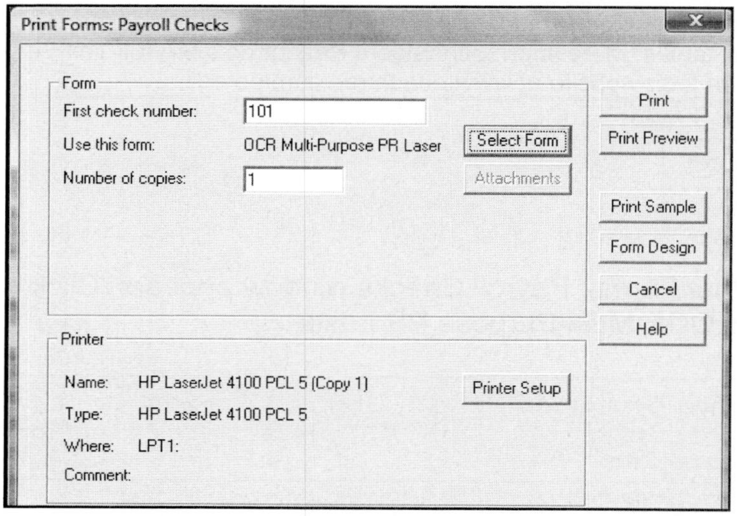

15. Click Print. Your check starts to print.

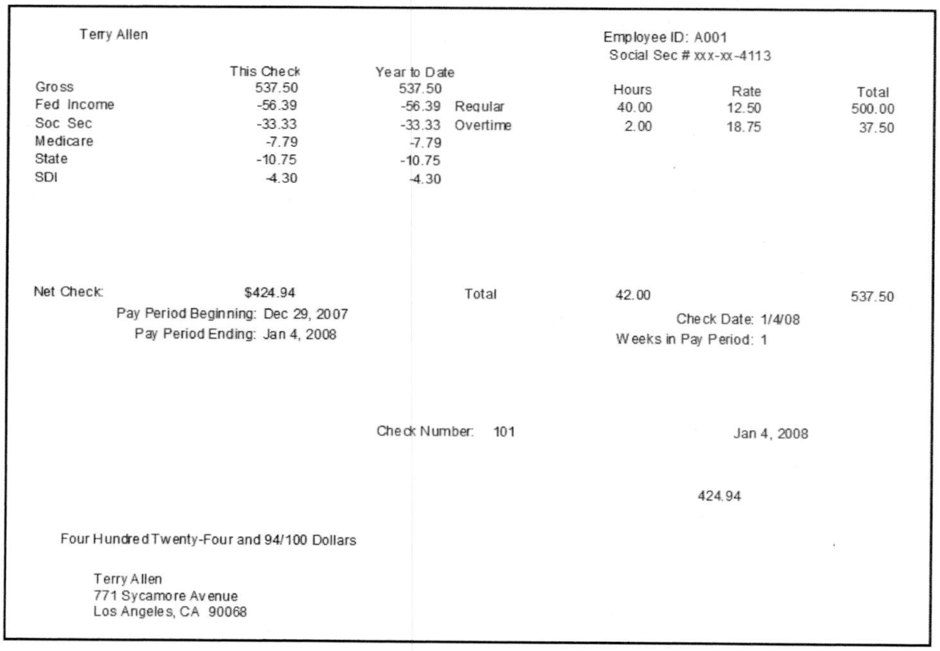

Terry Allen

Employee ID: A001
Social Sec # xxx-xx-4113

	This Check	Year to Date		Hours	Rate	Total
Gross	537.50	537.50				
Fed Income	-56.39	-56.39	Regular	40.00	12.50	500.00
Soc Sec	-33.33	-33.33	Overtime	2.00	18.75	37.50
Medicare	-7.79	-7.79				
State	-10.75	-10.75				
SDI	-4.30	-4.30				
Net Check:	$424.94		Total	42.00		537.50

Pay Period Beginning: Dec 29, 2007
Pay Period Ending: Jan 4, 2008

Check Date: 1/4/08
Weeks in Pay Period: 1

Check Number: 101

Jan 4, 2008

424.94

Four Hundred Twenty-Four and 94/100 Dollars

Terry Allen
771 Sycamore Avenue
Los Angeles, CA 90068

16. Make the selections to pay Ms. Goode on January 4, 2008. She worked 40 regular hours for Susan's Service Merchandise.

17. Print Check No. 102.

Lynn Goode

Employee ID: G001
Social Sec # xxx-xx-8900

	This Check	Year to Date		Hours	Rate	Total
Gross	500.00	500.00				
Fed Income	-21.92	-21.92	Regular	40.00	12.50	500.00
Soc Sec	-31.00	-31.00				
Medicare	-7.25	-7.25				
State	-1.72	-1.72				
SDI	-4.00	-4.00				
Net Check:	$434.11		Total	40.00		500.00

Pay Period Beginning: Dec 29, 2007
Pay Period Ending: Jan 4, 2008

Check Date: 1/4/08
Weeks in Pay Period: 1

Check Number: 102

Jan 4, 2008

434.11

Four Hundred Thirty-Four and 11/100 Dollars

Lynn Goode
123 Highland Avenue
Los Angeles, CA 90026

18. Make the following payroll entries for Terry Allen and Lynn Goode.

Date	Name	Hours Worked	Overtime	Check No.
1/11/08	T. Allen	40	1	103
	L. Goode	40	1	104
1/18/08	T. Allen	40		105
	L. Goode	40		106
1/25/08	T. Allen	40		107
	L. Goode	40		108

After recording the paycheck information, type the check number, then click 

to post. You do *not* need to print the paychecks.

19. Close the Payroll Entry window.

PRINTING THE PAYROLL JOURNAL

Follow these steps to print the Payroll Journal:

1. From the Recently Used Employee Reports area of the Employees & Payroll page, link to <u>Print</u> the Payroll Journal.

2. Make the selections to print.

Susan's Service Merchandise
Payroll Journal
For the Period From Jan 1, 2008 to Jan 31, 2008
Filter Criteria includes: Report order is by Check Date. Report is printed in Detail Format.

Date Employee	GL Acct ID	Reference	Debit Amt	Credit Amt
1/4/08	77500	101	500.00	
Terry Allen	77600		37.50	
	23400			56.39
	24000			33.33
	24200			7.79
	23600			10.75
	23650			4.30
	24100			33.33
	24400			7.79
	23500			4.30
	23700			18.28
	23800			0.54
	72510		33.33	
	72520		7.79	
	72530		4.30	
	72540		18.28	
	72550		0.54	
	10300			424.94
1/4/08	77500	102	500.00	
Lynn Goode	23400			21.92
	24000			31.00
	24200			7.25
	23600			1.72
	23650			4.00
	24100			31.00
	24400			7.25
	23500			4.00
	23700			17.00
	23800			0.50
	72510		31.00	
	72520		7.25	
	72530		4.00	
	72540		17.00	
	72550		0.50	
	10300			434.11
1/11/08	77500	103	500.00	
Terry Allen	77600		18.75	
	23400			53.58
	24000			32.16
	24200			7.52
	23600			9.63
	23650			4.15
	24100			32.16
	24400			7.52
	23500			4.15
	23700			17.64
	23800			0.52
	72510		32.16	
	72520		7.52	
	72530		4.15	
	72540		17.64	
	72550		0.52	
	10300			411.71
1/11/08	77500	104	500.00	
Lynn Goode	77600		18.75	
	23400			23.80
	24000			32.16
	24200			7.52
	23600			2.10
	23650			4.15

Susan's Service Merchandise
Payroll Journal
For the Period From Jan 1, 2008 to Jan 31, 2008
Filter Criteria includes: Report order is by Check Date. Report is printed in Detail Format.

Date Employee	GL Acct ID	Reference	Debit Amt	Credit Amt
	24100			32.16
	24400			7.52
	23500			4.15
	23700			17.64
	23800			0.52
	72510		32.16	
	72520		7.52	
	72530		4.15	
	72540		17.64	
	72550		0.52	
	10300			449.02
1/18/08	77500	105	500.00	
Terry Allen	23400			50.77
	24000			31.00
	24200			7.25
	23600			8.85
	23650			4.00
	24100			31.00
	24400			7.25
	23500			4.00
	23700			17.00
	23800			0.50
	72510		31.00	
	72520		7.25	
	72530		4.00	
	72540		17.00	
	72550		0.50	
	10300			398.13
1/18/08	77500	106	500.00	
Lynn Goode	23400			21.92
	24000			31.00
	24200			7.25
	23600			1.72
	23650			4.00
	24100			31.00
	24400			7.25
	23500			4.00
	23700			17.00
	23800			0.50
	72510		31.00	
	72520		7.25	
	72530		4.00	
	72540		17.00	
	72550		0.50	
	10300			434.11
1/25/08	77500	107	500.00	
Terry Allen	23400			50.77
	24000			31.00
	24200			7.25
	23600			8.85
	23650			4.00
	24100			31.00
	24400			7.25
	23500			4.00
	23700			17.00
	23800			0.50
	72510		31.00	
	72520		7.25	
	72530		4.00	
	72540		17.00	

Susan's Service Merchandise
Payroll Journal
For the Period From Jan 1, 2008 to Jan 31, 2008
Filter Criteria includes: Report order is by Check Date. Report is printed in Detail Format.

Date Employee	GL Acct ID	Reference	Debit Amt	Credit Amt
	72550		0.50	
	10300			398.13
1/25/08	77500	108	500.00	
Lynn Goode	23400			21.92
	24000			31.00
	24200			7.25
	23600			1.72
	23650			4.00
	24100			31.00
	24400			7.25
	23500			4.00
	23700			17.00
	23800			0.50
	72510		31.00	
	72520		7.25	
	72530		4.00	
	72540		17.00	
	72550		0.50	
	10300			434.11
			4,561.97	4,561.97

ACCOUNT RECONCILIATION

In Chapters 11-14, you worked with Peachtree's accounts payable, accounts receivable, inventory, and payroll systems. PCA's general ledger is integrated with the other parts of the program. For example, when a vendor is paid, that entry is recorded in *both* the general ledger, La Brea Bank *and* Accounts Payable accounts, and the individual vendor's account. In other words, the subsidiary ledger (vendor ledger) works together with the general ledger.

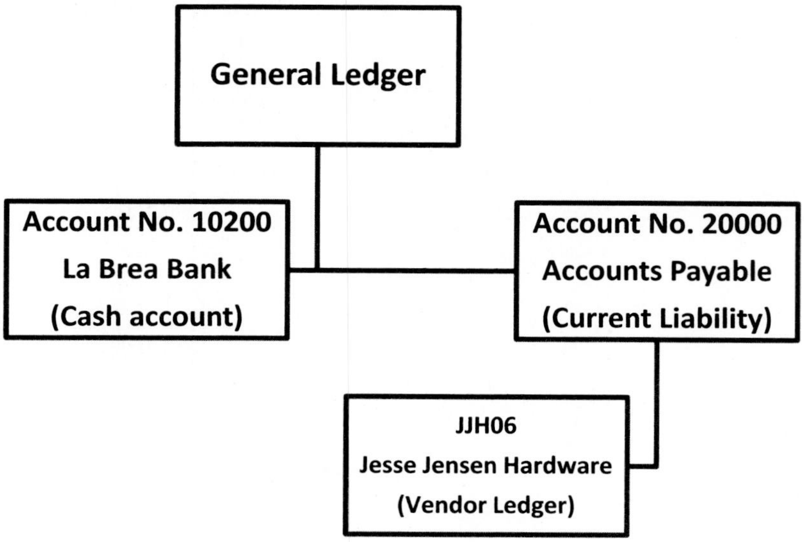

To see how this works, you are going to reconcile two bank statements.

- The January 31, 2008 bank statement from La Brea Bank on this page and page 550.
- The January 31, 2008 bank statement from the Payroll Checking Account, page 550.

Then, you are going to check the accounts receivable, accounts payable, and merchandise inventory account balances against the general ledger. This shows you that Peachtree's subsidiary ledgers (customer ledgers, vendor ledgers, and inventory valuation) are in agreement with the associated general ledger accounts.

La Brea Bank Statement

You may want to review the steps for Account Reconciliation in Chapter 9, pages 292-294.

Statement of Account La Brea Bank January 1 to January 31, 2008		Account No. 82183-44-01		Susan's Service Merchandise 7709 Wilshire Boulevard Los Angeles, CA 90060	
REGULAR CHECKING					
Previous Balance		12/31/07	71,500.00		
8 Deposits(+)			3,606.88		
11 Checks (-)			9,446.63		
Service Charges (-)		1/31/08	18.00		
Ending Balance		1/31/08	**65,642.25**		
DEPOSITS					
1/15/08	324.00	1/24/08	1,404.00	1/29/08	693.88[4]
1/22/08	324.00	1/25/08	324.00	1/30/08	216.00
1/23/08	105.00	1/26/08	216.00		
CHECKS (Asterisk * indicates break in check number sequence)					
		1/5/08	Transfer	6,500.00	
		1/1/08	3030	160.00	

[4]On January 28, 2008, two deposits were made–53.88 + 640 = 693.88. (Refer to page 483, Cash Receipts Journal.)

	1/24/08	3031	41.00	
	1/24/08	3032	107.65	
	1/27/08	3033	72.14	
	1/27/08	3034	500.00	
	1/27/08	3035	500.00	
	1/28/08	3036	370.44	
	1/31/08	3037	392.00	
	1/31/08	3038	117.60	
	1/31/08	3039	685.80	

Payroll Checking Account Bank Statement

Statement of Account Payroll Checking Account January 1 to January 31, 2008	Account No. 391-4388123		Susan's Service Merchandise 7709 Wilshire Boulevard Los Angeles, CA 90060	
REGULAR CHECKING				
Previous Balance	12/31/08	0.00		
1 Deposits(+)		6,500.00		
6 Checks (-)		2,552.02		
Service Charges (-)	1/31/08	15.00		
Ending Balance	1/31/08	**3,932.98**		
DEPOSITS				
	1/5/08	6,500.00		
CHECKS (Asterisk * indicates break in check number sequence)				
	1/8/08	101	424.94	
	1/8/08	102	434.11	
	1/14/08	103	411.71	
	1/14/08	104	449.02	
	1/14/08	105	398.13	
	1/31/08	106	434.11	

Printing Reports: Account Reconciliation, Accounts Receivable, Accounts Payable, and Inventory

1. Print the La Brea Bank account reconciliation report.

Susan's Service Merchandise
Account Reconciliation
As of Jan 31, 2008
10200 - La Brea Bank
Bank Statement Date: January 31, 2008

Filter Criteria includes: Report is printed in Detail Format.

Beginning GL Balance				71,500.00
Add: Cash Receipts				5,982.88
Less: Cash Disbursements				(3,946.63)
Add (Less) Other				(6,518.00)
Ending GL Balance				67,018.25
Ending Bank Balance				65,642.25
Add back deposits in transit				
	Jan 30, 2008	01/30/08	2,376.00	
Total deposits in transit				2,376.00
(Less) outstanding checks				
	Jan 30, 2008	3040	(500.00)	
	Jan 30, 2008	3041	(500.00)	
Total outstanding checks				(1,000.00)
Add (Less) Other				
Total other				
Unreconciled difference				0.00
Ending GL Balance				67,018.25

2. Print the Payroll Checking Account reconciliation report. (*Hint:* On the Accounting Reconciliation Select a Report or Form window, click 

. In the Select a filter filed, select Account No. 10300, Payroll Checking Account.)

Susan's Service Merchandise
Account Reconciliation
As of Jan 31, 2008
10300 - Payroll Checking Account
Bank Statement Date: January 31, 2008

Filter Criteria includes: Report is printed in Detail Format.

Beginning GL Balance				
Add: Cash Receipts				
Less: Cash Disbursements				(3,384.26)
Add (Less) Other				6,485.00
Ending GL Balance				3,100.74
Ending Bank Balance				3,932.98
Add back deposits in transi				
Total deposits in transit				
(Less) outstanding checks				
	Jan 25, 2008	107	(398.13)	
	Jan 25, 2008	108	(434.11)	
Total outstanding checks				(832.24)
Add (Less) Other				
Total other				
Unreconciled difference				0.00
Ending GL Balance				3,100.74

3. Print the General Ledger accounts 10200 and 10300. (*Hint:* On the General Ledger Select a Report or Form window, click 

. On the Modify Report - General Ledger window, select the filter GL Account ID. Select One or more, then place a checkmark in the boxes next to 10200 and 10300. Click OK.) Observe that Account No. 10200, La Brea Bank; and Account No. 10300, Payroll Checking Account agree with the Ending GL Balances shown on the account reconciliation reports on pages 551 and 552: $67,018.25 and 3,100.74, respectively.

Susan's Service Merchandise
General Ledger
For the Period From Jan 1, 2008 to Jan 31, 2008
Filter Criteria includes: 1) IDs: Multiple IDs. Report order is by ID. Report is printed with shortened descriptions and in Detail Format.

Account ID Account Description	Date	Reference	Jrnl	Trans Description	Debit Amt	Credit Amt	Balance
10200	1/1/08			Beginning Balance			71,500.00
La Brea Bank	1/4/08		GEN	La Brea Bank		6,500.00	
	1/14/08	Invoice 103	CRJ	Phil Merchant	324.00		
	1/21/08	Invoice 101	CRJ	Alice Peters	324.00		
	1/22/08	Invoice 104	CRJ	Judy Prince	105.00		
	1/23/08	3030	CDJ	Dave Heinrich		160.00	
	1/23/08	3031	CDJ	U.S. Post Office		41.00	
	1/23/08	3032	CDJ	Century City Office		107.65	
	1/23/08	3033	CDJ	RCT Phone Co.		72.14	
	1/23/08	Cash	CRJ	Cash	1,404.00		
	1/24/08	3034	CDJ	Joe Greene		500.00	
	1/24/08	3035	CDJ	Susan Currier		500.00	
	1/24/08	3036	CDJ	Lyle Lewis Product		370.44	
	1/24/08	Invoice 106	CRJ	Alice Peters	324.00		
	1/26/08	Invoice 108	CRJ	Phil Merchant	216.00		
	1/28/08	3037	CDJ	Jesse Jensen Hard		392.00	
	1/28/08	3038	CDJ	Ronald Baker Fabri		117.60	
	1/28/08	Invoice 105	CRJ	Betty Barton	53.88		
	1/28/08	Invoice 102	CRJ	Doris Conlin	640.00		
	1/29/08	Cash	CRJ	Harriet Wilson	216.00		
	1/30/08	3039	CDJ	TMI Mortgage Co.		685.80	
	1/30/08	3040	CDJ	Joe Greene		500.00	
	1/30/08	3041	CDJ	Susan Currier		500.00	
	1/30/08	Cash	CRJ	Cash	2,376.00		
	1/31/08	01/31/08	GEN	Service Charge		18.00	
				Current Period Cha	5,982.88	10,464.63	-4,481.75
	1/31/08			**Ending Balance**			**67,018.25**
10300	1/1/08			Beginning Balance			
Payroll Checking Acc	1/4/08		GEN	Payroll Checking A	6,500.00		
	1/4/08	101	PRJ	Terry Allen		424.94	
	1/4/08	102	PRJ	Lynn Goode		434.11	
	1/11/08	103	PRJ	Terry Allen		411.71	
	1/11/08	104	PRJ	Lynn Goode		449.02	
	1/18/08	105	PRJ	Terry Allen		398.13	
	1/18/08	106	PRJ	Lynn Goode		434.11	
	1/25/08	107	PRJ	Terry Allen		398.13	
	1/25/08	108	PRJ	Lynn Goode		434.11	
	1/31/08	01/31/08	GEN	Service Charge		15.00	
				Current Period Cha	6,500.00	3,399.26	3,100.74
	1/31/08			**Ending Balance**			**3,100.74**

4. Print the general ledger account balance for Account No. 11000, Accounts Receivable.

Susan's Service Merchandise
General Ledger
For the Period From Jan 1, 2008 to Jan 31, 2008
Filter Criteria includes: 1) IDs: 11000. Report order is by ID. Report is printed with shortened descriptions and in Detail Format.

Account ID Account Description	Date	Reference	Jrnl	Trans Description	Debit Amt	Credit Amt	Balance
11000	1/1/08			Beginning Balance			
Accounts Receivable	1/6/08	101	SJ	Alice Peters	324.00		
	1/6/08	102	SJ	Doris Conlin	640.00		
	1/6/08	103	SJ	Phil Merchant	432.00		
	1/6/08	104	SJ	Judy Prince	486.00		
	1/9/08	105	SJ	Betty Barton	53.88		
	1/14/08	CM103	SJ	Phil Merchant		108.00	
	1/14/08	Invoice 103	CRJ	Phil Merchant - Inv		324.00	
	1/19/08	106	SJ	Alice Peters	324.00		
	1/19/08	107	SJ	Doris Conlin	320.00		
	1/19/08	108	SJ	Phil Merchant	216.00		
	1/20/08	109	SJ	Betty Barton	81.00		
	1/21/08	Invoice 101	CRJ	Alice Peters - Invoi		324.00	
	1/22/08	Invoice 104	CRJ	Judy Prince - Invoi		105.00	
	1/24/08	Invoice 106	CRJ	Alice Peters - Invoi		324.00	
	1/26/08	Invoice 108	CRJ	Phil Merchant - Inv		216.00	
	1/28/08	Invoice 105	CRJ	Betty Barton - Invoi		53.88	
	1/28/08	Invoice 102	CRJ	Doris Conlin - Invoi		640.00	
				Current Period Cha	2,876.88	2,094.88	782.00
	1/31/08			**Ending Balance**			**782.00**

5. Compare the general ledger's accounts receivable balance to the customer ledgers balance.

Susan's Service Merchandise
Customer Ledgers
For the Period From Jan 1, 2008 to Jan 31, 2008
Filter Criteria includes: Report order is by ID. Report is printed in Detail Format.

Customer ID Customer	Date	Trans No	Type	Debit Amt	Credit Amt	Balance
ap001	1/6/08	101	SJ	324.00		324.00
Alice Peters	1/19/08	106	SJ	324.00		648.00
	1/21/08	Invoice 101	CRJ		324.00	324.00
	1/24/08	Invoice 106	CRJ		324.00	0.00
bb002	1/9/08	105	SJ	53.88		53.88
Betty Barton	1/20/08	109	SJ	81.00		134.88
	1/28/08	Invoice 105	CRJ		53.88	81.00
dc003	1/6/08	102	SJ	640.00		640.00
Doris Conlin	1/19/08	107	SJ	320.00		960.00
	1/28/08	Invoice 102	CRJ		640.00	320.00
jp004	1/6/08	104	SJ	486.00		486.00
Judy Prince	1/22/08	Invoice 104	CRJ		105.00	381.00
pm005	1/6/08	103	SJ	432.00		432.00
Phil Merchant	1/14/08	CM103	SJ		108.00	324.00
	1/14/08	Invoice 103	CRJ		324.00	0.00
	1/19/08	108	SJ	216.00		216.00
	1/26/08	Invoice 108	CRJ		216.00	0.00
Report Total				**2,876.88**	**2,094.88**	**782.00**

6. Print the general ledger account balance for Account No. 20000, Account Payable. (A minus sign in front of a general ledger balance means it is a credit balance.)

Susan's Service Merchandise
General Ledger
For the Period From Jan 1, 2008 to Jan 31, 2008
Filter Criteria includes: 1) IDs: 20000. Report order is by ID. Report is printed with shortened descriptions and in Detail Format.

Account ID Account Description	Date	Reference	Jrnl	Trans Description	Debit Amt	Credit Amt	Balance
20000	1/1/08			Beginning Balance			
Accounts Payable	1/2/08	56JJ	PJ	Jesse Jensen Hard		300.00	
	1/14/08	112	PJ	Taylor Sales and S		512.00	
	1/20/08	90	PJ	Lyle Lewis Product		432.00	
	1/20/08	210	PJ	Ronald Baker Fabri		120.00	
	1/20/08	78JJ	PJ	Jesse Jensen Hard		500.00	
	1/24/08	VCM90	PJ	Lyle Lewis Product	54.00		
	1/24/08	3036	CDJ	Lyle Lewis Product	378.00		
	1/28/08	VCM78JJ	PJ	Jesse Jensen Hard	100.00		
	1/28/08	3037	CDJ	Jesse Jensen Hard	400.00		
	1/28/08	3038	CDJ	Ronald Baker Fabri	120.00		
				Current Period Cha	1,052.00	1,864.00	-812.00
	1/31/08			**Ending Balance**			**-812.00**

7. Compare the general ledger's accounts payable balance to the vendor ledgers balance.

Susan's Service Merchandise
Vendor Ledgers
For the Period From Jan 1, 2008 to Jan 31, 2008
Filter Criteria includes: Report order is by ID.

Vendor ID Vendor	Date	Trans No	Type	Paid	Debit Amt	Credit Amt	Balance
JJH06	1/2/08	56JJ	PJ			300.00	300.00
Jesse Jensen Hardware	1/20/08	78JJ	PJ	*		500.00	800.00
	1/28/08	VCM78JJ	PJ	*	100.00		700.00
	1/28/08	3037	CDJ		8.00	8.00	700.00
	1/28/08	3037	CDJ		400.00		300.00
LLP07	1/20/08	90	PJ	*		432.00	432.00
Lyle Lewis Products	1/24/08	VCM90	PJ	*	54.00		378.00
	1/24/08	3036	CDJ		7.56	7.56	378.00
	1/24/08	3036	CDJ		378.00		0.00
RBF08	1/20/08	210	PJ	*		120.00	120.00
Ronald Baker Fabrics	1/28/08	3038	CDJ		2.40	2.40	120.00
	1/28/08	3038	CDJ		120.00		0.00
TSS09	1/14/08	112	PJ			512.00	512.00
Taylor Sales and Service							
Report Total					**1,069.96**	**1,881.96**	**812.00**

8. Print the general ledger account balance for Account No. 12000, Merchandise Inventory.

Susan's Service Merchandise
General Ledger
For the Period From Jan 1, 2008 to Jan 31, 2008
Filter Criteria includes: 1) IDs: 12000. Report order is by ID. Report is printed with shortened descriptions and in Detail Format.

Account ID Account Description	Date	Reference	Jrnl	Trans Description	Debit Amt	Credit Amt	Balance
12000	1/1/08			Beginning Balance			27,740.00
Merchandise Inventor	1/2/08	56JJ	PJ	Jesse Jensen Hard	300.00		
	1/6/08	101	CO	Alice Peters - Item:		100.00	
	1/6/08	102	CO	Doris Conlin - Item		216.00	
	1/6/08	103	CO	Phil Merchant - Ite		120.00	
	1/6/08	104	CO	Judy Prince - Item:		150.00	
	1/14/08	CM103	CO	Phil Merchant - Ite	30.00		
	1/14/08	112	PJ	Taylor Sales and S	512.00		
	1/15/08	JG	INAJ	lighting		128.00	
	1/19/08	106	CO	Alice Peters - Item:		100.00	
	1/19/08	107	CO	Doris Conlin - Item		108.00	
	1/19/08	108	CO	Phil Merchant - Ite		60.00	
	1/20/08	90	PJ	Lyle Lewis Product	432.00		
	1/20/08	210	PJ	Ronald Baker Fabri	120.00		
	1/20/08	78JJ	PJ	Jesse Jensen Hard	500.00		
	1/23/08	Cash	CO	Cash - Item: 001ha		100.00	
	1/23/08	Cash	CO	Cash - Item: 002w		300.00	
	1/24/08	VCM90	PJ	Lyle Lewis Product		54.00	
	1/28/08	VCM78JJ	PJ	Jesse Jensen Hard		100.00	
	1/29/08	Cash	CO	Harriet Wilson - Ite		60.00	
	1/30/08	Cash	CO	Cash - Item: 002w		300.00	
	1/30/08	Cash	CO	Cash - Item: 001ha		400.00	
				Current Period Cha	1,894.00	2,296.00	-402.00
	1/31/08			**Ending Balance**			**27,338.00**

9. Compare the general ledger's merchandise inventory account balance to the Inventory Valuation Report's item value. (*Hint:* From the Reports list, select Inventory; Inventory Valuation Report.)

Susan's Service Merchandise
Inventory Valuation Report
As of Jan 31, 2008
Filter Criteria includes: 1) Stock/Assembly. Report order is by ID. Report is printed with shortened descriptions.

Item ID Item Class	Item Descriptio	Stocking U/M	Cost Method	Qty on Han	Item Value	Avg Cos	% of Inv Valu
001hardware Stock item	hardware	each	Average	87.00	4,350.00	50.00	15.91
002wall Stock item	wall	each	Average	125.00	3,750.00	30.00	13.72
003floor Stock item	floor	each	Average	201.00	10,854.00	54.00	39.70
004lights Stock item	lighting	each	Average	131.00	8,384.00	64.00	30.67
					27,338.00		**100.00**

PRINTING THE GENERAL LEDGER TRIAL BALANCE

1. In the Reports list, select General Ledger. In the General Ledger: Account Information list, select General Ledger Trial Balance.

2. Make the selections to print.

Susan's Service Merchandise
General Ledger Trial Balance
As of Jan 31, 2008

Filter Criteria includes: Report order is by ID. Report is printed in Detail Format.

Account ID	Account Description	Debit Amt	Credit Amt
10200	La Brea Bank	67,018.25	
10300	Payroll Checking Account	3,100.74	
10400	Worldwide Savings & Loan	20,000.00	
11000	Accounts Receivable	782.00	
12000	Merchandise Inventory	27,338.00	
13000	Supplies	1,750.00	
14000	Prepaid Insurance	2,400.00	
15000	Furniture and Fixtures	5,000.00	
15100	Computers & Equipment	7,500.00	
15500	Building	100,000.00	
20000	Accounts Payable		812.00
23100	Sales Tax Payable		429.99
23400	Federal Payroll Taxes Payable		301.07
23500	FUTA Tax Payable		32.60
23600	State Payroll Taxes Payable		45.34
23650	State Disability Insurance		32.60
23700	SUTA Payable		138.56
23800	SETT Payable		4.08
24000	FICA Employee Taxes Payable		252.65
24100	FICA Employer Taxes Payable		252.65
24200	Medicare Employee Taxes Payabl		59.08
24400	Medicare Employer Taxes Payabl		59.08
27000	Long-Term Notes Payable		20,500.00
27400	Mortgage Payable		74,412.05
39006	Joe Greene, Capital		70,195.00
39007	Joe Greene, Drawing	1,000.00	
39008	Susan Currier, Capital		70,195.00
39009	Susan Currier, Drawing	1,000.00	
40000	Sales-Hardware		2,550.00
40200	Sales-Wall		2,700.00
40400	Sales-Floor		960.00
40600	Service Fees		124.89
50000	Cost of Sales-Hardware	850.00	
50500	Cost of Sales-Wall	810.00	
57000	Cost of Sales-Floor	324.00	
57050	Cost of Sales-Lights	128.00	
59500	Purchase Discounts		17.96
62000	Bank Charges	33.00	
67500	Interest Expense	97.85	
70000	Maintenance Expense	160.00	
72510	FICA Expense	252.65	
72520	Medicare Expense	59.08	
72540	SUTA Expense	138.56	
72550	SETT Expense	4.08	
73500	Postage Expense	41.00	
75500	Supplies Expense	107.65	
76000	Telephone Expense	72.14	
77500	Wages Expense	4,000.00	
77600	Overtime Expense	75.00	
	Total:	**244,074.60**	**244,074.60**

PRINTING THE FINANCIAL STATEMENTS

1. Print the <Standard> Balance Sheet.

Susan's Service Merchandise
Balance Sheet
January 31, 2008

ASSETS

Current Assets				
La Brea Bank	$	67,018.25		
Payroll Checking Account		3,100.74		
Worldwide Savings & Loan		20,000.00		
Accounts Receivable		782.00		
Merchandise Inventory		27,338.00		
Supplies		1,750.00		
Prepaid Insurance		2,400.00		
Total Current Assets				122,388.99
Property and Equipment				
Furniture and Fixtures		5,000.00		
Computers & Equipment		7,500.00		
Building		100,000.00		
Total Property and Equipment				112,500.00
Other Assets				
Total Other Assets				0.00
Total Assets			$	234,888.99

LIABILITIES AND CAPITAL

Current Liabilities				
Accounts Payable	$	812.00		
Sales Tax Payable		429.99		
Federal Payroll Taxes Payable		301.07		
FUTA Tax Payable		32.60		
State Payroll Taxes Payable		45.34		
State Disability Insurance		32.60		
SUTA Payable		138.56		
SETT Payable		4.08		
FICA Employee Taxes Payable		252.65		
FICA Employer Taxes Payable		252.65		
Medicare Employee Taxes Payabl		59.08		
Medicare Employer Taxes Payabl		59.08		
Total Current Liabilities				2,419.70
Long-Term Liabilities				
Long-Term Notes Payable		20,500.00		
Mortgage Payable		74,412.05		
Total Long-Term Liabilities				94,912.05
Total Liabilities				97,331.75
Capital				
Joe Greene, Capital		70,195.00		
Joe Greene, Drawing		(1,000.00)		
Susan Currier, Capital		70,195.00		
Susan Currier, Drawing		(1,000.00)		
Net Income		(832.76)		
Total Capital				137,557.24
Total Liabilities & Capital			$	234,888.99

2. Print the <Standard> Income Stmnt (Income Statement).

Susan's Service Merchandise
Income Statement
For the One Month Ending January 31, 2008

	Current Month		Year to Date	
Revenues				
Sales-Hardware	$ 2,550.00	40.25	$ 2,550.00	40.25
Sales-Wall	2,700.00	42.62	2,700.00	42.62
Sales-Floor	960.00	15.15	960.00	15.15
Service Fees	124.89	1.97	124.89	1.97
Total Revenues	6,334.89	100.00	6,334.89	100.00
Cost of Sales				
Cost of Sales-Hardware	850.00	13.42	850.00	13.42
Cost of Sales-Wall	810.00	12.79	810.00	12.79
Cost of Sales-Floor	324.00	5.11	324.00	5.11
Cost of Sales-Lights	128.00	2.02	128.00	2.02
Purchase Discounts	(17.96)	(0.28)	(17.96)	(0.28)
Total Cost of Sales	2,094.04	33.06	2,094.04	33.06
Gross Profit	4,240.85	66.94	4,240.85	66.94
Expenses				
Bank Charges	33.00	0.52	33.00	0.52
Interest Expense	97.85	1.54	97.85	1.54
Maintenance Expense	160.00	2.53	160.00	2.53
FICA Expense	252.65	3.99	252.65	3.99
Medicare Expense	59.08	0.93	59.08	0.93
FUTA Expense	32.60	0.51	32.60	0.51
SUTA Expense	138.56	2.19	138.56	2.19
SETT Expense	4.08	0.06	4.08	0.06
Postage Expense	41.00	0.65	41.00	0.65
Supplies Expense	107.65	1.70	107.65	1.70
Telephone Expense	72.14	1.14	72.14	1.14
Wages Expense	4,000.00	63.14	4,000.00	63.14
Overtime Expense	75.00	1.18	75.00	1.18
Total Expenses	5,073.61	80.09	5,073.61	80.09
Net Income	$ (832.76)	(13.15)	$ (832.76)	(13.15)

3. Print the <Standard> Cash Flow.

Susan's Service Merchandise
Statement of Cash Flow
For the one Month Ended January 31, 2008

	Current Month	Year to Date
Cash Flows from operating activities		
Net Income	$ (832.76)	$ (832.76)
Adjustments to reconcile net income to net cash provided by operating activities		
Accounts Receivable	(782.00)	(782.00)
Merchandise Inventory	402.00	402.00
Accounts Payable	812.00	812.00
Sales Tax Payable	429.99	429.99
Federal Payroll Taxes Payable	301.07	301.07
FUTA Tax Payable	32.60	32.60
State Payroll Taxes Payable	45.34	45.34
State Disability Insurance	32.60	32.60
SUTA Payable	138.56	138.56
SETT Payable	4.08	4.08
FICA Employee Taxes Payable	252.65	252.65
FICA Employer Taxes Payable	252.65	252.65
Medicare Employee Taxes Payabl	59.08	59.08
Medicare Employer Taxes Payabl	59.08	59.08
Total Adjustments	2,039.70	2,039.70
Net Cash provided by Operations	1,206.94	1,206.94
Cash Flows from investing activities		
Used For		
Net cash used in investing	0.00	0.00
Cash Flows from financing activities		
Proceeds From		
Used For		
Mortgage Payable	(587.95)	(587.95)
Joe Greene, Drawing	(1,000.00)	(1,000.00)
Susan Currier, Drawing	(1,000.00)	(1,000.00)
Net cash used in financing	(2,587.95)	(2,587.95)
Net increase <decrease> in cash	$ (1,381.01)	$ (1,381.01)
Summary		
Cash Balance at End of Period	$ 90,118.99	$ 90,118.99
Cash Balance at Beg of Period	(91,500.00)	(91,500.00)
Net Increase <Decrease> in Cash	$ (1,381.01)	$ (1,381.01)

BACKING UP CHAPTER 14 DATA

Follow these steps to back up Chapter 14 data:

1. From the Company page, link to Back up.

2. Click Back Up.

3. Accept the default for backing up to the hard drive or make the selections to back up to another location. Type **Chapter 14** in the File name field.

4. Click Save.

5. When the window prompts that This company backup will require approximately 3.40MB, click on OK. When the Back Up Company scale is 100% complete, you have successfully backed up to the current point in Chapter 14.

6. Continue or click on File, Exit to exit Peachtree.

INTERNET ACTIVITY	
1.	From your Internet browser, go to the book's website at http://www.mhhe.com/yacht2008.
2.	Link to Student Edition.
3.	In the Course-wide Content list, link to Part 3 Internet Activities for Chapters 11-14. Open or Save. (You can also choose Chapter 14, then link to Internet Activities. If you Choose a Chapter, observe that other chapter-specific links are available; for example, Quizzes, PowerPoints, and Going to the Net Exercises.)
4.	Complete the SALARY WIZARD-Chapter 14 exercise. Read steps 1-5.
5.	Follow the steps shown on the book's website to complete this Internet activity.
6.	Using a word processing program write a brief summary of what you find. Include all appropriate website addresses.

SUMMARY AND REVIEW

SOFTWARE OBJECTIVES: In Chapter 14, you used the software to:

1. Explore the Payroll Setup Wizard.
2. Enter initial payroll fields.
3. Enter employee and employer default information.
4. Journalize and post Payroll Journal entries.
5. Print paychecks.
6. Reconcile La Brea Bank Account and the Payroll Checking Account.
7. Compare the vendor ledgers, customer ledgers, and inventory valuation report to the associated general ledger accounts.
8. Print the financial statements.
9. Make four backups: two for Susan's Service Merchandise; two for the end-of-chapter exercises.

WEB OBJECTIVES: In Chapter 14, you did these Internet activities:

1. Used your Internet browser to go to the book's website.
2. Went to the Internet Activity link on the book's website. Then, selected WEB EXERCISES PART 3. Completed the fourth web exercise in Part 3— Salary Calculator.
3. Used a word processing program to write a summary of the websites that you visited.

GOING TO THE NET

Access the Employer Reporting and Instructions website at http://www.ssa.gov/employer/. Link to General W-2 Filing Information, then answer these questions.

1. What are dates that employers must send W-2 information to the Social Security Administration? (Include the dates for *both* electronic and paper filing.)
2. When must employers give employees their W-2?
3. What two forms do employers send to the Social Security Administration?

Multiple-Choice Questions: In the space provided, write the letter that best answers each question. (*The questions that follow assume PCA 2008, Educational Version, payroll tax amounts were used.*)

_____1. The cash account to credit when disbursing checks for Susan's Service Merchandise employees is:

a. Account No. 10200, La Brea Bank.
b. Account No. 10300, Payroll Checking Account.
c. Account No. 23200, Wages Payable.
d. Account No. 77500, Wages Expense.
e. None of the above.

_____2. The amount withheld from employees' paychecks depend on:

a. How many employees a company has.
b. The amount withheld changes on every paycheck.
c. There are no withholdings.
d. The number of withholding allowances.
e. None of the above.

_____3. Guidelines for employee and employer withholdings are found in the following IRS publication:

a. Circular E, Employer's Tax Guide.
b. Circular E, Employee's Tax Guide.
c. Circular F, Employee/Employer Tax Guide.
d. Both a. and b.
e. None of the above.

_____4. On the Maintain Employees/Sales Reps window, you enter the following types of information:

a. Employee name, address, and telephone number.
b. The way an employee is paid.
c. Tax filing status and withholding allowances.
d. All of the above.
e. None of the above.

_____5. Terry Allen received a January 4 paycheck in the amount of:

a. $495.00.
b. $424.94
c. $400.00.
d. $550.00.
e. None of the above.

_____6. The entry in the General Journal for the transfer of funds on January 4, 2008 is:

a. Debit, Account No. 10200, La Brea Bank, $6,500; Credit, Account No. 10300, Payroll Checking Account, $6,500.
b. Debit, Account No. 10300, Payroll Checking Account, $6,500; Credit, Account No. 10200, La Brea Bank, $6,500.
c. Debit, Account No. 10400, LA Savings & Loan, $6,000; Credit, Account No. 10200, La Brea Bank, $6,000.
d. Debit, Account No. 10200, La Brea Bank, $6,500; Credit, Account No. 10400, LA Savings & Loan, $6,500.
e. None of the above.

_____7. All of these payroll tax deductions are subtracted from an employee's gross pay EXCEPT:

a. Federal income tax (FIT).
b. Social security tax (FICA).
c. Medicare tax.
d. Federal unemployment tax (FUTA).
e. None of the above.

_____8. The Gross Pay Account is:

a. Account No. 72000, Payroll Tax Expense.
b. Account No. 23400, Federal Payroll Taxes Payable.
c. Account No. 77500, Wages Expense.
d. Account No. 24000, FICA Employee Tax Payable.
e. None of the above.

_____9. Lynn Goode received a January 11 paycheck in the amount of:

a. $449.02.
b. $338.59.
c. $430.00.
d. $360.00.
e. None of the above.

_____10. The unemployment percent used for Susan's Service Merchandise is:

a. 3.4%.
b. 5.4%.
c. 4.5%.
d. Since no one is collecting unemployment compensation, Susan's Service Merchandise does not have to pay this tax.
e. None of the above.

Exercise 14-1: Follow the instructions below to complete Exercise 14-1. Exercises 11-1, 11-2, 12-1, 12-2, 13-1, and 13-2 must be completed before starting Exercise 14-1.

1. Start PCA. Open the company that you set up in Exercise 11-1, Your Name Sales & Service.

2. Restore your data from Exercise 13-1. You made this back up on page 521. To make sure you are starting with the correct data, display the General Ledger Trial balance and compare it to Exercise 13-2, step 5, page 521.

3. Journalize and post the following General Journal entry:

01/04/08	Transferred $5,450 from Account No. 10200, Eugene Bank, to Account No. 10300, Payroll Checking Account.

4. Print the January 4, 2008 General Journal.

5. Use the following information for the Payroll Setup Wizard:

   State in which you pay most of your employees: OR
   Unemployment Percent for Your Company: 3.40%
   Enter the Locality: Tri-Met

   Tri-Met is an abbreviation for the tri-metropolitan area located in Eugene, Oregon. In order for Peachtree to compute local payroll taxes properly, you must have Tri-Met in the locality field.

   Do You Want to Record Employee Meals and Tips? No

Gross Pay Acct:	77500 Wages Expense
Tax Liability Acct:	23400 Federal Payroll Taxes Payable
Tax Expense Acct:	72000 Payroll Tax Expense

   Your business does not offer a 401(k) plan, and vacation and sick time are not tracked.

6. Set up the Pay Levels for your employees using Account No. 77500 for Regular wages and Account No. 77600 for Overtime wages.

7. Use the following EmployEE Fields:

   For Fed_Income, accept the default for Account No. 23400, Federal Payroll Taxes Payable.

   Soc_Sec, Account No. 24000, FICA Employee Taxes Payable

   Medicare, Account No. 24200, Medicare Employee Taxes Payable

   State, Account No. 23600, State Payroll Taxes Payable

8. Use the following EmployER Fields:

	Liability column	*Expense column*
Soc_Sec_ER	24100, FICA Employer Taxes Payable	72510, FICA Expense
Medicare_ER	24400 Medicare Employer Taxes Payable	Add Account No. 72520, Medicare Expense (Expenses)
FUTA_ER	23500, FUTA Tax Payable	72530, FUTA Expense
LIT_ER	Add Account No. 25000 Local Payroll Taxes Payable (Other Current Liabilities)	Add Account No. 72535, Local Payroll Taxes Expense (Expenses)
SUI_ER	23700, SUTA Payable	72540, SUTA Expense

9. Add the following employees.

   Employee ID: C50
   Name: Richard Cooke
   Accept the default for Employee
   Address: 1341 Farrington Road, Apt. 1D
   City, ST Zip: Eugene, OR 97406
   Telephone 1: 541-555-8891
   E-mail: cooke@email.com
   Social Security #: 409-00-3182
   Type: FULL
   Hired: 1/2/08

Withholding Info:

Filing Status:	Single for Federal, State, and Local
Allowances:	1 for Federal, State, and Local

Pay Info: Hourly, $12.50/hour; $18.75/hour, overtime; paid weekly

Employee ID:	M60
Name:	Mindy Miller
Accept the default	for Employee
Address:	19 North First Avenue
City, ST Zip:	Eugene, OR 97401
Telephone 1:	541-555-2022
E-mail:	mindy@email.com
Social Security #:	841-99-2138
Type:	FULL
Hired:	1/2/08

Withholding Info:

Filing Status:	Married for Federal, State, and Local
Allowances:	1 for Federal, State, and Local

Pay Info: Hourly, $12.50/hour; $18.75/hour, overtime; paid weekly

10. Print an employee list. (*Hint:* Reports & Forms; Payroll, Employee List.)

11. Make a backup of your work. (Use **Exercise 14-1** as the file name.)

12. Exit PCA or continue.

Exercise 14-2: Follow the instructions below to complete Exercise 14-2.

1. Start PCA. Open your company.

2. If necessary, restore your data from Exercise 14-1.

3. On January 4, 2008, issue payroll check 6050 to Richard Cooke. Mr. Cooke worked 40 regular hours. Issue paychecks from the Payroll Checking Account. Type **6050** in the Check Number field. To post, save after each payroll transaction.

4. On January 4, 2008, issue payroll check 6051 to Mindy Miller. Ms. Miller worked 40 regular hours. (The company paid each employee a full week's wages on January 4. The two new employees helped set up merchandise prior to the January 2 grand opening.)

5. Make the following payroll entries for Richard Cooke and Mindy Miller.

Date	Name	Hours Worked	Overtime	Check No.
1/11/08	R. Cooke	40		6052
	M. Miller	40	1	6053
1/18/08	R. Cooke	40	2	6054
	M. Miller	40		6055
1/25/08	R. Cooke	40		6056
	M. Miller	40	1	6057

After recording the paycheck information, type the check number, then post. You do *not* need to print paychecks 6050–6057.

6. Print the Payroll Journal. Continue with account reconciliation on pages 570-571.

7. Complete account reconciliation for Eugene Bank.

Statement of Account Eugene Bank January 1 to January 31, 2008		Account No. 833-122-1900		Student Name Service Merchandise Student Address Student City, State, Zip	
REGULAR CHECKING					
Previous Balance		12/31/06	$60,500.00		
6 Deposits(+)			6,815.00		
8 Checks (-)			6,835.57		
Service Charges (-)		1/31/08	12.00		
Ending Balance		1/31/08	**60,467.43**		
DEPOSITS					
1/15/08	340.00	1/24/08	255.00		
1/22/08	450.00	1/25/08	900.00		
1/23/08	470.00	1/31/08	4,400.00		
CHECKS (Asterisk * indicates break in check number sequence)					
		1/15/08	Transfer	5,450.00	
		1/15/08	2020	392.00	
		1/24/08	2021	235.20	
		1/24/08	2022	125.00	
		1/27/08	2023	41.00	
		1/27/08	2024	145.72	
		1/27/08	2025	46.65	
		1/30/08	2026	400.00	

8. Complete account reconciliation for the Payroll Checking Account.

Statement of Account Payroll Checking Account January 1 to January 31, 2008	Account No. 163-3577909		Student Name Service Merchandise Student Address Student City, State, Zip	
		REGULAR CHECKING		
Previous Balance	12/31/08	0.00		
1 Deposits(+)		5,450.00		
6 Checks (-)		2,381.09		
Service Charges (-)	1/31/08	15.00		
Ending Balance	1/31/08	**3,053.91**		
		DEPOSITS		
	1/5/08	5,450.00		
	CHECKS (Asterisk * indicates break in check number sequence)			
	1/8/08	6050	376.98	
	1/8/08	6051	403.48	
	1/14/08	6052	376.98	
	1/14/08	6053	417.18	
	1/14/08	6054	402.99	
	1/31/08	6055	403.48	

9. Print the account reconciliation report for Eugene Bank.

10. Print the account reconciliation report for the Payroll Checking Account.

11. Print the Customer Ledgers; Vendor Ledgers; and Inventory Valuation report.

12. Print the General Ledger Trial Balance.

13. Print the following financial statements: Balance Sheet, Income Statement, and Statement of Cash Flow.

14. Make a backup. (Use **Exercise 14-2** as the file name.)

CHAPTER 14 INDEX

Project 2 Stanley's Sports

In Project 2, you will complete the Computer Accounting Cycle for Stanley's Sports, a merchandising business. Stanley's Sports sells mountain bicycles, road bicycles, and children's bicycles. It is organized as a corporation.

It is the purpose of Project 2 to review what you have learned in Part 3 of the book, Peachtree Complete Accounting for Merchandising Businesses. Accounts payable, accounts receivable, payroll, and inventory transactions are included in this project. Account reconciliation is also completed.

Vendors offer Stanley's Sports a purchase discount of 2% 15, Net 30 days.

A checklist is shown listing the printed reports that you should have at the end of this project. The step-by-step instructions also remind you to print reports at certain intervals.

Follow these steps to complete Project 2, Stanley's Sports:

Step 1: Start Peachtree.

Step 2: If a company opens, from the menu bar, select File; New Company; OK, Next. (*Or,* from the startup window, select Create a new Company.)

Step 3: Complete the following company information:

Company Name:	Stanley's Sports (use your last name, then the company name; for example Smith's Sports)
Address Line 1:	1635 Grand Avenue
City, State, Zip:	Phoenix, AZ 85031
Country:	USA

Telephone:	602-555-3230
Fax:	602-555-3234
Business Type:	Corporation
Federal Employer ID:	22-8482233
State Employer ID:	29-7831315
State Unemployment ID:	299148-6
Web Site:	www.stanleysports.com
E-mail:	mail@stanleysports.com

Step 4: Accept the default for Use a sample business type that closely matches your company.

Step 5: Scroll down the list. In the Detailed types list, select Retail Company.

Step 6: Accept the default for Accrual accounting.

Step 7: Accept the default for Real Time posting.

Step 8: Accept the default for 12 monthly accounting periods.

Step 9: The Choose the first period of your fiscal year window appears. If necessary, select 2008 as the year.

Step 10: At the You are ready to create your company window, click [Finish]. When the Have you started using credit cards for your Business? window appears, click [OK].

Step 11: When the Peachtree Setup Guide window appears, click on the box next to Don't show this screen at startup to place a checkmark in it. Close the Setup Guide window.

Step 12: Change the accounting period to 01-Jan 01,2008 to Jan 31, 2008—[Period 1 - 01/01/08-01/31/08].

General Ledger

1. Delete the accounts shown on the next page.

10000	Petty Cash
10100	Cash on Hand
10300	Payroll Checking Account
11500	Allowance for Doubtful Account
14200	Notes Receivable-Current
15400	Leasehold Improvements
15500	Building
15600	Building Improvements
16900	Land
17400	Accum. Depreciation - Leasehold
17500	Accum. Depreciation - Building
17600	Accum. Depreciation - Bldg Imp
19000	Deposits
19200	Note Receivable-Noncurrent
19900	Other Noncurrent Assets
23000	Accrued Expenses
24200	Current Portion Long-Term Debt
60500	Amortization Expense
63000	Charitable Contributions Exp
63500	Commissions and Fees Exp
65000	Employee Benefit Programs Exp
66000	Gifts Expense
68000	Laundry and Cleaning Exp
89000	Other Expense

Change these account names:

10200	Regular Checking Accounting to Phoenix Bank
10400	Savings Account to Arizona Savings
12000	Product Inventory to Inventory-Mountain Bicycles
14000	Prepaid Expenses to Prepaid Insurance
23300	Deductions Payable to Medicare Employee Taxes Payabl
23800	Local Payroll Taxes Payable to Medicare Employer Taxes Payabl
24000	Other Taxes Payable to FICA Employee Taxes Payable
24100	Employee Benefits Payable to FICA Employer Taxes Payable
24800	Other Current Liabilities to Short-Term Notes Payable
27000	Notes Payable-Noncurrent to Long-Term Notes Payable
40000	Sales-Merchandise to Sales-Mountain Bicycles
50000	Cost of Goods Sold to Cost of Sales-Mountain Bicycle
72500	Penalties and Fines Exp to FUTA Expense
73000	Other Taxes to SUTA Expense
74000	Rent or Lease Expense to Rent-Mall Space

Add these accounts:

12020	Inventory-Road Bikes	Inventory
12030	Inventory-Children's Bikes	Inventory
40020	Sales-Road Bikes	Income
40030	Sales-Children's Bikes	Income
50020	Cost of Sales-Road Bikes	Cost of Sales
50030	Cost of Sales-Children's Bikes	Cost of Sales
73200	FICA Expense	Expenses
73300	Medicare Expense	Expenses

2. Click [Account Beginning Balances]. (*Hint:* Record beginning balances as of December 31, 2007.)

3. You purchased Stanley's Sports in December of 2007. Use the Balance Sheet below and on the next page to record the chart of account beginning balances.

Stanley's Sports, Balance Sheet January 1, 2008		
ASSETS		
Current Assets		
Phoenix Bank	$ 80,400.00	
Arizona Savings	11,500.00	
Inventory-Mountain Bicycles	6,000.00	
Inventory-Road Bikes	8,250.00	
Inventory-Children's Bikes	4,050.00	
Prepaid Insurance	2,400.00	
Total Current Assets		$112,600.00
Property and Equipment: Furniture and Fixtures	6,000.00	
Other Assets: Organization Costs	500.00	
Total Property and Equipment and Other Assets		6,500.00
Total Assets		$119,100.00
LIABILITIES AND STOCKHOLDERS' EQUITY		
Short-Term Notes Payable	4,000.00	
Long-Term Notes Payable	5,500.00	
Total Liabilities		$9,500.00

Stockholder's Equity: Common Stock		109,600.00
Total Liabilities and Stockholders' Equity		$119,100.00

4. You may want to backup your work. The suggested filename is Stanley's Sports Starting Balance Sheet.ptb. This is an *optional* backup.

Accounts Payable

Follow the instructions below to set up vendor information for Stanley's Sports.

1. Set up the following vendor defaults.

   Standard Terms: Due in number of days
   Net due in: 30 days
   Discount in: 15 days
   Discount % 2.00
   Credit Limit: 15,000.00

   GL Link Accounts:

   Expense Account: 12000 Inventory-Mountain Bicycles
   Discount GL Account: 59500 Purchase Discounts

2. Set up the following vendors.

   Vendor ID: ABC111
   Name: ABC Mountain Bicycles
   Contact: Aaron Carlin
   Mailing Address: 830 Moorpark Blvd.
   City, ST Zip: Los Angeles, CA 90088
   Vendor Type: mountain
   1099 Type: Independent Contractor
   Expense Account: 12000, Inventory-Mountain Bicycles
   Telephone 1: 213-555-2344
   Fax: 213-555-2138
   E-Mail info@abcmountainbicycles.biz
   Web Site: www.abcmountainbicycles.biz

Purchase Info:

Tax ID Number:	28-9832192

Vendor ID:	ERB112
Name:	Elton's Road Bikes
Contact:	Kevin Elton
Mailing Address:	67100 Aspen Road
City, ST Zip:	El Paso, TX 76315
Vendor Type:	road
1099 Type:	Independent Contractor
Expense Account:	12020, Inventory-Road Bikes
Telephone 1:	915-555-0603
Fax:	915-555-0605
E-mail:	elton@roadbikes.com
Web Site:	www.roadbikes.com

Purchase Info:

Tax ID Number:	71-3166403

Vendor ID:	TTW113
Name:	Tiny Tots Wheels
Contact:	Michael Sanders
Mailing Address:	1501 Reardon Road
City, ST Zip:	Flagstaff, AZ 86001
Vendor Type:	children
1099 Type:	Independent Contractor
Expense Account:	12030, Inventory-Children's Bikes
Telephone 1:	928-555-3489
Fax:	928-555-3491
E-mail:	info@tinytotswheels.biz
Web Site:	www.tinytotswheels.biz

Purchase Defaults:

Tax ID Number:	59-3377418

Accounts Receivable

Follow the instructions below to set up customer information for Stanley's Sports.

1. Set up the following customer defaults.

Standard Terms:	Due in number of days
Net due in:	30 days
Discount in:	0 days
Discount %:	0.00
Credit Limit:	5,000.00
GL Sales Account:	40000 Sales-Mountain Bicycles
Discount GL Account:	49000 Sales Discounts

2. Use the Sales Tax Wizard to set up a new sales tax. (*Hint:* Refer to Chapter 12, pages 450-453.)

   a. In the Sales Tax field (last column), click on the down arrow.

   b. Click 

.

   c. Use the Sales Tax Wizard to Set up a new sales tax. (*Hint:* Refer to Chapter 12, pages 450-453.

Total rate/sales tax rate:	7.00%
Sales tax agency ID:	AZ
Sales tax agency name:	Arizona Dept. of Revenue
Account to track sales taxes:	23100, Sales Tax Payable
Sales tax name:	Arizona sales taxes

3. Set up the following customers.

Customer ID:	DB001
Name:	David Barson
Billing Address:	901 County Line Road
City, ST Zip:	Phoenix, AZ 86006
Sales Tax:	AZ
Customer Type:	MAR (for Maricopa County)
Telephone 1:	602-555-1239
Fax:	602-555-8913
E-mail	barson@phoenix.com
Web Site:	www.phoenix.com/barson

Sales Info:

GL Sales Acct:	40000, Sales-Mountain Bicycles

Customer ID:	RL002
Name:	Rick Lender
Billing Address:	643 83rd Street
City, ST Zip:	Mesa, AZ 86046
Sales Tax:	AZ
Customer Type:	MAR
Telephone 1:	480-555-2913
Fax:	480-555-2915
E-mail:	rick@mesa.com
Web Site:	www.mesa.com/lender

Sales Info:

GL Sales Acct:	40020, Sales-Road Bikes

Customer ID:	SW003
Name:	Susan Winter
Billing Address:	20031 University Avenue
City, ST Zip:	Tempe, AZ 85235
Sales Tax:	AZ
Customer Type:	MAR
Telephone 1:	480-555-9299
Fax:	480-555-3705
E-mail:	winter@valley.net
Web Site:	www.winter.net/susan

Sales Info:

GL Sales Acct:	40030, Sales-Children's Bikes

Payroll

1. Set up the following Employee defaults.

State:	AZ
Unemployment Percent for Your Company:	3.4
Do You Want to Record Employee Meals and Tips:	No

Gross Pay Acct: 77500 Wages Expense
Tax Liability Acct: 23400 Federal Payroll Taxes Payable
Tax Expense Acct: 72000 Payroll Tax Expense

2. Accept the following defaults:

   401(k) plan not offered
   Vacation time not tracked
   Sick time not tracked

3. Click 

to exit the Payroll Setup Wizard.

4. Complete the following employee defaults. Click on the Pay Levels tab. For Salary Pay Levels, select Account No. 77000, Salaries Expense as the G/L Account.

5. Click on the EmployEE Fields tab. Select the following accounts:

   Accept the default for Fed_Income, Account No. 23400, Federal Payroll Taxes Payable

   Soc_Sec, 24000, FICA Employee Taxes Payable

   Medicare, 23300, Medicare Employee Taxes Payable

   State, 23600, State Payroll Taxes Payable

6. Click on the EmployER Fields tab. Select the following accounts:

	Liability column	*Expense column*
Soc_Sec_ER	24100, FICA Employer Taxes Payable	73200, FICA Expense
Medicare_ER	23800, Medicare Employer Taxes Payable	73300, Medicare Expense
FUTA_ER	23500, FUTA Tax Payable	72500, FUTA Expense
SUI_ER	23700, SUTA Payable	73000, SUTA Expense

7. Click 

.

8. Add the following employee.

Employee ID:	1ML
Name:	Manny Lopez
Accept the default for Employee	
Address:	3144 Main Street
City, ST Zip:	Phoenix, AZ 85033
Telephone 1:	602-555-3150
E-mail:	manny@email.net
Social Security #:	214-00-2390
Type:	FULL
Hired:	1/2/08

Withholding Info:

Filing Status:	Married for Federal, State, and Local
Allow:	2 for Federal, State and Local
State–Additional Withholding:	5.04 (Type 5.04 in the State, Additional Withholding column.)

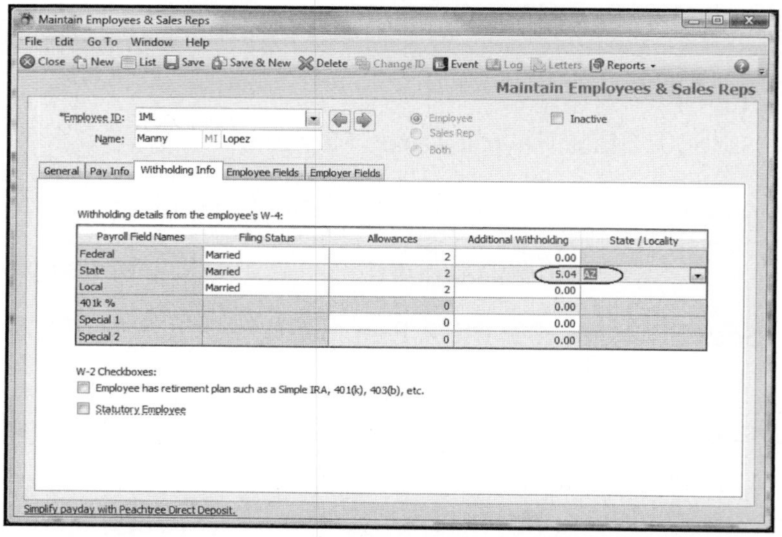

Pay Info: Salary, $500 per week. (*Hint:* Remember to select Salary as the Pay Method. Weekly is the default.)

Employee ID:	2JW
Name:	Janet Williams
Accept the default for Employee	
Address:	5190 Rural Road, Apt. 6B
City, ST Zip:	Phoenix, AZ 85021
Telephone 1:	602-555-1389
E-mail:	janet@mail.net
Social Security #:	000-02-4513
Type:	FULL
Hired:	1/2/08

Withholding Info:

Filing Status:	Single for Federal, State, and Local
Allow:	1 for Federal, State and Local
State–Additional Withholding:	11.68 (Type 11.68 in the State, Additional Withholding column.)

Pay Info: Salary, $500 per week.

9. Close.

Inventory

1. Set up the following inventory defaults. Click on the GL Accts/Costing tab.

2. Set up LIFO as the inventory costing method.

3. Set up the following Inventory items.

Item ID:	mbicycles
Description:	mountain bicycles
Item Class:	Stock item
Description for Sales:	mountain bicycles
Price Level 1:	300.00
Last Unit Cost:	150.00
Cost Method:	LIFO
GL Sales Acct:	40000 Sales-Mountain Bicycles
GL Inventory Acct:	12000, Merchandise Inventory-Mountain Bicycles
GL Cost of Sales Acct:	50000, Cost of Sales-Mountain Bicycles

Item Tax Type:	1
Item Type:	mountain
Stocking U/M:	each
Minimum Stock:	10
Reorder Quantity:	5
Preferred Vendor ID:	ABC Mountain Bicycles

Beginning Balances: mountain bicycles

Quantity:	40.00
Unit Cost:	150.00
Total Cost:	6,000.00

Item ID:	rbikes
Description:	road bikes
Item Class:	Stock item
Description for Sales:	road bikes
Price Level 1:	150.00
Last Unit Cost:	75.00
Cost Method:	LIFO
GL Sales Acct:	40020, Sales-Road Bikes
GL Inventory Acct:	12020, Inventory-Road Bikes
GL Cost of Sales Acct:	50020, Cost of Sales-Road Bikes
Item Tax Type:	1
Item Type:	road
Stocking U/M:	each
Minimum Stock:	10
Reorder Quantity:	5
Preferred Vendor ID:	Elton's Road Bikes

Beginning Balances: Road Bikes

Quantity:	110.00
Unit Cost:	75.00
Total Cost:	8,250.00

Item ID:	cbikes
Description:	children's bikes
Item Class:	Stock item
Description for Sales:	children's bikes
Price Level 1:	90.00

Last Unit Cost:	45.00
Cost Method:	LIFO
GL Sales Acct:	40030, Sales-Children's Bikes
GL Inventory Acct:	12030, Inventory-Children's Bikes
Cost of Sales Acct:	50030, Cost of Sales-Children's Bikes
Item Tax Type:	1
Item Type:	children
Stocking U/M:	each
Minimum Stock:	10
Reorder Quantity:	5
Preferred Vendor ID:	Tiny Tots Wheels

Beginning Balances: children's bikes

Quantity:	90.00
Unit Cost:	45.00
Total Cost:	4,050.00

4. Make a backup. Use **Stanley's Sports Begin** as the filename.

Journalize and post the following transactions:

Date	*Description of Transaction*
01/04/08	Issued pay checks 5001 and 5002 to Manny Lopez and Janet Williams. (*Hint: Select Phoenix Bank as the cash account for payroll checks. Type the check number, then post the payroll entry.*)[1]
01/07/08	Invoice No. 74A was received from ABC Mountain Bicycles for 10 mountain bicycles at $150 each.
01/07/08	Invoice No. 801 was received from Tiny Tots Wheels for 15 children's bikes at $45 each.
01/07/08	Invoice No. ER555 was received from Elton's Road Bikes for 12 road bikes at $75 each.

[1]Stanley's Sports paid each employee a full week's salary on January 4. The employees helped set up merchandise prior to the January 2 grand opening.

01/10/08 Deposited cash sales of $2,670, plus sales taxes of $186.90: 4 mountain bicycles, $1,200; 5 road bikes, $750; 8 children's bikes, $720. Cash sales are deposited in the Phoenix Bank account. (*Hint: Make sure the correct Sales account is credited.*)

01/11/08 Deposited cash sales of $1,950, plus sales taxes of $136.50: 5 children's bikes, $450; 4 road bikes, $600; and 3 mountain bicycles, $900.

01/11/08 Issued pay checks 5003 and 5004 for Manny Lopez and Janet Williams. (*Hint: If necessary, complete the Check Number field.*)

01/14/08 Sold one mountain bike to David Barson on account, Sales Invoice 101. (*Hint: Type the invoice number in the Invoice # field.*)

01/17/08 Deposited cash sales, $1,920, plus sales taxes of $134.40: 3 children's bikes, $270; 2 mountain bicycles, $600; 7 road bikes, $1,050.

01/18/08 Issued pay checks 5005 and 5006 for Manny Lopez and Janet Williams.

01/21/08 Issued Check No. 5007 to ABC Mountain Bicycles in payment of purchase Invoice No. 74A. Complete the Check Number field. Issue checks from the Phoenix Bank account. (Make sure that the Discount Account field shows 59500 for Purchase Discounts.)

01/21/08 Issued Check No. 5008 to Elton's Road Bikes in payment of purchase Invoice No. ER555.

01/21/08 Issued Check No. 5009 to Tiny Tots Wheels in payment of purchase Invoice No. 801.

01/22/08 Deposited cash sales of $3,810, plus sales taxes of $266.70: 6 mountain bicycles, $1,800; 8 road bikes, $1,200; 9 children's bikes, $810.

01/22/08 Issued Check No. 5010 to Arrowhead Rentals for $1,350 in payment of mall space rent for Stanley's Sports. (*Hint: Remember to complete the Check Number field.*)

01/22/08 Sold one children's bike to Susan Winter on account, Sales Invoice 102. (*Hint: Type the invoice number in the Invoice No. field.*)

01/24/08 Invoice No. 88A was received from ABC Mountain Bicycles for three mountain bicycles at $150 each.

01/24/08 Invoice No. 962 was received from Tiny Tots Wheels for five children's bikes at $45 each.

01/24/08 Invoice No. ER702 was received from Elton's Road Bikes for five road bikes at $75 each.

01/25/08 Deposited cash sales of $3,240 plus sales taxes of $226.80: 6 mountain bicycles, $1,800; 6 road bikes, $900; 6 children's bikes, $540.

01/25/08 Issued pay checks 5011 and 5012 for Manny Lopez and Janet Williams.

01/29/08 Issued Check No. 5013 to Sara Dowling for $245 in payment of Short-Term Notes Payable.

01/29/08 Issued Check No. 5014 to Phoenix Bank for $175.80 in payment of Long-Term Notes Payable.

01/29/08 Issued Check No. 5015 to Southwest Utilities for $225.65 in payment of utilities.

Complete account reconciliation for the Phoenix Bank account. The January 31, 2008 bank statement is on the next page.

Statement of Account Phoenix Bank January 1 to January 31, 2008		Account No. 146903-2118		Stanley's Sports 1635 Grand Avenue Phoenix, AZ 85031	
		REGULAR CHECKING			
Previous Balance		12/31/06	$80,400.00		
5 Deposits(+)			14,541.30		
8 Checks (-)			7,699.86		
Service Charges (-)		1/31/08	15.00		
Ending Balance		1/31/08	**87,226.44**		
		DEPOSITS			
1/12/08	2,856.90	1/23/08	4,076.70		
1/15/08	2,086.50	1/27/08	3,466.80		
1/18/08	2,054.40				
		CHECKS (Asterisk * indicates break in check number sequence)			
		1/8/08	5001	434.79	
		1/8/08	5002	399.30	
		1/15/08	5003	434.79	
		1/15/08	5004	399.30	
		1/22/08	5005	434.79	
		1/22/08	5006	399.30	
		1/27/08	5007	1,470.00	
		1/28/08	5008	882.00	
		1/28/08	5009	661.50	
		1/29/08	5010	1,350.00	
		1/29/08	5011	434.79	
		1/29/08	5012	399.30	

Print the following reports:

1. Print the General Ledger Trial Balance.
2. Print the Account Reconciliation report for the Phoenix Bank.
3. Print the Inventory Valuation Report.
4. Print the financial statements: Balance Sheet, Income Statement, and Statement of Cash Flow.

5. Print the Customer Ledgers and Vendor Ledgers.

6. Make a backup of Project 2, Stanley's Sports. Use **Stanley's Sports January** as the file name.

	CHECKLIST OF PRINTOUTS, Stanley's Sports
	General Ledger Trial Balance
	Account Reconciliation – Phoenix Bank
	Inventory Valuation Report
	Balance Sheet
	Income Statement
	Statement of Cash Flow
	Customer Ledgers
	Vendor Ledgers
	OPTIONAL PRINTOUTS
	Chart of Accounts
	General Ledger
	Customer List
	Vendor List
	Purchase Journal
	Cash Disbursements Journal
	Sales Journal
	Cash Receipts Journal
	Payroll Journal
	Cost of Goods Sold Journal

Student Name________________________________**Date**___________

CHECK YOUR PROGRESS: PROJECT 2, Stanley's Sports

1. What are the total debit and credit balances on your General Ledger Trial Balance? __________

2. What are the total assets on January 31? __________

3. What is the balance in the Phoenix Bank account on January 31? __________

4. How much are total revenues as of January 31? __________

5. How much net income (net loss) is reported on January 31? __________

6. What is the balance in the Inventory-Mountain Bicycles account on January 31? __________

7. What is the balance in the Inventory-Road Bikes account on January 31? __________

8. What is the balance in the Inventory-Children's Bikes account on January 31? __________

9. What is the balance in the Short-Term Notes Payable account on January 31? __________

10. What is the balance in the Common Stock account on January 31? __________

11. What are the total expenses reported on January 31? __________

12. Were any Accounts Payable incurred during the month of January? (Circle your answer.) YES NO

Project 2A Student-Designed Merchandising Business

In Chapters 11, 12, 13, 14 and Project 2, you learned how to complete the Computer Accounting Cycle for merchandising businesses. Project 2A gives you a chance to design a merchandising business of your own.

You will select the type of merchandising business you want, edit your business's Chart of Accounts, create an opening Balance Sheet and transactions, and complete PCA's computer accounting cycle. Project 2A also gives you an opportunity to review the software features learned so far.

You should think about the kind of business you want to create. In Chapters 11, 12, 13 and 14 you worked with Susan's Service Merchandise, a partnership form of business; and Your Name Sales & Service , a sole proprietorship. In Project 2, you worked with Stanley's Sports, a corporate form of business. You might want to design businesses similar to these. Other merchandising businesses include: jewelry store, automobile dealer, convenience store, florist, furniture dealer, etc.

Before you begin, you should design your business. You need the following:

1. Company information that includes business name, address, telephone number, and form of business.
2. One of PCA's sample companies.
3. A Chart of Accounts: 80 accounts minimum, 110 accounts maximum.
4. A Balance Sheet for your business.
5. One month's transactions for your business. These transactions must include accounts receivable, accounts payable, inventory, and payroll. You should have a minimum of 25 transactions; a maximum of 35 transactions. Your transactions should result in a net income.
6. A bank statement.
7. Complete another month of transactions that result in a net loss.

After you have created your business, you should follow the steps of PCA's computer accounting cycle to complete Project 2A.

After completing the Student-Designed Merchandising Business, you should have the following printouts.

CHECKLIST OF PRINTOUTS Student-Designed Merchandising Business	
	General Ledger Trial Balance
	Account Reconciliation Report
	Inventory Valuation Report
	Balance Sheet
	Income Statement
	Statement of Cash Flow
	Customer Ledgers
	Vendor Ledgers
	OPTIONAL PRINTOUTS
	Chart of Accounts
	General Ledger
	Customer List
	Vendor List
	Purchase Journal
	Cash Disbursements Journal
	Sales Journal
	Cash Receipts Journal
	Payroll Journal
	Cost of Goods Sold Journal

Part 4 Advanced Peachtree Complete 2008 Applications

In Part 4 of the book, you complete four chapters and three projects:

Chapter 15, Customizing Forms, shows how to change the preprinted forms included with the software.

Chapter 16, Import/Export, shows how to use PCA 2008 with a word processing program.

Chapter 17, Using Peachtree Complete Accounting 2008 with Microsoft Excel and Word, shows how to use Peachtree with two Microsoft Office applications. You need Microsoft Office 2000 or higher to complete the Excel and Word exercises in Chapter 17.

Chapter 18, Write Letters, Use Templates, and Peachtree Online, shows you how to use Peachtree's write letters feature, create templates, and explore Peachtree's website.

Projects 3 and 4 complete your study of *Computer Accounting with Peachtree Complete 2008, 12th Edition*. All features of the software are included for review in these projects.

Project 4A gives you an opportunity to add another month's worth of transactions to any of the projects that you have already completed.

The chart below shows the size of the backups made in Part 4--Chapters 16, 17, Project 3 and Project 4. You may back up to external media, the hard drive, or network. (In Windows Vista, backup to the desktop or other hard drive location then copy to external media.) There is no data saved in Chapter 15. *The Exercise 6-2 backup is used in Chapters 15-17 of the textbook.*

Chapter	File Name	Kilobytes	Page No.
16	customer.csv	35 KB	624-625
	customer.lst.txt	35 KB	627
17	balance sheet.xlsx	13 KB	639
	balance sheet and income statement.xlsx	20 KB	642
	Bellwether Garden Supply.doc	26 KB	643
18	Customer Letters.doc	3,741 KB	652
	Bellwether Sales Special.doc	578 KB	654
	Exercise 18-1.doc	571 KB	663
	Exercise 18-2.doc	571 KB	663
Project 3	Verde Computer Club.Begin.ptb	940 KB	671
	Verde Computer Club January.ptb	959 KB	672
Project 4	BJW Mftg Starting Balance Sheet.ptb	948 KB	678
	BJW Mftg Begin.ptb	979 KB	688
	BJW Mftg January.ptb	1,067 KB	693

The size of your backup files may differ from the amounts shown on the table.

The letter templates included with PCA 2008 are .doc files.

Extensions that end .xlsx, are saved in the 2007 version of Microsoft Office.

Chapter 15 Customizing Forms

SOFTWARE OBJECTIVES: In Chapter 15, you use the software to:

1. Define Peachtree forms.
2. Customize a form (invoice).
3. Print a practice form.
4. Use design tools.
5. Use the Financial Statement Wizard.

WEB OBJECTIVES: In Chapter 15, you do these Internet activities:

1. Use your Internet browser to go to the book's website.
2. Go to the Internet Activity link on the book's website. Then, select WEB EXERCISES PART 4. Complete the first web exercise in Part 4–Academic Websites.
3. Use a word processing program to write summaries of the websites that you visited.

You have used many different kinds of forms: invoices, statements, checks, etc. There may be times when you want to create your own form or customize one of the formats that come with PCA. You can customize forms with PCA's Form Designer.[1]

PRINTING FORMS

There are three types of documents that can be accessed from the Reports & Forms menu:

- Reports
- Financial Statements
- Forms

---

[1]You need a mouse to use the Form Designer.

The rules for each type of document are different for printing and designing. This chapter will explain the rules for designing forms.

WHAT IS A FORM?

A form in Peachtree is a document that you exchange with customers, vendors, or employees. The forms that come with PCA include checks, tax forms, invoices, statements, mailing labels, quotes, and collection letters.

Usually, these documents are printed on preprinted forms, but you can also design a form and print to blank paper. When you are ready to print or design a form, you select Reports & Forms then select Forms. Select the appropriate form from the Forms submenu. The illustration below shows the Checks selection. From the Forms list, additional selections can be made.

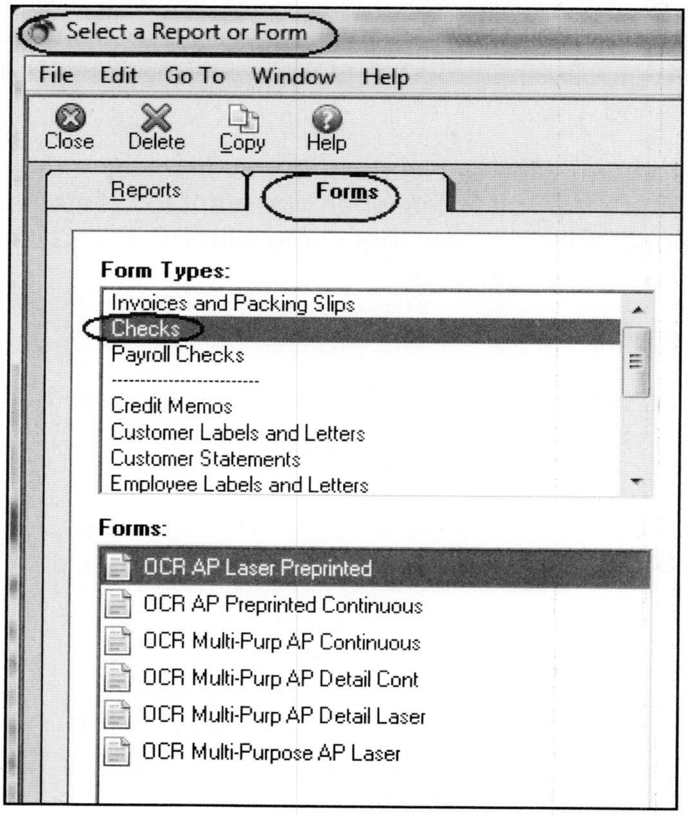

The following table lists the forms that can be printed or edited:

Accounts Receivable	Accounts Payable	Payroll
Invoices	Disbursements checks	Payroll checks
Statements	1099 Forms	W-2's
Customer Mailing Labels	Purchase Orders	940 and 941 Forms
Quotes	Vendor Mailing Labels	State Quarterly Tax Forms
Collection Letters		Employee Mailing Labels

Preprinted paper forms require special attention because the forms must be aligned in the printer correctly and the printer must be configured to accommodate the form. That is why forms cannot be displayed on your screen prior to printing. You can print practice forms to test alignment and printer configuration, or you can view the layout of the form in the Form Designer.

GETTING STARTED

In this chapter, you are going to use Bellwether Garden Supply (the sample company that you used in Chapters 1 through 7).

1. Start Peachtree.
2. Open the sample company, Bellwether Garden Supply. (The instructions in this chapter assume that you are using data from the Exercise 6-2.ptb backup made on page 204. No new data was added in Chapter 7.)

> **Comment**
>
> You can use beginning Bellwether Garden Supply data or any subsequent Bellwether backup. To install Bellwether's starting data, restore the bgs.ptb backup file. Steps for restoring the bgs.ptb backup file are on pages 26-30.

3. To verify Exercise 6-2 data, display the balance sheet. Compare your balance sheet with the one shown in Chapter 7, pages 215-216. (If you restored the bgs.ptb backup file, your balance sheet will differ.)

CUSTOMIZING A FORM

1. From the Navigation Bar, select 

. In the Recently Used Customer Reports area, link to View All Customer & Sales Reports. The Select a Report or Form window displays.

2. Select the Forms tab. In the Forms Types list, Invoices and Packing Slips is highlighted.

3. In the Forms list, select Invoice. Observe that the Report Description box explains says to Use with plain paper.

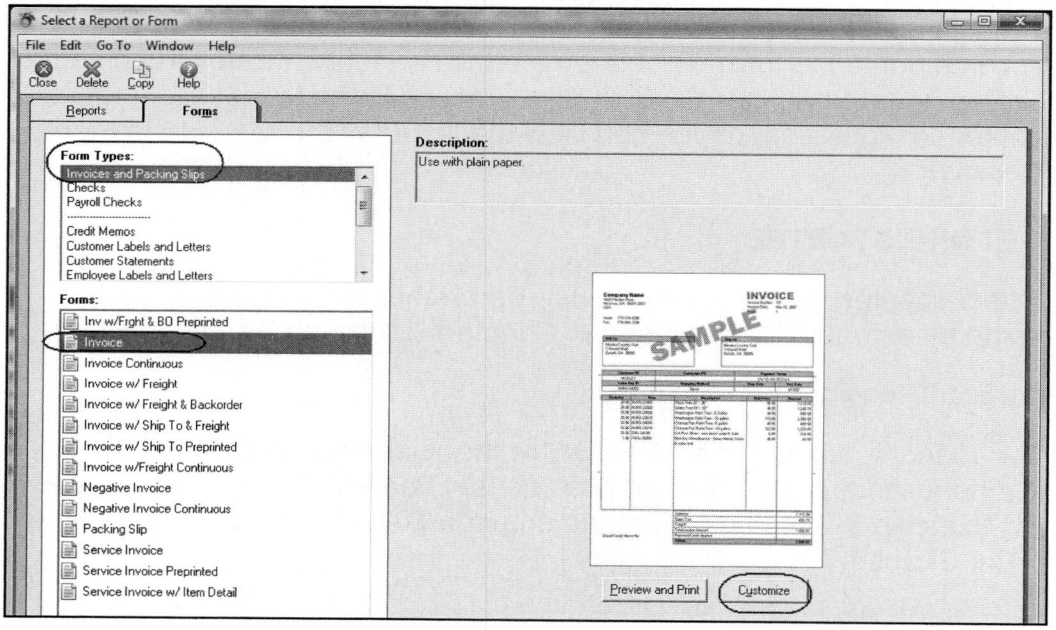

4. Click 

. The Form Designer window appears. A partial Form Designer window is shown on the next page.

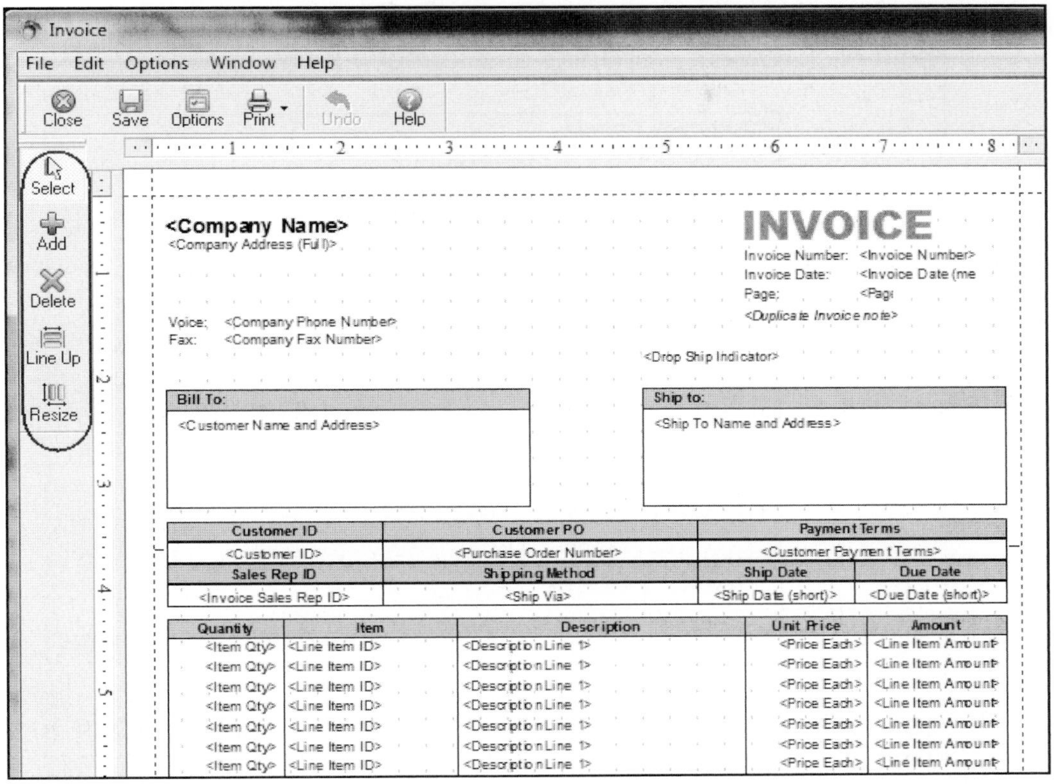

You have several options available for customizing the form. To the left of the Forms Design window (by default) are design tools: Select, Add, Delete, Line Up, Resize. These assist in selecting and adding various types of form objects.

You can also design forms in certain task windows (for example, Sales/Invoicing, Payments, and Payroll Entry) by selecting the Print button, then Form Design on the Print dialog.

5. To select an object for customizing, use the Selection tool []. With your mouse pointer, you can drag and drop objects to move them around. Click . Then move your mouse cursor to the inside of the form (inside the red outline). Click on the <Company Name> field to select it (field selection is indicated by a box).

6. With the <Company Name> field selected (blue box is around it), right-click. Object properties and format options appear.

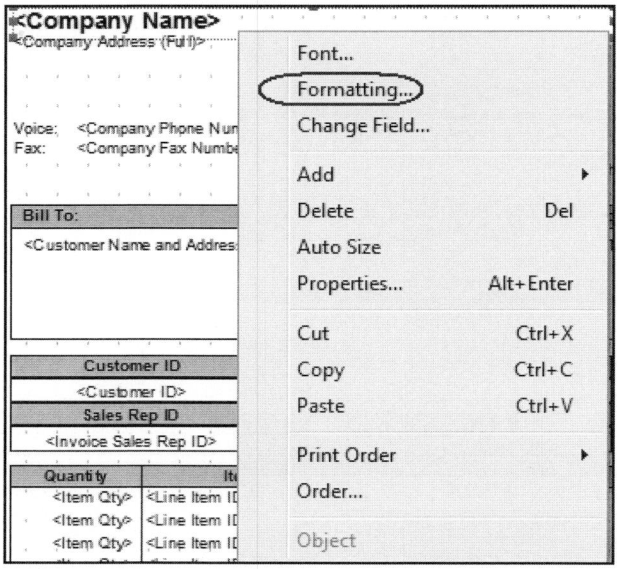

7. Left-click Formatting. The Data field Options window appears. In the Text alignment field, select Center.

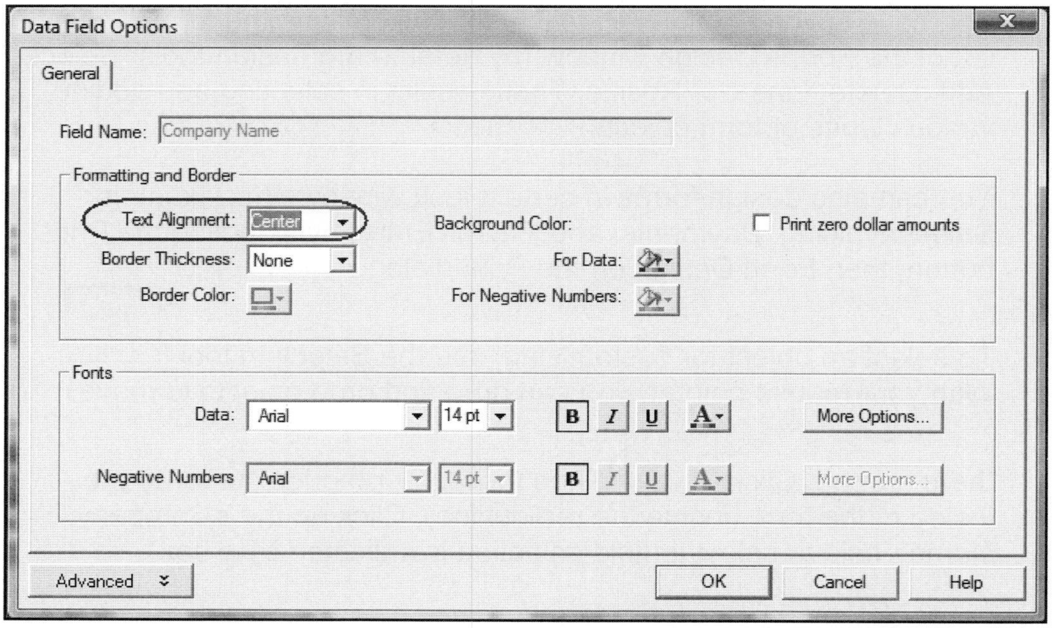

8. Click OK. Observe, the <Company Name> field moves to the center. Right-click on various fields and make changes such as font size, alignment, etc. You might delete a field or two as well.

9. Click Add. Observe that you can add a Logo or image, Data from Peachtree, Text, Shape, Line, Column to table, and Other object.

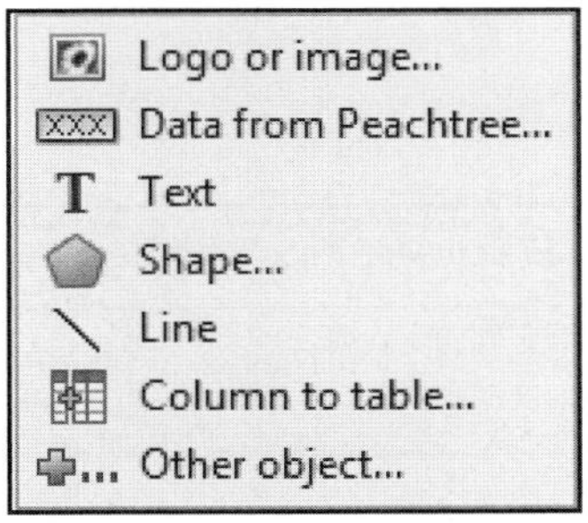

10. On the icon bar of the Forms Designer, click Options. The Forms Design Options window appears.

    Select the Display tab to select various display options. Select the Grid/Copies tab to adjust grid options and specify a default number of copies for this form.

11. Click OK to close the Forms Design Options window.

12. When finished designing the form, select Save. The Save As window appears.

13. Type **Practice** in the Form Name field. Observe that the Filename field shows the path for this form. Compare your Save As window with the one shown on the next page.

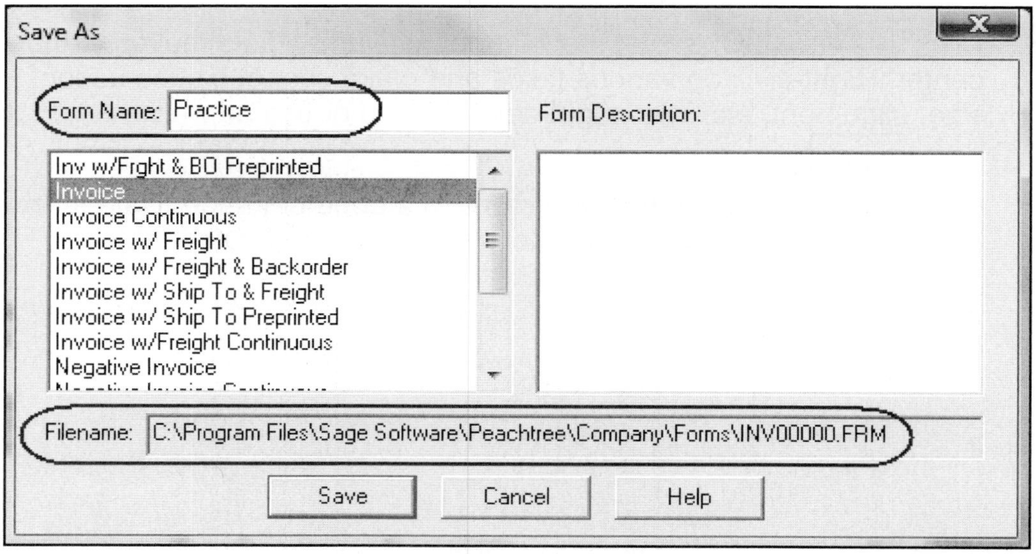

14. Click [Save]. Click [Close]. Observe that Practice is shown on the Forms list. Select Practice.

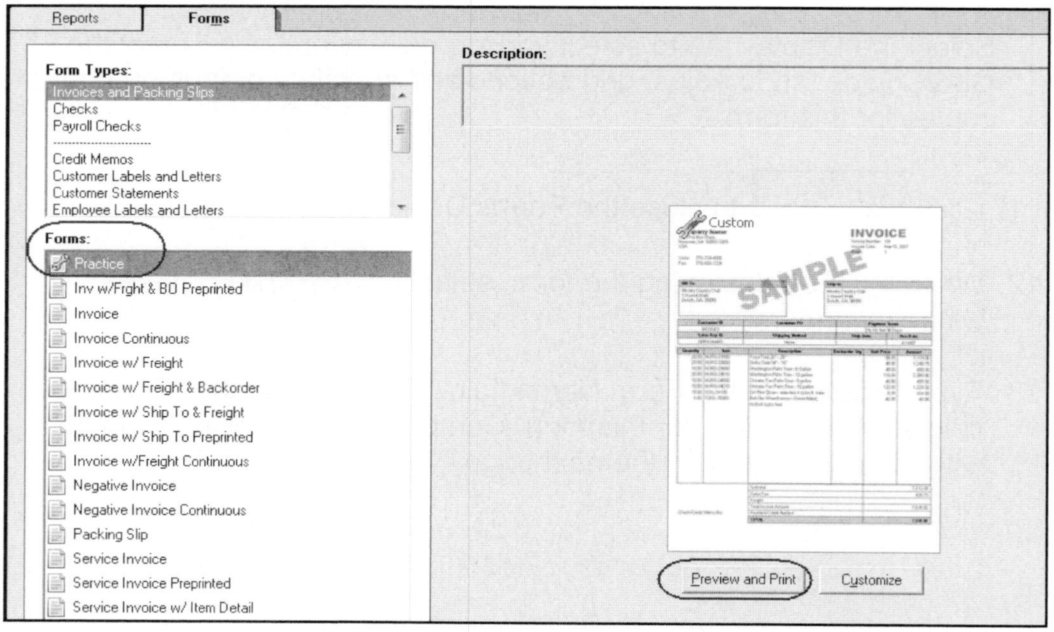

15. Click [Preview and Print].

PRINTING CUSTOMIZED FORMS

The Preview and Print Invoices and Packing Slips window should be displayed. Follow these steps to see the redesigned Invoice.

1. Make the following selections on the Preview and Print Invoices and Packing Slips window

   a. The Invoices to Print/e-mail field shows Unprinted invoices through Mar 15, 2007.
   b. The Number of the first invoice field shows 103.
   c. The Use this form field shows Practice.
   d. In the Delivery method field shows Print and e-mail.
   e. Click 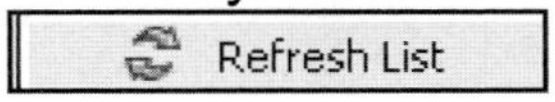

.

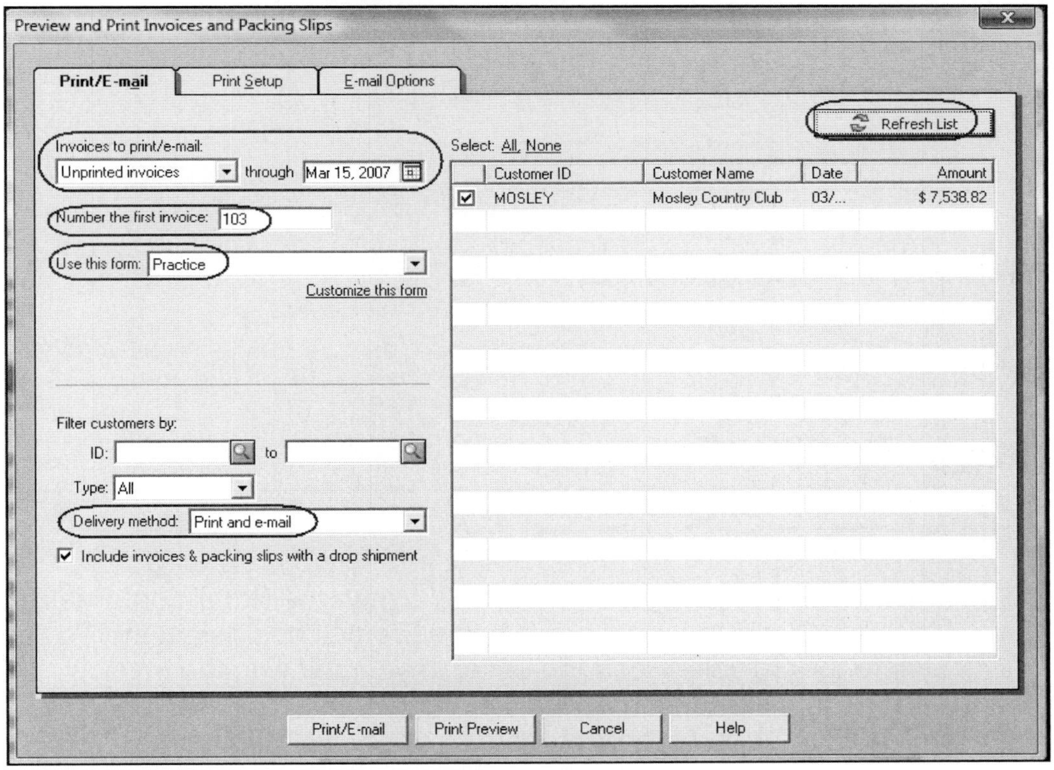

2. Click Print Preview. Notice that Bellwether Garden Supply, and its address information has been moved, along with Voice and Fax numbers. Your Invoice may differ depending on which fields you changed. A partial Invoice is shown below. (*Hint:* The author centered the heading, moved the Voice and Fax numbers, increased the font size in the Bill To field, and deleted the "duplicate" field and Ship to fields.)

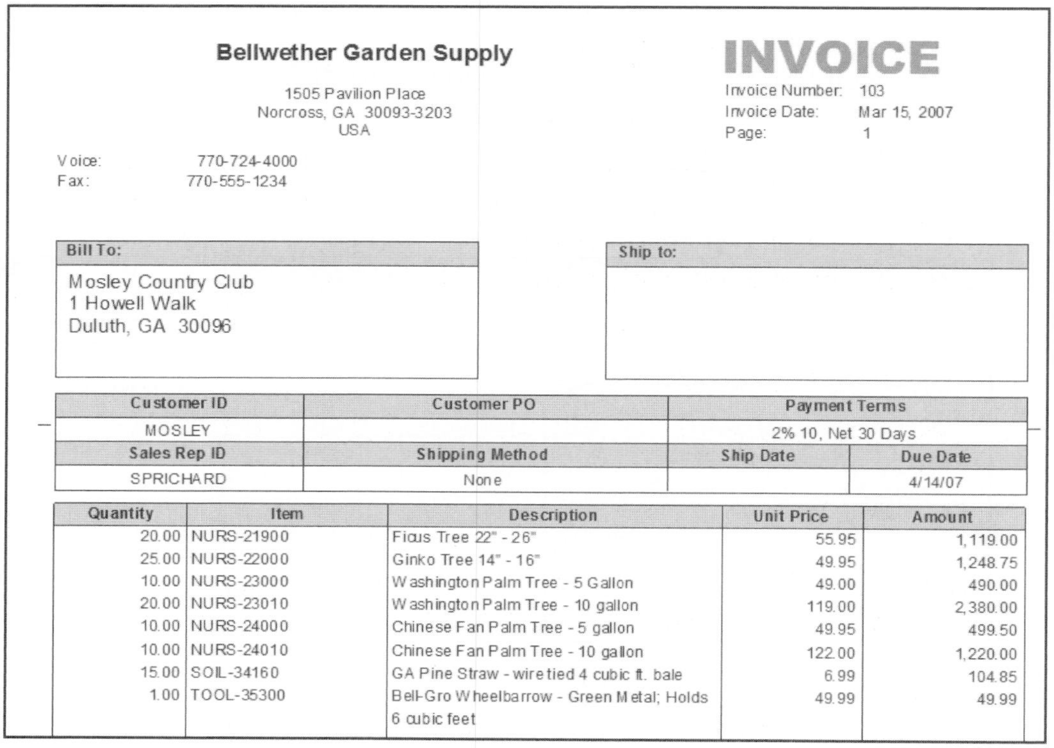

Bellwether Garden Supply

1505 Pavilion Place
Norcross, GA 30093-3203
USA

Voice: 770-724-4000
Fax: 770-555-1234

INVOICE

Invoice Number: 103
Invoice Date: Mar 15, 2007
Page: 1

Bill To:
Mosley Country Club
1 Howell Walk
Duluth, GA 30096

Ship to:

Customer ID	Customer PO	Payment Terms	
MOSLEY		2% 10, Net 30 Days	
Sales Rep ID	**Shipping Method**	**Ship Date**	**Due Date**
SPRICHARD	None		4/14/07

Quantity	Item	Description	Unit Price	Amount
20.00	NURS-21900	Ficus Tree 22" - 26"	55.95	1,119.00
25.00	NURS-22000	Ginko Tree 14" - 16"	49.95	1,248.75
10.00	NURS-23000	Washington Palm Tree - 5 Gallon	49.00	490.00
20.00	NURS-23010	Washington Palm Tree - 10 gallon	119.00	2,380.00
10.00	NURS-24000	Chinese Fan Palm Tree - 5 gallon	49.95	499.50
10.00	NURS-24010	Chinese Fan Palm Tree - 10 gallon	122.00	1,220.00
15.00	SOIL-34160	GA Pine Straw - wire tied 4 cubic ft. bale	6.99	104.85
1.00	TOOL-35300	Bell-Gro Wheelbarrow - Green Metal; Holds 6 cubic feet	49.99	49.99

3. Click Print to print Invoice No. 103. When the Email Job: Peachtree Accounting window appears, type your email address in the To field. Delete the Cc field. Send the email to yourself with the Invoice #103.PDF file attached. (*Hint:* Read the email. You may need to download Adobe Acrobat Reader to open the attachment.)

4. Click Yes at the screen prompt. Go to your email account to open the attachment and print the invoice.

5. Close the Select a Report or Form window.

EDITING A FORM DESIGN

1. From the menu bar, select Reports & Forms; Forms, Invoices and Packing Slips.

2. In the Forms list, select Practice.

3. Click 

. Select the fields you want to change.

4. On the Practice window's icon bar, click 

. Select the Display tab to select various display options. Select the Grid/Copies tab to adjust grid options and specify a default number of copies for this form.

5. When through, click 

.

6. Save the form. Use the same filename, Practice.

DESIGN TOOLS

The Form Designer window includes design tools: Select, Add, Delete, Line Up, Resize. These terms are defined as follows:

Object Toolbar

Select: Select this to use the Selection tools to highlight or select one or more form objects.

Add: Select Add to add an object to the form. You can add an image or log, data field, text field, column field, shape, line or other object using this tool.

Delete: Select Delete to delete the object or objects that you have selected on the form.

Line Up: Select Line Up to align the objects that you have selected on the form. You can Line Up-Left, Right, Top, bottom.

Resize: Select Resize to resize the objects that you have selected on the form. You can resize the width and height.

1. Click  to return to the Select a Report or Form window. Close to return to the menu bar.

Formatting Toolbar

Use the formatting toolbar to change the format of the selected object on your form. Use this toolbar to change the font, color, and background color of the selected object. If you have selected a text object, you can click the Edit Text button to change the text. Clicking the Properties button will open the corresponding property window, where you can modify the object's properties. The Fonts section of the Data Field Options window is shown below.

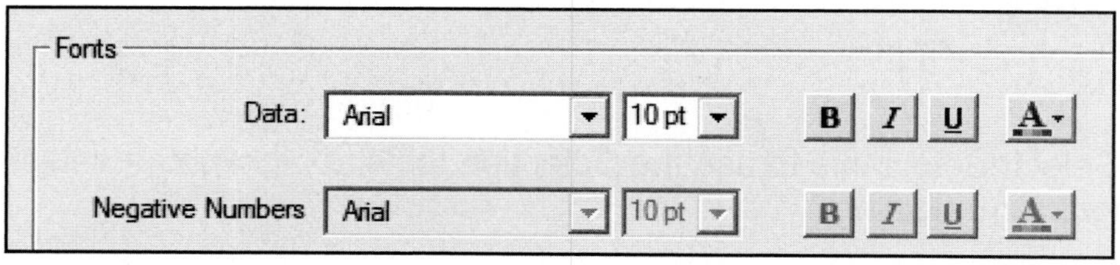

You may want to experiment with the Practice form to see some of these design features.

FINANCIAL STATMEMENT DESIGN TOOLS

When you design a financial statement, use the financial statement Design Tools window. It has three major areas: the toolbar at the top of the window, the design toolbar at the side of the window where you select the type of fields you want to place on the designer, and the design area where you actually create the financial statement.

When you create a financial statement, you work with five areas: 1) the header; 2) lines of text; 3) columns; 4) totals; 5) footer. Follow these steps to see the designing tools that are available on the Statement of Cash Flow.

1. From the Reports & Forms menu, select Financial Statements, <Standard> Cash Flow.

2. Click 

. The <Standard> Cash Flow window includes the design tools necessary for customization. Compare yours with the one shown on the next page.

   The information that follows is for explanation purposes only. You may want to experiment with some of the design tools to make changes to Peachtree's <Standard> Cash Flow.

   When designing a new form or modifying an existing one, you need to save the form to record your changes. If you change one of the standard forms (those that came with Peachtree), you must rename the form before saving your changes. You cannot save changes to the standard forms using the original form name. This allows you to keep the standard form in case you make a design error and need to start over.

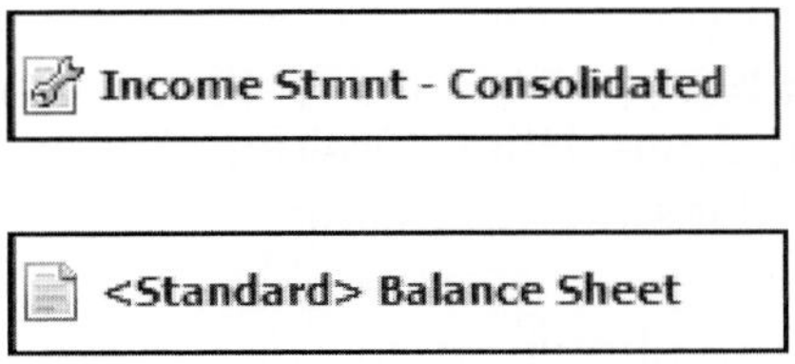

A custom form appears on the report list with a different icon than a <Standard> form.

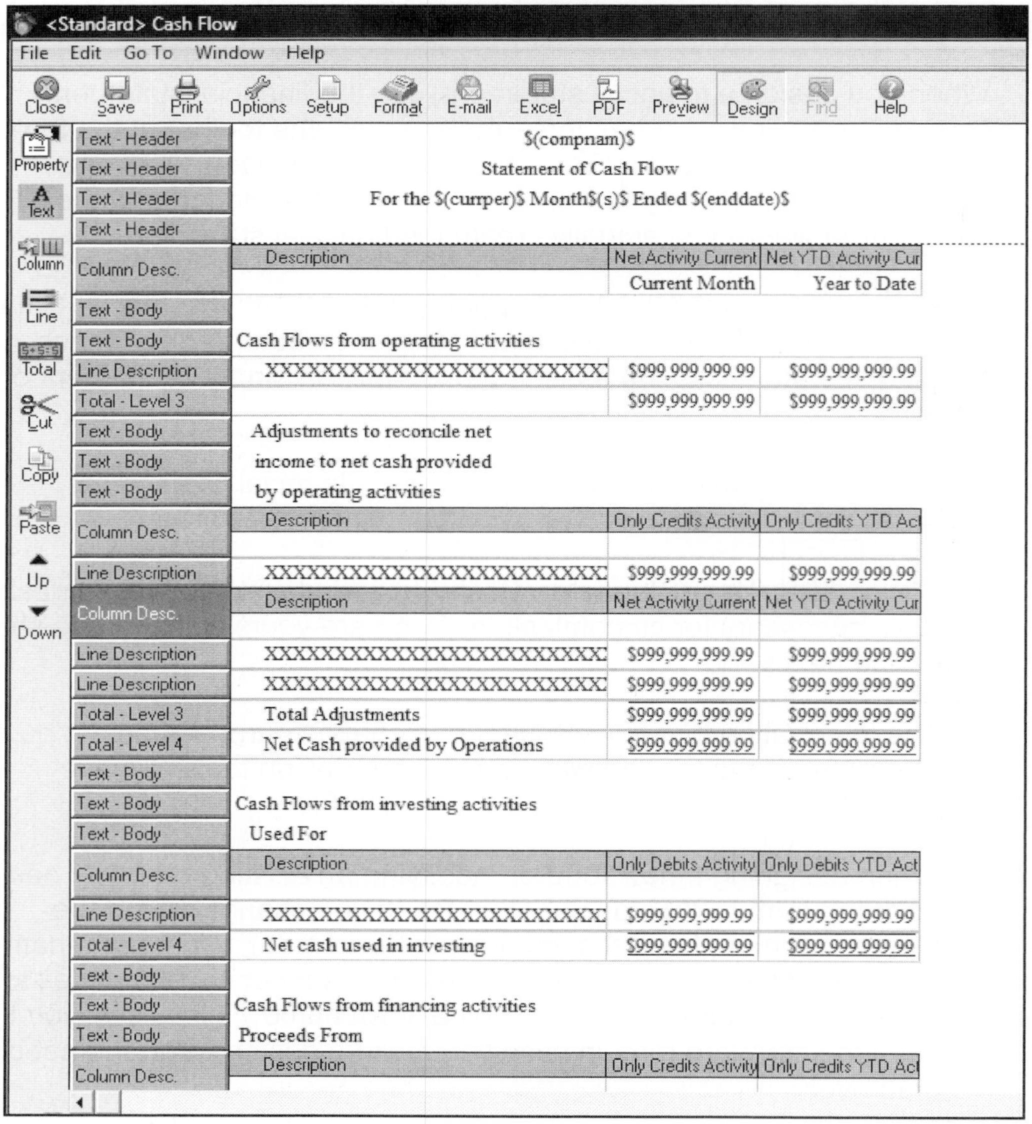

At the side of the designer window, observe that each row has a button next to it that defines the row; for example, Text – header, Column Desc., Text – Body, etc. The icon bar at the top of the window contains the following buttons: Close, Save, Print, Options, Setup, Format, E-mail, Excel, PDF, Preview, Design, and Help.

The financial statement design tools are shown on the next page.

Use the Property tool to work with the properties window for the selected row type. For example, if you select a text row, the text window opens.

Use the Text tool to insert text that will you not change from statement to statement (for example, section headings).

Use the Column tool to define columns, enter a title for each column, select the alignment of each column title (left, right, or center) and select the style, size and color of the text.

Once the columns are defined, use the Line tool to define what data to put in each row of a column. Line objects are placed below column objects.

Use the Total tool to tell the program how to calculate totals and subtotals.

Use the Cut tool to remove the selected row and copy it to the Windows Clipboard.

Use the Copy tool to copy the selected row to the Windows Clipboard.

Use the Paste tool to insert the current row from the Windows Clipboard.

Use the Up tool to move the selected row up one position in the list of rows.

Use the Down tool to move a selected row down one position in the list of rows.

You can select multiple rows in the window and then apply the cut, copy, and paste functions to all of them. To select multiple rows, hold down the Ctrl key, and then with the cursor select the buttons that define the rows you want.

FINANCIAL STATEMENT WIZARD

The Financial Statement Wizard walks you through the process of designing financial statements. Follow these steps to use the Financial Statement Wizard.

1. If necessary start Peachtree. Open Bellwether Garden Supply.
2. From Navigation Bar, select 

; link to View All Financial Statements. The Select a Report window appears.
3. Link to Financial Statement Wizard.

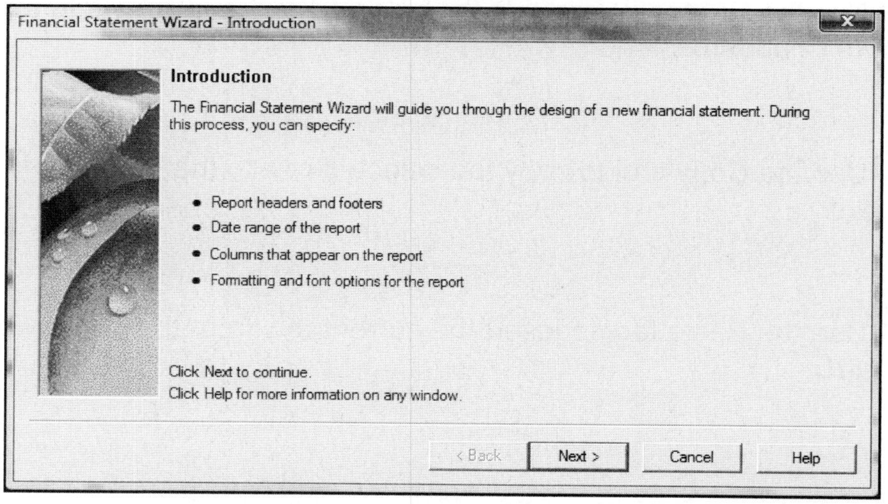

4. After reading the information on the Introduction window, click 

.

5. Make sure <Standard> Balance Sheet appears in the Financial Statement Template field.

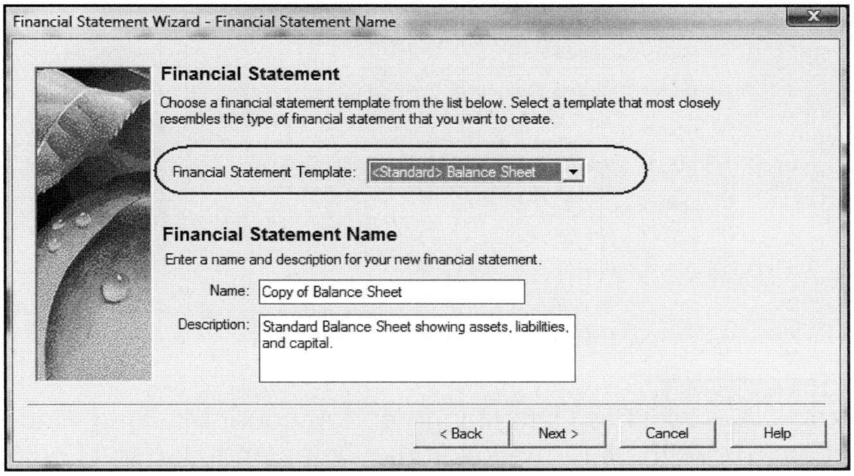

5. After reading the information on the Financial Statement window, click 

. The Headers and Footers window appears.

6. The Headers and Footers window allows you to change information at the top and bottom of the balance sheet. For purposes of this exercise, click on the Header 1 line, then type **your name** followed by a comma and a space.

7. In the Header 3 line, click on the beginning of the line, then click 

(down arrow next to Insert). Select Today's Date from the drop-down list. Type a comma after $(Date)$, then put a space between the $(Date)$ and $(enddate)$ comments.

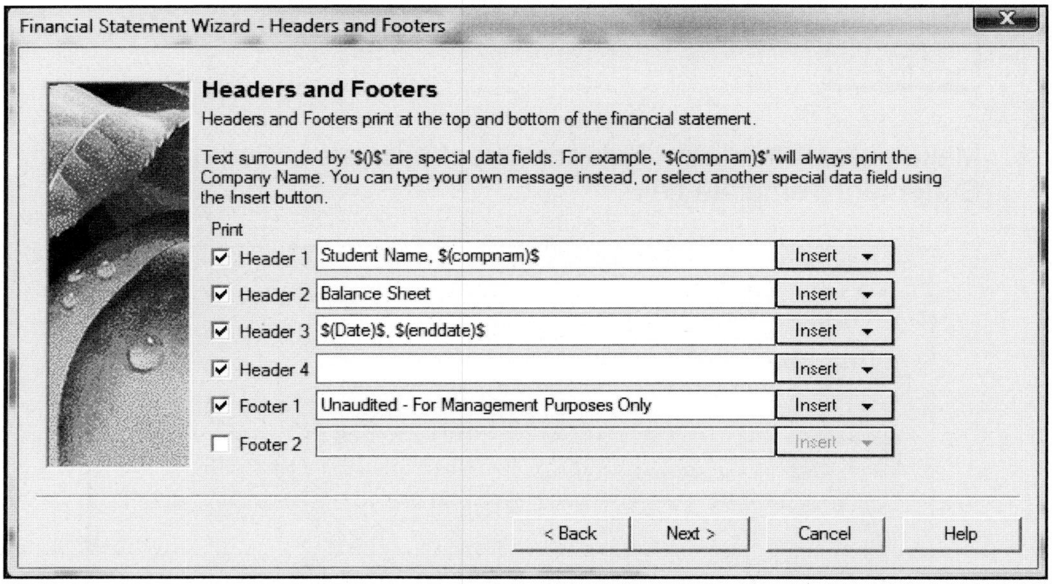

8. Click . The Date Range and Account Masking window appears. Read the information in the Dates and General Ledger Account Masking sections. Accept the defaults on this window, by clicking on .

9. Accept the defaults on the Column Properties window by clicking on .

10. Accept the defaults on the Column Options window by clicking on .

11. Unless you want to change fonts, accept the defaults on the Fonts window by clicking on .

12. Accept the defaults on the Formatting and Default Printer window by clicking on .

13. The Congratulations window appears. To display your new financial statement, click Finish. The Copy of Balance Sheet window appears, click OK.

Compare your balance sheet to the one shown below. Observe that the header shows your name on line one; today's date is shown on line 3 before March 31, 2007 (your current date will differ). If you are using a different chapter's backup data, your balance sheet amounts may differ.

A partial balance sheet appears below. This balance sheet is from the Exercise 6-2.ptb backup file. In Chapter 7 on page 215, you printed Bellwether Garden Supply's balance sheet.

Line 1 of and Line 3 of header changed

Student Name, Bellwether Garden Supply
Balance Sheet
September 26, 2007, March 31, 2007

ASSETS

Current Assets		
Petty Cash	$ 327.55	
Cash on Hand	1,850.45	
Regular Checking Account	9,046.52	
Payroll Checking Account	9,093.25	
Savings Account	7,500.00	
Money Market Fund	4,500.00	
Accounts Receivable	174,940.73	
Other Receivables	7,681.84	
Allowance for Doubtful Account	(5,000.00)	
Inventory	12,021.41	
Prepaid Expenses	14,221.30	
Employee Advances	3,000.65	
Notes Receivable-Current	11,000.00	
Other Current Assets	120.00	
Total Current Assets		250,303.70
Property and Equipment		
Furniture and Fixtures	62,769.25	
Equipment	38,738.33	
Vehicles	86,273.40	
Other Depreciable Property	6,200.96	
Buildings	185,500.00	
Building Improvements	26,500.00	
Accum. Depreciation-Furniture	(54,680.57)	
Accum. Depreciation-Equipment	(33,138.11)	
Accum. Depreciation-Vehicles	(51,585.26)	
Accum. Depreciation-Other	(3,788.84)	
Accum. Depreciation-Buildings	(34,483.97)	
Accum. Depreciation-Bldg Imp	(4,926.28)	
Total Property and Equipment		223,378.91

14. Close the balance sheet window and Select a Report or Form window. Exit Peachtree or continue.

INTERNET ACTIVITY	
1.	From your Internet browser, go to the book's website.
2.	Link to Student Edition.
3.	In the Course-wide Content list, link to Part 4 Internet Activities for Chapters 15-18. Open or Save. Choose Chapter 15 to complete Quizzes, PowerPoints, and Going to the Net exercises.
4.	Complete the ACADEMIC WEBSITES exercise. Read steps 1–6.
5.	Follow the steps shown on the book's website to complete this Internet activity.
6.	Using a word processing program write summaries of what you find. Include all appropriate website addresses.

SUMMARY AND REVIEW

SOFTWARE OBJECTIVES: In Chapter 15, you have learned to use the software to:

1. Define Peachtree forms.
2. Customize a form (invoice).
3. Print a practice form.
4. Use design tools.
5. Use the Financial Statement Wizard.

WEB OBJECTIVES: In Chapter 15, you did these Internet activities:

1. Used your Internet browser to go to the book's website.
2. Went to the Internet Activity link on the book's website. Then, selected WEB EXERCISES PART 4. Completed the first web exercise in Part 4— Academic Websites.
3. Used a word processing program to write summaries of the websites that you visited.

GOING TO THE NET

Access press releases about the Peachtree Accounting Product Line at http://smallbusiness.sagesoftware.com/press/press_releases_peachtree.cfm.

1. Select two recent product news articles.

2. Write a brief summary (no more than 100 words for each article). Identify the name and date of the articles and the website address in your answer.

Multiple-choice questions: In the space provided, write the letter that best answers each question.

_____1. The definition of a form in Peachtree is:

a. Preprinted paper forms that can be displayed on your screen.
b. A document that you exchange with customers, vendors, or employees.
c. Reports that are selected from the menu bar.
d. Options selected from the menu bar.
e. None of the above.

_____2. The three types of documents accessed from the Reports & Forms menu are:

a. Reports, Financial Statements, Forms.
b. Payroll Checks, Disbursements Checks, Invoices.
c. Sales Invoices, Purchase Invoices, Cash Receipts.
d. Filter, Forms Designer, Report List.
e. None of the above.

_____3. The Accounts Payable forms that can be printed or edited are:

a. Payroll Checks, W2s, 940's and 941's, State Quarterly Tax Forms, Employee Mailing Labels.
b. Disbursement Checks, 1099 Forms, Purchase Orders, Vendor Mailing Labels.
c. Invoices, Statements, Customer Mailing Labels, Quotes, Collection Letters.
d. All of the above.
e. None of the above.

_____4. The Accounts Receivable forms that can be printed or edited are:

a. Payroll checks, 940's and 941's.
b. Purchase Orders, 1099 Forms, Disbursement Checks, Vendor Mailing Labels.
c. Invoices, Statements, Customer Mailing Labels, Quotes, Collection Letters.
d. All of the above.
e. None of the above.

_____5. To use Peachtree's form designer window, make this selection:

a. Customize.
b. Select.
c. Customers & Sales.
d. View All customer & Sales Reports.
e. None of the above.

_____6. These buttons are called design tools:

a. Select.
b. Add.
c. Delete.
d. Line Up and Resize.
e. All of the above.

_____7. The default location for saving the Practice form is:

a. C:\Program Files\INV00000.FRM
b. C:\Program Files\Practice
c. C:\Program Files\Peachtree Software\Invoice\Practice.
d. C:\Program Files\Sage Software\Peachtree\Company\Forms\INV00000.FRM
e. None of the above.

_____8. To add an object to the form, make this selection:

a. Select.
b. Add.
c. Delete.
d. Resize.
e. All of the above.

_____9. This selection walks you through the process of designing financial statements.

a. Customizing forms.
b. Financial statement wizard.
c. Financial statement template.
d. The Navigation Bar selection, Company.
e. None of the above.

_____10. The top and the bottom of financial statements include the following:

a. Object toolbar.
b. Formatting toolbar.
b. Design tools.
c. Fonts selections
d. Headers and footers.
e. None of the above.

Exercise 15-1: Use PCA's Form Designer to experiment with different formats and type fonts.

Exercise 15-2: Print the form that you designed in Exercise 15-1.

CHAPTER 15 INDEX

Chapter 16 Import/Export

SOFTWARE OBJECTIVES: In Chapter 16, you use the software to:

1. Export information from Peachtree to a word processing program. (In this chapter Microsoft Word 2007 and Windows Vista is used.)
2. Select the customer list from Bellwether Garden Supply to export.
3. Save two files.

WEB OBJECTIVES: In Chapter 16 you do these Internet activities:

1. Use your Internet browser to go to the book's website.
2. Go to the Internet Activity link on the book's website. Then, select WEB EXERCISES PART 4. Complete the second exercise in Part 4—Women's Business Center.
3. Use a word processing program to write summaries of the websites that you visited.

Importing translates data from other programs into a format that Peachtree can use. The diagram below shows how importing works.

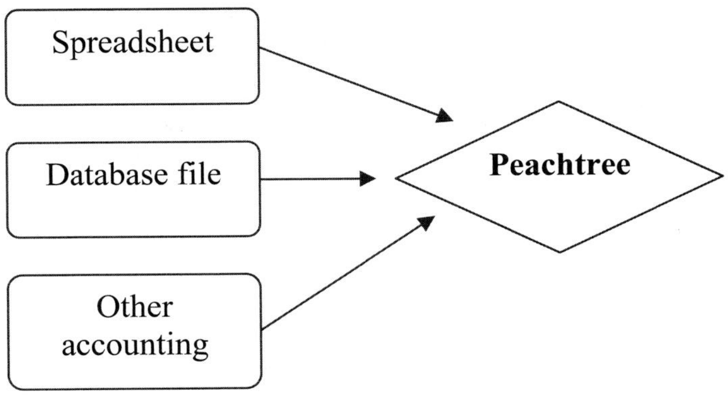

Exporting copies Peachtree data into a format that other programs can read and use. The diagram below shows how exporting works.

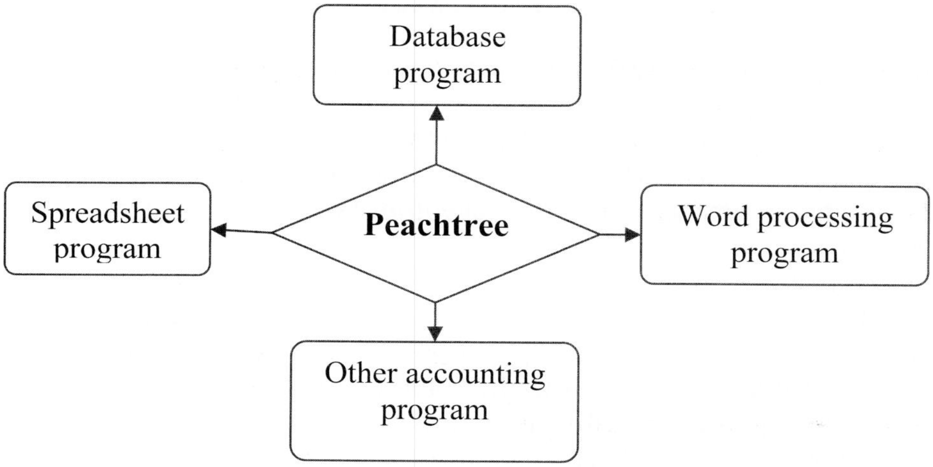

The chart below shows how Peachtree organizes data.

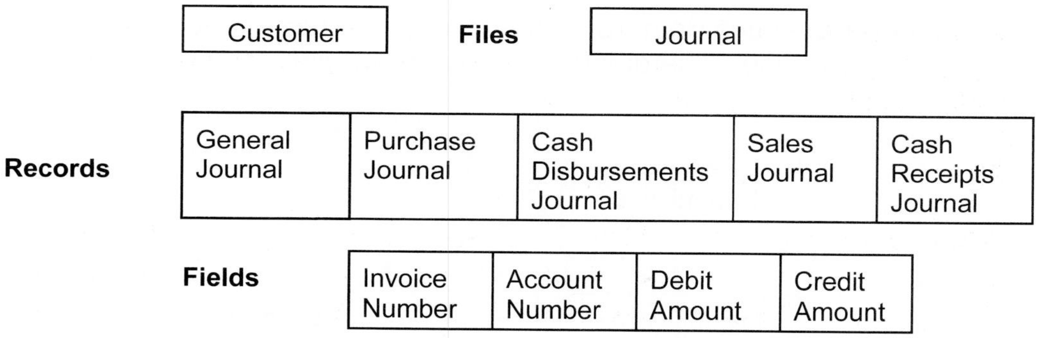

- ***Files*** are a group of related records; for example, customer files and journal files.
- ***Records*** are a group of fields that contain information on one subject; for example, the general journal, purchase journal, cash disbursements journal, sales journal, or cash receipts journal.
- ***Fields*** are an individual piece of data; for example, invoice numbers, account numbers, debit amount, credit amount.

Files

When you import or export files, you use templates to format the data. The templates included in Peachtree are:

- Accounts Receivable: Customer List, Sales Journal, and Cash Receipts Journal
- Accounts Payable: Vendor List, Purchase Journal, and Cash Disbursements Journal
- Payroll: Employee List
- General Ledger: Chart of Accounts and General Journal
- Inventory: Inventory Item List
- Job Reports: Jobs List

Records

When you select a file to export, you can define which information you want. For instance, when you select the Customer List, you can select which customers you want to export.

Fields

When you export in Peachtree, you export individual fields of information. You can see what fields are exported by selecting the Format folder tab. You may uncheck fields to exclude them from being exported or move fields around to change their order.

When you export, the information is exported in a comma-separated format. This means that the fields for each record are written in one line, with commas between them. You see how this works when you export one of Peachtree's customer lists into Microsoft Word 2007.

The file created during the export process is an ***ASCII*** file, which contains only text characters. Each record is on a separate line. ASCII is an acronym for American Standard Code for Information Interchange. It is one of the standard formats used for representing characters on a computer. Most word processing, spreadsheet, and database programs can read ASCII files.

GETTING STARTED: EXPORTING

1. Start Peachtree.

2. Open Bellwether Garden Supply. (In this chapter data is used from the Exercise 6-2.ptb backup file made on page 204.)

3. From the Navigation Bar, select 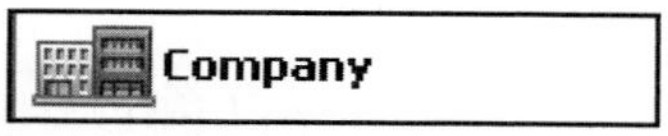

; link to Import and Export. The Select Import/Export window appears.

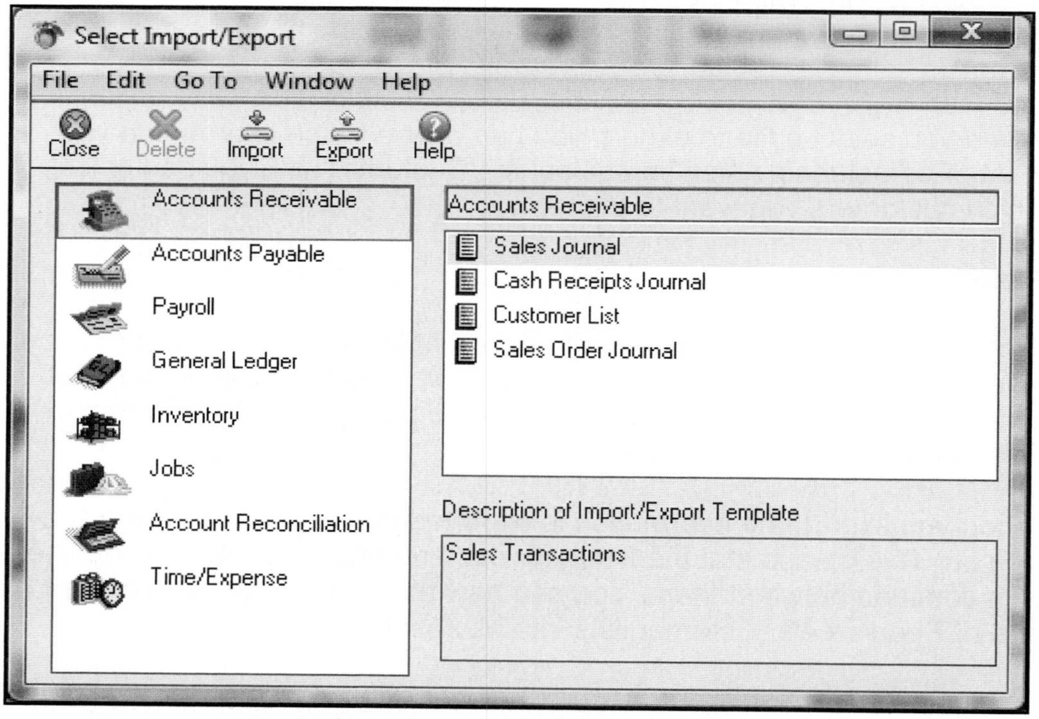

4. In the Accounts Receivable list, highlight Customer List.

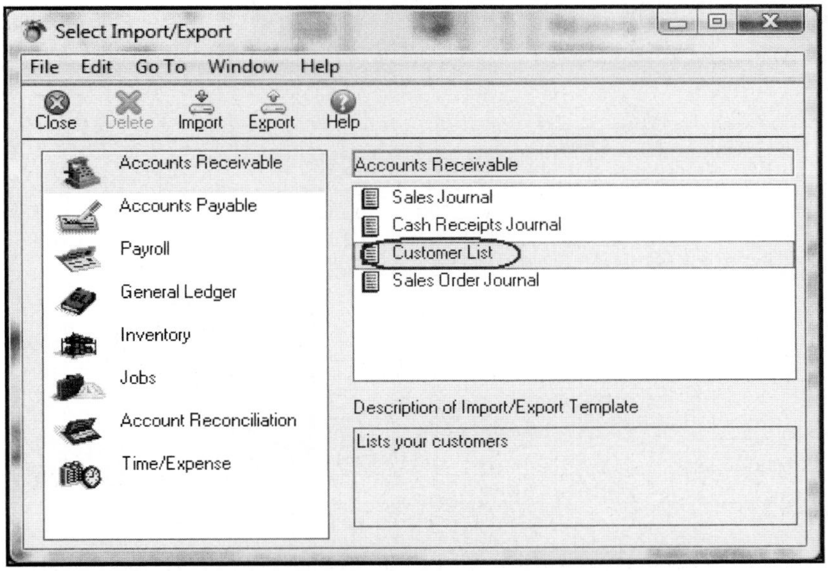

5. Click 

. The Customer List window appears.

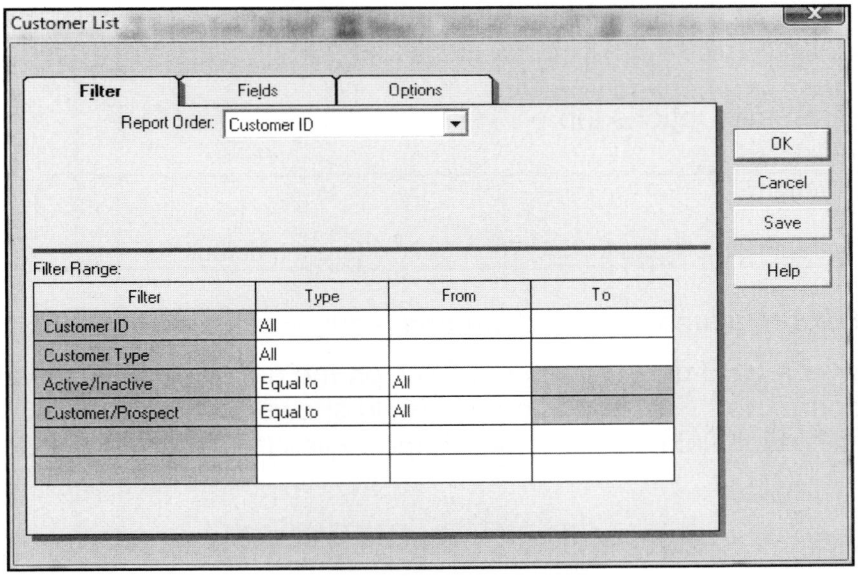

6. Click on the Fields tab, then click 

.

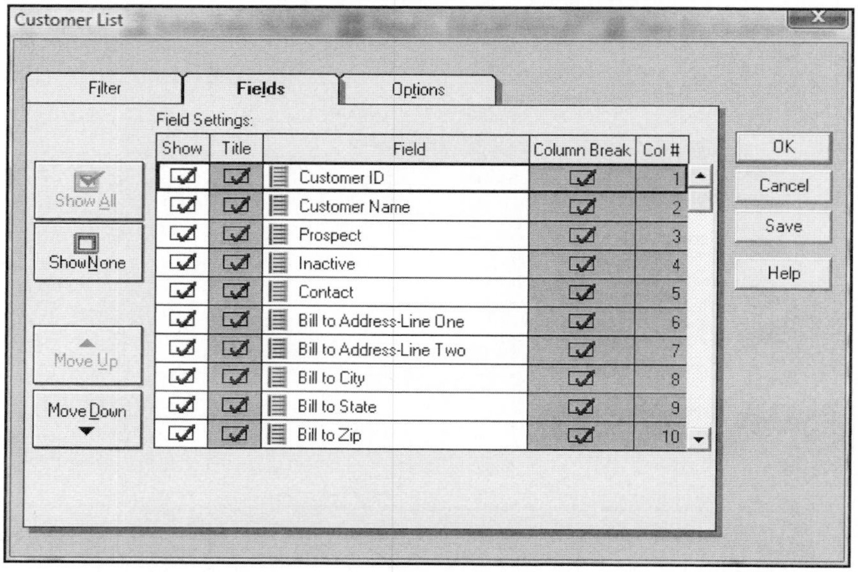

Comment
Show All places a check mark in all the fields.

7. Click on the Options tab.

Comment
The radio button next to Ask, Then Overwrite is the default.

8. Put external media in the appropriate drive. In the example that follows a USB drive was used. Click on the arrow  underneath Import/Export File. The File name field shows CUSTOMER.CSV; the Files of type field shows Import/Export Files (*.CSV).

9. Select the appropriate drive letter. In the example that follows drive H is shown. Then click 

.

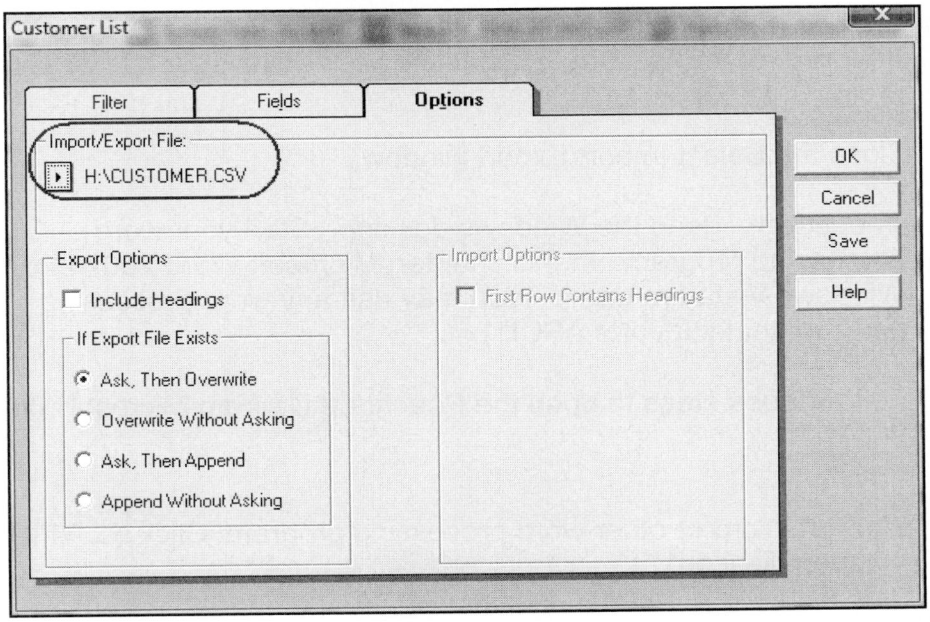

Observe that H:\CUSTOMER.CSV is shown next to the arrow  underneath Import/Export File.

10. Click 

. The Save As window appears. Type **Customers** in the Name field.

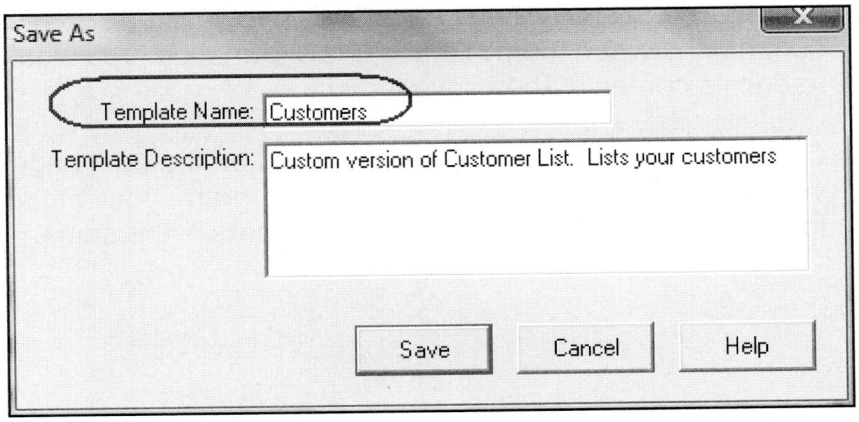

11. Click Save.

12. You are returned to the Customer Options window. Make sure that the Customer Options window shows X:\CUSTOMER.CSV as the Import/Export File name. (Substitute your drive letter for X.) Click OK.

13. Close the Select Import/Export window.

14. If necessary, go to the Windows desktop. Start your word processing program. In this chapter, Microsoft Word 2007 and Windows Vista are used. (You may use any word processing program that supports ASCII.)

15. Follow these steps to open the Peachtree file from Microsoft Word 2007.

    a. Start Word or other word processing program. Click  (the open file icon).

    b. In the Look in field, select the appropriate location of the CUSTOMER.CSV file.

    c. Highlight the CUSTOMER.CSV file, then click Open. (*Hint:* If a convert file window appears, select Plain Text.)

    The data on your window was exported in a comma-separated format. The fields for each record are written in one line, with commas between them. To use this information, you would need to edit its contents, then save it.

    Compare your window to the one shown on the next page. If you used a different word processing program, your window will look different but the text portion of the data is the same.

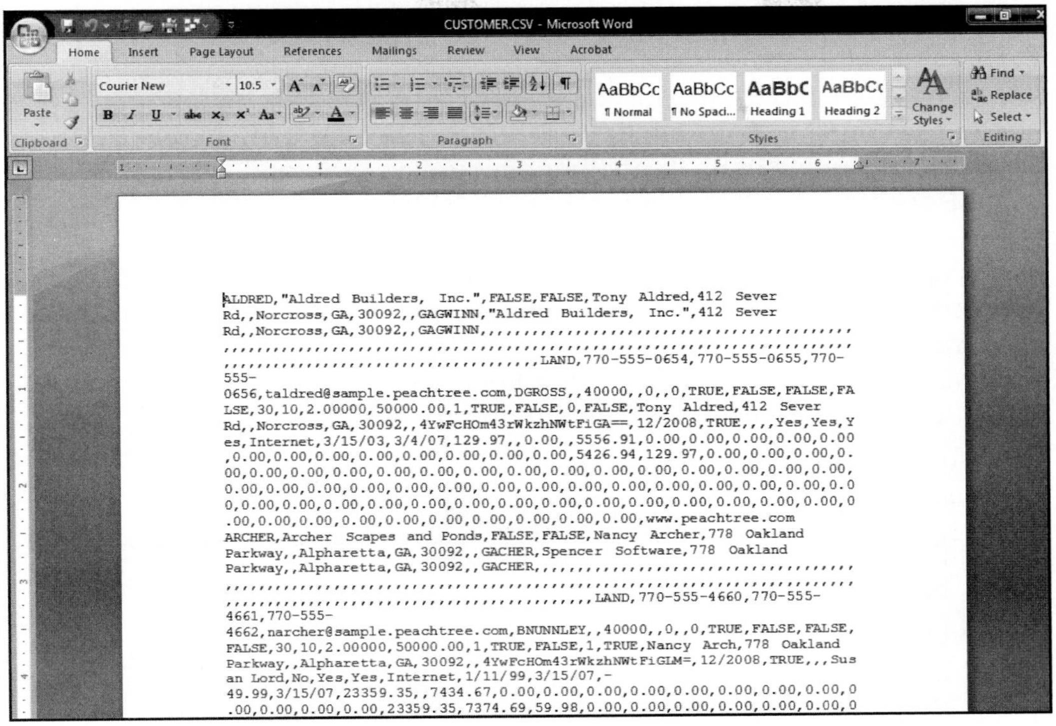

d. To keep the original ASCII file, use Word's Save As command and rename the file **CUSTOMER.lst**. When you save, the file will convert into a text document file from its original ASCII format.

e. Exit your word processing program.

IMPORTING

Importing data from another accounting, database, or spreadsheet program into Peachtree works similarly to exporting. Any information that is entered in Peachtree during setup and maintenance can be imported.

When you use the Select Import/Export command, you can:

- Select specific fields to import from other programs, such as Quicken.

- Create templates for importing. When you create a template, you can exclude information from the imported files or change the order of the imported fields.

➢ You can import all the files for a fiscal year.

Importing is an important tool, especially if you are switching from another accounting program to Peachtree. For example, if you have a Chart of Accounts set up in another accounting program, you can import it into Peachtree.

In this chapter you saw the steps for exporting data from Peachtree to Microsoft Word 2007. Since importing works similarly to exporting, you may want to try to import data from another accounting program into Peachtree. Remember to select the Import icon on the Select Import/Export window to start the import process.

INTERNET ACTIVITY	
1.	From your Internet browser, go to the book's website at http://www.mhhe.com/yacht2008.
2.	Link to Student Edition.
3.	In the Course-wide Content list, link to Part 4 Internet Activities for Chapters 15-18. Open or Save. Choose Chapter 16 to complete Quizzes, PowerPoints, and Going to the Net exercises.
4.	Complete the WOMEN'S BUSINESS CENTER exercise. Read steps 1 – 4.
5.	Follow the steps shown on the book's website to complete this Internet activity.
6.	Using a word processing program write summaries of what you find. Include all appropriate website addresses.

SUMMARY AND REVIEW

SOFTWARE OBJECTIVES: In Chapter 16, you have used the software to:

1. Export information from Peachtree to a word processing program. (In this chapter Microsoft Word 2007 and Windows Vista is used.)

2. Select the customer list from Bellwether Garden Supply to export.

3. Save two files.

WEB OBJECTIVES: In Chapter 16, you did these Internet activities:

1. Used your Internet browser to go to the book's website.

2. Went to the Internet Activity link on the book's website. Then, selected WEB EXERCISES PART 4. Completed the second exercise in Part 4—Women's Business Center.

3. Used a word processing program to write summaries of the websites that you visited.

GOING TO THE NET

Access the article "Peachtree by Sage Premium Accounting for Nonprofits 2008 Now Available" online at
http://www.sagesoftware.com/newsroom/news/index.cfm/fuseaction/news.detail/id/896

Answer the following questions.

1. What trusted accounting system is offered by Peachtree by Sage Premium for Nonprofits 2008? Explain the performance enhancements.

2. List six features built into Peachtree Premium Accounting for nonprofits.

Multiple-Choice Questions: In the space provided, write the letter that best answers each question.

_____1. A group of related records is called a/an:

a. File.
b. Record.
c. Field.
d. Balance Sheet.
e. All of the above.

______2. A group of fields that contains information on one subject is called a/an:

a. File.
b. Record.
c. Field.
d. Income statement.
e. All of the above.

______3. An individual piece of data such as an account number or customer's name is called a/an:

a. File.
b. Record.
c. Field.
d. Income statement.
e. All of the above.

______4. Exporting copies Peachtree data into a format that the following programs can read and use:

a. Spreadsheet programs.
b. Database programs.
c. Accounting programs.
d. Word processing programs.
e. All of the above

______5. Importing allows you to translate data from the following types of programs:

a. Spreadsheet programs.
b. Database programs.
c. Accounting programs.
d. None of the above.
e. All of the above.

______6. Information that appears on Peachtree's reports can be:

a. Imported.
b. Exported.
c. Formatted into an ANSI file.
d. A macro.
e. None of the above

______7. The name of the company from which you exported data is:

a. Jon Haney Design.
b. Mary Albert, Accountant.
c. Stanley's Sports.
d. Susan's Service Merchandise.
e. None of the above.

______8. When you import or export files, you use one of the following to format the data:

a. Template.
b. File.
c. Field.
d. Record.
e. None of the above.

______9. The type of file that is exported into a word processing program is called a/an:

a. DOS text file.
b. ANSI file.
c. ASCII file.
d. WordStar file.
e. None of the above.

_____10. The data on your window was exported in the following format:

a. Comma separated.
b. Line separated.
c. Field separated.
d. File separated.
e. None of the above.

Exercise 16-1: Follow the instructions below to complete Exercise 16-1.

1. Select one of the companies that have a vendor list.

2. Export the vendor list to a word processing program.

3. Open the vendor list.

Exercise 16-2: Follow the instructions below to complete Exercise 16-2.

1. Select one of the companies that have a customer list.

2. Export the customer list to a word processing program.

3. Open the customer list.

CHAPTER 16 INDEX

Chapter 17 Using Peachtree Complete Accounting 2008 with Microsoft Excel and Word

SOFTWARE OBJECTIVES: In Chapter 17, you use the software to:

1. Copy Peachtree report data to an Excel spreadsheet.
2. Copy Peachtree report data to Word.
3. Save Microsoft Excel and Word files.

WEB OBJECTIVES: In Chapter 17 you do these Internet activities:

1. Use your Internet browser to go to the book's website.
2. Go to the Internet Activity link on the book's website. Then, select WEB EXERCISES PART 4. Complete the third exercise in Part 4–Web Development.
3. Use a word processing program to write a summary of the websites that you visited.

If you have Microsoft Office 2000 or higher, you can use PCA 2008 data in numerous ways. For example, you can add data to an Excel spreadsheet. Or, you can add Peachtree financial statements to a Microsoft Word document that can be used for year-end reports.

This chapter describes several procedures for adding Peachtree data to Microsoft Office applications. In this chapter, you see how to insert Peachtree report data into a Microsoft Excel spreadsheet or a Word document. Then you can view or format that data using the features of Excel or Word.

GETTING STARTED

If you have Microsoft Excel 2000 (or higher) installed on your computer, you can copy a PCA report or financial statement to an Excel spreadsheet.

1. Start PCA.

2. Open the sample company, Bellwether Garden Supply.

COPYING PEACHTREE REPORT DATA TO MICROSOFT EXCEL

Bellwether Garden Supply's should be opened. Follow these steps to copy Bellwether's balance sheet and income statement data to Excel.

1. Restore the Exercise 6-2.ptb file. (This backup was made in Chapter 6 on page 204.)

> **Comment**
>
> If you no longer have your back up disk from Exercise 6-2, use starting data for Bellwether Garden Supply. If you use Bellwether's starting data, the illustrations will differ from those shown in this chapter. If necessary, refer to Chapter 1, pages 26-30.

2. The title bar shows Peachtree Accounting: Bellwether Garden Supply.

Balance Sheet

1. From the menu bar, select Reports & Forms; Financial Statements, <Standard> Balance Sheet.

2. Click 

; then click 

. The <Standard> Balance Sheet Options window appears. Click 

.

> **Comment**
>
> Microsoft Office 2007 and Windows Vista are used for the illustrations in this chapter. If you are using another version of Microsoft Office you may notice some differences with the illustrations shown in Chapter 17.

3. The Copy Report to Excel window appears.

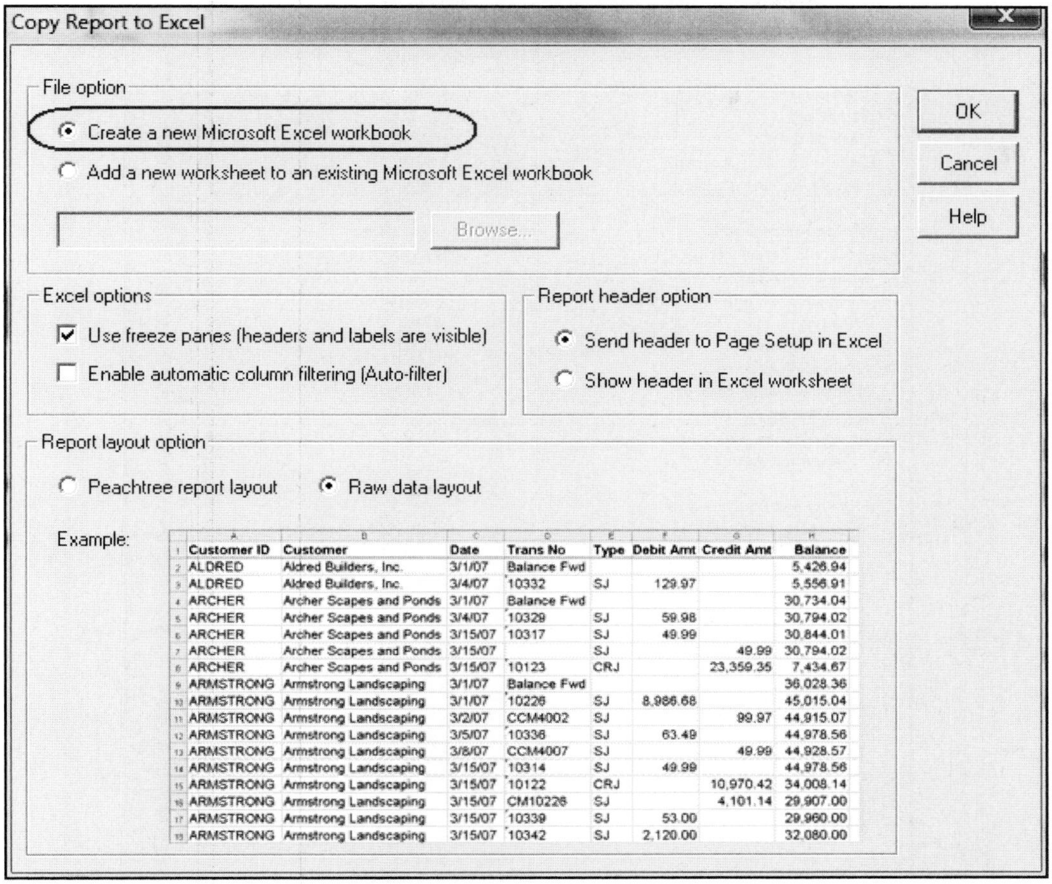

4. Accept the default for Create a new Microsoft Excel workbook by clicking on OK. Peachtree will start the Excel program and copy Bellwether's balance sheet into a blank worksheet. (If you are using Bellwether's starting data, your balances will differ.) The ASSETS section of the Balance Sheet is shown on the next page.

	A	B	C	D
1				
2	ASSETS			
3				
4	Current Assets			
5	Petty Cash	$ 327.55		
6	Cash on Hand	1,850.45		
7	Regular Checking Account	9,046.52		
8	Payroll Checking Account	9,093.25		
9	Savings Account	7,500.00		
10	Money Market Fund	4,500.00		
11	Accounts Receivable	174,940.73		
12	Other Receivables	7,681.84		
13	Allowance for Doubtful Account	(5,000.00)		
14	Inventory	12,021.41		
15	Prepaid Expenses	14,221.30		
16	Employee Advances	3,000.65		
17	Notes Receivable-Current	11,000.00		
18	Other Current Assets	120.00		
19				
20	Total Current Assets		250,303.70	
21				
22	Property and Equipment			
23	Furniture and Fixtures	62,769.25		
24	Equipment	38,738.33		
25	Vehicles	86,273.40		
26	Other Depreciable Property	6,200.96		
27	Buildings	185,500.00		
28	Building Improvements	26,500.00		
29	Accum. Depreciation-Furniture	(54,680.57)		
30	Accum. Depreciation-Equipment	(33,138.11)		
31	Accum. Depreciation-Vehicles	(51,585.26)		
32	Accum. Depreciation-Other	(3,788.84)		
33	Accum. Depreciation-Buildings	(34,483.97)		
34	Accum. Depreciation-Bldg Imp	(4,926.28)		
35				
36	Total Property and Equipment		223,378.91	
37				
38	Other Assets			
39	Deposits	15,000.00		
40	Organization Costs	4,995.10		
41	Accum Amortiz - Organiz Costs	(2,000.00)		
42	Notes Receivable- Noncurrent	5,004.90		
43	Other Noncurrent Assets	3,333.00		
44				
45	Total Other Assets		26,333.00	
46				
47	Total Assets		$ 500,015.61	

5. To see the header for the report, from Excel's menu bar, click , Print, Print Preview. Observe that Bellwether's header information is included. To see page 2 of the balance sheet, click Next Page. Click Next Page to see page 3 of the balance sheet. Close the print preview window.

Now that Bellwether's balance sheet is in Excel format, you can use

Excel's features to make changes to this report. (*Hint:* Excel 2007 and Windows Vista is used for the illustrations in this chapter.)

6. From Excel's menu bar, click File, Save As.

7. In the Save in field, select the appropriate drive.

8. The File name field displays Book1.xlsx. (*Hint:* In Excel 2003 and lower, the extension is .xls.) The Save as type field displays Microsoft Excel Workbook. Highlight the file name. Type **balance sheet** in the File name field.

9. Click 

. Excel automatically adds the extension .xlsx to the file name. (For Excel 2000-2003, the extension is .xls.)

10. Minimize the Excel window. Bellwether's Select a Report or Form window appears. (*Hint: You can also click* 

on the taskbar.)

Income Statement

1. From the Select a Report window, highlight <Standard> Income Stmnt.

2. Click 

; then 

. When the <Standard> Income Stmnt window appears, uncheck the Print Page Numbers and Show Zero Amounts boxes. Then click 

.

3. At the Copy Report to Excel window, you have *two* choices. Create a new Microsoft Excel workbook *or* Add a new worksheet to an existing Microsoft Excel workbook. Select Add a new worksheet. A partial Copy Report to Excel window is shown on the next page.

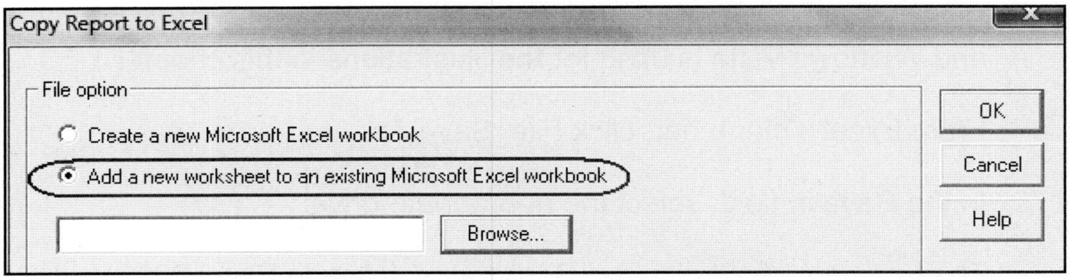

4. Click  and go to location where you saved the balance sheet. Click on the balance sheet file to highlight it. Make sure that the File name field shows balance sheet.xlsx (or balance sheet.xls). Then, click  . The Browse field shows X:\balance sheet.xlsx (substitute the X for your drive letter). Click  .

5. If necessary, from the taskbar click  . The Excel spreadsheet for Bellwether's income statement appears. (If you are using Bellwether's starting data, your account balances will differ.) Observe that you have two sheet tabs (at the bottom of the Excel worksheet). The active sheet, **Income Stmnt,** is shown. Compare the Income Statement to the one shown on the next page.

	A	B	C	D	E
1		Current Month		Year to Date	
2	Revenues				
3	Sales	$ 295.00	0.34	$ 295.00	0.11
4	Sales - Aviary	7,172.71	8.16	51,697.86	18.43
5	Sales - Books	149.75	0.17	7,293.10	2.60
6	Sales - Equipment	17,838.82	20.30	60,192.31	21.46
7	Sales - Food/Fert	1,006.96	1.15	5,204.15	1.86
8	Sales - Hand Tools	729.67	0.83	7,058.12	2.52
9	Sales - Landscape Services	17,467.43	19.88	26,975.53	9.62
10	Sales - Miscellaneous	0.00	0.00	45.00	0.02
11	Sales - Nursery	33,625.13	38.27	67,467.21	24.05
12	Sales - Pots	7,504.68	8.54	11,069.11	3.95
13	Sales - Seeds	1,457.43	1.66	8,661.39	3.09
14	Sales - Soil	655.02	0.75	9,082.55	3.24
15	Other Income	100.00	0.11	25,600.00	9.13
16	Sales Discounts	(145.72)	(0.17)	(155.62)	(0.06)
17					
18	Total Revenues	87,856.88	100.00	280,485.71	100.00
19					
20					
21	Cost of Sales				
22	Product Cost	(68.50)	(0.08)	(68.50)	(0.02)
23	Product Cost - Aviary	2,210.60	2.52	20,954.25	7.47
24	Product Cost - Books	14.27	0.02	2,361.37	0.84
25	Product Cost - Equipment	7,402.55	8.43	24,159.05	8.61
26	Product Cost - Food/Fert	398.80	0.45	2,060.04	0.73
27	Product Cost - Hand Tools	287.15	0.33	2,813.85	1.00
28	Product Cost - Pots	2,984.45	3.40	3,259.45	1.16
29	Product Cost - Seeds	584.45	0.67	3,450.65	1.23
30	Product Cost - Soil	283.22	0.32	4,048.47	1.44
31	Direct Labor - Nursery	1,750.00	1.99	3,062.50	1.09
32	Materials Cost	1,567.45	1.78	1,567.45	0.56
33	Materials Cost - Nursery	5,387.40	6.13	9,617.50	3.43
34	Subcontractors - Landscaping	335.50	0.38	335.50	0.12
35					
36	Total Cost of Sales	23,137.34	26.34	77,621.58	27.67
37					
38	Gross Profit	64,719.54	73.66	202,864.13	72.33
39					
40	Expenses				
41	Freight	0.00	0.00	50.00	0.02
42	Advertising Expense	1,325.00	1.51	1,325.00	0.47
43	Auto Expenses	274.56	0.31	274.56	0.10
44	Bad Debt Expense	1,341.09	1.53	1,341.09	0.48
45	Bank Charges	18.00	0.02	18.00	0.01
46	Depreciation Expense	2,761.30	3.14	8,394.00	2.99
47	Legal and Professional Expense	150.00	0.17	510.00	0.18
48	Licenses Expense	150.00	0.17	150.00	0.05
49	Maintenance Expense	75.00	0.09	75.00	0.03
50	Office Expense	479.89	0.55	479.89	0.17
51	Payroll Tax Exp	5,849.42	6.66	16,110.84	5.74
52	Rent or Lease Expense	550.00	0.63	1,100.00	0.39
53	Repairs Expense	125.00	0.14	3,694.00	1.32
54	Supplies Expense	2,928.17	3.33	2,928.17	1.04
55	Utilities Expense	303.45	0.35	303.45	0.11
56	Wages Expense	51,086.42	58.15	140,705.46	50.16
57	Other Expense	464.90	0.53	464.90	0.17
58	Purchase Disc- Expense Items	(10.11)	(0.01)	(10.11)	(0.00)
59					
60	Total Expenses	67,872.09	77.25	177,914.25	63.43
61					
62	Net Income	($ 3,152.55)	(3.59)	$ 24,949.88	8.90

6. Scroll down the window to see the rest of the income statement. Or, click File, Print Preview to see it.

7. Save the income statement. Use **balance sheet and income statement** as the file name.

8. Exit Excel.

9. Close the Select a Report or From window, then exit Peachtree; or continue with the next section.

COPYING PEACHTREE REPORT DATA TO MICROSOFT WORD

A displayed PCA report or financial statement can be copied to the Windows clipboard. Then you can paste that data into other applications, such as Microsoft Word or another word processing program. The steps that follow show you how to copy and paste a report using Microsoft Word 2000 or higher.

1. If necessary start PCA. Open the sample company, Bellwether Garden Supply.

2. If necessary restore the Exercise 6-2. ptb file. If you do not have that backup, use Bellwether's starting data. Refer to pages 26-30, Using Peachtree's Restore Wizard.

3. From Bellwether's menu bar, select Reports & Forms; Financial Statements; <Standard> Retained Earnings.

4. Click 

. The Statement of Retained Earnings displays.

5. Click 

. Uncheck Print Page Numbers and Show Zero Amounts. Click 

.

6. From the menu bar, click Edit, Copy.

7. Start Microsoft Word or other word processing program. From Word's menu bar, click Edit, Paste. Bellwether's statement of retained earnings appears. You need to format the statement in order for it to look like the one below. (These account balances reflect data from the Exercise 6-2.ptb backup file. If you are using a different back up file, your account balances will differ.)

Bellwether Garden Supply
Statement of Retained Earnings
For the Three Months Ending March 31, 2007

Beginning Retained Earnings	$	189,037.60
Adjustments To Date		0.00
Net Income		24,949.88
Subtotal		213,987.48
Ending Retained Earnings	$	213,987.48

For Management Purposes Only

8. Click , Save As. In the Save in field, select the appropriate drive. Accept the file name Bellwether Garden Supply.docx. Observe that the File as type field shows Word Document.

9. Click 

.

10. Exit Word.

11. Exit PCA.

INTERNET ACTIVITY	
1.	From your Internet browser, go to the book's website at www.mhhe.com/yacht2008.
2.	Link to Student Edition.
3.	In the Course-wide Content list, link to Part 4 Internet Activities for Chapters 15-18. Open or Save. Choose Chapter 17 to complete Quizzes, PowerPoints, and Going to the Net exercises.
4.	Complete the WEB DEVELOPMENT exercise. Read steps 1 and 2.
5.	Follow the steps shown on the book's website to complete this Internet activity.
6.	Using a word processing program write a brief summary of what you find. Include all appropriate website addresses.

SUMMARY AND REVIEW

SOFTWARE OBJECTIVES: In Chapter 17, you have used the software to:

1. Copy Peachtree report data to an Excel spreadsheet.
2. Copy Peachtree report data to Word.
3. Save Microsoft Excel and Word files.

WEB OBJECTIVES: In Chapter 17, you did these Internet activities:

1. Used your Internet browser to go to the book's website.
2. Go to the Internet Activity link on the book's website. Then, select WEB EXERCISES PART 4. Complete the third exercise in Part 4—Web Development.
3. Used a word processing program to write a summary of the websites that you visited.

GOING TO THE NET

Access the Microsoft Office website at http://office.microsoft.com. To answer the questions below, link to the appropriate Microsoft Office program. Click on the Products tab; link to the appropriate desktop program.

1. What is the website address for Word?
2. After linking to the Word website, briefly describe what kind of information can be obtained. If you link to other websites, include the appropriate address(es) in your answer.
3. What is the website address for Excel?
4. After linking to the Excel website, briefly describe what kind of information can be obtained. If you link to other websites, include the appropriate address(es) in your answer.

Short-Answer Questions: Write an answer to each question in the space provided.

1. Explain what Peachtree feature you use to export report data to an Excel spreadsheet.

2. What data do you use if you do not have the recommended back up file?

3. In Chapter 17, do you create a new Microsoft Excel workbook or add a new worksheet to an existing Microsoft Excel workbook?

____

4. In Chapter 17, it is recommended that you use data from what Bellwether back up file?

____

____

5. Why do you use Excel's Print Preview feature?

____

____

6. What extension does Word automatically add to saved files?

____

____

7. When you save the Peachtree data in Microsoft Word, what file name is automatically given to the report?

____

____

8. What extension does Excel automatically add to saved spreadsheets?

9. After copying the Peachtree data to Microsoft Word, do you need to format the document?

10. In Chapter 17, what Peachtree report do you use with Microsoft Word?

Exercise 17-1: Copy Peachtree data to Microsoft Excel. Experiment with different PCA reports.

Exercise 17-2: Copy Peachtree data to Microsoft Word. Experiment with different PCA reports.

CHAPTER 17 INDEX

Chapter 18 Write Letters, Use Templates, and Peachtree Online

SOFTWARE OBJECTIVES: In Chapter 18, you use the software to:

1. Use Peachtree's Write Letters feature.
2. Use Peachtree's letter templates.
3. Save Word files.
4. Extract the PAWMail.zip folder.
5. Explore Peachtree's website.

WEB OBJECTIVES: In Chapter 18, you do these Internet activities:

1. Go to the Internet Activity link on the book's website.
2. Select WEB EXERCISES PART 4. Complete the fourth exercise in Part 4–Additional Accounting Sources.
3. Use a word processing program to write summaries of the websites that you visited.

Peachtree's write letters feature allows you to send information to a large number of people quickly. For example, you can send personally addressed letters to all the company's customers. The Tasks menu and the Reports menu include a selection for write letters. You can use Peachtree's write letters feature to create mailings or e-mail messages from existing or custom letter templates using customer, vendor, and employee information. A ***template*** is a document pattern or part of a document that you keep stored so that it can be used again.

You can create mailings such as newsletters, announcements, collection letters, individual letters, e-mail messages, and other types of mailings. Peachtree integrates with the Microsoft Word mail merge feature, using Word to edit and create custom templates, then generates mailings using selected Peachtree information.

GETTING STARTED

1. Start Peachtree. Open Bellwether Garden Supply.

2. If necessary, restore the Exercise 6-2 file. This back up was made on page 204.

> **Comment**
>
> If you no longer have your Exercise 6-2 back up file, use starting data for Bellwether Garden Supply. Refer to pages 26-30, Using Peachtree's Restore Wizard, to restore Bellwether's starting data.

CREATE A MAILING TO CUSTOMERS

Follow these steps to use one of Peachtree's Write Letters templates.

1. From the Tasks menu, select Write Letters; Customer Letters.

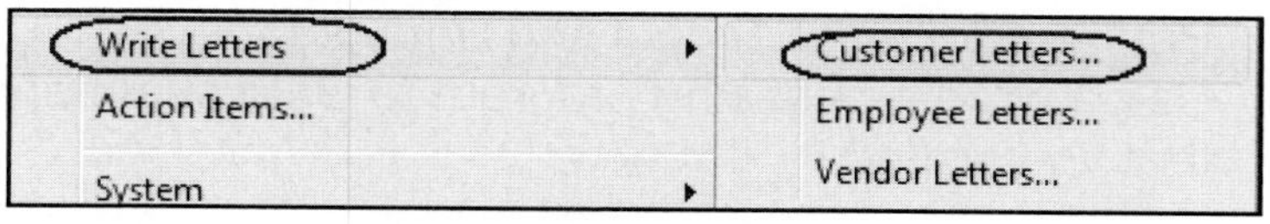

2. The Select a Report or Form window appears. Observe that the Form Types list shows Customer Labels and Letters highlighted. The Forms list shows Bellwether Sales Special selected. The Description field shows 2nd Qtr Sales Promotion letter.

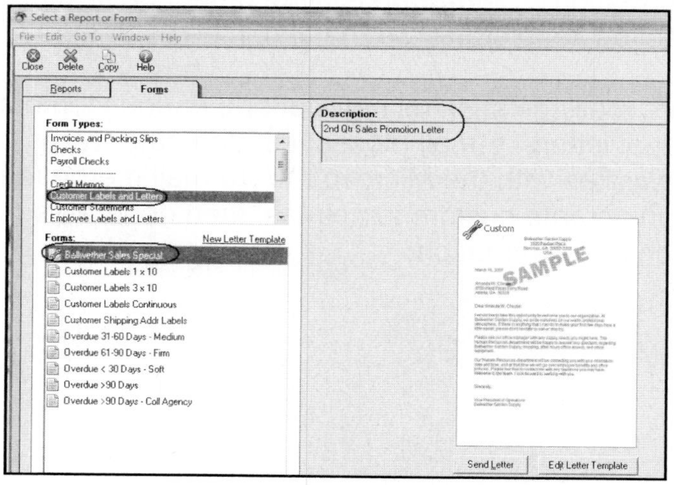

3. Click [Send Letter]. The Write Letters - Bellwether Sales Special Select Recipients window appears. Observe that you can select Word or E-Mail. Click [Word]. Wait a few moments for the first customer letter to appear. Observe that the taskbar shows Page 1 of 33– [Page: 1 Page: 1 of 33]. This means there are 33 customer letters. The Aldred Builder's, Inc. letter is shown below. Read the letter.

BELLWETHER
GARDEN SUPPLY
1505 Pavilion Place
Norcross, GA 30093-3203
770-724-4000

BUY ONE ITEM GET THE 2nd ITEM 50% OFF PROMOTION!!!

Aldred Builders, Inc.
412 Sever Rd
Norcross, GA 30092

Dear Tony Aldred:

As one of our loyal customers, we would like to ***thank you*** by extending you a ***special offer***. Buy any item in our catalog at the regular price and receive any **2nd** item (at an equal or lesser value) for ***50%*** off.

This offer is also good for purchases made online!! Check us out on the web at **www.peachtree.com.**

Again, thank you for your continued business.

Regards,

Derrick P. Gross
Sales Representative

4. Go to pages 2, 3, etc. Observe that each customer receives an individually addressed letter.

5. To save the letter, select File; Save As. The suggested filename is Customer Letters.doc. (*Hint:* Peachtree's letter templates are .doc files).

6. To close the document, select File; Close.

7. On the taskbar, click 

to return to the Select a Report window.

EDIT LETTER TEMPLATES

Follow these steps to create a letter template from the promotion letter shown on page 651.

1. From the Select a Report window, make sure Bellwether Sales Special is selected. (If necessary, select Tasks; Write Letters, Customers Letter.)

2. Click 

. The Edit Letter Template – Bellwether Sales Special window appears. Observe that the Letter Template Description shows 2nd Qtr Sales Promotion Letter.

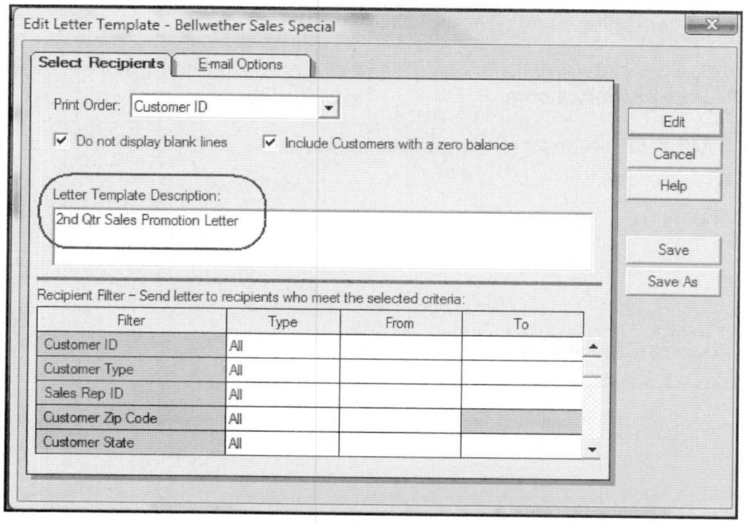

3. Review the information on the Edit Template window. Click Edit. The letter appears with fields identified. A partial letter is shown below.

«Company_Address_Line_1»
«Company_Address_Line_2»
«Company_City», «Company_State» «Company_Zip_Code»
«Company_Telephone_Number»

BUY ONE ITEM GET THE 2nd ITEM 50% OFF PROMOTION!!!

«Customer_Name»
«Customer_Full_Address»

Dear «Customer_Contact»:

As one of our loyal customers, we would like to ***thank you*** by extending you a ***special offer***. Buy any item in our catalog at the regular price and receive any **2nd** item (at an equal or lesser value) for ***50%*** off.

This offer is also good for purchases made online!! Check us out on the web at **«Company_Website_Address»**.

You can use this letter as a template or model to create a similar letter. Observe that the information in the letter is the same as the customer letter shown on page 651, *except* for the customizable information—((Company_Address_Line_1)), etc.

4. To add a date to the letter, click on a line or two above ((Customer_Name)). Select Date & Time [Date & Time] from Word 2007's Insert selections. Select the appropriate format and the date is inserted.

BELLWETHER
GARDEN SUPPLY
«Company_Address_Line_1»
«Company_Address_Line_2»
«Company_City», «Company_State» «Company_Zip_Code»
«Company_Telephone_Number»

BUY ONE ITEM GET THE 2nd ITEM 50% OFF PROMOTION!!!

Current Date — Today's date

«Customer_Name»
«Customer_Full_Address»

Dear «Customer_Contact»:

As one of our loyal customers, we would like to **thank you** by extending you a **special offer**. Buy any item in our catalog at the regular price and receive any **2nd** item (at an equal or lesser value) for **50%** off.

5. Save the template. The suggested filename is Bellwether Sales Special.doc. (*Hint:* Peachtree's letter templates are .doc files.)

CUSTOMER TEMPLATES

Follow these steps to see some of Bellwether's customer templates.

1. From Word's menu bar, select [Office button]; Open (File; Open). A list of letters appears. This is shown on the next page.

   Hint: If File; Open does *not* show a list of letter templates, select File; Save or File; Save As. (Another way to open the templates is to extract the PAWMail.zip folder. See page 656-667.)

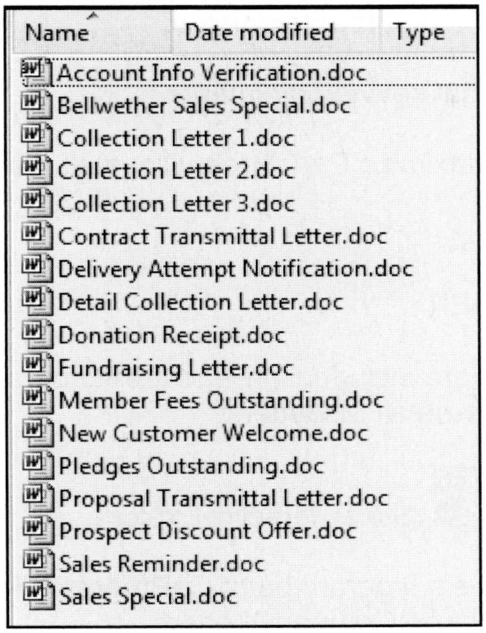

Name	Date modified	Type
Account Info Verification.doc		
Bellwether Sales Special.doc		
Collection Letter 1.doc		
Collection Letter 2.doc		
Collection Letter 3.doc		
Contract Transmittal Letter.doc		
Delivery Attempt Notification.doc		
Detail Collection Letter.doc		
Donation Receipt.doc		
Fundraising Letter.doc		
Member Fees Outstanding.doc		
New Customer Welcome.doc		
Pledges Outstanding.doc		
Proposal Transmittal Letter.doc		
Prospect Discount Offer.doc		
Sales Reminder.doc		
Sales Special.doc		

2. Observe these letters end in a .doc extension which means that the Peachtree customer templates have been saved as Word 97-2003 files. Double-click Contract Transmittal Letter. The letter template for contracts appears. Observe the fields that this letter includes.

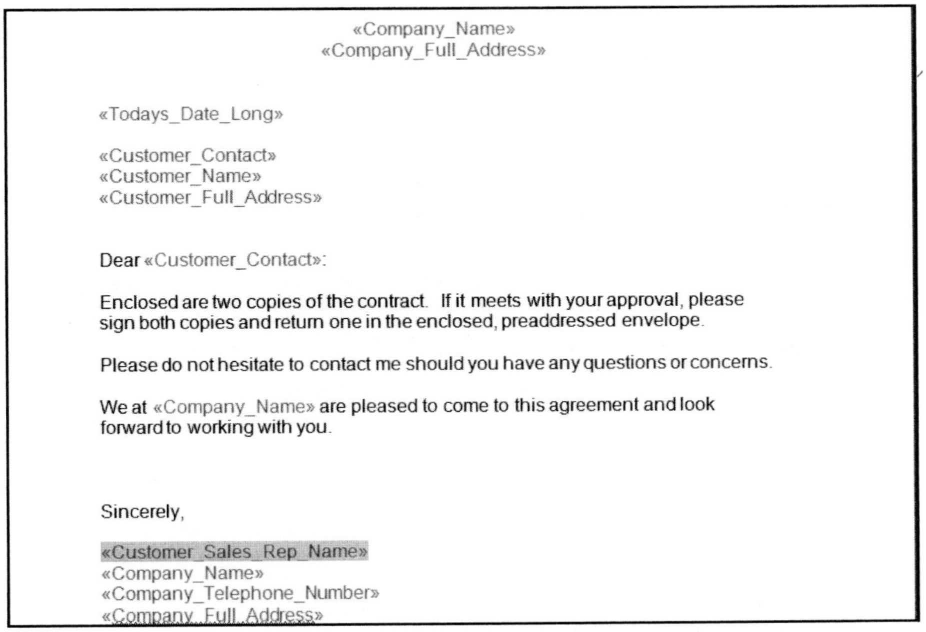

«Company_Name»
«Company_Full_Address»

«Todays_Date_Long»

«Customer_Contact»
«Customer_Name»
«Customer_Full_Address»

Dear «Customer_Contact»:

Enclosed are two copies of the contract. If it meets with your approval, please sign both copies and return one in the enclosed, preaddressed envelope.

Please do not hesitate to contact me should you have any questions or concerns.

We at «Company_Name» are pleased to come to this agreement and look forward to working with you.

Sincerely,

«Customer_Sales_Rep_Name»
«Company_Name»
«Company_Telephone_Number»
«Company_Full_Address»

3. Look at some of the other templates.

4. Exit Word without saving documents.

5. If necessary, maximize Peachtree. Close all windows.

6. Exit Peachtree.

PAWMail.Zip FOLDER

The letter templates are included in Peachtree program path. Follow these instructions to see all the letters.

1. Right-click  (Start); left-clickExplore.

2. Go to Peachtree's program path: C:\Program Files\Sage Software\Peachtree\Company\Letters.

3. Copy the PAWMail.zip folder to your desktop.

4. Extract the files. You can also open the templates from the following folders: Customer; Employee; Vendor.

   a. The Customer folder includes these documents:

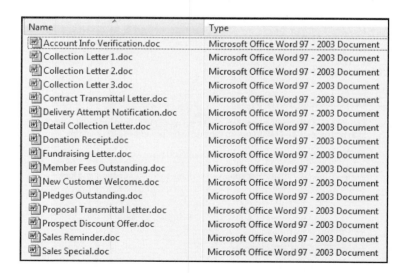

Name	Type
Account Info Verification.doc	Microsoft Office Word 97 - 2003 Document
Collection Letter 1.doc	Microsoft Office Word 97 - 2003 Document
Collection Letter 2.doc	Microsoft Office Word 97 - 2003 Document
Collection Letter 3.doc	Microsoft Office Word 97 - 2003 Document
Contract Transmittal Letter.doc	Microsoft Office Word 97 - 2003 Document
Delivery Attempt Notification.doc	Microsoft Office Word 97 - 2003 Document
Detail Collection Letter.doc	Microsoft Office Word 97 - 2003 Document
Donation Receipt.doc	Microsoft Office Word 97 - 2003 Document
Fundraising Letter.doc	Microsoft Office Word 97 - 2003 Document
Member Fees Outstanding.doc	Microsoft Office Word 97 - 2003 Document
New Customer Welcome.doc	Microsoft Office Word 97 - 2003 Document
Pledges Outstanding.doc	Microsoft Office Word 97 - 2003 Document
Proposal Transmittal Letter.doc	Microsoft Office Word 97 - 2003 Document
Prospect Discount Offer.doc	Microsoft Office Word 97 - 2003 Document
Sales Reminder.doc	Microsoft Office Word 97 - 2003 Document
Sales Special.doc	Microsoft Office Word 97 - 2003 Document

b. The Employee folder includes the Employee Welcome.doc file.

c. The Vendor folder includes two documents: Disputed Charte.doc and Request Credit Increase.doc.

5. Open the Request Credit Increase.doc.

«Company_Name»
«Company_Full_Address»

«Todays_Date_Long»

«Vendor_Name»
«Vendor_Full_Address»

Re: Request for increase in credit limit

Dear «Vendor_Contact»:

«Company_Name» has enjoyed doing business with your company for the past twelve months. We are very happy with your product, and are looking forward to a continued business relationship. After reviewing the past year's records, I would like you to consider increasing our credit limit. An increase of available credit in the amount of $500.00 should suffice.

Thank you for your consideration in this matter. If you have any questions, please feel free to contact me at my direct extension.

Sincerely,

Office Manager
«Company_Name»

6. Close Windows Explorer.

PEACHTREE ONLINE

Peachtree includes numerous resources on its website at www.peachtree.com. It is important to remember that websites are time and data sensitive. What that means is that home pages will change over time. You should regularly check Peachtree's website to see what new information is added.
During your study of Peachtree, you have accessed various websites. This chapter will show you some additional online resources.

1. Go online to www.peachtree.com.

2. Link to PRODUCTS. As of this writing, there are links to General Accounting, Industry Solutions, Add-on Products & Services, Outgrowing Peachtree, Online Accounting, Request More Information, Enhancement Requests, Peachtree Updates (*not* available with Educational Version.), and Product Reviews.

3. Select the Industry Solutions. Observe that Peachtree includes specific products for:

    - Accountants
    - Construction
    - Distribution
    - Manufacturing
    - Nonprofits

4. Link to Construction. Then in the Industry Solutions area, link to

    - Product Features
    - Features Tour
    - Frequently Asked Questions
    - Outgrowing Peachtree

5. Continue to explore the various Peachtree products for Distribution, Manufacturing, Accountants, and Nonprofits.

6. Observe there is a Services selection menu. Select SERVICES, Peachtree Passport Services, Create a New Passport Account.

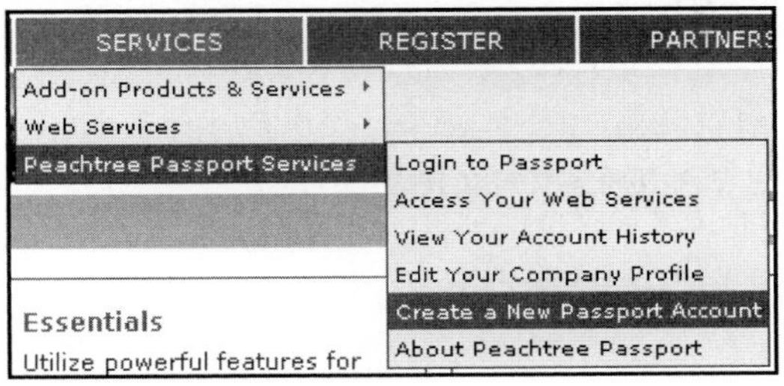

Create a Peachtree Passport Account to use Peachtree's Knowledgebase. Peachtree's knowledgebase includes numerous documents to help you in your study of PCA 2008.

Follow the screen prompts to Create a New Passport Account. Once you create a Passport account, you receive an email that allows you to log on for the first time. Once your log in information is available, you can use your Passport account to search Peachtree's knowledgebase.

Explore other links on Peachtree's website to learn more about accounting software that you have used in the textbook.

INTERNET ACTIVITY	
1.	From your Internet browser, go to the book's website.
2.	Link to Student Edition.
3.	In the Course-wide Content list, link to Part 4 Internet Activities for Chapters 15-18. Open or Save. Choose Chapter 18 to complete Quizzes, PowerPoints, and Going to the Net exercises.
4.	Since this exercise was started in Chapter 17, continue to explore the WEB DEVELOPMENT links.
5.	Using a word processing program write a brief summary of what you find. Include all appropriate website addresses

SUMMARY AND REVIEW

SOFTWARE OBJECTIVES: In Chapter 18, you have used the software to:

1. Use Peachtree's Write Letters feature.
2. Use Peachtree's letter templates.
3. Save Word files.
4. Extract the PAWMail.zip folder.
5. Explore Peachtree's website.

WEB OBJECTIVES: In Chapter 18, you did these Internet activities:

1. Go to the Internet Activity link on the book's website.
2. Select WEB EXERCISES PART 4. Complete the fourth exercise in Part 4–Additional Accounting Sources.
3. Use a word processing program to write summaries of the websites that you visited.

GOING TO THE NET

Access the MSDN Online Library website at http://msdn.microsoft.com/library/. Answer the following questions.

1. What is the MSDN library?
2. Type **What are templates?** in the Search for field. Click .
3. Link to an article of interest about templates. Write a brief essay about what you find (minimum length is 75 words; maximum length 150 words). Include website addresses in your answer.

Short-answer questions: Write an answer to each question in the space provided.

1. What does the Write Letters feature do?

____

____

2. How many customers does Bellwether Garden Supply have?

____

____

3. What type of promotion is Bellwether offering its customers?

____

____

4. How do customers receive this special offer?

____

____

5. What toolbar is used to change or add template fields?

____

____

6. What is a template?

____

____

7. What is the program and data path for Bellwether's letter templates?

____

____

8. List four customer letter templates.

____

____

____

____

Exercise 18-1: Follow the instructions below to complete Exercise 18-1.

1. Print the sales promotion letter to Chapple Law Offices. Use March 15, 2007 as the date. (*Hint:* Use the Bellwether Special letter template. Send a letter to Chapple Law Office.)

2. Save the file as Exercise 18-1.doc.

Exercise 18-2: Follow the instructions below to complete Exercise 18-2.

1. Print a sales promotion letter to Cummings Construction. (Use the current date.)

2. Save the file as Exercise 18-2.doc.

CHAPTER 18 INDEX

Project 3 Verde Computer Club

In Project 3, you complete the computer accounting cycle for Verde Computer Club which is located in Denver, CO. Verde Computer Club is a nonprofit business organized as a corporation.

Because Verde Computer Club is a nonprofit business, observe that there are some differences in its Chart of Accounts and some of its transactions. For example, revenues are derived from membership fees and seminars. Club members also contribute computers to local schools. When you work with this project, you see how these transactions are handled.

The club sponsors a trip to the Consumer Electronics Show (CES), a trade show in Las Vegas, Nevada. The trip involves expenses for bus rental, motel rooms, meals, and entrance fees to the trade show. Since so many club members attend the CES, a special rate is offered to them.

In this project you complete the accounting cycle for the month of January 2008. Verde Computer Club's Balance Sheet, checkbook register, and bank statement are provided as source documents.

At the end of this project there is a Checklist that shows the printed reports you should have. The step-by-step instructions also remind you when to print. Your instructor may ask you to turn in these printouts for grading purposes. Remember to make backups at periodic intervals.

Follow these steps to complete Project 3, Verde Computer Club:

Step 1: Start Peachtree.

Step 2: Make the selections to create a new company.

Step 3: The company information for Verde Computer Club is:

Company Name:	Verde Computer Club
Address Line 1:	1500 E. Cedar Avenue, Suite 10
City, State, Zip:	Denver, CO 80207
Country:	USA
Phone:	303-555-7211
Fax:	303-555-7233
Business Type:	Corporation
Federal Employer ID:	41-8755323
State Employer ID:	71-3149987
State Unemployment ID:	713342-7
Web Site:	www.computerclub.com
E-mail:	verde@computerclub.com

Step 4: Accept the default to Use a sample business that closely matches your company.

Step 5: Select Non-Profit Organizations. (*Hint:* Scroll down the Detailed types list.)

Step 6: Accept the default for Accrual accounting.

Step 7: Accept the default for Real Time posting.

Step 8: Accept the default for Choose an accounting period structure, 12 monthly accounting periods per year.

Step 9: The Choose the first period of your fiscal year window appears. If necessary, select January 2008.

Step 10: At the You are ready to create your company window, click 

. This will take a few moments. When the Have your started using credit cards for your Business window appears, click OK. The Peachtree Accounting: Verde Computer Club title bar is shown.

Step 11: When the Setup Guide appears, select Don't show this screen at startup. Then, close; click OK.

Step 12: Change the accounting period to Period 1 – 01/01/08 to 01/31/08 - Period 1 - 01/01/08-01/31/08.

Step 13: Delete, add, and change the following General Ledger accounts in the Chart of Accounts:

Delete these accounts:

Acct. #	*Account Name*
10000	Petty Cash
10100	Cash on Hand
10300	Payroll Checking Account
10500	Special Account
10600	Cash-Restricted Fund
10700	Investments
11400	Other Receivables
11500	Allowance for Doubtful Account
12100	Inventory-Kitchen
12150	Inventory-Golf & Tennis
12200	Inventory-Snack Stand
14100	Employee Advances
14700	Other Current Assets
15200	Automobiles
15300	Other Depreciable Property
15400	Leasehold Improvements
15500	Building
15600	Building Improvements
16900	Land
17200	Accum. Depreciation-Automobi
17300	Accum. Depreciation-Other
17400	Accum. Depreciation-Leasehold
17500	Accum. Depreciation-Building
17600	Accum. Depreciation-Bldg Imp
19000	Deposits
19150	Accum. Amortiz. - Org. Costs
19200	Note Receivable-Noncurrent
19900	Other Noncurrent Assets
23000	Accrued Expenses

23100	Sales Tax Payable
23300	Deductions Payable
23400	Federal Payroll Taxes Payable
23500	FUTA Tax Payable
23600	State Payroll Taxes Payable
23700	SUTA Payable
23800	Local Payroll Taxes Payable
24000	Other Taxes Payable
24100	Employee Benefits Payable
24200	Current Portion Long-Term Debt
24800	Other Current Liabilities
24900	Suspense-Clearing Account
27000	Notes Payable-Noncurrent
27100	Deferred Revenue
27400	Other Long-Term Liabilities
40200	Sales-Kitchen/Dining Room
40400	Sales-Golf & Tennis
40600	Sales-Snack Stand
40800	Sales-Other
41000	Contributions-Unrestricted
41200	Grants
41400	Program Service Revenue
41800	Investment Income
42000	Realized gain in Investment
42200	Miscellaneous Income
42400	Contributions-Restricted
42600	Investment Income-Restricted
43000	Other Income
48000	Fee Refunds
58000	Cost of Sales-Other
59000	Purchase Returns and Allowance
60000	Default Purchase Expense
60100	Grant and Allocation Exp.
61500	Bad Debt Expense
65000	Employee Benefit Programs Exp
65500	Other Employee Benefits
72000	Payroll Tax Expense
76500	Compensation of Officers
77000	Salaries Expense
89000	Other Expense

Change these accounts:

Acct. #	*Account Name*	*New Account Name*
10200	Regular Checking Account	Stockmen's Bank
12000	Inventory-Bar	Inventory-Computers/Schools
14000	Prepaid Expenses	Prepaid Rent
15100	Equipment	Computer Equipment
17000	Accum. Depreciation-Furnitur	Accum. Depreciation-Furn & Fix
17100	Accum. Depreciation-Eq.	Accum. Depreciation-Comp Equip
20000	Accounts Payable	Credit Card Payable
40000	Sales-Bar	Fees-Seminars/Classes
66000	Supplies Expense	Office Supplies Expense
67500	Occupancy Expense	Rent Expense
70000	Travel Expense	Bus Rental-CES
72500	Depreciation Expense	Depr. Exp.-Furniture & Fixture

Add these accounts:

Acct. #	*Account Name*	*Account Type*
39002	Membership Contributions	Equity-doesn't close
60000	Advertising Expense	Expenses
60400	Bank Service Charge	Expenses
70010	Meals-CES	Expenses
70020	Motel-CES	Expenses
70030	Fees-CES	Expenses
72520	Depr. Exp.-Comp Equip	Expenses

Read Me: How do I show my name on printouts?

Follow these steps to add your name to the company name.

1. From the menu bar, select Maintain; Company Information. The Maintain Company Information window appears.
2. Type your first and last name after Verde Computer Club. The Company Name field shows: Verde Computer Club—Your first and last name.
3. Click .

Step 14: Use Verde Computer Club Balance Sheet to record the chart of accounts beginning balances.

Verde Computer Club Balance Sheet January 1, 2008		
ASSETS		
Current Assets		
Stockmen's Bank	$15,250.00	
Inventory-Computers/Schools	500.00	
Inventory-Office	1,500.00	
Total Current Assets		$17,250.00
Property and Equipment		
Furniture and Fixtures	1,200.00	
Computer Equipment	3,000.00	
Total Property and Equipment		4,200.00
Other Assets: Organization Costs		300.00
Total Assets		$21,750.00
LIABILITIES		
Credit Card Payable	250.00	
Total Liabilities		250.00
CAPITAL		
Retained Earnings		21,500.00
Total Liabilities and Capital		$21,750.00

Step 15: Back up your data. The suggested file name is Verde Computer Club Begin.ptb.

Step 16: The checkbook register that follows provides you with the information necessary for Verde Computer Club's Cash Receipts Journal and Cash Disbursements Journal entries for January.

Check Number	Date	Description of Transaction	Payment/Dr. (-)	Deposit/Cr. (+)	Balance
					15,250.00
	1/2/08	Deposit (membership dues)[1]		2,850.00	18,100.00
8001	1/8/08	Payment - Credit Card	250.00		17,850.00
8002	1/8/08	Dean Advertising	205.00		17,645.00
8003	1/9/08	Denver Office Supplies	155.65		17,489.35
8004	1/17/08	Meals-CES	800.00		16,689.35
8005	1/17/08	Bus Rental-CES	600.00		16,089.35
8006	1/17/08	Entrance Fees-CES	725.00		15,364.35
8007	1/17/08	Motel Rooms-CES	835.27		14,529.08
8008	1/26/08	Mountain Telephone	41.76		14,487.32
8009	1/26/08	U.S. Post Office	41.00		14,446.32
	1/29/08	Deposit (seminar fees)		800.00	15,246.31

Step 17: *Additional journal entry*: On January 31, a club member donated a computer system and printer to the club. The value of the computer and printer is $250. (Debit, Inventory - Computers/Schools; Credit, Membership Contributions. Use the General Journal for this entry)

Continue with step 18 on next page.

[1]For each deposit shown on the check register, type the date of the transaction in the Deposit ticket ID field. For each check, use Banking; Write Checks.

Step 18: Verde Computer Club's bank statement is shown below. Journalize and post the entry for the bank service charge. Then complete the Account Reconciliation for the checking account.

Statement of Account Stockmen's Bank Jan. 1 to Jan. 31, 2008		Account #189-926390	Verde Computer Club 1500 E. Cedar Ave., Ste 10 Denver, CO 80207	
		REGULAR CHECKING		
Previous Balance	12/31/07	$ 15,250.00		
2 Deposits(+)		3,650.00		
7 Checks (-)		2,887.68		
Service Charges (-)		12.00		
Ending Balance	1/31/08	**$ 16,000.32**		
		DEPOSITS		
	1/3/08	2,850.00	1/31/08	800.00
		CHECKS (Asterisk * indicates break in check number sequence)		
	1/10/08	8001	250.00	
	1/11/08	8002	205.00	
	1/17/08	8003	155.65	
	1/26/08	8004	800.00	
	1/28/08	8005	600.00	
	1/29/08	8007*	835.27	
	1/31/08	8008	41.76	

Step 19: Make a backup. The suggested file name is Verde Computer Club January.ptb.

Your instructor may want to collect this project. A Checklist of Printouts is shown on the next page.

	Checklist of Printouts, Project 3: Verde Computer Club
	Chart of Accounts
	Account Reconciliation
	Cash Account Register – Stockmen's Bank
	Cash Disbursements Journal
	Cash Receipts Journal
	General Journal
	General Ledger Trial Balance
	General Ledger
	Balance Sheet
	Income Statement
	Statement of Cash Flow
	Statement of Changes in Financial Position
	Statement of Retained Earnings

Student Name________________________________**Date**______________

CHECK YOUR PROGRESS: PROJECT 3
VERDE COMPUTER CLUB

1. What are the total debit and credit balances on your general ledger trial balance? __________
2. What is the total amount of checks outstanding? __________
3. How much are the total expenses on January 31? __________
4. How much are the total revenues on January 31? __________
5. How much is the net income (net loss) on January 31? __________
6. What is the account balance in the Membership Contributions account on January 31? __________
7. What are the total assets on January 31? __________
8. What is the ending retained earnings on January 31, 2008? __________
9. What is the balance in the Credit Card Payable account on January 31? __________
10. What is the balance in the Office Supplies Expense account on January 31? __________
11. Is there an Increase or Decrease in cash for the month of January? __________
12. Was any Credit Card Payable incurred during the month of January? (Circle your answer) YES NO

Project 4 BJW Manufacturing, Inc.

In Project 4, you complete the computer accounting cycle for BJW Manufacturing, Inc. This company manufactures backpacks, sleeping bags, and tents.

BJW Manufacturing, Inc. offers its customers a sales discount of 2% 15, Net 30 days. Vendors offer BJW Manufacturing a purchase discount of 1% 15, Net 30 days.

Follow these steps to complete Project 4, BJW Manufacturing, Inc.

Step 1: Start Peachtree.

Step 2: Make the selections to create a new company.

Step 3: Type the following company information for BJW Manufacturing:

Company Name:	BJW Manufacturing, Inc. (*use your initials, then Manufacturing, Inc.*)
Address Line 1:	7108 Montgomery Avenue
City, State, Zip:	Philadelphia, PA 19120
Country:	USA
Phone:	215-555-2332
Fax:	215-555-2334
Business Type:	Corporation
Federal Employer ID:	41-4825312
State Employer ID:	20-8844221
State Unemployment ID:	203207-4
Web Site:	www.phila.net/bjwmftg
E-mail:	bjwmftg@phila.net

Step 4: Accept the default for Use a sample business type that closely matches your company.

Step 5: Scroll down the list. In the Detailed type list, select Manufacturing Company.

Step 6: Accept the default for Accrual accounting.

Step 7: Accept the default for Real Time posting.

Step 8: Accept the default for 12 monthly accounting periods.

Step 9: The Choose the first period of your fiscal year window appears. If necessary, select January 2008 as the year.

Step 10: At the You are ready to create your company window, click Finish.

Step 11: When the Have you started using credit card sales for your Business? window appears, click OK. When the Peachtree Setup Guide window appears, click on the box next to Don't show this screen at startup to place a checkmark in it. Close the Setup Guide Window.

Step 12: Change the account period to 01-Jan 01,2008 to Jan 31,2008—Period 1 - 01/01/08-01/31/08.

General Ledger

1. Delete the following accounts:

10100	Cash on Hand
10400	Savings Account
10500	Special Account
10600	Investments-Money Market
15400	Leasehold Improvements
16900	Land
17300	Accum. Depreciation-Other
17400	Accum. Depreciation-Leasehold
24800	Other Current Liabilities

2. Change these account names:

10200	Regular Checking Account to Franklin Bank
10300	Payroll Checking Account to Philadelphia Savings & Loan
14000	Prepaid Expenses to Prepaid Insurance
15100	Equipment to Computers & Equipment
15200	Automobiles to Trucks/Autos
17100	Accum. Depreciation-Equipment to Accum. Depreciation-Comp & Equ
17200	Accum. Depreciation-Automobil to Accum. Depreciation-Trucks/Aut
23300	Deductions Payable to Medicare Employee Taxes Payabl
24000	Other Taxes Payable to FICA Employee Taxes Payable
24100	Employee Benefits Payable to FICA Employer Taxes Payable
27000	Notes Payable-Noncurrent to Mortgage Payable
40000	Sales #1 to Sales-Backpacks
40200	Sales #2 to Sales-Sleeping Bags
40400	Sales #3 to Sales-Tents
72500	Penalties and Fines Exp to Employer FUTA Expense
73000	Other Taxes to Employer SUTA Expense

3. Add these accounts:

Acct. ID	*Acct. Description*	*Account Type*
12010	Inventory-Backpacks	Inventory
12020	Inventory-Sleeping Bags	Inventory
12030	Inventory-Tents	Inventory
22000	Credit Card Payable	Other Current Liabilities
23350	Medicare Employer Taxes Payabl	Other Current Liabilities
23650	Employee SUI Taxes Payable	Other Current Liabilities
73200	Employer FICA Taxes Expense	Expenses
73300	Employer Medicare Expense	Expenses

4. You purchased BJW Manufacturing in December 2007. Use the Balance Sheet on the next page to record the chart of account beginning balances.

BJW Manufacturing, Inc. Balance Sheet January 1, 2008		
ASSETS		
Current Assets		
Franklin Bank	$65,650.00	
Philadelphia Savings & Loan	31,300.00	
Investments-Cert. of Deposit	14,500.00	
Inventory-Backpacks	1,612.50	
Inventory-Sleeping Bags	1,760.00	
Inventory-Tents	2,679.60	
Prepaid Insurance	3,600.00	
Total Current Assets		$121,102.10
Property and Equipment		
Furniture and Fixtures	2,500.00	
Computers & Equipment	6,000.00	
Trucks/Autos	25,000.00	
Building	105,000.00	
Total Property and Equipment		138,500.00
Organization Costs		1,000.00
Total Assets		$260,602.10
LIABILITIES AND STOCKHOLDER'S EQUITY		
Credit Card Payable	15,900.00	
Mortgage Payable	97,500.00	
Total Liabilities		$113,400.00
Stockholder's Equity: Common Stock		147,202.10
Total Liabilities and Stockholder's Equity		$260,602.10

5. Backup. The suggested filename is **BJW Mftg Starting Balance Sheet.ptb**.

Accounts Payable

1. Set up the following vendor defaults.

Standard Terms:	Due in number of days
Net due in:	30 days
Discount in:	15 days
Discount %	1.00
Credit Limit:	20,000.00

GL Link Accounts:

Expense Account:	12010 Inventory-Backpacks
Discount GL Account:	59500 Purchase Discounts

2. Set up the following vendors:

Vendor ID:	dd22
Name:	David and Dash Fabrics
Contact:	Jay Dash
Mailing Address:	211 East Third Street
City, ST Zip:	Hartford, CT 06108
Vendor Type:	slpg bgs
1099 Type:	Independent Contractor
Expense Account:	12020 Inventory-Sleeping Bags
Telephone 1:	860-555-1234
Fax:	860-555-1270
E-mail:	jay@ddfabrics.com
Web Site:	www.ddfabrics.com

Purchase Info:

Tax ID Number:	36-7993838

Vendor ID:	ep33
Name:	Ellison Products
Contact:	Kathy Ellison
Mailing Address:	1413 Heights Boulevard
City, ST Zip:	Cleveland, OH 44192
Vendor Type:	tents
1099 Type:	Independent Contractor

Expense Account:	12030 Inventory-Tents
Telephone 1:	216-555-1341
Fax:	216-555-1342
E-mail:	kathy@ellisonproducts.com
Web Site:	www.ellisonproducts.com

Purchase Info:

Tax ID Number: 43-2281390

Vendor ID:	rk44
Name:	RK Supplies
Contact:	Roslyn Kalmar
Mailing Address:	200 Main Street
City, ST Zip:	Trenton, NJ 07092
Vendor Type:	backpack
1099 Type:	Independent Contractor
Expense Accounting:	12010 Inventory-Backpacks
Telephone 1:	609-555-8900
Fax:	609-555-8999
E-mail:	info@rksupplies.net
Web Site:	www.rksupplies.net

Purchase Info:

Tax ID Number: 22-1384187

Accounts Receivable

1. Set up the following customer default settings:

Standard Terms:	Due in number of days
Net due in:	30 days
Discount in:	15 days
Discount %:	2.00
Credit Limit:	15,000.00
GL Sales Account:	40000 Sales-Backpacks
Discount GL Account:	49000 Sales Discounts

2. Enter the following customer records:

Customer ID:	001BOS
Name:	Benson's Outdoor Suppliers
Contact:	Vicky Benson
Billing Address:	3102 West Ninth Street
City, ST Zip:	Tucson, AZ 85711
Customer Type:	AZ (for Arizona)
Telephone 1:	520-555-3288
Fax:	520-555-0613
E-mail:	info@bensonoutdoor.biz
Web Site:	www.bensonoutdoor.biz

Sales Info:

G/L Sales Acct:	40000, Sales-Backpacks
Resale Number:	6832551-7

Customer ID:	002SCS
Name:	Sharon's Camping Store
Contact:	Sharon Clarke
Billing Address:	18 West 12th Street
City, ST Zip:	Portland, OR 97218
Customer Type:	OR (for Oregon)
Telephone 1:	503-555-3223
Fax:	503-555-3001
E-mail:	sharon@campingstore.biz
Web Site	www.campingstore.biz

Sales Info:

G/L Sales Acct:	40200, Sales-Sleeping Bags
Resale Number:	8091293-2

Customer ID:	003WST
Name:	West's Store
Contact:	Jane West
Billing Address:	2041 Princeton Street
City, ST Zip:	Cincinnati, OH 45227
Customer Type:	OH (for Ohio)
Telephone 1:	513-555-2902

Fax: 513-555-2904
E-mail: jane@weststore.com
Web Site: www.weststore.com

Sales Info:

G/L Sales Acct: 40400, Sales-Tents
Resale Number: 8719803-4

Payroll

1. Enter the following employee defaults:

   State: PA
   Unemployment Percent for Your Company: 3.4
   Enter the locality: Phila
   Enter the locality tax rate: 1.00
   Do you want to record employee meals and tips?: No

   Gross Pay: **51000 Direct Labor Costs**
   Tax Liability: 23400 Federal Payroll Taxes Payable
   Tax Expense: 72000 Payroll Tax Expense

2. Accept the following defaults: 401(k) plan not offered, Vacation time not tracked, Sick time not tracked.

3. Click 

 to exit the Payroll Setup Wizard. Close the Peachtree Help window.

4. Go to the Employee Defaults screen. Observe that the State / Locality area shows PA (for Pennsylvania) as the State, and Phila (for Philadelphia) as the locality.

5. Select the Pay Levels tab. In the Salary Pay Levels table, select G/L Account 77000, Salaries Expense, for the salaried employee, Elaine King.

6. Select the following EmployEE Fields:

   The Fed_Income line displays Account No. 23400, Federal Payroll Taxes Payable, for FIT.

   Soc_Sec, 24000, FICA Employee Taxes Payable

   Medicare, 23300, Medicare Employee Taxes Payable

   State, 23600, State Payroll Taxes Payable

   Local, 23800, Local Payroll Taxes Payable

   SUI, 23650, Employee SUI Taxes Payable

7. Select the following EmployER Fields:

	Liability column	*Expense column*
Soc_Sec_ER	24100, FICA Employer Taxes Payable	73200, Employer FICA Taxes Expense
Medicare_ER	23350, Medicare Employer Taxes Payabl	73300, Employer Medicare Expense
FUTA_ER	23500, FUTA Tax Payable	72500, Employer FUTA Expense
SUI_ER	23700, SUTA Payable	73000, Employer SUTA Expense

8. Enter the following employee records:

Employee ID:	EK40
Name:	Elaine King
Accept the default for Employee	
Address:	1215 North 75th Street
City, ST Zip:	Upper Darby, PA 19112
Telephone 1:	215-555-7143
E-mail:	elaine@mail.net
Social Security #:	444-00-1111

Type:	FULL
Hired:	1/2/08

Pay Info: Salary, $1,000. Ms. King is paid monthly.

Withholding Info:

Filing Status:	Single for US Federal, State, and Local
Allow:	1 for US Federal, State and Local

Employee ID:	JS50
Name:	Janice Sullivan
Accept the default for Employee	
Address:	1341 Farrington Rd.
City, ST Zip:	Philadelphia, PA 19191
Telephone 1:	215-555-1023
E-mail:	janice@mail.net
Social Security #:	207-00-0011
Type:	FULL
Hired:	1/2/08

Pay Info: Hourly, $9.75 per hour; Overtime, $14.63. Ms. Sullivan is paid weekly.

Withholding Info:

Filing Status:	Married for Federal, State, and Local
Allow:	3 for Federal, State, and Local

Employee ID:	LS60
Name:	Lee Smith
Accept the default for Employee	
Address:	8192 City Line Avenue
City, ST Zip:	Philadelphia, PA 19122
Telephone 1:	215-555-8201
E-mail:	lee@mail.net
Social Security #:	010-00-1234
Type:	FULL
Hired:	1/2/08

Pay Info: Hourly, $9.75 per hour; Overtime, $14.63. Mr. Smith is paid weekly.

Withholding Info:

Filing Status:	Single for Federal, State, and Local
Allow:	1 for Federal, State, and Local

Employee ID:	OW70
Name:	Oscar Watson
Accept the default for Employee	
Address:	1490 Broad Street, Apt. 1003
City, ST Zip:	Philadelphia, PA 19135
Telephone 1:	215-555-5231
E-mail:	owen@mail.net
Social Security #:	300-00-2233
Type:	FULL
Hired:	1/2/08

Pay Info: Hourly, $9.75 per hour; Overtime, $14.63. Mr. Watson is paid weekly.

Withholding Info:

Filing Status:	Married for Federal, State, and Local
Allow:	2 for Federal, State, and Local

Inventory

1. Make sure that FIFO is the default inventory costing method.

2. Set up the following inventory items:

Item ID:	backpacks
Description:	backpacks
Item Class:	Stock item
Description for Sales:	backpacks
Price Level 1:	150.00
Last Unit Cost:	37.50
Cost Method:	FIFO
GL Sales Acct:	40000 Sales-Backpacks

GL Inventory Acct:	12010, Inventory-Backpacks
GL Cost of Sales Acct:	50500, Raw Material Purchases
Item Tax Type:	2 Exempt
Item Type:	backpack
Stocking U/M:	each
Minimum Stock:	10
Reorder Quantity:	5
Preferred Vendor ID:	rk44, RK Supplies

Beginning Balances:	backpacks
Quantity:	43.00
Unit Cost:	37.50
Total Cost:	1,612.50

Item ID:	sleeping bags
Description:	sleeping bags
Item Class:	Stock item
Description for Sales:	sleeping bags
Price Level 1:	105.00
Last Unit Cost:	27.50
Cost Method:	FIFO
GL Sales Acct:	40200, Sales-Sleeping Bags
GL Inventory Acct:	12020, Inventory-Sleeping Bags
GL Cost of Sales Acct:	50500, Raw Material Purchases
Item Tax Type:	2 Exempt
Item Type:	slpg bgs
Stocking U/M:	each
Minimum Stock:	10
Reorder Quantity:	5
Preferred Vendor ID:	dd22, David and Dash Fabrics

Beginning Balances:	sleeping bags
Quantity:	64.00
Last Unit Cost	27.50
Total Cost:	1,760.00

Item ID:	tents
Description:	tents
Item Class:	Stock item

Description for Sales:	tents
Price Level 1:	175.00
Last Unit Cost:	47.85
Cost Method:	FIFO
GL Sales Acct:	40400, Sales-Tents
GL Inventory Acct:	12030, Inventory-Tents
GL Cost of Sales Acct:	50500, Raw Material Purchases
Item Tax Type:	2 Exempt
Item Type:	tents
Stocking U/M:	each
Minimum Stock:	10
Reorder Quantity:	5
Preferred Vendor ID:	ep33, Ellison Products

Beginning Balances:	tents
Quantity:	56.00
Unit Cost:	47.85
Total Cost:	2,679.60

Jobs

1. Set up the following job records:

Job ID:	13-221
Description:	backpacks
For Customer:	001BOS
Start Date:	1/2/08
End Date:	12/31/08
Job Type:	backpack

Job ID:	14-331
Description:	sleeping bags
For Customer:	002SCS
Start Date:	1/2/08
End Date:	12/31/08
Job Type:	slpg bgs

Job ID:	15-441
Description:	tents
For Customer:	003WST

Start Date:	1/2/08
End Date:	12/31/08
Job Type:	tents

2. Backup your data. Use **BJW Mftg Begin.ptb** as the filename.

3. Exit or continue.

Journalize and post the following transactions:

Date	*Description of Transaction*
01/04/08	Invoice No. 315 was received from David and Dash Fabrics for 15 sleeping bags @ $27.50 each for a total of $412.50. Post invoice 315.
01/04/08	Invoice No. 45 was received from RK Supplies for 20 backpacks @ $37.50 each for a total of $750.00. Post invoice 45.
01/04/08	Invoice No. 800 was received from Ellison Products for 16 tents @ $47.85 each for a total of $765.60. Post invoice 800.

01/04/08 Pay the factory employees for 40 hours of direct labor. Select Account No. 10300, Philadelphia Savings & Loan, as the Cash Account. In the Check Number field, type **101** for Ms. Sullivan's paycheck. The check numbers for Mr. Smith and Mr. Watson will be automatically completed. (Do *not* print the payroll checks.) Remember, click 

to complete the following:

Check No.	*Employee*	*Job*	*Hours*
101	Janice Sullivan	15-441	40
102	Lee Smith	14-331	40
103	Oscar Watson	13-221	40

Remember to click 

after each payroll entry.

01/11/08 Sold 20 backpacks on account to Benson's Outdoor Suppliers for a total of $3,000.00, Job 13-221. In the Invoice # field, type **101**.[1] Post sales invoice 101.

01/11/08 Sold 12 sleeping bags on account to Sharon's Camping Store for a total of $1,260.00, Job 14-331. Post sales invoice 102.

01/11/08 Sold 20 tents on account to West's Store for a total of $3,500.00, Job 15-441. Post sales invoice 103.

01/11/08 Pay the factory employees for 40 hours of direct labor. *Remember to post each payroll entry.*

Check No.	*Employee*	*Job*	*Hours*
104	Janice Sullivan	15-441	40
105	Lee Smith	14-331	40
106	Oscar Watson	13-221	40

01/16/08 Issued Check No. 1001 to RK Supplies in payment of purchase Invoice No. 45. Select Account No. 10200, Franklin Bank as the cash account. In the Check Number field, type **1001**. Do *not* print vendor checks. In the Discount Account field, make sure that Account No. 59500, Purchase Discounts is shown. Post Check No. 1001 in the amount of $742.50.

01/16/08 Issued Check No. 1002 to David and Dash Fabrics in payment of purchase Invoice No. 315. Post Check No. 1002 in the amount of $408.37.

01/16/08 Issued Check No. 1003 to Ellison Products in payment of purchase Invoice No. 800. Post Check No. 1003 in the amount of $757.94.

01/18/08 Invoice No. 328 was received from David and Dash Fabrics for 15 sleeping bags @ $27.50 each for a total of $412.50. Post invoice 328.

---

[1]Since you are not printing sales invoices, it is necessary to complete this field.

01/18/08 Invoice No. 900 was received from Ellison Products for 20 tents @ $47.85 each for a total of $957.00. Post invoice 900.

01/18/08 Pay the factory employees for 40 hours of direct labor. *Remember to click on Save after each payroll check is recorded.*

Check No.	*Employee*	*Job*	*Hours*
107	Janice Sullivan	15-441	40
108	Lee Smith	14-331	40
109	Oscar Watson	13-221	40

01/25/08 Received payment from Benson's Outdoor Suppliers for sales invoice 101. Select Account No. 10200, Franklin Bank, as the cash account. Use the date of the transaction in the Deposit ticket ID field. In the Reference field, type **Inv. 101**. Post this receipt in the amount of $2,940.

01/25/08 Received payment from Sharon's Camping Store for sales invoice 102. In the Reference field, type **Inv. 102**. Post this receipt in the amount of $1,234.80.

01/25/08 Received payment from West's Store for sales invoice 103. In the Reference field, type **Inv. 103**. Post this receipt in the amount of $3,430.

01/25/08 Sold 25 sleeping bags on account to Sharon's Camping Store for a total of $2,625.00, Job 14-331. In the Invoice # field, type **104**. Post sales invoice 104.

01/25/08 Sold 21 tents on account to West's Store for a total of $3,675.00, Job 15-441. Post sales invoice 105.

01/25/08 Pay the factory employees for 40 hours of direct labor. *Remember to click on Save after each payroll check is recorded.*

Check No.	*Employee*	*Job*	*Hours*
110	Janice Sullivan	15-441	40
111	Lee Smith	14-331	40
112	Oscar Watson	13-221	40

01/25/08 Pay the salaried employee, Elaine King. In the Salary Amounts table, make sure that account 77000, Salaries Expense, is shown in the Account column. If not, select that account. *Post Check No. 113.*

01/31/08 Issued Check No. 1004 to Franklin Bank for $709.23 in payment of Mortgage Payable; split the mortgage payment between principal in the amount of $584.06, and interest in the amount of $125.17. In the Check Number field, type **1004**. (Use the Write Checks task and the split feature. Make sure that account 10200, Franklin Bank, is selected as the Cash Account.) Post Check No. 1004.

01/31/08 Issued Check No. 1005 to Philadelphia Savings & Loan for $800 in payment of Credit Card Payable. Post Check No. 1005.

01/31/08 Issued Check No. 1006 to the Power Company for $204.75 in payment of utilities. (Debit Utilities Expense, Account No. 78000.) Post Check No. 1006.

01/31/08 Issued Check No. 1007 to Eastern Bell for $189.10 in payment of telephone bill. Post Check No. 1007.

01/31/08 Received payment from West's Store for sales invoice 105. In the Reference field, type **Inv. 105**. Post this receipt in the amount of $3,601.50.

Continue with Account Reconciliation on pages 692 and 693.

Account Reconciliation

Complete the bank reconciliation for Franklin Bank and Philadelphia Savings & Loan. The January 31, 2008, bank statements are shown on this page and page 693.

Statement of Account Franklin Bank January 1 to January 31, 2008		Account #30312	BJW Manufacturing, Inc. 7108 Montgomery Avenue Philadelphia, PA 19120	
REGULAR CHECKING				
Previous Balance	12/31/07	$65,650.00		
2 Deposits(+)		11,206.30		
3 Checks (-)		1,908.81		
Service Charges (-)	1/31/08	22.00		
Ending Balance	1/31/08	**$74,925.49**		
DEPOSITS				
	1/28/08	7,604.80		
	1/31/08	3,601.50		
CHECKS (Asterisk * indicates break in check number sequence)				
	1/30/08	1001	742.50	
	1/30/08	1002	408.37	
	1/31/08	1003	757.94	

Statement of Account Philadelphia Savings & Loan January 1 to January 31, 2008		Account #606-8771321	BJW Manufacturing, Inc. 7108 Montgomery Avenue Philadelphia, PA 19120	
		PAYROLL CHECKING		
Previous Balance	12/31/07	31,300.00		
Deposits(+)				
9 Checks (-)		2,946.15		
Service Charges (-)	1/31/08	20.00		
Ending Balance	1/31/08	**28,333.85**		
		DEPOSITS		
		CHECKS (Asterisk * indicates break in check number sequence)		
	1/12/08	101	339.36	
	1/12/08	102	309.67	
	1/12/08	103	333.02	
	1/19/08	104	339.36	
	1/19/08	105	309.67	
	1/19/08	106	333.02	
	1/27/08	107	339.36	
	1/27/08	108	309.67	
	1/27/08	109	333.02	

Back up your data. Use **BJW Mftg January.ptb** as the file name.

Your instructor may want to collect this project. A Checklist of Printouts is shown below.

CHECKLIST OF PRINTOUTS, BJW MANUFACTURING, INC.		
	1	Account Reconciliation Report: Franklin Bank
	2	Account Reconciliation Report: Philadelphia Savings & Loan
	3	Cash Account Register: Franklin Bank
	4	Cash Account Register: Philadelphia Savings & Loan
	5	General Ledger Trial Balance
	6	General Ledger
	7	Balance Sheet
	8	Income Statement
	9	Statement of Cash Flow
	10	Statement of Changes in Financial Position
	11	Statement of Retained Earnings
	12	Customer Ledgers
	13	Vendor Ledgers
	14	Job Ledger
	15	Job Profitability Report
	16	Inventory Profitability Report
	17	Payroll Register
Optional printouts, BJW Manufacturing, Inc.		
	18	Chart of Accounts
	19	Customer List
	20	Vendor List
	21	Payroll Journal
	22	Purchase Journal
	23	Cash Disbursements Journal
	24	Sales Journal
	25	Cash Receipts Journal
	26	Cost of Goods Sold Journal
	27	General Journal

Student Name__________________________________**Date**__________

CHECK YOUR PROGRESS: PROJECT 4
BJW MANUFACTURING, INC.

1. What are the total debit and credit balances on your General Ledger Trial Balance? __________

2. What are the total assets on January 31? __________

3. What is the balance in the Franklin Bank account on January 31? __________

4. What is the balance in the Philadelphia Savings & Loan account on January 31? __________

5. What is Sharon's Camping Store account balance on January 31? __________

6. What are the direct labor costs on January 31? __________

7. How many backpacks were sold during the month of January? __________

8. How many sleeping bags were sold during the month of January? __________

9. How many tents were sold during the month of January? __________

10. What is the ending retained earnings amount on on January 31? __________

11. What are the total expenses reported on January 31? __________

12. Was any Accounts Payable incurred during the month of January? (Circle your answer) YES NO

Project 4A Student-Designed Project

You have completed four projects: Mary Albert, Accountant; Stanley's Sports; Verde Computer Club; and BJW Manufacturing, Inc. In each project you completed the Computer Accounting Cycle for one month.

It is the purpose of Project 4A, to have you write the next month's transactions for one of the four projects. You pick the project and complete the accounting cycle: Project 1, Mary Albert, Accountant, a service business; Project 2, Stanley's Sports, a merchandising business; Project 3, Verde Computer Club, a nonprofit business; or Project 4, BJW Manufacturing, Inc., a manufacturing business. At the end of your month's transactions, you are required to complete adjusting entries.

Good luck! It is your turn to create the transactions for another month and complete the Computer Accounting Cycle. Remember to back up periodically.

Appendix A Troubleshooting

Appendix A, Troubleshooting, includes the following.

VISTA OPERATING SYSTEM INSTALLATION

Peachtree Complete Accounting 2008 uses the Pervasive database. If you are using Windows Vista, you may need to install a service utility from the Pervasive website.

If you start your computer and a W3DBSMGR Information Error window appears that says:

> "W3DBSMGR (5.22.1.1.8): Error 8520. A timeout occurred during the initialization of SRDE engine." Click OK.

Follow these steps to run the Pervasive service utility wizard.

1. Close all windows.

2. Go online to www.pervasive.com.

3. Click on the Developers tab. From the drop down list, select Component Zone.

4. Link to Tools/Utilities.

5. Link to Pervasive PSQL Service Utility for Windows Vista. When the Wizard starts, follow the prompts to download. (*Hint:* Click Next until the Install button appears.)

6. Close your browser.

7. Restart your computer.

8. Start Peachtree; open a company.

PROBLEM BACKING UP TO USB DRIVE OR OTHER EXTERNAL MEDIA

When I back up to USB media (thumb or flash drive), the following message appears:

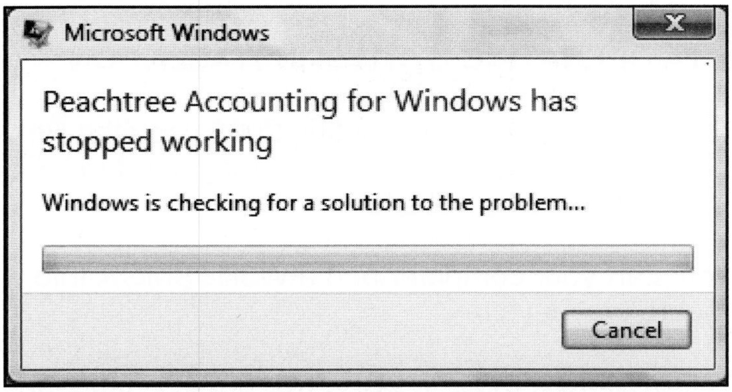

Then, this window appears:

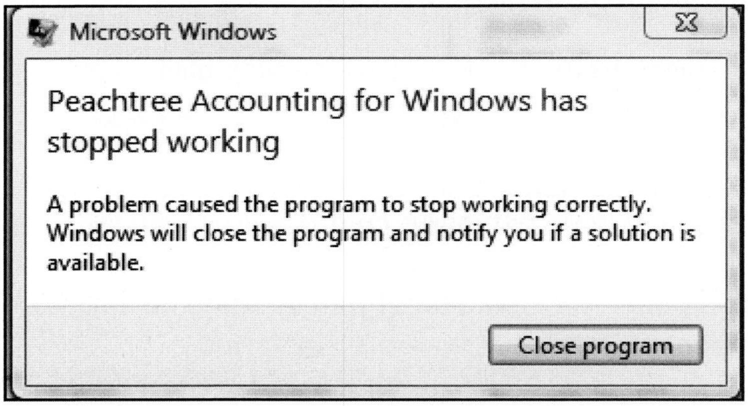

Click 

. You are returned to the Windows desktop.

Make a backup, using your Desktop as the destination for that backup. Then, copy the backup to a USB drive. Follow the steps shown below to do that.

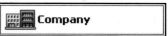

1. From the Navigation Bar, select Company; <u>Back up</u>.
2. Click Back Up.
3. In the Save in field, select Desktop.
4. In the File name filed, type the appropriate file name. (In the example below Chapter 3 is shown.)

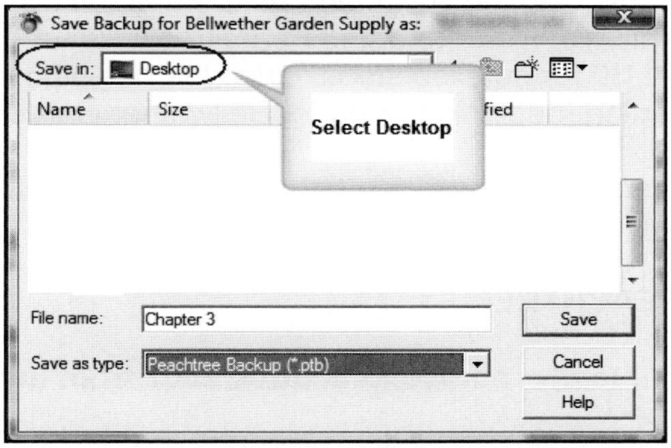

5. Click Save.
6. When This Company backup will require approximately X.XXMB window appears (substitute correct number for Xs.), click OK. When the Back Up Company scale is 100% complete, you have successful backed up. Minimize Peachtree to go to your desktop. The Chapter 3.ptb file is shown on the Windows desktop.
7. Right click on the Chapter 3.ptb file; left-click Copy.

8. Right click on the Start button; left-click Explore.

9. Go to your USB drive location. Right-click on the USB drive; left-click Paste.

RESTORING STARTING DATA FOR THE SAMPLE COMPANIES: BELLWETHER GARDEN SUPPLY AND STONE ARBOR LANDSCAPING

To start the sample companies from the beginning (before any data was added), restore these files:

1. In Chapter 1, on pages 18-21, you backed up Bellwether Garden Supply. This back up was made *before* any data was added. estore the bgs.ptb file. Refer to Using Peachtree's Restore Wizard on pages 26-30 for detailed steps. Once the bgs.ptb file is restored you have starting (beginning) data for Bellwether Garden Supply.

2. In Chapter 8, on pages 239-240, you backed up Stone Arbor Landscaping. Restore the Chapter 8.ptb file.

DELETING PEACHTREE

How do I completely remove Peachtree 2007 from my system?

1. Uninstall Peachtree via the Peachtree CD.

2. Go to Start; Control Panel, Add/Remove Programs and remove Pervasive.

3. Go to My Computer, the C: drive and delete the PVSW and PVSWARCH folders.

4. Double-click on WINDOWS or WINNT, for Windows 2000 and delete the "PeachtInst" folder.

5. Go to the C:\Documents and Settings\users folder name\Application Data and delete the Peachtree folder.

6. Go to C:\Program Files\Common Files\and delete the “Peach” and “Pervasive Software Shared” folders.

7. Click the Back button to return to the Program Files folder. Rename any folders labeled “Sage Software” or “Peachtree” to “oldSage Software” or “oldPeachtree.”

8. Go to Start; Run and type in “regedit” and click on OK.

9. Locate these keys and delete them:

   HKEY_CURRENT_USER\Software\Peachtree
   HKEY_CURRENT_USER\Software\PEACHW Release (10, 9, 8, or 7)
   HKEY_LOCAL_MACHINE\Software\Peachtree
   HKEY_LOCAL_MACHINE\Software\Pervasive
   HKEY_LOCAL_MACHINE\Software\Pervasive Software
   HKEY_LOCAL_MACHINE\Software\PEYX489ZK

10. Go to Start; Search, All Files and Folders (For Files and Folders in Windows 2000). In “All or Part of the File Name” type in p*.ini and click Search. Once the search is over, click on Name at the top of the page to alphabetize the list and look for PFA140.ini, PAW140.ini, PCW140.INI, PPA140.ini, PPAC140.ini, PPAM140.ini, PPAD140.ini, PPAN140.ini, PPAA140.ini, PTX140.ini, or PTXA140.ini. If you see any of these files, delete them.

11. Go to Start; Run, type in %temp% and click OK. Delete everything in this folder that can be deleted. (NOTE: There are some files and folders that cannot be deleted.)

12. Go to Start; Run, type in C:\Windows\Temp and click OK. Delete everything in this folder than can be deleted. (NOTE: There are some files and folders that cannot be deleted.) Close the window.
13. Reboot PC to complete removal of the Peachtree program.

How do I remove Peachtree Release 8.0 and Peachtree 2002 through 2006?

To check your software version, start Peachtree, open any company, and then click on Help, About Peachtree Accounting. To delete Peachtree Complete Accounting Release 8 and higher, do the following:

Step 1: Make a backup of any data files that you have created.

Step 2: Close Peachtree Complete Accounting.

Step 3: From the Start menu, select Control Panel, then Add or Remove Programs.

Step 4: Select Peachtree Complete Accounting from the list; then click Add/Remove Programs.

Step 5: Select remove to confirm that you want to remove Peachtree Complete accounting program files. (If necessary, click Yes to All to delete shared files.)

Step 6: Once the program has been removed, click 

.

Step 7: If necessary, delete the c:\windows\pcweXXX.ini file. (Substitute the appropriate numbers for XXX; for example Peachtree Complete Accounting 2008, Educational Version, Release 15.0 is c:\windows*pcwe140.ini*.)

How do I delete Peachtree 3.0, 3.5, 5.0 or 7.0 from my system?

Step 1: Delete the PAWxx.ini file. The xx stands for a number; for example, PAW35.ini; PAW36.ini, PAW50.ini, PAW70.ini. The PAWxx.ini file is a subdirectory of Windows; for example, c:\windows\PAW70.ini.

Step 2: Delete the program path; for example, c:\paw7edu. If you do not know where the Peachtree is installed, follow these steps.

a. Right-click on Peachtree's desktop icon. Then, left-click on Properties.

b. If necessary, select the Shortcut folder tab. The Target box shows where Peachtree is installed; for example, C:\paw7edu. The subdirectory identified as \peachw.exe is the executable file for the program.

Step 3: Empty the Recycle bin.

Step 4: Restart your computer.

Once you have deleted the .ini file(s), install Peachtree Complete Accounting 2008, Release 15, Educational Version. If you do not get the Standard install option, you did not delete the two files shown in steps 1 and 2.

SERIAL NUMBER IN USE; YOU CANNOT USE PEACHTREE BECAUSE IT HAS REACHED ITS MAXIMUM NUMBER OF USERS

If you are receiving Serial Number in use, Another Peachtree user is using the same serial number, or Peachtree has reached its maximum number of users, do the following to correct this.

1. If necessary, exit Peachtree.

2. Go to Task Manager by pressing the CTRL+ALT+DEL keys and on the Processes tab look for W3DBSMGR.EXE, click to highlight and choose End Task.

   The W3DBSMGR.EXE file is the Pervasive database which sometimes takes time to end. You may have exited Peachtree, then tried to start it *before* Pervasive stopped running.

3. Restart Peachtree.

SYSTEM REQUIREMENTS WARNING

If a System Requirements window warns RAM is not large enough or processing speed is too slow, you may continue installation but Peachtree 2008 may run slower.

The minimum requirements for Peachtree 2008 installation are 256 MB of RAM and 1 GHz processor speed. The author installed with .8 GHz processor speed and 504 MB of RAM on a Windows XP Service Pack 2 computer.

Appendix B Review of Accounting Principles

Computer Accounting with Peachtree Complete 2008, Release 15, 12th Edition is for students who are studying accounting or have used accounting in business. Some of you may have completed one or two semesters of accounting using *Fundamental Accounting Principles*, 18e, Wild et al., McGraw-Hill/Irwin, 2008, or another accounting textbook. Appendix B is a review of basic accounting principles and procedures.

Accounting is concerned with how transactions and other economic events should be described and reported. The Computer Accounting Cycle is shown below. This series of steps is repeated each month for a business's transactions.

Peachtree Complete Accounting Computer Accounting Cycle	
1.	New Company Set up and the chart of accounts.
2.	Analyze transactions.
3.	Journalize entries.
4.	Post to the ledger.
5.	Print general ledger trial balance (unadjusted).
6.	Account reconciliation.
7.	Journalize and post adjusting entries.
8.	Print the general ledger trial balance (adjusted).
9.	Print the financial statements.
10.	Change accounting periods.
11.	Interpret accounting information.

In the service businesses featured in this book, you used the Cash Payments Journal and Cash Receipts Journal for business transactions. Then you post these transactions to the General Ledger. In a merchandising business you use Peachtree's Accounts Payable system and Accounts Receivable system. Special journals are used in conjunction with the Accounts Payable and Accounts Receivable ledgers. The special journals include: Cash Receipts Journal, Sales Journal, Cash Disbursements Journal, and Purchases Journal. The General Ledger, Accounts Payable Ledger and Accounts Receivable Ledger systems are taught in Parts 1, 2 and 3 of *Computer Accounting with Peachtree Complete 2008, 12e.*

Standard accounting procedures are based on the double-entry system. This means that for each business transaction, one or more debits and one or more credits must be made in a journal and posted to the ledger. The debits must equal the credits.

The double-entry accounting system is based on the following premise: each account has two sides–a debit (left) side and credit (right) side. This is stated in the ***accounting equation*** as:

Assets = Liabilities + Owner's Equity

Assets are the economic resources and other properties that a business owns. Asset accounts include: Cash, Accounts Receivable, Office Supplies, Equipment, Land, Buildings, etc.

Liabilities are the business's debts. Liability accounts include: Accounts Payable, Loans Payable, Unearned Rent, etc.

Equity is the difference between the organization's assets and liabilities. Equity accounts for organizations that are sole proprietorships or partnerships include: Capital and Withdrawals. Equity accounts for organizations that are corporations include contributed capital accounts like common stock which represent external ownership and retained earnings and dividends accounts which represent internal ownership interests. Temporary equity-related accounts known as revenue and expense accounts recognize an organization's income activities during the period.

Since assets are on the left side of the accounting equation, the left side of the account increases. This is the usual balance, too; assets increase on the left side and have a debit balance. Liabilities and Equity accounts are on the right side of the equation. Therefore, they increase on the right side and normally carry credit balances.

Another way to show the accounting equation and double-entry is illustrated below.

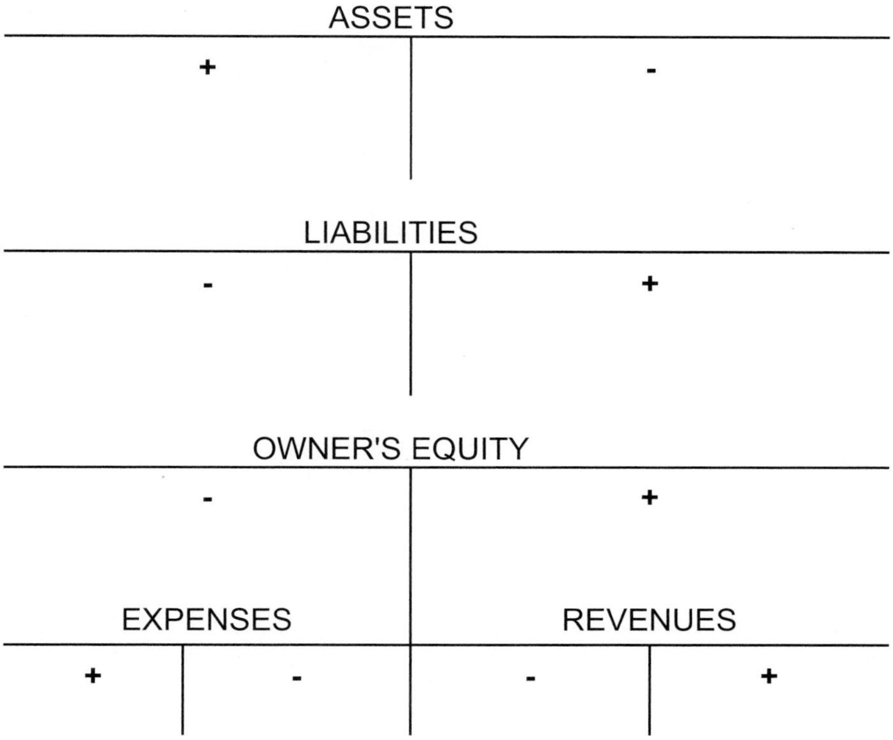

Each element of the accounting equation, Assets, Liabilities, and Equity, behaves similarly to their placement in the equation. Assets have debit balances; Liabilities have credit balances; Equities have credit balances; Expenses have debit balances because they decrease equity; and Revenues have credit balances because they increase equity.

In computerized accounting it is important to number each account according to a system. This is called the Chart of Accounts. The Chart of Accounts is a listing of all the general ledger accounts. The Chart of Accounts identifies accounts with a number (five digits in Peachtree's detailed chart; four digits in Peachtree's simplified chart). The account number is shown in the Account ID column; the name of the account in the Account Description column; the next column shows whether account is Active; and the Account Type column classifies accounts for the financial statements. On Peachtree's chart of accounts, the Account Type column classifies accounts as cash, accounts receivable, inventory, fixed assets, accumulated depreciation accounts, liability accounts, etc. A partial chart of accounts is shown below.

Page: 1

BJW Manufacturing, Inc.
Chart of Accounts
As of Jan 31, 2008

Filter Criteria includes: Report order is by ID. Report is printed with Accounts having Zero Amounts and in Detail Format.

Account ID	Account Description	Active?	Account Type
10000	Petty Cash	Yes	Cash
10200	Franklin Bank	Yes	Cash
10300	Philadelphia Savings & Loan	Yes	Cash
10700	Investments-Cert. of Deposit	Yes	Cash
11000	Accounts Receivable	Yes	Accounts Receivable
11400	Other Receivables	Yes	Accounts Receivable
11500	Allowance for Doubtful Account	Yes	Accounts Receivable
12000	Raw Materials Inventory	Yes	Inventory
12010	Inventory-Backpacks	Yes	Inventory
12020	Inventory-Sleeping Bags	Yes	Inventory
12030	Inventory-Tents	Yes	Inventory
12050	Supplies Inventory	Yes	Inventory
12100	Work in Progress Inventory	Yes	Inventory
12150	Finished Goods Inventory	Yes	Inventory
14000	Prepaid Insurance	Yes	Other Current Assets
14100	Employee Advances	Yes	Other Current Assets
14200	Notes Receivable-Current	Yes	Other Current Assets
14300	Prepaid Interest	Yes	Other Current Assets
14700	Other Current Assets	Yes	Other Current Assets
15000	Furniture and Fixtures	Yes	Fixed Assets
15100	Computers & Equipment	Yes	Fixed Assets
15200	Trucks/Autos	Yes	Fixed Assets
15300	Other Depreciable Property	Yes	Fixed Assets
15500	Building	Yes	Fixed Assets
15600	Building Improvements	Yes	Fixed Assets
17000	Accum. Depreciation - Furnitur	Yes	Accumulated Depreciation
17100	Accum. Depreciation-Comp & Equ	Yes	Accumulated Depreciation
17200	Accum. Depreciation-Trucks/Aut	Yes	Accumulated Depreciation
17500	Accum. Depreciation - Building	Yes	Accumulated Depreciation
17600	Accum. Depreciation - Bldg Imp	Yes	Accumulated Depreciation
19000	Deposits	Yes	Other Assets
19100	Organization Costs	Yes	Other Assets
19150	Accum. Amortiz. - Org. Costs	Yes	Other Assets
19200	Note Receivable-Noncurrent	Yes	Other Assets
19900	Other Noncurrent Assets	Yes	Other Assets
20000	Accounts Payable	Yes	Accounts Payable
22000	Credit Card Payable	Yes	Other Current Liabilities
23000	Accrued Expenses	Yes	Other Current Liabilities
23100	Sales Tax Payable	Yes	Other Current Liabilities
23200	Wages Payable	Yes	Other Current Liabilities
23300	Medicare Employee Taxes Payabl	Yes	Other Current Liabilities
23350	Medicare Employer Taxes Payabl	Yes	Other Current Liabilities
23400	Federal Payroll Taxes Payable	Yes	Other Current Liabilities
23500	FUTA Tax Payable	Yes	Other Current Liabilities
23600	State Payroll Taxes Payable	Yes	Other Current Liabilities
23650	Employee SUI Taxes Payable	Yes	Other Current Liabilities
23700	SUTA Payable	Yes	Other Current Liabilities
23800	Local Payroll Taxes Payable	Yes	Other Current Liabilities
23900	Income Taxes Payable	Yes	Other Current Liabilities
24000	FICA Employee Taxes Payable	Yes	Other Current Liabilities
24100	FICA Employer Taxes Payable	Yes	Other Current Liabilities
24200	Current Portion Long-Term Debt	Yes	Other Current Liabilities
24400	Deposits from Customers	Yes	Other Current Liabilities
24900	Suspense-Clearing Account	Yes	Other Current Liabilities
27000	Mortgage Payable	Yes	Long Term Liabilities
27100	Deferred Revenue	Yes	Long Term Liabilities
27400	Other Long-Term Liabilities	Yes	Long Term Liabilities
39003	Common Stock	Yes	Equity-doesn't close
39004	Paid-in Capital	Yes	Equity-doesn't close
39005	Retained Earnings	Yes	Equity-Retained Earnings
39007	Dividends Paid	Yes	Equity-gets closed
40000	Sales-Backpacks	Yes	Income
40200	Sales-Sleeping Bags	Yes	Income
40400	Sales-Tents	Yes	Income

Peachtree includes over 75 sample companies from which you can copy default information, including detailed and simplified Chart of Accounts examples. If you want to see which sample companies are included in Peachtree, select Help from the menu bar, then select Contents and Index. If necessary, select the Contents tab; then double-click Help about Your Specific Type of Business. Double -click on the A-Z List of Business Types. An alphabetic list of company types displays. Move your mouse to a company that you want to see and single click. To see the chart of accounts, click on Display a sample chart of accounts for this type of business. If you want a printout, click 

. Click 

to select another business type; or click  on the title bar to close the Peachtree Help screen.

Report information in the form of financial statements is important to accounting. The Balance Sheet reports the financial position of the business. It shows that assets are equal to liabilities plus equity—the accounting equation. The Income Statement shows the difference between revenue and expenses for a specified period of time (month, quarter, year). The Statement of Cash Flow reports the operating, financial, and investing activities for the period.

Peachtree tracks income and expense data for an entire year. At the end of the year, all revenue and expense accounts are closed to equity. All you need to do is select Tasks, System, then Year-End Wizard. This step closes all revenue and expense accounts to equity. The income and expense accounts have zero balances and you are ready to start the next year. Peachtree includes 24 periods so it is possible to accumulate data for two years.

In accounting you learn that asset, liability, and equity accounts are included on the balance sheet. Revenue (income) and expense accounts are placed on the Income Statement. The Cash Flow Statement shows the sources of cash coming into the business and the destination of the cash going out.

The most important task you have is recording transactions into the appropriate accounts. Peachtree helps you by organizing the software into Business Status, Customers & Sales, Vendors & Purchases,

Inventory & Services, Employees & Payroll, Banking, and Company navigation centers. You record transactions into the right place using easy-to-complete forms. Once transactions are entered, the data is organized into journal entries, ledgers, reports, and analysis capabilities. Another important task is deciding how to enter transactions. Recording and categorizing business transactions will determine how Peachtree uses that information. For instance, observe that the chart of accounts for BJW Manufacturing, Inc. shows Account 10200 – Franklin Bank, classified as the Account Type, Cash; Account No. 11000, Accounts Receivable, classified as Accounts Receivable. The Chart of Accounts Account Type column classifies the account for the financial statements—Assets, Liability, and Equity accounts go on the balance sheet; Income, Cost of Sales, and Expense accounts go on the Income Statement.

As you work with Peachtree, you see how the accounts, recording of transactions, and reports work to provide your business with the information necessary for making informed decisions.

Another important aspect of accounting is determining whether the basis for recording transactions is cash or accrual. In the cash basis method, revenues and expenses are recognized when cash changes hands. In other words, when the customer pays for their purchase, the transaction is recorded. When the expense is paid the transaction is recorded. In the accrual method of accounting, revenues and expenses are recognized when they occur. In other words, if the company purchases inventory from a vendor on April 1, the transaction is recorded on April 1. If inventory is sold on account on April 15, the transaction is done on April 15 *not* when cash is received. Accrual basis accounting is seen as more accurate because assets, liabilities, income, and expenses are recorded when they actually happen.

The charts on the next two pages summarize Appendix B, Review of Accounting Principles.

ACCOUNTING EQUATION:	Assets =	Liabilities +	Owners Equities +	Revenues –	Expenses
Definition:	Something that has future or potential value "resources"	Responsibilities to others "Payables" "Unearned"	Internal and External ownership	Recognition of value creation	Expired, used, or consumed costs or resources
Debit Rules:DR	Increase	Decrease	Decrease	Decrease	Increase
Credit Rules:CR	Decrease	Increase	Increase	Increase	Decrease
Account Types and Examples	**Current Assets:** Cash, Marketable Securities, Accounts Receivable, Inventory, Prepaids **Plant Assets:** Land, Buildings, Equipment, Accumulated Depreciation **Noncurrent Assets:** Investments, Intangibles	**Current Liabilities:** Accounts Payable, Unearned Revenue, Advances from Customer **Noncurrent or Long-term Liabilities:** Bonds Payable, Notes Payables, Mortgage Payable	**Sole Proprietor:** (both internal and external) Name, Capital; Name, Withdrawals **Partnership:** (both internal and external) Partner A, Capital; Partner A, Withdrawals, etc. **Corporation**: External: Common Stock, Preferred Stock, Paid-in Capital Internal: Retained Earnings, Dividends	**Operating Revenue:** Sales: Fees Earned, Rent Income, Contract Revenue **Other Revenue:** Interest Income	**Product/Services Expenses:** Cost of Goods Sold, Cost of Sales **Prepaid Expenses:** Selling Expenses, Administrative Expense, General Expense, Salary Expense, Rent Expense, Depreciation Expense, Insurance Expense **Other Expenses:** Interest Expense

T-Account Rules

	Assets		Liabilities		Owners Equities		Revenues		Expenses	
T-Account Rules	Acquire resources	Consume resources	Pay bills Recognize earnings	Buy on credit Receive cash or other assets before earning it	Internal: Net Loss External: Owners reduce ownership thru withdrawals or dividends	Internal: Net Income External: Investment made by owners in company	Sales returns Sales discount given	Sales Earned Income	Resources used consumed expired	
	increase	*decrease*	*decrease*	*increase*	*decrease*	*increase*	*decrease*	*increase*	*increase*	*decrease*

Basic Financial Statement Rules:

Income Statement

Revenue=Net Income (NI) or Net Loss (NL)

(*Prepare first*)

Statement of Equity

Beginning* +NI or –NL–(Withdrawals)=Ending*

*for Sole Proprietors and Partnerships use Capital; for Corporations use Retained Earnings

(*Prepare second*)

Balance Sheet

Assets=Liabilities+Owners Equities

(*Prepare third*)

Statement of Cash Flows

Operating+/-Investing+/-Financing+Beginning Cash=Ending Cash

(*Prepare last*)

Appendix C Glossary

Appendix C lists a glossary of terms used in *Computer Accounting with Peachtree Complete 2008, Release 15, 12th Edition*. The number in parentheses refers to the textbook page. Appendix C is also included on the textbook website at www.mhhe.com/yacht2008, link to Student Edition, then Glossary.

accounting equation	The accounting equation is stated as assets = liabilities + owner's equity. (p. 708)
accounts payable	The money a company owes to a supplier or vendor. (p. 382)
accounts payable ledger	Shows the account activity for each vendor. (p. 406)
accounts payable transactions	Purchases of merchandise for resale, assets, or expenses incurred on credit from vendors. (p. 382)
accounts receivable	Money that is owed by customers to the business. (p. 446)
accounts receivable ledger	Shows the account activity for each customer. (p. 458)
accounts receivable transactions	Credit transactions from customers. (p. 446)
activity items	An item class for time and billing. (p. 231)

ASCII	An acronym for American Standard Code for Information Interchange. A standard format for representing characters on a computer. Most word processing, spreadsheet, and database programs can read ASCII files. (p. 622)
assets	The economic resources and other properties that a business owns. (p. 708)
audit trail	The path from the source document to the accounts. (p. 175)
average cost	A method of computing inventory. (See weighted-average method). (p. 411)
backing up	A copy of a data file typically stored on the hard drive or external media. (p. 18)
balance sheet	Lists the types and amounts of assets, liabilities, and equity as of a specific date. (p. 267)
bank reconciliation	The process of bringing the balance of the bank statement and the balance of the cash account into agreement. (p. 294)
batch posting	Journal entries are held in temporary storage on your disk and not made part of the permanent records of the company until you decide you are satisfied with them and select Post from the icon bar. After you post, the General Ledger and all other accounting reports are updated. (p. 110)
business status center	When you open a company, the Business Status Center appears. Like a car's dashboard it tells you what you need to know in one place. (See dashboard.) (p. 6)

case sensitive	Refers to the use of lowercase and uppercase letters. When coding a customer or vendor, you must use either a capital or lowercase letter. For example, a vendor code that is A002 will not be recognized if a002 is typed. (p. 67)
cash disbursements journal	All payments of cash are recorded in the cash disbursements journal. In Peachtree, the Payments task is the cash disbursements journal. (p. 412)
cash receipts journal	In Peachtree the receipts task posts to the cash receipts journal. (p. 458)
charge items	An item class for time and billing. (p. 231)
chart of accounts	A list of all the accounts used by a company, showing the identifying number assigned to each account. PCA has over 70 sample charts of accounts. (p. 154)
coding system	A combination of letters and numbers that are used to identify customers and vendors. The coding system is case sensitive, for example, A002 is not the same as a002. (See case sensitive.) (p. 66)
credit memos	Refunds for merchandise that is returned by a customer. Also known as a credit invoice. (p. 120)
customer ledger	Shows account activity for each customer. (p. 451)

dashboard The Business Status Center shows you in one place what you need to know about the business—data relating to account balances, who owes you what and what bills need to be paid, who your most profitable customers are, etc. (p. 6).

default Information that displays in windows or information that is automatically used by the system. You can change the default by choosing another command. (p. 330)

desktop Depending on how your computer is set up, various icons appear on your desktop when you start Windows. (p. 7)

dialog box A window that appears when the system requires further information. You type information into dialog boxes to communicate with the program. Some dialog boxes display warnings and messages. (p. 3129)

drill down The act of following a path to its origin for further analysis. In certain Peachtree reports, you can click transactions to drill down to the task window. For example, from financial statements, you can drill down to the general ledger report; then you can drill down to the task window. (p. 7975)

drop-down list The down arrow means that this field contains a list of information from which you can make a selection. Many of PCA's windows will have drop down lists. When you click on the arrow next to a field, the list appears. You can press **<Enter>** or click your mouse on an item to select it from the list. (p. 11)

ellipsis (...)	A punctuation mark consisting of three successive periods (...). Choosing a menu item with an ellipsis opens a dialog box. See glossary item, dialog box. (p. 31)
equity	The difference between the assets and liabilities or what the business has left after the debts are paid. (p. 708)
exemptions	These are withholding allowances claimed by the employee. The number of exemptions or withholding allowances usually includes one for the employee, one for the employee's spouse, and one for each dependent. (p. 524)
expense tickets	Used to track and aid in the recovery of customer-related expenses. (p. 230)
exporting	Copies Peachtree data into a format that other programs can read and use. (p. 620)
external media	Examples of external media include floppy disks; CD-R; DVD-R; USB flash drive; Zip disks. External media of this type can be used for backing up Peachtree data. (p. 18)
FICA taxes	This deduction from wages is also called the social security tax and provides qualified workers who retire at age 62 or older with monthly payments from the federal government. A portion of this tax is for Medicare. (See Medicare.) (p. 524)
fields	An individual piece of data, for example, the account number for sales or a customer's name. (p. 620)
FIFO	First in, first out method of inventory assumes that the items in the beginning inventory are sold first. (p. 497)

files	A group of related records; for example, customer files and journal files. (p. 620)
filter	Filtering allows you to select specific types of activities and events. (p. 10)
global options	Settings that affect the entire program. When you set global options for one company, you set them for all companies. You can access these settings from the Options menu. (p. 15)
graphical user interface (GUI)	Consists of procedures which enable you to interact with PCA. The key is the Windows environment: the menus, dialog boxes, and list boxes. A mouse simplifies use of the GUI, but it is not required. (p. 1)
home page	The Business Status page is also known as the home page. (p. 13)
HTML	HTML is an abbreviation for Hypertext Markup Language. Peachtree's Help topics are displayed in HTML. (p. 154)
icons	Small graphic symbols that represent an application or command. Icons appear on the screen when Windows programs are used: file folder, eraser, clock, hour-glass, etc. (p. 1)
icon bar	The icon bar shows pictures of commands or additional information that pertain to the window. Some icons are common to all windows while other icons are specific to a particular window. (p. 9)

internal control	An integrated system of people, processes, and procedures that minimize or eliminate business risks, protect assets, ensure reliable accounting, and promote efficient operations. (175)
importing	Translates data from other programs into a format that Peachtree can use. (p. 619)
Internet	The worldwide electronic communication network that allows for the sharing of information. To read about the differences between the Internet and the World Wide Web, go to www.webopedia.com/DidYouKnow/Internet/2002/Web_vs_Internet.asp. (p. 44)
invoice	A bill that shows an itemized list of goods shipped or services rendered, stating quantities, prices, fees, and shipping charges. (p. 446)
liabilities	The business' debts. (p. 708)
LIFO	Last in, first out method of inventory assumes that the last goods received are sold first. (p. 497)
line items	These rows appear on many of Peachtree's windows. On color monitors, a magenta line is placed around the row you select. (p. 10)
line objects	You can draw lines or rectangles on your forms. (p. 601)

lookup field Lookup fields are indicated by an icon with a magnifying glass. When you are in the text field portion of the lookup field, the cursor changes to an I-bar with a plus sign and question mark, **<** I +? **>**. In a lookup field, you can either select from a list of records, such as vendors, customers, accounts, etc. or you can type a new record. (p. 11)

masking The ability to limit information on the report to a single division, department, location, or type code. Masking allows you to departmentalize financial statements. (p. 217)

Medicare A portion of FICA taxes (also called social security taxes) deducted from wages of qualified workers. Retirees receive medical benefits called Medicare after reaching age 65. (p. 524)

merchandise inventory Includes all goods owned by the business and held for resale. (p. 497)

merchandising business Retail stores that resell goods and/or perform services. (p. 497)

modem The word modem is an abbreviation of Modulator/Demodulator. A modem is a device that translates the digital signals from your computer into analog signals that can travel over telephone lines. There are also DSL (digital subscriber lines), wireless, and cable modems, as well as T-1 lines for faster connections. (p. 44)

mouse A pointing device that is used to interact with images on the screen. The left mouse button is used in PCA. (p. 1)

navigation bar	The navigation bar appears on the left side of the Peachtree main window and offers access to seven navigation centers: Business Status; Customers & Sales; Vendors & Purchases; Inventory & Services; Employees & Payroll; Banking; and Company. Also called a dashboard. (p. 17)
navigation centers	Each navigation bar selection takes you to the navigation center pages, which provide information and access to the Peachtree program. (p. 17)
net income	A net income results when revenues exceed expenses. (p. 209)
net loss	A net loss results when expenses exceed revenues. (p. 209)
option button	Circles in dialog boxes which toggle options on and off. Options signal an either or choice. For example, there are two option buttons on the Maintain Employees dialog box: Salary or Hourly pay. You select one or the other; you cannot select both. (p. 39)
payroll journal	In Peachtree, the Payroll Entry window is also the payroll journal. The Payroll Entry window posts to the General Ledger and to the Employee file. (p. 540)
PCA	Abbreviation for Peachtree Complete Accounting. (p. 1)
perpetual inventory	In a perpetual inventory system, an up-to-date record of inventory is maintained and the inventory account is revised each time a purchase or sale is made. (p. 153)

posting	The process of transferring information from the journal to the ledger. (p. 247)
purchase discount	Cash discounts from vendors in return for early payment of an invoice, for example, 2% 10 days, net 30. (p. 53)
purchase journal	In the Purchase Journal, or Purchases/Receive Inventory window, you can enter invoices received from vendors or enter and print purchase orders. In manual accounting, a Purchase Journal is a multi-columnar journal in which all purchases on account are recorded. (p. 405)
purchase orders	The business form used by the purchasing department to place an order with a vendor. Purchase Orders, abbreviated P.O., authorize the vendor to ship the ordered merchandise at the stated price and terms. (p. 57)
queue	A list of files waiting to be printed (p. 35)
radio button	Commands that can be turned on from a list of choices in a dialog box or window. (p. 39)
real-time posting	Journal transactions are posted to the General Ledger at the time they are entered and saved. Peachtree Software recommends real-time posting for networked computers. (p. 110).
records	A group of fields that contain information on one subject, for example, the general journal, purchase journal, cash disbursements journal, sales journal, or cash receipts journal. (p. 620)
restore	Previously backed up data can be restored or retrieved with the File, Restore selection. (p. 18)

sales discount	A cash discount that is offered to customers for early payment of their sales invoices. For example, Bellwether Garden Supply offers Teesdale Real Estate a 5% discount for payments received within 15 days of the invoice date. In PCA the discount period (number of days) and discount percentage can be changed. (p. 101)
sales journal	The Sales/Invoicing task in Peachtree is the sales journal. (p. 457-458)
service invoice	An alternative to the standard invoice. Use it when you want to create an invoice without inventory items. (p. 466)
shortcut keys	Enable you to perform some operations by pressing two or more keys at the same time. For example **<Alt> + <F4>** closes an application window. (p. 4)
source documents	Written evidence of a business transaction. Examples of source documents are sales invoices, purchase invoices, and a check register. (p. 252)
statement of financial position	Another name for a balance sheet. (See balance sheet.) (p. 267).
tabs	There are various tabs shown on Peachtree's windows. For example, in the Maintain Customers/Prospects window there are tabs for General, Sales Defaults, Payment Defaults, Custom Fields, and History. You can select one of these tabs to open a window so that more information will display about a customer. (p. 11)
taskbar	In Windows XP, the Start button and taskbar are located at the bottom of your screen. (p. 8)

template	A document pattern or part of a document that you keep stored so that it can be used again. (p. 649)
time tickets	Used to record time-based activities such as research or consultations. A record of activities of either a vendor or an employee. (p. 230)
title bar	The top line of every window is a bar which contains the name of the application or menu in that window. (p. 7)
trackball	A device that works like a built-in mouse. (p. 1)
unearned revenue	A liability account used to report advance collections from customers. (p. 341)
user interface	The user interface is also called the graphical user interface. Refer to glossary term, graphical user interface. (p. 1)
vendor credit memos	Returns to vendors. (p. 78)
vendor ledger	Shows the account activity for each vendor. (p. 406)
vendors	In PCA, this term refers to businesses that offer credit for merchandise or assets purchased or expenses incurred. (p. 382)
W-2 forms	An annual report of an employee's wages subject to FICA and federal income tax that shows the amounts of these taxes that were withheld. (p. 524)

weighted-average method	This method of inventory pricing divides the cost of the inventory purchased by the quantity of merchandise purchased. This unit cost is multiplied by the ending inventory. (p. 411)
WIMP	The acronym, WIMP, stands for Windows, Icons, Menus, and Pull-downs. This acronym is used to describe the way personal computer software looks and works. (p. 1)
windows	A visual (instead of typographic) format for computer operations. (p. 1)
withholding allowances	Exemptions claimed by the employee. The number of exemptions or withholding allowances often includes one for the employee, one for the employee's spouse, and one for each dependent. (p. 524)
World Wide Web (WWW)	A way of accessing information over the Internet. To read about the differences between the Internet and the World Wide Web, go online to www.webopedia.com/DidYouKnow/Internet/2002/Web_vs_Internet.asp. (p. 44)

Index